THE POLITICS OF EUROCOMMUNISM

THE POLITICS OF EUROCOMMUNISM

SOCIALISM IN TRANSITION

EDITED BY
CARL BOGGS AND DAVID PLOTKE

SOUTH END PRESS   BOSTON

Library of Congress Card Catalog Number: 79-66993
ISBN paper: 0-89608-051-x
ISBN cloth: 0-89608-052-8

Cover Design By Michael Prokosch
Typeset and Paste-Up by the South End Collective

HX
238.5
P64

Please Note: In the typesetting of this manuscript defective chemical pre-
servatives were employed. As a result many pages faded and density
varied considerably even within paragraphs throughout the volume.
Within the available limits set by time and finances we have endeavored
to minimize the impact of this unusual accident. We hope the density
variability that remains is not too great an inconvenience to the reader.

South End Collective

South End Press, Box 68, Astor Station
Boston, Mass., 02123

Contents

PREFACE

We began work on this book in the fall of 1977, when discussions and debates about the meaning of Eurocommunism were in full swing. Both of us, out of a longstanding interest in issues of Marxist theory, European politics, and socialist strategy, took part in these exchanges in the pages of *Socialist Review* and elsewhere. We felt that, while the discussions raised many important questions and suggested certain directions for analysis, they lacked depth and systematic elaboration. Too many issues were ignored or sidestepped; a priori assumptions, generally stemming from doctrinaire political viewpoints, often substituted for serious theoretical inquiry and historical analysis. It was out of a desire to move beyond such an impasse that this volume was conceived.

As we started thinking about the direction of our project, we were quickly forced to make a basic decision: was Eurocommunism a passing phenomenon, likely to disappear within the space of a few years, or might it represent some kind of fundamental break within the Marxist and Communist traditions? We concluded that it does mark a significant departure in both the history of the left on an international scale and in the development of European politics.

Moving from this premise, we approached the large number of problems suggested by the emergence of strong Eurocommunist parties in France, Italy, and Spain. We wanted the contributors to write essays that would go beyond the narrow boundaries of academic disciplines, and would address the range of political questions that preoccupy socialists of whatever orientation. On the one hand, we were committed to an anthology that would not be merely a topical discourse on Eurocommunism; we wanted to generate theoretical perspectives and insights that would have a more or less lasting value. On the other hand, we did not want to obscure the concretely political dimension of the subject matter; to this end, we encouraged analysis of a variety of specific topics and problems related to Eurocommunism—but not too many, we hope, to overwhelm the central themes that hold the volume together.

In carrying out a project of this type, where all of the essays were written originally for inclusion in this anthology, the editors find that they are indebted to an unusually large number of people for their assistance and support. Such help greatly facilitated the editorial process, improved the quality of the final text, and provided us with a rare learning experience.

First of all, we wish to thank the contributors to *The Politics of Eurocommunism*. In every case we encountered nothing but cooperation and a comradely spirit of helpfulness—in the willingness to listen to our suggestions and criticisms that sometimes spanned several drafts of manuscripts, in the patience shown throughout the long editing enterprise, in the sensitivity toward our perpetual (and sometimes capricious) deadlines, and in the great care taken in the preparation of final manuscripts. If the editors often imposed difficult demands upon the authors, complaints were surprisingly rare. Given our effort to integrate the widely-varying contributions so as to provide an overall unity to the volume, the many authors are certainly entitled to blame any remaining defects in their essays on the failures of their editors.

Secondly, we would like to express our gratitude to the many people who read and commented on one or more of the essays. Their criticisms and suggestions were invaluable, even if they often disagreed—sometimes strongly—with the perspectives and arguments that worked their way into the final text. These readers include: Michael Albert, Doug Appel, Sandra Chelnov, Harry Chotiner, Barbara Easton, Andrew Feenberg, Allen Hunter, Paul Joseph, Denis Lacorne, Billy Pope, and members of the *Socialist Review* collective.

We also owe much thanks to South End Press, which has given us the opportunity to work with a publisher that shares our political goals. The comradely relationship that developed over a year and a half meant that we did not have to drain our energies over the sorts of intellectual and political struggles that often occur at commercial and academic houses. More than that, the South End collective has succeeded in creating a process that brings authors into virtually all aspects of both editorial and production decision-making. The result is an end product that, for better or worse, is very much the expression of our own designs, preferences, and aesthetic tastes.

Finally, we wish to thank those who have given their time to assist us in producing this volume, including preparation of manuscripts, research, and translation. Among these are Sandra Chelnov, Temma Kaplan, Michele Prichard, Jose Rodriguez-Ibañez, Flo Westoby, and members of the Peoples Translation Service.

And there are others—far too numerous to mention here—who contributed in countless ways toward the realization of this project.

—Los Angeles, California
—Berkeley, California
   May, 1979

INTRODUCTION

THIS VOLUME WAS assembled with the intent of exploring the overall development of Eurocommunism, defining and analyzing its main features, and assessing its long-term relevance for socialist polities—not only in Western Europe, but in the United States and elsewhere. Our point of departure is the increasingly powerful role of the Communist parties in France, Italy, and Spain, and the way that role has evolved in relation to changing domestic and international conditions. The geographical focus is dictated in part by the strength of the common traditions and problems in Southern Europe; the emphasis on a single region is intended to provide a clear frame of reference within which a specific range of problems can be identified and studied.

We should enter the normal disclaimer at the outset: whatever the importance of developments in France, Italy, and Spain, "Eurocommunism" is something more far-reaching in its political and geographical scope than any particular set of events which may occur in those countries. And whatever the ultimate historical significance of Eurocommunism, it is evident that a process of major proportions is underway. This process is in many respects quite new—the term itself only appeared in the vocabulary of contemporary politics in the mid-1970s. For this reason, the anthology is not premised on arriving at any final conclusions; it is thus deliberately varied both in its theoretical and political orientations and in its styles of presentation.

While all of the authors approach the topic as socialists, sharp differences nonetheless exist. Some of the essays reflect a straightforward sympathy for the Eurocommunist parties; others, while supportive of their general direction, make sharp criticisms of particular aspects of party strategy, tactics, leadership, or organization; still others question whether these parties can ever play a major role in the transition to socialism. In every case, however, the contributors share the view that the politics of Eurocommunism may well dramatically alter the European social and political landscape. There is fundamental agreement that fresh approaches are needed to confront questions too often evaded or ignored by a left tradition long inhibited by Stalinism and (in a different way) by the mystique of Lenin and the Bolshevik Revolution. And there is further agreement that some of the objectives advanced by the Eurocommunist parties are crucial for socialists, whether or not those values are actually realized in the practice of those parties. In this spirit, we have tried to put together a collection of essays that would have an enduring value beyond any narrow partisanship.

THE MEDITERRANEAN COMMUNIST parties have been profoundly shaped by a series of global events during the past two decades. Among such events have been, in the first place, a number of schisms that have unsettled the world Communist movement, beginning with the Sino-Soviet split and reflected today in the increasing erosion of Soviet hegemony over the left in both Eastern and Western Europe. Perhaps never before has such a complex and fragmentary situation confronted the left on a world scale. In crucial respects, the appearance of large and relatively popular Eurocommunist parties both expresses and deepens this conflict, threatening to open a rupture between Western Communist parties and the Soviet Union that could be irreversible.

At the same time, Eurocommunism has evolved in a period when the massive power of the United States has been in crisis. The economic, political, and military strength of the U.S. is still sufficient to permit it to influence events in the Mediterranean countries; it can still hope to dictate, openly or covertly, the terms of left-wing participation in such governments. But its power is more fragile than at any time since the immediate postwar years, and the options available to U.S. foreign policy appear to be more and more restricted in the aftermath of the Vietnam defeat and the weakening of American economic domination in Western Europe and other regions. While this fragility clearly does not rule out the exercise of power, or preclude major intervention in moments of desperation (as in Chile), it does impose new limits on the American capacity to impede change in Western Europe.

Finally, Eurocommunism has strengthened its presence at the very time of rapidly-advancing economic and political integration within Western Europe. This process has been skillfully engineered by international monopoly capital, presided over by the multi-national corporations, the EEC, and such institutions as the International Monetary Fund. Even as the traditional language of proletarian internationalism within the world Communist movement is discarded, the difficulties of charting a strategy confined to the boundaries of a single nation-state have sharpened. The pressures toward European integration form a novel terrain for the unfolding of social and political struggles in the coming years.

It is this historical setting in which the left opposition—especially in the advanced capitalist countries—must begin to redefine its overall purposes and rethink its strategic orientation. Today, the left in general and Marxism in particular appear to suffer from a profound lack of ability to sketch a convincing alternative to liberal capitalism in North America, Western Europe, and elsewhere. Old approaches have become obsolete or have been soundly defeated, but new ones—at least politically *effective* ones—seem to be agonizingly slow in taking shape.

Eurocommunism—insofar as it has arrived at a coherent sense of identity—presents itself as a political formation that, in the midst of evolving crisis, can fill this void and transcend the failures and limitations of the past. In its groping for a socialist way out of the present impasse, it embraces a range of ideological and strategic themes that would appear to set it apart from both classical Leninism and the various forms of social democracy: rejection of traditional insurrectionary politics, the vanguard party, and the myth of the "dictatorship of the proletariat"; attachment to the idea of constructing a "social bloc" of forces, based upon a multi-class transition to socialism rather than a strict proletarian focus; involvement in political struggles that take place within existing representative institutions; commitment to building a mass party that would continuously press anew the goal of socialism; and a principled support of social and political pluralism—not only for the present, but in any future socialist order.

None of these themes is entirely new; all can be traced back to various sources and periods in the history of the left. Their novelty stems from the way the entire range of concerns and priorities has been integrated into a unified strategic, if not programmatic, format rooted in the peculiar situation of Mediterranean (and European) capitalism in the 1970s, in the serious thrust toward democratization and autonomy of parties within the world Communist movement, and in the first really comprehensive and overt departures from the Soviet model of bureaucratic centralism. It is a novelty that defies simplistic theoretical or historical parallels with earlier movements and tendencies. It is a novelty, moreover, that is rooted in the specific *political* conjuncture of forces at work in European history in the wake of a long sequence of events and processes: the Sino-Soviet split, the emergence of the new left in the 1960s, the Soviet intervention in Czechoslovakia, the overthrow of Allende in Chile, and the secular decline of right-wing hegemony in Southern Europe (the end of the Salazar regime in Portugal, the erosion of Francoism in Spain, the eclipse of Gaullism in France, and the disarray of Christian Democracy in Italy).

THE RELATIONSHIP BETWEEN socialism and democracy, which has presented a major problem for the left since the time of Marx and Engels, is a motif that permeates most of the essays in this book. Here the Eurocommunist parties—like other Communist parties with origins in the Third International—share a common history: initial rejection of social democracy and adoption of Leninist vanguardism; a period of left sectarianism in the late 1920s; the Popular Front politics of the 1930s; clandestine struggle against fascism during the late 1930s and 1940s (or, as in the case of the Spanish party, until very recently); and, finally, growing postwar involvement in the structures and norms of parliamentary democracy.

This history, of course, was until very recently shaped by the overwhelming power of the Soviet Union. The cold war years in particular were characterized by a rather strict subordination of the Western parties to the global interests of the USSR; the degree to which the various national Communist parties could adapt to changing indigenous conditions was therefore severely restricted, impeding any real attempt to combine the goals of socialist transformation with even the limited forms of parliamentary democracy. As early as 1956, however, this subordination began to erode. Following the twentieth CPSU Congress and the first stirrings of de-Stalinization in the USSR, the events in Hungary and other Eastern European countries, and PCI leader Palmiro Togliatti's call for "polycentrism" within international Communism, the outlines of a new strategy grounded in Western European experience started to appear. Along with the concept of "peaceful coexistence," the Soviet leadership encouraged the development of "national paths" and the "peaceful road" to socialism. The PCI, under the innovative guidance of Togliatti, seized upon this opportunity to develop—cautiously at first—its version of "advanced democracy" through a strategy of structural reforms. What the PCI envisaged was an organic process of change that abandoned civil insurrection in favor of a gradual internal democratization of the existing state apparatus. Implicit in this vaguely-defined model was a turning away from Leninism as the basis of Western political strategy and a challenging of Soviet hegemony over the world Communist movement—central elements in what would later be called "Eurocommunism." Already by the late 1950s, therefore, the PCI was groping its way toward a critique of the single-party state (as embodied in the historical reality of the USSR and Eastern Europe) for its negation of any semblance of democracy.

Once this process was set in motion, it did not take long for other parties to begin exploring new terrain. For Communist parties in Western Europe and elsewhere, the 1960s became a period of internal crisis and searching: old methods, strategies, and political alliances were questioned, new ones entertained and debated. It was a time of theoretical (not to mention political) doubt and self-reflection, not only among the party leaderships but among the rank-and-file. What emerged was a renewed concern for the role of distinctly national forces and traditions, and—by extension—a commitment to merging the objectives of democracy and socialism.

But the Western parties, for the most part, lacked any coherent or long-range strategy that could make sense of their new predicament and new opportunities; they were essentially limited to tactical, day-to-day responses. In part still confined to Leninist orthodoxy, the parties in fact undertook little in the way of new theoretical departures. This impasse was perhaps most profoundly revealed by the appearance of a large and dynamic new left in countries like Italy and France. Not only did the new left directly challenge the revolutionary pretensions of the Communist parties, it raised vital issues (for example, those of workers' control and feminism) that had been obscured within the Communist tradition. Most significantly, it suggested a vision of socialism that involves an extension of democracy into all spheres of social, economic, and political life.

Yet the crises and disruptions that appeared to immobilize the Western parties in the 1960s produced not degeneration but rather a new cycle of adaptation and rejuvenation. By the 1970s, memberships and popular support were increasing; the Mediterranean parties (notably the PCI) were expanding their political presence within the electoral arena, the trade unions, local government, and even the popular movements such as feminism. Inevitably, such rejuvenation—coinciding with the mounting long-term structural crisis of European capitalism—generated more elaborate theoretical and strategic formulations. The conflicts and tensions of the interregnum ultimately seem to have been resolved in favor of what we can now loosely refer to as "Eurocommunism." What this has meant since the mid-1970s is an even more explicit rejection of Leninism and the Soviet pattern of development; a more positive assessment of pluralist democracy; a reaching out to diverse social forces beyond the traditional proletariat (including Catholicism and the "new middle strata" of technical workers, civil servants, professionals, and intellectuals); and relaxation of internal party discipline associated with "democratic centralism." And it has meant, probably more than anything else, firm emphasis on the viability of elections and parliamentary forms in the transition to socialism.

Whether this strategic orientation actually constitutes an alternative to the limitations of past Marxist approaches remains to be seen. The new adaptation to changing social reality by the Eurocommunist parties promises a more effective socialist presence in the respective countries; at the same time, such adaptation can easily lead to a narrowing of political vision and a moderating of mass involvement that could in the long run have integrative rather than revolutionary consequences. The test of Eurocommunist strategy, of its efforts to intensify the contradictions between democracy and capitalism—assuming that it will sooner or later bring such parties to power—may not arrive for some time. And while the production and legitimation crises of Mediterranean capitalism are almost certain to produce further leftward shifts in France, Italy, and Spain, the long-range impact and fate of the Communist parties within these growing formations is surely difficult to predict.

While the various crises of Mediterranean capitalism persist, it is not certain that they will automatically generate further shifts to the left in France, Italy, and Spain. Nor, even if such shifts occur, are the long-range impact and fate of the Communist parties within a growing left easy to predict. In the few years since the emergence of Eurocommunism as a recognizable tendency, it has become clear that the simple adoption of Eurocommunist positions is no guarantee of political success in even the most narrow electoral terms. In several countries, such as Japan and Mexico, Communist parties that have been identified with such perspectives have played an increasingly important political role, though neither party is close to national power. In France, Italy, and Spain the emergence of Eurocommunism has encouraged electoral advances, but nothing resembling a dramatic victory. Nor are such victories likely to occur in the near future. It may be argued that had these parties not adopted a Eurocommunist strategy they might have suffered major political defeats and entered into processes of rapid decline. Whatever the case, it is clear that formal adoption of Eurocommunist positions is not enough to prevent sectarianism (for example, the PCF's behavior in the 1978 elections), or resolve the dilemmas of participation in regional and local government in the absence of a national power leverage (the PCI).

The test of Eurocommunist strategy, of its efforts to deepen the tensions between democracy and capitalism, may not arrive for some time. Its meaning, consequently, cannot be determined only by watching the short-term electoral results that it yields; a much more comprehensive approach, one which situates such outcomes within the framework of the general direction of the Eurocommunist parties and evaluates other potential strategic approaches, is necessary.

ALTHOUGH EVERY CONTRIBUTOR to this volume agrees that the most visible Eurocommunist initiatives are historically significant, there are major disagreements around the strategic meaning of such initiatives. There is above all the question of whether (and to what extent) the changes we are now observing anticipate some new form or model of revolutionary transformation in the advanced capitalist countries. Many of the essays, with varying emphases, suggest that the Eurocommunist break with past orthodoxy does in fact open the way to a new kind of transition to socialism. Other essays, while skeptical of the strategic and/or tactical choices of particular party leaderships, still entertain hopes for a renewal of party life and theoretical vision commensurate with the needs of revolutionary mobilization. And some of the essays argue that the abandonment of traditional models is likely to lead not to a new and more effective socialist opposition but to an unleashing of the most conservative tendencies within the parties—tendencies that might well transform them into agencies of bureaucratic rationalization or (conditions permitting) social-democratization along the lines of the Northern European systems.

Despite such differences, every treatment rests on the assumption that Eurocommunism is apt to remain a powerful force on the left in the Mediterranean for a considerable period, and that a judgment of its meaning cannot be rendered on the basis of old doctrinal formulas.

The following essays fall into roughly four categories. The first category encompasses those contributions which focus primarily on the *strategic* direction of the parties, within the framework posed by the general problem of the transition to socialism. These include the pieces by George Ross, Joanne Barkan, and Jose Rodriguez-Ibañez. The second type of essay stresses the relationship between the Communist parties and other social and political forces—for example, the women's and ecology movements, elements of the new left, Socialist Parties, national or regional movements, and terrorist organizations. This is the emphasis of the essays by Temma Kaplan, Suzanne Cowan, Andrew Feenberg, Annarita Buttafuoco, and Louise Bealieu and Jonathan Cloud. In the third group are contributions that examine the development of Euro-communism within the *international* context (the global crisis of capitalism, the response of American policy-makers to the left challenge, the fragmentation of the world Communist movement, and European integration). The treatments of Fred Block, Paul Joseph, Louis Menashe, and Diana Johnstone fit into this category. Finally, there are the exploratory efforts to arrive at a general assessment of the historical *meaning* of Eurocommunism, with reference to the concerns of Marxist theory, the development of the Communist tradition, and the political implications for the left in the United States and elsewhere. This is the motif that underlies the concluding essays written by the editors.

The structure of this anthology permits a comprehensive and detailed treatment of a wide variety of topics from a wide range of perspectives. We have chosen not to organize the volume according to specific institutional areas—the relationship of Eurocommunism to the trade unions, the state, regional politics, but rather according to general issues: the problem of strategy, the development of class alliances, the role of international forces. Our hope is that this approach will call attention to questions concerning the overall historical evolution of Eurocommunism. One unavoidable consequence of this editorial strategy is a certain amount of overlap and repetition from essay to essay, though we have sought to reduce this as much as possible.

Stylistically, too, we have tried to encourage diversity over uniformity. Some of the treatments are largely journalistic in format and tone; others are primarily historical, while still others focus on the theoretical dimension. Put another way, each essay combines the various emphases—journalistic, historical, and theoretical—in a distinct fashion. We feel that such diversity helps to broaden political dialogue, and also corresponds more fully to the complexity and openness of the subject matter.

Since Eurocommunism is a relatively new phenomenon, any attempt to establish final conclusions is necessarily premature. Ongoing changes in the class and power structures of the advanced capitalist societies, in the character of the global economy, and within the Marxist tradition itself will no doubt shape this emergent political force in ways that can at present only be dimly envisioned. That is why the trajectory of Eurocommunism cannot be grasped through a doctrinal matrix rooted in the political experiences of earlier phases of capitalist development or even of the recent past. If Eurocommunism now reflects more than anything else the end of the Bolshevik legacy in the West, it also represents a socialism in transition—in which new opportunities will be accompanied by new dilemmas and pitfalls, in which the very fate of the Eurocommunist parties will be at stake.

PART I

STRATEGIC ORIGINS
AND PERSPECTIVES

chapter 1

THE PCF AND THE END
OF THE BOLSHEVIK DREAM

George Ross

MOST OBSERVERS would agree that "Eurocommunism" is one of the great political changes of our time. But there exists little agreement on what Eurocommunism means. Establishment analysts either salute it as the long-awaited conversion of dangerous West European revolutionaries to safe liberalism or see it as an enormously subtle ruse to mislead the naive (a vision of Eurocommunists as wolves in sheep's clothing). On the left, Eurocommunism is seen either as the final corrupting culmination of "revisionism"—Communist surrender to the capitalist *status quo*—or as a welcome rejuvenation of genuine working-class radicalism. In the heat of such complex, and often ideologically-inflated discussions, two important points are often lost, however. The first is that the term "Eurocommunism" is something of a misnomer. There have been parallel changes in most Western European Communist movements in the last two decades. These changes have occurred in Communist parties characterized from the outset by strong national peculiarities. And since, more than anything else, Eurocommunism has meant a new attachment on the part of European Communists to the contours of their own national societies, the result of such change has been even deeper individuation between parties. Secondly, and more importantly, Eurocommunists are but part of the vast process of change involving the left everywhere in the world—that of de-Stalinization. Because de-Stalinization is a *process*, and because it has only just begun in earnest, most attempts to provide a final definition of Eurocommunism are bound to be ephemeral. The essay which follows tries to address these two questions for the French Communist Party. What, broadly speaking, are the particular characteristics of *French* Eurocommunism? And where is French Communism presently situated in the unfolding process of de-Stalinization?

PARTY FORMATION IN FRANCE: LENINISM, STALINISM AND THE BOLSHEVIK DREAM

FRENCH COMMUNISM WAS BORN out of the collapse of the Second International in 1914, the agonizing effects of World War I on the French labor movement (notably the left backlash caused by the collaboration of many of its leaders in the wartime *Union Sacrée*), and the success of the Bolshevik Revolution in Russia in 1917.[1] All of these events, worked out against the background of a French left and labor movements which had never been able to decide between insurrectionary and reformist politics,[2] led to the foundation of the *Parti Communiste Francais* (PCF) and a PCF-oriented labor union organization (the *Confédération Générale du Travail-Unitaire*) in the years 1920-21. Both party and union movement were set up with the backing of a substantial amount of rank-and-file support. (The PCF split from the SFIO, France's social democratic party, with a majority of its Congress delegates, while the CGTU did the same with a bare majority of delegates from the reformist *Confédération Générale du Travail*).

A heterogeneous group of people flocked to the PCF and the CGTU in these early years. To the PCF came pacifists and other objectors to the war, those who had opposed socialist participation in the wartime *Union Sacrée,* anarcho-syndicalists and left social democrats, all surrounding a core of dedicated "Zimmerwaldians" who were rather more in touch with, and committed to, Lenin's practices and intentions.[3] On the union side a similar spectrum of people were attracted to the CGTU, plus numbers of unionists (including many in newer, mass production areas of the economy) who objected to the ever more-pronounced reformism being espoused by the CGT leadership.[4] Forming such amorphous masses into an effective "new type" Leninist party and labor organization was the goal of "Bolshevization" in France, undertaken in the mid-1920s. The core of Bolshevization was the submission of French Communism to Lenin's 21 conditions for affiliation to the Communist International.[5] Among other things, this involved a drastic organizational shift to factory-based cells and away from the geographically based *sections* which had characterized earlier French socialist movements, the introduction of a rigorous "democratic centralism" to govern the internal life of the party, and the insertion of the PCF into the Third International as the French section of the world Communist movement. These changes did create a tightly-disciplined, highly-centralized party composed of toughened, dedicated *cadres* whose loyalty to the International became second nature. However, the harshness of such changes, together with the often-sectarian policies pursued by the PCF during the later 1920s, forced many of the PCF's original sympathizers out of the fold— anarcho-syndicalists, left social democrats, pacifists, virtually everyone but the Leninist "unconditionalists" moved off in other directions from both party and union movement (soon to be followed by the sympathizers of Trotsky). Thus the price of organizational Bolshevization was the relative decline of Communist party and union strength in France.

As processes of organizational change in French Communism, Bolshevization and Stalinization flowed one into the other. One consequence of Stalin's victory over his Soviet opponents in the 1920s was the rapid transformation of PCF democratic centralism into centralism *tout court*. Top-down leadership and authority patterns, modeled on those which came to prevail in the Soviet party, were instituted. Lively debate and discussion about theory and strategy among the rank-and-file, which informed and bound the party leaders, was replaced by a unified decision-making that increasingly centered around a small group of Politburo leaders. Eventually even this system of collegial authoritarianism at the top gave way to the absolute domination of party affairs by the Secretary-General (Maurice Thorez) and his immediate coterie. In such circumstances the primary tasks of ordinary Communists became the enthusiastic ratification and implementation of decisions—in the making of which they had no real part. Autocratic centralism, living off the profound and genuine desire of French workers for a new socialist society, became the PCF's norm in France.

Stalinization also involved a dramatic change in the French party's position in the international Communist movement. Stalin's victory in the Soviet Union brought a strategic shift in the Third International towards the "Socialism in One Country" line. This meant that all of the national constituent parties of the Comintern were henceforth charged with the primordial task of protecting and preserving the Soviet experiment. For the PCF and its mass organizations, this meant relegating national objectives to second place in their order of priorities. This critical transformation was reinforced by parallel changes in the organization of the international movement itself. In Lenin's eyes the International was to be a global front of Communist parties representing an international working class, united by common strategic concerns arrived at through democratic debate. Under Stalin, democratic debate between national parties was replaced by Soviet domination; this meant that with the emergence of fascism in the 1930s, the International increasingly became the vehicle for implementing Soviet foreign policy.[6] Organizationally it meant that the Russians increasingly gained overriding power in the internal lives of Communist parties. As the Secretary-General of the PCF increasingly dominated the deliberations of French Communism, Stalin—through his manipulation of the Comintern—came to dominate the Secretary-General of the PCF! The price the PCF and its mass organizations paid for such capitulation and for the particular policies they adopted (the "class against class" line of the late 1920s and 1930s) was clear. By the early 1930s, the PCF and CGTU had momentarily declined to the status of left-wing sects.

Such organizational change involved the adoption of new perspectives on revolutionary change, prompted again by the Soviet experience. The basic intellectual model for the PCF's class analysis was Lenin's *Imperialism,* as elaborated in Soviet writing and in the strategies of the International.[7] Advanced capitalism was entering the throes of its final crisis, in which the revolutionary working class would ultimately unify under Communist leadership, with intermediary social groups (primarily the *petite bourgeoisie* and small-holding peasants) going over to the side of the workers. The *grande bourgeoisie* presumably would be isolated and a revolutionary situation would ensue. The PCF foresaw a growing, ultimately decisive, class polarization leading to a revolutionary insurrection which could generate a new social order modeled on the Soviet Union. The early PCF handled the major problem in this scenario— namely, its own lack of strength among workers and the persistence of social democratic power—in a characteristic manner. The right-wing social democrats of the SFIO were "agents of the bourgeoisie" whose function was to misdirect the proletariat and stave off inevitable revolution. The policies that followed involved for the most part scathing, often vicious, denunciations of reformists as misleaders and traitors, along with militant attempts to organize the social democratic rank-and-file out from beneath its leadership. What was most striking, obviously, was the PCF's belief that there were no profound social reasons for the continuing reformism of French workers.

The revolutionary scenario which the PCF foresaw at this point was simplicity itself, and was shaped directly by the Soviet events of 1917. When class polarization reached its critical point, bourgeois society would begin to fall apart. In particular, as the legitimacy of bourgeois political institutions was undermined, the ruling class would have more and more difficulty staying in power. In such a chaotic situation the working class and its class allies in intermediary strata, led by the PCF, would be able to "seize power." The party of the working class would then install a single party "dictatorship of the proletariat," through which the bourgeois state would be "smashed" along with counter-revolutionary elements, of all types; it would proceed to create social and political institutions patterned on the Soviet model, including centralized economic planning, state ownership of the means of production, distribution and exchange, and collectivization of agriculture.

From its inception, the PCF conceived of itself as Leninist—as a collective of "professional revolutionaries" whose task it was to intervene in various social processes (in particular those where the working class was involved) in order to hasten and politicize the class polarization of its theoretical vision. First, the PCF insisted that there was only *one* working class in France, which meant that ethnic, occupational, regional, and religious differences were much less important to workers than their common proletarian bonds. Beyond this, it held that the interests of this working class were clearly identifiable. The PCF's most important class-forming lesson followed: the one French working class needed a vanguard—the PCF itself—to articulate working-class problems, the dynamics of imperialism, and the needs and interests of the international workers' movement. Broadly speaking, such interests would be advanced through class polarization and the promotion of alliances with "progressive" classes beyond the workers, the success of a Communist-led insurrection, the establishment of a "dictatorship of the proletariat," and the creation of a Soviet-type society. Super-imposed on these interests, in a somewhat contradictory way, was the duty of the French working class to commit itself to the preservation of socialism in Russia.

THE DILEMMAS OF THE BOLSHEVIK DREAM

THE BOLSHEVIK DREAM—that combination of theoretical, strategic, and organizational outlooks which came to characterize the PCF—was to prove burdensome for French Communism. The sociology beneath the dream was derived from inaccurate perceptions of capitalist development. The revolutionary scenario of insurrectionary politics that formed its core was an inappropriate generalization from Russian events to European conditions. The model for socialist society which it proposed was alien to most French people. The organizational forms of Stalinism employed by the PCF were effective in certain limited ways, but in others they created huge barriers to success. Beyond all of this, however, the PCF—as it matured—began to engage in *reformist* politics. Thus its theory, political rhetoric, model for social change, organizational behavior and actual political practices, taken together, added up to a muddle of contradictions.

France in the years between the two World Wars and in the immediate aftermath of World War II was a troubled and conflicted society. However, it was not a society in the terminal stage of capitalist crisis, as the extrapolations from Lenin's *Imperialism* expected. Rather it was a capitalist society in the throes of a painful, but ultimately successful, transition from its competitive stage to what the Communists themselves were to call, much later, "state monopoly capitalism." French capitalism in this period was thus not self-destructing towards *le grand soir,* but advancing into a new phase of development.[8] For this kind of society a revolutionary scenario borrowed from Soviet experience made very little sense.

Russia in 1917 was in the midst of a catastrophic transition to capitalism from its own peculiar forms of late feudalism. Here there existed three different social worlds, each out of phase with the other, all inserted into the explosive sphere of European imperialism. On the land was a peasantry isolated from urban changes, increasingly battered and bewildered by the incursion of capitalism and its markets into traditional social structures which were ill-prepared to handle them. The cities were enclaves where modern capitalist enterprise of a particularly brutal kind had begun to flourish and where a small but highly militant working class existed in a context of incipient rebellion. Above and out of touch with both of these turbulent social worlds was the political structure of Tsarism which was quite unable to perform, even in untroubled times, the integrative functions necessary to keep such a disjointed and rapidly changing social order from exploding. Beyond this, of course, Russia's destiny had passed out of its control by virtue of its integration into the dynamics of imperialism. In Lenin's famous formulation, Russia was the "weakest link in the imperialist chain." The paroxysm of imperialism in World War I was sufficient to break the chain at its weak point, and the rest of the story is familiar. Workers rose in the cities, peasants rebelled in the countryside, and the bourgeoisie proved too weak to reintegrate Russian society after Tsarism fell. The opportunity thus presented itself for the Bolsheviks to "seize power," which they proceeded to do.

The contrasts between Russia in 1917 and the situation faced by French Communism were obvious. Whereas Russia on the eve of revolution was a society riven by contradictions and falling apart at the seams, capitalist France was relatively well-integrated; capitalism, and the omnipresence of market relations, were not new intrusions into a traditional social order in France but had two full centuries to emerge as a daily frame of reference for elites, workers, peasants, and intermediary groups. Hence a degree of cultural solidarity, missing in Russia, had come to prevail, firmly resting upon the "fetishism of commodities" produced by shared life-situations within the capitalist market. And, as the PCF approached maturity, advancing French capitalism was developing new and vitally important mechanisms for reinforcing such solidarity: extended universal schooling, a popular press, and, ultimately, the electronic media. By the 1930s, the French had grown accustomed to living within capitalism. The immense social energy created by the pain of transition to capitalism had been spent. The French would have to transcend capitalism, if they wished to, from within a functioning capitalist society. The Russian option to refuse capitalism before it had had time to establish its hegemony was no longer present. Moreover, the French state functioned at least to the point where social order could be maintained and a necessary minimum of legitimacy established.

Beyond all this, the development of French social classes did not conform to the PCF's theories. In some very abstract sense there *was* one working class in France, but the abstraction was at a very high level. Divisions within the working class were real, and they had definite behavioral consequences, whatever the PCF thought. In addition, new categories of the "middle class" were emerging to fit the professional, technical and bureaucratic needs of the new monopoly order. As the old intermediary strata were threatened by change, newer ones arose which seemed, initially, to be the beneficiaries of this change; rather than becoming simpler and more polarized, French class structure was in fact becoming more complex. More important, the differential rewards and promises of capitalist expansion—along with the emergence of new intermediary groups—gave social democracy a firm anchoring, even during a difficult time of transition. In contrast to what the PCF believed, social democratic reformism in France was not simply a question of "misleadership" but had deep social roots.

Sociological observations provide only one key to understanding the question of social democracy. One form of cultural solidarity which united a majority of the French (and even segments of the working class) was a belief in the principles of democracy. France, after all, was the country of successive bourgeois democratic republics: 1789, 1848, 1871. It was also a society in which democratic changes had been won by repeated struggle conducted by coalitions of workers and middle-class groups. Even if it was evident that certain sectors of the French ruling class pledged only the most formal allegiance to this great national democratic heritage, the heritage ran deep nonetheless. In its class-forming activities the PCF could insist all it wanted that "bourgeois democracy" was a sham. General belief in parliamentarism, electoral and other conflict between contending political parties, civil liberties, and free and open discussion was a vital part of French life. *La France Republicaine* was located not only in important sectors of the working class but also in much of the traditional *petit bourgeoisie* and in the "new middle classes."[9]

Try as it might to expose "bourgeois democracy" by contrasting it to "proletarian democracy" which, it claimed, existed in the Soviet Union (and which it proudly advertised within the PCF itself), the PCF leadership ran up against a stone wall as soon as it reached out beyond its own working class constitutencies. However conscious many French people were that existing Republican institutions were more the promise than the actuality of democracy, they also realized the drastic shortfall between promise and performance in the "proletarian democracy" vaunted by the PCF. Here it was a question of simple cost-benefit analysis. While the PCF successfully persuaded certain large fractions of the working class (beginning in the 1930s) that the benefits of proletarian democracy outweighed its costs, other groups of workers and the middle strata reached different conclusions. However imperfect, French democracy had some important virtues; its very existence made it theoretically possible for some of the imperfections to be removed through further struggle. Against these considerations was the denial of elementary civil liberties in the Soviet Union, its lack of any open political conflict, its rule by a party which claimed to represent the working class but over which this same class had little influence, its periodic resort to bloody purges of opponents, its erection of Stalin to demigod status, and so on. To many French people, then, the price to be paid for the "proletarian democracy" advocated by the PCF was too high.

All of these considerations led to the same conclusion. French society was not going to follow the Soviet scenario. The types of extreme social polarization and dislocation that created openings for insurrection were not likely in France. France was an *advancing* capitalist society where revolutionaries could not count on the emergence of chaotic social contradictions to substitute for a revolutionary politics appropriate to French social relations themselves. Beyond this, many French people (including large numbers of workers) had too much to lose in the kind of revolution that the PCF anticipated. The PCF needed, but did not have, a theory based on the realities of advanced European capitalism.

POLITICAL SCHIZOPHRENIA: BOLSHEVIK DREAMS AND REFORMIST POLITICS

EVEN WEIGHED DOWN by such liabilities, the PCF was able to count new successes beginning in the 1930s. Behind such successes lay a tactical shift of the party (and Comintern) away from "class against class" towards the "United Front Against Fascism." Prompted mainly by the Soviet leadership's belated recognition of the Nazi threat and a desire to use the Comintern to forward Soviet anti-Nazi diplomatic goals, this shift nonetheless proved advantageous domestically to the PCF. In the complex of events surrounding the French Popular Front of the mid-1930s the PCF made great gains in membership, electoral support and trade union strength, at which point it abandoned the "dual union" approach to the labor movement and collapsed the CGTU into the CGT.[10] From a beleaguered, if dedicated, sect, the PCF became a force to be reckoned with, acquiring a substantial working-class base. The effects of the Nazi-Soviet pact of 1939 were momentarily catastrophic, but the party's ultimate shift towards the Resistance in 1941 (in which it became the major component) allowed it to capitalize on popular mobilization around Liberation. The PCF thus emerged from World War II even stronger than it had from the Popular Front. In the immediate postwar years it was the strongest party in France electorally; it attained its largest membership yet, and it wrested control over the CGT from the reformists who split to form their own union in 1947 in response to the cold war.[11]

The fact behind such successes was that the PCF, while abandoning neither its neo-Bolshevik theory and rhetoric nor its Stalinized internal organizational life, had begun to practice a radical reformist politics somewhat more in touch with the realities of French society. The party did not give up its objective of a socialist transformation of France; rather, its adjusted strategic vision focused on promoting a cumulative series of structural reforms that would progressively break the back of French capitalism. At the core of this new politics lay the systematic courting of allies to the PCF's immediate right—namely, socialists and left liberals. To woo such new friends, the PCF first had to accept their right to exist and stop denouncing them as "agents of the bourgeoisie," "social traitors" and the like. It had also to uncover issues of common concern around which a solid alliance might be constructed. In doing this, the PCF was obliged to present itself more moderately. The party became more "French," adopting the slogans and symbols of Jacobin Republicanism. It gave more respect to the institutions and procedures of "bourgeois democracy," seeing in them incomplete popular victories within an on-going class struggle—victories to be deepened and broadened through socialism. The PCF even assumed a nationalist character, contesting the claims of the right to a monopoly on national virtue by asserting that the left more truly represented French national interests than a bourgeoisie which had been willing to make an ignominious peace with fascism.

The PCF's new united frontism, which originated in the Popular Front period, became a full-fledged new strategy for socialist change in France during the immediate post-World War II years. Henceforth, at least in the eyes of the PCF, the construction of socialism would be a two-stage process. The first stage involved the promotion of a united front alliance in which the PCF would deploy its organizational strength to mobilize the masses and persuade potential allies to unite around a program of structural reforms. The next task was to promote the electoral success of this new front, with the aim of bringing it to power. This would be followed by the most difficult moment of the first stage— the implementation of the front's program of reforms in such a way as to shift the balance of power to the left while at the same time increasing the PCF's own power and hegemony within the left. The first stage, then, was a dedicated reformism designed to lead to a more thorough-going radicalism of stage two. Carrying out stage one successfully would make revolution a concrete possibility. Thus, if during the first stage the PCF put its Bolshevik uniform temporarily in the closet and decked itself out in the tricolor raiment of the *sans-culottes*, it was with the hope of being able to do a quick change back to Bolshevik clothes during stage two.

Those familiar with French events up the mid-1960s know that the PCF's united frontism rarely progressed beyond the earliest steps of stage one. For reasons to be discussed, allies were hard to come by, and where they existed they tended to part company with the Communists long before any system-transforming changes could be initiated.* It is worth noting, however, that those brief periods, when even the most tentative united front arrangements came into being, still stand as the *only* moments of significant social reform in recent French history. In the Popular Front period French workers won paid vacations, the 40-hour week, a number of changes at the factory level, and several structural reforms in the economy. And in the 1944-47 period several important nationalizations occurred, an advanced social security program (with social insurance and health care provisions) was created, the statute covering French civil servants was radically redrawn, shop committees for worker representaion were set up, and a subtle apparatus for economic planning (which later proved of vital importance in the resuscitation of what looked to be a moribund capitalism) was establish-ed.[12]

POLICY VICTORIES and increases in PCF strength notwith-standing, the party's newfound radical reformist politics were riven by profound contradictions. In the first place, the PCF's fervent public desire for allies and its real behavior toward such allies (potential or actual) tended to work at cross purposes. This was so because the PCF fully intended to use the political and social contiguity of any concluded alliances to organize a large part of its allies' rank-and-file support out from under its leaders and into the PCF's own fold (an intention which the PCF put into practice with great success in finally winning hegemony over the CGT in 1944-47). The PCF wanted allies, in part, in order to *use* them, to undermine their strength and, ultimately, to discard them. Since other forces on the French left and center were able to understand this, the PCF found it difficult to make firm united front allies (indeed, Socialist and Radical knowledge of PCF intentions served to encourage

*Within the Popular Front itself, the Socialists moved quickly to the right once the mobilization of 1936 had subsided, leaving the PCF isolated. In the 1944-47 period the Socialists did not agree to an alliance with the PCF alone, preferring always a tripartite arrangement that included Christian Democrats as a hedge against Communist pressure. And, of course, the Communists were literally thrown out of the postwar government and into isolation that would not end until the early 1970s.

both of these groups to pursue analogous goals towards the PCF itself, with the purpose of neutralizing the Communists and using them as a *force d'appoint*). Knowledge of the PCF's longer-term intentions did nothing to assuage the wariness of united front allies either. Here the PCF's continuing "insurrectionary" rhetoric and its adherence to the Soviet model were strong deterrents to groups well aware of the fates which the "party of the working class" reserved for them in a Soviet-model "dictatorship of the proletariat."

The PCF also geared its domestic goals tightly to the objectives of Soviet foreign policy, a practice which made united frontism even more complicated and contradictory.* Because of its devotion to Soviet diplomacy, the PCF was obliged to pursue two separate strategic and tactical lines simultaneously. On the one hand it promoted a united front reformist project for domestic change in France. On the other it attempted to use its domestic influence over other political forces to shape the international posture of France in ways which furthered Soviet international goals. And as perhaps *the* most loyal member of the Comintern (and later the Cominform), the PCF participated in the international Communist movement with deadly seriousness. Consequently it was the goal of supporting Soviet foreign policy which was usually most prominent in the strategic calculations of the PCF. All of this placed actual and potential united front allies in a doubly unpleasant situation. If they decided to collaborate with the PCF they risked being colonized and swallowed up by the Communists domestically, while at the same time being manipulated into serving the international purposes of the Soviet Union.

Thus united frontism, which seemed at first sight to be a sensible recognition of French reality, was really a genuine muddle for the PCF. The potentially conciliatory effects of radical reformist politics were nullified by a whole series of factors. Stalinist organizational practices within the PCF and its mass organizations made the party's "presentation of self" distasteful. Its obvious intention to subvert allies and reforms to its own ends hardly promoted solid alliances. Its continuing

---

*During the Popular Front period, the PCF's relationship to the Comintern led the party to gear its domestic goals to the promotion of French participation in a diplomatic coalition of "bourgeois democratic" states against Hitler, with the hope of deflecting Hitler's attention away from military action against the USSR. That the PCF's efforts failed takes nothing away from the energy they committed to this task. In the Liberation and postwar periods the PCF's united frontism was directed first toward promoting the war effort of the Grand Alliance and then toward preserving this alliance into the postwar era. This policy also failed, even though once again the PCF tried very hard to make it suceed. Similar analyses would be apporopriate during the 1940s and 1950s.

use of insurrectionary rhetoric, allegiance to insurrectionary goals, and unswerving commitment to Soviet-style socialism contradicted its re- formist practices and further scared allies. Finally, the strategic subor- dination of the PCF's domestic goals to Soviet foreign policy had two effects. As we have just noted, it provided allies and potential allies with further reasons, if they were needed, to mistrust the party leadership. Secondly, the thrust of Soviet foreign policy often ran directly counter to that of PCF domestic strategy. Thus in both the Popular Front and post-Liberation periods the PCF's allegiance to Soviet foreign policy objectives prompted the party to moderate its domestic reformist scenario and limit popular mobilization for change. Later, in the cold war years, PCF devotion to Soviet foreign policy led to the party's isolation and contributed to the virtual disenfranchisement of its members and supporters. Thus, given the enormous *a priori* difficulties which any serious reformist strategy inevitably must face, the PCF's contradictory conversion to reformism in the 1930s was doomed from the start.

THE PCF'S CONVERSION TO EUROCOMMUNISM

THE PCF'S LIFE after its eviction from the government in 1947 and during the cold war was not easy. The party and its mass organizations were isolated until the early 1960s. The PCF's membership declined from a high of one million in 1946 to less than 200,000 in the late 1950s. The CGT membership (five million in 1946) declined to 1,500,000 in the same period. From its brief moment as *le premier parti de Fance* in 1945 (with 26 percent of the vote), the party's support at the polls dipped under 20 percent in the first years of the Fifth Republic. The greater part of this resulted from an incredible onslaught of anti-Communism during the cold war and would have occurred whatever course the party chose to pursue. Some was brought on by the party itself, however. Its Zhdanovism in the realm of culture and ideology (Zhdanov was the Soviet cultural czar who, with Stalin's blessing, dictated a caricature of socialist realism to the world Communist movement) was zealous to a fault during the cold war, a fact that won the PCF no new friends and created sectarian habits which lingered for many years.[13] Its attempts to use the CGT and the labor movement as political clubs to oppose American foreign policy— attempts that often denied the specific rhythms of the French labor market—weakened the ability of labor to resist a process of economic modernization being carried on, to a great extent, at its expense.[14] Its theoretical life grew poverty-stricken in the extreme. During the deep cold war years, all of the old theoretical certainties of the interwar Comintern were upheld with addenda from the genial Stalin himself. Imperialism was staving off class polarization in its homelands by warmongering, with the ultimate goal of destroying the socialist camp. The entire Communist movement had but one duty, that of opposing imperialist foreign policy whatever the consequences of such oppostion for the domestic positions of specific Communist parties such as the PCF. As the threat of war receded in the mid-1950s, the PCF's own genial leader Maurice Thorez delivered some of the more inappropriate theoretical pronouncements in all of socialist history. Thorez claimed, at a moment when French capitalism was beginning to provide substantial and regular increases in per capita income to workers, that the working class was undergoing ever-greater relative and absolute "pauperization."* The complete implausibility of these views did not prevent their being used as the PCF's guiding light for understanding French social dynamics into the early 1960s.

The inner party life and international attachments of the PCF proceeded along similar late Stalinist lines. The growing insecurity of the Thorez leadership led to periodic high-level purges conducted in a completely undemocratic way (for example, the Marty-Tillon and Lecoeur *affaires* in the earlier 1950s and the Servin-Casanova purification in 1960-61).[15] As the period wore on the PCF's unswerving devotion to Soviet foreign activities proved quite costly, both inside and outside the party. When Soviet policies led to uprisings in Eastern Europe, to which the Russians responded with political and military intervention, the PCF did not flinch in its support. Indeed, along at least one dimension, the PCF proved itself even less flexible than the Russians themselves. When, after the 20th Soviet Party Congress in 1956, "de-Stalinization" became the order (or at least the slogan) of the day throughout much of the Communist movement, the PCF responded by simply denying for an intolerably long time that Khrushchev's "secret speech" on Stalin's crimes was authentic. Beyond this, Thorez actively threw his support to Khrushchev's collegial opponents both in the USSR and international Communism in order to block the processes of de-Stalinization which had begun.[16]

The irony of all this was that, except for the worst cold war years of 1947-1953, the PCF maintained its general commitment to united front reformism. Indeed its eager search for allies in the post-1954 period

---

*The "pauperization" articles appeared in 1955 at a time when the French economy was beginning to demonstrate its postwar vitality. Apparently they were meant to counteract the influence of Pierre Mendes-France and his reformist "modernism." Mendes-France went down to defeat, but the pauperization analysis lived on. The continued reliance of the PCF on a theory which ran so obviously against fact and common sense was a very good index of the party's internal paralysis in the last years of the Thorez leadership.

(when chances for the left seemed good) led it to underwrite momentarily the launching of the bloody Algerian war.* Despite its eagerness to find united front friends, however, it was unable to persuade anyone to its immediate right to join in preventing the demise of the Fourth Republic and General de Gaulle's accession to power in 1958. In fact, its decision in 1958 to support a Republic that it opposed for so long and with such vituperation left its most loyal electoral and trade union supporters completely behind, and the party suffered its worst electoral setbacks since the war.

With the 1960s came the beginnings of PCF Eurocommunism. Internationally, the PCF's hands were greatly freed by the conversion of the Soviet Union to a foreign policy of peaceful coexistence and *détente*. With this, Soviet interest in mobilizing the world Communist movement to devote its energies to promoting Soviet diplomatic success declined. Moreover, the Russians' power to coordinate international Communism was progressively reduced as first the Chinese and then the European Communists insisted on greater foreign policy autonomy. At the same time, the prestige of the Soviet model declined precipitously. Western parties belatedly discovered the lack of democracy and civil liberties along with the economic shortcomings of the Soviet system. The left in the third world, inspired by the Chinese, Cuban and Indochinese examples, also began to look for a socialism that better suited agrarian societies. The Soviet system ceased to stand as the exclusive blueprint for the construction of socialism. Instead, specifically indigenous paths to socialism adapted to the particularities of national societies became the order of the day, even in France.

New domestic circumstances leavened PCF change as well by greatly enhancing possibilities for alliance politics. The Fifth Republic, which had arrived so disastrously for the PCF in 1958, proved to be a blessing in disguise. By the early 1960s it was becoming quite clear that French politcal life would be dominated by a center-right majority around the Gaullist party for some time to come. This meant, in turn, that the "Third Force" center left-center right coalition politics between social democrats, Radicals and Christian Democrats which had characterized the Fourth Republic (and isolated the PCF) was no longer possible. Gaullism promoted left-right polarization. The Socialists, in

---

*In an attempt to woo the Socialists to the left after the 1956 legislative elections (which strengthened the left), the PCF voted "special powers" for the Algerian Minister-Resident—a vote that legitimated the vicious policy of repression in Algeria that followed. To the PCF's credit, it must be said that it consistently opposed the Algerian War and that this momentary action was one of the party's few opportunist slips.

particular, found their habitual Fourth Republic road to power blocked by the new situation. They were therefore faced with a choice between *attentisme*—waiting for the Gaullist formation to fall apart and new prospects for the center-left to open up—and united front cooperation with the PCF. The PCF sensed the Socialists' dilemma very early in the 1960s (beginning with the end of the Algerian War in 1962) and engaged itself in what became a dedicated quest for a new united front. The Socialists, hedging their bets, moved only very slowly towards a *Union de la Gauche*. However, beginning with the May-June 1968 explosion and continuing to the present, the PCF's united front drive was dramatically reinforced by the emergence of the first major economic crisis of French capitalism since World War II. With political and economic circumstances favoring the success of PCF policies, the Communists were propelled toward significant changes of doctrine and behavior in order to prove their worth and reliability as allies.[17]

ONE OF THE more important areas of Eurocommunist change within the PCF has been that of theory. Here the old Leninist-Stalinist perspective which posited drastic class polarization in the terminal agony of imperialism leading to an insurrectionary situation was jettisoned, replaced by a vision that recognizes the specificity of "state monopoly capitalism" and remaps the PCF's class analysis of French society in ways that give new sociological support to radical reformist politics.[18] The new theory abandons the primacy of progressive working class immiseration and the scenario of social chaos and a "seizure of power" by the "party of the working class." Instead it focuses on the economic domination of French society by the monopoly sector, the use of state power by the "monopoly caste" to stave off declining profit rates and the differential effects of both processes on various groups in the French population. Stress is placed on the relative social costs paid by different strata for monopoly rule and the barriers monopoly rule places in the way of genuine advance towards abundance, justice and liberation which the "raw materials" of French society now make theoretically possible. State monopoly capitalism analysis is meant to open up the prospect of a socialism specific to a highly advanced productive system, a socialism of wealth and freedom rather than one that stresses socialist accumulation."

In the new social class map of the state monopoly capitalist analysis it is, of course, the productive industrial working class that pays the highest price in terms of exploitation and injustice. State monopoly capitalism produces the greatest change, however, for various intermediary strata. For those professional, technical and bureaucratic employees usually labelled "new middle class" (although the PCF does not use this term), general submission to *salariat* subjects them to processes of severe wage compression and work rationalization as the monopoly sector seeks to cut overhead costs. Although most such employees are not strictly speaking, workers (they do not produce surplus value), they do thereby come to share certain basic life-situations and dilemmas with the working class. As part of the "collective worker" of advanced capitalism, some parts of the "new middle classes" are being proletarianized.* It is generally true of such intermediary groups, whether they are becoming proletarianized or not, that older "middle class" notions of social prestige and status are becoming ever more difficult to sustain. "Independent producer" middle strata (the old *petite bourgeoisie* and small-holding peasants) suffer from the imposition of industrial models of organization and work in the spheres of commerce and circulation, as the monopoly sector tries to cut the overhead costs of distribution. Finally, according to the PCF, even small and middle-sized capitalist groups are negatively affected by state monopoly capitalism.

From all of this there emerges a new picture of class dynamics in French society. State monopoly capitalism is producing a potential coalition of the working class, new and old intermediary strata, and certain elements of the non-monopoly bourgeoisie; the boundaries between workers and middle strata are becoming less dramatic. The monopoly bourgeoisie and its defenders are increasingly isolated. Despite growing social contiguity between aggrieved groups, however, each one has its own specific perceptions of its situation and its own interests. What is new, in the PCF's eyes, is the general focus of these perceptions and interests on the need to transcend monopoly capitalism. State monopoly capitalism thus makes possible the creation of an anti-monopoly social front based on the highest common denominator of reformist enthusiasm shared by the groups involved. The PCF's practical task then becomes promoting anti-monopoly sentiment in general and the forging of a formal political alliance around a specific program of anti-monopoly reforms. This was, of course, the meaning of the PCF's constant prodding towards a Common Program of the Left throughout the 1960s and its agreement to such a program in June, 1972 with the Socialists and Radicals.[19]

---

*"Collective worker" is an expression borrowed from Marx to designate the value-producing unit created in an industry characterized by a highly-advanced division of labor—one in which engineers, technicians, line workers, transportation workers, and other occupational groups combine to produce commodities.

THEORETICAL CHANGE and doctrinal modifications went hand-in-hand. As the development of a French variety of Euro-communism progressed, a whole series of formerly untouchable dogmas about socialism and how to get there were dropped. In the early 1960s the PCF initiated this process by advancing the notion that a one-party dictatorship of the proletariat was an "abusive generalization" from the Soviet experience, suggesting that a multi-party transition to socialism was desirable for France. The party then added that, in all likelihood, any French transition to socialism would be peaceful, i.e., that the insur-rectionary perspective of earlier years was no longer to be taken seriously. Next came agreement that not only the transition to socialism but socialism itself, would flourish best in a multi-party system. Later, in the 1970s, when the *Union de la Gauche* had become a serious electoral threat, the party declared that it would fully respect democratic rules should a left government lose its electoral majority—i.e., should it step down in such an eventuality. Then in the mid-1970s the PCF issued a series of ringing declarations about its commitment to specific civil and economic liberties, particularly in a socialist France.[20]

The PCF's 22nd Congress in 1976—at which the party aban-doned its committment to the need for a Dictatorship of the Proletariet—marked a turning point in this transformation.[21] In itself, state monopoly capitalism analysis had asserted only that the social conditions existed out of which an anti-monopoly, multi-class alliance might be created that, in turn, might be prodded towards socialism. Moreover, all the various doctrinal changes up to the 22nd Congress amounted to a rather incoherent patchwork, united only by the PCF's desire to become a more plausible united front partner. However welcome and necessary this was, it did not really bring the party up to date in a France where strong demands for economic and political decentralization were being made, where workers' control, women's liberation, and strivings for a freer cultural life were as prominent as direct anti-monopoly protest. The 22nd Congress brought a new approach that, at least theoretically, promised to make the PCF's new identity more coherent. State monopoly capitalism had reached a critical point, according to the Congress, where its further evolution was in direct conflict with the development of democracy in France. French society therefore faced a profound "crisis of democracy," with capitalism and democracy in sharp opposition; it followed that the struggle to extend and deepen democracy would undermine state monopoly capitalism.

The 22nd Congress thus definitively cut the PCF's ties with Soviet theory. Promoting democracy—not setting up classic Soviet-style insti-tutions—was the road to socialism. Unfortunately for the PCF, at least in the short run, this important change in direction occurred mainly in the realm of high principles. What the "crisis of democracy" position signified in less general terms was left to time and experience for elaboration. This meant that the party, as it approached the critical 1978 elections, was quite unclear about a number of things. In the realm of theory, for example, the party had abandoned a fully-articulated theory of the transition to socialism and substituted for it only the vaguest of good democratic intentions. In the absence of further clarification about the "crisis of democracy" and its connection to the transition, French Communists were left in great confusion about the theory of the state. On a more mundane level, the tactical meaning of the "crisis of democracy" was unclear. Did it mean simply that the party should begin to open itself to new issues which up to 1976 it had shied away from—*autogestion*, feminism, ecology and so on? Or did it mean that the party should continue along pre-1976 lines, advocating economic democracy, changes in political institutions, and increased civil liberties? The months after 1976 brought little clarification. Both the PCF and CGT, especially as the 1978 elections dawned, found new sympathies for *autogestion*, and there was greater discussion of lifestyle and cultural issues among PCF members (many party sections created *"commissions feminines"* to debate feminist issues relevant to internal party life). But there were no drastic changes in directions.

In this context, the PCF's turn towards open criticism of Soviet society and government should not have been surprising. The Euro-communist PCF had to begin ridding itself of the burdens of its earlier attachment to the Soviet model. By 1975 the PCF was as quick as any other party to condemn most Soviet political aberrations. Thus when Western television showed scenes from a Soviet labor camp for political dissidents in 1975, the PCF, rather than following its earlier course of denying such film's validity, issued a public statement abhorring the USSR's treatment of dissenters. Since then, on the many occasions when the Russians have taken brutal steps to eradicate internal opposition, the PCF has often protested. Indeed, by June 1978 during the Scharansky-Ginzburg trials in Moscow, the PCF actively encouraged its militants to participate in public demonstrations over which the party had no control whatsoever (a significant departure from earlier practices). Even thorny issues of the Soviet past have been treated recently with much greater candor. When French television broadcast Costa Gavras' film, *Confession*, which represents the Slansky trials in Czechoslovakia with great frankness, Jean Kanapa (the PCF's foreign affairs specialist at the time) acknowledged the veracity of the film and thoroughly deplored the events of Stalin's last years. And while the PCF has not yet completely faced the responsibilities which it bears itself in acquiescing to Stalinist brutalities, there have been some tentative steps in this direction.

In foreign policy, however, the PCF's leave-taking from the Soviet Union has been more complicated. In recent years the PCF leadership has assumed a front-line position in rejecting Soviet attempts to impose political lines on Western European Communist parties. This was most true in the period leading to the 1976 East Berlin Conference of European communist parties. Here, when the CPSU tried to gather in the threads of a decentralizing Communist movement and reassert its control, the PCF directly confronted the Soviets and frustrated their intentions.[22] On a number of lesser questions where conflicts developed between Soviet foreign policy goals and the domestic interests of the PCF, the party stood its ground. And on certain general issues of Soviet policy, where CPSU initiatives seriously compromised the PCF's position in France (as in the Soviet armed intervention in Czechoslavakia in 1968), the PCF has not hesitated to condemn Soviet actions. But the general picture here is murky. Where the vital interests of the PCF are threatened by Soviet behavior, the French party will now refuse to sacrifice its domestic strategy for the alleged greater good of the socialist camp. Beyond this, however, the PCF's new position is much less one of disavowing Soviet goals than of simple avoidance of open interest in them. The PCF is no longer strategically subordinate to the Soviet Union in the realm of foreign affairs, but there is still little evidence that the PCF generally differs from the Russians on overall foreign policy orientation.

THE PCF HAS CHANGED significantly. The party has abandoned its beliefs that the Soviet experience could or should be replicated in France. It has dropped its neo-Leninist catastrophe theories and its rhetoric of insurrectionary politics. Party ideology no longer holds that the domestic pursuits of French Communism should be subordinated to the imperatives of Soviet foreign policy. Eurocommunism, in its specially tailored French variant, is a reality. At its core are a new radical reformist theory, a refined united frontism, a new national identity, and a degree of real independence within the international Communist movement. The Bolshevik dream, which was at times a nightmare for the PCF (and for its opponents), is no more. Now French Eurocommunism must be evaluated on its own terms. What are its prospects, then?

THE DILEMMAS OF UNITED FRONTISM: THE 1978 ELECTIONS

THE PCF'S EUROCOMMUNIST changes render the party's radical reformist united front strategy more feasible. With certain exceptions the PCF can now pursue its domestic goals without being stymied in advance by the contradictions that beset it earlier. To say this, however, is only to indicate that the PCF is now in a better position to confront the difficulties involved in pursuing a thorough-going reformist strategy. Eurocommunism does not remove these difficulties; it simply makes them clearer.

The PCF's modern united frontism is a complex strategy. In its initial stages it involves promoting alliances between groups and parties all of whom are interested in some change, but few of whom are interested in thorough change. It is the PCF's primary task at this point to persuade its allies to go as far as they can be prodded towards such change without jeopardizing the alliance. At the same time, to ensure that this initial stage of reform does not lead simply to social innovations which will strengthen French capitalism, but rather open possibilities for greater change, the PCF must see to it that reforms strengthen those forces in French politics and society committed to further change. In part this means advancing reforms so that they genuinely pay off for major social groups in France in order that the contrast between the pre- and post-reform situations will lead to mass pressure for further change. In part it also means achieving reforms that enable those political and social organizations most dedicated to greater change—which the PCF sees as itself and its mass organizations—to emerge strengthened. In other words, the PCF view of the first stage of united frontism is that it should ideally strengthen the left and broaden PCF power within the French left. Success at this is the *sine qua non* for passage to the second stage of united frontism, when more thorough-going change towards socialism becomes possible.

The first stage of the PCF's scenario can be understood better by references to the party's recent activities. Throughout much of the early and mid-1960s the party devoted most of its energy to the task of persuading the Socialists to collaborate with the PCF, primarily around electoral occasions (the 1962 and 1967 General Elections and the 1965 Presidential campaign of Francois Mitterrand). At this early point the party was mainly concerned with laying the groundwork for alliance, developing habits of unified action, and initiating discussion about program. After the May 1968 crisis, which temporarily re-divided the left but ultimately brought Communists and Socialists closer, the party pushed more strongly for a broad agreement on the left around a full program of structural reform. This step was completed in 1972 with the Common Program, in which one finds a catalogue of specific measures to which the *Union de la Gauche* pledged itself in the event of a left electoral victory. Here the core of PCF structural reformism becomes clear. The Program proposes a long list of social welfare-type measures which, taken together, would lead to a considerable redistribution of income. To sustain such a redistribution economically, the Program then proposes a series of nationalizations of finance and industry (most of French banking, plus nine industrial groups, all of which are virtual monopolies and all of which are of strategic economic importance). Then to ensure that the power of the left to mobilize popular support will be enhanced, a series of reforms promoting greater democracy and allowing workers (through their unions, primarily) greater power within firms is proposed. After 1972 the PCF's goal was to promote the electoral success of the left, to solidify commitment to the Common Program, and to increase the strength of the PCF within the left. As is now well known, the PCF succeeded in the first endeavor but did much less well in the second and third of these tasks.

As recent events have underlined, the PCF's conversion to Euro-communism has not removed the many pitfalls of such a radical reformist scenario. The core of everything for the PCF lies in persuading other political forces to promote more, and different, changes than they really want, at least initially. The PCF must lead its allies, each with their own projects for change (with which the PCF may disagree) to the point where they will accept changes of the kind the PCF desires. The PCF's new united frontism, therefore, ultimately comes down to a conflicted relationship. Either the PCF has the political skill and resources to persuade its allies to do things which *a priori* they don't want, or these same allies will succeed in using the PCF to support their own projects. If the first course is followed, then a radical reformist road to socialism may open up in France. If the second course is pursued—i.e., if the PCF fails—the united frontism will lead to left management of French capitalism.

Illustrative of this are the stormy days of fall and winter 1977-78. The PCF had undertaken its modern united front offensive with the goal of promoting left unity while simultaneously strengthening the party within the left, enabling it therefore, to be the driving force in a left government. As the *Union de la Gauche* progressed towards the critical 1978 elections, its success was evident. The left stood a good chance of winning. However, left union proved to be much less a success for PCF strategy. The left increased its strength within France, but the PCF did not increase its strength commensurately within the left. Such a situation was very dangerous for the PCF, as it turned out. Were the left to have come to power in 1978, the Socialists would have been firmly in control of a left government. Beyond this, the change in relative strength within the left encouraged an evolution within the Socialist Party of which the PCF could not approve. From its beginnings in the early 1970s, the new Socialist Party had been an unstable amalgam of different political tendencies grafted onto the old French Socialist Party (the SFIO) which had declined after World War II into a group of social democratic careerists mainly interested in coalition-mongering to obtain ministerial posts. What the PCF had hoped for was a decisive shift to the left in the new PS towards some form of genuine socialism. Such hopes were not unfounded, since some of the forces at work within the PS were truly leftist (primarily the CERES group—*the Centre d'Etudes et Recherches Socialistes*—which built a powerful rank-and-file organization, particularly in Paris) and the very fact of left union put a number of older social democratic leaders on the defensive. The electoral dynamic of left unity that favored the socialists, however, tended also to strengthen social democratic tendencies within the PS, much to the PCF's dismay. As the 1978 elections approached (and particularly after the 1977 Socialist Congress), the Socialist left was isolated and the Mitterrand leadership, backed by centrist and social democratic elements, reigned supreme. For the PCF, this translated into what the Communists came to call a Socialist "turn to the right." Socialist leaders began to retreat from the positions they had earlier taken in the Common Program. Simultaneously they began to talk about further increasing their electoral strength at the expense of the PCF itself.

The dangers in the 1978 electoral situation were thus clear to the PCF. "Strengthening the left, strengthening the PCF within the left" had failed. The left had become strong enough to make a claim on power, but the PCF had not increased its own strength commensurately. This would have given the PS considerably more resources than the Communists once the left came to power. There were also disturbing signs that the Socialists might well start eating away at the PCF's own electoral base were things to continue as they had.[23] Hence, as the electoral period approached, the PCF had to face two delicate dilemmas. How could it avoid becoming a simple support group for the Socialists if the left came to power? How could it avoid losing part of its traditional electoral base to Socialist raids?

The PCF answered the first dilemma—that of disequilibrium between it and the PS within the *Union de la Gauche*—by opting to force the Socialists to agree on policy for a future left government before the 1978 elections. The occasion for this was the long-scheduled meeting among the left parties to "update" the Common Program that began in the summer of 1977. In these "actualization" talks the PCF stuck firmly to its programmatic guns; major income redistributions were necessary and could only be economically sustained if the structural reforms proposed in the 1972 Common Program (primarily nationalizations) were carried out to the fullest. The Socialists, in contrast, had actually retreated from the position on redistribution advanced by the 1972 Program and desired a much narrower range of nationalizations than the PCF. The logic of the Socialists' position was clear. They were more interested in using a left political victory to provide the government with more effective power over investment decisions in order to re-launch economic growth than in using such power to initiate a breakthrough towards socialism. The Socialist leaders justified their new timidity by pointing to the economic crisis that a left government would have to face. To the PCF, such explanations only increased suspicions that the Socialist leadership's real goal was to "manage capitalist crisis." The two parties also disagreed profoundly over foreign and defense policies, with the PCF more "nationalist" and the Socialists more "European" and "Atlantic." Given such deep disagreements, along with the PCF's relatively weak bargaining position, the Communists had only one major weapon for achieving compromise with the Socialists before the 1978 elections—the threat of disrupting pre-electoral left unity. When it became clear that the Socialists would, under no circumstances, accede to PCF demands, the Communist leadership was pushed to employ this weapon. On the night of September 22, 1977, only a few months before the elections, left unity came to an end.

The 1978 electoral campaign unfolded in the shadow of this disunity. PCF attacks on the Socialists for their "right turn" grew increasingly brutal as the weeks wore on, reminding many observers of the "class against class" and cold war periods when Communists spared nothing to excoriate the evil "right-wing Social Democrats." The Communist purpose was, of course, to escalate such attacks in order to raise political costs to the Socialists for not conceding programmatic points, but the Socialists did not budge. It may be that the Socialist leadership came to believe that the split with the PCF might actually help its own cause, since it was preoccupied with winning "new middle class" voters away from the center; a hard Socialist stand against Communist demands might strengthen their attraction to the middle strata. The Socialist leadership may also have felt, erroneously, that the PCF had ultimately nowhere to go but back towards unity as the election approached. The fact that the Socialists did not concede can be explained by the ideological orientation of the Mitterand leadership, which emphasized crisis management. Beyond this, however, French public opinion polls consistently gave the divided left substantial leads right up to election day; since this fed Socialist optimism that the left could win despite its disunity, PCF tactics inevitably lost most of their teeth. The left remained divided through the first round of the elections in March, 1978.*

---

*The reason why Socialist threats to the PCF's traditional electorate were credible follows mainly from the tradition of the left "protest" vote in France. For

The PCF dealt with its second electoral dilemma, that of Socialist threats to its electoral power, by designing its own campaign to ensure that such threats were repelled. It did so by pitching its entire electoral appeals around those issues most salient to its traditional working-class base (and particularly to its less affluent segments): these included an emphasis on "soaking the rich," overcoming "poverty and misery," securing massive raises in the minimum wage, and so on. Such an approach did present the PCF as a strong defender of working-class material interests and it did pay dividends. The PCF maintained its percentage of the vote and its control over the traditional Communist electorate. The party's choice of campaign tactics, however, had one distinct disadvantage. It made the PCF electorally incomprehensible to anyone else but workers, thus undermining any long-term Communist attempt to construct a multi-class electoral base that the party would ultimately have to develop to mobilize the politcal resources necessary for it to initiate change. Thus the PCF's campaign tactics were successful on one level—"social democracy" was thwarted and the party retained its electoral postion. But such victories were defensive at best, especially since the left, owing to its disunity, wound up losing the general elections.[24]

De-Stalinization or not, Eurocommunism or not, the strategic problems of a thorough-going radical reformist politics persist for the PCF, how it deals with such problems will provide the key to its newly-emerging identity. If it resolves them by abandoning the radical cutting-edge of its politics, if it ceases to prod its allies constantly beyond the limits of their own predispositions, then it will become a simple partner in liberal coalition politics—to the great joy of its opponents. This would in fact amount to the "social democratization" of the PCF. The problems faced by the *Union de la Gauche* in updating its Common Program and in contesting an election would indicate that the PCF has not yet succumbed to such degeneration. Yet the constant temptation to succumb is the central issue in a radical reformist strategy. To pursue united front politics effectively, the PCF needs allies; but such potential

---

decades, at least since the cold war, a certain percentage of the total PCF vote came from such "protest" voters—people whose allegiance was to the left rather than to the PCF as such. As long as the PCF remained the only major political force clearly representing the left, this vote came faithfully to the party. *Union de la Gauche,* however, began a process of legitimating the Socialists as truly a party of the left. As this process unfolded, former Communist "protest" voters began to think about supporting the Socialists. The party first grew wary of this phenomenon in the 1974-75 period. It was during the municipal elections of 1977, however, that the party first realized that it would have to do something or lose a certain percentage of its traditional base.

allies will disagree with the PCF's goals, to the degree that such goals are genuinely radical. At critical moments, then, the PCF may have to choose between fidelity to such goals and its alliance prospects. Choosing allies over principles would minimize the risk of Communist isolation, but it would also mean that PCF reformism would no longer threaten French capitalism. Of course reformism is a process rather than a single event. Thus the PCF, given its Eurocommunist option, will constantly be faced with such dilemmas. Even if it retains its radical cutting-edge at one point, the seductive possibilities of renouncing it at a later point will remain. Moreover, the likelihood of strategic and tactical errors or incorrect assessments of political situations might reinforce the dangers of social-democratization. It is in the nature of a radical reformist strategy that while evidence to prove social-democratization may be easily obtained, evidence to demonstrate the opposite—that a reformist party still maintains its radical goals—can never be definitive, at least until the transition to socialism is finally begun.

THE CONTRADICTIONS OF INCOMPLETE EUROCOMMUNISM

THE DANGER OF capitulation to liberal coalition politics does not constitute the only problem for the PCF. In certain areas, in particular that of internal party organizational life, de-Stalinization has been incomplete. "Democratic centralism" in the PCF has traditionally been long on centralism and short on democracy.* In the past (the 1950s, in particular) the lack of internal channels for real discussion has had disastrous consequences. While the party has recently made claims for the existence of a new internal democracy, hard evidence for real change is still thin. Major decisions are still made by a very small number of leaders and, apparently, in a top-down way. The decision to abandon the "dictatorship of the proletariat," for example, was announced by General-Secretary Georges Marchais on French television before any real debate about it had taken place in the party. And purges of party officials whose only visible sin has been disagreement with the leadership have occurred as recently as spring 1970, when Roger Garaudy was driven from his leadership posts. While there are strong indications that

* One commonly hears PCF members use the "apartment house" metaphor to discuss the problem of democratic centralism. The party is portrayed as a multi-story apartment house with a central stairway between floors, in which the leadership resides at the top while the lower levels of the party reside on the lower

the "cult of personality" has been reduced—for example, Georges Marchais has not been automatically getting his way in recent years among Polit Bureau colleagues—more in-fighting at the top does not mean more democracy at the rank-and-file level.

The issue of the de-Stalinization of inner party and mass organizational life is not simply one of political theory (after all, the internal life of most French parties and mass organizations is distinctly undemocratic, if in different ways from that of the PCF). To begin with, the persistence of an old-style, neo-Bolshevik "proletarian democracy" within the PCF and its affiliated organizations clashes with the party's desire to promote an "advanced democracy" in France. This clash inevitably has had negative effects on the PCF's search for allies, not to mention its electoral appeal, especially given the eagerness of PCF enemies to saddle the Communists with the legacy of Stalinism whenever possible. Beyond this, however, bureaucratic centralism in the PCF and its mass organizations has serious implications for the political performance of both. In its neo-Bolshevik distortions, Leninism has been historically prone to "vanguardism", in which the vanguard party becomes a surrogate for the working class and assumes that its will and desires, however determined, are those of the class itself. In France, the debilitating effects of vanguardism (to which the PCF has definitely been prone) have been clearest in the party's mass mobilization efforts. Without a degree of democratic feedback it has been (and will undoubtedly continue to be) difficult for the party to be in proper touch with rank-and-file problems.

Two central issues are thus involved in the discussion of inner-party democracy. Because of inadequate leadership consultation with various constitutencies, PCF attempts to mobilize support for party goals may not work; alternatively, such attempts may fail because of the bureaucratic manner in which they are carried out. On a quite different plane, lack of sufficient democratic feedback may lead the party to discourage any popular mobilization that expresses genuine discontent. This could embarrass the party, especially if the discontent is broad-based, since it would be caught on the wrong side of a popular protest. Or it could blunt the development of movements that, once stimulated, might advance the party's objectives. Here of course we are talking about questions of degree. The PCF's history demonstrates that, despite recurrent problems

floors. Democratic centralism, so the story goes, gives the leadership the freedom to pour buckets of water down the central staircase to the rank-and-file, while at the same time giving the rank-and-file the freedom to pour their buckets of water up the staircase to the leadership.

of authority and democracy, it is far from being indifferent to the world around it. More often than not it is quite close to the mark in its mobilization aims. But the neo-Bolshevik model of inner-party authority and all that it implies for relations between the party and the outside world has been, at times, a serious liability. And it is evident that the success of a radical united frontism like the PCF's will depend upon a Communist party able to promote serious, sustained, and deeply-rooted popular mobilization.

The issue of incomplete internal de-Stalinization arose in dramtic ways after the failure of the left in the 1978 elections. The post-electoral period naturally lent itself to reflection and self-criticism within every part of the French left, as organizational reflexes—long taut from continous mobilization—were allowed to relax. Initially, party discussions of the election were strategically-oriented; but during the course of the reflection, a number of strong criticisms of the party's electoral course emerged among the rank-and-file.* How had the situation which led to a split in September 1977 come about? Why had the PCF failed to increase its own strength over the years as the *Union de la Gauche* had grown? Why had it failed to build any substantial new multi-class base of support in the 1970s, despite its theoretical and strategic commitment to do so? Why had it been so insensitive to the new middle strata themes of self-management, feminism, and ecology? From one minority within the party came the inevitable queries about why disagreements with the Socialists were allowed to become so divisive. A different segment raised the issue of why the PCF had become so completely attached to the *Union de la Gauche* in the first place.

The PCF leadership responded to this outpouring of sentiment from below by asserting that the party had no reason to question its own behavior, that the left's electoral failure had been entirely the doing of the Socialists, and that the PCF had followed the correct strategy. Moreover it refused to allow rank-and-file discussion to be carried out in

---

*The French legislative elections take place in two rounds on consecutive Sundays. In the first round, candidates from all parties compete for places in the following week's runoff. Only candidates receiving more than a specified percentage of votes are allowed to enter the runoff (although if a candidate achieves an absolute majority in the first round he is automatically elected). It has been customary for candidates both of the left and of the right to withdraw from the runoff in favor of better-placed candidates from their end of the spectrum. This means that the runoff is usually a left-right confrontation.

In order to allow this to happen in 1978, Communists and Socialists, who had been attacking one another without restraint until the previous evening, concluded an electoral agreement on March 13 to exchange runoff support. The agreement resolved none of the issues between the two parties.

Humanité, the party daily newspaper. Partly as a result of this (and partly because the establishment press was eager to embarrass the PCF in the aftermath of a disastrous election) critics within the PCF began to publish their letters and treaties in *Le Monde* and other "bourgeois" locations. Here, in particular, the articles of Jean Elleinstein and Louis Althusser, the PCF's leading "right" and "left" dissenters, were important.[25] The leadership responded by attempting to isolate and discredit the critics as quarrelsome intellectuals. Petitions were signed by hundreds of militants, however, demonstrating that such criticism was not merely the province of individualistic Parisian literati.* The leadership's effort to stifle debate did not succeed; what it did was to shift the focus of debate around the party's internal life and, more specifically, around the unfinished nature of the PCF's de-Stalinization.

What had in effect occurred was an explosion of important new contradictions in the PCF's life—contradictions between the party's Eurocommunist posture towards the external world and the relatively slow pace of change in the party's internal habits. When the party faced the outside, particularly after the 22nd Congress, it tended to stress the "crisis of democracy" in France. For PCF militants, to take advantage of the opportunities that advanced capitalism continues to present to the French left is the critical question.

CONCLUSIONS:
EUROCOMMUNISM AND CLASS-FORMATION

THE PCF'S ADOPTION of a radical reformist united front strategy raises fundamental issues for the party's class-forming goals. In the days of Stalinism, PCF mobilization politics was designed to prepare workers for Soviet-style revolution and for allegiance to Soviet foreign

---

Le Monde printed petitions from initial groups of 100 Parisians, 300 Communists in the provinces (this petition which came from Aix-en-Provence, was in time signed by many hundreds more), and several tens of distinguished Communist scientists. All affirmed that the party's strategic conduct before and during the elections deserved open debate and discussion and that the party's structure made such discussion difficult. The petitions inspired the leadership to accuse unidentified "comrades" of "fractional" activity (i.e. organized, horizontal contact outside the established party structures). In fact, the petitions were quasi-"fractional" activities, indicating the degree to which party dissidents felt that their views ought to be heard. It should be added that Georges Marchais announced in the weeks following the election that no exclusions would result from party debates—an announcement that may have undermined some rank-and-file reverence for the rules of democratic centralism.

policy. With Eurocommunism, however, many of the class-forming certitudes of the Stalinist past are gone. For the PCF there is still only *one* working class: it has clearly-identifiable interests, is situated in direct conflict with the French bourgeoisie, and is ultimately committed to basic social change. Yet, according to the PCF's new state monopoly capitalist vision, the boundaries of this class have become less rigid, while the distance between it and other social groups has diminished considerably. The one working class is no longer isolated in a class ghetto in modern France; it has class allies whose social existence has brought them closer to that of the workers. And in a number of ways the PCF's class-forming practices have been modified to fit this transformed Eurocommunist class map of French society. The central change lies in the role of the working class in this new period. As the group most advanced in its understanding of the need for basic change, it must now conciliate its immediate class interests with the differing, and more moderate, interests of its class allies. If it remains in the interests of French workers to abolish capitalism in the long run, the path to this is an anti-monopoly alliance of workers, "salaried intermediary strata," and independent producers. Since the non-working class sectors of this alliance cannot yet be expected to identify their long-range class interests with socialism, workers will probably have to restrain themselves in order to accommodate these less radical groups.

The result is a pronounced change in the PCF's guiding class-forming message to its own forces. In form, the message is the same—the problems of French workers can only be solved by basic political change. But the context is new. For example, appeals to socialism are downplayed. The task of carrying out the first stage of the PCF's united front scenario is now primary. The enactment of the Common Program or something similar is now presented as the most profound aspiration of workers. In effect the PCF has been telling French workers for more than a decade that the road to socialism is through reformism. But in the new discourse the character of socialism is rarely discussed, while the road to it has become all important. The working class is called upon to hold, simultaneously, a long-term revolutionary perspective and a powerful reformist vision for the immediate future—with overwhelming stress on the latter. Thus to the degree that PCF's class-forming activities in the Eurocommunist era are successful (and it must be remembered that the PCF is only one class-socializing agency among many in France), such activities may well promote a deeper commitment to reformism—as opposed to revolutionary radicalism—among workers. The danger is that such a deepened reformism will have an impact on the PCF's own deployment of resources. Thus even if the PCF attunes itself to a broader revolutionary agenda, in which initial reformist moderation is only one part, the party may encounter a mass of rank-and-file supporters who see reformism as the key to political action. Should this be the case, the PCF might have to moderate its approach even more to promote the success of its united front strategy. And, of course, its ability to mobilize mass support in a way that goes beyond simple reformism will be the critical variable in building socialism in France.

Final assessment of the PCF's Eurocommunization thus remains inconclusive. Through its recent changes, French Communism has cleared its decks for pursuit of a realistic strategy of radical reformism. The problems it faces are the problems of all such strategies. Radical reformism and simple coalition politics commonly look the same. In both cases, the construction of alliances involving different political forces and requiring compromise is the means of achieving results. Simple coalition politics necessitates compromise to achieve power with fundamental questions of social change put aside. Radical reformism involves the promotion of reforms that progressively undermine the status quo and lead to its transformation. So far, there is considerable evidence that PCF-style Eurocommunism is of the latter type. Yet the success of radical reformism depends upon Communist adherence to principle in its dealings with allies so that programs and tactics which promise genuine change remain at the center of the united front. Simple coalition politics, on the other hand, would be the easiest way for the PCF to make friends. The ultimate question then is which of these two paths the PCF will follow. One leads to comfortable social democratization, while the other leads to combat, struggle, and at times, isolation. The most difficult part of this question is that the Eurocommunist PCF must answer it anew every day.

Notes

1. On the early history of the PCF, see Annie Kriegel, *Aux Origins du Communisme Francaise* (Paris: Mouton, 1964); Robert Wohl, *French Communism in the Making, 1914-1924* (Stanford, Calif.: Stanford University Press, 1966); the PCF's own *Histoire du PCF* (Paris: PCF Press, 1964); Ronald Tiersky, *French Communism, 1920-1972* (New York: Columbia University Press, 1974) part one, ; and Jacques Fauvet, *Histoire du PCF* (Paris: Fayard, 1977), second edition.

2. On this period see Bernard H. Moss *The Origins of the French Labor Movement* (Berkeley: University of California Press, 1976); Val Lorwin, *The French Labor Movement* (Cambridge: Harvard University Press, 1954), chapters 1-4; and Alfred Rosmer, *Le mouvement ouvrier pendant La Guerre* (Paris: Librarie du Travail, 1936).

3. The Zimmerwald Conference was held in September 1915. Lenin and Trotsky were key figures, and several French anarcho-syndicalists, later to be key figures in the PCF, attended and signed the Zimmerwald Manifesto which condemned both the war itself and Social Democratic support of the war.

4. On the CGT and its reformism, see Georges Lefranc, *Le Mouvement sous la Troisième Republique* (Paris: Payot, 1967), and Leon Jouhaux, *Le Syndicalisme de la CGT* (Paris: Editions de la Sirene, 1920).

5. On the history of the Comintern, see Fernando Claudin's magnificent *The Communist Movement* (New York: Monthly Review Press, 1975), volume 1.

6. Claudin, op. cit. chapters 3 and 4.

7. On such questions, see Frederic Bon's excellent essay "Structure de l'ideologie communiste," in Bon, et. al., *Le communisme en France* (Paris: Armand Colin, 1968).

8. This point is one of Nicos Poulantzas' central concerns in his *Classes in Contemporary Capitalism* (London: New Left Books, 1975).

9. On the Republicanism of the traditional *petite bourgeoisie*, see Christian Malemort, Roger Establet, et. al., *la petite bourgeoisie en France* (Paris: Francois Maspero, 1974).

10. On the *Front Populaire*, see Claude Willard et. al. *le Front Populaire* (Paris: Editiones Sociales, 1972); Daniel Brower, *The New Jacobins* (Ithaca: Cornell University Press, 1968); and Annie Kriegel and Michelle Perrot, *le socialisme francais et le pouvoir* (Paris: EDI, 1966). On the CGT, see Antoine Prost, *la CGT a l'Epoque du Front Populaire* (Paris: Armand Colin, 1964).

Although insufficient documentation makes generalization difficult, it seems that PCF pressure on the Comintern (and particularly that applied by Maurice Thorez) played a major part in the shift to Popular Frontism.

11. On the PCF in this period see Alfred Rieber, *Stalin and the French Communist Party* (New York: Columbia University Press, 1962); Tiersky, *op. cit.* chapter 5; Fauvet, *op. cit.*; and Francois Billoux, *Quand Nous Etions Ministres* (Paris: Editions Sociales, 1972). On the CGT, see George Ross, *The Confédération Générale du Travail: French Workers and French Communism* Unpublished Ph.D. dissertation, Harvard University, 1972), and Ross, "Party and Mass Organization: the Changing Relationship of the PCF and CGT," in D.L.M. Blackmer and Sidney Tarrow, eds., *French and Italian Communism* (Princeton, N.J.: Princeton University Press, 1975).

12. On the interesting story of French economic planning, see Stephen Cohen, *Modern Capitalist Planning: the French Model* (Berkeley: University of California Press, 1977).

13. Recently several important participants in the PCF's cultural life of this period have written memoires. While in each case the books are written by apostate PCFers, together they paint an interesting and probably accurate picture of the extremes of PCF Zhdanovism. See Pierre Daix, *J'ai Cru au Matin* (Paris: Robert Laffont, 1976); Paul Noirot, *la Memoire Ouverte* (Paris: Stock, 1976); and Dominique Desanti, *les Staliniens* (Paris: Fayard, 1975).

14. See Ross, Confederation Generale du Travail, chapter 2, and Michel Branciard, *Societe Francaise et Lutte de Classes* (Paris: Editions Ouvrieres, 1967), volume 1.

15. Both the Marty-Tillon and Lecoeur *affaires*, which occurred in the early 1950s, seemed to have been aimed mainly at high party cadres who had been impossible to work with (although in the case of Charles Tillon, this seems to have been less the case). For Marty-Tillon, the PCF made use of the paranoid anti-Titoist atmosphere created in the East by Stalin to eliminate potential national Communists from Eastern European party leaderships (for example, through the Slansky and Rajk trials) to clean up its own house. In both cases, to be sure, threats to the Thorez leadership had been posed. See Philippe Robrieux, *Maurice Thorez* (Paris: Fayard, 1975), chapter 7; *PCF Histoire, op. cit.,* pp. 536-540; Andre Marty, *L'Affaire Marty* (Paris: Editions des Deux Rives, 1955); and Auguste Lecoeur, *L'autocritique attendue* (Paris: Girault, 1955) The Servin-Casanova purge was more directly political in essence; the group advocated a change towards more "Krushchevian" positions against Thorez' rigidity. Thorez managed to win the Soviet leadership over to his side, carried out the purge within the party, and soon initiated the PCF's shift towards what was to become "Eurocommunism." In other words, Thorez—like Stalin before him—purged his opponents and then coopted their support by implementing many of the policies they advocated. See Robrieux, *op. cit.,* and Francois Fejto, *The French Communist Party and the Crisis of International Communism* (Cambridge: MIT Press, 1967).

16. See Robrieux, *op. cit.*, chapter 8.

17. On the unity question, see Robert Verdier, *PS, PC, une lutte pour l'entente* (Paris: Seghers, 1976), and Jean Poperen, *L'unité de la Gauche* (Paris: Fayard, 1975).

18. The state monopoly capitalism analysis was developed by the *Economie et Politique* group and its first thorough statements came from that journal, with Paul Boccara the dominant intellectual figure. The most important codification of the theory is to be found in the *Section Economique* of the Central Committee's *Traite d'Economie Marxiste (le capitalisme monopoliste d'état)* (Paris: Editions Sociales, 1971), two volumes. See also Paul Boccara, *Etudes sur le capitalisme monopoliste d'état, sa crise et son issue* (Paris: Editions Sociales, 1974).

19. See *Programme Pour un Gouvernement d'union Populaire* (Paris: Editions Sociales, 1972). For PCF internal documents on party discussion around the Program, see Etienne Fajon, *L'Union est un combat* (Paris: Editions Sociales, 1975).

20. See PCF, *Vivre Libres* (Paris: Editions Sociales, 1975).

21. See PCF, *Le Socialisme Pour la France* (Paris: Editions Sociales, 1976), the *comptes rendus* of the 22nd Congress in *Cahiers du Communisme*, March 1976. For critical but fraternal views on the "dictatorship" issue, see Etienne Balibar, *la Dictature du Proletariat* (Paris: Marspero, 1976), and Louis Althusser, *XXII Congress* (Paris: Maspero, 1977).

22. See Fernando Claudin, *l'Eurocommunisme* (Paris: Maspéro, 1977).

23. On the "actualization" negotiations, see Pierre Juaquin, *l'actualization a livre ouvert* (Paris: Editions Sociales, 1977). This book consists of a transcript of the negotiations. Since it comes from a member of the PCF·*Bureau Politique*, one is entitled to suspect its accuracy. From what I have been able to determine, after consulting various documents on the negotiations (in particular the working papers submitted by the Socialist leadership for the talks), Juaquin's version is substantially correct.

24. For a more detailed discussion of the left and the 1978 elections, consult George Ross, "How to Lose an Election," in *Working Papers for a New Society*, August 1978. See also *le Monde*, "les elections de mars 1978," in its *Dossiers et Documentation* series, April 1978. For a brief description of the election as lived by a PCF cell, see George Ross and Jane Jensen, "Life in a Communist Cell, *in Canadian Dimension*, Nov.-Dec. 1978.

25. The Elleinstein articles were in *Le Monde*, April 13, 14, and 15. The Althusser essays appeared in the same paper on April 25, 26, 27, and 28, and later appeared in a small book entitled *ce qui peut plus durer au PCF* (Paris: Maspero, 1978). At about the same time two very interesting books on life in the party were authored by Communists who disagreed with many aspects of the PCF but who intended to stay in the party and work for change. See Gerard Molina and Yves Vargas, *Dialogue a l'interieur du parti communiste* (Paris: Maspero, 1978), and Jean Rony, *trente ansadu parti* (Paris: Christian Bourgeois, 1978).

26. For an account of the origins and development of the PCF's crisis, see George Ross, "The Crisis of Eurocommunism: the French Case," in the *Socialist Register 1978* (London: Merlin, 1978), edited by Ralph Miliband and John Saville.

chapter 2

ITALIAN COMMUNISM
AT THE CROSSROADS *

Joanne Barkan

"A PARTY OF STRUGGLE, a government party" became the Italian Communists' slogan in 1976, just as Eurocommunism was beginning to generate a great deal of discussion in the United States and elsewhere. As an organization that wins 12 million votes, counts almost 1,800,000 members, and claims commitment to an independent, national road to socialism, the PCI has attracted particular attention. Yet questions about its political character are still being posed: is it a revolutionary party that has developed a new strategy for the socialist transformation of Italian society, or is it disguising its reformism (traditional or new style) under a cloak of rhetoric? To suggest an answer, this investigation will explore the PCI's day-to-day mode of operation, its internal structure, and its relationship to the working class, mass movements and the state since World War II. The gradual shift of the PCI from a class-oriented mass party to a more socially heterogeneous electoral force, its organizational decline through the 1960s and subsequent gain in strength, its traditionally weak links with the most politically militant sectors of society—all of these are consequences of the party's moderate strategy and reformist presuppositions. Now, after more than 30 years as a legal political force, the PCI faces a series of problems that its strategy seems unable to resolve. The PCI's future as a party both of struggle and of government has been thrown into question. To understand how this developed, we must go back to the immediate postwar period.

*An earlier version of this essay, which was originally written for this volume, appeared in *Radical America*, October 1978. I would like to thank Frank Brodhead, Alan Charney, Jon Friedman, Larry Miller, Robert Proctor, Paul Sweezy, George Vickers, and Victor Wallis for their very helpful comments on the draft of that version. Thanks also to Giovanni Forti for the information he sent from Rome.

During the armed Resistance in Italy, many partisans and workers expected the PCI leadership to escalate the anti-fascist struggle into an insurrection to seize power at the close of the war. Instead, party secretary Palmiro Togliatti returned from the USSR in 1944 and outlined a gradualist strategy with plans to participate in a coalition government that included all non-fascist political parties. Although many cadres were surprised and believed this was a ruse to distract the Italian ruling class and the Anglo-American forces, the decision had its origin in the Yalta agreements in which Roosevelt, Stalin, and Churchill divided Europe among the great powers. Since Italy was assigned to the Western camp, any attempt at revolution could have precipitated a brutal reaction from the Allies (as in Greece in 1948) with little prospect for Soviet aid. Until then, the policies of the Communist International had strongly influenced the major decisions of the leadership. Thus it was not surprising that Togliatti rejected the possibility of an insurrection at the end of the war.

The English and American forces, which occupied Italy at the close of the war, were well aware of the militancy and strong revolutionary currents within parts of the Resistance movement and the industrial working class in the North. It is clear from military maneuvers in 1943 and 1944, as well as from various documents and statements, that the Allies were determined to prevent a revolution in Italy.[1] At the same time, the Italian ruling class was in disarray as workers and other popular forces seized the political initiative. Armed workers occupied factories in the industrialized North, while National Liberation committees formed an embryonic state apparatus in the vacuum created by the collapse of the fascist state. At this juncture, the PCI surely could have won significant political and economic concessions from the capitalists and the non-socialist political parties—concessions that would have placed the workers and popular forces in a much stronger position during postwar reconstruction.

Yet the PCI leadership did not press for these concessions. Its overriding concern after the end of the war was to avoid a confrontation with the Italian bourgeoisie and other conservative forces. The party feared doing anything that might alienate the middle strata and create the conditions for a resurgence of fascism. The PCI leadership argued that the working class was not yet strong enough to impede or withstand political reaction. The PCI's proposed strategy was to play a primary role in the consolidation of a progressive democratic state that would enact structural reforms and allow for the gradual and peaceful transformation of Italy into a socialist society. Toward this end, the leadership committed itself to working with all non-fascist parties within the arena of parliamentary democracy. The Communists helped author the new constitution and participated in the national unity governments of the immediate postwar period. Concerns of national unity rather than class struggle dominated the PCI's rhetoric, and the protection of civil liberties became a principle objective. Party tactics were essentially defensive, which was one factor helping the bourgeoisie regain the upper hand. The Christian Democrats emerged during these years as the dominant political force in Italy. It must not be forgotten that the United States government played an active—and successful—role in strengthening the Christian Democratic Party (DC) and in undermining the left opposition. Yet even the PCI leadership admitted by 1951 that it had made too many concessions to the ruling class.[2] To understand this strategic context, we should first turn to the PCI leadership's basic conception of political organization and to the early postwar development of the party.

THE PCI AS MASS PARTY

AFTER THE LONG YEARS of clandestine activity and exile under fascism, the PCI emerged from the war not as a small organization of professional cadres, but as a mass party of 1,718,836 members which grew to 2,252,446 by 1947.[3] Togliatti, leader of the party from 1926 until his death in 1964, established the model for the PCI's postwar development. The party would function not simply as an electoral force, but would build roots in every community and workplace among the millions of Italians who sought change. In theory, the PCI was to give these popular aspirations an organized form and lead Italians in struggles for specific objectives. This was the party of struggle that occupied a central position in the PCI's early postwar strategic formulations.

Here it might be useful to introduce Otto Kirchheimer's distinction between "mass party" and "catch-all party" for our analysis of the PCI.[4] The political organization envisaged by the PCI leadership was that of a European-style mass party. As a class-oriented political force, the mass party has an explicit and coherent ideology as well as some kind of global program for social transformation. It acts in the interest of specific groups, and gives priority to this rather than to winning as many votes as possible. Electoral activity is just *one* of its functions—and often not even its primary function. The party constantly initiates non-electoral political activity and mobilizes its supporters in demonstrations, rallies, strikes, and so on. Moreover, it plays a role in the everyday life of the workplace and the community, emerging as a major force in the cultural, moral, and intellectual development of its base. Because of its ideological thrust and its strategic (as well as tactical) cohesiveness, the mass party attracts a relatively homogeneous class membership. Hence its electorate tends to be relatively stable. In contrast, the catch-all party has no organic program for transforming society. It limits itself to electoral activity and changes its program to meet demands of the moment. The catch-all party does not penetrate into the daily life of the individual and cannot mobilize its constituency for non-electoral purposes. It presents no long-term objectives or fundamental principles, and its electorate tends to fluctuate. The goal of the catch-all party is to obtain the maximum number of votes, and so it directs its electoral campaigns to all social classes (much along the lines of the Democratic Party in the U.S.).

To create a mass party, the PCI leadership devoted primary attention during the early years to building party organization. The "territorial section," which draws members from a geographical area (for example, a neighborhood) became the basic structural unit. One slogan of these early years was "a section for every bell-tower." The PCI placed great emphasis on recruitment, and party militants devoted much of their energy to membership drives and creating new sections around the country. Here the PCI was quite successful. By 1964, it had penetrated even some of the smallest and most remote communities and counted 9,569 sections and 1,578 nuclei (sections of less than 20 members). Only 14.7 percent of the cities and towns in Italy were without a section or nucleus.

The PCI also satisfied many of the other "mass party" criteria. Its ideological orientation and strategic goals were explicit, even if it never really developed a program of specific short-term and intermediate objectives with well-defined tactics to achieve them. The PCI attracted members who identified with its ideology and strategy, and therefore its social composition was fairly homogeneous. In 1954, urban workers (industrial and service sector) made up 48.6 percent of the membership with farm workers accounting for 21.7 percent; overall, workers thus comprised more than 70 percent of the PCI's base. Small farmers and sharecroppers accounted for 19.7 percent, artisans and merchants 6.4 percent, and students less than 1 percent. The PCI's electorate was fairly stable—its share of the votes increasing only 4.32 percent from 1953 to 1968 (from 22.64 percent to 26.96 percent). In contrast to its membership base, the party's electoral support has always been socially heterogeneous, but this is not unusual for an electorally successful mass party.

As for intervening in everyday life and playing a direct role in the intellectual and cultural transformation of its base, the PCI put out daily newspapers, weekly periodicals, and theoretical journals and operated its own publishing house. It gained control over the cooperative movement, carried on commercial activities, ran recreational and cultural centers, organized popular festivals, and held administrative posts in the local governments of certain cities, towns, and provinces.

The PCI succeeded in maintaining its identity as a mass party from the end of the war until the early 1970s. Yet as a party of struggle—a force that would lead millions of Italians in the battle for structural reforms—the PCI had little success. The explanation for this is two-fold: it involves both early postwar tactical choices and the party's mode of operation on a day-to-day basis. There is no doubt that U.S. intervention in Italian affairs, along with the cold war, created an extremely difficult situation for the PCI. The party was forced to contend with the breaking-up of the unified trade union confederation in the late 1940s, the political strings attached to the Marshall Plan and the European Recovery Program, steady anti-communist propaganda, and the organized repression of the working class (with the government denying the right to assemble in the factory and to hold certain types of strikes, militant workers and unionists losing their jobs, police often attacking picketing workers). Yet it is true that the PCI leadership could have won more for the popular forces in the political arena and could have developed a greater capacity for mass mobilization.

THE CONSEQUENCES OF MODERATION

ONCE THE PCI HAD committed itself to postwar reconstruction within the boundaries of the capitalist system, class struggle increasingly revolved around the criteria for conversion of the war-time economy. The question was how much leverage the competing class forces would have and how much each would pay in terms of their own economic interests. As instruments of struggle, the working class had the PCI and the Communist-dominated union—the Confederazione Generale Italiana del Lavoro (CGIL). But since the aim of the PCI leadership was to avoid direct class confrontation, it did not utilize these instruments very aggressively. For example, the first taxes established after liberation were direct deductions from workers' salaries rather than taxes on excess corporate profits from speculation and the war. The party proposed no general agrarian reform program, and in September 1945 the CGIL agreed to mass industrial layoffs. By August 1946, northern workers were demonstrating against the policies of the Communist Treasury Minister, Epicarmio Corbino. In general, the PCI put a brake on worker militancy while trying to win limited reforms for the rural petty bourgeoisie and working class (for example, land reform in the south). The CGIL refused to lead strikes in factories that were still operating, while the occupation of plants that were shut down did not greatly undermine the capitalists at that time. In 1950, moreover, the CGIL accepted an accord that gave management a free hand in individual layoffs. The ruling class used this measure effectively over the next decade to weed out militant workers and maintain an orderly labor force.

The key sectors of the Italian economy were converted for peacetime production by 1950, with the bourgeoisie reconsolidating its control. Thus just five years after liberation, the PCI could do no more than rhetorically denounce the monopolists for pursuing a course that favored foreign capital to the detriment of the national economy. With restructuring firmly in the hands of the bourgeoisie, the remaining economic battles to be fought by the working class were over the distribution of wealth and the creation of jobs. Here too, the PCI failed to secure any victories. From 1950 to 1955, profits soared 86 percent while real wages rose only 6 percent and the unemployment rate remained over 8 percent. The PCI suffered a significant defeat in the political arena as well, when DC Prime Minister Alcide De Gasperi resigned in May 1947 and then formed the first postwar cabinet without the Communists or Socialists. With financial and propagandistic support from the U.S., the DC won an absolute majority in the April 1948 elections, and from then until the early 1970s the exercise of state power was no longer a practical issue for the PCI.

All this could only discourage and disillusion the most radical sectors of the working class which had continued to struggle after the war. After 1948, this struggle ceased to intensify and in the 1950s tapered off. By 1951, the consequences of the PCI's strategic and tactical choices were becoming clear. The party leadership had assumed that, as a party of struggle, the PCI would forge a strong bond with the most combative sectors of the working class. But this presupposed that the party would develop alongside these sectors while sustaining its organizational presence in the factories. Instead, the PCI's involvement as a force of moderation served to weaken its ties to the most militant strata of workers.

A VARIETY OF data demonstrates this trend. The non PCI-dominated union confederations (which tended to stress the specific interests of various sectors rather than class unity) began to increase their strength at the expense of the CGIL. As early as 1951, the former won 25 percent of the vote in some large factories. By 1953, they achieved further gains, and in 1955 the CGIL actually lost its majority at Fiat—the historic heart of the Italian workers' movement. The PCI also lost strength in the large northwestern cities where the organized industrial working class was concentrated and where revolutionary sentiment had been strong at the end of the war. The party's vote in Milan, for example, fell from 24.9 percent in 1946 to 20.5 percent in 1953. The "rate of adhesion" to the party (the percentage of PCI members in the entire voting age population) in cities of more than 200,000 inhabitants dropped from 7.2 percent in 1949 to 6.8 percent in 1952 and then declined to a low point of 2.6 percent in 1971. As for the PCI's organizational presence at the point of production, the number of factory cells fell from 11,495 to 3,013 between 1954 and 1967.

The cold war, accompanied by a general rightward political shift, is not enough to explain the PCI's predicament. After all, some strata of the working class had been prepared for insurrection only a few years before. Moreover, the PCI's electoral strength increased slightly from the late 1940s to the early 1950s, indicating that Italians were not withdrawing their votes from the PCI because of the cold war. Instead, the party's tactical choices probably discouraged a large enough part of the workers' movement to adversely affect membership, rate of adhesion, presence in the factories, and CGIL strength.

A further reason for the PCI's lack of success as a party of struggle involves the character of its internal organization and its day-to-day practice.* Party membership after the war required little more than signing up and paying dues, and only a small proportion of the members regularly participated in organizational activities and duties. As mentioned earlier, the territorial section drawing members from a neighborhood or municipality was the PCI's basic organizational unit. Most activists worked through these "street" sections rather than through workplace cells or sections. The sections performed mainly the routine work of membership drives, fundraising, distribution of newspapers, and so on, which was interrupted periodically by electoral campaigns and major national and international events. The latter often sparked political discussion at the base, but the leadership tended to dominate these discussions and often treated such events as "current events" separate from the experiences and activities of party members and therefore unconnected to the tactics and strategy of the party. On rather exceptional occasions, PCI sections did organize a mass response to political issues. In 1952, for example, the party led a successful campaign against the *legge truffa* (a law promoted by the DC that would have given almost two-thirds of the seats in parliament to any party winning 50 percent plus one vote). Yet this kind of call to mass mobilization was directed at the entire population, to all Italian citizens. The sections were not able to build a class movement that brought together the most militant and politicized groups around class (rather than civic) themes.

---

*The following description applies to the PCI today as well as during the earlier postwar period.

At the intermediate level, within the federation, the PCI once again devoted much of its time and energy to routine matters involving budgets, membership, publications, and electoral campaigns—the activities most related to the party's institutional maintenance and self-perpetuation. The strongest of the more than 100 federations also ran cooperatives and sponsored community and cultural events, while those in the "red zones" (where the PCI was part of local government) exercised a range of administrative activities. Although these activities rooted the party solidly in the social fabric of a given area, they also resulted in the party's emergence as a progressive and equilibrating institution within the existing system. Such tasks promoted bureaucratization, since functionaries (full-time party employees) worked at this level and became professional city councilpersons, unionists, and cooperative directors who depended on the party for their jobs. Now lacking time for "creative" politics and for building class movements, many functionaries came to perceive this kind of activism as opposed to party (and self) interests.

The highest levels of PCI leadership (the central committee, politbureau, directorate, and secretariat) were responsible for elaborating the political line, articulating positions on specific issues, directing parliamentary activity, and overseeing the work of the lower levels of the party. The national leadership also assumed the function of establishing the PCI's formal relationship with whatever movements and struggles existed. Yet given the organizational—and in many cases political—gap between the party hierarchy and these movements, the methods used to build this relationship were bound to be extremely indirect. They included programmatic platforms (often presented as legislative proposals), conferences on particular issues, and publicity work. From so great a distance, the PCI leadership could not easily forge a class movement, and the organizational structures, methods of work, and political cadre necessary for bridging the gap did not exist.

As might be expected, the PCI's deficiencies as a party of struggle took their toll in terms of organizational strength. Thus in the period between 1954 and 1968, party membership dropped by 650,000 or 30 percent, the rate of adhesion slipped from 6.9 percent to 4.2 percent, and the PCI youth organization (FGCI)—always an indication of party strength among young people—lost over 70 percent of its members. The number of recruits each year varied between 96,000 and 160,000, but the number of members not rejoining was even higher, fluctuating between 115,000 and 306,000. The length of time members remained in the party was often very short, indicating an instability in the party's membership base. Between 1956 and 1967, moreover, the number of sections and nuclei fell by 300, and the percentage of Italian municipalities without a PCI section or nucleus increased from 16.9 to 22.1. By the late 1950s, this organizational erosion was of urgent concern to the leadership, but in spite of all efforts to rebuild the membership base (including recruitment contests between federations), the decline continued.

Here it is important to note that although the PCI's organizational strength diminished, the characteristics of a mass party (explicit ideology, consistent strategic goals, socially homogeneous membership base, and stable electorate) were maintained through the late 1960s. After that, there were some significant changes, but in order to explain these changes, we must look at the party's relationship to the two cycles of militant class struggles that took place in Italy during the 1960s.

CRISIS AND ADAPTATION IN THE SIXTIES

THE PCI HAD CLEARLY grown out of touch with changes in the structure of both the Italian economy and the industrial working class. The party was caught off-guard by the wave of militant struggles that swept through the factories of the north from 1960 through 1962, signalling a reawakening of the Italian working class. Young workers and "immigrant" workers from the south had been pulled onto the assembly lines by the tens of thousands as the economy expanded. Unlike previous generations of skilled workers, the new "mass" workers generally did not belong to a political party or union, but their common experiences in the factory generated a level of unity and militancy not seen in Italy for many years. The PCI, which did not initiate or lead the struggles of 1960-62, was forced to respond to this situation as it developed. This was indicative of the party's relationship to the working class and to the most advanced social forces. Thus, it is not surprising that the PCI benefited little in terms of organizational strength from these developments.

The same kind of separation characterized the initial relationship between the PCI and the student and workers' movements that shook the country in the late 1960s. From the occupation of Milan's Catholic University in October 1967 through the "hot autumn" of workers' struggles around contract negotiations in 1969, the PCI had to deal with autonomous movements that questioned all forms of authority, hierarchy, and representative democracy as well as capitalist relations of production. The movements, which were centered in the large northwestern cities (Milan, Turin, Genoa, etc.), generated a kind of cultural revolution throughout the entire society. The PCI leaders, who were still committed to a party of struggle, had to establish and maintain a relationship with the popular movements. This was especially true since elements of both the party leadership and base (perhaps 15-20 percent) saw these struggles as a positive sign that a new strategy for revolution was necessary and feasible. The PCI therefore kept an "open" attitude and even went along with certain specific demands. At the same time, however, it tried to control the movements and slow them down; by late 1969, it had succeeded to a great extent. Meanwhile, there was a shift in power relations within the party hierarchy. By 1968, both the left position (led by Pietro Ingrao), which favored a more militant and activist line, and the right (lead by Giorgio Amendola), which held a fairly conservative social democratic position, were defeated. The centrist "middle generation" (led by Enrico Berlinguer) emerged victorious and consolidated its hold on the party.

The period 1968-1970 marked a watershed for the PCI in three significant ways. First, the long-term trend of organizational decline was reversed, while the party's subsequent growth had a somewhat different character. Second, there was a shift in tactics. Third, the PCI took on the role of a government party, which necessarily affected its relationship with the other political forces in Italy as well as its own base.

CONSIDERING FIRST THE PCI's organizational strength, there is no doubt that the movements of the late 1960s were instrumental in reversing the downward trend. After 1968, the number of recruits increased while the number of members not rejoining decreased, reflecting greater membership stability. Altogether the PCI grew by 301,935, reaching a total of 1,797,597 in 1976, while the rate of adhesion increased from 4.2 percent in 1968 to 4.7 percent in 1976. The number of sections also grew during this period. Still, it should be remembered that those figures represent the reversal of a trend and not record high levels; the PCI was far from achieving the membership and rate of adhesion levels of the late 1940s. In addition, the percentage of Italian municipalities without Communist sections continued to rise, indicating that the party was gaining strength in the areas of its greatest organizational presence.

In contrast to what many observers have assumed, the movements of the late 1960s did not channel themselves into institutional forms and "flow into" the PCI once their momentum began to subside. The PCI made few and in some cases no gains in those geographical areas where popular movements were the strongest or among those workers and young people who had been the protagonistists of the struggles. Instead, the late 1960s increased the general level of political consciousness in Italy and shifted whole sectors of the population leftward. It was in the geographical periphery of the movement (the cities of the northeast, south, and central regions—except for the "red zones"—and the provincial towns of the north) that the PCI made its strongest gains. Between 1969 and 1971, the PCI lost members in the large cities of the northwest but made gains in the provinces of the same region. The rate of adhesion in Milan—the "capital" of the same movement—was actually lower in 1976 than it had been in 1968. Yet in five traditionally Catholic and DC-dominated cities of the North (Venice, Verona, Brescia, Trieste, and Padua), the rate of adhesion grew after 1968, and by 1976 was stronger in these areas than in Milan. The same was true for many cities in the South.

Looking at industrial workers, the same trend holds. Between 1968 and 1974, the percentage of PCI members who were industrial workers in the northwest dropped from 51.9 to 49.9 percent, whereas in the central region there was an increase from 37.2 to 39.1 percent, and in the south from 32.5 to 35.1 percent. Meanwhile, the PCI continued to make little headway among young people. At the high point of the movement in 1969, the youth organization suffered a near collapse, losing almost half of its already small membership—sinking to a low of 68,648 in comparison with 125,438 in 1968 and 463,954 in 1951. Although recovery began in 1971, the FGCI still had fewer members in 1976 than it had a decade earlier.

Another indication of the PCI's failure to incorporate the most politicized groups was the growth of political forces to the party's left after 1968. Throughout most of the 1960s, the "left opposition" had been extremely fragmented and dispersed. Then three organizations were born out of the movements, each maintaining a base of thousands of activists. The new left, or "revolutionary left" as it is often called, attracted many of those who participated in the struggles of the late 1960s, especially young people from the student movement. Until 1977, this political area to the left of the PCI was generally considered the strongest and best organized new left of any advanced capitalist country.

Although the PCI did not win over the protagonists of the late 1960s, it did continue to make significant headway among the various middle strata. By 1974, the party's social composition had markedly changed from its early postwar character. As the chart below demonstrates, the middle strata (artisans, merchants, white collar employees, teachers, and professionals), which comprised only 8.9 percent of the base in 1950, accounted for more than 22 percent by 1974.

	urban workers service & industrial	farmworkers	artisans and merchants	small farmers and sharecroppers	teachers, professionals, white collar employees	students
1950	50.4	21.6	5.2	18.5	3.7	0.6
1974	59.9	6.7	12.3	8.2	10.3	2.6

This change in the PCI's social composition reflects demographic changes in Italian society as a whole. Over the last 20 years, many Italians working in the countryside "immigrated" to urban areas to find jobs. At the same time, the middle strata have increased in size. The PCI's more heavily middle class base, therefore, does not in itself indicate that the party has become less proletarian than the larger society. To understand how the social composition of the party is changing, an analysis of the rate of adhesion of various social groupings is necessary. (The rate of adhesion indicates how many out of every 100 workers or artisans or students belong to the PCI). As the chart below demonstrates, the rate of adhesion among urban workers did increase from 1968 to 1976 but, proportionately, adhesion increased a great deal more among the middle strata.

	urban workers service & industrial	farmworkers	small farmers & sharecroppers	artisans	merchants	teachers, professionals, white collar employees	students
1968	7.07	11.23	6.47	5.27	1.47	1.45	1.45
1976	8.44	8.08	5.12	7.30	3.37	3.64	4.12
	19.4%	-28.0%	-20.9%	38.5%	129.3%	151.0%	184.1%

A comparison of the social composition of the party leadership with that of its membership sheds some light on the relative weight of the various social strata. For example, urban workers made up 59.9 percent of the membership in 1974 but only 26.2 percent of the federation committees in 1975. In 1972, 34.6 percent of the committee members were workers, while in 1947 this figure was even higher (38.7 percent). Professionals, teachers, white collar employees, and students accounted for 12.9 percent of the party membership in 1974, but they held 65 percent of the federation committee posts in 1975, only 53 percent in 1972, and 50.4 percent in 1947. In 1976, only 8.7 percent of PCI parliamentary deputies and only 5.2 percent of its senators came from the industrial working class. In the 1978 directorate, there was not a single leader of working-class origin.

THE SEVENTIES: ELECTORAL ADVANCES AND TACTICAL SHIFTS

THE PCI MADE ITS GREATEST electoral gains during the 1970s. In the administrative (regional, provincial, and municipal) elections of 1972, the party polled a national average of 27.5 percent, which it then increased to 32.4 percent in the 1975 elections—a tremendous victory in a country where a two-percent shift in the vote is considered a major change. The PCI followed this by winning 34.4 percent in the parliamentary elections of 1976. There is no definitive information as to who the new PCI voters are. One hypothesis is that they come mainly from the middle strata; another is that they are Catholic workers who shifted to the left after the movements of the late 1960s. Given the increased weight of the middle strata in PCI membership, it seems likely that the party also attracted many new middle strata voters and that the first hypothesis as well as the second holds true.

Since 1970, the PCI has grown faster electorally than it has organizationally. Considering the nature of both kinds of growth since 1945, it seems clear that the party has developed steadily over the years into a tremendous electoral force, while struggling—and for a long period failing—to maintain its organizational strength. When this is added to the fact that the PCI gained most after 1970 among those social strata least rooted in the mass movements, it might be concluded that the party has lost in some measure its identity as a mass party and has taken on some of the characteristics of a catch-all party. While there is some truth to this, it is not the case that the PCI has become *simply* a catch-all party or that it no longer functions as a mass party.

The growth and transformations analyzed so far are closely related to a shift in party tactics and to the PCI's new role as a government party. Party Secretary Berlinguer first clearly articulated the shift in tactics after the September 1973 military coup in Chile. He proposed that the Communists assume direct responsibility for administering the Italian state by reentering the national government in the near future. This in itself was not a change; the definition of the PCI's "national role" after 1947 presupposed the party's eventual re-entry into some kind of coalition government. The new elements in Berlinguer's proposal involved the kind of coalition sought and the class alliances envisioned for Italy's future development.

It had been previously assumed that the Communists would wait until the DC was split or badly shaken before going into the government. In this way, the PCI could play a dominant role and build the "advanced democracy" that would allow for Italy's transformation into a socialist society. The party had conceptualized a grassroots alliance of social forces (the "new historic bloc") including Communists, Socialists, and Catholics that would be the foundation of a new coalition government that was not premised on any erosion of the DC. Moreover, no alliance of social forces existed to serve as the foundation. The leadership spoke of a possible shift to the left of the entire Christian Democratic Party, but the PCI pursued the coalition even when this shift never materialized. As for class alliances, the PCI had previously called for a bloc of all anti-monopoly forces, including small and medium-sized entrepreneurs. In the mid-1970s it proposed an alliance of the working class and progressive capitalists (those who claimed an interest in rationalizing the economy and working with organized labor). This alliance would include the monopolies; its goal would be to eliminate parasitism and waste while reordering the economy to meet the needs of both classes.

Shaken by events in Chile, the PCI leadership concluded that the Popular Unity government had moved too quickly, alienating the middle strata and provoking a reaction. In a speech shortly after the coup, Berlinguer announced the party's objective of a coalition government with the DC, calling it the "historic compromise."[5] By governing with the Christian Democrats, the PCI could share in state power and at the same time avoid full responsibility for the awesome task of resolving Italy's economic and social problems. For the leadership, the historic compromise also provided a way of avoiding a break or confrontation with the capitalists and middle strata, since the coalition government would presumably represent their interests as well. The DC was in a weakened position, discredited by a generation of inefficient and corrupt rule and plagued by internal conflicts and divisions. The Communist leadership, however, reevaluated the potential role of the DC and, in the wake of Chile, concluded that a split in the DC would precipitate a chaotic and uncontrollable reaction from the right. After 1973, therefore, the PCI avoided pressing any issue that might exacerbate internal divisions within the DC.

POLITICS OF THE HISTORIC COMPROMISE

THE CONTEXT FOR THE NEW TACTICS was the general shift to the left that had taken place after the late 1960s. The PCI found itself in a more hospitable climate, as shown by the party's electoral successes. Because of the DC's inefficiency and corruption, the declining influence of the Catholic Church, and the lessened impact of virulent anti-communist campaigns, there was a growing and generalized demand for reform. During the early 1970s, the PCI was increasingly identified with progressive change, efficiency, and honesty; the Communists pointed to their showcase administration in Bologna, where they had been the major government party since the war, as a model of what could be done throughout Italy. In addition, working-class strength had grown in the aftermath of the struggles of the late 1960s. Beyond increases in wages and benefits, Italian workers had wrested unprecedented concessions from the ruling class, including control over the organization and pace of factory work, over lay-off policies, and—on paper at least—over production choices and investment decisions. They also won more egalitarian salary policies and the right to study on company time. For a while, it appeared that capitalist relations of production were being thrown into question.

Given this situation, along with PCI electoral gains and a more favorable climate for the left in general, the party leadership now felt compelled to escape from its immobile position. The direction chosen was determined by a deeply-entrenched concern to avoid confrontation with the bourgeoisie and a reaction from the right. By transforming the PCI into a government party, the leadership could promise both reforms to the general population and protection of working-class interests; at the same time, it also hoped to keep the popular movements from erupting out of control. Since these movements had already reached a level of militancy and anti-capitalist consciousness that threatened the system, the PCI leadership could not allow the struggles to escalate without risking a break with the ruling class that would jeopardize its new tactics. What emerged from this dynamic was the PCI's mediating role in the parliamentary arena.

This role made it difficult for the PCI to organize ongoing and unified class movements based in the most radical sectors of the population. Instead, the party tended to support—while often moderating—particular struggles and demands. The party was flexible and successful enough in this limited kind of involvement never to alienate completely its working-class base. As party leaders began to direct most of their energies and resources toward reentering the government, they tried to explain policies in terms of a double identity—a party of struggle, a government party. Yet, as we shall see, the line pursued by the leadership threw the PCI's identification as a party of struggle into question as never before.

DEFINED BY PCI LEADERS as a long-term tactic, the historical compromise is fraught with contraditions. First there is the relationship to the Christian Democratic Party. After the war, the DC built an intricate, nationwide system of patronage reaching down into the smallest communities. Its power rests on this system and on its control of the various government ministries, departments, and agencies. Since the early 1960s, the DC has also become the major party of big capital as more and more industry (now about 50 percent) fell under state control. Since the PCI program for sharing state power involves streamlining the public bureaucracy, eliminating corruption and parasitism, and rationalizing the administration of state industry, the entire power structure of the DC is under direct threat. The Christian Democrats would have to hand over ministries and agencies to their Communist partners, thereby relinquishing a nearly unrestricted hold on the state. For these reasons, a faction of the DC has been adamantly opposed to this historic compromise from the outset. Since acceptance of the pact has always presupposed the DC's inability to govern without the Communists, it seems clear that at the first opportunity the Christian Democrats would scuttle the partnership. The relationship of the bourgeoisie to the historic compromise is similar to that of the DC. It would accept Communist participation in the government only to the extent that it was no longer capable of managing the economic situation itself and needed the PCI to keep the labor force in line.

The result is that the historic compromise puts the Communists in an extremely difficult position: the PCI hopes to carry out a reform program in alliance with a party that has always opposed reform. (Beginning in 1964, the Socialist Party entered a series of coalition governments with the same goal and failed abysmally.) Meanwhile, the PCI's electoral constituency would expect reforms and workers would expect their interests to be protected.

From the start, much of the PCI membership was surprised and confused by the historic compromise; many were jolted when the leadership proposed an alliance with a political force that had been seen as the enemy for so long. The debate on the new line began almost immediately. New left organizations either condemned the historic compromise as a policy that would lead to a working class defeat or hoped that the PCI would carry it out and then be justly discredited. As was always the case with a new controversial policy, PCI leaders and functionaries made efforts to explain the tactic through roundtable discussions, speeches, and articles in various publications. Since party loyalty and discipline are strong, most members were willing to follow the leadership, many taking a "wait-and-see" attitude. During the period from 1974 through the elections of 1976, the PCI's image in the country as a whole was greatly enhanced, generating new expectations about what the Communists would do once in government. As the left in general and the PCI in particular gained social acceptance, leftist politics became almost stylish (one trivial but indicative example was the appearance of Berlinguer's picture on the cover of personality magazines). This new credibility, however, was built around the PCI's potential role as a progressive-reformist force, a party that would be far more honest and efficient than the DC.

The PCI's 1975 electoral victory (32.4 percent) surprised even optimistic party members. While the rank-and-file mood was triumphant, the attitude of the leadership was somewhat ambivalent; the historic compromise was materializing faster than anticipated. The party now had to assume local administrative responsibility in about half the regions and many additional provinces and municipalities. At the same time, the economy was in a severe crisis. The leadership seemed worried about the party's ability to handle the situation, and, as if to prepare its constituency, warned that changes could not be made too quickly. Events, however, continued to accelerate. The government fell and parliament was dissolved in the spring of 1976. In the June elections that followed, the PCI polled 34.4 percent of the vote to the DC's 38.8 percent. For the first time since 1947, the Christian Democrats were unable to form a government unless the Communists abstained on the initial vote. This marked a turning point in post-war Italian politics.

After June 1976, the PCI took on some of the functions of a government party. Party policies and actions since then demonstrate both the contradictions of the historic compromise and the inadequacies of the PCI's overall strategy. The Communists were in the unusual position of keeping the DC government afloat, but at the same time they were not a formal part of the new cabinet or the parliamentary majority. The PCI constituencies expected the party to use its leverage to push through far-reaching reforms. Instead the leadership devoted all its efforts to working out a formal agreement with the DC, backing down on major issues in order to keep negotiations going. During the year of the "government of the abstentions," the DC passed a series of measures that served its own interests: Large sums of money were allocated to industry (ostensibly for an "industrial conversion" program) with no stipulations as to how the money would be spent; the government covered the deficits of state-owned conglomerates but refused to investigate the questionable practices of those industries; prices for the basic consumer goods, public transportation, and utilities were raised; and cost-of-living escalator mechanism (*scala mobile*), which protects the organized working class against inflation, was partially dismantled.

THE POLITICAL CRISIS ESCALATES

BY FEBRUARY 1977, the so-called "marginalized" strata (students, youth, women, the unemployed) were in revolt, frustrated by the lack of jobs and the refusal of the government to enact significant social and economic reforms. Their protests were often directed at the PCI. Small groups within these "emergent" movements armed themselves, and demonstrations inevitably ended in violence. The Communist leadership reacted to the new situation by taking a law-and-order stand that was sometimes more rigid than that of the DC. The result was to widen the gap between the new movement and the organized working-class movement. In June 1977, the situation was tense enough to force the DC leadership to sign a political accord with five other parties, including the PCI. Yet it was the DC that managed to dictate the terms of the agreement: there was no economic reform program, and the parties committed themselves to following the guidelines set by the International Monetary Fund (lowered labor costs, austerity measures to reduce inflation and the balance of payments deficit, cut-backs in public spending). The accord also stipulated a hiring freeze in the public sector and patient fees for medication that had been free under the national health program. In addition, the parties agreed to a series of law-and-order measures for parliament to consider: police would be allowed to hold suspects for 24 hours without making an arrest, to question them without the presence of a lawyer, and to use wiretaps more extensively.

Once this agreement was signed, the PCI was one step closer to having a share of governmental power. Yet the DC continued to dominate the political situation. The mass base of the PCI was clearly dissatisfied, but most members accepted the leadership's argument that the party had to join a government coalition before it could move ahead. By December, however, the most militant sector of the organized working class—the metal workers—was disgruntled enough to organize a mass demonstration against the government's policies. This was also an indirect protest against the PCI. As in the past, the party leadership knew that it could not ignore a widespread dissatisfaction without alienating its base. The day after the 200,000 metalworkers, women, and students marched in Rome, the PCI declared that the existing political arrangement was inadequate, thus initiating the long negotiations for the party's entry into the government. The Carter administration in the U.S. made it clear that an Italian cabinet with PCI ministers was unacceptable. Since most of the DC leadership was equally hostile to this solution, a compromise was worked out: The Communists would enter the parliamentary majority but not the government (cabinet) itself. On March 16, just a few hours after prominent DC leader Aldo Moro was kidnapped by left-wing terrorists, parliament voted the PCI into the majority with practically no debate.

ALTHOUGH THE MORO KIDNAPPING dominated the political situation in Italy for two months, the PCI's conduct as a government party became clear. The necessity of maintaining a precarious alliance with the DC conditioned Communist policies. A good illustration of this was the maneuvering around the politically-charged abortion law. The DC proposed amendments to make the new legislation more restrictive; the PCI abstained, allowing the changes to go through. Parliament then passed the modified and weakened measure with the DC voting against it. While deliberations were going on, thousands of women, including those belonging to the PCI affiliated *Unione Donne Italiane* (Italian Women's Union), were demonstrating outside parliament. Five days after Moro was kidnapped, the DC cabinet imposed as temporary decrees those law-and-order measures contained in the 1977 accord. In May, the parliamentary majority voted them into law. During the next few months, parliament also passed long-delayed legislation on health care and rent control, but in a form acceptable to DC interests. The economic situation continued to deteriorate, but the majority parties took no steps toward developing a comprehensive reform program.

In those areas where the PCI entered the local government in 1975, Communist performance was equally disappointing for several reasons. First, the party's general policy was to avoid pushing the DC too hard for fear of upsetting political negotiations at the national level. As a result, the DC continued to manipulate local politics. Second, the national government in Italy controls almost all local funding and the DC controls most of the banks. As a result, funds for reforms on the local level were often blocked. Third, the PCI found it did not have enough trained or experienced cadre to administer health care, welfare, sanitation, housing, urban renewal, and so on. The party shifted many of its functionaries and activists into specialized administrative positions where they had to train themselves on the job. This left the sections and federations understaffed and overworked in terms of party duties, meaning that the PCI was less able to respond to local initiatives around specific issues.

Thus three years after stepping into the national arena as a government party, the PCI was not yet able to effectively shape the political and economic situation in Italy. The PCI's membership is for the most part well aware of the contradictions and failures of the party's tactics. As in the past, dissatisfaction is having a negative effect on the party's organizational strength. After years of recruitment success, membership levelled off in 1977 and declined by 20,000 in 1978. This trend was especially strong in the northwest: between 1976 and the end of 1977, party membership dropped in Milan, Turin, Genoa, Rome and Naples. Moreover, the Communist youth organization lost 10.6 percent of its members during the same period. According to a DOXA poll (the Italian equivalent of Gallup) conducted in September 1977, about one-third of PCI members did not approve of party policies toward the government.

The Communist electorate has also begun to show signs of disaffection. An example is the May 1978 provincial and municipal elections, which involved about 10 percent of the Italian voters.* Comparing these returns with those of the June 1976 parliamentary elections in the same localities, the PCI lost an average of 9.1 percent—dropping from 35.6 percent to 26.5 percent—and barely surpassed the 1972 level of 25.7 percent. In contrast, the DC's average share of the votes increased from 38.9 percent to 42.5 percent. (A sympathy vote because of Moro's death probably added to the DC gain.) The new left did relatively well in those localities where it ran candidates, and more than doubled its share of the votes, taking over 3 percent. After the elections, the PCI leadership admitted that it had lost votes to the far left in certain cities. Meanwhile, the Socialists were able to reverse their long-term electoral slide, winning an average of 13.3 percent of the 1978 vote as compared to 9.2 percent in 1976.

Signs of dissatisfaction with PCI policies since 1976 are evident. Yet the party—up to the present at least—has seemed locked into tactical choices that were bound to guarantee its continued failure as both a reformist government party and a party of struggle. One can explain the PCI's dogged pursuit of this course only in terms of its *operative* theoretical assumptions (its assumptions in practice) and its consequent choice of class alliances and strategic perspective.

THE PCI'S TACTICAL PREMISES

ON VARIOUS OCCASIONS DURING the last several years, the Communist leadership has affirmed that no socialist revolution is possible in Italy in the present historical period given the existing national and international balance of forces. Of course the PCI operated on this same assumption during the 1950s and 1960s, but its position has become more explicit with the escalation of class struggle after 1968 and the intensification of the economic crisis after 1974. What the PCI leadership proposes as an alternative to revolution—at least for the present—is to build working-class strength through a variety of economic, social, and institutional reforms. The long-term political mechanism for achieving this is the historic compromise; the short-term goal is

---

*Although comparing local electoral results with national parliamentary outcomes does not provide a completely accurate measure of shirts in popular support, it is nonetheless true that any election in Italy can function as a political barometer indicating broad shifts and trends.

to pull Italy out of its severe economic crisis. Once the balance of power shifts in favor of the working class, and once other strata swing over to the left, the socialist transformation of Italian society can presumably move ahead—given a more favorable international context.

Underlying this approach is the assumption that capitalists and workers can function together politically to meet their separate needs. What the PCI leadership has in mind is an alliance of the working class and the progressive sectors of capital in order to relaunch the Italian economy. In theory, this alliance would guarantee increased worker productivity and high profits for the capitalists while simultaneously redirecting production and revenues to meet social needs. In the early 1970s, the PCI emphasized the national role of the working class to maintain order and a high level of productivity in the factories. Then once the economy went into severe crisis, the leadership insisted that the workers would have to make sacrifices in order to stave off complete collapse. Just as the party hopes to avoid direct confrontation with the ruling class, it also hopes to avert economic breakdown. The only solution it envisions for the present historical period, therefore, is a rebuilding of capitalism. As a result, the PCI's general economic plan has been essentially the same as that of the bourgeoisie. It conforms to the usual two-phase schema: first create the conditions for a new cycle of investment (increased productivity, labor mobility, higher profits); then allow the new investments to generate jobs, increased income, and the surplus necessary for reforms.

This plan contradicts the analysis of many economists, who argue that relaunching capitalism in Italy will requires the working class to give up much of its previously-won control over the labor process and lay-off policy as well as wage and benefit gains. They maintain that labor mobility (laying off workers in certain factories with the promise of employing them elsewhere) would probably translate into long-term unemployment and that there is no guarantee new investments would generate many new jobs since a large proportion of the capital would go toward increased automation. Accordingly, the needs of the bourgeoisie are seen as necessarily conflicting with those of the working class— especially given the severity of the economic crisis in Italy. This conflict is intensified, from the viewpoint of these economists, by vriute of the fact that world capitalism is in a long-term structural crisis that will enable the strongest national economics to maintain their domination at the expense of the weaker countries like Italy. Since Italy is particularly poor in raw materials and energy resources and has also imported much of its advanced technology since the war while allowing domestic agriculture to decline, the country is quite dependent on exports in order to import what it needs. Thus prospects for sustained economic growth during a long-term international downswing are very limited.

THE PCI COUNTER THIS perspective by arguing that as a government party it can influence investment choices to promote production for social needs, for agriculture, and for development of the south. It claims that a period of austerity and sacrifice on the part of the working class will make possible a rationalization of the economy.

The PCI's economic analysis has generated skepticism for years. After the 1976 elections, both the party's constituency and its political opponents pressured the leadership to present a concrete economic program. The leadership finally published its *Proposal for an Intermediate Project (Proposta di proggetto a medio termine)* in July 1977. (This 115-page text covers industrial and agricultural conversion, employment, the role of private enterprise, the public sector, government financing, planning, labor policy, education, health, welfare, state reform, worker participation and control, local government, the credit system, state-controlled industry, the European Economic Community, detente, and the new international economic order.) General reaction to the proposal was disappointment over its vagueness. The program does little other than outline Italy's economic and social ills and specify a few generic solutions; there is no elaboration of how to move from the status quo to a more progressive system of industrial management, health care, or international relations. There is no connection between programmatic goals and the concrete framework of Italian politics. The program offers no timetable or well-defined stages of development, although it does insist that the more serious aspects of the Italian crisis can be overcome within three to five years. The text stresses that private enterprise—including the multinationals, so long as they function in Italy's interest—has an important role to play in future development. The vision is of a rationally ordered system providing for both human needs and profits. Yet there are no indications, either from concrete experiences since 1976 or from a general economic and political analysis, that the PCI's reform program is viable.

The PCI national leadership is worried about the recent organizational and electoral losses of the party. Since late 1976, the debate at several central committee meetings has been more conflictual than usual. Some members of the national leadership are concerned that the party is losing touch with its base, has been alienating young people, and is less combative than before. Party president Luigi Longo argued this position on several occasions. Recently there have been open discussions about political and organizational problems; the focus has been on the PCI's dual identity as a party of struggle and a government party and the relationship between party organization and the masses.[6] The national leadership admits that the sections are less able to mobilize the base and link up with the daily needs of people in the communities and workplaces. Since 1975, local leaders and functionaries have been spending most of their time performing administrative tasks and working with the other political parties. There is a strong trend toward bureaucratization among the younger (under 40) cadre who have constituted the bulk of the intermediate level leadership since the mid-1970s. (It is interesting to note that many of these did not enter the party until after 1969.) They relate primarily to the higher levels of the party hierarchy and tend to be out of touch with the local workplaces and the neighborhoods. The national leadership also admits that the PCI has not developed the capacity to deal with the multiplicity of issues (the environment, urban renewal, the universities, and so on) that have emerged in the urban areas since 1970. There is also great concern about the diminishing weight of working-class cadre in the party; of the nearly 12,000 PCI sections in 1978, only 800 were in workplaces.

INTERNAL PARTY DEMOCRACY: THEORY AND PRACTICE

THE TOP LEADERSHIP discusses these problems frankly but, publicly at least, has ended up reaffirming the correctness of the established political line. So far, dissatisfaction within the party has not shaken the control of the most powerful figures. The leadership often lays blame for political and organizational difficulties on an inadequate assimilation and implementation of the line by the intermediate and base levels of the party. They are commonly accused of carrying out the party line without much vigor or conviction. When this phenomenon is added to the membership and electoral losses since 1976, two important questions emerge: First, if the PCI base and elements of the leadership are dissatisfied, why have they not been able to modify or even radically change the party's line? Second, who exactly formulates PCI strategy? These questions cannot be answered without analyzing the PCI's internal structure and its degree of internal democracy. Although the party claims to function democratically, and although some formal mechanisms for broad participation exist, there is still a great discrepancy between theory and practice.*

The PCI operates according to a somewhat rigid form of democratic centralism, which can be summarized as follows: once an issue is debated

---

*It should be kept in mind that the limited internal democracy of the PCI is still greater than that of the DC and the PSI, both of which are plagued by factional infighting and maneuvering and demonstrate even less membership involvement.

throughout the party as a whole, the minority accepts and carries out the decision of the majority; within the organizational pyramid, the higher bodies have authority over the lower ones; and no organized political tendencies or factions are permitted.*

In theory (and by statute), the national congress held every three of fours years establishes the party line, which the central committee then carries out. The central committee is thus supposed to be the main leadership structure. (An assembly of delegates elects the central committee, which in turn chooses the directorate, which then chooses the secretariat.) In practice, the debate at national congresses is limited to documents agreed to by top leaders ahead of time. They present the documents to the delegates as components of a party line to be defended, and the congress inevitably approves what the leadership has decided. The directorate and secretariat also end up controlling who is nominated and elected to the central committee, the directorate, and the secretariat; in general, only 10 to 20 percent of the leadership changes after the assembly of delegates holds elections.

THE CENTRAL COMMITTEE meets too infrequently (every three months) and it is too large to play its assigned leadership role. So, in effect, formulation of the party line, decision-making, and power remain in the hands of directorate and secretariat. The important debates take place within the directorate (which meets every week), but neither the topics discussed nor the content of the debate is made public. When open debate reaches the central committee, as it has several times since 1976, it means that the directorate is divided. Although there are greater possibilities for dissent and debate at the PCI's base (the sections and cells), local leadership tends to dominate discussions, and many members feel too inhibited to participate. Opposition to the party line can develop in one section, but most often it is horizontally isolated from other sections and stifled vertically by the party's bureaucratic structure. The result is that the base plays no role in formulating strategy and has little

---

*The national leadership of the PCI includes the secretariat (nine members), the directorate (37 members), and the central committee (182 members). In 1975, the party abolished the politbureau in order to give more authority to the directorate. Below the central committee is the regional organization; each of the 20 regions has a secretariat, directorate, and regional committee. Next is the provincial level which includes about 100 federations (practically all of which correspond to a province), and they too have a secretariat, directorate, and federation committe. Below the federations are party sections which cover either a particular geographical area (for example, a neighborhood) or a specific sector of the population (for example, a large workplace or university). Cells are generally smaller units that affiliate with a section. This and the following two figures vary slightly from year to year. The numbers given are for 1978.)

chance of modifying the line. Major shifts in strategy take place only when there is a significant break at the highest echelons of party leadership.

CONCLUSION

SINCE THE END OF the Second World War, the PCI's strategy has remained fundamentally unchanged, and party policies have consistently reflected a gradualist approach to social transformation as well as certain reformist assumptions. Yet these politics embody significant tensions and a great deal of ambiguity: The party claims to be steering a course that follows neither the Bolshevik model for revolution nor the social democratic path of reforms. At times, the leadership maintains that socialism is not possible in Italy in this historical period, implying that a very different set of national and international circumstances must first exist. Yet there is also the implication that the present PCI course will eventually—and without a major break of any kind—result in a workers'-controlled socialist society. In both cases, socialism has become a vague goal, relegated to an unforseen future. What does seem clear is that the PCI does not have an adequate strategy for pulling the working class, the "emergent" strata, and the most politically advanced groups together into a unified and dynamic class movement while effectively dealing with the DC, middle strata alliances, and the issue of state power.

The 1970s presented the PCI strategy with its most important test since the war. As the decade began, the working class had achieved a level of political consciousness, militancy, and organization unsurpassed in any advanced capitalist country. Other groups, such as women, young people, and the unemployed, had been politicized and continued to struggle—as did the workers. The ruling class was on the defensive, and its largest party (the DC) was weakened and beset by internal divisions. These conditions gave the PCI an exceptional opportunity to swing the balance of power even further toward the working class and popular strata by unifying a large anti-capitalist movement around the most advanced economic, political, and social demands possible at the time. The PCI rejected this course in all the ways and for all the reasons that we have seen. What became more evident than ever during this period was the profound separation between the party's stated goals and its tactics, between its theoretical program and its practice.

The PCI constituency has grown increasingly dissatisfied since 1976, and the leadership—always sensitive in the long run to base reaction—has responded recently by taking a harder line toward the DC. But given the premises of the current PCI leadership as well as the nature of the party's internal structure and mode of operation, it is not clear whether the Italian Communists will be able to devise a new and more adequate strategy in the short run. Success here would involve a kind of cultural as well as political revolution within the party itself—a revolution that would radically alter the relationship of the leadership to the mass base, the working class, mass movements, and the state.

It is difficult to know exactly what the impetus for these changes would be. They might grown out of the extreme dissatisfaction of the party rank and file, perhaps out of a new wave of radicalization and mass movements, or perhaps out of the provocations of the right. It is hard to imagine the most politically advanced sectors of Italian society quietly resigning themselves to a repeal of past victories or to additional sacrifices that would only help rebuild ruling class economic and political hegemony. If the PCI continues to frustrate its own constitutency and if those who try to transform the organization and its strategy fail, then the party may end up dividing its own base and creating a situation where part of the working class and other groups accept defeat while others begin mobilizing in opposition to the PCI. Should this happen, the leadership role may pass to a new political force (or forces) better able to provide a revolutionary strategy for Italy.

Notes

1. John Hewetson, *Italy After Mussolini* (Pamphlet printed by *Radical America*, Somerville, Mass.).

2. Giorgio Galli, *Storia del partito comunista italiano* (Milano: Schwartz, 1958).

3. All of the data on PCI membership, rate of adhesion, party organization, and social composition contained in this paper can be found in Marzio Barbagli and Piergiorgio Corbetta, "Partito e movimento: aspetti e rinnovamento del PCI," in *Inchiesta,* January-February, 1978.

4. See Otto Kirchheimer, "The Transformation of the Western European Party Systems," in Joseph Lapalombara and Myron Weiner, eds. *Political Parties and Political Development* (Princeton, N.J.: Princeton University Press, 1966).

5. Enrico Berlinguer, "Reflections after the Events in Chile," in *The Italian Communists* (Foreign Bulletin of the PCI), no. 5, 1973.

6. Paolo Franchi, ed., "Il partito oggi: il rapporto con le istituzioni e con le masse," in *Rinascita*, January 6, 1978.

chapter 3

SPANISH COMMUNISM
IN TRANSITION

Jose Rodríguez-Ibañez

After nearly 40 years of clandestine activity, the Spanish Communist Party (PCE) has emerged as the third largest electoral force in the country and now seeks to improve its political image and social influence by adopting a "Eurocommunist" strategy that still remains to be fully elaborated. The PCE's endorsement of democracy, its detachment from the Soviet Union, and, most importantly, its recent dropping of the "Marxist-Leninist" label have indeed placed it in the forefront of this tendency. But such a development stands in powerful contrast to the entire PCE tradition, which for years was associated with orthodox, rigid positions closely identified with the Soviet leadership. The PCE's recent shift toward Eurocommunism really began in 1968, when the party leadership condemned the Soviet invasion of Czechoslovakia; this shift is still evolving, insofar as the PCE now operates in a transitional period between its Stalinist past and a future that is open and uncertain. To illustrate this process, it will be useful to sketch the history of orthodoxy, out of which the current positions have evolved.

Old Premises, New Realities

WE MIGHT START with the famous polemics carried out in 1964 between Fernando Claudin and the PCE leadership, culminating in the expulsion of Claudin and other leading militants (for example, Jorge Semprún) from the party for their "dark and muggy pessimism," "counterrevolutionary" attitudes, "opportunistic subjectivism," "vulgar rightism," etc.[1] Such polemics might be seen as the PCE's rejection of perspectives that could be labelled "pre-Eurocommunist"; in 1964, the PCE was quite intolerant of alternatives that would in fact later represent in some way its own line. This paradox symbolizes the internal contradictions and difficulties of the PCE's recent development.

The main premise of the party dissidents at that time was that the PCE leadership (for years exiled in Paris) had little awareness of the changes that were occurring in Spanish society, especially in the 1960s. This lack of awareness functioned to produce a strategy that was politically irrelevant. The dissidents argued, moreover, that the new conditions urgently required an internal democratization of party organization.

By the time of Claudin's expulsion from the party (in 1965), the PCE still maintained the fiction that Francoism was a weak political force which could be overthrown by the unified and decisive action of popular forces. Many within the PCE leadership looked to a general strike, which would be the catalyst of a new phase of development—the "democratic, anti-monopolist revolution." This phase would rapidly bring the working class and the popular masses to hegemonic positions, with the party itself emerging as the leading force because of its clandestine legacy and the relative absence of competing leftist movements. In the PCE's words: "The establishment in Spain of universal suffrage, political freedoms, and democratic institutions will mean the creation of a *revolutionary situation....In a situation of political freedoms, the workers' movement will take giant strides forward within days or even hours*; what today already appears as a great force will then become a true power able to carry out a democratic, anti-feudal and anti-monopoly revolution. In that situation, our party, which is potentially the majority party among the workers, will surface *in every corner of Spain,* in the towns and in the countryside, with no force that can stop it. No other Spanish politial party has the potential for making the same progress in such a short period of time."[2]

Beyond this, the PCE was virtually blind to the massive industrial-urban transformation of the country[3]—for example, it ascribed far too much weight to the peasant movement, characterizing "the peasant, along with the industrial proletariat, [as] the fundamental revolutionary force of Spain, not only in this period but also in future ones."[4]

AGAINST ALL THOSE trumpeting theses reflecting the PCE's flagrant misunderstanding of Spanish social reality, Claudin argued that the growing oppositional movements in the country were not the symptom of a definitive crisis of monopoly capital but were more accurately the symptom of a political crisis that monopoly capital could survive if it chose to adopt new forms of domination. Thus: "The matter is not a crisis of the state monopoly capitalist system, but a crisis of its political forms of domination.... We are not facing a national revolutionary crisis but a political crisis that will be solved by struggles 'from below' and initiatives 'from above' through a building of phases and partial political and economic reforms following a gradual and relatively peaceful path."[5]

According to Claudin's analysis, Spain was becoming a modern industrial society in which the peasant sector was progressively declining because of enforced migration abroad and the absorption of the labor force by a growing industrial sector. Claudin understood this process as leading to a change of consciousness within the working class—a shift from Civil War radicalism to contemporary consumerism. This did not reflect a strict process of "embourgeoisement" but rather the rejection by most workers of violent tactics at a time of relative prosperity, when few wanted to see a repeat of the terrible past. Meanwhile, Claudin concluded, there were growing numbers of the middle classes now in favor of democracy, but not committed to revolution as such, although they would surely be indispensable to any coherent leftist strategy in the future. On this basis Claudin proposed what later came to be known as a "Eurocommunist" strategy: "The impending tasks of the democratic revolution will develop as follows: *first*, the liquidation of the fascist form of the state; *second*, successive democratic transformations, both political and economic, imposed by the struggle of anti-monopoly forces during the immediate period following the liquidation of Francoism, although monopoly capital (or any of its representative groups) will maintain the fundamental core of political power; *third*, a period of taking power by an anti-monopoly coalition led by the working class, that is the most radical phase of the democratic revolution and of the beginning of its change toward socialist revolution."[6]

At a later point, Claudin added: "The first important step toward the solution of the problems proper of the democratic revolution is the liquidation of fascist political forms and the conquest, through a series of phases or partial advances, of a democratic political regime that will remain the form of monopoly capital power (although this power may be shared with other bourgeois groups), but where the working class and the popular masses will weigh considerably and will obtain a variety of political and economic reforms."[7] Here Claudin was anticipating the popular struggles of the late 1960s and 1970s, as well as the emergence of a younger generation of rightists able to revitalize the old Francoist political class. The latter included Adolfo Suárez Union of Democratic Center (UCD), a coalition of former Francoist politicians, conservative Christian Democrats, social democrats, and liberals representing an evolving right wing which incorporates a moderate opposition to Francoism, and which seems to represent the interests of monopoly capital in a form appropriate to new conditions.

Claudin envisaged this new right as fundamentally Christian Democratic and supported by "broad sectors of the party and middle urban bourgeoisies; middle, rich, and even poor peasants; certain sectors of the working class; some intellectual and academic groups; technocrats, civil servants, and professionals; and a large number of women."[8] In 1964, he envisioned the formation of a spontaneous kind of multi-class conservative party, but this developed since the evolution of the right in fact became much more of an administered operation. At the same time, Claudin's central argument about the rise of a new "civilized" right was insightful.

Claudin was more or less accurate in predicting that the future counterpart of the Christian Democrats would be a renewed social democratic party presumably organized as a reconstituted Spanish Socialist Workers' Party (PSOE), which had been the dominant force on the left for nearly a century (and whose Leninist dissidents founded the PCE in 1921). The PSOE was very influential during the Second Republic and the Civil War, but was little more than a symbolic presence after the 1939 defeat and the massive repression that followed. Claudin argued that the PSOE's revitalization was a logical consequence of Spanish neocapitalist development and was, furthermore, the kind of stabilizing force that the conservatives preferred. In contemporary Spain this political framework of two main, contending forces—a moderate right and a moderate left—is an established reality, though not in the precise terms anticipated by Claudin. But in 1964, the PCE denied this prospect, supporting its contention not with political analysis but with prejudicial irony and scorn. Curiously, such irony had a boomerang effect, since the judgments presented as mocking reductions *ad absurdum* of Claudin's theses now merely reinforce the accuracy of the latter's analysis and the weakness of the PCE's position during that period. Consider the following example, which is indeed a matter of repressed anticipation: "Monopolist oligarchy, today in power, will achieve the wonder of transforming from above the fascist regime into a democratic one without abandoning its power. Claudin, willfully or not, aligns himself with those who defend the idea of 'revolution from above'. From the phoenix bird's ashes of monopoly dictatorship will rise the phoenix of monopolist 'democracy'."[9]

The Renewal of the PSOE

THE BROAD POLITICAL appeal of the PSOE stems from its tradition of being a genuinely national leftist force—a party that from the beginning has shown a considerable degree of flexibility. Founded as a Marxist workers' party, it has incorporated many different tendencies, ranging from radical to Fabian. Historically it has shown a capacity for shifting its basic positions. For example, while it effectively organized the general strike of 1917 and was in the leadership of many other mass actions, such as Asturias' revolution of 1934, it chose to collaborate with the Primo de Rivera dictatorship in the 1923-30 period.

After 1939, the exiled PSOE leadership developed a strong anti-Communist perspective and played a very limited role within the underground opposition to Franco. In the mid-1950s, a group of young intellectuals led by Tierno Galván tried to link the "interior" to the dormant but still dominant group that had grown old in exile. New Socialist groups later formed and began to spread (especially at the universities), making contact with the older (isolated and scarcely organized) militants of the PSOE and its labor union, Unión General de Trabajadores (UGT). By 1974, the young Socialists were strong enough to revitalize the PSOE and take power in the Congress of Suresnes (France), where Felipe González (an obscure lawyer from Seville at that time) was elected Secretary General. The defeated faction denounced this Congress and tried to hold on to the traditional strategy within a parallel PSOE. Other Socialists, concerned with the problem of decentralization and regional autonomy, founded the Federation of Socialist Parties, which was composed of autonomous groups from every Spanish nationality and region. Finally, Tierno Galván formed an allegedly more radical socialist party—the PSP (Socialist Popular Party). These efforts, however, were condemned to failure; following the general elections of 1977, all of these groups wound up merging with the PSOE.

At present, the Socialist Party contains an internal pluralism rooted in the differences among its militants. While supported by a large percentage of the electorate,[10] it lacks experienced leaders or cadres as well as the organizational capability that the PCE possesses—the consequence of a broad gap between veteran militants and a new generation of leaders. The PSOE base is composed of intellectuals, professionals, civil servants, middle classes, and of course sectors of the working class (which generally have a strong Socialist tradition). In the 1978 Spanish labor union elections, the UGT won only 31 percent of the vote against the 38 percent of the Communist-dominated *commisiones obreras* (workers' commissions). The main significance of the PSOE today is political; it constitutes a powerful electoral force that can present itself as an alternative to the existing government.

Given its goal of winning elections and forming a new government, and given its diverse ideological and social composition, the PSOE is compelled to moderate its program as it seeks the broadest possible mass support. The dynamic reached its extreme development when Gonzalez declared that he will propose, at the next party congress, to delete the term "Marxism" from the PSOE statutes, arguing that it was only included at the last (1976) congress, and that, furthermore, the Spanish Socialists need the cooperation of groups such as the progressive Christians and liberals who could never agree to join a "Marxist" party but who would support a socialist party with the openness and diversity of the PSOE. This question is not purely verbal; it hides important problems that are reflected in ongoing polemics within the party as well as the Spanish media. Whereas the PSOE contends that "Marxism" connotes anti-democratic practices and that its inclusion is tactically wrong, some elements within the party—notably within the Socialist Youth groups— argue that such a move would parallel the conservative move of the German Social Democratic Party at its Bad Godesberg Congress in 1959. Such a "social democratization" of the PSOE would help to reinforce the PCE's democratic and parliamentary, yet Marxist, role in Spain. The convergence of both parties around democratic goals, with differing emphases and commitments, helps to stimulate cooperation between them. At present the PSOE is not interested in any real alliance with the Communists since it feels strong enough to govern or at least present an alternative by itself. In the case of the PCE, however, and despite some reservations on the part of the leadership which are the residue of ancient debates, the base seems cooperative and has even forced an additional paragraph on alliances in the resolutions of the Ninth Congress.

RETURNING TO the Claudin polemics—an approach that permits us to examine the antcedents of the PCE's Eurocommunist strategy—we might note his insistence upon a broadening of the party's previously narrow conception of the working class and a transcendence of the ideological limitations of "prolet-cult." Claudin's viewpoint was that the PCE could easily be surpassed in the future by newly-emerging leftist forces more rooted in the changing social conditions of Spain—an assessment that proved to be particularly correct for the PSOE, and one which shaped Eurocommunist perspectives at a later time. In this respect, the PCE now defends the concept of an alliance between the "forces of work and culture" and outlines a notion of the "mass party" that is accessible to broad sectors of the population. Claudin hence advocates a democratization of the PCE's internal orgnization.[11] Of course he realized that underground political conditions impeded any perfect democratic functioning of party structure, but he insisted that anti-democratic practices prevalent at the time—appointed leaders, absence of criticism motivated by fear, careerism, and hierarchy—existed even under non-clandestine conditions (for instance, at party meetings that were held in exile) and persisted as regressive features well into the present period. In this context, Claudin also proposed a radical departure from Stalinist practices in general and from a Soviet orthodoxy that undermined any revolutionary ethos. The PCE had unconditionally supported the Soviet line, even to the extent of affirming that "international detente (and) coexistence (are) a revolutionary factor." For the PCE, the de-Stalinization process that was set in motion by Khrushchev's "thaw" at the Twentieth CPSU congress in 1956 was sufficient.

It is within this framework that the PCE began to take on its Eurocommunist character. I wish to turn now to a general treatment of that evolution in the years following Claudin's expulsion. Here it is crucial to keep in mind the caution of party leadership, especially vis-a-vis the older generations of militants, as well as the absence of any real self-critical posture.*

The PCE's Evolution Toward Eurocommunism

THE DEPARTURE of Spanish Communism from the Soviet model is perhaps the most visible sign of the party's Eurocommunist evolution. We have already suggested that in 1964-65 the PCE accepted Soviet leadership with no reservations. This situation changed in 1968, when the party leadership felt compelled to attack the Soviet Union for its invasion of Czechoslovakia. The PCE leadership began to understand the dangers of being a puppet party in terms of its future prospects as a legal and democratic force in Spain. At the same time, the implementation of the doctrine of "national roads to socialism"—along with the feeling that socialism must be the extension and not the supercession of democracy— were the motivating factors behind this condemnation. Also in 1968, Manuel Sacristán, a leading PCE philosopher and ideologist, included in his forward to Dubcek's *Czechoslavak Road to Socialism*[12] a strong

---

*I can offer a personal testimony. During the 48-hour political gathering organized by the PCE in Madrid, in October 1977, Carrillo spoke in a closing speech. Prior to his intervention, testimonies of solidarity from abroad were read. I was surprised by a group of old-fashioned Communists. Applause was generally only polite after the reading of each message, but after the Soviet message was read the applause was long and particularly loud. And this despite the hostile Soviet position toward the PCE leadership, which was already obvious by this time, and which would become even more virulent a few days later when at the Fiftieth Anniversary of the Russian Revolution in Moscow. Carrillo was not allowed to speak.

defense of the "Prague Spring," referring to it as an example of Leninist self-critique (which was a tribute to the still untouchable "Marxism-Leninism" label) and, most importantly, a necessary step toward socialist democracy in a period of consolidated economic welfare—a position that the USSR had completely rejected.

In 1973, Manuel Azcárate (the PCE's "foreign minister") developed a more explicit and political critique of the USSR. In a report approved by the Central Committee, he argued that "the great socialist countries" (that is, the USSR and China) do not practice a revolutionary policy but simply a politics of superpower interests. In his words: "Revolution disappears from the horizon of the great socialist countries' foreign policy...A contradiction arises: when the crisis of imperialism is more than evident, the most important Communist parties in power adopt *defensive* attitudes in contrast to the exigencies of anti-imperialist struggles...When the leaders of those countries speak about international questions, they generally do so only as statesmen; they do not express a vanguard, fighting view...(but) ideas and words molded in most cases by diplomatic considerations that do not reach the revolutionaries. There is an enormous gap between the potential of the existing means and the potential of revolutionary thought."[13] Subsequently, the polemics between the USSR and the PCE intensified, reaching their peak during the November 1977 celebration of the Fiftieth Anniversary of the Russian Revolution.

As far back as the late 1960s, however, the Soviet leadership was disconcerted enough with the PCE to create a dissident Spanish Communist Party—led by Enrique Líster, former general of the Republican Army and one of the legendary figures of the Civil War. This attempt, however, ended in dismal failure. Líster now lives in Spain and heads the recently-legalized PCOE (Spanish Communist Workers' Party), which has little political strength. On the whole, there has been no large-scale defection of militants from the PCE, with even the most staunchly old-guard elements choosing to remain within the party.

The PCE presently advocates a policy of national independence, which among other things means opposition to the balance of terror and superpower competition. This is why it is opposed to Spain's entry into NATO, arguing that such involvement would reinforce tensions between the Eastern and Western military blocs—blocs which the PCE equally rejects. Concerning U.S. military bases in Spain—a dangerous presence that de facto allies Spain with NATO—the PCE has not taken very radical positions; it contends that the bases will disappear when international military blocs themselves disappear, thus dissolving the problem of U.S. military penetration in Spain into the larger problem of the struggle against global military blocs.[14]

New Anti-Monopoly Alternatives

THE SECOND CHAPTER of the PCE's evolution is its revision of anti-monopoly strategy. We have already seen that in the 1960s the party identified the conquest of political freedoms and the defeat of fascism in Spain with the period of transition to socialism. The PCE regarded both moments as phases of a very rapid process. Now it argues the necessity of a preliminary period of advanced social and political democracy whose inner logic and progressive maturity would create the conditions for the transition to socialism. Let us examine the PCE's change in this respect as well as concrete steps it proposes for reaching the stage of advanced democracy.

A good point of departure is the PCE's Eighth Congress in 1972, where its stance vis-a-vis the European Common Market was debated. A resolution proposed by Juan Gómez, and finally approved by the Congress, favored the entry of Spain into the EEC. Gómez argued that while few people could deny that the EEC is indeed a monopoly and imperialist organization, it was also true that the Spanish economy could only channel its products through Europe, and that under such conditions it would not be realistic to ignore the Community. The end of monopoly, then, was no longer considered an immediate goal.[15] A few months later, Gómez also elaborated a new "long march" anti-monopoly strategy. He defined the 1973 energy crisis as a scheme by monopoly capital against which anti-monopoly forces in Spain should mobilize themselves by means of expanded democratic and popular control of public institutions.[16]

More recently, "M.C." (Tomás García, now a Communist parliamentarian who chose at that time to remain anonymous) outlined a concept of structural transformation within the sphere of anti-monopoly struggle—the beginning of a transformation seen as the only valid, non-maximalist response to the world crisis of capitalism: "The question is to elaborate a platform of measures...through the phase that the PCE conceives of as a period of *political and social democracy*. In this phase, the task will not be the building of socialism which demands political and social conditions not present in Spain, but putting in practice some fundamental changes that will solve the crisis of the system: nationalization of financial and insurance firms; socialization of large monopolies; land for the people who work it; fiscal reform; self-determination of nationalities comprising the Spanish state; administrative autonomy; democratic planning; development of the public sector; public aid to non-monopoly forms of industry; aid to small and middle trade; improvement of workers' social conditions, including forms of self-management..."[17]

This statement actually outlines the main goals of a program that the PCE would later approve as its Manifesto-Program in Septemeber 1975, and which is still a foundation of the party's overall program today. In it, the PCE refers to "the great tasks of social and political democracy," elaborating upon the points that "M.C." had condensed. The Manifesto also recognizes that in the phase of social and political democracy "the immense majority of bourgeois owners—the bourgeois class—will survive," although some bourgeois sectors, along with the working class, the middle classes, and the intellectuals, will ally against the power of monopoly capital. The first task, therefore, would be the isolation of, and struggle against, monopoly oligarchies—a gradual struggle that requires political pluralism and ideological debate.[18]

The resolutions of the Ninth Congress have tempered the measures of the Manifesto; they still recognize the "full validity" of the latter, but the measures are no longer viewed as immediate priorities—they are conceived of as objectives to be realized only following a long series of progressive transformations, beginning with the consolidation of democracy. The urgency assigned to democratic transformation of the state is supported by the notion that "[at present] it would be artificial to drastically separate the political from the economic. Indeed, a transformation of the state in a profoundly democratic sense can be the main economic reform, the most efficient and safest method of curbing and later ending the existing power of the capitalist monopolies."

As examples of "transformations that are being pushed forward even now," the resolutions cite the establishment of political liberties, the creation of a federal structure of the state, the abolition of the death penalty,* nationalization of the banks, tax reform, educational and health reform, and assistance to small and medium-sized enterprises. These are all vital issues of parliamentary debate—especially those in the realm of education and economics, where governmental and rightist opposition are strong. Taking this into account, the PCE has cautiously restricted its proposals to democratization and popular control of public enterprises, nationalization of the energy sector with special emphasis on nuclear plants, aid to small businesses, agrarian reform, and a solid program of investment in education, science, and technology.

Agrarian reform is perhaps the area where the PCE's caution is most visible. In the final years of the Franco regime, when the nature of political change was not clearly predictable and the left thought that democracy would entail some kind of rupture, the PCE favored a comprehensive program of land reform that sought to abolish the *latifundio*—a system of landed property typical of southern Spain, where enormous holdings are concentrated in just a few hands and where the majority of peasants work only during limited periods (for example, during the harvest of grapes and olives). The PCE maintains

---

*The Spanish Constitution abolishes the death penalty, although it leaves open the possibility of maintaining it in the military code of justice.

its anti-*latifundio* position, of course, but only as a general aim; the resolutions refer only to "an advancement of agrarian reform measures."

THE PCE INSISTS upon the democratic character of this advanced stage prior to the transition to socialism. The Ninth Congress resolutions hold that in cases where socialist forces gain a majority and then are defeated in subsequent elections, "they would have to leave the government and enter into the opposition in order to gain anew the country's confidence." The PCE's "political and social democracy" is a combination of parliamentary democracy and new forms of "direct" democracy—the latter representing the fulfillment of democracy at the local and communal levels within a scheme of progressive decentralization and self-management. Apart from stimulating workers' participation within enterprises and at places of work, the PCE cites the prospects of implementing direct democracy through the popular movements that have spread in Spain within the spheres of education, health care, urban housing, and ecology. The party advocates a balance between traditional democratic forms and the new qualitative, grassroots movements of the sort that have enriched opposition in the advanced capitalist countries. The PCE model is anticipated in the Ninth Congress resolutions as follows: "Political and social democracy would mean the putting into practice of an articulated system of democracy that will have its basis in parliament as a representative popular will but which will be supported at the same time by a complex system of organs deeply rooted in the popular masses. This articulation will not weaken the role of the political parties, elections, and parliament; on the contrary, it will favor them since the entire country will develop an intense political life. Moreover, representative democracy will heighten the meaning of all forms of self-management and direct democracy in the political, social, and cultural spheres."[19]

This commitment to the integrity of social movements could be interpreted as a tactical effort by the PCE leadership designed to enhance the party's political influence outside the strictly electoral and parliamentary realm and thus, indirectly, bolster its modest electoral strength. According to such a ploy, the PCE would be backed by a series of increasingly significant popular movements—notably the workers' movement—that would operate according to an extraparliamentary dynamic. The PCE itself denies this motivation:[20] still, it is evident that the party wants to become a hegemonic force within these movements, and it has already done so within the *comisiones obreras* and some neighborhood associations which are highly influential in local politics. The important thing here is that, whatever the tactical realities, the PCE's involvement at this level reflects its absorption of new sensibilities and the development of new ideological perspectives—its democratic commitment being vital to this process.

The Problem of Internal Democracy

WE HAVE SO far considered two major aspects of the PCE's transition from orthodoxy to Eurocommunism. The third aspect concerns the way in which the party adopts internally democratic methods consistent with the values and practices it advocates for society as a whole. Here the measures taken by the PCE are presented as adaptations to new social realities rather than as a recognition of past mistakes. As I have already suggested, a thoroughgoing self-criticism would be difficult for the older generation of militants. Hence, the avoidance of internal criticism and the maintenance of an official tone remains typical of leadership discourse—the historical sections of Carrillo's *Eurocommunism and the State* perhaps best illustrate this approach.* With respect to internal democracy, it is true that even though Claudin denounced anti-democratic practices within the party in 1964, in 1976 the PCE leadership insisted that the appointment system was still the only possible approach for providing in the underground situation the most qualified and responsible people—a "natural selection."[21]

The legacy of centralized and hierarchical leadership poses one of the main obstacles to the PCE's internal democratization—an obstacle reflected in the conflicts and contradictions of the Ninth Congress that built up between the initial proposals of the leadership and the final resolutions that were approved after intense pressure was exerted by the younger militants. The crisis of the PSUC (Catalan Communist Party) in the province of Tarragona also expressed these same conflicts, as did the angry atmosphere of the PCE's Asturias Conference and the widespread dissidence reflected at the Madrid Conference which discussed the proposals of the Ninth Congress.**

---

*Carrillo assesses the historical evolution of the PCE in order to locate the precedents for his current Eurocommunist positions. In this respect, he emphasizes the PCE's support of Republican legality during the Civil War. In an initial attempt at self-criticism, Carrillo recalls a dark episode (the assassination of Andreu Nin—a prominent Trotskyist leader of the Catalan Worker's Party of Marxist Unification, POUM), which took place during the Civil War and is commonly attributed to the PCE. Carrillo admits that perhaps some rank-and-file party members were responsible, but he adds that they acted as individuals and not as party members. At any rate, whether they were responsible or not, the wartime circumstances were very confusing. This is a perfect example of an "official explanation" that fails to give a full picture of events.

**In Tarragona, reportedly almost 100 members out of a total of 399 quit the party, citing incompatibility with the authoritarian local committee. At the Asturias Conference, 113 delegates (of approximately 500) left the gathering at the inaugural session when they realized that the chairperson was impeding any possibility of open debate. These delegates, however, did not want to resign from

Similar conflict has broken out in Euskadi (the Basque Country), where the PCE suffered a massive electoral failure and the long-time party Secretary, Ramón Ormazábal, has been replaced by a young physician, Roberto Lertxundi, who is more familiar with Basque reality and who formerly belonged to the armed revolutionary organization ETA (the *Euskadi Ta Azkatasuma*, or Basque Country and Freedom). Lertxundi is presumably more popular and acceptable to broad sectors of the Basque population. In Catalonia, where the electoral outcome was more favorable, Gregorio López Raimundo, exiled since the Civil War until very recently, left his PSUC Secretary General position and was replaced by Antonio Gutiérrez, a prestigious leader long involved in the anti-Franco opposition. Gutiérrez is now also a minister (*conseller*) of the provisional Catalan government.

Concerning the problem of the "untouchable" leaders, many PCE members are convinced that the party's legendary President, Dolores Ibarruri, has been obstinately kept in her post despite her extreme fragility and old age. They argue that it would be more reasonable to allow *La Pasionaria* to assume an honorary position and turn the presidency over to a more vigorous political leader. There has also been some disenchantment with Carrillo's sometimes authoritarian political style; indeed, rumors have been floating around for some time to the effect that once Ibarruri dies Carrillo might be "up-graded" to the position of President, which would leave room for a younger and more dynamic Secretary General. For the moment, however, Carrillo's status has been reaffirmed by the Ninth Congress.

The PCE's recently approved statutes affirm that free speech and open debate are fully acceptable within the party, so long as "unity of action" and "political homogeneity" are preserved. "Fractional activity" and "organized tendencies" remain forbidden.[22] Here it is interesting to note the extent to which the PCE is now downplaying the conspiratorial aura commonly associated with Communist parties. As a legal party, the PCE no longer strictly defines the Communist militant as a "professional cadre" whose role is somehow "mysterious"; at present, differing degrees of militancy and involvement are accepted within the party. Accordingly, the statutes replaced the traditional organizational unit—

the party but pushed their viewpoints through various internal mechanisms. During the Madrid Conference, an important sector of the delegation denounced the PCE's triumphalistic prose in the proposals and contested the local Madrid leaders.

One of the most significant cases was that of Vilar, a journalist and author of a book on Francoism. Vilar authored a piece in the Madrid newspaper *El Pais* which noted the distance between professed Communist ideas and social reality. A militant of the PSUC, Vilar, criticized the authoritarian practices of local party cadres and wound up leaving the organization in March 1978.

the cell—with a more diffuse structure called the *"agrupacion,"* which is composed of party members at the same workplace. The statutes also include a measure that is original among Communist parties—one that establishes a "constitutional court" as an organ of internal arbitration. Of course the scope and applicability of all these declarations will have to be tested in the future.

Political Change and Party Identity

SINCE THE LATE 1960s, the PCE has conspicuously tried to break with the narrow conception of a workers' party by appealing to the middle strata, professionals, and intellecuals. Aware that advanced capitalism has generated a range of economic and social transformations that require a strategic departure from the classic theory of a unified proletariat as absolute revolutionary subject, the party leadership supported the idea of an alliance between the "forces of work and culture." The concept increasingly attracted sectors of professional people who are now mainly in their late twenties and early thirties and who are of diverse ideological origins—in many cases having joined the PCE after abandoning an earlier left-wing communism. It was these younger "new wave" groups that confronted the older generation of leaders at the Ninth Congress,[23] challenging the old-fashioned triumphalism which, for example, viewed the 1977 electoral results as a moderate victory even though the PCE won little more than nine percent of the vote and elected only 20 candidates to the Congress. (Carrillo himself stated publicly before the elections that he would be happy with nothing less than the election of 30 candidates.) The party, moreover, maintained its optimism despite the fact that the Communist vote was very unevenly distributed—with not a single PCE candidate elected from the highly-industrialized Basque Country, and with no significant electoral support in any rural province except Andalusia.

The PCE attempted to present Adolfo Suárez' party as a real centrist party, whereas everyone knows that it is nothing more than a renovated right. The Communists also tried to exaggerate their own potential role in Spanish politics in order to conceal their electoral failure; for example, they contended that the realization of semi-autonomous regional governments now depends upon the presence of PCE parliamentary representation in each region—regardless of the significant national and cultural differences that shape each area. Moreover, the PCE showed a sort of "guilt," by going to great lengths to justify minimal tactical steps, like the endorsement of Juan Carlos' Monarchy and the adoption of the traditional Spanish flag (which many people still identify with Franco).

The final resolutions of the Ninth Congress present a more realistic image of the Spanish political situation than did the initial leadership proposals. For one thing, the resolutions conceded that a genuine democratic break did not occur with the eclipse of Franco and that the electoral outcome should not be viewed as a victory but as a tentative first step toward further political development. Nor did they exaggerate the PCE's potential role in regional governments, offering instead to collaborate with other forces in order to achieve a decentralized Spanish state. Also, the government's party is located on the right, and the lengthy, "guilty" paragraphs have disappeared.

The leadership proposals concerning culture amounted to a reflection of the continuing residues of traditionalism within the PCE hierarchy. This applied especially to the incredible thesis on youth, where the party employed a sermon-like tone aimed at convincing young people that the party alone can be the medium for channeling juvenile unrest. Alienation from conventional politics, "hip" lifestyles, and so forth were portrayed as a kind of disease molded by drugs, "nihilism," and even vandalism. In its final formulation, the resolution on youth eliminates such dusty language and outmoded tone, while analyzing the problems of Spanish youth, admitting that classical Marxism has lost its appeal to young people, and offering a more sympathetic interpretation of emerging leftist and countercultural movements.

In the case of women's liberation, the steps taken at the Congress went even futher. The final text even admits that Marxism in general lacks a perspective on feminism and notes that many PCE members, women included, are not fully aware of the specificity of women's oppression, arguing that the party must support autonomous feminist movements in the future. It also calls for a deep cultural revolution that eradicates machismo elements from the language and from everyday life.

Such examples reflect a ferment within the PCE's popular base, especially among youth. But it cannot be concluded that the Ninth Congress expressed any real open conflict within the party between the traditional leadership and the new generation. The leading personalities were all re-elected. It could be argued that a new balance was reached at the Congress. One things seems clear at this point: the party's evolution henceforth will depend as much upon its own internal needs and requirements as upon tactical exigencies, and the leadership knows this.

Paradoxically, the most controversial resolution—that rejecting Leninism—was approved without significant textual changes. This signifies a convergence between the leadership's initiative (along with its disciplined old-fashioned supporters) and the "new wave" base concerning the issue of democratization—which in the long run seems to be the real meaning of the PCE's "de-Leninization." Indeed, prior to the

Congress the PCE had introduced significant ideological declarations praising democracy, criticizing the orthodox impulse to scorn civil liberties, and presenting socialism as a deep democratic achievement. Illustrative of this was Carrillo's statement that "the generation of Marxists who have lived the painful experience of fascism and, in another sphere, Stalinist degeneration, appreciate the concept of democracy differently [than Lenin], not in opposition to socialism and communism but as a road to and a *principled component* of the latter."[24]

If "Leninism" means a monopoly of the vanguard party, "dictatorship of the proletariat," and an insurrectional seizure of power, then a Eurocommunist perspective based on broad social alliances, evolutionism, and respect for democracy could no longer maintain an ideological fidelity to the "Leninist" label. But "Marxism-Leninism" still functions as sacred terminology. This is why the PCE's abandonment of Leninism takes place within an elaborated official formula that changes the former Manifesto-Program declaration that the party is "inspired by the principles of Marxism and Leninism." The resolutions of the Ninth Congress affirm that the PCE is a "Marxist, democratic, and revolutionary party, inspired by the theories of social development elaborated by the founders of scientific socialism, Marx and Engels." Lenin is excluded from the "founding fathers." However, the document adds that the party incorporates the "Leninist contribution as far as it proves to be valid, like any other revolutionary contribution, but on the basis that at present it is not possible to maintain the restrictive idea that 'Leninism is the Marxism of our time'."

The central idea of the resolution departing from Leninism is that while the latter had as its *raison d'etre* its role as bearer of the legacy of the Bolshevik Revolution, it cannot be used as a valid strategy for the advanced capitalist countries. In other words, the PCE rejects Leninism because of its obsolescence in contemporary Spain. The party thereby safeguards the validity of traditional Leninism, which it carefully distinguishes from Stalinism. Moreover, it is able to preserve its political identity since it contends that the post-World War I adoption of Leninism by European Communist leaders, which justified a break with social democracy, was necessary to preserve the genuine socialist objective that had been perverted by social democracy. In the PCE version, therefore, Leninism *was* necessary, even though it must be superseded today.

The party has thus chosen the easiest path for transforming its tactics without endangering its own history and image. Had Leninism been criticized more radically (for instance, by arguing that the roots of Soviet authoritarianism and technocracy were already present in the Leninist strategy), the party would have had to admit to its own past errors, and, more importantly, to the flimsy basis of its split with the PSOE in the 1920s. The PCE's Eurocommunist remodelling, while preserving the party's ideological "dignity," also implies a deep change in its political character, which is now moving closer and closer to that of the Socialists. It was not a matter of random choice that both the PCE and the PSOE have used similar electoral slogans—"socialism in freedom" for the former, "socialism is freedom" for the latter. Both parties appear to be converging around the notion of a plural, democratic, and parliamentary road to socialism; only the degree of radicalism would now seem to separate them. Indeed, convergence is a goal emerging within the *base* of the two parties—moving beyond the leadership's colder, more manipulative stances. In this regard, the Socialist Youth organization angrily reacted when the PSOE Secretary General announced that he was willing to eliminate the word "Marxism" from the party statutes. This militancy of young Socialist members and supporters has its Communist counterpart in the conciliatory attitude that opposed Carrillo's harsh critique of the Socialists in his opening speech to the Congress.

The PCE and the Spanish Left

MUTUAL ANTAGONISMS between Socialists and Communists presumably will not die easily in the near future. For the moment, however, it is the prospect of convergence that is most interesting. It must be noted that the PCE now supports the idea of a "new political formation" that would include groups favoring socialism and advanced democracy. This suggests an atmosphere of collaboration in which the short-term difficulties are clear: the PSOE really does not need alliances because of its political strength, while the popular movements do not fully trust the PCE's claimed "neutrality" since Communist efforts to control popular struggles born outside of the party are well-known. The point here is that the PCE now understands that its influence depends upon the support of a popular majority and not simply a narrow stratum of the working class. This is why it accepts parliamentary democracy in the context of a "long march" strategy where structural changes are no longer viewed as magical solutions but as requiring a complementary cultural transformation.

Such a parliamentary and "plural" or "inter-class" focus is the reason why groups to the left of the PCE increasingly associate the party with "supporters of the bourgeoisie" in general instead of stressing its "revisionism." Hence it could be said that antagonisms within the Spanish left develop more and more between parliamentary and extra-parliamentary tendencies. The PCE is still the object of leftist attacks for its support of the monarchy and for its collaboration with the government through the "Moncloa Pact," which among other things, seeks to ensure that the *comisiones obreras* (as well as the socialist union, UGT) do not develop a strategy of mass mobilization and radical demands.

WHAT ARE THE major groups to the left of the PCE today? First, there are the extreme-left nationalist movements that demand independence from Spain—for example, the Basque *abertzale* left grouped within the organization KAS (Koordinatora Abertzale Socialista) and the Galician AN-PG (Alianza Nacional do Pobo Galego). These forces regard themselves as liberation movements linking independence with socialism. They do not espouse violent tactics (although they do not condemn them either) but do advance a militant political line that posits no transitional stage and emphasizes the role of popular mobilization. The Basque ETA shares the above objectives but also stresses armed action (many examples of which if has already furnished). These groups are not particularly large, but their impact on public opinion is great. Their supporters are normally students, with some support in other popular sectors, especially in the Basque Country, where an independentist electoral coalition won two seats in parliament, something the PCE was not able to achieve.*

Another far left group, FRAP (*Frente Revolucionario Anti-fascista Patriotico*) advocates violence and expresses itself politically through a "Marxist-Leninist" Communist Party, which has only an insignificant appeal. The Trotskyist Communist Revolutionary League attacks the PCE's concept of a mass party and insists that a true communist party must never abandon its character as a proletarian party. Trotskyists too play a very modest political role in Spain, although their presence within some working-class organizations is significant—for example, in the *comisiones obreras,* where they function as a minority opposition to the PCE's dominant role. The recently-formed MC (Communist Movement) performs a similar if smaller role. The PT (Labor Party) presents itself as an effort to build a mass working-class alternative to the PCE. While its political influence is also marginal, its labor union, the CSUT (*Confederacion de Sindicatos Unitarios de Trabajadores)* is a growing force in the Southern regions of Andalusia and Extremadura, where rural unemployment is extreme and agriculture is structured according to the model of the *latifundio.* The PT-CSUT has organized symbolic land occupations and may yet take an active role in the southern agrarian conflicts that

*The Basque left vote virtually skipped from the PSOE to the extreme left. This not only reflects the widespread radicalism of the area but can also be interpreted as the legacy of the PCE's traditional centralism that has been modified only in Catalonia.

many observers expect in the near future. Finally, the Revolutionary Workers' Organization presents itself as a Marxist-Leninist party that follows the thought of Stalin and Mao Tse-tung. It is "pro-Chinese," with origins that lie in a progressive Christianism, and whose power resides in several workers' communities, especially in Madrid.

Despite the collective strength of these leftist forces, the PCE's traditional support has remained more or less intact. A disciplined working-class base still constitutes the core of the PCE, whose support among other social sectors (and various regions with little Communist tradition) has been quite weak. Much of this is explained by the PCE's orthodox past, the powerful anti-Communist campaign of the Franco regime, and the strong competition of the PSOE. This situation, however, might change should the Socialists move closer to classic social democracy. The Communists could further broaden their base if they can demonstrate through concrete action that the Ninth Congress resolutions are more than mere rhetoric. In this respect, the PCE's Eurocommunism has already generated new sources of support among Catholics, who now feel that they can join the party since it has jettisoned its critique of religion.*

*The PCE now accepts religious believers and even priests within its ranks. One priest, F. Garcia Salve, is a member of the Central Committee who only recently abandoned the priesthood in order to marry. There are other prominent Catholic figures who are not leaders of the PCE but who openly support the party, such as Father Llanos—a pioneer of the worker-priest movement. This phenomenon is of great importance in Spain, where Communism has traditionally been described by the right as anti-Catholic. In *Eurocommunism and the State*, Carrillo praises the emerging democratic consciousness of the Church as one of the most important forces undermining the Franco dictatorship. Moreover, the Ninth Congress resolutions state that the PCE should not interfere with its members' private religious beliefs. The growing democratic consciousness of the Catholic leadership during the late 1960s and 1970s deprived the Franco regime of one of its important legitimizing weapons. Yet it is clear that in the present transitional situation, the Spanish Church evinces only a moderate democratic faith and has by no means renounced its traditional privileges. Although the Church is no longer the reactionary force it once was, it still claims for itself an important role in Spanish public affairs. In this regard, the Church (assisted by the right) remains a powerful social force, especially in the realm of education. Still, the tension deriving from the struggles around Catholicism has abated; today, the Church operates like any other interest group in Spanish politics, and the old "religious question" that has traditionally generated conflict in Spain seems to have run its course.

CONCLUSIONS

AMONG THE GREATEST obstacles to fundamental change in the PCE remains the ideological and organizational weight of the past. If for reasons of prestige and tradition, the party can feel secure in its working class support, the prospects for mobilizing other sectors are much less certain.* The PCE needs to win the support of groups such as the professionals and small landowners, but these strata prefer to wait for the actualization of Eurocommunist measures before moving to support the Communists. In the meantime, it is clear that the PSOE is still the main political force identified with democratic socialism. Images can change rapidly, however, and it must not be forgotten that the PCE has already succeeded in building a base among certain professional and middle class sectors in Catalonia.

The problem of image and identity is crucial for the PCE. In fact, the party's desire to be both a "party of struggle and of government," a popular force but also a national force, needs to be clarified in a way that overcomes the present ambiguity. The Ninth Congress resolutions are a massive step forward in this sense; but questions such as the party's internal restructuring, its relation to other popular movements, its commitment to decentralization and self-management, and its ability to incorporate new cultural sensibilities are still unclear.

A further issue shaping the PCE's strategy and present predicament is the world crisis of capitalism, which can impede the party's attempt to establish broad alliances and win the support of the non-monopolist bourgeoisie. The latter stratum naturally fears instability, and this could easily push it in the direction of monopoly "order"—a shift that occurred during the capitalist crisis of the 1920s and 1930s—rather than toward an alliance with broad popular forces. At a theoretical level, however, the

---

*At the same time, the *comisiones obreras* have to compete not only with their Socialist rival, the UGT, but with other unions that have been increasing in strength (for example, the CSUT in the south). There are other unions, such as the anarchist CNT (National Confederation of Labor), that exert considerable influence only in particular regions like Catalonia.

PCE's Gramscian effort to create a popular hegemonic "bloc," articulated in terms of social forces and not in terms of a single-party dictatorship, seems appealing. At this point, in any case, we can conclude that after several years of legality which have included electoral tests and the proceedings of the Ninth Congress—the PCE has clearly departed from the classical strategy it endorsed for so long. The party's Eurocommunist perspective—until now a matter of definitions and declarations—will have to inspire a period of sustained political activity. New issues will certainly be posed and new opportunities may arise that will put the PCE's Eurocommunism to its first real test.

Notes

1. Fernando Claudin, *Documentos de una divergencia comunista* (Barcelona: Viejo Topo, 1978). This work includes Claudin's two reports to the Executive Committee, and the official responses to the first of them published in the PCE's political and theoretical journal, *Neustra Bandera*—the second report, a 161-page document, having been officially ignored. The importance of these polemics lies in Claudin's authority as a theoretician that has been demonstrated in his *Crisis of the Communist Movement* and *Eurocommunism and Socialism.* Claudin's analysis is reinforced by his experience as a political militant. He was a prominent member of the PCE leadership until his expulsion in 1965, and he is still politically active in Spain as an independent leftist. As for Semprún, his importance is more literary than theoretical; he is the author of some celebrated novels, such as *The Long Journey,* which chronicles his experiences as a Nazi prisoner at the age of 16, and screenplays like *Z* and *La guerre est finie.* He also did considerable underground work in Spain during the 1950s and early 1960s, which he novelized in his *Autobiografía de Federico Sánchez,* a highly controversial book that won the prestigious Spanish Planeta award and has been considered outrageous by the PCE.

2. Claudin, *op. cit.*, pp. 242 and 245. Excerpts are from the PCE's responses, with the party's emphases.

3. For a brief summary of the sociological processes of contemporary Spain, see my "The Cultural Thaw in Spain," *Telos*, no. 30, winter 1977.

4. *Ibid.,* p. 287.

5. *Ibid.,* pp. 46-47.

6. *Ibid.,* p. 11.

7. *Ibid.,* p. 47.

8. *Ibid.,* p.152.

9. *Ibid.,* p. 248.

10. This has been confirmed by the May 1978 partial elections to the Senate in the provinces of Asturias and Alicante, where two Socialist candidates were elected.

11. "Against the dogmatic, authoritarian and bureaucratic degeneration of centralism, the essential requirement for creating the kind of mass communist party capable of a valid theoretical perspective is the enforcement of internal democracy." Claudin, *op. cit.* p. 183.

12. Aleksandr Dubcek, *La via checoslavaca al socialismo* (Barcelona: Ariel, 1968).

13. Manuel Azcarate, *Informe aprobado por el Comite Central del PCE*, September 1973, *PCE Publication*, p. 18. Author's emphasis.

14. PCE, *Resoluciones del Noveno Congreso* (Ninth Congress resolutions), Madrid, 1978. Resolution 13, Section 7.

15 Juan Gomez, "Sobre el Mercado Comun Europeo," in *VIII Congreso del PCE*, Bucherest, 1972, pp. 207-215.

16. Juan Gómez, "La crisis del petróleo y la crisis general del capitalismo," *Nuestra Bandera*, no. 73, January-February 1974.

17. "M.C.", "La crisis mundial del capitalismo y las perspectivas politicas de los comunistas," *Nuestra Bandera*, nos. 79-80, March-June 1975, p. 80. Author's emphasis.

18. *Manifesto-Programa del PCE*, Madrid, 1977, pp. 36-50.

19. For this and other quotations referring to the Ninth PCE Congress resolutions, see *Resoluciones...*, *op. cit.*, pp. 14-18 (resolution no. 6).

20. "[It would be a mistake] to think that if other political forces control the state, we [the PCE] will control social movements." See *Resoluciones*, p. 36.

21. Santiago Carrillo, *De la clandestinidad a la legalidad*. Report to the PCE Central Committee, Rome, 1976, pp. 35-37.

22. *Estatutos del PCE*, article 11, f, Madrid, 1978.

23. PCE, *Proyectos de propuestas políticas y de estatutos al IX Congreso*, Madrid, 1978.

24. Santiago Carrillo, *Eurocommunism y Estado* (Barcelona: Grijalbo, 1977), pp. 115-116. Author's emphasis.

PART II

THE PARTIES
AND POPULAR MOVEMENT

chapter 4

DEMOCRACY AND THE MASS POLITICS OF THE PCE *

Temma Kaplan

THE SPANISH COMMUNIST PARTY (PCE) is struggling to defeat fascism and to create a democratic state in Spain. Hitler's Reich lasted more than a decade, but Franco's authoritarianism—albeit without Franco and with a new constitution—remains structurally intact after forty years. Until the elections of April 1979, all mayors, provincial governors, judges, police and army officials were fascist appointees. The King retains Franco's power to rule by decree, which has been invoked in the Basque Country, where near civil war between the local people and the army has threatened to provoke an army coup.

Fear of another civil war, more than Eurocommunist policy, defines PCE strategy. No one yet knows whether Operation Galaxia, an attempted military coup repressed by the government in November 1978, was merely a dry-run to see who would remain silent or whether the centrist government of Adolfo Suárez actually was in control of the army. The PCE announced that it would call a general strike should the military attempt to seize power. In such a struggle, the Communist dominated labor unions known as the workers' commissions would play a leading role, but right now they (and the smaller independent and Socialist unions) are not even permitted to organize in factories. Within this context, the PCE has defined the replacement of a fascist state by a stable bourgeois democracy to be the first step in the struggle for socialism.

*As always, I am grateful for Jon Wiener's friendly criticism.

SPONTANEOUS RESISTANCE TO the Franco dictatorship arose among industrial workers, urban consumers, and regional autonomists as early as the late 1940s. The clandestine PCE, a classic Leninist party with limitations on internal democracy created both by its underground status and its attachment to Soviet orthodoxy, organized among all these resistance groups. Pressure by the left in the streets forced some relaxation of repression following Franco's death in November 1975. This has given the PCE the opportunity to unite diverse groups around a coordinated political strategy.

By placing itself at the head of the popular movement for democracy, the PCE has established itself as one of the most powerful forces on the left. However, the autonomous groups will ally with the PCE only to the extent that it gives up its old Leninist structure and becomes a mass democratic party, replacing its bureaucratic centralism with participatory democracy.

The future of the PCE lies in its identification with the mass movement, as its past reputation lay with its support of the struggle against Franco. To hold the workers' commissions and win allegiance from the new sections of the mass movement, the PCE must become a new kind of party. It must provide structures through which feminists, tenants, ecologists, factory workers, and regionalists can participate in formulating party policy and resolve antagonisms among themselves democratically. The party must be able to overcome conflicts between the workers' commissions, which oppose terrorism, and the Basques, who need a statute of autonomy to give them regional control over police and soldiers; between traditional male workers and feminist groups; between industrial unions and the "new working class" of state employees and service workers, whose interests are not necessarily the same. All this requires participatory democracy in place of party infallibility based on doctrinal orthodoxy.

At the same time, the PCE must make sure the bourgeoisie at the center holds firm in its weak resolve to create democratic state institutions which would guarantee civil rights and take institutional power away from the army and the fascists. To this end, the PCE has argued that the struggle for democracy is prior to the struggle for socialism. Nowhere in Spain except among the far left is this disputed. What is a source of conflict between the current party leadership and the larger popular movement is whether struggles should be waged in the street through direct action or through the few representative political bodies that exist. The workers' commissions, by conforming to the social pact of Moncloa and by opposition to the Basque terrorists of ETA (Basque Homeland and Freedom) have shown that they agree with the party leadership about the need for peaceful transition and the danger of provoking a coup. The rest of the mass movement, including groups to the left of the PCE, argue that limited forms of direct action through mass demonstrations will secure improvements immediately, and that without them the Cortes (Parliament), King, and Prime Minister would not have moved at all.

Much political conflict centers around the Basque Country. Forty years of military occupation has convinced its population of the necessity of a statute of autonomy, which in fact would give it fewer powers than an American state. Despite a statute of pre-autonomy, which is barely a statement of intention, the Basques do not have control of the regional army and the police according to the Constitution of 1978. In the summer of that year the King decreed martial law in the Basque Country for the third time since Franco's death in 1975. Alleged terrorists of ETA can be held more than 72 hours (during which time many are tortured). There are no rights of *habeas corpus,* and any house can be invaded to pursue suspects.

The army looms above all political discussion, a dark shadow commanded by Franco's cronies, made up of younger officers who have never fought against anyone but the Spanish civilian population. No one knows what the army will do to "defend" public order and the integrity of the nation. The army has opposed mass demonstrations (more than 20 demonstrators have been killed since Franco's death in 1975); limited decentralization, modeled on the federalist system of the U.S.; free speech (especially when it is critical of the army); and the legalization of left parties.

What follows is not a new theory of mass parties but an historical analysis of the concrete political situation in Spain today and an examination of the role the PCE seems to be playing in it. It remains to be seen whether the PCE can persuade the Spanish bourgeoisie and state functionaries that their interests lie with democracy rather than fascism at the same time that it democratically restructures its own party apparatus and procedures.

HISTORICAL DEVELOPMENT OF THE PCE

THE PCE THAT HAS emerged since Franco's victory in 1939 has defined itself in relationship to anti-fascist struggle, which it has for the most part led. After 1939, PCE General Secretary José Diaz favored pursuing the war in Spain along the lines the Chinese Communists were developing. (Between 1939 and 1952, independent groups of leftists tried to carry on guerilla war from the mountains around Asturias, Madrid, and Andalusia.) Stalin vetoed this strategy, and Diaz disappeared in

Russia during World War II. At the Potsdam Conference, Stalin and Truman wanted to overthrow Franco, but Churchill feared a socialist Spain.[1] Following the Second World War, PCE activities were directed by Santiago Carrillo from his office in Paris.

The struggle against Franco in the postwar period began spontaneously with strikes in Barcelona and the Basque Country. In 1949, female textile workers organized the first strikes in Franco Spain, even though strikes were punished as insurrections in military courts. That same year, housewives catalyzed a general strike in the Basque Country that was soundly defeated. Municipal fare increases in Barcelona in 1951 provoked students to initiate a bus boycott that drew thousands into a general strike. Additional wage squeezes in 1956 provoked strikes in the Basque Country and Catalonia, where workers were joined by students.[2]

Out of these spontaneous student, worker, consumer, and neighborhood struggles, the PCE recruited underground party members in the 1950s. The PCE was so impressed with the militance of the Spanish population that they themselves attempted to develop a strategy of the peaceful general strike to topple Franco. Against the growing scepticism of the PCE underground leaders such as Jorge Semprún and Fernando Claudin, the party pursued a policy that succeeding in decimating its Spanish operatives. Simón Sanchez Montero, an underground leader in Madrid, was arrested in 1959, tortured, and incarcerated for sixteen years. Julian Grimau, another leader, was tortured and assassinated by the fascist police.[3]

Semprún and Claudin blamed these defeats on the ignorance and rigidity of Santiago Carrillo and the PCE leadership in exile in France. So long as the general stikes were spontaneous, the police could only react. Once the PCE tried to organize and control them, they risked infiltration that could only reduce their chance for success. Semprun and Claudin, who worked underground in Spain, knew that Franco had carried out a revolution from above that had, with the help of the United States and international capital, transformed Spain from a backward, underdeveloped agrarian country to a major industrial capitalist center. As difficult as it would have been for a revolution to overthrow Franco before the 1953 Mutual Defense Treaty with the U.S. that exchanged bases for investments, it was increasingly difficult afterwards.[4]

The Spanish economic miracle began in the 1950s. The World Bank and International Monetary Fund followed the U.S. into Spain to take advantage of a labor force whose wages were kept miserably low by the fascist labor syndicate, to which all workers and their bosses had to belong. Until 1958 the syndicate set wages unilaterally. They were so low that in 1954 the buying power of a Spanish worker was half what it had been in 1936.[5] International capital's development plan for Spain, organized through the National Industrial Institute, called for construction of new centers of electronic, chemical, and metallurgical industries, away from traditional areas of labor militance in Catalonia and the Basque Country. They built plants close to large supplies of cheap labor in Galacia, Navarre, Old Castile, and Andalusia. British Leyland, Fiat, and Ford constructed auto plants in the Pamplona, Avila, and Valencia. Dow Chemical and I.G. Farben constructed chemical plants in Huelva and Zaragosa. New metallurgical industries in Madrid provided the basis for a large proletariat, which transformed Madrid into one of Spain's major centers of working class militance.

SEMPRÚN AND CLAUDIN, the party's chief theorists, attempted to convince the PCE leadership meeting in Bohemia in 1964 that Spain was no longer a semi-feudal agrarian backwater, but was now characterized by new class relations that required a new political strategy. They argued for democratic decision-making, self-criticism, and the formulation of a new strategy appropriate to the social transformation that had taken place under fascism; all of these points were labeled defeatist by an angered PCE leadership which expelled them from the party in 1965.[6] (Antoni Lopez Raimundo, one of the few contemporary PCE leaders willing to comment upon the expulsion, has recently argued that the party knew at the time that Semprún and Claudin were correct. But he claims it was impossible to reveal to workers that they might have to face twenty more years of struggle against Franco.)

Militant workers organized secret committees around the coal mines and iron foundries of Asturias beginning in 1957 and 1962, but these were brutally repressed.[7] In 1964, metal workers in Madrid formed factory committess to improve shop conditions that survived repression. They also spread word to other regions and consolidated the committees into district and provincial commissions that nevertheless retained autonomy. Their leaders were old militants of every political persuasion, some of whom—like Marcelino Camarho—were members of the underground PCE. At the same time, the Communists decided to run militants as representatives in the fascist labor syndicates. In 1967 and 1968, municipal workers in Madrid and Barcelona led general strikes against further declines in real wages. The police repressed the commissions and imprisoned most of the PCE militants. Between 1969, when a State of Exception was decreed, and 1975, many were tortured repeatedly. This history of struggle has won the PCE recognition as the leader of anti-fascist struggle in Spain.

In unquestioning support for the Soviet Union, only the Communist parties of Bulgaria and the United States had outdone the PCE. Stalin used the PCE in his attack on Tito in 1949. In 1956, the PCE denounced the Hungarian Revolution and the uprisings in Poland and East Germany. When the Asturian miners in 1957 struck against Franco and Poland broke the strike by shipping coal to Spain, the PCE remained silent.[8] In 1967, during the Sino-Soviet split, Carrillo became a spokesman for a villification campaign against Mao. But the invasion of Czechoslavakia in August 1968 was a turning point. In Spain, the PCE was trying to promote a "movement of national reconciliation" among liberals and leftists to form an opposition movement to Franco. Carrillo and the party were forced to condemn the Soviet invasion or kiss goodby the hope of PCE credibility with liberals. The Soviet Union attempted to use Enrique Lister, a Civil War general and central committee member, to split the PCE and overthrow Carrillo. When he was unsuccessful, Lister formed a splinter party, but Carrillo was able to keep Dolores Ibarurri (La Pasionaria) and the rest of the Central Committee on his side. From 1970 on, the PCE began to depend upon the Italian Communist Party for the financial and political support it could no longer expect from the Soviet Union.[9]

EUROCOMMUNISM AND THE MASS MOVEMENT

THE POLICY OF seeking to transform the state apparatus from a fascist to a bourgeois democratic structure began with the "movement of national reconciliation" in the 1950s. The proposed alliance of center and left is the bulwark of the PCE's program for the peaceful destruction of fascism. Many trace this strategy to Claudin and Semprún, but their dispute was more about internal party democracy than about political tactics. Claudin and Semprún attempted to create a PCE which would admit mistakes, acknowledge the opinions of militants, and reformulate policy when necessary. They objected to Stalinist practices of labeling all dissenters factionalizers as if there could never be honest disputes within the party. They wanted sweeping self-criticism of the party's tactic of the peaceful general strike. Debate about how disagreement ought to be resolved in a democratic party continues to preoccupy activists in the mass movement and in the growing left wing of the party itself.

Outside Spain one of the most controversial activities of the PCE and other Eurocommunist parties has been their willingness to participate in social pacts that impose wage ceilings, currency controls, tax reforms, and a variety of readjustments in the capitalist systems that are wracked by inflation. Spain, like other major capitalist countries, is suffering major economic crisis, which forced the government to devalue the currency by 20% in 1977. That autumn, all the parties represented in the Cortes agreed to the Moncloa Accords, which placed ceilings on wages. By limiting wage hikes, it helped reduce inflation in 1978 from a projected 30% to 25%; by increasing agricultural productivity by 7%, it managed to cut the balance of trade deficit due in large measure to petroleum imports. It also attempted to revamp Spain's tax structure, no easy matter since fewer than two percent of those earning the equivalent yearly income of $15,000 or more pay any income taxes at all. State revenues come largely from excise and payroll taxes imposed on salaried workers. The PCE signed these accords, and when they were discussed at the PCE congress in April 1978, they met with no opposition.[10]

Like other advanced industrial countries, including the United States, Spain seems able to reduce trade deficits by increasing agricultural exports. As consolidation, mechanization, and the use of chemical fertilizers and insecticides have made Spanish agriculture more productive than ever before, its labor requirements are lower.[11] Labor demands in Andalusia, which contains one-sixth of the Spanish population, have declined at the same time that tens of thousands of migrant workers to northern Europe from this region have been sent home, as German, Swedish, Dutch and Swiss industry no longer require their labor. Communist leaders are reluctant to discuss the consolidation of land carried out by Franco whose IRYDA (National Institute of Agricultural Reform and Development) already gives the state control of vast land areas. They certainly would not favor dividing it up into small parcels farmed cooperatively. That program is left to the Maoist Spanish Labor Party (PTE), which has won popular support in Andalusia where agricultural unemployment means destitution for nearly one-half million people.[12] Yet the PCE's workers' commissions for agrarian workers won over 100,000 adherents in Andalusia among landless laborers and peasants in the spring 1978 union elections.[13]

THREE MAIN GROUPS have defined what democracy will mean in a transitional period to socialism. The first is centered in the workers' commissions, many of whose members became Communists because the PCE supported their work as autonomous militants. They are related to the neighborhood associations, which began spontaneously as agencies that beginning in the early 1970s forced Franco to provide some necessary public services to the new working class suburbs that had sprung up, particularly around Madrid, Barcelona, Bilbao, and Valencia. Often dominated by working-class housewives, these Associations of Neighbors have defined many of the social issues, including environmental controls, that the PCE now supports.[14]

The second major arena of mass politics is the movements for regional self-determination. The Basque and Catalan claims to autonomy date back to the Middle Ages, but recent interest in self-determination has emerged in every major Spanish province. The government has been forced to grant statutes of pre-autonomy not only to Basques and Catalans, but also to Andalusians. Traditional Communist statism generally turns it against regionalist movements in capitalist states, and the PCE was no exception. But the Third International recognized PSUC United Socialist Parties of Catalonia) as a Communist Party autonomous from the PCE. Judged by electoral success in the 1977 and 1978 Cortes elections, PSUC is far stronger than the PCE. (This has led some Catalans to suggest that the PCE call itself "PSUC's branch in Spain")[15]

PSUC strength derives from the role Catalan cultural nationalism has played in the struggle against Francoism. After the fascist triumph, Franco destroyed the Catalan schools and provincial government that had flourished under the Second Republic. After 1939, it was illegal to speak Catalan, to dance the traditional dances, to sing the regional songs. Jordi Pujol, now a Catalan centrist, spent two years in jail following police torture for leading a theater audience in the Catalan national anthem during Franco's visit to the province in 1962. A repressed language, along with military occupation well into the 1960s, in a region that produces one-third of the entire Spanish GNP made Catalan nationalism a potent strategy in the anti-facist struggle.[16] The earliest and largest general strikes took place in Catalonia where not even Francoist repression could destroy communal customs rooted in language. The PSUC recruited among workers and students engaged in the struggle against Franco. The workers' commissions of Catalonia have been more thoroughly Communist than commissions elsewhere. In March 1966, moving to support Barcelona students striking for a democratic association in the university, thirty Catalan intellectuals and artists — many of them Communists — barricaded themselves in a local monastery from which they were forcibly removed by police. Neighborhood associations, protest singers, and world famous painters such as Pable Picasso, Antoni Tapies, and Joan Miro, all linked by the Catalan language, gave support to their native Communists' attempts to win democratic reforms for the mass movement in the 1960s. Catalan nationalism is far stronger than Communism, but regional self-consciousness among the Catalans contributes to the power of the PSUC.[17]

Outside of Catalonia, regional branches of the PCE do not have as much autonomy as they would like. The PCE has been particularly blind in its treatment of Basque regionalism, and they have paid the price. There are fewer party members proportionally in the Basque Country than in any other industrialized area of Spain. The question of human rights in Euskadi is taken up by the ETA terrorists; by bringing repression upon themselves, they mobilize the population against the state, and are supported in their goals, if not their tactics, even by Basque centrists. Many Basques believe that the PCE is more eager to establish its non-violent credentials than to fight for Basque rights. When Nicolas Sartorius (a member of the 1978 Central Committee close to the workers' commissions) addressed the PCE congress, he claimed that terrorism (rather than the army) was the greatest threat to Spanish democracy, and he was widely acclaimed, particularly by non-Basque members of workers' commissions.[18] Elsewhere in Spain, in areas where social struggles have been less violent, the PCE's concern with creating a moderate federalist structure that would give Spanish provinces rights to issue permits and licenses, run schools and public services (all of which are now controlled by the central state) has won the party supporters.

Feminists are the third major part of the mass movement in contemporary Spain. Through demonstrations to decriminalize adultery for women and win rights to disseminate birth control materials, the feminist movement has won in the streets the repeal of laws that brutally discriminate against women. They have kept up pressure on the Cortes for a divorce law. Now they increasingly devote their efforts to exposing organized violence against women, including rape. They have forced police and judges to prosecute rapists, and in the process, have pushed for democratization of the fascist judiciary. They have stressed the need for birth control clinics and free abortions, and have generally drawn attention to Spain's inadequate and expensive medical system. They work with women in the neighborhood associations to establish clinics and popular universities, and to mobilize for parks, better sewage and toilets, ecological controls and against nuclear power[19]. As in the United States, the women's movement largely takes the form of local organizations which in Madrid, Barcelona, and Zaragoza have formed umbrella associations. They have no unified strategy and do not force members to conform to a feminist line. All the left parties have female cadres who work on women's issues. Increasingly, whatever their other ties, feminists have declared primary loyalty to the women's movement.

Many PCE and PSUC women have been active in feminist organizations from the beginning. Some feminists oppose activity in the PCE and other mixed left groups of men and women, but significant numbers of militant feminists remain in the PCE. Many of them, believing that feminism is a revolutionary ideology, are nudging the PCE to recognize the need to extend universal civil liberties to women. The chief opponents of integrating feminist issues into the party are male workers, who through the workers' commissions, have thus far occupied a privileged position within the party. Many of them view feminism as frivolous. Others denounce it as bourgeois and want to limit the party's commitment to "feminism of the class." Some are afraid to raise issues that might arouse antagonism between male and female militants.

The 1978 PCE Congress

THE PCE'S NINTH Party Congress held in April 1978 deserves scrutiny not only because it was open and public but because many disputes were resolved through participatory democracy. Conflict with the leadership is a sign of vitality and of commitment, at least on the part of the base, to make views known. General Secretary Santiago Carrillo's repeated statement that under his leadership the party may have made mistakes provoked one delegate to request that Carrillo drop "may have" from his statement. The delegates applauded wildly.[20] Arguments took place in front of reporters. The proceedings, including attacks on party leaders, were printed in party organs. The enforced unanimity and deference to authority associated with some other Communist parties were absent from this congress.

Three proposals aroused great conflict and thus point to the lines of fissure in the mass movement and the PCE. Article 6 raised questions about the shape of the party and the democratic state it hopes to create. Article 15, characterized in the western press as a retreat from Leninism, in fact concerned the relation of the workers' commissions to other groups. Article 8, which dealt with feminism and the PCE, was totally rewritten in committee after intense debate. Detailed consideration of these three controversial issues helps bring into focus the procedures by which the PCE may accommodate itself to various elements in Spain's mass movement.

Debates at the congress had less to do with Marxist theory than with recent Spanish history. Article 6 of the platform claimed to distinguish Eurocommunism in Spain from social democracy as practiced by the PSOE (Spanish Socialist Workers Party), the historic social democratic party in Spain. In 1977 and 1978 the Communists had concentrated their attacks not upon the King or Prime Minister but upon the PSOE and its leader Felipe Gonzalez. PCE leaders criticize the PSOE for refusing to enter the government, for dissenting so strongly about the Constitution written in secret, and for ultraleft grandstanding about the Constitution written in secret, and for ultra left grandstanding about Spain's proposed entrance into NATO and the EEC.[21] The leftist bear, since thier own relentless moderation is based on fear of the anti-Communist army, which never denounces nor attacks the PSOE. Felipe is one of the few major Spanish leftists who has never been exiled or jailed.[22]

The greatest difficulty that the PSOE poses for the PCE is competition for the same popular base of support. The PSOE is the largest party in Spain today. Electoral gerrymandering kept it from winning the appropriate number of seats in parliament, but it will almost surely run the government in the very near future.[23] Critics of the PCE outside

Spain accuse it of pursuing a narrowly parliamentary strategy, but in fact it combines work in the Cortes with attempts to build its strength in broad institutions where the PSOE works.[24] In the period following Franco's death, the Barcelona workers' commissions led a losing battle for unified left unions. Had they won, all Socialist, Communist, and far-left workers would have been united in a single, democratically run labor confederation. PCE leadership helped defeat this aim, but the PSOE deserves part of the blame. Carrillo opposed diluting the strength of Communists in the workers' commissions by merging them with other workers' groups even though that would have meant that more than 90 percent of all industrial workers would have been united. Felipe felt the same way and was willing to have the Socialist General Union of Workers (UGT) come in second to the commissions in the 1978 union elections, as they did, rather than provide a forum where Communists could try to recruit Socialist workers.

PCE leadership stresses the issue of party democracy in its conflict with the PSOE. In its theoretical statements about how it differs from social democrats, it attempts to outflank the PSOE on the left with the argument that its party is more democratic, hence more socialist. Felipe and a few PSOE leaders make decisions on their own without consulting popular autonomous organizations. PSOE is unabashedly an American-style electoral party, though its financial support comes from the German Social Democrats.[25] Like an American party, it has affiliations with unions, women's groups, and ecology associations, but it does not integrate them into decision-making. Sometimes it appears as if the PCE leaders envy Felipe his power. He and the PSOE will for the foreseeable future have greater electoral strength in the Cortes and in municipal governments than the PCE, and the PSOE stresses its refusal to make pacts with the Communists. The Communists' access to power lies in their ability to build up the workers commissions, women's groups, neighborhood associations, and environmental movements and work through them, as it did during the clandestine period before 1977. The PCE must therefore vie for power in these popular institutions and its political life depends upon the party's ability to be sufficiently democratic to hold leftists from the autonomous organizations.

Discussion of energy policy came up in the context of democratization at the PCE congress of 1978 where the debate demonstrated another revolt of the Catalans. PSUC speakers succeeded in reversing the energy policy favored by Carrillo. Spain's petroleum shortages affect not only automobiles but refining and chemical industries, key growth sectors. Against growing mass opposition to the proliferation of nuclear energy in private hands, PCE leadership had supported the government's program to develop it without controls. The Catalan proposal presented by

Joaquim Sempere won the day and committed the party to support nuclear construction only through the public sector and with community controls, if at all. The party agreed to initiate public debate about the comparable merits of nuclear, thermal, and solar energy. At the same time, it called for rigorous health and safety controls on old installations, and for community review of whether and where new installations should be constructed. The PCE strongly endorsed the growing ecology movement, and pledged to use party organizations to promote greater consciousness of environmental problems.[26]

Around the issue of the mass party, the delegates discussing Article 6 made further attempts to refine their notions of democracy, especially in relation to the "new working class." In *Eurocommunism and the State*, Carrillo argued that salaried workers, including teachers, technicians, bureaucrats, and professionals now join the proletariat in its opposition to the fascist state, which is run in the interests of monopoly capitalism. He claimed that the principal contradiction in contemporary society is between the multinationals, which control the state apparatus, and everyone else—not between the bourgeoisie and the proletariat, as many members of the commissions and their supporters (especially in Catalonia and Asturias) still argue.[27] Carrillo and the party leadership employ the phrase "forces of labor and culture" as shorthand for their class analysis.

PSUC, which of all the Communist sections is most staunchly tied to the workers' commissions, attempted to force the party to define the relative weights it gives to "labor" and to "culture." In committee debate around Article 6, the PSUC had unsuccessfully attempted to win support for its suggestion that "democracy of the base," meaning political control through workers' commissions, be substituted for the more amorphous call for "direct democracy" that the convention finally approved. By voting for "direct democracy," two-thirds of the delegates in effect voted against giving the workers' commissions priority in the party, even though the commissions won four times as many votes in the union elections of early 1978 as the party had won in the previous year's national elections.

QUESTIONS OF PARTY commitment to internal democracy were at the root of the conflict around Article 15—the so-called retreat from Leninism—at the April 1978 party congress. By defining itself as "a revolutionary Marxist democratic party," the PCE broke with a long tradition among Communist parties which claimed that "Leninism is the Marxism of today." The PCE is attempting to win PSOE supporters by convincing them that the Communists are not dominated by the Soviet Union, are deeply committed to democracy, and can meet the needs of working people in contemporary Spain. Several years ago, when chastised for his lack of discipline with regard to the CPSU, Carrillo rsponded, "I am not a Russian, I am a Spaniard." As with previous Eurocommunist decisions to drop the term "dictatorship of the proletariat," the PCE's decision to drop Lenin indicates much more about what kind of party it already is than what it plans to be and do in the future.

There was substantial opposition to dropping Lenin's name, but this was once again over the relationship of the workers' commissions to other party members, and over the tactics the party leadership used to achieve its victory. No one in the PCE argued that it ought to imagine itself as a monolithic single party capable of becoming the state of the future. No delegate argued for a directly insurrectionary politics. The debate is nothing like the debate over Leninism that occurred among American leftists in the 1970s.

In the pre-convention regional party meetings, Carrillo's "anti-Leninism" aroused the most vociferous opposition from the Asturian miners.[28] Carrillo claimed that only the "intellectuals" at the university opposed dropping Lenin. But he underestimated the doctrinal sophistication and orthodoxy of the miners organized into the workers' commissions. No group in the PCE is admired more than the mine and metallurgical workers of Asturias. In 1934 they rose up against a reactionary government and held the province for two weeks. The government repressed them with Moroccan troops led by Colonel Francisco Franco, and imprisoned or exiled more than 30,000 of the striking workers. When Franco and the Nationalists rebelled against the Republic in July 1936 and attempted to carry out a coup that resulted in the three-year-long Civil War, the miners of Asturias as dynamiters became the folk heroes of revolutionary struggle on the Madrid Front. Their sons organized the first factory committees in Franco Spain, and when they went to parliamentary elections in 1977, they elected the most famous person from their region, La Pasionaria, as their delegate to the Cortes. One source of their strength in the fierce struggle against Franco was their unquestioning and rigid belief in Marxism Leninism, and many of them remain Leninist fundamentalists.[29]

In February 1978, at the regional meeting in Asturias prior to the April 1978 convention of the PCE, the miners defended Lenin against Carrillo and the party leadership. After heated debate over whether Carrillo was watering down the revolutionary potential of the party, 113 delegates (representing 25 percent of the PCE members in Oviedo) marched out. None of these was "invited" to come to Madrid in April. But many who share their views did not walk out, and they fought for their position at the Ninth Party Congress.[30]

Francisco Frutos, longtime leader of PSUC, also spoke against dropping "Leninism." He argued that it is compatible with a commitment to democracy secured by the working class. The people for whom Frutos spoke became known as the "Leninists," which is ironic insofar as they were calling for open debate within the party about key issues. Many members of the minority want the party to discuss support for the King, which Carrillo has unilaterally declared. They want to open debate concerning high unemployment among youth and develop a program for how jobs ought to be divided. The Basques and Andulusians want more local party control over Communist policy toward their regions, exercised through the workers' commissions. The "Leninists" actually come close to Trotskyist demands for dual power through the Party and the workers' commissions. Their side won 248 votes while the majority got 968; they did not even win many of the 734 workers who were delegates to the congress, though they did win a significant number of those from Asturias, Catalonia, and the Basque Country.[31]

LENINISM HAS USUALLY acknowledged the need for broad alliance strategies, but does not identify these social blocs with narrowly parliamentary strategies. The arguments within the PCE concern which groups within an alliance ought to take precedence, and which groups ought to be treated as opponents. The "Leninists" want to preserve the industrial working-class character of the clandestine PCE. Although they lost their doctrinal struggle, those who want power in the party to rest primarily with the commissions won indirectly by forcing the party to add five representatives of the workers' commissions to the Executive Committee.[32] The Catalan PSUC, which overwhelmingly backed the "Leninists," has tremendous power in the PCE. The largest section of the Spanish working class is in Catalonia. Although the majority are migrants from Andalusia, Extremadura, and Galacia, many of them helped build the anti-fascist workers' commissions of Catalonia. Continued party recognition of the centrality of industrial workers gives PSUC leverage over other party decisions; rather than a cult of personality, the Catalan branch of the party has a "cult" around the commissions. Since the PSUC won 22 percent of the popular vote in Catalonia in the national elections of March 1979 compared to the PCE's 11 percent in the rest of Spain, the party can hardly ignore the PSUC's wishes.

Carrillo and the majority in the PCE seem to favor a broader alliance strategy than the PSUC and many industrial workers in the party are willing to accept. Carrillo and the leadership have attempted to construct a democratic liberal center coalition capable of transforming the fascist state. The effort, generally known as "cultural work," seeks to win people like the 25,000 functionaries who until 1977 were employed by the fascist National Syndical Confederation. The PCE claims that these people are not fascists, but along with other workers would fight for free trade unions, expanded social security programs, and welfare reforms, if only the party can convince them that future employment lies with the strength of these new institutions. The authoritarian centralist state Franco created brought government bureaucracy to new heights and provided jobs for hundreds of thousands. To dismantle the fascist state requires restructuring work opportunities for them as well as for the returned migrant laborers and youth that swell the ranks of the million unemployed.

The strategy of party leaders also entails securing support from the national bourgeoisie. These include textile manufacturers, steel producers, ship builders, retailers, and farmers, who lack power in the state. Opposed to them and the democractic forces are Franco's family and friends who have made their fortunes in construction, banking tied to international finance capital, and as managers for the multinationals in the auto, chemical, and metallurgical sectors. This group and those who run the large estates and mines which were nationalized under Franco, are known familiarly as "the oligarchy." These are the people who control the fascist apparatus through government agencies and whose enterprises the PCE speaks of nationalizing.[33]

The party is playing a dangerous game for the army, police, and courts are still dominated by Francoists. The PCE hopes to avoid a Chilean situation by allaying the fears of farmers, merchants, and industrialists right now, but no group is more conservative than the industrialists. In late winter 1978, the large corporations opposed attempts at moderate economic reforms to obtain some public control over energy and steel. The corporate leaders won support among small and medium capitalists, and together they forced the government to discharge the official who wrote the proposal for reforms including a moderate income tax.[34]

Feminism and Communism

THE GREATEST TEST of the PCE's alliance with popular movements is its relation to feminism, an interclass movement of opposition to Francoist repression. The neighborhood associations that emerged in working-class suburbs thoughout Spain in the early 1970s have provided the main institutional structure for feminism outside the universities. The chief tactic feminists employ is the mass demonstration, which they have used to force the government to abridge laws that oppress women. Spanish feminists place their faith in direct action in the streets, a strategy with which the PCE leadership is not entirely comfortable.

If there are stages in the development of the feminist movement, Spain has shuffled through them very quickly. The economic miracle of the 1960s absorbed male workers who, with their families, swelled the new industrial suburbs. Inadequate public services, including transportation, medical facilities, schools, sewage, garbage collection, and, most of all, the high cost of bread, drew women of Catalonia and the Basque Country into the first massive demonstrations against Franco. The growth of the Spanish economy following American investment in the 1950s permitted some women to enter the universities where, in the mid- and late-1950s, they fought in student demonstrations for reforms including liberalization of curriculum, improved facilities, and an end to forced membership in the fascist student organization.

Spanish women have suffered from the patriarchal organization of fascism. Until recently, all Spanish women between the ages of 16 and 34, unless married or nuns, had to serve six months in some social service organization of the fascist party. Without a certificate of completion, for which a course in fascist principles of female service and motherhood was required, no woman could enter the university, get a driver's license, or apply for a civil service job. Until 1973, no Spanish woman under 25 could legally leave her paternal home to live except to marry or become a nun.[35]

Until 1961, women by law were excluded from professional training, so those women who entered the university were largely in humanities, the center of the first student struggles. Many daughters of the bourgeoisie—the only women who could get a university education until the late 1960s—joined the parties of the left, including the clandestine PCE. From this group came the Democratic Movement of Women in 1966, which led amnesty campaigns for political prisoners from the clandestine workers' commissions.

The radical feminist movement, which stresses male supremacy over class oppression, developed in the early 1970s even before Franco's death.[36] Feminist organizations such as the Feminist Collective of Barcelona were made up of a cross-section of the female population. Members ranged from labor lawyers, who defended men in the commissions, to neighborhood housewives angry about slum housing and lack of schools. (There were a half-million more children than school places in Madrid in 1976). At the core were young, university-trained professionals and students. The women's movements in Catalonia and Madrid extended their political work for amnesty to include women. They demanded the decriminalization of adultry, the right to divorce, the end to imprisonment for victimless crimes such as prostitution, homosexuality, and teaching birth control. They publicized the conditions of female prisoners, especially those imprisoned for alleged terrorist activities. Focusing upon women's rights to control their bodies, the Women's Liberation Front formed in Madrid in the early 1970s. Other groups, generally preoccupied with single issues, developed throughout Madrid and Barcelona, with scant representation elsewhere. When these groups attempted to hold a national feminist conference to which noted European feminists were invited in 1974, the police arrested its leaders and cancelled the meeting. Finally, in late 1975, following the death of Franco, the first feminist conference in 36 years was held in Madrid.[37]

Since that time, the feminist movement has increasingly worked in the neighborhood associations and in the streets. The most notable legal form of repression of women was the 1889 law against adultery which specified that only women could be punished. A man could be charged as a criminal adulterer only if he moved another female into his home or if he had sexual relations with a woman he knew was married to someone else. On the other hand, a woman absent from home without her husband's permission and found in the company of another man could be accused of adultery. There were very few cases in which the law was enforced until the rise of the women's movement. Before the 1970s if a father or his parents wanted custody of a child, they would threaten the woman with an adultery suit and, rather than face public shame, fines and a possible jail sentence of up to six years, she gave up her child.

THE WOMEN'S MOVEMENT, including many members of the PCE, pursued several of these cases in 1976 and 1977 in Barcelona, Madrid, and Zaragoza. They persuaded women threatened with adultery suits to confront them in court. Massive demonstrations of 5,000 included working class women and children from the neighborhood associations who wore placards around their necks that proclaimed "I too am an adulterer." The police often attacked them, but they fought on and in 1978 the government bowed to this pressure and modified the law. The PCE has commitments to reform the fascist legal system, but they have been slow to acknowledge that the feminists have begun to do it through direct action.

Birth control is a more touchy subject in Catholic Spain, although the decline in the birth rate from 21.9 per 1000 women in 1960 to 19.4 in 1972 indicates that family limitation practices are widespread.[38] Recent surveys show that a majority of Spanish women favor the use of birth control, especially the pill, which until 1978 was imported from France. Most middle class women have the name of London abortionists, but outside the big cities and middle class strongholds, birth control is hard to find. Not a single labor union or political party working in Andulusia includes birth control information among its services, despite the fact that these women are literally dying in their thirties from excessive childbirth.[39] Outside of feminist circles, no group on the left views this as a form of fascist oppression.

Like other fascist governments, the Francoist state encouraged women to stay home and raise large families. Beginning with the third child, the family received government subsidies, important income to poor women in the agricultural areas. With each additional child, the subsidy increased so long as the mother did not work outside the home. Under such circumstances, reproduction was a source of family income. In countries such as Spain in which there are few if any schools for poor children, extra children earn extra money for the family, and in the south of Spain it is quite common for the poorest women to marry at 16, have six or seven children, and be worn-out wrecks by 30.[40]

Even so, it is estimated that 300,000 illegal abortions took place in Spain in 1978 for want of other forms of birth control. Repeated amateur abortions probably account for the high rate of uterine cancer suffered by poor Spanish women. Recently the women's movement has won modification of the laws on birth control devices, to permit their legal sale. Through militant street demonstrations they will get free distribution of birth control through state operated clinics. The struggle for abortion on demand will take longer to win, although some "therapeutic" abortions, carried out under the most humiliating conditions, have begun. Males and non-feminists in the PCE and other left groups have not yet been convinced that this systematic oppression of women during the past forty years in Spain is part of the systematic organization of fascism, which must be overcome before feminists can speak of "democratization."

Spanish feminists now emphasize transforming the judiciary and common law practices in the treatment of women by attacking rape and other forms of violence against women. The fascist penal code makes it difficult to prosecute rapists, since women are not full citizens and crimes against them are crimes only if, as property of men, they are disabled. The victim is responsible for proving that she resisted, did not know the man who raped her prior to the attack, and, if unmarried, that she was a virgin. As in the United States until recently, rape victims are ashamed to go to the authorities for fear of the humiliation to which they are forced to submit. The Spanish feminists have bypassed the judicial system by holding popular tribunals against rapists in the streets of Madrid and Barcelona.

Communist and non-Communist feminists have increasingly engaged in political action with the women of the Association of Neighbors, many of whom are the wives of men in the workers' commissions. The basements of new tenements are often taken over for meetings and for instruction in birth control. Popular universities for women of the neighborhood have emerged in some of these centers from which has come support for the creation of parks and controls over food prices. These groups have demonstrated to win environmental controls on chemical factories such as the ones built by DOW, which have made life in Huelva insufferable. These women have joined anti-nuclear demonstrations in Catalonia, Euskadi (the Basque Country), and Galacia, and have been leaders of the opposition to constructing a nuclear plant near Donana, the largest wildlife and bird sanctuary in Europe.[41] In their community organizations, women represent a popular democratic institution that the PCE has tapped only indirectly, through the workers' commission members who live in such housing developments.

The more democratic the party becomes, the more difficulty party leadership has in juggling its constituencies, some of which—like the largely male workers' commissions (among industrial wage laborers) and the feminist movement—are antagonistic. Throughout the spring of 1977 prior to the first national elections in June, Communist Party rallies included one obligatory female speaker to address "women's issues" such as housing, medical care, and public services. These female party members addressed the need for wage parity between men and women, but they scarcely considered birth control and never spoke about abortions. Militants at these and subsequent rallies in 1979 generally ignored the female speakers. Two nights before the first elections, Carrillo made a dramatic appeal on television for birth control and the right of abortion, infuriating his feminist comrades, many of whom had been required to soft-pedal their demands for female reproductive rights during the campaign.[42]

THE PCE'S USUAL BLEND of opportunism and sensitivity to new constituencies led the drafting committee of Article 8 of the 1978 PCE platform to make the exaggerated claim that the PCE was "a feminist party, the party of women's liberation."[43] Acrimonious debate in committee revealed hostility between representatives of industrial workers and feminists.

The argument over feminism demonstrated conflict within the party over Eurocommunist strategy. Delegates from Euskadi, after Catalonia the most industrialized region of Spain, suggested that the party not give blanket support to feminism but endorse only proposals that affect working class women. Since feminism is a universalist movement, dedicated to achieving equal civil rights for all, it unites women across classes, a process male industrial workers reject. A representative from the Asturian miners suggested that feminism could divide working class men and women, and therefore ought to be avoided. Eduardo Saborido Galan, a leader of workers' commissions who has been in the party for 20 years and now serves on the Central Committee, spoke for many workers when he argued that the party could not consider gender oppression to be as important as class oppression.[44]

Debates led some delegates to propose new areas of research, especially around the condition of peasant and working women in the rural areas. Some participants called for a party analysis of the patriarchal family and authoritarian practices in the private sphere.[45] The committee brought forth a new Article 8 which acknowledges (on paper at least) that the struggle for equality of the sexes is inseparable from the campaign to secure democratic institutions to replace fascist ones. It affirms that "masses of women fighting for liberation represent a revolutionary potential that embellishes the vision of labor and cultural forces...The liberating power of feminist struggle will enrich the common fight of all those who aspire to transform society."[46] The party platform that was accepted calls for women's freedom to obtain divorce, practice birth control, follow sexual preferences, enjoy equal education, and earn wages equal to men's.

Artilce 8 began what many feminists in the party hope will be an on-going debate about the comparable importance of class oppression and gender oppression. The party accepted the burden of struggling to raise consciousness about how capitalism uses women and why destroying the fascist state will not entirely solve their problems. "It is certain that to abolish discrimination against women, it is necessary to destroy capitalism; it is also true that socialism cannot be won without the total transformation of society, including the destruction of all forms of social and sexual domination."[47] Feminists' suggestion that more women be promoted to the inner councils of party power was not taken up at the congress or since.

The feminist movement poses a challenge to the PCE, which claims to be building an inter-class alliance to overthrow fascism by substituting democratic institutions for analogous parts of the present state. Although the PCE never claims that the party is the embryo of a new state, female militants—like male workers commission members—sense that their position in the future would be more secure if they had more power in the party now. The workers' commissions gained five new positions on the Central Committee in 1978, but feminists have none. Party leaders still raise Stalinist objections against "factionalism," by which they mean the representation of special interests. They oppose any suggestion of structural reform, by which neighborhood associations, workers commissions, and representatives of other interest groups among the mass movements would debate differences and contribute to party decision-making on an ongoing basis.

Without real power within the party as feminists, female party members refuse to abandon their tried and true strategy of massive street demonstrations, which inadvertently forces the party to make decisions that favor them. By these actions, feminists have already brought a variety of reforms in institutions the PCE claims to want to tackle, such as the universities and the legal system. Many feminists have withdrawn from active membership in the PCE, and others are certain to follow.

THE ETA TERRORISTS AND BASQUE REGIONALISM

COMMUNIST PARTIES in industrially-developed countries have failed to come to terms with the persistence of nationalist and regionalist sentiments because of a deep-rooted statism that is part of their orthodox tradition. Much of contemporary left theory on the national question analyzes colonialism in its classical forms and then argues by analogy to the underdeveloped regions within the state. But the two places in Spain where there have been autonomist movements for centuries—Catalonia and the Basque Country—also happen to be, along with Madrid, the most industrial areas of Spain.

Eurocommunism as practiced by the PCE has tended to include support for regionalist movements that have emerged in Spain in opposition to fascist centralism. Nowhere more than in the Basque Country, known as Euskadi, has the party been forced to honor this commitment, and nowhere has it more clearly failed. The four Basque Provinces lie in a region of deep valleys and high mountains, west of the Pyrenees, in northern Spain. Due to topography, they were never conquered by the Romans and not Christianized until the thirteenth century. A native rural artisan metal industry of the early nineteenth century gave way to the development of heavy industry later in the century. Next to Catalonia and Madrid, Euskadi and its two and one-half million people form the major center of industrial capitalism in Spain. Bilbao (Spain's Pittsburgh) gives ample proof of the vitality of Basque capitalism and its national bourgeoisie.[48]

Three of the four Basque provinces held firm against Franco during the Civil War. Both Catalonia and the Basque Country had secured statutes of autonomy from the Second Republic (1931-1939) that gave them some control of schools, police, and provincial government. Both regions spoke languages different from Castilian, which under Franco was the only language permitted. The rugged terrain of Euskadi was no protection against the Nazi bombers of the Condor Legion, which bombed the Basque center at Guernica to terrorize the civilian population into surrender. At the close of the war, Basque priests, the only group of Spanish clergy who in any significant numbers opposed Franco, were marched in chains from one village to the next. Many of them were executed along with civilian anti-fascists. Euskadi and Catalonia lost their autonomy and were subjected to the law of Franco's armies of occupation, which jailed hundreds of thousands following the war.[49]

Euskadi was ruled by the hated domestic army known as the Guardia Civil (Civil Guard). Created in the nineteenth century as a rural police force against bandits, the Guardia Civil was a standing army in the countryside. The growth of working-class suburbs in formerly rural areas surrounding the big cities of Spain has led to struggle between the working class and the Guardia Civil, particularly in the Basque Country.

Basque nationalists, who wanted home rule and an end to police brutality, organized ETA (Basque Homeland and Freedom) in the late 1950s. In it, the old Basque nationalist exiles allied with liberals seeking civil rights and young Basques who had grown up under fascism. A portion of the movement became socialist and began to argue that only through the overthrough of capitalism as well as Franco could Basques hope to gain their freedom. Police brutality, experienced by the entire civilian population of Euskadi, fell hardest on the workers believed to belong to the underground workers' commissions. Arrests generally meant prolonged periods of torture, during which many prisoners died even before friends and relatives had discovered their whereabouts.

The strategy of reprisals against police for the torture of Basques was initiated by one of the socialist groups within ETA. The Guardia Civil responded by increasing its attacks on Basque nationalists, workers' commission members, and suspected terrorists. In late 1970, Franco staged a show trial in military court in Burgos of ten alleged ETA terrorists. The courts condemned them to death, but massive protests throughout Europe forced Franco to commute them to life sentences in a dramatic New Year's Eve reprieve.

NEAR CIVIL WAR in the Basque Country has posed the single most important military challenge to Spanish fascism since 1939. Since most ETA members are between 18 and 30, youth itself is suspect. Even bourgeois parents face searches of their homes without warrants and seizure of their children as the police, driven mad by ETA assassinations, attempt to pursue their enemies. Working-class parents in the Basque Country face additional torment since the police often carry out reprisals against their whole families if a child is a suspected ETA terrorist.

In a daring and politically significant exploit in December, 1973, ETA terrorists in Madrid assassinated Admiral Luis Carrero Blanco, Franco's designated successor. As the Prime Minister was leaving Mass in his limousine, a charge under the street blew him onto the roof of a neighboring convent. It is hard to find Spanish leftists whatever their views of terrorism who question that the course of contemporary Spanish

history would have been worse had Carrero Blanco not been assassinated.[50]

Repression and reprisal led to pitched battles in Bilbao, Vitoria, and
Pamplona. In 1975 the government decreed sweeping anti-terrorist laws
(renewed in 1978) that effectively denied everyone in Euskadi of their civil
rights. When that failed to end terrorism, Franco—despite pressure from
Western European governments—executed five young men, three of
them alleged ETA terrorists. The execution in October, 1975, was
Franco's last major political act before he died in November.

At Franco's death, more than half of Spain's political prisoners were
Basques. Finding the limited amnesty King Juan Carlos decreed upon
Franco's death insufficient, ETA pursued its struggles with substantial
Basque popular support through demonstrations of up to 200,000 people
in five cities. The government continued to terrorize the entire population
in its frustration about its inability to end terrorism. Amnesties dribbled
out, but as late as May 1977, one month before the first national
elections, large numbers of suspected ETA terrorists were still in prision.
In the previous decade, the PCE had perfected the mass demonstration
for the release of political prisoners who were in the workers' commissions. But now they avoided demonstrations for Basque amnesty. The
PCE, legalized in April 1977, argued that terrorists would provoke a
confrontation with the army which could not be won. They opposed the
mobilization for Basque amnesty organized throughout Euskadi the first
week in May 1977. Hundreds of thousands marched in the major Basque
cities and were attacked by the Guardia Civil, resulting in dozens of
wounded and three deaths. The entire Basque region threatened to
boycott the national elections, forcing the government of Prime Minister
Adolfo Suárez to free most of the political prisoners just one month
before the elections.

Struggle over the new constitution and its failure to include a statute
of autonomy acceptable even to the liberal Basque Nationalist Party
(PNV) provoked ETA to renewed violence. In the period before the
national referendum and the King's signing of the constitution in
December 1978, ETA assassinated a liberal journalist and increased its
attacks on police. ETA's chief theorist, José Miguel Benaran (Argala),
died on December 21, 1978 in a gangland-style murder, widely attributed
to the police. Before the end of the year, and scarcely a month after the
government had repressed an army coup, ETA assassinated a general and
a colonel in Madrid. Many feared that civil war was imminent, and
nowhere was it feared more than in the workers commissions and in the
PCE, which mobilized peace demonstrations throughout Spain (including the Basque Country). The first months before the national
elections of March and the municipal elections of April 1979 demon-

strated that the ETA's practice of assassinating police and capitalists will continue until either the movement is smashed or Basque autonomy is secured.

ETA regards terrorism as an appropriate tactic when engaged in armed struggle, which the PCE and the masses of the population want to avoid. The attacks on a liberal Basque journalist who had attempted to mediate between ETA and the government, and on centrist army officials, who the government had replaced with more right wing officers reveals that ETA's strategy is to keep Spanish politics polarized. All groups to the left of the PCE are impatient with the slow liberalization program Suárez and the King have pursued, but even the Trotskyists and the Maoists urged people to support the new constitution, which is quite conservative. A left journalist wrote that he plannd to vote "yes" so that his purist friends could vote "no" and Spain could nevertheless have a constitution, which it desperately needs. ETA fears this kind of meliorist view, although it has not begun to assassinate people on the left.

Ironically, the Basque movement—of which ETA is only the most extreme arm—is exactly the kind of alliance Carrillo and the PCE leadership favor, since it includes workers, youth, middle strata, part of the national bourgeoisie, and women. But the PCE has never fully understood the Basque need to confront the fascist state directly. The PCE paid for its failures in Euskadi in 1977 when, despite the strength of workers' commissions and the working class in general, not a single PCE delegate was elected. They also paid in certain red suburbs of Madrid, where thousands of Basques who work in the capital cast their first ballot in 40 years against the Communists and for the Socialists. Nearly a year later at the PCE Ninth Party Congress, a leading Basque Communist from the workers' commissions attacked Eurocommunist notions of national reconciliation and reminded the delegates that Euskadi had waged war on fascism for nearly two decades. He argued that without a real statute of autonomy, which would permit the legalization of outlawed political parties and guarantees of civil rights, it would be impossible to defeat terrorism. The Basque speaker warned that so long as the PCE took its stand with Suárez and against the Basques, it would be opposed in Euskadi.[51] The mass peace demonstrations of late 1978 and early 1979 revealed that the Basque population does not want ETA to provoke civil war, but the March 1979 Cortes elections demonstrated that, despite the PCE's peace program, the Basques prefer the Socialists and the Basque Nationalist Party, which stress the desperate need for Basque autonomy.

THE CHANCE FOR DEMOCRACY

IF THERE IS no military coup, the PCE could conceivably make dramatic advances in the near future. One prospect is that it will be able to help dismantle the fascist state piecemeal, by substituting democratic agencies such as free trade unions for the fascist corporate union structure. To succeed in this process, the PCE will have to democratize itself in order to assume leadership of the autonomous mass movements. It might adopt an entirely novel course of establishing democratic party structures in communities and workplaces through the workers' commissions, neighborhood associations, and autonomous women's groups. Out of these popular organizations, an executive and central committee of the party might be chosen. It is unlikely that the current party leaders would accept such structural change, but their pragmatism has already led them to support other improbable revisions of Marxist-Leninist orthodoxy.

The PCE can lead what is now an autonomous movement for democracy and socialism only if it democratizes its internal structure. Spain's militant mass movement can be most effective if its actions are part of a coordinated strategy, but it is too diverse and too autonomous to accept Stalinist discipline and doctrine. The PCE's 1978 Congress took steps in a democratic direction, but they were only first steps. If the party does not expand the process of internal democratization, it will condemn itself to remain a minor force in Spanish politics, leaving it to the Socialists and the government's centrist party (UCD) to construct a post-Franco Spain.

Notes

1. Herbert Southworth, "The Divisions of the Left," in *Times Literary Supplement* (London), 9-VI-1978, pp. 649-650; Jose Yglesias, "The Franco Years" (new York, 1977), p. 43.
2. Temma Kaplan, "Turmoil in Spain," in *Radical America* (March-April 1977), Vol. 11, no. 2, pp. 53-73; pp. 55-56.
3. This period has been the subject of debate recently as former Communists attempt to make the party come to terms with its history. No two works have done more to criticize the leadership while upholding the heroic history of the mass base than Jorge Semprún's *Autobiografía de Féderico Sanchez* (Barcelona, 1977) and Fernando Claudin's *Documentos de una divergencia comunista. Los textos del debate que provoco la exclusion de Claudin y Jorge Semprún del PCE* (Barcelona, 1978).
4. Claudin, *Documentos*, p. 105; Alison Wright, *The Spanish Economy, 1959-1976*, (London, 1978).
5. Ricardo Soler, "The New Spain," in *New Left Review*, 58 (November-December 1969), pp. 17-20; *Organization de Cooperation et de Development Economiques: L'Evolution demographique de 1979 à 1985 dans les pays membres de L'OCDE* (Paris, 1974), p. 102; Wright, *Spanish Economy*, p. 67.
6. See Semprún, *Autobiografía*; Claudin, *Documentos*; Ramon Roca, "Classe et Avant Garde dans le 'Mesetaria': 1960-1975," *Les Temps Modernes*, 357 (1976), pp. 196-199; and for Santiago Carrillo's side of the story see his *Dialogues on Spain* (London, 1976), pp. 115-118.
7. Yglesias, *The Franco Years*, pp. 48, 52; Faustino Miguelez, *La lucha de los mineros Asturianos bajo el Franquismo* (Barcelona, 1976).
8. Yglesias, *The Franco Years*, pp. 33; 48; 52.
9. I reviewed this situation in my article, "The PCE and the Mass Movement in Spain," in *Socialist Revolution* 34 (July-August 1977), pp. 29-36.
10. *Nuestra Bandera: Revista teorica y politica del Partido Comunista de Espana* (Madrid), 93 (April 1978), pp. 49-52.
11. Jose Luis Leal, Joaquin Leguina, Jose Manuel Nardo, Luis Tarrafeta, *La agricultura en el desarrollo capitalist espanol, (1940-1970)*, (Madrid, 1975).
12. Manuel Castells, "Immigrant Workers and Class Struggle in Advanced Capitalism" in *Politics & Society*, Vol. 15, no. 1 (1975), 33-66; V. L. Alonso, J. Calsada, J.R. Huerta, A. Langreo, J.S. Vinas, *Crisis a ararias y luchas campesinas* (1970-1976), (Madrid, 1976); Juan Baldrich Caballe, *Programas agrarias de partidos pliticos espanoles* (Madrid, 1977); see also the special issue on Andalusia in *Cambio 16* (Madrid), 12-III-1978.
13. *Cambio 16*, 12-III-1978, p. 17.
14. Manuel Castells, *Ciudad, democracia y socialismo* (Madrid, 1978); Jane Carbonell, et. al., *La lucha de barrios en Barcelona*, (Madrid, 1976).
15. For PSUC's program see *PSUC, Una proposta democratica i socialista per a Catalunya* (Barcelona, 1976).

16. Ramon Trias Fargas, *Introduccion a la economia de Cataluna* (Barcelona, 1972).
17. *Cambio 16*, 14-V-1978, pp. 116-117.
18. *Nuestra Bandera*, 93, pp. 25-26; *Cambio 16*, 30-IV-1978, pp. 55-56.
19. For a cross-section of feminist activities in Spain see *Vindicación feminista* (Barcelona), numbers 1-25, 1975-.
20. *Cambio 16*, 30-IV-1978, p. 58.
21. *Cambio 16*, 30-IV-1978, pp. 55-56.
22. *New York Times*, 4-VII-1978.
23. *Los Angeles Times*, 4-IV-1978; Temma Kaplan and Jon Wiener, "The Spanish Left: Divided but Surprsingly Strong," in *Working Papers* (January-February 1978), pp. 20-24.
24. Yglesias, *The Franco years*, p. 60.
25. *New York Times* 4-VII-1978.
26. *Nuestra Bandera*, 93, p. 62.
27. Carrillo, *'Eurocommunism' and the State* (London, 1977), pp. 22, 24. For a critique of this see Fernando Claudin, *Eurocommunism and Socialism* (London, 1978).
28. *Cambio 16*, 9-IV-1978.
29. Yglesias, *The Franco Years*, pp. 32-33; Miguelez, *La Lucah.*
30. *Cambio 16*, 9-IV-1978, pp. 32-33.
31. *Nuestra Bandera*, 93, pp. 67-70.
32. *Cambio 16*, 30-IV-1978, pp. 56;58.
33. Carrillo, *'Eurocommunism' and the State*, 24-26; 76-81.
34. *Newsfront International*, People's Translation Service, no. 213 (April 1978).
35. Lourdes Beneria, "Women's Participation in Paid Production under Capitalism," in *The review of Radical Political Economics*, Vol. 8, no. 1 (spring 1976), 18-33; 33. See also her *Mujer economia y patriarcado durante la Espana Franquista* (Barcelona, 1978).
36. News about these different groups appears monthly in "Mujeres del Mundo" section of *Vindicación.*
37. Amparo Moreno, *Mujeres en lucha. El movimiento feminista en Espana* (Barcelona, 1978).
38. Beneria, "Women's Pariticpation," p. 33.
39. *Cambio 16*, 12-III-1978, p. 19.
40. Bel Carrasco, "Amar sin Miedo," in *La Calle* (Madrid), 28-III-1978, pp. 39-
41. *Vindicación*, 22 (April 1978), pp. 52-53; *Cambio 16*, 28-V-1978, pp. 125; 127; Imre de Boroviczeny, "A fight to save ethereal Donana and its wildlife," in *Smithsonian* (Washington, D.C.) Vol. 9, no. 3 (June 1978), pp. 72-79.
42. Kaplan and Wiener, "The Spanish Left," p. 23.
43. *Proyectos de propuestas politicas y de estatutos al IX Congreso del Partido comunista de Espana* (Madrid, 1978), p. 17.
44. *Nuestra Bandera*, 93, p. 72.
45. *Ibid.*, p. 71.
46. *Ibid.*, p. 74.
47. *Ibid.*, p. 76.
48. Juan Pablo Fusi, *Politica obrera en el Pais Vasco, 1880-1923* (Madrid, 1975).
49. Herbert Southworth, *Guernica! Guernica!* (Berkeley, 1977).
50. Julen Agirre, (Transl. Barbara Probst Solomon), *Operation Ogro: The Execution of Admiral Luis Carrero Blanco* (New York, 1974).
51. *Nuestra Bandera*, 93, pp. 27; 29.

chapter 5

FRANCE: THE NEW MIDDLE STRATA AND THE LEGACY OF THE MAY EVENTS

Andrew Feenberg

IN MAY OF 1968 ten million French workers transformed a student protest into a revolutionary movement by joining it in the streets. In the short space of a month France was overthrown and restored, but not without suffering a shock which resounds to this day. Like many unsuccessful revolutions before it, the May Events triumphed in the political culture of the society that defeated it in the streets. In the perspective of ten years, it now appears that May '68 inaugurated a new era in French political life, which still continues.

The May Events lay at the intersection of two histories: not only did the new left of the 1960s peak in France in 1968, but France gave the first signal of the political instability that has overtaken much of Southern Europe in the 1970s. In 1968 no one imagined that the Events would be relayed by an electoral movement such as Eurocommunism. Then the talk was of all the "senility" and "sclerosis" of the official opposition parties. In fact the May Events overthrew not the Gaullist state, but the narrow ideological horizons of the old left it challenged in attacking capitalism in new ways. The Events transformed the popular image of socialism in France, contributing to the collapse of moribund Stalinist and social democratic traditions, and to the rise of an aggressive Eurocommunist movement that threatens to take power. Some of the most important ideas of May continue to live through this movement.

FROM THE MAY EVENTS TO EUROCOMMUNISM
THE LEGACY OF THE MAY EVENTS

THE PARADOXICAL SURVIVAL of themes and hopes from the sixties in the mainstream politics of France in the seventies testifies to the need for a new interpretation of both the May Events and their Eurocommunist successor.[1]

What happened during May? The Events began with student protests, some of them against the war in Vietnam, which led to the closing of the university system. Similar occurrences in other countries had resulted in nothing more remarkable than large headlines; but the French government was uniquely vulnerable. De Gaulle's authoritarian style and technocratic reformism had provoked widespread opposition in every class and region. If Gaullism survived, this was primarily due to the divisions of its enemies, who could not mount a convincing electoral challenge to it. When the regime finally came up against the student movement, the many currents of opposition crystallized around the struggle in the streets. Within a few weeks, the struggle had escalated into the largest movement of the 1960s, the only movement of that period in the West to achieve the proportions of a national crisis through the simultaneous uprising of students, large sectors of the middle strata, and a majority of the working class.

At first the most powerful opposition force, the Communist Party, rejected the student movement on the grounds that its leaders were ultra-left provocateurs, preventing good students from doing their work and passing their exams. But on the night of May 10, tens of thousands of students and young workers built barricades in the Latin Quarter, fought the police against all odds and were brutally beaten. The event caused a shockwave of indignation throughout France. The Communists were obliged to subdue their attacks on the student movement, and offered some support for the more moderate student demands. The Communists helped to mobilize an enormous solidarity strike and demonstration on May 13, in which nearly a million people, many of them workers, marched through the streets of Paris to protest police repression.

To cut off the growing movement, the government offered concessions to the students, including the reopening of the Sorbonne. Coming from a regime as intransigent in its authoritarianism as de Gaulle's, these concessions were interpreted by the population as signs of weakness. When the students trouped back into the Sorbonne, it was not with the intention of returning to their books and their exams. They had glimpsed a more exciting future than the one promised by a diploma. "Socialist Revolution" and not "University Reform" was now the slogan that mobilized them and, surprisingly, they received an answering call from workers who began to strike and occupy their factories all over France.

After a decade of repression and defeat, the French working class was on the offensive: the red flag was quite literally raised over the gates to the proudest bastions of French capitalism.

A general strike affecting nearly ten million workers paralyzed the country, spreading through the factories, the bureaucracies, and the mass media. Swept up in the movement, the Communist party and its unions contributed to generalizing it. The first step toward revolution was taken: everyone ceased to obey, to conform to their social and economic roles. But for this crisis to become a successful revolution, the people in revolt would have had to unite behind an alternative to Gaullism—an alternative that integrated their various demands in a coherent program, and which focused the popular will to change on the overthrow of the weakened, but still menacing state apparatus.

It was precisely this element that was lacking in May. The students, knowing their own weakness all too well, did not propose their own revolutionary candidacy, but called on the workers to seize power. The student strategy involved the transformation of the general strike into an "active strike" in which the workers would set their factories back in motion on their own account. Then, with the economy beginning to turn again, but for the workers and not for their former bosses, the state would succumb in impotence, to be replaced by a democratic socialist regime based on self-management. This strategy for socialism responded not only to the students' belief in the injustice of both the exisitng capitalist and socialist societies, but also to their deep revulsion for the bureau-cratic occupations to which they were destined by their studies.

SOME WORKERS joined with the students in attempting to implement this strategy, but the vast majority turned to the Communist Party to press the movement forward to victory. The party responded by discouraging revolution. Instead, it negotiated a favorable economic settlement with management and the government and tried to initiate a massive return to work on that basis. It was May 27, and the movement seemed about to die. To the astonishment of nearly everyone, French workers massively rejected the proposed settlement. They wanted not just Samuel Gompers' famous "More!"; they wanted something "other," a different kind of life entirely. Four hectic days followed, in which France seemed on the verge of socialist revolution.

The Communist Party maneuvered desperately in this period. It briefly participated in the call for de Gaulle's resignation and the formation of a "popular government," but quickly retreated when the President-General mobilized his troops at the end of May. With its defection the revolutionary movement was once again without leadership and focus, and it gradually succumbed to the very disorganization and paralysis it had opposed to the power of the state. During June the Communists struggled mightily to end the strike movement and to win the legislative elections called by the regime as a sop to its critics. They succeeded only in terminating the movement; along with all the other left parties, they lost votes and deputies in the elections.

It is the penultimate moment of this story that is most significant, the moment in which the workers and their allies demanded the resignation of a government that could no longer even control the state bureaucracy, much less provide for the normal pursuit of economic activity. In this moment the nation hung in suspense while the workers and the government took each others' measure and considered the significance and potential of the movement. In this moment of hesitation at the end of May, the movement became something more than a mere collection of struggles for economic gains. The workers gave a deeper meaning to their refusal to work. Massive disobedience to authority in every sphere, whatever its immediate occasion, set off a chain reaction in the crucible of which a political will was formed.

To call the May Events a "revolution," it is not necessary to show that the government could have been overthrown by an insurrection at this point. The defining characteristic of a revolution is not that it is stronger than the existing society, but that it abruptly calls the existence of that society into question in the minds of millions, through a common struggle in which they participate. Precisely this is what happened during May. Social forms were as though liquified into their human basis in the individuals whose willingness to cooperate within their framework had made possible the old society. In dissolving society into its component parts, even if only briefly, the May Events set in motion a process of cultural change that still continues.

THE MAY EVENTS destabilized French society at its roots, in the collective imagination of both advocates and adversaries of revolution. It brought to mass consciousness themes of struggle and discontent that had formerly been the exclusive property of a few intellectuals. As Jean-Paul Sartre explained at the time, the May Events had "enlarged the field of the possible." What has happened in France since 1968 can only be understood against the background of this profound transformation in the popular sense of what is and what might be.

Of all the cultural changes initiated by the Events, the most important is in the popular image of socialism in France. Before 1968 socialism meant to most of the French what it still means to the majority of Americans today: more social justice, but at the price of a stronger state, more planning, more bureaucracy. One could be for socialism or against it, but there was no doubt about what it was. This was the influence of the Russian model, which still predominated through the propaganda of the Communist Party. But since 1968, self-management, the central demand of the May movement, has gradually penetrated French political culture, where it appears as a democratic alternative to the older image of socialism, an alternative based on the idea of self-determination in economic and social life. This change in the image of socialism has helped the left to overcome its divisions, and bridged the gap between the political aspirations of workers and the middle strata.

The rest of this article will be concerned with measuring the extent of this change as well as the continuing resistance to it. To prevent any misunderstanding, I want to anticipate my conclusions here. I do not believe, as Louise Beaulieu and Jonathan Cloud suggest I do in their contribution to this volume, that the PCF is the "heir" of the May Events. This would mean, at the very least, that the Party has become the principal bearer of the hopes born in 1968 for a new type of revolutionary transformation of French society. My argument is that only the French people itself can play the role of creating a self-managed socialist society. However, I do contend that the PCF, and still more the Socialist Party, have been drawn into a larger process of cultural change which they further by their rhetoric and some of their activities. This process of change rests ultimately on mass aspirations and actions, but the parties contribute by giving these an articulate form and a national resonance. The most important question is thus not whether the parties of the left are sincerely revolutionary, or whether they have changed as much as they "ought" to have changed since 1968. Posed in this form, the answers must be negative. More significant, however, is the fact that in spite of their dubious commitment to socialism and their still regressive positions on many issues, the parties have become functional elements in a mass social offensive they can only contain politically through a rhetoric and style that unwittingly enlarges and deepens the cultural base of the movement. How important one regards this cultural impact will depend on several factors—for example, on whether one has a spontaneist theory of revolutionary development, or whether one considers (as I do) that political parties play an important role in socializing the beliefs and attitudes underlying oppositional practices that could lead to a movement capable of effecting major transformations.

It is this background which explains why, in spite of its electoral victory, the French Establishment has run scared since May. It first attempted to coopt as much of the reformist content of the movement as it could. De Gaulle was to be the "Imagination in Power" for which the students had called. The failure of this bizarre experiment led to de

Gaulle's fall from power. The more conservative Pompidou regime which followed was wracked by scandals, as though there was no time left for the slow honest path to riches. Giscard d'Estaing represents what may be a last fling at liberal reformism in France, but the projeted Swedenization of the society remains a rhetorical flourish of a regime that in most domains continues Gaulllist policies without the authority of the preceding governments.

THE TRANSFORMATION OF THE FRENCH LEFT

WHILE THE MAY EVENTS caused a profound crisis in French ruling circles, they also opened up opportunities for the left. At first, of course, it too was in disarray. In the immediate aftermath of the Events, their bitter lesson seemed to be that the left itself was the main obstacle to socialism in France. Thus at the very moment when frightened voters fled the ranks of the left to shore up the tottering state, tens of thousands of veterans of the May movement ignored the parties and swarmed into radical extra-parliamentary groups to challenge their hegemony. These groups spurred on the social offensive which continued after May, in the schools, factories and other institutions of French society.

But in the years that followed, the constellation of left forces gradually changed. The extra-parliamentary groups declined and the weakened parties revived. The signing of the Common Program of the left in 1972 marked a turning point by demonstrating to the population at large the parties' will to claim the political leadership of the continuing social movement. From adversaries of the movement in 1968, the parties finally became advocates of many of its ideas, popularizing the new themes and images far beyond the range reached by the May Events in its few brief weeks of struggle. So the Communist and Socialist Parties, under intense pressure from the grass roots, were gradually transformed from antiquated repositories of cold war ideology into the popular representation of a mass social movement for a new kind of socialism. The testing of the limits of this transformation will no doubt occupy the years to come.

The rejuvenated French left is now within striking distance of political power. In the last two local elections, the alliance of the left received a majority of the vote and, while it lost the recent legislative elections, it is generally believed that it could easily have won them had it stuck together through the campaign. In the past the left was always defeated by anti-Communist scare tactics, or by the cooptative rhetoric of reform. For the first time its defeat is due only to itself. This is no doubt small comfort for those who hoped that it could win in 1978, ten years after the May Events, but it does indicate the depth of the change in French politics in those ten years.

The dynamics of the breakdown in the alliance can now be reconstructed. There is, of course, a political basis for the present problems, reflected in serious differences between the parties concerning many issues. However, these political differences have always existed and do not explain the failure of an alliance that for so long had overcome them. The breakdown occurred not because of new and greater political differences between the parties, but because of a change in the balance of power between them. As the Socialist Party became the biggest vote-getter, it attempted to assert its dominance in the alliance, and this proved an intolerable strain on PCF good will.

At first it seemed that the PCF had acted with the utmost cynicism simply to weaken a growing rival. Yet matters are in fact more complicated. The Communists can claim much of the credit for the growth of the Socialist Party that, without the support of an increasingly moderate PCF after its near collapse in 1969, would doubtless have remained a minor force like the Italian Socialist Party. Ironically, the strengthened Socialists wanted to assign the Communists a role in the alliance proportional to their minority influence with the voters. Yet the foundation of the entire left edifice was the willingness of the PCF to support the kind of positions that made its Socialist allies credible to their voters! The PCF learned too late that its moderate image did not strengthen it, but rather strengthened the more moderate parties to its right. The leadership of the PCF cut this gordian knot expeditiously by bringing the alliance crashing down around its own head.. It remains to be seen whether this extreme reaction will sit well with the majority of PCF members and the mass of its voters. Already there are signs of serious opposition in the Party, and the leadership is too weak and exposed to purge its ranks of dissidents.

THE LONG-TERM prospects of the French left are now uncertain. The Fifth Republic has always been haunted by nostalgia for a return to the centrism of the Fourth. Giscard occasionally suggests reviving a center-left politics that would freeze out both Gaullists and Communists. This would spell the death of the Union of the Left. But it is doubtful that Giscard really represents a reformist center movement with which the Socialists could ally themselves. Thus in spite of much talk of a break-up of the left, its parties are condemned to resolve their differences and prepare together for the Presidential elections of 1981.

No one can predict whether the alliance will recover its *élan* by then or whether it will continue in its present crippled form. In any case, the legislative elections have taught a lesson: the *sine qua non* of full cooperation between the parties of the left will be the mutual recognition of their equality in the alliance. It is difficult to imagine a left victory, at least one of any lasting significance, that would not be based on such a recognition, and the revival of a common program of government reflecting the parties binding commitments to each other and to the voters. It is too soon after the recent defeat to say whether this will occur, and at what price in terms of changes in the parties and their leadership. But it is still a real possibility that must be kept in mind as a corrective to the triumphalist propaganda of the victorious bourgeoisie. The tenacity of the left voters may yet be rewarded by an eventual reconciliation of the parties representing them and the formation of a left government. This possibility continues to inform every political discourse and decision in France, as it will for years to come.

In any case, what is certain is that the cultural changes inaugurated by the Events and furthered by the parties while they fought for the Common Program will permanently mark French politics. The May Events and the subsequent electoral movement have had a cumulative effect in France, without parallel in the United States, where the old left was too weak and sectarian to capitalize on the struggles of the 1960s. The partial confluence of "old" and "new" left strategies which characterizes the present French scene, is not yet a real possibility here. However, even if Eurocommunism is no model of strategy for the American left, it does promise something still more significant. The popular image of socialism in America, both for the left and for everyone else as well, is profoundly influenced by the example of what others have done in its name. The success of the European left in one or several countries would be a truly momentous historical event, altering the conception of socialism everywhere. An image based on the possibilities of a rich and democratic society would replace models based on the experience of poor countries without democratic traditions. Such an example might rekindle the difficult but vital dialogue between the left and the American people begun in the 1960s and interrupted in large part by the inability of the left to offer Americans an acceptable image of a socialist future.

CULTURAL CONTRADICTIONS OF THE LEFT

THE PRIMARY ACQUISITION of the May Events is the new and more democratic image of socialism that has largely replaced the old Stalinist and social democratic images in the popular imagination. However, in other domains the heritage of 1968 has not always been so thoroughly assimilated. Among the most radical goals of the May Events were two on which I will focus here: the replacement of *hierarchical social organization* and *consumer society* by an *egalitarian society* emphasizing *public models of consumption* of a new type. Understanding of these goals is spreading but it is not yet sufficiently generalized for the left to have a cultural program really corresponding with the political rupture it intends. Typically, these goals are best assimilated where they can be formulated in political terms; for example, the one kind of anti-hierarchical struggle that is well understood concerns struggle for workers' control of management through elected boards of directors. The struggle against the division of mental and manual labor, which cannot be formulated in these simple political terms, is still a marginal concern. Thus the cultural side of the movement is far less developed than the political side; time will tell if this is to be a permanent source of contradictions in the left, or whether the growth of a radical sensibility will eventually bridge the gap.

There is no doubt that the May Events began to make people aware of these cultural themes on a large scale for the first time. For example, the May Events made *social domination*, alienation, a theme of socialist struggle, in contrast with the traditional emphasis of Stalinists and social democrats alike on narrowly conceived political and economic struggles. By challenging technocratic bureaucracy—East and West—and by calling into question the division of labor associated with modern industrial societies, the May Events reclaimed for Marxist socialism a major and nearly forgotten aspect of its heritage: its debt and contribution to the idea of freedom. With the May Events it became possible once again for millions of people to see in socialist revolution a promise of increased freedom.

THERE IS PLENTY of evidence of the popular and hence potentially "left" character of the demand for socialism with freedom. There is, for example, the fact that this demand is associated with attempts by workers to democratize the unions in order to make of them more militant instruments of struggle against capitalist power in the workplace. (One union federation, the CFDT, has accepted the general principle of workers' "self-management" of strikes.) Since 1968 workers have carried out many such struggles, the best known of which was at the Lip watch factories in 1973, in the course of which the workers seized their workplace and continued to produce and distribute watches for many months.[2]

What this amounts to is the recovery, by the workers themselves, of the struggle against alienation which the parties and unions ignored and even suppressed so long as the workers were weak. It is in the context of this renewed social struggle that the left's interest in political freedom can best be understood: only if the power of the socialist state is limited can a revolutionary social dynamic based on mass initiatives unfold in society at large.

Awareness of the working-class struggle against alienation has had a deep influence on the other post-May social movements in France. There as here in the United States, such movements indicate the various concrete dimensions in which freedom must be won in the course of the struggle for socialism. But in France the simultaneous co-existence of strong working class offensives has imprinted these movements with a socialist character from the very start. Thus veterans of the May Events have spawned movements by and for women, high school students, migrant workers, prisoners, and for the environment, all in the hope of an eventual merging of these movements with the struggle of workers for a self-managed socialist society. To be sure, the junction of these struggles in the socialist movement has yet to be made. There is resistance to some of these movements in the official left parties, and the harsh criticism is often reciprocated. But despite these tensions, the overall impression one retains is of a gradual education of opinion in the broader socialist constituency that may eventually affect party policy.

The women's movement, for example, does not seem to have succeeded in making great changes in the left parties. Yet it has won legislative victories (notably on abortion) that testify to changes in the general climate of opinion, and certain measures contained in the Common Program, such as the massive expansion of the day care system, would contribute to increasing political participation by women. Similarly, while the environmental movement has had little programmatic impact on the left so far, its electoral candidates withdraw on the second round of voting in favor of the left, from which it attracts a majority of its fairly impressive support.

In sum, the movements inspired by the May Events to broaden the scope of the left have had some considerable success. Yet they are far from having become a fully integrated and self-evident dimension of the left, on a par with such things as union struggles, or demands for better public transport. The future of the French left may well depend on it achieving this goal.

Less hopeful are the results of the critique of American-style consumer society in France. During the May Events the French Socialist and Communist parties were accused of wanting to universalize consumer society rather than wanting to abolish it in favor of new and liberating models of social consumption. This theme was closely related to the critique of the official left's fixation on electoral power. Voting was denounced by the radical left as the supreme act of passive consumption and liberal authoritarianism. One leaflet argued that "the instrument of capitalist power...no longer resides so much in this latter [the state] as in the submission of the workers to models of consumer society and to all the differentiated forms of authority which assure its functioning."[3]

The official left regards these charges as utopian. It argues that the system cannot be transformed overnight, that a transitional regime under socialist leadership is needed as a prelude to bigger and better things. Parties that reject "consumer society" when workers are just beginning to participate in it, or that challenge aspects of the hierarchical social organization from which large strata of potential socialist voters still benefit, can never hope to build an electoral base for a transitional government.

THIS IS WHY the Common Program took for granted the persistence of so many regressive features of the established society. The Communists and Socialists argue that they are attempting to build socialism with "people as they are, not as they should be." More radical demands would be objectively counterrevolutionary because they would confuse and divide the potential electoral base for socialism.

Indeed, how can one attack the automobile, that prime example of "false" gratification under capitalism, when so many French workers have only recently acquired this mixed blessing? It is easier for prosperous revolutionaries living in desirable sections of Paris or in green suburbs to dispense with this questionable luxury than for those who live in dreary industrial slums. Similarly, an attack on the privileges, the status, and the incomes of the middle strata has a clear ultra-left content. Like "middle peasants" in the Chinese Revolution, these groups must be drawn into alliance with the left for it to succeed in France. It is difficult to see how support can be mobilized by criticism of their role in the capitalist hierarchy from which they profit in small ways. These sorts of arguments are familiar to many Americns who went through the experience of the new left, frequently criticized by liberals for their "counterproductive" methods. Yet the problem in France is perhaps more complicated than it was here. Some real struggles have dramatized the tension between the radical critique of advanced capitalism and the potential social base for its overthrow.

In May '68 many students felt betrayed by the working class, which transformed its general strike into a major wage offensive instead of mobilizing a direct assault on the state. Was this (as many students believed) a sign of the "integration" of the working class, of a definitive collapse of its socialist aspirations under the combined pressure of consumer society and the Communist Party? Or was it an illustration of Rosa Luxemburg's dictum: 'Every great political mass action, after it has attained its political highest point, breaks up into a mass of economic strikes."[4] If it were the latter, there would have been no betrayal, no defect in the will to socialism, but only a defect in the power to obtain it.

Whatever the answer (I incline to the latter), it is certain that many workers were insulted by student criticism of their attempts to meet their economic needs, which are still mediated by the wage system and the market in consumer goods.

There was a later attempt by the CFDT, under the influence of radical left activists, to promote anti-hierarchical wage struggles, designed to diminish the economic gap between different categories of employees. This offensive apparently met with strong resistance from better-paid workers and members of the middle strata. The majority of those groups felt threatened by movements that reduced their relative advantage, so that "anti-hierarchical" strikes split rather than united the workers. This result was particularly frustrating for the organizers, who had initiated the struggles precisely to overcome the divisive effects of the wage differentials established by capitalism. The Communist-led CGT anticipated just this and opposed such struggles from the beginning. It argued that capital could well afford to redistribute the same size wage bill more fairly among the labor force, especially if as a result the better-paid workers were bound more tightly than ever to the system in defense of their interests. The CFDT eventually abandoned this strategy.

These conflicts and failures are ominous because the problems would be intensified in a transitional regime. If the radical left critique cannot be successfully embodied in practice today, when will it ever be? Once in power the socialist movement seems likely to grow even more committed to the mechanisms of social differentiation and control made available by capitalism and which it will then command. It may find these mechanisms essential to its continued power and gradually create not socialism but social democracy, not just because it is politically conservative, as its critics charge, but still more because it depends on a cultural base in contradiction with its politcal goals. In this case the "transitional" regime would prove to be simply a more humane way of defusing social conflict and reproducing something much like the established system.

Supporters of the official left might reply that they intend a major shift away from capitalist culture, and point to the more radical chapters of the Common Program in their defense. What better start in the struggle against generalized and wasteful private consumption than reforms such as the proposed development of public transport and child care, changes in city planning and public housing, decentralized financing of culture, and democratization of education which the left has proposed? Taken together and developed consistently, such reforms promise a collective orientation toward consumption and a more favorable terrain of struggle for socialism generally.

The Common Program promised an attack on hierarchy as well. According to its provisions workers in the enlarged state sector would wield considerable power. The management of nationalized companies would be democratized and decentralized, with the local representatives of workers and consumers holding a majority of seats on the boards of directors. This measure would bar the way to the sort of centralized planning and administration characteristic of the Soviet model, and might also prove incompatible with the traditional social democratic subordination of nationalized industries to the needs of those still in private hands. In other areas as well, administration would be subjected to more democratic controls. Elected councils would govern the social security system, which administers both pensions and medical insurance. Tenant's unions would be recognized and would hold a majority of seats on the administrative councils of public housing projects. Educational institutions would be freed of rigid state control. And so on.

One interesting group of proposals contained in the Common Program shows a certain awareness of the need for changes in capitalist technology and labor organization to deal with problems of disqualification and environmental pollution. The Common Program proposes to legislate work pace, limit night shifts, and restrict the length of time a worker can be assigned to the hardest and most dangerous work. Workers employed at the most painful and boring jobs will benefit from a reduced work load at equal pay, and the time freed can be used for job training in more interesting work. Research on more humane technologies will begin. Science and technology will be enlisted in the struggle against pollution and for the preservation of the environment, and businesses that damage the environment will be held accountable for repair cost. Polluting technologies will be replaced when alternatives are available or can be developed. These are only modest first steps, however, and the official left has proved unresponsive to more drastic suggestions, such as ending the nuclear generation of electric power.[5]

THE MAY EVENTS promised to institute a new model of civilization by rapid and illegal means. Are the pretentions of the parties to initiate the transition to such a new society through legal reforms really plausible? The answer must remain in doubt for the present. One senses that this long-range goal is not a live issue for the leaders of the left, whatever their contribution to making their constituents aware of it. The Common Program and the electoral propaganda of the left may hint at some very radical changes, but it does not actually propagandize for action to initiate these changes now, nor does it succeed in summoning up a vision of a truly different model of civilization. Thus the left parties play some role in generalizing radical concerns, but it is a muted role.

The effective combination of the new and the old themes of struggle has not yet occurred. The resulting ambiguity of the movement is reflected in the title of the first chapter of the Common Program, "To Live Better, To Change Life." The first phrase, taken from the Communist Party Program of 1971, refers to all the traditional demands of the left for a better life for workers. But the second phrase has an entirely different history. *"Changer la vie"* was a slogan of the May Events derived ultimately from the French poet Rimbaud by way of surrealism. It signifies the desire to make of the Revolution a "joyous celebration" and through it to release the aspiration toward social creativity. It is good that the official left should attempt to coopt such a slogan, but it cannot really claim to be the prime mover in this area.

There is nothing to surprise us in this. Culturally as well as politically the French left runs behind its troops and not in front of them. The possibility of revolutionary political change depends ultimately on the ability of the French to make the kinds of cultural changes discussed above; socialism cannot do better than capitalism at providing the fruits of a capitalist culture.

POLITICAL CULTURE AND POLITICAL STRUCTURE
THE FUNCTION OF THE LEFT

AGAINST THE BACKGROUND of the May Events, the alliance of the French left appears profoundly inadequate. It is true that it has attempted in many ways to modernize its structures and programs, but it remains after all completely committed to an electoral path to socialism. Many French radical leftists are deeply hostile to the parties which participated in the restoration of order in '68; these leftists see little hope that once elected these same parties will play a revolutionary role. The radicals condemn the existing parliamentary institutions as essentially bourgeois, the inevitable antagonist of the self-managed regime they wish to create.

Yet the turn toward renewed electoral struggle is more than a revival of social democratic illusions about the neutrality of parliamentary institutions, but reflects a realistic evaluation of the May Events by the millions of workers who participated in them. After May, French workers knew that they were capable of closing down the country in a few days' time, but they had also discovered that this is insufficient to overthrow the capitalist system. Everything that has happened in France since 1968 lies under the shadow of this dilemma: the economy is already in principle hostage to the working class, but the state still lies beyond its reach as the dominant institution of the society. Discovering themselves blocked on one path—the path of revolution—the workers have proceeded to move along another one. The attack on capital simply changed in form, proceeding no longer by violence but by primarily electoral means. This explains why, for broad sectors of the population, the Common Program could become a powerful means for delegitimizing the established society, a catalogue of politically realizable aspirations and demands against which the achievements of conservative governments could be measured.

These considerations help to explain the great popularity of the alliance of the left with French voters, who do not simply support it because their leaders tell them to, but who are, rather, even more committed to it than these leaders. It is this popularity of the alliance that has obliged radical activists to come to terms with it despite their misgivings. In fact, as the official left has prospered over the last ten years, the alliance has become more and more the natural audience and sounding board for more radical groups, attempting to bring their movements and concerns to the attention of the general public. Thus over the years it has become nearly impossible to separate electoral from radical activist components of the French left, so complex are the alliances and complicities that have drawn them all into the orbit of the official electoral movements to one degree or another.

For these reasons most of the critics of the Union of the Left finally decided to support it with their votes. Sceptical, even cynical they may be, but it is apparent that the election of a left government is something the whole constituency of the left insists upon—not a mere tactic that could be dismissed as a mistake or a manipulation of a few political leaders. Many who were at first contemptuous of the parties and saw in them the main enemy in the wake of the May Events, now expect an electoral victory to improve the terms of the struggle for socialism. In this view, if a revolutionary mobilization is ever to occur again on the scale of the May Events, it will have to be *after* the election of a left government.

It is too early to tell whether this nuanced view will survive the recent debacle of the parties. It is only to the extent that these parties appear sincerely committed to taking power by electoral means that they can hold their troops in line; a loss of credibility by the official left might provide the terrain on which radical activists could develop more successful and independent movements. It is also possible that the aggressive right wing counter-offensive which began in the wake of the elections could provoke large-scale defensive movements by the mass base of the left, altering drastically the relations of force between these masses and their electoral representatives.

In any case, this complex dialectic of the French left is very different from the image of French politics that is widely held in the United States. A common viewpoint here seems to be that we are witnessing the culmination of a long process of social democratization in the French and

European Communist movement generally. Critics are no doubt correct in arguing that parties like the PCF do not follow a revolutionary line, but whether the impact of these parties will be "social democratic" in the critics' sense will depend less on their line than on the actions of the social forces they attempt to lead. These latter have evolved in remarkable ways in the last decade. This evolution can only be understood through an analysis of the changes in political culture and the new forms of class alliance emerging not only in France but throughout Southern Europe, the implications of these changes and alliances for future struggles, and the international balance of power conditioning these struggles.

Such an analysis reveals potentialities ignored by the critics, with their primary focus on doctrinal considerations and analogies with the past. It is, of course, impossible to say whether the actualization of this potential is imminent. Rather than attempt to make predictions, I will present the general outlines of a *structurally possible* alternative to those entertained in the debate over Eurocommunism up to this time. I want to make clear that in doing so I am not "endorsing" Eurocommunism, in the sense of sharing its illusions, not the least of which is the promise of a gradual and legal transition to socialism. I will not argue, for example, that the French left has a clear idea of how to initiate the transition to socialism, through electoral politics, nor that the abandonment of the concept of the dictatorship of the proletariat is theoretically defensible from a Marxist standpoint. But the decisions of the parties are not the only factors to be considered. The *function* they ultimately serve in the mass movement they represent may be very different from their own intentions and expectations. It is in this light that I will now evaluate some of the arguments for the social democratization thesis, and develop an alternative to it. Unless this alternative is considered, the French situation cannot be accurately evaluated.

THE QUESTION OF SOCIAL DEMOCRACY

PERHAPS THE MOST interesting socialist critique of Eurocommunism published in the United States is that of Carl Boggs.[6] His argument appears less dogmatic than that of other critics because he does not rely on doctrinal points, but on methodological assumptions about socio-economic development that are widely shared by American social scientists. These assumptions, I will argue, do prejudge the case against Eurocommunism, even if at first they appear to be quite neutral. The methodological approach to which I refer consists in regarding "Northern Europe," with its "integrated" working class, as the universal model of advanced capitalism while analyzing the "Southern European" left as a symptom of economic backwardness. The stage is then set for analogies with post World War I Germany, where a reformist left contributed to "modernization" instead of revolution. Presumably, contemporary class struggles in Southern Europe will most likely accomplish the same modernization that was earlier accomplished in the North. The imposition of this North/South schema, overlaid by the parallel modernized/backward schema, "contains" the Eurocommunist movement in a familiar and disappointing theoretical framework.

Like other theories of modernization, this one presupposes what it sets out to prove, namely that apparently different societies are converging around a single model that is normative for them all.[7] This is a a "functionalist" approach in the sense that it evaluates social forces and events in terms of their role in the development of an ideal-typical "integrated" social system. Such a functional model of development necessarily abstracts from the balance of force between classes in determining the ultimate significance of reforms in specific, real societies. Naturally, the bourgeoisie would like Communist participation in governance to be the first step toward a "Northern" solution to the social problem. This outcome is not, however, a foregone conclusion. A favorable constellation of class forces might lead from this first step to revolutionary results. In the final analysis, it will be class power that determines the place of reforms in the reproduction of society, and not the reforms themselves that will somehow automatically "co-opt" the working class and integrate the system. Functionalism overlooks the ambiguous role played by strategies of reform in the competition for class power, and so arrives conveniently at the very conclusion it presupposes.*

Although Boggs is primarily concerned with Italy, his use of the concept of modernization raises a serious problem to the extent that he by implicaton criticizes Eurocommunism as a whole. Not all of the countries of southern Europe are backward and in need of modernization. Doubtless like many other critics, Boggs writes primarily about Italy because he knows it best and because the Italian Communist Party has long taken positions only recently adopted by others. These are legitimate reasons for setting out from the Italian example. However, there is a risk in this approach. The critic may distort the entire presentation of the case against Eurocommunism by ascribing charac-teristics of one or several countries of that region to Southern Europe as a

---

*The fact that the ruling class succeeds in "integrating" reform does not show it to have failed, but rather defines what we mean by calling something a "reform" instead of a revolutionary break. The class that rules ultimately determines the place of any reform in the reproduction of the system. Reforms cannot, therefore, be analyzed in terms of their more or less "revolutionary" character, but must be considered in relation to their effect on class power.

whole. But where the relations of international and class force are very different, as in France, apparently similar policies may have quite different meanings.

FRANCE IS NOT a backward country by any reasonable standard. Italy is much poorer and more deeply dependent than France. It is more politically backward, with a powerful Christian party and significant fascist movements. France is far wealthier, has far greater international power and prestige, and an as yet untested potential for translating these advantages into means of economic survival on the world market, where Italy is relatively helpless. Hence the French left has a much better chance of overcoming the obstacles of domestic reaction and international financial pressures than has the Italian left.

These considerations help to explain why, in spite of many common Eurocommunist positions, the Italian and French Parties have adopted very different strategies of class alliance—the former pursuing a "historic compromise" with sectors of the bourgeoisie, the latter building a class front of wage earners. The policies of the PCI are compatible in principle with capitalist strategies of modernization in the present constellation of forces, and so can be proposed as reforms that under certain constraints bourgeois parties could accept.   French Eurocommunism, however, has emerged within an already modernized capitalist system. There the presence of a strong left cannot be regarded as an expression of economic backwardness, and it can play no further role within capitalist strategies of development. The Common Program is thus supported mainly by wage earners, and its measures are not necessarily compatible with the survival of anything resembling a healthy capitalist system. (The French left cannot play the store-minding role of the British Labour Party—an alternative "functional" role to the "modernizing" one—given the lack in France of a consensus supportive of private property.)

In sum, the French left has the potential to threaten capitalist control of the sources of reproduction of the society; the Italian left is not yet in such a strategically strong position, but must work to achieve it. To go beyond the sort of reforms that would contribute to this goal, the Italians will probably need foreign support. Could such support come from France? Conceivably, the Italian left could go rapidly beyond a "modernizing" strategy with French support, and it may be that the PCI is quite consciously preparing for this eventuality. In any case, the French left stands a chance of carrying through a strategy of rupture with capitalist development, which places it in a unique position within Southern Europe. The French case will thus require an independent analysis. What is more, such an analysis will affect our evaluation of socialist prospects in other countries of Southern Europe, insofar as the French left may alter the relations of force conditioning struggles throughout the region.

IF WE REJECT a functionalist approach to Eurocommunism, based on developmental classifications, how shall we explain what is happening in Southern Europe? I would argue that what we are witnessing is less the social democratization of the Southern European left than the crisis of the bourgeois order in that region. It is the political system of several Southern European countries that is most directly affected. This system is shaped by the failure of the bourgeoisie to win cultural hegemony over the working class—the normal precondition for admitting workers' parties to a consensual competition for political power, as in Britain and West Germany. The outcome is the exclusion of workers from political participation in governance by shifting alliances of parties representing small and large property owners. Under such conditions workers have been able to perpetuate autonomous organizations and ideology from the period of competitive capitalism down to the present, even under fascist attack in some countries. But this system has entered into crisis today due to changes in the class composition of advanced capitalism that will be discussed below.

A new international setting intensifies this crisis dramatically in the more democratic countries of Southern Europe. The postwar "Atlantic" system in France and Italy has been based on the ability of pro-American bourgeoisies to produce electoral majorities behind American policy. The building of such majorities rested in turn on the sharp wedge driven through the heart of the left by the cold war. So long as no stable alliance of Socialists and Communists was possible, both bourgeois power and American influence was assured. But the policy of *detente* and the ending of the cold war have removed the principal ideological bulwark against a natural regrouping of the left around class positions. In countries with a strong Communist party, the result has been the typical Eurocommunist move toward broad electoral alliances in an attempt to bring Communist representatives into the government. In France and Italy this strategy threatens the "Atlantic" system already; in Spain and Portugal it may do so in a few years' time.

At present we do not have an adequate theory of this Southern political system, and this is one of the reasons for the great confusion over the significance of its crisis. The Southern system is typically viewed as a product of backwardness. In fact it cuts across such developmental classifications: in France it is not symptomatic of backwardness, but of a special kind of modernity, different from that of Northern "models" like

Great Britain. Of course normative theories of development may dismiss the French case as an anomaly, due to vestigial survivals of an earlier era. Such an ad hoc explanation protects the status of West Germany or Great Britain as universal models of advanced capitalist society in the face of an obvious counter-instance.

It is not at all clear why socialists should wish to adopt this approach. After all, Marxism concerns the possibility and consequences of modernity without "integration," and such a signal example as France ought to be taken quite seriously for its implications for Marxist method. What needs to be explained is how, in France, the Southern political system has been successfully reproduced at higher and higher stages of economic and social development, even after the decline of a number of the most important factors usually associated with it, such as a very large peasantry and a politically active and influential Catholic Church. An understanding of the social mechanisms through which the French left has reproduced itself would also contribute to evaluating the prospects of strategies such as the historic compromise, which have similar intentions.

I would like to suggest an analytic hypothesis that may help to explain the remarkable persistence of the Southern political system, in the face of all the claims and predictions of modernization theory. An adequate theory of capitalist democracy must be able to describe both the Northern and Southern types in systemic terms, independently of developmental considerations. We now need a polycentric theory of capitalist development in which there is no single pole or model, just as we have long ago accepted polycentrism in our discussions of socialist development.

Northern political systems have a familiar binary structure, based on alternation in power of two competing parties or alliances of parties, one of which has the primary loyalty of workers and the other of the middle classes and the bourgeoisie. Alternation in power is possible without threat to the regime because the bourgeoisie tolerates independent political expression by workers, and workers' parties do not attempt to destroy the social and economic bases of the capitalist system when in power. These are the conditions of what is customarily called "consensual pluralism." It is widely assumed that consensual pluralism is the normal outcome of economic advancement, due to the growing prosperity of workers and their consequent loss of revolutionary fervor.

The Southern system of such countries as France and Italy has a ternary structure in which a multiplicity of parties ultimately fall into three categories—right, left and center. Here the conditions of consensual pluralism are lacking because the working-class parties, while allowed to participate in parliament, do not accept the foundations of the property system and so are not normally admitted to alternation in executive power. The country is ruled by shifting alliances of center and right parties, representing the middle classes and the bourgeoisie, respectively (often with some significant working-class support, especially where the influence of the Church is strong).

In spite of the political exclusion of workers in the Southern system, the governing parties are occasionally responsive to parliamentary pressures and frequently to extra-parliamentary mobilization by workers. In responding, those in power arrive at legislative solutions to social problems similar to those developed by Northern systems. Thus workers obtain such benefits as the right to unionize, social security, and so on, even though workers' parties may never participate in power, or may do so only very briefly in periods of unusual social crisis.

It is a commonplace now to argue that in contemporary capitalism state intervention in the resolution of social and economic problems legitimizes the established order precisely by managing its contradictions. In the Northern system social reforms do clearly legitimize the capitalist system and its political institutions, reducing working class antagonism to the property system. However, in the Southern system of France, similar reforms have not produced the same integrative consequences. It is precisely the failure of cooptative strategies in the Southern system which raises serious questions about any normative model of development.

I would suggest that in Southern systems state-sponsored reforms and concessions to workers fail to legitimize the established order because workers' believe them to be the product of militant mobilization. Working-class political culture includes the notion that state action on behalf of workers is due exclusively to the relations of force between classes, and not to any intrinsic virtue of the system. The claims to legitimacy the ruling groups would like to make on the basis of their reformist efforts are simply dismissed by the intended audience. As a result the state may fail to acquire any credit for its cooptative policies, and the Southern system reproduces itself *politically* even though the *social* integration of workers proceeds apace. From the standpoint of this analytic framework, Eurocommunism can be understood in part as an attempt to move from a typical ternary structure toward a new type of binary structure, without surrender to the claims of legitimacy of the state and the capitalist system. In France this "bipolarization" dissolves the old right, left and center into two competing blocs.

ANY THEORY which takes Northern models as normative will see in this shift further proof that the path of modernization leads inevitably to a system like the British one, with a fully integrated labor party competing for power with a conservative bourgeois party within the framework of "consensual pluralism." But this hypothesis is not confirmed by actual contact with the facts of French political life. It is not conservative changes in workers' attitudes, but the radicalization of large portions of the middle strata that makes possible the bipolarization of French politics today. There is no evidence of the emergence of a new conservative social consensus concerning the property system, but there is an observable breakdown of capitalist hegemony in the middle strata, which will be discussed more fully below. The consequent leftward drift of important center parties, such as the Socialist Party, has made it possible for workers to pursue socialist goals through the established political system to an unprecedented and as yet uncertain degree.

In spite of the binary shift in the French political system, this latter does not appear to be converging with the "consensual pluralist" model. Instead, the French left may attempt to form a government without first conceding the legitimacy of the fundamental property relations on which the political structure is ultimately based. A welfare statist compromise between workers' parties exercising political power and capitalists still in comfortable control of the economy is by no means assured. The question of whether some original accommodation between workers and the capitalist system will be found, or whether there will be a head-on confrontation between the two, cannot yet be answered. What remains for us is to try to better understand the conditions under which the traditional French political system is collapsing, so that the structural potentialities inscribed in the present crisis can be specified. To this end I will focus now on some of the changes in the attitudes of the middle strata on which, as I have indicated the present movement depends.

THE MIDDLE STRATA

PERHAPS THE SINGLE most surprising thing about the May Events was the emergence of militant revolutionary opposition to capitalism at relatively privileged levels of the labor force, among the employed middle strata. The Events demonstrated the political volatility of the middle strata and revealed the issues and appeals that could provide a basis for an alliance between these groups and workers. It is no doubt true, as sceptics remark, that the middle strata as a whole are still to the right of the workers in France, that they are deeply divided politically, and that in the upper levels of the technocracy there are many who support the left out of fear or ambition. But major social movements among these strata since 1968 indicate that they have a revolutionary potential the limits of which have not yet been tested. Already it is clear that the old pessimistic analyses of white collar labor (for example, by C. Wright Mills) are outdated. The middle strata as a whole are no longer committed to a "politics of the rearguard," nor have technocratic ambitions completely replaced their traditional conservatism. Most basically, the modern middle strata are not afraid of losing a capital they do not in any case possess, and so in the context of the Southern political system large sectors of them can enter into a principled alliance with workers for socialism.

The May Events provide the most convincing empirical evidence for this assertion. During May many teachers, scientists, journalists, and other cultural workers openly and enthusiastically supported the most radical goals of the movement: the overthrow of the state and the institution of a council communist regime. Powerful strike movements also hit the government bureaucracies during May, and there were even some business executives, medical personnel and other traditionally quite conservative professionals who supported this movement. In France the revolutionary potential of these strata was revealed for the first time as the students found their own revolt embedded in the much broader movements of those occupational groups most dependent upon university degrees.

The May Events produced a flowering of theories to explain this phenomenon, from "new working class" interpretations to a vigorous reassertion of the traditional Communist view that assigned these groups to the petty bourgeoisie. (This is not the place to review such discussions. Terminologically, I prefer to evade the issue by referring to the groups in question by the neutral term used in French sociology, "the employed middle strata.") The perspective on their role in the May Events proposed here does not resolve the theoretical problem, but it can teach us how the middle strata understood themselves and acted in support of a developing revolutionary movement. This is precious information for evaluating their political potentialities, along with the potential of a Euro-communism based on an alliance of workers with these strata.

There is one basic theoretical conclusion that can be drawn from the study of the middle strata in the May Events that I want to emphasize here. Most theories of the middle strata attempt to deduce their political potentialities from their function in the capitalist system, defining them as more or less conservative petty bourgeois where this function is seen as primarily repressive, or, on the contrary, as more or less revolutionary where their function is seen as little different from that of other workers. This methodological approach is refuted by the May Events, during which the middle strata themselves called into question their function and suggested ways of transforming it. Thus, far from being restricted to political roles growing out of their function in capitalist society, the middle strata proved to be the most articulate critics of their functional insertion into that society. This is not to say that the French middle strata felt useless or guilty about their privileges, but rather that they felt *misused* by those in command of the society. Their radical stand is best understood as an appeal to the working class and to the general population to reorganize and redirect their work into more humane and productive channels. Some examples may make this clear.

1. *Education*. During the May Events high schools and universities in solidarity with the movement declared their "autonomy" from the government. As one leaflet explained it, "The autonomy of public education is a political act of seccession from a government which has definitively failed in its task of defending the real interests of the community in the educational sphere."[8] But how was "autonomy" to be understood? Did the university in revolt hope to isolate itself from society? In fact, the students concretized their demand for "autonomy" with proposals for "permanent education for all" and invitations to workers to help plan the reform of the university. Autonomy was thus not an end in itself: it was precisely *through* autonomy that the university was to reverse its class allegiance. Such formulations imply that the relation of the university community to the working class is asymmetrical. While the automobile industry would certainly have to be restructured as part of a socialist revolution, teachers and students could claim no special right to participate in this process on the grounds that they had been unjustly excluded and deprived of its products in the past. They might be consulted as citizens or as experts, but not as a social category with a special interest in the change.

2. *Communications*. The communications industry was also thrown into turmoil during May. The nationalized sector was struck by employees demanding "a radio and television in the service of all and not of a party."[9] This was the counterpart of student-faculty demands for a democratization of education. And like the students, the workers in radio-television saw increased autonomy as the means of better serving the people, as well as of their own liberation from the stifling supervision of the Gaullist state. In the context of the May Events, the "objectivity" demanded by the strikers had a fairly clear class significance: it meant mirroring back to the revolution its own activities and thereby contributing to its unfolding.

3. *Civil Service*. Many government ministries were closed during May by employees who were on strike in solidarity with the movement. The pattern of protest was similar in every case: a combination of demands for more democratic working conditions internally, and an end to policies judged by the civil servants to be opposed to the interests of the people. The events at the government ministries showed the power of

attraction of the movement even in relatively elevated strata of the state apparatus. There the civil servants simply re-enacted the model of the student movement, complete with occupations, general assemblies and reform commissions. As one participant in the strike noted, "there was a very great solidarity vis-a-vis the students, and through this solidarity. ...there began to be still diffuse but real feelings of solidarity toward the striking workers. 'Those people,' it was said, 'Those people are like us.'"[10] In cases like these the very language of the professional ideology of "public service" glides imperceptibly into the Maoist rhetoric of "service to the people." Civil servants, like students and communications workers, attempted to include the previously excluded, and to reverse their allegiances from the state to the "people."

4. *Business Executives.* As far as can be determined, most business executives were hostile to the movement, although a significant minority expressed their solidarity with it. As one commentator noted:

> In the Loire-Atlantique the *cadres* were in solidarity with the workers in impressive numbers, something which had never before been seen. But support for wage demands was not the essential: it was the theme of management methods which cemented the union. The *cadres* are frustrated by the excessive centralization of public enterprises: they remain in their offices signing papers, but they have no power of decisions.[11]

On May 20th 1500 *cadres* met at the Sorbonne and declared their sympathy with the movement. Several hundred seized the Paris head-quarters of the conservative union of executives and engineers, issuing a call for a general strike of executives. In a leaflet issued on May 24th, they demanded "The elaboration of concrete solutions for the democratization of management and of the general economic decision-making process. The goal of fulfillment of the personality, in work as well as in leisure, must be substituted for the usual goals of profitability and expansion."[12]

5. *Technical Experts.* A case study made during the Events of a strike in a government supported think-tank illustrates our theme especially well. The researchers earned good livings making surveys and studies for government ministries, usually concerning public works projects. Yet they suffered, even before May, from a distinct malaise. They were aware that for the most part their work, once it became the "property" of the purchasing ministry, served to justify pre-established policies or was ignored where it conflicted with them. Often the researchers felt these policies were not in the best interests of the populations they had been called on to study and analyze. The problem is not confined to France. Henry Kissinger once said, "Intellectuals are

called in not because any one cares about their opinion but because they are judged useful in defending policy elsewhere."[13] This is an alienating situation and during May, as the authors' of the case study note, "It suddenly seemed intolerable that the researcher have in the final analysis no control over the product of his work."[14] Yet this control was not claimed for the sake of personal satisfaction. No sooner had the researchers gone on strike than they attempted to link up with the people whose interests they wished to serve. Their union declared: "The workers of the National Union of Social Sciences affirm their will to see their work placed in the service of the workers and not in the service of management and the capitalist state apparatus."[15] Concretely, they provided financial assistance to poorer strikers and, most significantly, agreed to make a free study of employment in the Paris suburbs at the request of the local unions with which they had contact.

How can such movements be explained? It is not enough to point to such motivations as the proletarianization of the middle strata, although in the absence of discontent they would obviously remain politically passive. What is needed is a theory of the structural position of these groups, enabling us to understand the forces that influence their political reactions and their search for solutions to social problems. What such a theory must explain is how the self-perception and behavior of these strata is rooted in the class struggle of workers and capitalists, not only in their occupational roles.

A NEW ALLIANCE STRATEGY

MUCH RECENT DISCUSSION of the structural position of the middle strata is shaped by reified Weberian theory, which sees bureaucracy as an integrated functional element of industrial society. In terms of such a model, what happened in May is simply inexplicable, except perhaps through dubious psychological speculations. In fact, the Weberian model is relevant only to societies where class differences are so immense that the middle strata can feel no solidarity with workers, or where class divisions are so muted that the issue of allegiances simply never arises. In a sharply class-divided advanced capitalist society such as France, the political behavior of the middle strata cannot be deduced from their functional role in capitalism, but must be studied in its relation to class struggle.

IN FRANCE, the middle strata are evidently capable of becoming conscious of what Erik Wright has called their "contradictory location" in the social relations of production[16] Instead of regarding themselves as an autonomous "middle class," as in the United States, these groups become aware of their radical dependency within the class structure. The middle strata are, in fact, composed of individuals who have been hired, after meeting requirements such as educational credentials, for the purpose of serving certain social needs, as defined by laws and administrative regulations. Unlike other classes in capitalist society, which arise from an "organic" economic process, the middle strata acquire their class identity through a process of selection. This curious social position becomes problematic to the middle strata themselves insofar as the legitimacy of their selection and orientation is questioned in the course of class struggle.

The customary way members of the middle strata define their own position in the class structure is through the notion of professionalism. In professionalist ideology the middle strata are the "agents" or "representatives" of "client" individuals and groups in whose interests they act, and for whom they perform services. The belief that their work is not just an ordinary element in the social division of labor is reinforced by the fact that in providing these services, professionals often exercise considerable control over their clients. Interaction with the "consumer" of services is thus not a simple market relation, but has a semi-political character.

In advanced capitalist societies, this political aspect of professional activity serves the specific reproductive needs of the system. Those at the top of the bureaucracies ensure that "service" to the people is also service to capitalism and its elites. To this extent the "representative" status felt by members of the middle strata is a real and contradictory one, not just a product of professionalist ideology. It signifies the mediating role of the middle strata in serving the needs of the community within the limits of the capitalist system.

Where class struggle is weak or ideologically inarticulate, a technocratic self-conception arises from the misperception of this contradiction. But in the May Events mass strikes by workers appear to have made many members of the middle strata aware of this contradiction and forced them to take sides in a struggle between its aspects. When the "clients," rose in the streets, the legitimacy of capital and the state to represent the public interest was visibly challenged; the repressive aspects of their work, as it was organized and shaped by elite purposes, became clear to many in the light of resistance from below. The working class then appeared as an ally through which the middle strata could be reconstituted and their "selection" reconfirmed under a different class hegemony and for different social purposes. The "people" or the working class appeared to be a substitute source of legitimacy once the capitalist organization of social life had been rejected.

This formulation reflects the experience of the May Events and helps to explain the subsequent rise of the electoral alliance of the Communist Party, primarily representing workers, and the Socialist Party which today represents a large fraction of the the middle strata. While there are still theoretical debates about the nature of the middle strata, they are generally evaluated more positively by French social theory today than they were previous to this historical experience. In 1971, when the PCF revised its attitude toward the middle strata, its theoreticians emphasized their political potentialities to an unprecedented degree.

> Only a part of them can be placed in the working class; in their totality, they cannot be purely and simply assimilated to the unsalaried middle strata [the petty bourgeoisie]. It is certainly a matter of diversified social strata, but the workers who make them up are united by a common trait of decisive importance. Even if their activity is not directly productive, these are all salaried workers, exploited individually and collectively...
>
> Before these transformations emerged, the support for working class struggles by the middle strata and especially by intellectuals appeared as a rallying to the proletarian cause. Today there is no longer any question of individuals rallying to the cause, but of an entente to be established between social strata having common interests and which can build a democratic future together.[17]

It is equally significant that Poulantzas' more hostile analysis of the middle strata comes to a similar conclusion. In his *Classes in Contemporary Capitalism*, Poulantzas suggests the decline of the traditional strategy of the worker-peasant alliance, and its replacement by an alliance of workers and what he calls the "new petite bourgeoisie" (the middle strata). Poulantzas argues that this shift in alliance strategy "provides the new historic possibility for the socialist revolution in France."[18]

SOCIALISM IN FRANCE?

A NEW MODEL OF TRANSITION

IN THE REMARKS that follow I would like to develop this approach in relation to the French situation *not* as a prediction of the consequences of an electoral victory of the left, but rather to enlarge the range of possibilities to be considered in evaluating the prospects of Eurocommunism. This will involve sketching a revolutionary process in many ways unlike those for which we have successful precedents in countries like Russia and China. However, the model of transition discussed below is not without a basis in past revolutionary experience, especially that of the May Events. Furthermore, it reflects the significant changes in the Marxist understanding of the middle strata, inspired no doubt by their recent and unprecedented participation in progressive struggles. It is this foundation that justifies the attempt to project actual tendencies (which may or may not be realized, depending on circumstances).

I intend now to consider the case in which the political and cultural divisions of the left were at least partially overcome and a left government formed on that basis. I think we can safely assume that at the outset such a government would attempt to limit its own impact on the economic "health" of the nation, perhaps seeking (and obtaining) large loans from international financial institutions to shore up the economy. Conceivably, the entire enterprise could be contained within this framework for several years. However, if and when the French left encountered economic blockade, the panic flight of capital and widespread attempts to disrupt the economy, matters would probably take a very different course.

Under these circumstances, French workers would probably respond to the economic crisis to some extent independently of governmental initiatives. During the May Events the "active strike" was supposed to have this character: workers would occupy the factory and continue to function on their own, arranging distribution and exchange of raw materials and food directly with other workers. Such strikes occurred in some sectors in 1968 and occasionally thereafter, and constitute part of French political culture.

THIS TACTIC WOULD no doubt be revived and applied throughout the country as a riposte to a frontal assault on the government by capital. As businesses closed their doors, workers would seize and occupy them, prevent their owners from removing tools, equipment, documents and materials, and appeal to the government for immediate nationalization.* The workers would no doubt also request the help of already nationalized enterprises which, under the system of democratic manage-

---

*This possibility is apparently anticipated in a passage of the Common Program which suggests what I have called a "flight-forward" strategy of socialization. The Program declares, "The progress of nationalizations will be linked to economic development and the demands of the masses who must assume the broadest responsibilities. This is why when the workers express the will to see their enterprise enter the public or nationalized sector, the government can propse this to the "Parliament." (pp. 114-115)

ment proposed in the Common Program, might very well have the administrative independence and the will to offer it, whatever the fears or hesitations of the government. For example, the railroads—run by a board of directors dominated by workers—might decide to provide free services to industries sabotaged by their owners, as an act of revolutionary solidarity. Such things occurred on the initiative of railroad workers during the May Events. If such a strategy were widely adopted by the workers themselves, it is difficult to see how the government could avoid being swept up in the wave, offering whatever help it could.

However, as workers seized power in their companies, they would quickly discover both the impossibility of overcoming the economic crisis on the basis of the old methods of management, and also the limits of their own capacity to innovate new ones. Typically, they would identify the need for more direct and voluntaristic approaches, yet at certain points their dependence on a specialized administrative personnel is inscribed in the very division of labor. The workers would appeal for help to the middle strata and would doubtless receive it to some degree, at which point the struggle would take on a different character. The middle strata would become pivotal in the contest between capital and labor, the former urging them to go on strike, the latter attempting to involve them in a socialist experiment. The willingness and availability of large numbers of technical and adminstrative personnel for this experiment might well be decisive for its victory. The massive defection of the middle strata in such a crisis would, on the contrary, produce a generalized climate of political reaction and contribute to a total economic collapse which might be the prelude to an electoral defeat or a military coup.

It is in the context of such an advanced socio-economic alliance of workers and the middle strata that their electoral alliance might take on a revolutionary significance. While electoral outcomes alone do not make the government omnipotent, in the context of a crisis such as that described above it would have the power to make enormous and progressive changes in the personnel, organization and orientation of the administrative superstructures of the society. The bureaucracies are composed of a personnel with an ambiguous class position; the willingness of this personnel to support radical change stems from the resolution of this ambiguity in favor of socialism through immensely complex ideological and political struggles. The initiatives of the government will obviously play an important and perhaps decisive role in these struggles. A left government could encourage active solidarity between the administration and workers, protect members of the middle strata from both ultra-left and rightist attack, and intervene in the internal power struggles within the bureaucracies in support of a fundamental shift in their class orientation. These efforts would sharpen the split in the middle strata in ways that would retain the support of its majority and ensure this majority a revolutionary leadership. Without such support from above, it is difficult to imagine the rapid success of such a massive reorientation.

While the formal authority of the government could play a decisive role in resolving ambiguities in the bureaucracy, its influence on the army is more questionable. The mere fact that the government leadership supports a policy may influence administrative personnel unsure of their class loyalties, but the same may not be true for military officers whose loyalties are assured by a much more ideologically rigorous training and selection. Thus I think the critics of Eurocommunism are correct to emphasize its lack of a military strategy, and to point out that in this domain elections are a secondary factor. At the same time, military aspects of revolutionary struggle are ultimately determined by political relations between classes and not the contrary. No revolutionary movement, even a guerrilla movement with its own troops, can hope to defeat a united army with good morale. But unity and morale in the army are based on the class relations in which officers and soldiers are involved as members of society at large. Armed struggle is thus not an alternative to political and cultural struggle, but rather a domain in which the results of shifting class relations are worked out to their logical conclusion. This may involve twenty years of bloodshed where the adversaries are confident, vigorous, and well-armed. But in other cases, it may be a matter of a few riots, a show of disobedience by the troops, and faltering support from foreign allies.

The conditions for a left success in the military domain must be secured in the economy, essentially in the stability of the alliance between workers and the middle strata in the maintenance of economic activity. Only on this basis can the left hope to keep the nation at work, and insure a climate in which fascist opinion and movements would remain relatively weak and isolated. Success in the economic domain would greatly intensify the traditional divisions within the French army, polarizing it in ways favorable to the left. During the May Events draftees were consigned to quarters in some areas, so suspect were their loyalties in the eyes of the conservative state that armed them.* Since 1968 the morale and loyalty of these soldiers has if anything deteriorated. While the small French professional military would be a powerful, perhaps overwhelming adversary if it retained its unity, it might be paralysed by divisions if the left were generally successful and exercised a strong ideological influence on ordinary soldiers from an early point.

---

*In the city of Nantes, workers actually seized power for a little over a week during the May Events. Tannick Guin writes: "Abandoned by its professional

It is possible to construct a model of a new kind of revolutionary process that would initiate a transition to socialism on the basis of a combination of electoral and mass action.* While I have assumed that mass action would play a leading role, the government, in constantly renegotiating the relation of the working class to the middle strata, would also play an essential part. This model raises some crucial questions concerning the traditional Marxist theory of revolution.

THE EVALUATION OF Eurocommunism within the theoretical framework of Marxism requires some major innovations. The practitioners of Eurocommunism themselves offer us policy statements primarily intended to win votes, and these are more striking for their disingenuousness and pragmatism than for their theoretical originality. The models of revolutionary class struggle worked out in the Leninist tradition to explain events in poor countries with peasant majorities have no direct application to advanced capitalist ones. Similarly, the theories of counter-revolution and social integration in advanced capitalism developed by the Frankfurt School do not account for what is occurring

politicians, could the lawful authorities hope for help from the army? In this domain the Prefect had also to give up. The troops stationed in the Nantes barricks...turned out ill-inclined to obey the orders of the government and to enter on the path of repression. In effect the draftees were largely recruited in the Western region....These young people were thus perfectly aware of the workers' problems and their appearance in the streets would have ended in nothing but a disastrous fraternization. The Prefect therefore limited himself to having the rails watched and the ORTF transmitter guarded by career soldiers who never approached the town." *La Commune de Nantes* (Paris, Maspero, 1969, pp. 101-102.)

*What role might radical left forces play in these events? This is very difficult to say. The radical left in France has been in steady decline since shortly after its apotheosis in the May Events. The phases of this decline are instructive. First, the spontaneously formed action committees that emerged during the May Events distintegrated the next year under the impact of political disagreements among their sectarian components. Ultra-left Maoist sects became famous but soon declined in the face of severe repression and their own failure to spark a replay of the May Events. The radical survivors of this initial shakedown were the transformed PSU, which traded its rather intellectualist pre-1968 image for a militant one, various Trotskyist groups, and many single issue or local groups the most visible of which are the ecology and feminist movements. Many radical leftists are also active in the CFDT union. It is certain that these surviving links with the non-party left of May '68 will be found in the midst of any future mass mobilization.

in countries where capitalism is threatened by a combination of traditional class forces and an original type of social crisis. In sum, we need new models of revolution that have yet to be elaborated.

The approach to this task taken here has been based on several hypotheses. The first is that the model of a totally polarized capitalism in which an immense majority of proletarians overthrow a system sustained by a tiny minority of capitalists is *in principle* without strategic application. Lengthy historical experience shows that no matter how large the proletariat, its strength is always greatly diminished by ideological divisions that persist through the period of the revolution; moreover, capitalist strategies of development invariably maintain a small independent middle class while inflating the employed middle strata.

Given the impossibility of homogeneous class polarization, class alliances are not accidental or contingent components of the struggle, but are structurally essential aspects of it. Class alliances thus cannot be conceived as mere auxiliary support for an independent proletarian strategy that might be modified slightly to offer "concessions" to these supporters. Rather, working class struggle itself is first and foremost the struggle for the constitution of a bloc of social forces capable of overthrowing the established system. Furthermore, the correct structure of alliances in each instance is dictated by the level and type of development of the society, and is not a matter of political choice or opportunity.

The conclusion I draw from these premises is that alliance structure determines strategy rather than vice-versa. The working class does not choose allies as a function of certain strategic objectives, but rather, having realized the possible and necessary alliances through which it can advance its cause, it then finds before it a limited range of strategic choices. What is more, the significance of these strategic choices must be evaluated in terms of their functions within the configuration of class forces opposing the capitalist sytem. The same strategic choice—for example, formation of a left government—may therefore have a radically altered significance at different stages of development. Such a question cannot be settled once and for all by reference to the debates over "revisionism" at the beginning of this century. In fact, given the new class alliance in advanced capitalism, the formation of a left government in France might well have a progressive function.

RECONSTITUTION FROM WITHIN

IS THIS A "SOCIAL DEMOCRATIC" position? The Second International often viewed the state apparatus as a neutral instrument of the government; it was argued that the proletariat could change the class nature of the entire state by changing the class character of its elected leadership. Soon thereafter Lenin argued in theory and demonstrated in practice that the state is not neutral, but is rather the enemy which must be overthrown and "smashed." These two contrary positions have historically shared the field in socialist debates, and indeed they continue to dominate assessments of Eurocommunism. However, on the basis of the French experience since 1968, it is possible to sketch out a position somewhat different from both traditional social democratic reformism and Leninist insurrectionism. According to this position, the state—at least in Southern political systems—is neither neutral nor hostile, but a contradictory terrain of struggle on which the left can advance its own positions in conflict with conservative forces.[19] From this standpoint the election of a left government is seen as a precondition for winning struggles within the state apparatus that might be initiated by major mass movements in society at large.

The contrast between this position and the classical social democratic one should be clear. However, its relation to Lenin's position is much more complex. It is true that for Lenin the state is an "enemy" to be destroyed, not a position to be captured; but the modalities of this destruction are differentiated according to the class character of different state institutions, and according to the very different problems raised by the twofold (military and economic) nature of the revolution.

Revolutionary movements take power at two distinct levels. First, a military showdown must be prepared and carried through, establishing a new balance of force in the society favorable to revolutionary change. This military aspect of the struggle is not, of course, the revolution itself, but only the moment of struggle in which the bourgeoisie loses the capacity to resolve the revolutionary crisis by authoritarian means. The revolution proper must proceed primarily at the second level—that of the economy. There, in the sphere of production, power must be shifted downward from the bourgeoisie and its managerial representatives to the organized working class, usually through direct action legalized *a pos teriori*. This economic takeover can be considered a success when: 1) economic production has been restored under workers' control; 2) the working class has gained the cooperation of sufficient managerial and technical personnel to operate the economy, and; 3) the subordination of these personnel to the goals of the revolutionary movement has been institutionalized in the framework of a reconstituted state apparatus. The military and economic victory of the revolution constitutes the "smashing" of the state and the "expropriation of the expropriators" that Marx regarded as defining characteristics of socialist revolution.

For Lenin, the position which holds that the state is a terrain of struggle accurately describes the military aspect of revolution. Lenin regarded the military not as uniformly bourgeois, but as a contradictory, class-divided institution that might be split by a subversive appeal in the context of militant social struggles. His military strategy therefore involved not only arming the workers, but still more importantly splitting the army along class lines.

IF LENIN NEVERTHELESS regarded the state as adversary, this was because at all its commanding heights and throughout its bureaucratic superstructure he expected and encountered implacable hostility. No movements of lower-level bureaucrats for socialism paralleled the remarkable struggles of ordinary soldiers; the entire administrative corps of Russian society was opposed to the revolution, and this had telling effects on the economic phase of the struggle not just during the civil war, but for at least a generation. The solution, then, did not involve ideological appeals to discontented bureaucrats, but the reconstitution of something resembling the old administrative superstructure with a hostile personnel, won over by bribery and fear, and subject to constant political and police supervision.

This difference between the military and economic levels of the struggle in Russia was foreseeable on the basis of the different class origins of the army and the bureaucracy. The Russian Revolution was based on an alliance of workers and peasants, who made up the bulk of the soldiery, while Russian administrators were, by their class status and consciousness, firmly allied to the bourgeoisie. It is precisely this constellation of class alliances which differs in contemporary France, indicating the need for a new look at the question of the state in that instance.

The French left is not based on a worker-peasant alliance, but on an alliance of workers and the middle strata, the very groups that populated the administrative superstructures of French society. The actual experience of the May Events indicates that this alliance structure sharply divides the bureaucracies; in a revolutionary crisis they would be a terrain of contradictory class initiatives, much like the military. But if the divisions sharpened by the revolution cut across the bureaucracies instead of dividing them from the people, then the "smashing" of the state called for in the Marxist classics could take a novel form: not the shattering of the old administrations from without, but rather their reconstitution *from within*, on the initiative of the middle strata themselves in the context of a mass movement of workers. The result would be a new type of socialist revolution.

Notes

1. This discussion of the May Events is condensed from Andrew Feenberg and James Freedman, *The Changing Image of Socialism: The May Events of 1968*, (Boston: South End Press, forthcoming).

2. For a more detailed analysis of the Common Program, see Andrew Feenberg, "Socialism in France? The Common Program and the Future of the French Left," *Socialist Revolution*, no. 19.

3. "Quel est le Sens des Elections Qui Nous Sont Imposé," published in early June by the Comité d'Action du Laboratoire de Sociologie Industrielle. This and other documents of the May Events cited below are available on microfilm at the library of San Diego State University.

4. Rosa Luxemburg, "The Mass Strike, the Political Party and the Trade Unions," in *Rosa Luxemburg Speaks*, edited by Mary Alice Waters (New York: Pathfinder, 1970), p. 185.

5. See the *Programme Commun de Gouvernement du Parti Communiste et du Parti Socialiste,* introduction by Georges Marchais (Paris: Editions Sociales, 1972).

6. Carl Boggs, "Italian Communism in the Seventies," *Socialist Revolution*, no. 34. Cf. also, "The New Reformism," *Monthly Review*, June 1976.

7. For a more complete presentation of my position on modernization theory, see Andrew Feenberg, "Transition or Convergence: Communism and the Paradox of Development," in Frederick J. Fleron, ed. *Technology and Communist Culture* (New York: Praeger, 1977).

8. *Le Mouvement,* no. 3, Censier, June 3, 1968.

9. For more on the strike of the ORTF, see *Teleciné,* no. 143, July 1968.

10. "Greve Sur Place au Ministere de l'Equipement (20 Mai-8 Juin)," *Cahiers de Mai,* no. 2, July 1968.

11. "Toute une Ville Decouvre le Pouvoir Populaire," *Cahiers de Mai,* no. 1, May 15, 1968, p. 6.

12. "Manifesto," a leaflet which exists in several versions with different authors is apparently due to the Comité de Coordination des Cadres Contestataires.

13. Quoted by Samuel Sharp in "Unity or Struggle of Opposites, *Newsletter on Comparative Studies of Communism.* Vol. VI, no. 2, Feb. 1973, p. 12.

14. "Les Bureaux de Recherches," *Action,* June 24, 1968.

15. Ibid.

16. Erik O. Wright, "Intellectuals and the Class Structure of Capitalist Society," in *Between Labor and Capital* (Boston: South End Press, 1979).

17. *Le Capitalisme Monopoliste d'Etat* (Paris: Editions Sociales, 1971) vol. 1, pp. 239-40.

18. Nicos Poulantzas, *Classes in Contemporary Capitalism* (London: New Left Books, 1975), p. 333.

19. Nicos Poulantzas, interviewed by Henri Weber, "The State and the Transition to Socialism," *Socialist Review,* no. 38, March-April, 1978.

chapter 6

TERRORISM AND THE ITALIAN LEFT

Suzanne Cowan

The kidnapping and assassination of five-time Prime Minister of Italy Aldo Moro represents the most clamorous and daring act of political terrorism to occur in that country since the end of the Fascist period, and one of the most extraordinary exploits to take place in all of Europe during the postwar era. In a country where social tension and instability are common elements of everyday life, and where political kidnappings, physical attacks and assassinations occur with chilling regularity, the violence of this crime is not particularly noteworthy in itself. What distinguishes the Moro case from others which preceded it is the fact that, in choosing their victim, the terrorists carried out the objective proclaimed in their official communiques: namely, to launch "an attack at the heart of the state." Because Moro occupied a crucial position within the political machinery of the country at a moment when a thirty-year struggle for power seemed to be entering its decisive phase, his death contributed to unsettling a very tenuous equilibrium of forces. The long-range effects of this disruption may not be predictable; however, it does appear to have rather grave implications for the strategy and tactics of the Italian Communist Party, and thus for its relationship to other western parties comprising a potential Eurocommunist "bloc."

The Erosion of Ruling Class Hegemony

BY EMPHASIZING THE enormity of the Moro assassination, people often fall into a conventional trap, a habit conditioned largely by the western press: namely, the tendency to give a great deal of weight to such actions because of the stature and prestige of their single victims, forgetting that in Italy (as in nearly every nation marked by intense class conflict and social struggle) political terrorism is a long-established tradition, generally perpetrated by right-wing forces against the left. This being the case, and particulaarly since the victims of ultra-right terrorism tend to be collective and "anonymous" rather than well-known public figures, the major organs of the mass media commonly ignore them. It is true, nonetheless, that Moro held a unique position within postwar Italian politics, playing a role that had become particularly vital for the ruling class at the very moment of his kidnapping. It is worthwhile to discuss this role briefly, because examining the significance of Moro's career helps clarify the major tendencies and developments of Italian society and politics over the past thirty years.

In broad terms this period can be characterized by the existence of continuous, militant class struggle and open social conflict, coupled with a gradual deepening and broadening of popular consensus around the movement for democratic reform and renewal led by the major mass-based party of the Italian left—the Communist Party (PCI). This trend has logically implied a progressive weakening of established political power (mainly at the local and regional levels), but even more, a loss of ideological hegemony and what might be called ethical leadership on the part of the ruling Christian Democratic Party (DC).

The Christian Democrats have retained their economic and political power over the past three decades primarily through the following means: a vast network of patron-client relationships bolstered by the maintenance of enormous and inefficient (partly or wholly) state-run enterprises which represent veritable fiefdoms for DC party retainers; the *"sottogoverno"* or "sub-government," which consists of an overwhelming, swollen state administrative bureaucracy employing a multitude of petty officials who remain loyal to the party and much more responsible to the privileges of its top DC bosses than to the real needs of the population; support of the Vatican and the vast political-economic power base it controls; complicity of major industrialists, bankers, and landowners who are permitted to engage in practically uncontrolled speculation as well as a myriad of illegal and corrupt forms of self-enrichment, in return for guaranteeing the continued loyalty (in the form of votes) of the areas under their political control; tacit or open support from top members of the armed forces, police, legal establishment, and the Mafia; and finally, massive financial support and encouragement, not exclusive of direct political intervention, by the United States—which, of course, means loans from the International Monetary Fund, World Bank, and other financial entities controlled by the U.S.

Although these sources of power and control have been rigorously maintained during the postwar period, the mass left—with its meticulously honest system of local administrations, leadership of the large and militant working-class movement, great cultural and ideological prestige, and ability to mobilize significant sectors of the youth and unorganized workers, as well as "progressive," "open-minded" elements of the middle class (students, journalists, intellectuals, artists and "cultural workers" in various spheres, many young professionals, feminists, scientific and technical workers, significant numbers of white-collar employees, and even new recruits from lower and middle-level corporate management positions) has attained an ever-growing share of national power over the past thirty years, and directly challenged significant areas of the DC power base. To accomplish this the PCI has been obliged to develop a power base of its own, which has meant the establishment of a sort of *counter-clientele* in competition with the one maintained by the DC. In Italy, where the majority of the population is acquainted with the often squalid necessities of day-to-day survival, no power can be achieved by persuasion alone: if a party wants to lead, it has to "deliver the goods." As reporter Jane Kramer observed, in a rather cynical but nonetheless accurate statement, "Italians regard their citizenship as a kind of bad deal with the devil. They do not really believe that their rights as citizens entitle them to fair treatment from the government; they expect their rights to be honored in direct proportion to the power of the particular party that protects them."[1] What makes PCI "protection" qualitatively different from DC protection is that it is generally honest, clean, and allotted not to a mass of indifferent and unqualified hacks, but to young activists sincerely committed to meaningful, lasting social reforms.

The influence of these reforms and the real power of the left has come to bear increasing weight on Italian society since the late 1950s, a fact which could not help influencing the policy of the Christian Democrats. Although the party has maintained its essentially conservative stagnant posture throughout this period, on the parliamentary level it has made some significant bends, mainly to the left. It was in this area, i.e., in the realm of inter- and intra-party politics, that Aldo Moro made his influence felt most directly over the past several decades.

Unlike most of his fellow party members, Moro was not an ex-Fascist. His anti-communism, deep-seated though it was, could probably best be understood as an ethical and philosophical mistrust largely conditioned by his southern Catholic roots (he came from the city of Bari, in Puglia, and drew some of his strongest support from the peasants of that region) rather than in terms of pure class antagonism. His political ideology was that of a somewhat detached, pessimistic Catholic conservative. Although he always remained a loyal Christian Democrat, he was known for his quiet independence and personal integrity—a notable quality in DC politicians—and was one of the few who attained a position of national leadership through skill and patient work rather than pure opportunism. In the face of blatant corruption and ineptitude on the part of his colleagues, he preferred to maintain a bemused, tolerant silence, taking their active defense only when absolutely necessary in order to avoid damaging the party. Rather than participate in the chorus of anathemas hurled against the PCI by fellow Christian Democratic leaders, Moro was content to work quietly and doggedly, usually behind the scenes, to improve his party's national image. Naturally, this meant observing an anti-communist line. But once it became clear that the DC would have to come to terms with an increasingly strong, serious adversary, he realized that virulent anti-communism was both anachronistic and threatening to DC power. From the late 1950s, therefore, he defined his own position as one of cautious compromise and openness toward the left.

An idealistic, meditative Christian, he expressed the following thought during the dramatic student-worker demonstrations of 1968: "On the deepest level, it is a new humanity which wants to come into being, it is the irresistible movement of history."[2] Moro's sensitivity to the growing power of the PCI as a force of opposition, and to the genuine impetus toward reform which this power represented, was reflected in a remark which he made in the same year: "[We have learned that] we must undertake a serious self-criticism; that to a certain extent, we must become a force of opposition ourselves."[3]

Representing the moderate-progressive wing of the DC, Moro helped to bring about the center-left coalition: a decade-long parliamentary alliance between the DC and Socialist Party, formed when it became impossible for the Christian Democrats to continue ruling alone or with the sole support of a flanking constellation of small, "secular" parties (Republicans, Liberals, Social Democrats, etc.). Known as the major architect of the DC's "opening to the left," he bears primary credit for restoring the prestige of his party, which had been seriously eroded from 1968 to the mid-1970s. The essential stages of the DC's recuperation of power after this point coincide with the stages of Moro's advancement in the ranks of governmental power. He played a leading role in the 1975 divorce referendum, helping to quell the fears and hesitations of those Catholics who dissented from the official Party and Vatican position. He also led the 1976 electoral campaign, and worked tirelessly to reorganize the DC after this election, making it more open to voices of dissent and reform, more responsive to pressure from certain areas of the left—in short, a more effective and authentic concentration of all those forces committed to preserving the *status quo* in Italy.

Moro's leadership and unobtrusive but persistent maneuvering revived the DC as a global force encompassing both party and state. With his election to the presidency of his party on October 14, 1976 (a title which, although usually just a formality, acquired a much deeper significance when he assumed it), Moro was consecrated in his role of supreme moderator, catalyst in the unavoidable "confrontation" between the DC and the PCI. He maintained this role throughout the governmental crisis of January 1978 and was primarily responsible for bringing the PCI into the parliamentary majority which followed that event—a masterpiece of mediation which required the utmost in patience and tenacity. In describing the relationship between the two major parties, he used the cryptic term "parallel convergencies"—a logical paradox that, all the same, aptly corresponds to the paradoxical relationship of two huge political forces which cannot share power equally (at least not with the present conditions) and cannot possibly govern alone.

This was the political career and the life that were so brutally truncated by the Red Brigades on May 10, 1978. We have already mentioned that such instances of political terrorism are not a new phenomenon in Italy, a point which must be reiterated if we are to avoid falling into confusion between various different forms of political violence, or concluding (along with most of the media) that they are all basically the same.

Right-Wing Terrorism

MOST INSTANCES of political terrorism in Italy since 1945 have been directed from the right against forces of the working class and organized left. As such they can be seen essentially as a continuation of the type of right-wing violence used under Fascism. Although much remains to be discovered about those individuals who finance neo-fascist groups, and much information remains sealed up within special "classified" files of the Italian police and armed forces, these groups are known to enjoy the support of large industrialists both in Italy and abroad. Their troops are recruited mainly from the upper middle class: sons and daughters of wealthy professionals and old aristocratic families, many of them former fascists who attribute the country's problems to an excess of democracy and lack of solid control from the top. There is also a large representation of the petty bourgeoisie—small property owners and struggling independent entrepreneurs—among the ranks of the neo-fascists. Much of their organizational groundwork is carried out at universities and high schools. For example, certain departments of major universities, such as Padova and Rome, are known as fertile terrain for the cultivation of new right-wing activists; and escalating cynicism and frustration among university students, particularly those of the lower middle class, has made right-wing recruiting there very fruitful indeed.

In recent years, notably since 1969, deployment of arms and the use of terrorism has fallen into a certain rather predictable pattern. This "strategy of tension"—represents a coordinated and inherently logical plan to destabilize the already tenuous balance of social and political forces in the country by creating a climate of tension and violence that is designed to frighten people into demanding that greater and greater power be given to the forces of "law and order." The end result would be the installation of an authentically right-wing, authoritarian regime that would put an end to strikes, factory occupations, and all forms of militant social protest.[4]

Right-wing attempts at "destabilization" have taken place with alarming frequency since the late 1960s, at the rate of nearly one each day. Preferred targets include PCI section headquarters, labor union halls, recreation centers frequented by left-wing actiists, schools known to have politically militant student body or faculty members, publishing firms, editorial offices of left-wing papers and magazines, individual militants, and mass meetings called by left organizations. The most extreme of these attacks took place in a crowded downtown square in Milan on December 12, 1969, when a bomb exploded in the *Banca Nazionale dell 'Agricoltura*, killing sixteen people and wounding eighty-eight. Following this event were others of similar ferocity: several bombs were set off in the course of political rally-demonstrations called by the PCI in the main square of Brescia in 1974, killing six persons; another bomb was detonated in the express train *Italicus* as it approached Bologna, massacring the passengers of several wagons, in the summer of that same year; in July, 1976, Judge Vittorio Occorsio, who had been pursuing a judicial investigation of the activities of a well-known fascist group called *Ordine Nuovo,* was machine gunned to death in Rome, finally in March of 1978 there was the seemingly gratuitous murder of two young students (both sympathetic to the left, but hardly radical leaders) as they were on their way to a jazz concert in Milan.

The general response to these terrorist actions on the part of the authorities has been to crack down on the left. Following the 1969 Milan bank bombing the police ordered an immediate roundup of left-wing militants; throughout the country, members of "extra-parliamentary" organizations (and numerous PCI activists as well) were arrested and brought to police headquarters for identification. Many were held for days without bail or legal assistance of any kind. Accusations for the crime were shortly brought against three unfortunate anarchists, who were kept in prison awaiting trial for nearly four years while police scrupulously accumulated and hid away documents pointing toward the incontestable guilt of persons belong to a fascist group. It was mainly the painstaking and dogged work of the left that, in such an atmosphere, brought out the real facts of the case. When the facts did emerge, they led to the conclusion that the bombings of Piazza Fontana (site of the *Banca dell 'Agricoltura*) had been planned and executed by a neo-fascist organization. In itself, this revelation would not have come as a particular surprise. However, it eventually became clear that the fascists were only one piece in a large, complicated jigsaw puzzle which, when partially assembled, revealed an intricate network of relationships.

The December 12 bombings, and similar crimes of lesser magnitude, had been committed by right-wing groups working with the protection and complicity of international fascist and paramilitary organizations, large industrialists, the armed forces, secret service, police, law courts, and sectors of the government itself, which in many cases were supported by the U.S. Central Intelligence Agency. Moreover, despite pressure from the left, neo-fascist parties such as the MSI (*Movimento Sociale Italiano*) and DN (*Destra Nazionale*) have been permitted to recruit new members and run candidates in local and national elections. These parties contributed directly to financing and planning many "destabilizing" actions, taking careful steps to protect those who actually carried them out. In more than one case, parliamentary deputies from these parties, clearly identified as responsible for various acts of violence, could not even be brought to trial because they benefit from parliamentary immunity. In the complex network of responsibility and complicity surrounding right-wing terrorism in Italy, it is significant that no member or faction of the Christian Democratic Party has been directly implicated. As the major political party, in fact, the DC has found it advisable to be very circumspect about allying itself too openly with elements of the far right; in general it has been content to provide cover for them by exerting indirect pressure on the police and law courts, so as to sabotage any serious attempts to interfere with their operations.

What emerged from the bombings, then, was the picture of a systematic campaign of violence and terror, in which "small" fascists (like those who were eventually tried and imprisoned for the 1969 massacre) figured as little more than errand-boys at the service of much higher authorites. This helps explain why big-time fascist conspirators, such as General Miceli, have consistently emerged unscathed from their brief run-ins with the law:[5] why escalating terrorism carried out by the neo-fascist Italian Social Movement (MSI) over the past ten years has hardly ever led to trial, much less conviction, of the guilty parties; and why on January 24 1978 *Ordine Nuovo*—a self-proclaimed fascist organization which has committed, and admitted openly to, a long chain of physical attacks against leftist militants, various crowd bombings, coup plots and assassinations—was ruled to be a non-fascist organization and therefore immune from legal dissolution.*

If right-wing or neo-fascist terrorism thus fits into a rather historically consistent plan and corresponds to a long tradition of anti-communist, anti-working class, anti-progressive strategy, it is quite a different story for the outburst of "left-wing terrorism" which has aroused so much fervor throughout Western Europe in recent months. Not only in its historical development, but in its social and political roots and its immediate and long-range causes, left-wing terrorism occupies a very different category.[6]

Emergence of the Red Brigades

IT MUST BE emphasized that the nature and constituency of the left-terrorist groups (claimed to be more than 115, according to police estimates, in Italy at the end of 1978) is very difficult to assess. This is true for two major reasons.

First, these groups are probably infiltrated by a large number of right-wing provacateurs and adventurists. To cite only one of the few known examples, there is Silvano Girotti, alias "Brother Machine-gun," a self-proclaimed revolutionary priest who fought (so he says) alongside of Che Guevara in Bolivia, and took part in various other popular struggles in Latin America. He then returned to help out the Italian police by becoming a member of the Red Brigades—a collaboration which eventually led to the arrest and conviction of the leaders now imprisoned in Turin. An equivocal character if there ever was one. Brother Machine-gun was not content merely to help put away the *brigatisti* (in the name of what he describes as a higher, more socially responsible form of people's justice), but went on to divulge to the authorities information about other alleged left-wing terrorists, who actually had proved themselves through long and respected careers as combatants in the Resistance movement and leaders of a number of important working-class struggles. Girotti is only one of the visible infiltrators. But it is virtually impossible to state how many other, invisible ones there may be fomenting social violence and terrorism within far-left groups.

*Italian law expressly prohibits the re-constitution of fascist groups in any form.

It is also extremely difficult to study the internal organization of these groups because of their necessarily clandestine nature and decentralized structure. From what information the police have been able to accumulate (and they know precious little!), the Red Brigades, or BR, have a very tight, coherent structure, and even keep scrupulous records of their monthly expenses down to the last lira spent for gas and electric bills. They are apparently divided into "columns," established in different cities, which operate in highly synchronized conjunction with each other. Nevertheless, it is also believed that a sort of generation gap occurred between the older group of leaders (those now in prison) and the younger ones (those responsible for the kidnapping and assassination of Moro)— who espouse a different philosophy and set of tactics. Although both "generations" are firmly convinced of the necessity for "armed proletarian combat" and for clandestine structure (at least in the formative stages) of the new revolutionary party, it is probable that the older group placed greater emphasis on interaction and contact with the working-class base. Its concept of violence stemmed from a somewhat different analysis of the identity and nature of the class enemy, defined as those servants of capitalist oppression most readily identifiable by the masses (hence, the political justification for assassinations of major oppressors such as chiefs of police, right-wing jurists, etc.); whereas the "new" *brigatisti*, finding exponents of the hated "multinational corporate state" at every level and within every major institution of society, insist upon the political necessity of repeated, exemplary acts of violence such as "kneecapping," sequestration, kidnapping, etc.

Adding to the general confusion is that a single left-wing group has at times claimed credit for a certain action only to be denounced and contradicted by others claiming to be the legitimate representatives of that same group. During the time Moro was held prisoner, for example, a communique received by a major Rome newspaper and signed by the Red Brigades proposed an exchange of prisoners: the *brigatisti* locked up in Turin for Aldo Moro. Almost immediately following the publication of this message, another was sent to the same paper, signed by the Red Brigades and decrying the first communique as the work of impostors. The BR leaders awaiting trial in prison probably knew little or nothing about the operation being carried out by their comrades. Although they expressed jubilation at the news of the kidnapping, it was clear from the attentive curiosity with which they followed radio reports of the successive stages of the police investigation and other news related to the case that they were completely uninformed. Authorities have hypothesized that the Red Brigades and similar groups may be organized loosely and flexibly enough so that the moment one of their members is arrested, the others change their locations, equipment, and even leaders. Thus, any information "leaked" to police by captured militants (who, at any rate, steadfastly refuse to speak and cannot be forced to do so through legal means) will predictably be wrong.

Beginning then with a profound state of ignorance as to the organizational framework and membership of the left-wing terrorist groups, we can however make some general statements about their history, and about the political analysis and strategy that motivate them. Terrorist undercurrents can probably be traced back to the militant phase of the student-worker movement of the late 1960s, which culminated in the convulsive "hot autumn" of 1969. Extremist groups had some theoretical precedents in branches of the various "extra-parliamentary" left groups which flourished during that period: notably *Potere Operaio* and *Lotta Continua*, as well as certain smaller Maoist and self-styled Leninist organizations. The Red Brigades themselves, however, originated primarily in the highly radicalized sociology department of the University of Trento, known as a hotbed of militant agitation—as well as a leftist "think-tank" during the period of roughly 1968-1972. It also grew out of some circles of the left-wing Catholic movement, and took root in the early 1970s within certain northern industrial areas such as the Sit-Siemens factory near Milan, where a series of fire bombings, kidnappings of management executives, and acts of sabotage took place with notable regularity.

Like other, more recently formed groups of the radical left—*Autonomia Operaia* ("Working-class Autonomy") and the flamboyant counter-cultural militants known as "Metropolitan Indians"—the terrorist groups represent the evolution of a certain branch of the new left, which developed in reaction to the absence of leadership—on the part of the mass left parties. Whenever they established roots within the northern industrial plants and carried on their work there, it was, again, as a reaction to what they saw as compromise and immobilism on the part of the PCI, and to the extreme difficulty of consolidating a truly revolutionary opposition to the PCI within the labor unions. Nevertheless, it is important to draw a distinction between the authentic terrorist organizations such as the BR and NAP ("Armed Proletarian Nuclei"), on the one hand, and other militant left groups like the *Autonomia* and Metropolitan Indians. Whereas these latter groups advocate open, mass political violence carried out against the most visible perpetrators of the capitalist system (police, journalistic establishment, trade union "sell-outs," etc.), the BR and similar terrorist organizations operate strictly underground, engaging in actions which can only be carried out by a relatively small number of militants working in absolute secrecy and with meticulous planning. There is nothing "spontaneist" about the Red Brigades' strategy or philosophy. They reject both adventurist street confrontations with police and the open destructiveness of the urban guerrilla shock troops which scandalized a large part of Italian society during the violent demonstrations of the *emarginati*, or "marginal" people (unemployed, students, women, sporadically employed working-class youth, Yippee-style, counter cultural activists, etc.) in early spring of 1977.

It is true that these groups enjoy a certain amount of tacit, or even declared, support from what is called the general "Autonomous area," and given the extremely restless and heterogeneous nature of this formation it would be impossible to state precisely what, if any, lines of contact run between it and the Red Brigades. Nevertheless, insofar as one can judge from the goals and principles enunciated by spokespersons for the *Autonomia*, the two organizations disagree on a number of fundamental points. In particular, the question of violence: while the Autonomous groups accept the necessity of armed proletarian struggle, they make a fairly neat distinction between this and terrorism. The concept of insurrection espoused by the *Autonomia* has little to do with clandestine acts of violence, which must be planned and carried out in strictest isolation. Its leaders generally insist on the importance of working within and among the masses (although, to be sure, they have yet to provide a clear definition of the nature and function of this work), and maintain that armed violence, while an important component, is not the fundamental aspect of their political strategy. It is one thing for the *Autonomia* to consider BR members as revolutionary comrades who have adopted an essentially mistaken strategy and set of tactics, and therefore to refuse denouncing them (assuming their identity can be known) to the police, but another to offer them concrete support in the form of people and contributions. In fact, at the time of the Moro kidnapping, although there was some hesitation on the far left about what position to assume with respect to this sort of terrorism, it was not long before even the most "extremist" groups took their distance from the *brigatisti*. Spokespersons for the *Autonomia* eventually condemned BR as ultraleftist adventurists whose politics, divorced from the real interests or experience of the masses, ultimately serve only the interests of the state. Moreover, even if the *Autonomia* had reserved its criticisms, it is unlikely that it would have been chosen as primary terrain for recruitment by the Red Brigades; the entire Autonomous movement is infiltrated with so many spies and police agents that it has been compared, in the words of one observer, to "a rice-field full of land mines."

Insofar as the Autonomous organizations have a coherent political strategy, it is to engage greater and greater numbers of citizens in the sorts of "exemplary actions" which will mobilize the wavering masses of the oppressed and working class, immobilize the "reformist" left, and produce an overwhelming popular movement—that will virtually sweep the left into power. When subjected to critical scrutiny, this appears to be more a generalized clamor than a movement. Insufficient and infantile though this strategy may seem, it has widespread appeal among the masses of students and hundreds of thousands of perennially unemployed youth in Italy, frustrated by failure of other more traditional left-wing groups to fill the void in political leadership left by the PCI and to constitute a real opposition to the ruling party and its interests.

The political strategy and theory put forward by the Red Brigades, in the form of various communiques and position papers, seems more coherent—if not more convincing. They advocate the use of those sorts of "destabilizing" actions, such as kidnapping, assassinations and "knee-capping" of political figures that will force the reformist parties to reveal their "true face" by stepping into the camp of the repressive forces and allying themselves openly with the Christian Democrats and police. They perceive the real enemies of the working class, not as the most blatantly exploitative or repressive elements of capitalism, but as the upper- and middle-level technocrats who carry out the orders of what they call the "Imperialist State of the Multinationals." Since the multinational corporate state is all-encompassing and ubiquitous, its servants—and therefore the targets of BR attacks—may be as insignificant as simple newspaper reporters, middle-management executives, and ordinary cops, or as prestigious as Aldo Moro; they may be avowed fascists or progressive, democratic supporters of a PCI-DC coalition. Such actions, they believe, will gradually create a "strategic pole of resistance against the processes of imperialist counter-revolution," which will in turn become an "armed combatant party."[7] The function of this party must be to attack the vulnerable points of state power so as to reveal its contradictions and unmask the reactionary nature of its power before the eyes of the proletariat. In this process, they see themselves as a militant formation constituting an "anti-state," antagonistic and gradually becoming equal in power to the bourgeois state itself. These are the major points clearly enunciated in the message, transmitted to the Rome press, in which the Red Brigades announced the opening of their "people's trial" against Moro. This trial, calculated to coincide with the beginning of the trial of the BR members imprisoned in Turin, was intended as a reciprocal thrust, a game of "power against power," in a trial parallel to the one then being initiated in Turin by the bourgeois state.

The Response of the Left

ONE BASIC FACT is that the various actions planned and carried out by terrorist organizations over the past few years, culminating in the

Moro assassination, have had an effect diametrically opposite to the one envisioned by the Red Brigades. Specifically, their outcome has been not to expose the "true face" of bourgeois power, but to more successfully mask it and strengthen it by unifying a broad spectrum of popular sympathy and consensus around the ruling party, and to provide the government with a handy pretext for carrying out further repression against the left. The police dragnets and round-ups of leftist suspects on fatuous pretexts, the strengthening of emergency laws, lengthy interrogations, and all the rest are by now well-known.

It must be pointed out that oppressive measures have not been nearly as extreme as one might have expected, given the gravity of the actions and the extent of public outrage they aroused. If one thinks, for example, of the sweeping abrogation of civil liberties and basic legal rights carried out in West Germany—even before the kidnapping and assassination of Hans Martin Schleyer—in the name of combating terrorism, the Italian response seems relatively mild. The fact that it was not harsher must be attributed to the very genuine respect for democracy and safeguarding of democratic rights that the left has managed to impose, albeit insufficiently and inconsistently, upon the organs of state power. All the more reason then to feel distressed at the enthusiasm with which the mass-based left organizations have jumped onto the anti-terrorist bandwagon and shown their willingness to participate in the battle against political criminality, even at the cost of some dearly-won rights. To say that these rights have been irrevocably sacrificed is an exaggeration; to say that they have been compromised and eroded is a statement of fact. In a certain respect—and there is a sad irony here—one major goal of the Red Brigades has been fulfilled, if the Moro operation was intended to further expose and discredit the PCI by forcing it to take a "law and order" position, thereby tightening its embrace with the DC. But the terrorists' entire strategy rests on the assumption that this exposure will lead to a further crystallization of class antagonisms and to the strengthening of a "pole" of revolutionary proletarian combat. Thus far, the BR actions have utterly failed to accomplish this primary objective, and there is no indication that they will lead to the desired effect in the foreseeable future. Along the way, the left—the entire left, and not just the extremist or radical "fringe"—has been forced onto the defensive. In this fundamental respect, the BR action has been unquestionably counter-productive.

Under pressure of the general climate of hysteria and anger surrounding the Moro affair, most of the radical left groups condemned both the terrorists and the government, as the following statement by *Lotta Continua* confirms: "We totally condemn the means, the objectives, and the political conception of the *brigatisti*, which is based on terror. But we refuse to build, upon this state, the social basis for an increasingly repressive regime."[8] Careful to maintain the principled position that both the apparatus of the existing state and the terrorist tactics of the Red Brigades are fundamentally opposed to the interests of the working class and to the grassroots leftwing movement as a whole, most radical groups advocated negotiating with the BR to arrange for a release of prisoners in exchange for Moro's freedom—this position was pushed, not for humanitarian motives, but on the political grounds that refusal to negotiate was tantamount to upholding the sacred inviolability of "democratic institutions," which would be irrevocably compromised by any retreat in the face of terrorist violence and blackmail. For most far-left groups, this argument put forward by the major political parties constituted a grotesque obfuscation. They correctly pointed out that the institutions of this particular state have never been so democratic as to justify their defense at the cost of even a single human life. In any event, their appeal turned out to be fruitless, since the possibility of negotiations was never concretely or forcefully articulated by the Red Brigades, and furthermore was soon rejected out of hand by the major parties.

The slogan, "Neither the state nor the Red Brigades," so earnestly put forward by the radical left (and not only the radical left but also a number of trade union rank-and-file organizations articulated the same sentiment) nevertheless appeared almost pathetic in contrast to the thundering condemnation of terrorism issued by the Communists. There is a rather sad aptness to the slogan, which seems to have been adopted by the radical left almost half-heartedly—as if to say, "there's nothing better available, so we might just as well use this one." It is consonant with the general mood and level of the new left in Italy at present, in that it is both negative and abstract. To be sure, all slogans are abstractions, in the sense that they only gain vital substance from the movement and concrete political program which puts them forward. This is precisely why "Neither the state nor the Red Brigades" is perfectly suited to the radical movement: already splintered and debilitated before the current spate of terrorist attacks, it has become all the more so since Moro's kidnapping. In this national drama, the major parties definitely occupied center stage, with the fragments of the far left unceremoniously pushed back into the wings. Their slogan seems especially pathetic because it can suggest no alternative, no "third way" to replace the two poles that it rejects. In short, it implies the total lack of program—not so much for uprooting left-wing terrorism, but for rendering it impotent and irrelevant by building a militant, unified and effective revolutionary party. Given the general state of affairs in Italy, and the state of the radical left in particular, chances for creating such a party are now virtually nonexistent. If the slogan is inadequate, it is because there is no program, no real force, behind it. A better one could no doubt be invented, but this would not help to fill in the political vacuum. The PCI had hardly ever seemed so united, so firmly committed to a single principle: safeguarding the democratic institutions of the state. In calling down the just wrath of the authorities against the Red Brigades, PCI spokespersons sounded almost more indignant than the Christian Democrats themselves. The following quotation, taken from a fomal resolution issued by the Party leadership on the day after the discovery of Moro's body, may be taken as exemplary: "The assassination of Aldo Moro is a monstrous crime. Those who carried it out have revealed their full inhumanity and bestiality. They are enemies of civil society, of the Italian people, of republican democracy. The Communists lower their own banners in memory of Aldo Moro, and express their own sympathetic solidarity with his family and (with) the Christian Democratic Party. In this dramatic moment for the country, the workers, popular masses, and parties must reinforce their unity in defense of the Republic and its institutions. The unitary mobilization of the forces of labor, of all democratic forces, is the response which must be given to those who attack the anti-fascist Republic; to everyone who would like to set Italy back from the conquests that have been won and to throw it into chaos and adventurism."[9]

From such invective, an impartial observer might have almost thought the PCI was trying to outdo the Christian Democrats at their own rhetoric. This should come as no surprise, if one recalls the epithets hurled at far-left organizations by the party in recent years. The general tendency of the PCI—a tendency that appears logical in light of its over-all strategy of compromise and collaboration with the DC—is to lump together the *Autonomi*, various Maoist and Marxist-Leninist organizations, anarchists, "Metropolitan Indians," and other groups operating to its left with fascists, branding them indiscriminately as criminals and "enemies of the democratic state."

At the same time, the PCI's condemnation of the ultra-left is not as unanimous or unswerving as it appears on the surface: at every level within the party apparatus, and certainly on the "inside" at upper levels, the debate is more subtle. Many PCI cadres and officials realize that the root causes of left-wing terrorism are dialectically intertwined with the day-to-day operations, as well as the long-range strategy, of the party itself, and they debate these issues publicly and privately. Still, the essential PCI position on terrorism, and on the groups to its left, is articulated in its major journals, mass-distribution publications, and public statements. There can be little question that the prevailing idea is to equate almost any form of left-wing violence with terrorism, nearly all far-left groups with goon squads, and almost any type of political struggle which transcends established norms and institutionalized controls as "adventurist," "destructive," "criminal," etc. (This does not contradict the PCI's general strategy toward the far left, which has been to attempt to split its ranks, drawing part of it back into its own bosom. This plan has been quite successful, especially since the extreme left has continually suffered from a marked degree of disunity and internal conflict.)

As if wishing to deny that a state whose democratic institutions have been built mainly through the sacrifice of the popular masses since the fall of fascism could spawn its own native terrorist movement, the PCI largely supported the theory that the BR were actually operating under the direction of foreign power—most likely (recalling the example of Chile) the CIA. To be sure, various other theories of "outside control" have also been put forward. There is the "German hypothesis," according to which the BR draw their inspiration, and perhaps much of their equipment, from groups such as the Baader-Meinhof and *Rote Armee Fraktion* in West Germany; the "KGB hypothesis," which states that the Red Brigades may actually be financed and armed by the Soviet Union (this theory, articulated especially by certain small far-left groups maintains that the USSR would like to strengthen the Christian Democrats and prevent the PCI, which has been notably critical of Soviet internal policies, from attaining power); and finally, a terribly complicated hypothesis connecting the terrorists with a column operating actively in Czechoslovakia.

Of all these speculations, the only one that seems to hold a modicum of truth is the one positing some sort of right-wing matrix—either domestic or foreign or both—behind the actions of the Red Brigades. It certainly does appear that if the Moro kidnapping, coming at the precise moment and in the manner it did, was not the work of the far-right, it might just as well have been. It could not have been more perfectly calculated to confuse and weaken the left-wing movement throughout all of Europe, for it occurred just on the eve of a crucial election in France, which pitted the left against the center in a dramatic context. It also coincided in Spain with the important Ninth Congress of the Spanish Communist Party, in which certain fundamental policy decisions were to be worked out, and in West Germany with the opening of a series of hearings, bitterly opposed by conservatives, to investigate the widespread crackdown on the left. Most significantly, however, the kidnapping seemed perfectly timed to coincide with the formation of the first postwar Italian government in which the PCI was to participate, along with the Christian Democrats, in the parliamentary majority—a collaboration that surely could not have been welcome to right-wing forces.

Naturally, such an harmonious concert might have been purely accidental, and whether or not the terrorist group's activities are actually directed by neo-fascists remains for now confined to the realm of speculation. Whatever one may think on this subject, however, there is no doubt that the phenomenon of left-wing terrorism is a home-grown, Italian product; not a shred of evidence has appeared to lend strength to the theories of foreign intervention or control. Just as the BR's historical roots are different from those of the traditional right-wing terrorist organizations, so its motivations and logic are different from those of leftist groups elsewhere, from the Baader-Meinhof to the U.S. Weathermen. Whereas such organizations must be seen as an expression of frustrated moral and political opposition to systems that rest upon ideological consensus, Italian terrorism develops out of frustration with a system marked by continuous, bitter class struggle and social conflict—but a system where the traditional organs of the mass-based left appear unable and unwilling to lead the very real forces of opposition in a concerted struggle for radical change. This is the crux of both the campaign waged by the Red Brigades and other left-wing terrorist organizations in Italy, and the dilemma of the mass-based left itself.

The Predicament of the PCI

THE AGONIZING, UNCERTAIN situation in which the Italian Communists and, by extension, the forces to the left of the PCI now find themselves has, of course, been developing for some time. Exactly how long is a matter of debate. Some would maintain that it has been growing ever since the adoption of Togliatti's program for a peaceful "Italian road to socialism" back in the 1950s; others would say since the beginning of the so-called "economic miracle."* Still others would date the precipitation of the dilemma from the outburst of working-class militancy and intense grass-roots pressure for social reform that started in the late 1960s. Finally, it might be argued that the period of deepest crisis for the PCI began at the precise moment when it achieved its greatest political victories within the electoral and parliamentary framework, namely with the regional and municipal elections of 1975 and the general elections of June 20, 1976. In any case, although the dilemma of the left has been building up over a certain period, we may state that the Moro case had the effect of thrusting the dilemma to the forefront of public concern and action.

The fundamental quandary of the PCI, although extremely complex, may perhaps be summed up in one over-all question: What is to be

---

*Starting in the late 1950s, this was a period of growth and expansion from which the Communist Party and labor movement drew considerable benefits, while still retaining their political role as forces of opposition.

the relationship between a mass-based, democratic leftwing party—dedicated to a peaceful transition to socialism—and the institutional structures of the bourgeois capitalist state in which it operates? This theoretical question lies at the heart of one of the most animated debates to take place on the European left in several decades—a debate that has inspired Marxist intellectuals throughout the continent, and which has been a sharp focus of attention among all those Western European parties and forces attempting to develop that tendency known as Euro-communism. The question has presented itself with particular urgency in Italy over the past few years.

The PCI, along with other sectors of the "democratic left," have justifiably taken credit for the creation and defense of democratic institutions in Italy during the postwar period—institutions built up painfully, and against tremendous odds, on the ruins of fascist dictatorship. It must be emphasized that fascism established certain authoritarian institutional patterns and habits that have all too frequently been revived by the ruling forces whenever it has seemed that class struggle is bringing the left close to victory. As a party dedicated to the legal, constitutional ascent to power, the PCI has had to accomplish a truly Herculean task namely, to defend and strengthen the existing, democratic institutions while at the same time combating undemocratic measures called forth by the ruling class to defeat the workers' movement and its political leadership. The first contradiction lies precisely here: the left in general, and the working class movement in particular, knows quite well that the "democracy" so fervently touted both by the current generation of PCI leaders and by DC leaders has always been a *bourgeois* democracy, meaning that it has generally extended its protection and largesse to the ruling class. The Italian labor movement, unlike most of its American counterparts, has a long and accurate historical memory. It clearly recalls the covert and overt attempts to sabotage union organizing in the northern plants during the 1950s; the peaceful demonstrators shot down by police in the public squares; the union and party organizers rounded up, imprisoned, interrogated, and blacklisted; the Mafia killings of left-wing organizers in agricultural areas in the south; the assassinations for which the police never seemed able to find the criminals, even though everyone knew who they were; the barely-intercepted right-wing military coups; and then, of course, the steady stream of unpunished and uninvestigated right-wing terrorist attacks.

Given this background, large numbers of working-class people, including significant sectors of the PCI's own rank and file base, understandably feel dismayed and perplexed when party leaders extoll the supposed "autonomy" of state instituions—police, law courts, military establishment, mass media, and so forth—and vow to defend them despite their obvious imperfections. Following the Moro assassinations, the PCI presented itself as a zealous protector of law and order, launching a veritable anti-terrorist crusade that called for the expansion of the secret police (provided, of course, that it is expanded along with elements demonstrably democratic and loyal to the Constitution) and more vigorous suppression of political criminality.

The logical outcome of this position was the PCI's staunch opposition to abrogation of the *Legge Reale*, known colloquially as the "police law," an item of legislation the party had vigorously opposed when the law was first presented to Parliament in May of 1975. Several left-wing civil liberties organizations had launched a petition drive calling for a popular referendum on whether to retain it. Among its other provisions, the *Reale* law allowed frightening expansion of police powers by extending their right to arrest and detain citizens merely suspected of criminal acts, to shoot on sight anyone presumed to be fleeing or carrying a weapon, and to deny parole to persons accused of political terrorism. In June, 1978, prior to the referendum, the PCI emerged as one of the strongest forces in support of retaining the law—predictably, on grounds that it was necessary to combat political terrorism and reinforce the firm but rightful authority of the state. After having just stepped into a parliamentary majority in which it was pledged to cooperate with the DC, the Communists found themselves obliged not only to take credit for the development of state institutions, but to defend them as products of the "popular democratic mass movement" mobilized jointly by the PCI and enlightened sectors of the DC. The obvious contradiction between the Communists' former position with respect to the *Reale* law and their current stance was clearly felt by the PCI rank and file, and also revealed itself in the form of a certain embarrassment among party leaders themselves. The statement that perhaps most strongly demonstrates the acute discomfort felt by even some high-level PCI spokespersons appeared in the PCI newspaper *l'Unità* the day before the June 11 national referendum. The paper's editorial satirist, known by the pen name of "Fortebraccio" and justfly famous for his subtle, penetrating wit, made the following plea to readers: "The first duty to observe consists of never, in any case, betraying the party of the workers. [We must vote] no first of all and above all because this party demands it of us. All other reasons, valid though they may be, come later...we have no need to interrogate our own personal conscience, which gives precedence to the deeper and larger one of the party we belong to."[10]

As an expression of profound democratic convictions of the party leadership, such a statement needs little comment. It might be dismissed as a mere journalistic blunder. Unfortunately, it is serious and reflects the extent to which the party has become virtually impaled on the point of its own lance defending democratic institutions. These are institutions that, given the current economic and social crisis, and in the absence of a true political opposition, can only develop in the direction of greater authoritarianism. Through an ironically dialectical process, the PCI has agreed to become co-participant and collaborator in a regime whose fundamental contradictions are becoming daily more acute. In order to assume its position as assistant manager (it would be incorrect to say partner) of the DC in this system, it is ineluctably forced to take on the role of defender of law and order, of the status quo, of the existing state and form of power—which means, in the final analysis, relinquishing the very role of opposition force that gave it political strength and autonomy in the first place.

During the period of the 1950s and throughout most of the 1960s, the left was engaged in a frontal conflict with the Christian Democrats. It represented an authentic opposition, and therefore was able to block the most reactionary and authoritarian trends developing in Italy. However, since around 1969—that is, since the consolidation of its policy as co-participant, rather than opponent, of the DC—the party has adopted the position that "defense of republican institutions" is an indispensable goal, necessary to protect these institutions against terrorist attacks. This is the real heart of the contradiction: what might be called the illusion that an authoritarian, repressive direction in the legislative and police apparatus might be necessary, in fact indispensable, for defending the conquests of the working class and popular grassroots movements. There is absolutely nothing to justify this illusion. With respect to combating terrorism, it has proven a thoroughly bankrupt policy: from 1974 to the present, the authoritarian tendency has simply exacerbated the parallel increase of political and common crime, without diminishing or controlling it in the least.

Furthermore, the role adopted by the PCI—that of a pressure group working within and upon, rather than against, the hegemonic forces has simply permitted the Christian Democrats to maintain their monopoly over the government, actually going over to the counter-offensive and forcing both the labor movement and the PCI itself into an increasingly defensive position. Within the general context of this counter-offensive, the traditional roles have been reversed. Instead of the guilty party, the DC now assumes the status of a victim, and the guilty elements thus become permissiveness, social conflict, open demonstrations of anger and frustration; in short, any challenge to the established order. And it should not be forgotten that as soon as the PCI shows signs of overstepping its accepted boundaries and reclaiming its role as oppositional force, the DC, now in a position of arrogant inviolability, can turn against the Communists the accusation of fomenting violence. As a conservative Italian newspaper editor, Indro Montanelli, wrote in April, 1978:

> "[The responsiblity of the Christian Democrats for the average Italian's loss of faith in democracy] lies not so much in their having destroyed the state as in their having allowed the state to be destroyed by the Communist Party. Today the party has assumed a peaceful, legalistic, democratic mask. For 30 years, however, it has done nothing but sabotage all the institutions and infiltrate all the ganglia of social life— administration, education, mass media, judicial system, police and armed forces—corrupting them in the process...The sole political force that can substitute itself for democracy while pretending to defend it is the Communist Party, which is, in fact, renewing its pressure to be invited into the government ...Today the Communists are right when they say that they alone would be able to combat terrorism. That is true. But at the price of another—a legalized, institutionalized terror that would make our days more peaceful but our nights far more uneasy. I myself have received in my own body four Red Brigade bullets. But I prefer the Red Brigades to a Communist regime that would inevitably convert them into its secret police."[11]

To rantings of this nature the PCI, given its present stance, can do no more than protest in righteous indignation and reiterate once again its absolute dedication to democracy and order. This will not help. The Christian Democrats, and their various right-wing allies, have regained the upper hand. And the Red Brigades and other terrorist groups have aided them immeasurably in this by allowing them to assume the image of the ultimate bulwark of order, the responsible party, co-equal with the strong and responsible state.

In May, 1978, approximately ten percent of the voting population went to the polls to elect new municipal and regional governments in some parts of Italy. The results showed an alarming decrease in support for the PCI: a loss of fully one-fourth of its popular vote, when measured against the last parliamentary elections held in the same regions in June 1976. Of course, there is always a disproportion in popular support for the various parties between local or administrative elections, and parliamentary ones. Logically, political parties nearly always gather a higher percentage of popular votes in parliamentary than in local elections. When measured against its success in previous local elections held in the same areas, Communist Party votes actually increased very slightly (0.6%). The important point, however, is that the rate of decrease in voter support for the PCI was quite drastic, not only with respect to all previous defeats, but also compared to the results for all other major parties. The PCI was the only one which registered a truly dramatic setback from the June, 1976, parliamentary elections. In fact, with the sole exception of the neo-fascist MSI-DN, all the other major parties increased their electoral percentages. Moreover, the party which emerged unconditionally victorious on all local fronts was the DC, with a dramatic increase in votes—not only since the last parliamentary elections (3.8%) but since the last local ones as well (5.9%). The DC triumph was the salient fact of this election, and particularly noteworthy in that it signalled the reversal of a downward trend which had been rather steady for nearly a decade.

To be sure, this vote can be interpreted largely as a demonstration of sympathy with the Christian Democrats following Moro's assassination. Nevertheless, close analysis of the working-class vote in those cities and towns where local elections took place revealed that many constituencies of the traditional PCI base turned away from the party. (This fact was readily discernable to its officials, for almost immediately following the elections, a series of worried meetings took place at different levels, from the Secretariat and Central Committee to local and regional party headquarters. It was obvious, even from the guarded and laconic comments of party spokespersons, that some rather serious self-criticism took place at those sessions.) In general, the May 14 elections must be seen as symptomatic of a general affirmation of the center-right (with the DC in the lead) and a weakening of the Italian left.

The Christian Democrats, however, realize that they are not in a position to turn this relative victory into an all-out attack against the PCI, the unions, or the left in general. By itself, it would be nearly impossible for the DC to achieve a parliamentary majority, and if it attempted to constitute itself as a single-party government—the labor movement would still be capable of crippling the economy in retaliation. The elections of May, 1978, therefore, confirm Moro's strategy of cautious confrontation and parliamentary collaboration with the PCI. The resulting support accorded to it by the Communists and the labor movement (in the form of acceptance of at least a sizeable number of proposed "austerity measures") might evade the DC to attenuate the current economic crisis. All the merit for these slight, temporary improvements will accrue to the Christian Democrats, while the PCI stands to gain at most cautious praise for making serious attempts at self-criticism and correction of its general line.

CONCLUSIONS

THE DC CANNOT help but draw tremendous advantage from the

essential disappearance of an opposition which has done it great harm in past years. For some time, it thought that it would be hurt by granting partial legitimacy to the PCI, by accepting it as a partner in the government majority. But now it seems clear that, given the cautious, tolerant, "open" position espoused by Moro, such collaboration will not work to its detriment. Its traditional supporters will not abandon it, realizing clearly that the policy of "national unity" (collaboration with the Communists) is rendered absolutely necessary by its own electoral weakness. Once again, it appears that the DC is capable of playing a truly hegemonic role in defending public order and social tranquility.

It seems most unlikely that the PCI, in turn, will change direction or go beyond limited changes and corrections in immediate, short-range tactics, up to the point of transforming its basic strategy. The DC is likely to become more rigorous and demanding with respect to the Communist Party and labor movement; it is likely to ask for more concessions in the realms of the economy and social control. If this policy is successful, the Christian Democrats will in all likelihood try to obtain a double victory: first, by driving the PCI still further away from a position of effective power within the government, making it accept an increasingly subordinate role; and secondly, by weakening and wearing down the party without actually driving it back into the oppositon.

This is the bleak picture facing the mass left in Italy, and the real quandary out of which it must somehow find an exit. The dilemma also lays a great burden on the "extra-parliamentary" or radical left, which must now face the difficult work of recuperating its forces and rebuilding the bases for some sort of unitary strategy and program in the face of widespread confusion, mistrust, and apathy, not to speak of continued violence on both left and right. Finally, it has to reconstitute itself as a catalyst and leader for vast masses of the population that no longer can identify their interests with those of the mass-based left parties and labor organizations; and at the same time it must provide political direction for these forces to work directly on the institutions of the state—as well as indirectly on the leading left-wing formations, toward the goal of a truly democratic and socialist society. This is a long, exhausting task, requiring vast reserves of revolutionary patience.

SINCE THE ASSASSINATION of Aldo Moro, Italy has continued to live under the lengthening shadow of political terrorism, in a climate of deep social tension and malaise. The Moro crime proved to be just one link in a grotesque chain of threats, violent attacks and reprisals. On January 25, '79, for the first time in postwar Italian history, a Communist Party member and labor leader was the victim of left-wing terrorism. Guido Rossa, a Genoese representative to the powerful metal- and machine-workers' union (FLM), was machine-gunned to death by a Red Brigades commando, ostensibly in retaliation for his court testimony identifying a factory co-worker as a BR agent. In truth, Rossa, a highly principled and dedicated union militant, had simply acted according to the dictates of his conscience when summoned to appear at a preliminary hearing on a suspected terrorist. He affirmed that he had seen the man shortly after a pile of leaflets, signed by the Red Brigades, had been found in his wing of the plant. This hardly constituted enough testimony to condemn the suspect, but it proved more than sufficient to kill Rossa. The usual communique, sent to a newspaper shortly after his death, defined him as a spy, servent of the multinational oppressors, and traitor to the working class. His factory and party associates apparently did not agree: Rossa's funeral was attended by an enormous throng, composed mainly of working class people, and the prevailing mood was more angry than mournful—angry at the government, the Christian Democrats, and the entire present political situation.

Less than a week after this event, another left-wing attack—even more grim and disconcerting because of its lack of even minimal justification—claimed the life of a respected Milanese jurist named Emilio Alessandrini. It was Alessandrini's patient, tenacious work, carried out in near-total isolation and against tremendous obstacles, which had gradually exposed the "black trial" of complicity leading from the 1969 Milan bank bombing to the fascist group *Ordine Nuovo*, and from there to the highest echelons of the military intelligence service. For nearly a decade Alessandrini had continued to accumulate evidence and data on the conspiracy, a project which remained his major focus of interest. In recent months he had also presided at a few hearings on left-wing terrorist suspects, pronouncing sentences—minor ones, for the most part—and insisting on scrupulous observation of the civil and political rights of the suspects. His death was proclaimed a victory by *Prima Linea* (Front Line), a rival organization of the Red Brigades. The group's communique identified Alessandrini as a dangerous agent of the capitalist state, because he played an objective role as force of "legitimation" for one of its most oppressive institutions: the legal system. However, the leftist authorship of this crime is open to speculation. Shortly before his death Alessandrini claimed that he was on the brink of making the most spectacular series of revelations thus far concerning military and government involvement in the terrorist bombings of the late 1960s and early 1970s. It would seem logical that the forces most directly interested in preventing these facts from coming to light occupy the right of the political spectrum, whereas the hard-line "communist" organization claiming responsibility for the assassination could provide only the most spurious, insubstantial justification of it from a left-wing standpoint. At any rate, Alessandrini's death was greeted with shock and indignation, and the mass of mourners that turned out to honor his memory clearly identified him, through slogans and tributes, as a friend of the left.

Although terrorism was not the major cause of the Italian government's fall last January 26, it stood conspicuously in the background. Pressured, on the one hand, by the government's failure to take action on any of the promised reform measures, and on the other by repeated signs of restlessness among both its actual and potential supporters, the PCI finally withdrew its support from the majority, initiating the 38th governmental crisis in postwar Italy. Among the main reasons for his party's withdrawal, Enrico Berlinguer cited the lack of seriousness with which the PCI's often-repeated position on terrorism had been greeted by the other parties, particularly the DC. In the message presented to the parties of the "constitutional arc" (the non-fascist majority) on the occasion of the PCI's separation from the dominant parliamentary coalition, Berlinguer stated: "A campaign was conducted, mainly by the DC, against our party, singled out as ideologically and politically responsible for terrorism at the very moment when, during the Moro episode, we offered exemplary proof of firmness in the defense of democracy and solidarity toward the government and the DC itself, which had been stricken in the (person of) its most authoritative leader."

It seems clear, examining the text of Berlinguer's address, that it was meant not only as a dignified criticism of the DC, but also as a reassurance, directed toward the doubtful elements of its own base, that it did not intend to wait forever or to relinquish its heritage of popular struggle and opposition. "As far as we Communists are concerned," said Berlinguer toward the conclusion of his statement, "we maintain that we have given constant demonstrations of (our) sense of responsibility, commitment to unity, patience, and loyal support of the government. But...we must now ask ourselves whether you have not mistaken this sense of responsibility for willingness to back down; whether you haven't really believed that we were going to participate in the majority as a sort of apprenticeship or (proof of) democratic legitimacy; that in any case we would be contented and satisfied, no matter how things went, simply to belong to the majority. Whoever believed this has been seriously mistaken."

At this writing, the major problem for the PCI appears to be how, precisely, it will manage to convince the other parties and its own base that its opponents have been "seriously mistaken." As repeated efforts to constitute a new government satisfactory to all sides have thus far proved fruitless—and the DC shows itself more determined than ever to refuse granting the Communists their coveted cabinet posts—early elections seem to offer the only possible solution to the current political crisis. The PCI had fervently hoped to avoid them; polls indicate that it will be fortunate to maintain its previous electoral percentage without losing ground. If this turns out to be the case, the party will be working from a position of even less political leverage than before, and can offer faint hope for resolving the nation's acute problems or halting the upward spiral of political terrorism.

Notes

1. Jane Kramer, "A Reporter in Europe: Rome," *The New Yorker,* May 2, 1977.
2. Quoted in *l'Espresso,* May 14, 1978, p. 15.
3. *Ibid.*
4. The expression "strategy of tension" was first used by left-wing commentators, but quickly became part of the general political vernacular. It has always been applied to political tension within a right-wing matrix. To my knowledge, no analogous expression has yet been coined to refer to left-wing terrorism. An impressive array of documentary materials and reports is available on the "Strategy of tension." To cite only a few of the best-known public sources: Camilla Cederna, *Pinelli: una finestra sulla strage* (Milano: Feltrinelli, 1972); Marco Sassono, *La politica della strage* (Padova: Marsilio, 1973); Vincenzo Nardella, *Noi accusiamo: Contro requisitoria per la strage di Stato* (Milano: Jaca Book, 1971); Alessandro Colletti, *Anarchici e questori* (Padova: Marsilio, 1972); Corrado Stajano and Marco Fini, *La forza della democrazia* (Torino: Einaudi, 1977).
5. General Vito Miceli, co-founder of an extreme right-wing paramilitary organization called *La rosa dei venti*, helped plan a coup attempt in 1972, an abortive enterprise in which he was assisted by various other members of the military top brass and by certain sectors of the traditionally reactionary Roman aristocracy. Although called to trial for his part in the coup plot, Miceli was acquitted for lack of conclusive evidence that could be brought against him.
6. An excellent general left-wing assessment is *Sulla violenza: Politica e terrorismo—un dibattito nella sinistra* (Roma: Savelli, 1978).
7. Quoted in *l'Espresso,* March 26, 1978, p. 11.
8. Quoted in *Le Monde,* March 22, 1978.
9. *l'Unità,* May 10, 1978.
10. *l'Unità,* June 10, 1978.
11. Quoted in the *New York Times,* April 21, 1978, p. 27.

chapter 7

ITALY:
THE FEMINIST CHALLENGE

Annarita Buttafuoco

THE RELATIONSHIP between the Communist Party and the women's movement in Italy cannot be analyzed according to any clear-cut schema. Their historical pattern of interaction is so complex as to defy simple generalizations. For one thing, the "women's movement" as such doesn't really exist in Italy; it is a concept employed in a situation where hope prevails over reality, and thus serves to obscure rather than enhance political understanding. There is, however, a *feminist* movement, which is divided internally among several groups that often differ greatly over questions of analysis and strategy. First of all, there is the *Unione Donne Italiane* (UDI)—the Italian Women's Union—which is independent of the major political parties, but whose activists are primarily recruited from the ranks of the traditional left (the PCI and the Socialist Party) and whose relationship to the feminist groups has always been tense. In addition, there are the women's commissions attached to the political parties and trade unions, which have at times adopted positions critical of the dominant male orientation of these organizations.

A body of rich political and cultural experience is developing among Italian women. Awareness of the specific characteristics of women's oppression is growing, despite the social, economic, and political burdens that confine women to domestic life.

At the same time, there looms the presence of the PCI, which advances the legitimate claim that it has always taken up the "woman question" in its political strategy. Yet the PCI has often wound up sacrificing the deepest needs of women in favor of more "general" political issues, "broader" strategies, and mediations that have sometimes been disastrous for the advance of the masses of Italian women. From such sacrifices have emerged the complex and ambiguous relations between the PCI and women committed to the struggle for their emancipation and liberation—relations that are central to the theoretical debate now underway among women around the question of "the movement and institutions."[1]

THE PCI'S HARSH JUDGMENT

SINCE THE PCI is the most significant political force after the Christian Democratic Party, and is also, despite the transformation that it has undergone, a Marxist party, one would expect it to have advanced women's issues more effectively than has actually been the case. This expectation is based on a generally positive assessment of the PCI's potential long-range role in the transformation of Italian society. The PCI has often been reproached for ignoring, underestimating, and even disdaining women's struggles. While the party is accused of bartering away the most important women's goals through its "pacifying" line of compromise, the real problem may be that the PCI is—by virtue of its very identity—unable to incorporate the revolutionary aspects of the feminist movement. This is an image that the PCI has quite commonly reinforced in practice. For example, its reaction to the birth of the feminist movement was extremely cautious and distrustful; pointing to the movement's radical and American-influenced ideology and to its roots in the student movement of the 1960s, the party alluded to the "foolish idealistic aspirations" and "abstract extremist impatience" of Italian feminism. Thus PCI theorist Luciano Gruppi argues:

> Far from engaging in practical politics, a typical characteristic of these [feminist] movements is an existential experience that reaches the doorstep of politics without really penetrating inside. Since it is the personal that prevails (and perhaps also personal frustration, which is understandable and to be respected), the basis of these movements is too individualistic to bring about awareness of the need for a mass movement (and

for this reason, naturally, the activists cannot have a true understanding of the importance of building ties to the working-class parties, the unions, and the democratic women's organizations).[2]

Gruppi claims, moreover, that the feminists do not devote sufficient attention to the problems of female workers—a category used by the PCI to refer strictly to women employed outside the home (although many feminists argue that housewives should also be regarded as female workers). For Gruppi, such insensitivity is "indicative of these movement's social origins and their essential detachment from the working class. This creates a situation in which the family, procreation, and sexual concerns (which we all see as important) appear to a certain extent isolated from the struggle for jobs, for the rights of women workers, for a specific kind of economic development within which such problems can be effectively solved."[3]

The above quote expresses a rather revealing synthesis of the PCI's attitude toward the feminist movement. It is the petit-bourgeois and professional origins of the movement that, according to the PCI's somewhat schematic approach, impart to it an individualistic character. The feminist rejection of traditional political practice is seen by the PCI as the reason for the inability to link up with mass movements and, as a result, for women's withdrawal into feminist groups that only reinforce individual frustrations. The Italian feminist movement unquestionably has middle class origins, and its initial attitudes in some measure reflected those origins. However, the PCI's harsh judgment can be better understood once we appreciate that many of the groups evolved out of the student movement, were identified in the beginning with the new left, and were strongly critical of the PCI and its reformist strategy. The PCI somewhat clumsily interpreted the criticism of the latter groups as plain anti-communism—refusing to acknowledge any distinctions—and closed itself off from these groups, which represented the largest component of Italian feminism. This is not a banal psychological issue; it has been routine that the PCI react to similar criticism with distrust and rejection. While this attitude is rooted in part in the PCI's persecution, up until little more than a decade ago, it certainly has not helped to enrich its own internal debate.

One contradiction is that while the PCI reproaches feminism for its middle-class origins, the party has in recent years turned increasingly toward that very stratum. The PCI has been consistently attentive to the disquiet of the middle strata, which have traditionally exhibited neither a coherent ideology nor a unifying political line. In this context, the party has tried to present itself as a point of reference for every (even minimally) progressive tendency.

There is also a fear within the PCI that an openness to feminist concerns might set back considerably its strenuous effort to establish a dialogue with the Catholic masses. This fear persists, although those Catholics who accepted the innovative spirit of the Second Vatican Council have shown their openness to such feminist issues as a positive reevaluation of the human body (following centuries of the Church's anti-sexual obscurantism), of the individual's freedom of conscience around such issues as contraception (and even abortion), and of the desire to redefine family relations to remove sex roles that inhibit free expression. There are few such Catholics relative to the Catholic population as a whole, but the Party attributes to the Church mainstream a far more doctrinaire ideology than is actually practiced. The problem is that when the PCI speaks of Catholicism, it is often alluding to the Christian Democrats, who it sees (correctly) as representing the conservatism of large masses of people—attitudes that find their theoretical basis and ideological justification in Catholicism.

Gruppi's exhortation to feminists to overcome their detachment from the working class thus rings false, given the PCI's own stance in the present political context. His argument tends, moreover, to ignore the reasons why the feminist movement has come into serious conflict with the workers' movement, the protagonist in the overthrow of existing social relations. Because the feminist movement challenges even workers' hegemony (as traditionally understood) within those forces committed to transforming the present order, it raises questions about some of the deepest beliefs of the working-class movement itself.[4]

THE FEMINIST RESPONSE

THE SLOGAN popularized by the feminist movement that "the personal is political" contains the essence of the feminist critique of "haute politics." Feminist thought affirms the totality of the human being as opposed to the fragmentation imposed by captialist society—a fragmentation that reduces people to roles (such as worker, father, lover, comrade, etc.). The feminist critique points out that capitalist society, while emphasizing "public" roles, makes no attempt to analyze their interdependence with "private" roles. Women suffer in a specific way from this fragmentation. Except for reassuring myths such as that of the "sublime mission of motherhood," women are almost exclusively relegated to roles traditionally considered to have no social value. It is not by chance, therefore, that women themselves have initiated the revolt and that their theoretical debate has centered around the family as the main sphere of their oppression, where the free expression of their sexuality is contained in the interests of men and the society they represent.

It follows that the feminist insistence on women's control of their own bodies as "political entities" around which to build their liberation is not only political but also embraces an extraordinary revolutionary content insofar as it reveals the basic contradiction between the "human being" and "citizen." PCI spokesperson (and UDI leader) Marisa Rodano failed to grasp this when, in 1973, she wrote:

> The freedom to do as one pleases with one's own body is considered by feminists to be the fundamental—if not exclusive—condition for women's liberation. The emancipation of women is therefore seen in a frustratingly individualistic context, outside of all social relations and reduced in the end to *an attempt to overcome the specificity of women's oppression by having the condition of men serve as the ideal model.*[5]

Of course it would be ridiculous to imagine that a complete, well-defined, and well-articulated political theory could emerge from such a young movement. Biancamaria Frabotta correctly notes that when the left (PCI, PSI, and the far left) blames women for not being sufficiently politicized, for not engaging in direct struggles against capital, it devotes little attention to the impact of women's strong emotional ties with the male "adversary" on the long history of their struggles.[6]

MISTRUST AND theoretical misunderstandings aside, it is in political practice that the relationship between the PCI and the feminist movement (including the UDI) expresses itself most concretely. A good example of this has been the enactment of abortion legislation—the struggle for which has put women in a very painful and frustrating confrontation with the political and social institutions. Because the political forces involved in the abortion issue approach the struggle from different perspectives, the present law was passed only following great divisiveness and many frustrating attempts to reach a solution. The feminist movement went through this process by moving back and forth between periods of public demonstrations and internal debate, with abortion only one of the issues taken up. The abortion issue created the basis for initiating an overall analysis of sexuality, motherhood, sex-role differentiation, and the resulting subordinate position of women. In the feminist movement, the issue developed into a critique of reproduction—that is, of the reproduction of the labor force in capitalism, around which there exist deep antagonisms between classes, within classes, and between the sexes.

In certain sectors of the movement, this critique became so extreme that some collectives refused to participate in the struggles to legalize abortion because they felt that abortion actually reinforced a concept of genital reproductive sexuality dominated by men, and perpetuated male supremacy. In this view, abortion merely confirmed the power of men which, at this historical moment, has no need for an expanding labor force and is therefore disposed toward radical forms of birth control.

Aside from its theoretical discussions, the feminist movement expressed its strength in street demonstrations, in published documents, in collective meetings, and in the formation of women's groups concerned with health care, contraception, and abortion. An organization affiliated with the Radical Party—the Women's Liberation Movement (MLD)—started a petition campaign calling for a referendum designed to repeal the existing repressive legislation. As for the UDI—the only women's organization in which housewives, working class, and peasant women are a majority—while it sees the battle for abortion as a struggle against clandestine abortions (from which thousands of women die each year), it supported its legalization on grounds of its social value in protecting motherhood. The UDI has fought for the recognition of motherhood as a collective resposibility rather than as part of the private domain. But such responsibility does not mean that "control" should be exercised *over* women—simply that they should be free to decide for themselves whether or not to become mothers. The UDI position creates political difficulties, in that it wants the male-dominated institutions that manage Italian society to relinquish control of reproduction to women, which is precisely what men are least disposed to do for they know—whether consciously or not—that this control over reproduction guarantees their power over women.*

The UDI's struggle is virtually a solitary one, to the extent that it places itself between the feminist movement and the working-class parties. From within the former it advances certain "discoveries," such as that of personal politics, that it then reinterprets and offers for inclusion in the political platforms of the parties, as proposals that are more concrete than the (however profound) analyses of the feminist movement itself. The latter deeply mistrusts the UDI, whose history is closely bound

---

*On the other hand, the emphasis on the social value of motherhood grows out of the traditional base of the PCI and of the working class movement; the presence of the UDI, however, imparts a more revolutionary content to this movement to the extent that it places decisively at the center of political struggles the liberation of women—a process that means more than simply the protection of an already-existing motherhood.

up with the PCI's, and which is often regarded as the party's "transmission belt." The feminist movement is critical of the UDI for its excessive timidity, as well as for a political "tacticism" reminiscent of male-dominated political practice.

THE STRUGGLE FOR ABORTION RIGHTS

AS FOR THE PCI, the largest of the working-class parties, its involvement in the abortion struggle has been marked alternately by moments of reserve toward both feminism and the UDI (viewed by many party leaders as having become too feminist), and periods of almost exclusive preoccupation with the concerns of the Christian Democrats, who have assumed an increasingly important role within the framework of the "historic compromise." The PCI's first bill to "Regulate the Voluntary Interruption of Pregnancy," presented to Parliament in February 1975, further widened the gap between the party and the feminist movement. The guiding inspiration of this bill, and of others that followed, was the battle to eliminate clandestine abortions—which for working-class women have been the ultimate recourse to end unwanted pregnancies.[7] The bill called for free medical assistance in public facilities, going beyond the simple demand for depenalization of abortion—a demand that, if met, would keep the termination of pregnancy a private matter to be resolved either in luxurious clinics or in appallingly-hazardous conditions (depending upon the woman's social status).

In contrast to this inspiration were articles that specified the circumstances under which abortions can be performed. First, abortion would be permitted only in the case of a woman whose life or health is endangered by either the pregnancy or the delivery, whose pregnancy is the result of rape or incest, or where there is serious genetic deformity. If taken literally, these are very serious restrictions, even where possibilities for flexible implementation exist. In any case, this bill stipulated (and the present legislation also stipulates) that women who want abortions must demonstrate that the pregnancy or delivery constitutes an imminent danger to their physical or mental health.

Beyond this was another source of conflict between the PCI and the feminist movement—the provision that the final decision must be left up to a three-member commission composed of two doctors and a social worker. It is in this area that women's freedom of choice is most clearly undermined. More than that: after the feminist movement's persistent denunciations of the medical establishment's repressive practices toward women, this provision gave the medical profession vast discretionary powers (similar to a court of law) that constituted a virtually insurmountable obstacle. While the main purpose of the law was presumably to free poor and working-class women from the risk of death by abortion, the plague of clandestine abortions certainly would not be eliminated by placing working-class women (who are intimidated by the authority of the state) before a panel of three "experts" who have the task of ascertaining whether she is telling the truth about her health. (The *"mammana"** asks no questions, since her only interest is money.) For many women, however, the risk of death does not outweigh the risk of having another unwanted child.

The PCI's first bill was bitterly criticized even by women within the party, who felt that the desire to avoid clashes with the DC in parliament could never justify such compromises. At a later point the PCI fought to incorporate women's demands within the subsequent bill jointly written with the other political parties—notably the demand that women must have the right to make the final decision. In the ensuing dramatic events in parliament, the conflict between those favoring the legalization of abortion and those viewing it as a crime revolved around this principle of self-determination*, so much so that in the end, the bill was partially modified, at least in spirit, and the rights of minors were seriously restricted. (In the final version of the bill, the woman does have the final say, though she is required to appear before a commission.)

Further debate took place around an article of the final bill which enables all medical and nursing personnel to refuse to perform abortions on the grounds of conscience. The concept of "conscientious objection" was introduced into Italian legislation in 1972 in the context of military service; the law states that when clear and recognized moral and religious commitments make it impossible for citizens to accept military duty, they can be relieved in exchange for civil service work. This regulation explicitly recognizes the inherently violent nature of military battle. To introduce this kind of objection into abortion legislation suggests that the same criteria apply to the procedure of terminating pregnancies; abortion

---

*"*Mammana*" is a popular disparaging term that refers to women who, lacking medical qualifications, perform abortions with very rudimentary instruments: knitting needles, probes, grass-cutters, and so forth.

*There were reservations even among the most supportive parliamentarians—a fact that was revealed during the secret balloting in the Senate on June 7, 1977. It was following this balloting that the law suffered a setback, even though the vote count itself—computed on the basis of a roll call—created the impression of a narrow victory.

is thus seen as legalized state homicide, in which doctors and nurses are privileged to refuse to take part. Accordingly, while abortion was in principle no longer viewed as a criminal act, in practice it was considered to be such. As far as conscientious objection is concerned, the main problem revolves around the boundaries the state ought to establish in protecting the moral and religious beliefs of certain citizens when such beliefs run counter to the interests of the community at large. How is it possible for the state, in this situation, simultaneously to permit abortion and recognize the legitimacy of claims that abortion constitutes murder? This contradiction is not easily solved—nor, on another level, is that of guaranteeing women the right to secrecy (binding the doctor and the nursing staff to professional confidence), since this too tends to perpetuate the concept of abortion as a crime.

WHAT WAS THE PCI's approach to these issues? Not only did the party leadership fail to raise questions about the validity of including protection for "conscientious objectors," but it also included this formulation in its original proposals, without supplying any rationale. This clearly corresponds to the PCI's constant readiness to take into account the role of general interests as much as possible—in this case to gain credibility among Catholics, while establishing a point of convergence with the DC in parliament. In search of accord with the DC, the PCI consented stage-by-stage to changes within the Senate after the bill had already been approved in the Chamber.[1] These changes further weakened the abortion legislation. Although the final law was the result of a compromise among all the "lay" parties, it was the PCI's commitment to a policy of "broad consensus" that in the end prevailed. If today the Italians have an abortion law—which in itself is a great achievement—they owe it to the PCI. At the same time, they also owe *this* law to the PCI.

The bitterness and anger of women active in the feminist movement toward the PCI's maneuvering during parliamentary negotiations is understandable and justifiable, even though a more general analysis of party strategy would have revealed the risk women encountered in withdrawing from their efforts to put pressure on the political parties. The bitterness grew more acute when the Communist press characterized as huge victories those actions which were only small (if necessary) first steps. Yet it was hardly correct simply to accuse the PCI of compromising issues that are directly related to women's everyday lives. (Although as women we will have to fear the PCI's invitation to "sacrifices.") Such mediations are far more general and must be seen as part of a strategy having deep roots in the PCI's history. It is necessary to realize that the PCI's attitude toward the role of women has always followed its overall perspective, even if at times the party has appeared to extend itself more toward women's struggles than at others. The PCI's basic strategy must be systematically analyzed. The tendency to single out particular episodes and struggles opens up the risk of either uncritical glorification or total condemnation.

THE ORIGINS OF PCI STRATEGY

IT IS IMPORTANT to attempt a general overview of the development of the so-called "woman question" in the political line of the PCI. Such an effort might prove most fruitful if, alongside the analysis of writings and speeches of PCI leaders, it was possible to determine the degree of openness to particular issues within the base, and the nature of the dialectic between the leadership and the popular base. In other words, it would be interesting to know how much the still peasant-influenced patriarchal culture of Italy (a culture rather widespread among workers) was responsible for the PCI's foot-dragging and lack of understanding. Or, on another level, how much has the new consciousness among women (to the extent that such a consciousness has developed) been misinterpreted or held back by the party leadership? All this would require a research effort that Italian historiography has yet to take on; all we have, for the time being, are hypotheses.

IN THE EARLY 1920s, the PCI was faced with both the exhaustion of the suffrage movement and the dispersion of many of its supporters, after World War I, into either the Socialist Party or the newly-born Fascist Party, from which the suffragists hoped to secure the right to vote.[8] Moreover, the struggles of women workers—who had participated in working-class mobilizations during and after World War I—subsided following the expulsion of women from the work force to make room for veterans returning from the war. At that time the PCI's attitude toward women reflected two apparently contradictory, but in fact complementary positions: Lenin's perceptive analysis of women's oppression,[9] and the limited approach of the Third International. According to guidelines established by the Second Congress of the Comintern in 1920, a weekly column called "Women's Tribune" was started in the pages of *Ordine Nuovo* and assigned to Camilla Rivera.

The analysis contained in the "Tribune" during its two years of publication (1921-22) offers a good picture of the Italian political situation and indicates how stereotypes were established then that would be carried forward in the following years.[10] The women addressed by the "Tribune" (and through it by the PCI) were above all women working outside the home as part of a presumably "revolutionary" proletariat. Here the PCI did not regard the struggles of working women as in any sense "marginal;" on the contrary, it viewed them as *working-class* struggles. The fact that the protagonists were women was not particularly significant.[11]

Herein lies the fundamental and yet unresolved contradiction between a political practice that did not yet theoretically differentiate between men and women, and an approach relating specifically to the social existence of women. For the PCI, there was (and continues to be) a single fixed point: it is as a *producer* that an individual, whether man or woman, gains social value. It follows that female emancipation, which can ultimately occur only in a communist society, will develop out of the *economic* independence that women are able to attain. Hence: "Like a man, the woman must be prepared to become a productive and active member of society and to secure her economic independence."[12] The housewife must vanish, according to this analysis, because she is an isolated and unproductive worker:

> It is necessary to make women aware of the irrationality of today's individually-structured household, its resulting squandering of time and energy, and the feeling of submission associated with women's work. The present conditions, under which women exhaust themselves from morning to night without creating anything, must be contrasted with those of a communist society, with its communal kitchens, day-care centers, and all the other institutions serving to alleviate the burden of housework and freeing vast female energies to carry out production and cultural work.[13]

The early PCI followed a "workerist" policy toward women corresponding to the general lines of its political strategy. Meanwhile, the uncertainty and ambiguity of party messages directed to women reveal the difficulty involved in recognizing women *only* as workers. For there is yet another social reality for women. Whereas a man might be seen during those years as essentially a worker (insofar as the roles of husband and father could be fulfilled while the male was economically supporting his wife and children), for women quite the contrary was the case. Since a woman's social definition stems from her sexual role, she is above all a mother and a wife and only *secondarily* (perhaps) a worker. Herein lies the source of the PCI's lack of an organic policy toward women. Yet this uncertainty grew out of a searching process that was typical of all aspects of PCI activity during the early years.[14] It also grew out of the PCI's relationship to the Comintern, which expressed a similar ambivalence toward women's issues.

In the early 1920s, therefore, the PCI remained silent on the issue of women's suffrage, limiting itself to asking women to intensify their propaganda activity at election time. Not that the PCI hadn't confronted this issue; it did so, however, only within the terms laid down by the manifesto of the Comintern's Second Congress (which was reprinted in *Ordine Nuovo*). The manifesto begins with an invective against "those charlatans who seek to placate women with alms such as the right to vote." It continues:

> Do not let yourselves be swayed from your path. The political rights that bourgeois society may concede or promise you will not provide you with economic freedom. Only a victory of the working class will bring you and your (male) comrades true freedom and equality.

At the same time, the manifesto emphasizes that among the tasks of the Comintern must be that of "intensifying the development of propaganda for the conquest of women's civil rights."[15]

This contradiction reflected the nature of internal debate within the international Communist movement—a debate that became lively within the PCI, connected as it was to the question of participation within bourgeois parliaments.[16] From this manifesto, however, emerged a sharp critique of bourgeois feminism that was articulated through only a partial evaluation of the objectives and activities of the Italian women's movement, and which to this date has never been totally abandoned. Addressing this general point, Felicita Ferrerro was correct when she observed:

> In Germany women won the right to vote, which was a noteworthy moral conquest, and through their representatives in parliament women workers of Germany secured some reforms, but their social and economic status has not improved. And this teaches us that legislation protecting mothers, infants, and both female and child labor can be obtained from any bourgeois or social-democratic government, but the female worker will always find herself having to choose between an economically independent life (deprived, however, of the joys of family and motherhood) and a life at home (but economically subjugated to a man, if she no longer works, or oppressed by the work at the shop or office and by the weariness of housework).[17]

Yet to pass judgment on the *inadequacy* of emancipationist tactics within the bourgeois system does not mean that the feminist movement (which from the outset denounced the hypocrisy of formally proclaiming the right to "freedom" and "equality") should be so brusquely dismissed without a more extensive (even if critical) analysis. The PCI's rejection of bourgeois feminism was an expression of its rejection of any social phenomenon not perceived as grounded immediately in working-class experience. At the same time, the "feminism" proposed by Camilla Rivera, for example, goes much too far in its absolute faith in a communist revolution, especially in view of how rapidly social objectives concerning women and the family were subverted in Russia after the revolution. Ravera placed too much emphasis on the tasks that "nature" has presumably conferred on the two sexes. Though she insisted that male and female values are not unequal, but simply different, her argument is dangerous in that there will always be those ready to use any reference to "natural differences" against the female sex.

The issue of women's suffrage was taken up again in 1925, when Fascist minister Acerbo proposed to limit severely the voting rights of women.[18] The Communists immediately opposed such restrictions and countered with their own proposal:

> The Chamber affirms the equality of the sexes with respect to the administrative and political vote, based on the principle that all those who are producers and do not exploit others have the right to vote.[19]

Communist deputy Ruggiero Greco, in a speech before parliament, outlined a modified PCI position on the role of women which emphasized that "women's contribution to the productive process alone gives them the right to contribute to political life." But it also affirmed that women whose only work is housework—"the most tiring, least productive, most barbaric, and dreary of work"—also have the same right. In Grieco's speech there was a more egalitarian interest in the social condition of women, a new openness to life-experiences that are different from those of women employed in social production. Only a year later, however, Teresa Noce reaffirmed at the Third International Women's Conference in Moscow that women workers were more politically important than the wives of workers.[20]

THE LIMITS OF THE PCI'S EARLY POSITION

THE PCI'S EARLY position on the role of women was quite fragmentary. Two basic points—the family and motherhood—need to be more fully explored. The Russian Revolution had begun to redefine, in revolutionary terms, the relationship between men and women. Lenin claimed that "no democratic party in any of the most advanced bourgeois republics has done in ten years even one-hundredth of what we have accomplished in just the first year we were in power."[21] New social legislation transformed marriage rights so as to recognize the total equality between spouses while conceding the same rights to illegitimate as to legitimate children.[22] Beyond laws, however, there emerged a new moral posture toward love and sexual relations that Alexandra Kollontai expressed in her book *Communism and the Family*. The events that followed are well-known: Kollontai was subjected to violent attacks for her views, while many of the initial achievements were eventually limited or reversed. The following conception of communism could no longer be accepted in the climate of the New Economic Policy (NEP), which was designed to revitalize the domestic economy and therefore required the free labor of women in the household:

> Can the brief duration, the irregularity, the freedom of sexual relations be seen, from the perspective of working humanity, as a crime, as an act that must be punished? Obviously not. Freedom of sexual relations does not contradict the ideology of communism. The interests of the community are in no way harmed by the fact that a marriage is short or long-lived, that it is based on love, passion, or a passing physical attraction. The only thing that is damaging to the working community...is the element of material calculation that intervenes in the relationship between a man and a woman, both in the form of prostitution and in that of legal matrimony.[23]

Camilla Ravera accepted Kollantai's message in its specific denunciation of the invisible prostitution of women who, not being able to support themselves through their own wages, are forced to depend upon a man (father, brother, husband, or lover). Real prostitutes, Ravera noted, merely sell themselves more "honestly."[25] Ravera accepted an essentially conservative view of the family, seeing in it certain innate values—overlooking the socialist perspective (already advanced by Marx, Engels, and Bebel) that saw it as an ideological prop of the bourgeois state. For Ravera (and for the PCI), not even in a communist society would it be possible to abolish the family or women's role within it.[26]

An unsigned *Ordino Nuovo* article, "Socialist Revolution and Women," lamented the disappearance of the "domestic hearth" of peace and serenity that was presumably destroyed by capitalism, forcing women into the factories. Even if the article concludes with a reassuring tone based on the position that in a new society women's economic independence "would be a natural fact and not a feminist contrivance,"[27] the impression that remains is one of surrender to romantic idealizations of a family environment that in reality was characterized by severe abuses of power and violence against women.

On the issue of birth control, the PCI's stand was more flexible; it even hinted, ever so timidly, at the right to abortion. Yet it was still limited in comparison to Kollontai's approach. Motherhood as a matter of free choice was referred to only with respect to working women, so that the debate was not extended to all women. Once again, women were recognized only as producers. Even motherhood by choice—a theme that theoretically brought together women of all classes—was examined only from this partial viewpoint. Still, when viewed in the context of the (primarily economic) struggles of the time, the fact that the issue was raised at all is noteworthy. Above all, it is to the PCI's merit that it did recognize the social value of motherhood by questioning its isolated and privatized character, its "natural destiny," and the myth of sacrifice that surrounds it.

The PCI's general approach to women and the family remained essentially unchanged until 1944, when Palmiro Togliatti presented the basis of a more extensive and profound analysis. The rise of fascism in the 1920s had forced the party into a very selective political practice, and had meant that activity around what it perceived as less central issues (such as those relating to women) was set aside or suppressed.[28]

TOGLIATTI'S NEW POINT OF DEPARTURE

DURING THE RESISTANCE, women entered the political arena in large numbers. They apparently did so, however, without bringing to the mass struggles the range of feminist issues that might have reflected their new sense of dignity.[29] The testimony of women who were active during those years (1943-45) clearly reveals that they saw the end of fascism as a general catharsis that would tear away all forms of domination. The partisan struggles were carried out in the name of political and social liberation without the formulation of any specific objectives concerning the status of women. The enthusiasm of the Liberation was followed by a profound sense of disillusionment.

The only party to deal comprehensively with women's struggles was the PCI. Togliatti's speeches on this topic are still today considered by many to be the most advanced expression of Communist thought on this topic—notably his emphasis on the need for an autonomous women's organization that could develop a political understanding of the *specific* nature of women's oppression. Thus: "The emancipation of women cannot be the problem of one party, or even one class. The unity of all Italian women, who should be considered a social group with common interests, must be achieved."[30] The novelty of such a position for the PCI was obvious. Already at the end of the nineteenth century the women's suffrage movement had attempted to bring together all women regardless of their political persuasion, but it failed to do so.[31] It was precisely this approach that was later criticized by both the Socialists and (for reasons already cited) the PCI. But now, after having survived the underground and having lived through the experience of armed struggle in which women of all social strata and political viewpoints participated, the PCI was prepared for a break with the past. Togliatti gathered together this experience and directed it towards a specific policy that would free women to speak for themselves and promote their own struggles.

The *svolta* (turning point) of Salerno in 1944 called for the PCI's transformation into a new kind of party—from an organization based upon cadres or professional revolutionaries to one based upon the masses, "capable of inserting itself actively, broadly, and constructively into the political life of the country..."[32] Awareness that a truly popular party could not be built without the active participation of the female population drove Togliatti to resolve one of the "knots" in the party's political line. Women (not as workers but as women) were called on to claim their rightful place in the reconstruction of Italian society following the overthrow of fascism; this was part of the PCI's attempt to develop a broad democratic consciousness that would go beyond a strict class consciousness. Hence the PCI—alone among the major Italian parties— committed itself to the struggle for women's suffrage.* This meant proceeding at a pace appropriate to a slowly-evolving collective maturation process that would make allowances for the enormous disparities in custom, tradition, and culture throughout Italy as a whole. In short, it meant having respect for those who—still tied to old conceptions of the family and the role of women—feared abrupt changes, especially those imposed from above. At the same time, Togliatti's political vision entailed an ongoing commitment to formulating and diffusing new ideas and to realistic political action that would lead slowly to the radical transformation of Italian society.

Yet alongside this idealistic vision, the PCI's concrete political practice did not evolve through open debate and struggle but through a firmly-established leadership line that continued to accept the family

---

*Togliatti states: "Regardless of how women might choose to vote, they must attain the consciousness of this elementary right. Those women who today have not arrived at a particular solution to various problems must nevertheless vote according to their conscience and their convictions; we can never accept the idea that the Communist Party—a party of liberty and progress—is capable of imposing narrow party interests, or even the smallest barrier, in the path of mass female emancipation." *Op. Cit.* p. 47.

more or less as a "given." For Togliatti, the family would have to be renewed and transformed as part of destroying its "feudal" character; at the same time, in a country corrupted by fascism and destroyed by war, there would be a "need to defend the family unit."[33] In an attempt to stave off accusations of "immorality" levelled against the Communists, this statement closed ranks around traditional views in a way designed to cut off any debate around the question of the family—despite widespread hopes for postwar reforms (including divorce legislation). Moreover, the war-time reality of social dislocation, in which many families disintegrated as husbands and wives became separated and often wound up creating new families, appeared to encourage a more flexible position.

The passage of article 7 of the Italian Constitution, which was supported by the PCI and which in effect ratified the Concordat between the Italian government and the Vatican engineered by Mussolini in 1929, served for thirty years as a stumbling block to real collective debate around the issue of divorce.*

In reality, Togliatti's renewed emphasis on the family as the sphere where social consciousness is formed, as the basic structure of Italian society, marked the return to a viewpoint typical of the PCI's formative period—without, however, any critique of housework. The party did fight for article 29 of the Constitution, which would guarantee the legal and moral equality of spouses, and it did continue the struggle to give this article real content—which was finally realized with the passage of the family reform law in 1975. But there was still no intention of questioning traditional roles and, therefore, no attempt to raise the issue of women's domestic work.

All this is understandable in the context of the PCI's postwar self-definition; no longer in opposition to bourgeois democracy, it viewed itself as struggling within the electoral and parliamentary arenas, as seeking to win more freedom by fighting within them. One consequence of this was that the party no longer called into question the capitalist system, even though it continued to fight for the elimination of its most acute forms of exploitation.

---

*Nilde Jotti, in "I diritti della donna alla Costizuzione," *Donne e politica*, nos. 5-6, 1971, emphasizes, however, that to raise the question of divorce in 1946 would have been considerably premature given the underdeveloped conditions of women in the south and, in particular, the immediate postwar situation of demobilization.

THE PCI'S POSTWAR RETREAT

ONE OF THE main foundations of the capitalist economy—camouflaged by the ideology of women's "natural tasks"—is unpaid domestic labor, which reproduces the labor force both in the sense of the biological reproduction of children and as a guarantee of services (housecleaning, cooking, recreation, sex, etc.) that are needed by the male worker to alleviate his inevitable alienation within the capitalist organization of work. The PCI position, however, has ignored this fact: it has dwelled instead on the demand for social services that could remove some of the burden of female housework (especially in cases where women also work outside the home)—an approach far-removed from the viewpoint **developed by the PCI in the early 1920s. During the 1950s the parliamentary battles around such issues related specifically to protective** legislation for working mothers, the demand for publicly-financed daycare centers, the opening of new schools, and equal pay for equal work. These battles were generally supported by UDI-organized popular demonstrations of women throughout Italy.

The PCI's increasing parliamentary strength has enabled the party to shape decisively the content and success of social measures related to women's lives, even if many laws passed in legislative bodies were never fully implemented. At the same time, such successes have not been accompanied by any extensive debate within the party dealing with the specific nature of women's oppression or problems related to the "private sphere." Even the struggle against the repeal of the divorce law in 1974 was presented by the PCI as "anti-fascist" and "modernizing" rather than as a radical critique of family relations.* In fact, beginning in 1970 with the first stirrings of a referendum to repeal the divorce law, the PCI strenuously attempted to hold off the referendum on grounds that it might provoke a disastrous "religious war" and split the country in half. Throughout this campaign, the PCI continuously reafffirmed the integrity of the family against the "hypocrisy" of marriages held together merely on a legal basis.

*Adriana Seroni wrote, before the referendum: "We ask and will continue to ask all Italian women who have democratic sensibilities, and who have a sense of responsibility regarding national priorities, to reject the kind of dangerous designs proposed by the right wing within the framework of the referendum—on behalf of the struggle for a democratic order." In "Le donne italiane e il Referendum," republished in A. Seroni, *La Questione femminile in Italia, 1970-77 (Roma, 1977).*

As it turned out, the PCI's anticipation that the referendum would pass and overturn the divorce law failed to take into account the widespread change in customs that had been taking place in Italy. In this case, the party wound up directing too much attention toward pockets of traditionalism in its efforts to appear as a champion of stability and tradition. Thus:

> We Commmunists, expressing the profoundly wholesome conception of the family held by those workers, peasants and popular masses that we represent, want a vital and united family. Our sanction of the divorce law does not contradict this...The introduction of divorce has thus for us only one object: to permit the resolution of those situations where the family no longer exists and where it cannot be reconstructed.[34]

This position is meant to oppose "anarchistic individualism" and the "egoism of individuals" which, according to the PCI, characterize the approach to divorce of political forces such as the Radical Party.

The PCI's desire to avoid any clash with the most deeply-rooted traditions in Italy raises the issue of the role of the mass party—a formation that can bring together elements of an increasingly-diversified popular base. Should the party act as a proponent of progressive demands, while extending debate to the least responsive strata of the population, or should its role be to move ahead slowly, yielding to the latter's hopes for reassurance? In the case of divorce, the PCI chose the second path. For, even though it called on its militants to make a "progressive" choice, it defined that choice in strictly "anti-fascist"terms.

The resounding defeat of the referendum—coinciding with the PCI's "surprise" at discovering the importance of the women's vote in passing the divorce law—confronted the party with the need to redefine its main areas of political intervention. The problem, for the PCI, is how to mobilize women effectively without at the same time upsetting already existing political alliances. In particular, the success of the women's movement in raising the issue of sexuality has dramatically convinced the party leadership to take up actively the issue of birth control. At the outset, the PCI was reluctant to confront this problem. The repeal of fascist legislation designed to protect the "integrity and health of the race" (which also prohibited education dealing with methods of birth control), was once again perceived by the PCI as a dangerous occasion for clashes with conservative Catholics—clashes that might undermine its overall strategy of conciliation with the governing elites.

The major competing forces, however, are no longer simply the political parties: women are applying pressure from within institutions, and the PCI risks bearing the greatest responsibility for delays within the political system in addressing the wide range of issues posed by the new women's consciousness. The PCI confronted the issue of contraception not so much in terms of individual choice, but as part of what was generally understood as sex education. Together with the passage of the abortion law, it demanded that sex education be taught in all schools and that "*consultori*" (counseling centers) be opened for couples (rather than specifically for women, as the feminist movement sought).

Even here, however, the PCI's caution around the role of women in the *consultori* has generated considerable debate around the issue of women's medicine, self-help, and, above all, the extent to which the state ought to limit the participation of citizens in the management of public facilities. This debate is continuing today.

THE PROBLEMS OF FEMINIST STRATEGY

THE ITALIAN political situation has changed in many ways during the past few years. The feminist movement (and in certain ways the UDI itself) appears to have suffered. Many social goals seem to have been thrown aside by a pervasive attitude of diffidence; the demands themselves are commonly viewed as "alien" to other forms of struggle now taking place. New attitudes have emerged in the wake of the political violence that occurred during 1978. The result is that the feminist movement has shifted its focus, devoting more energy to concrete objectives such as implementation of the abortion law. In the process its character has begun to change as increasingly divergent groups of women (many of whom do not really identify with the feminist movement) are mobilized around these specific struggles.

The women's movement in Italy is therefore quite fluid and capable of moving in any number of directions. One conclusion that emerges from this essay is that it is extremely difficult for a single political party (even the PCI) to incorporate the totality of feminist demands, given the weight of party traditions, the requirements of managing a political strategy that takes into account a variety of social forces, and possibly even the very structure of the parties. Still the parties (again including the PCI) are faced with the political reality of having to recognize the vitality of the women's movement, and of having to adapt to a feminist critique without which the social transformation of **Italy** cannot be effectively accomplished.

NOTES

1. See "Movement and Institutions," in *Nuova Donna Woman Femme*, no. 4, 1977.
2. Luciano Gruppi, "Matrici ideali e sociali delle formazioni neo-femministe," in *Donne e politica*, no. 17, 1973. Reprinted in *Sezione Femminili PCI*: "Per l'emancipazione della donna: 3 anni di lavoro, di dibattito, di lotta." Roma, 1976.
3. Ibid.
4. Lidia Menapace, "Le cause strutturali del nuovo femminismo," in *Problemi del socialismo*, no., 4, 1976, p. 167.
5. Marisa Rodano, "Neo-femminismo: un modo sbagliato di fare i conti con la questione femminile," in *Donne e politica*, no. 17, 1973. The emphasis is mine.
6. Biancamaria Frabotta, *La Politica del femminismo* (Roma, 1976) p. 14.
7. *Atti Parlamentari*. Camera dei Deputati: Proposta di Legge no. 3474, February 14, 1975.
8. See F. Pieroni Bortolotti, *Femminismo e partiti politici in Italia, 1919-1926* (Roma, 1978).
9. Lenin, *L'emancipazione della donna*. Edited by E. Santarelli (Roma, 1970).
10. Examination of Communist materials related to women after the appearance of the "Tribune" would require a separate study. For information concerning the periodical *Compagna*, see P. Salvetti, *La stampa comunista da Gramsci a Togliatti* (Torino, 1975).

11. See A. De Perini, "Alcune ipotesi sul rapporto tra le donne e le organizzazioni storiche del movimento operaio," in A.A. V.V., *Dentro lo specchio* (Milano, 1977), p. 246.

12. "Il nostro femminismo," in *L'Ordine Nuovo*, March 10, 1921.

13. "La donna proletaria," in *L'Ordine Nuovo*, February 17, 1921.

14. See Paolo Spriano, *Storia del Partito Comunista Italiano*, vol. I (Torino, 1967).

15. "Le donne e l'internazionale Comunista," in *L'Ordine Nuovo*, February 10, 1921.

16. Spriano, *op. cit.*

17. F. Ferrerro, "Le teorie riformiste e l'emancipazione femminile," in *L'Ordine Nuovo*, September 29, 1921.

18. F. Pieroni Bortolotti, *op. cit.*

19. *Ibid.*, p. 235.

20. Teresa Noce, *Rivoluzionaria professionale* (Milano, 1974), and N. Spani e F. Camarlinghi, *La questione femminile nella politica del PCI, 1921-1963* (Roma, 1972), p. 18.

21. Lenin, *L'emancipazione della donna*, p. 47.

22. See E.H. Carr, *La rivoluzione bolscevica* (Torino, 1967) e *Il socialismo in un paese solo*, vol. I (Torino, 1968).

23. Cited in F. Pieroni Bortolotti, *op. cit.*, p. 147. See also Alexandra Kollontai, *Comunismo, famiglia, morale sessuale,* edited by M. Gramaglia (Roma, 1976).

24. See for example the article "Il pazzo gesto di un fidanzato," in *L'Ordine Nuovo* of March 29, 1921; also "Ragazza tredicenne picchia la madre," in the December 21, 1921 issue of the same journal.

25. "La concorrenza femminile nel lavoro," *L'Ordine Nuovo*, May 26, 1921.

26. Moreover:

> We cannot predict the nature of the innumerable innovations and changes of intellectual and moral life that would be created within the framework of a new society: the kind of mass psychology, the mode of thinking, judging, speaking. But basing ourselves upon those elements toward which we are already disposed...and departing from the conception that we have of the family today, we think that women will come to perform specific tasks which will be indispensible.
> Cited in *Il nostro feminismo*.

27. See *L'Ordine Nuovo*, June 2, 1921.

28. *Archivio Partito Comunista*. Relazione sull'attivita del segretariato femminile del PCd'I. March 15, 1925. Cited in N. Spano e F. Camarlinghi, *op. cit.*

29. See the collection of oral interviews edited by B. Guidetti-Serra, *Campagne* (Torino, 1977).

30. Palmiro Togliatti, *L'emancipazione femminile* (Roma, 1973), p. 41.

31. See F. Pieroni Bortolotti, *Alle origini del movimento femminile* (Torino, 1963) and *Socialismo e questione femminile, 1892-1922* (Milano, 1974).

32. Palmiro Togliatti, *op. cit.*

33. Togliatti, *op. cit.*

33. Togliatti, *op. cit.*, p. 39.

34. Enrico Berlinguer, "Divorzio, famiglia, societa," in *Comunisti e cattolici: stato e chiesa, 1920-71*. Roma: Sezione Centrale Scuola di Partito del PCI, 1972, p. 83.

chapter 8

POLITICAL ECOLOGY AND THE LIMITS OF THE COMMUNIST VISION

*Louise Beaulieu
and Jonathan Cloud*

THIS PAPER DEALS with the role of the French Communist Party in two broader contexts. The first is that of the changes occurring in European Communist Parties during the 1970s or "Eurocommunism." The second is that of the development of progressive politics in France since May 1968.

The term "Eurocommunism" first appeared in 1970; it was not coined by the European Communist parties themselves, but was applied in the Western media and subsequently by political analysts of the changes in the Communist parties of Italy, France, and Spain which had begun during the 1960s and were catalysed by the events of 1968-69. The term was, moreover, regarded with considerable suspicion by the parties, and was not used by them until 1976; it is still not widely used by the PCF today. For the purposes of analysis the term adequately refers to a set of new conditions that very broadly apply to all of the parties; but their responses to these conditions have differed in significant respects, and it would be a mistake to assume that Eurocommunism represents a coherent set of perceptions or policies shared by the three parties.

221

INTRODUCTION

THE SITUATION CONFRONTED by European Communist parties during the period from 1956 (and more importantly from 1968) to the present has involved, most importantly, the emergence of the European Communist parties from the isolation of the Cold War period, and their gradual assertion of autonomy from the Communist Party of the Soviet Union. What distinguishes the present period, and justifies the term "Eurocommunism," is the fact that these parties have gradually been obliged to define *for themselves* (independently of or in opposition to Soviet positions) their responses to the contemporary political and economic conditions of Western Europe. They have done so cautiously, hesitantly, and—at least in the case of the PCF—inadequately and with great reluctance; but one is nevertheless justified in speaking of Eurocommunism as that set of policies, positions and perceptions which has emerged during the period of the autonomy of the European parties.

The American left has tended to see in Eurocommunism a significant promise—the emergence of a radical alternative to social democracy which avoids the bureaucratic authoritarianism of existing Communist states. After the demise of the new left, the overthrow of Allende, the gradual hardening of the regime in Cuba, the disillusionment with the succession of Mao, and the documentation of atrocities and forced reconversions in Cambodia, Eurocommunism has appeared to offer the last possibilities for a renewal in contemporary Marxist practice. For some, such as Andrew Feenberg (writing in *Socialist Review*), there is a direct line from the events of May 68 to contemporary Eurocommunism involving the (at least partial) incorporation of the ideals of the New left into the last viable Communist parties in the West.

To even the most sympathetic European observer—and indeed to most members of the European Communist parties themselves—such a view would appear excessively optimistic. In all European countries, the Communist party remains hierarchically organized, ideologically disciplined, and politically cautious. As an idea, the Communist party is the repository of the Marxist revolutionary tradition; but where this tradition exists in a living, practical form—as opposed to merely providing a framework for academic analysis—it is, as all of its proponents are acutely aware, in crisis. This is not only a result of earlier theoretical errors, but is also the consequence of a series of defeats at the hands of bourgeois authorities and of the subsequent evolution of capitalist systems, coupled with the suppression of internal dissent on questions of tactics and strategy.

In France, the PCF has a long history of excluding its dissident intellectuals, endorsing Soviet repression in Eastern Europe, and collaborating with the French state to maintain or restore 'order.' Maurice Thorez (leader of the party from 1920 to 1964) outlasted the Soviets themselves in his commitment to Stalinism. The obstructive role of the PCF during the May events is well-known; recent attempts to suggest that the party was not wholly opposed to the worker-student alliances of 1968 serve not to cleanse the party of its past errors of judgment but merely to demonstrate its leaders' persistent cynicism. The PCF has, at other times, adopted progressive positions: during the period of the Popular Front of 1935-36, in organizing the French resistance, and in its virtually unwavering opposition to French intervention in Africa and Indochina. Important changes have occurred in recent years, most notably those confirmed by the 22nd Congress in 1976. But the defeat of the left in the 1978 elections has demonstrated the inadequacy of these reforms, and the bankruptcy of the strategies of the orthodox left as a whole for the last ten years. This defeat demands a radical rethinking of these strategies, and most particularly a reformulation of the positions and practices of the PCF. As of this writing, however, the leadership of the PCF has rejected efforts to initiate a thorough internal debate. Although the party no longer excludes dissident members, it has refused to publish critical writings in *l'Humanité* or other party publications, and has dismissed all external or internal criticisms of the party's strategies, leadership, or decision-making processes.

TO UNDERSTAND the present position and prospects of the PCF it is necessary to view the party's role in relation to the wider context of progressive political thought and action in France. In this context, the French Communist Party is only one element, and no longer, as it once was, the most important one. The role of the intellectuals, of the students, of the so-called 'extreme left' groups, of the Socialists, of the trade unions, and, more recently, of the women's groups, the ecologists, and the regional autonomists, along with the isolated experiments of workers and peasants in self-management and territorial defense, have all been more important than the PCF in shaping the present course of progressive politics in France. The evolution of the PCF has, for the most part, been reactive: the elements of its present position emerging in an ad hoc and frequently grudging fashion in response to these wider and diffuse movements, and to the changing character of the right, the evolution of the French state, and the changes in the French economy and society as a whole. One often has the impression that the Party remains locked in a struggle with the fading ghost of Gaullism, and has no comprehensive understanding of the political situation in France today. Communists and Gaullists have, in fact, approximately equal electoral strength and popular support, and share a similar political rhetoric, based upon the traditional class differences between the workers and the petit bourgeoisie. Similarly, the Socialists and the Giscardian technocrats share a 'modernist' perspective and rhetoric, seeking to appeal to the new middle class—the professionals, technicians, and managers of the postwar French economy. At the extremes, above and below these major blocs, are the ruling elite—controlling the financial, industrial, and bureaucratic institutions—and the dispossessed marginals: youth, women, migrant workers, peasants, and more or less isolated individuals such as artists and intellectuals.

This paper sketches some of the major elements of this evolving whole, as a basis for understanding the potential sources of progressive change. Any assessment of the possibilities for such change in France today must start from an adequate understanding of the May 1968 events, which represented a revolt against the cultural as well as the political repressiveness of French society. May 1968 gave rise to an abortive attempt to construct a radical left alternative in France, based partly on Maoism but involving also the creation or revitalization of small parties on the traditional revolutionary model—Leninist, Trotskyist, and anarchist. This attempt failed in the face of the growing repression of the technocratic state and the hostility of the older parties and class formations, and it left many disillusioned militants in its wake. It did, however, scatter the seeds for a variety of new ideas, movements, and specific-issue concerns which have developed during the 1970s, and whose manifestations can be found to varying degrees in the unions (particularly the CFDT), the PSU and the Rocardian faction of the Socialist Party, the feminist movement, the ecologists, the 'autonomes,' the so-called 'new philosophers,' and the struggles of the Lip workers and the peasants of the Larzac. The strongest autonomous force, in political terms, has been that of the ecologists—'les verts'—some of whom have sporadically (and so far unsuccessfully) sought to build a new radical alliance around the framework of political ecology. The future of these movements is of course uncertain, but it will be our contention that the locus of progressive political thought in France now lies outside both the orthodox and the 'extreme' left. The paper will conclude by comparing the potential of these movements for developing a new radical alternative with the possibilities for a genuine and revitalized Eurocommunism. Both may, indeed, be necessary if France is to evolve towards democratic socialism.

THE PCF AND THE FRENCH POLITICAL TRADITION

POLITICAL LIFE in France is unintelligible if not viewed in the perspective of social history, and of the self-conscious character of the political culture. Superimposed on a rationalistic, analytic temperament, the ideas and events of the past weigh heavily upon the present. Since the French Revolution, political discourse has repeatedly returned to its most fundamental starting-point, the self-constitution of the Republican polis. With the decline of imperial ambitions in Europe during the nineteenth century, embodied for France in the defeat of Napoleon, cultural integrity came to be seen as the essential foundation of the nation-state. Industrialization and overseas colonialism replaced European conquest as the means of expanding national wealth; liberalism and bourgeois democracy spread slowly through continental Europe, opposing the remnants of monarchy and feudalism on the one hand, and the ideas of socialism and anarchism on the other. No single vision or culture was dominant; no 'self-evident principles' united the people of any given nation; language and administration alone ensured the authority of the state. The struggle to maintain national boundaries, to win the allegiance of disaffected regions, and to strengthen the identification of the people with the national culture was paramount. With respect to other countries or peoples the aim of the French ruling class was never to expand 'the French way of life,' but was rather to assure the ascendancy of the unique and unreproducible French 'civilization,' with its emphasis on intellectualism and elite culture. The French language itself, with its highly literate, metaphorical, and efflorescent mannerisms, was originally evolved for use by the royal court, zealously guarded against impurity by the Academie Francaise, and not finally imposed upon the whole of the territory until the beginning of this century.

Until the Second World War, moreover, much of France remained agricultural and dominated by the local gentry, with industrialism spreading slowly in the north, Paris was the one major city in the country, a cultural, artistic, and financial center with links to the rest of Europe as much as to France itself. The class structure of the society retained its nineteenth century lines until well into the present century, with the growing presence of an industrial working class restricted to certain regions, and with sharp lines between the 'haute' and the 'petit' bourgeoisie and the peasantry. At the same time, the evolution of political life outside the capital favored increasing centralization through, on the one hand, the appeals of local populations for the protection of the central authorities against the depredations of the local 'notables,' and on the other, the deliberate policies of the central government to extirpate local cultures and traditions. In French public law today there is no such thing as 'local power': there is only the power of the indivisible Republic, transmitted down through departments and prefectures to the local level. The 'Republic,' moreover, does not consist of its people but of their 'genius' or spirit, which may be incarnated in an idea or in a single person; it was on this basis, for example, that de Gaulle was able to say, in the face of the total French capitulation to the Nazis, "*Je suis la France.*"

Following the defeat in the Franco-Prussian war of 1871, which was attributed to the lack of adequate diplomatic, technical, and military training for the elite, and the uprising of the Paris Commune, a conscious effort was made to develop a highly sophisticated political and bureau-cractic class, based on the system of the *grands écoles*, emphasizing military disciplines, engineering and technical knowledge, and an articulate grasp of 'high culture' and the humanities. That parts of this system had degenerated into pretentious bluster by the 1930s was recognized by the young de Gaulle, who spent the first half of his career advocating the modernization of the French army, and was finally demonstrated by the collapse of France under the German invasion; but this system, revised in the postwar years to incorporate new economic and managerial skills, remains essentially in place today. Virtually the entire political class—from the Socialists rightwards—is recruited from the *grands écoles*, creating a relatively homogeneous ruling group. This system is, moreover, separate from the universities, where the classical disciplines have given way grudgingly and painfully to the newer, 'American' social sciences in order to become the training-ground for the new middle class of professionals and technicians, and—as the oppressive character of the new technocratic state became evident—the breeding-ground for the radical discontent expressed in the events of May 1968.

THE HISTORY of the workers' movement in France stands in many respects in contrast and in opposition to this highly structured development, but it thereby draws some of its own features from it, and incorporates a Jacobin, provincial, and occasionally chauvinistic *ressentiment* against the evolving national order.

The PCF, created as the result of a split in the French section of the Second International (SFIO) at the Tours convention in 1920, over Lenin's proposals for the future direction of the movement, remains a unique institution. It is strongly anti-intellectual in its public image. Its leadership self-consciously displays its working-class credentials, however remote they may have become. The party performs not only at a national and international level but also at a local one, where its policies are almost invariably more progressive. It fosters economic development and political education in working-class neighborhoods; its officials and militants are authoritarian and paternalistic but also incorruptible. The party also performs important social and psychological functions for its members: "popular communism," as opposed to party communism, is based on folklore and camaraderie, on conviviality as well as commitment. It has been described, not altogether unfairly, by Georges Lavau as "an ideological-patriotic-republican-working-class syncretism, a sentimental and shallow attachment encouraged by a warm ambience and by frequent celebrations," such as the *fete de l'Humanité*, "a combination annual village fair and circus parade." Despite the derisory tone of these remarks, they indicate the party's attachment to popular culture, to the needs and views of the 'common people'; they can be seen, in fact, as part of the struggle of the *sens commun* against the dominant ideology and culture, and as an attempt to replace some of the functions of the church and the traditional community. The party also maintains an institutionalized intellectual counter-culture, including the Maurice Thorez Institute and several learned journals, dedicated to combating both bourgeois ideology and such 'deviations' as Illichism; but its principal orientation, in its literature, in the style of its demonstrations, and in its auxiliary organizations, is towards working-class and popular culture, with its values of simplicity, tradition, and family life. During its early years it displayed considerable sensitivity towards the regionalist and autonomist movements in Alsace, Lorraine, and Brittany, a posture that was, however, abandoned after 1944.

Politically, the PCF was founded on the acceptance of Lenin's 21-point program for the Communist International; this essentially amounted to a recognition of the moral leadership of the Soviet Union in the struggle to actualize a Communist Europe. At the time—in the heyday of European enthusiasm for the Russian Revolution—this could be seen as a progressive act, one that gave structure and substance to the revolutionary hopes of the French left, while affirming faith in international solidarity. It also tied the larger part of the French workers' movement to the positions of the Soviet state, and to its model of party organization. The progressive disillusionment with the Soviet experience in the West—of which the latest expression is concern with the issue of political freedom in Eastern Europe—has continually led the PCF into difficult struggles to redefine itself, especially so since the party leadership was often the last to recognize and adapt to the lessons of each new revelation. Thorez, a lifelong personal friend of Stalin's, refused to abandon Stalinism even after the Soviets had done so in 1956, and sought to align himself with the anti-Khrushchev CPSU. Playing out a surreal caricature of a Stalin without state power, but with total control over the party, Thorez remained its autocratic leader until his death in 1964. His successors, Waldeck Rochet and Georges Marchais, have each sought to distance themselves from these events, but without openly denouncing them; and the party retains a practice of bureaucratic centralism and closure to public debate that has repeatedly led to the alienation of its more able theoreticians.

During the 1920s and 1930s the PCF was the vital center of the French left, a vanguard party that united workers and intellectuals in a common struggle to understand and prepare for a revolutionary future. The PCF was one of the few French institutions to recognize the dangers of emergent fascism in Germany, Italy, and Spain; but it vacillated over the question of military support to the Republican side in the Spanish Civil War, and was unable or unwilling to bring about the changes in French industrial organization called for by the workers during the period of the *Front Populaire*. The strikes of 1935-36 were in fact a remarkable foreshadowing of the events of May 1968; they were an outpouring of popular resentment against the paternalism of the French bourgeoisie, against the emerging industrial order, as expressed in the speeding-up of the cadences in French factories, and against the petty despotism of the foremen; the mood of the strikes, as recounted by Simone Weil in several remarkable passages, was a festive, liberating one. Thorez, preoccupied with the problem of order, outflanked the Socialists on the right, and urged the workers to return to work.

The Stalin-Hitler pact of 1938, dutifully endorsed by the PCF, considerably weakened the struggle against fascism; and a period of remarkable quiescence preceded the war. Although it is not widely acknowledged today, the French people as a whole were not unsympathetic to Germany's expansionist aims; fully 90 per cent supported the Vichy regime in its search for an accommodation with the occupiers. The war halted the spread of industrialization, which threatened to engulf the traditional way of life of France's still extensive rural population. The Germans also spared Paris, and in Hitler's master plan, France was to remain an agricultural nation. The subsequent organization of the Resistance, in the face of the rising German demand for French workers in German factories, the deportation of the Jews, and the conduct of the war elsewhere, was largely the work of individual Communists and Socialists, with de Gaulle and his supporters outside the country 'speaking for France' to the Allied nations.

From this period dates the PCF's ambivalent attitude to de Gaulle. Thorez and Stalin viewed de Gaulle as representing the conservative, nationalistic strain in French thought, but his independence vis-a-vis the British and the Americans was regarded by Stalin as an important asset. The dissolution of the Communist International in 1943 marked the complete centralization of world Communist authority by Stalin, using the war as a rationale for linking the policies of national parties to the survival and international interests of the Soviet Union. In the immediate struggle de Gaulle was an ally; in the longer run, his anachronistic views of France's destiny would make him a thorn in the side of the capitalists.

This attitude towards de Gaulle was pursued throughout the post-war years; although he maneuvered to keep Communists out of 'sensitive' posts in the reconstruction government, and later campaigned against their proposals for a new constitution, the party refrained from attacking him openly, aware of the depth of his personal popularity. In 1958 the PCF indeed wished to oppose his magisterial return to power to settle the Algerian question, but was in no position to offer a credible alternative. The Algerian CP had been kept in a colonial position by the PCF; arguing for the primacy of the workers' struggle in the mother country rather than preoccupying itself with the local situation, it could not be a major force in the Algerian revolution. And the PCF itself, following Soviet priorities, had been more concerned with keeping the Germans disarmed and stopping plans for a European defense alliance than with colonial questions; it had argued for a French 'presence' in Algeria until very late. Since it appeared that de Gaulle would maintain such a presence if anyone could, the PCF had little to offer. In the 1958 referendum to ratify the Gaullist constitution of the Fifth Republic, the PCF found itself virtually alone in opposition and was wholly ineffective. The mounting criticism of the Gaullist regime in the 1960s within the rest of the political class—that it was a 'personalist' form of government—was also a delicate argument for the PCF, given Thorez' own pre-eminent position within the party. Finally, and perhaps most importantly, the Soviet Union remained favorable to de Gaulle's foreign policies; two members of the PCF, Servin and Casanova, were expelled from the party in 1961 for advocating a line of stronger opposition to Gaullism than Thorez was willing to pursue.

In government from 1944 to 1947, Communist ministers essentially accepted the inclusion of France into the Western camp, and agreed to its reconstruction along neo-capitalist lines. Many workers had had high hopes for increasing worker control of industry as the economy was reorganized, but Thorez went across the country making impassioned speeches urging them to put aside revolutionary ideals "for the moment" in the name of the larger national interest. Convinced of its ability to transform the society 'from the top down,' the party abandoned the line of mass action, accepted the dissolution of the popular militia, and advocated a peaceful road to socialism, stressing parliamentarism. The constitution which they proposed was one of the most democratic in French history, modelled upon that of the First Republic, and giving all power to the National Assembly; but by the time a compromise which fundamentally undermined it was finally approved after several referenda, the party was irrevocably committed to electoralism.

The PCF was also committed to a rapid return to industrial growth, supporting wage and production controls and advocating the nationalization of certain key sectors in the economy, including utilities, railways, and a number of financial institutions. Ironically, it was largely on the basis of these initial Communist plans for nationalization that the center-right parties were able to engineer France's postwar "economic miracle."

Finally, as an extension of their role in the Resistance and de Gaulle's evocation of patriotic sentiment, the Communists shifted to a policy of militant nationalism, dropping their support for regional autonomists, opposing German rearmament and U.S. proposals for European military and economic unification. This nationalism did not, however, exclude continuing support for Soviet policies, and during the Cold War, when they were effectively excluded from French political life, they were thrown back even more heavily upon their ties with the USSR. During this period the PCF turned inward, pursuing a more and more rigid ideological line. It supported Soviet 'firmness' in Eastern Europe and mounted an hysterical anti-Tito campaign; later it criticized the PCI for 'revisionism' and the Chinese for 'left extremism'; and throughout the period of Thorez' leadership it carried out 'white trials' modelled on the Moscow trials and expelled its dissidents. Most notable were the purges of Marty and Tillon, two prominent party men with good Spanish Civil War and Resistance records; of Pierre Hervé; and of Servin and Casanova (replaced on the Politburo by Garaudy and Marchais). Althusser has written: "There were real 'Moscow trials' right here in France. The death sentences were missing, but you can also make a man die of dishonor, by torturing him with the charge of being a 'police-agent,' 'crook,' or 'traitor'; by forcing all his old comrades-in-arms to condemn, shun, and calumniate him, renouncing their own past. That happened in France, between 1948 and 1965."[2]

It must be said that at the same time the party was subjected to an extensive campaign of anti-communist propaganda, was accused of subversive motives, and of being 'anti-French.' Jacques Duclos, a prominent party official, was arrested in 1952 for having a pigeon in his car, alleged to be a carrier-pigeon for sending secret messages to Moscow (when in fact it was his lunch). In order to 'rehabilitate' itself the party continually emphasized its commitment to the electoral process; and from 1958 on it sought a permanent alliance with the Socialists. From the point of view of legitimating itself in the political arena such decisions may appear to have been necessary; but their larger consequence was to turn radical working-class militants into political actors *within* the political system, thus strengthening that system. From an institutional point of view, the party can be seen as providing a vehicle for legitimating opposition within the French political context, but also stifling much of that opposition by channeling it along electoralist lines.

It also saddled the party with a tradition of autocracy and bureaucratic unresponsiveness which it retains to this day, no thorough critique of the party's past or of its decision-making practices has ever been accepted or carried out. The first real declaration of the PCF's independence from Soviet policies was in 1968, following the invasion of Czechoslovakia; but after registering its "surprise and disapproval" in the August 21 issue of *l'Humanité*, the PCF backed off, weakening its language. The PCF was also the first Western party to send representatives to Moscow after Prague, in November 1968, and officially disavowed Roger Garaudy's remarks to the Czech press agency opposing the invasion. Garaudy was ostracized; he subsequently published *Toute la verité* concerning the Czech events, and also wrote, a propos of his larger assessment of the crisis of Communism: "The reason why I now [in 1970] find myself obliged to conduct this argument in public is because, for over three years, not one of my suggestions has ever been allowed to break through the barrier of silence which surround the proceedings of the Politburo and the Central Committee."[3]

Significantly, the party leadership regarded August in Prague as more important than May in Paris; and its evolution since 1968 has reflected little of the spirit of those events. Althusser has spoken of the "astonishingly cold" Common Program put together with the Socialists in 1972; and any talk of radical social change, of emerging issues, or of direct action in the workplace was muted in the party from 1972 to 1978, in anticipation of the 'decisive' election. In view of this election, the PCF sought to distance itself further from Moscow; it dropped the phrase 'the dictatorship of the proletariat' from its platform, and announced that it had definitively abandoned Stalinism. It also did an abrupt about-face on the *force de frappe*, supporting an independent nuclear role for France and espousing a policy of defense *tous azimuts* (in all directions), without consulting the party membership. But this refurbishing of the party's image was too little, too late. Electorally, the party lost ground to the Socialists; and it broke with the Common Program six months before the election, thus virtually ensuring its defeat.

THE COLLAPSE OF GAULLISM

THE TRANSFORMATION of France into a highly industrialized, technologically sophisticated society is a remarkably recent phenomenon, dating from the postwar period. It occurred in a highly centralized and bureaucratic fashion, reinforced not only by the traditional structure of French administration, but also by the fact that significant financial resources and technological and managerial information were being channeled into the country from the outside. The political class that asserted itself after the war had, however, considerable difficulty adapting the political/governmental machine to its new tasks. The Fourth Republic (1947-58) suffered from endemic governmental instability, and one of de Gaulle's aims in drawing up the constitution for the Fifth Republic was to ensure greater institutional stability, in line with the requirements of managing a modern industrial state.

Although Gaullism was an essentially conservative political movement, drawing its support from middle and working-class nationalistic elements, and while de Gaulle himself was principally concerned with foreign policy and France's place in the postwar world, it was really under the Gaullist regime that France underwent its most dramatic modernization. Agricultural concentration, modernization and centralization of heavy industry, urban reconstruction, the development of new high-technology industries such as aerospace and computing, reconstitution of the defense forces and the development of an autonomous nuclear capability, were all guided through state control of key financial institutions and state planning. France surpassed the postwar growth rates of all its Western partners to become fifth in world industrial capacity, after the U.S., Russia, Japan, and Germany. This process enjoyed the support of virtually all sectors of French society. The PCF was certainly sympathetic to it; its leaders argued only for the democratization of its products, and for the expansion of the industrial labor force. That de Gaulle was head of state during the latter and most critical part of the process, symbolizing the greatness of France in its historical continuity, made the whole acceptable in otherwise reactionary quarters. Under de Gaulle a new generation of technocrats, often drawn from elite families as in the case of Giscard d'Estaing, consolidated economic power in both public and private corporations, moving freely from one to another at the higher levels of management (usually from government to private enterprise rather than vice versa, as is the case in the U.S.), and fostering the development of the new middle strata of professionals and technicians.

By the late 1960s, however, the costs of this socially-engineered "economic miracle" were becoming apparent: the industrial north had become an eyesore, workers were crowded into jerry-built suburbs, Paris was choking in automobile fumes and being mutilated with skyscrapers, in the universities students were being mass-programmed with alienating disciplines in order to fill alienating jobs, and the old lifestyles and patterns of interaction on which the French had long prided themselves were disappearing. It is in this context that May 1968 erupted.

The events of May 1968—a month of strikes, meetings, occupations, and protests on the part of students, workers, intellectuals, and some members of the middle class—clearly constituted an outbreak of profound revolutionary sentiment. It was an explosion born of frustration a protest in solidarity with the world student and youth movement against the war in Vietnam, and a revolt against the paternalism of French society exemplified by de Gaulle. But it was not, in the classical sense, a revolutionary act: it was not animated by a coherent vision; and it was not directed or fully comprehended by either the orthodox or the extreme left parties. Such an act is indeed barely conceivable in a modern industrialized society: the attempt to replace one social order with another, through concerted mass action aimed at the overthrow of the state, appears not only improbable but destined to end in a further and more total despotism. An articulation of revolutionary aspirations under advanced capitalism needs to be wider and more profound than that which is impossible in the rigidified language of the nineteenth-century ideologies. May 1968 could have no logical, agreed-upon outcome that would satisfy these aspirations. It was certainly not aimed at the coming to power of the left parties, whose rhetoric was openly opportunistic and productivist, and whose platforms promised only 'a transition to the transition.' In fact, the left parties reacted with growing alarm to the anarchistic, disruptive character of the May events. Later they sought to use them for their own narrow advantage, calling for an emergency government and demanding new elections—which is eventually what they got, and lost overwhelmingly. The working class reacted ambivalently.

The students first experienced and expressed the previously unrecognized political fact of the powerlessness of a dissatisfied people vis-a-vis the modern industrial state. As the revolt initiated by the students spread to include workers and other groups, however, they abdicated their initial leadership position and called on the workers to carry on the struggle, thus falling back on the reflexes of the European left. But some of the themes which grounded their understanding and motivated their actions went well beyond traditional Marxist analysis. Their revolt seemed to spring from a true horror of becoming cogs in the modern techno-industrial machine, of being caught in consumerism. Right-wing commentators on the events have tended to treat these aspects of the youth revolt with condescension, suggesting that it was all a function of the pampered baby-boom generation finding itself competing for too few outlets, misled by too literary (read: political) an education, the regrettable victims of change finding themselves out of step and giving vent to a transitory confusion. They even used the students' departures from traditional left rhetoric against them, claiming that their revolt was not genuine but self-indulgent. In this manner, the right appealed to the natural prejudices of other groups against them.

Yet the student radicals had obviously struck a chord of frustration in the working class, for in factory after factory the workers went on strike without benefit of the leadership of either unions or left parties. The CGT only endorsed the strike once it had become obvious that it represented a movement of considerable importance, and rapidly sought its resolution. Although the ultimate settlement which the unions negotiated as a return to work condition consisted of minor salary concessions, one suspects that the original motivating factors behind the workers' revolt were of a quite different order.

Teachers, cadres, technicians, and professionals of various kinds also joined in the events. Although these groups occupy a position of relative advantage, it is one of fairly recent origin. Many individuals had considerable sympathy for the cause of the students and workers; but these groups were also acting out of their own very real sense of frustration with everyday life. France is a hierarchical society, finely graded along class lines as well as those of professional position. Social roles are rigid and social interaction within and outside institutions, is highly formalized. One thus finds a profound ambivalence within the new middle class: on the one hand, a tendency to organize and present group demands, often in the guise of radical rhetoric, whose ultimate purpose is to protect and enhance the position of the group; on the other, a desire to shuck off many aspects of the oppressive social and cultural superstructure, which also finds its expression in radical political discourse. In its exuberance and spontaneity, May 1968 expressed this latter moment for these middle groups.

What a great deal of the analytic literature on May 1968 in France often overlooks is that the events were in parte a *fête*, a joyful occasion, a letting-go of the rigid rules of social intercourse. May 1978 saw a great wave of nostalgia sweep the Left in the country: "Were you there? wasn't it great?" It is no accident that the slogan which rallied the left for the 1978 legislative elections had nothing whatever to do with the Common Program: it was *vivre autrement; change la vie*. This is not to deny the political significance of May, but rather to point to its sources in people's immediate experience, in the frustration of fundamental affective and relational needs not only by a capitalist mode of social organization but also by the particular traits of French culture as it has evolved under capitalism. In this respect, widely-disseminated class consciousness may not be the revolutionary moving force that left analysis takes it to be. To be sure, class analysis furnishes critical tools with which to understand relations of power and the dynamics of oppression. But class consciousness as class identification also permeates the definitions of self and social reality in ways that may block change: your looks, the quality of your shoes, your accent, where you are from, are so many highly visible and consciously recognized determinants of who you are and who you can be. Class position is an integral part of the definition of self, and this is true not only in the bourgeoisie but also in the working class. The Communist militant, moreover, enjoys quite a comforting self-image, often based on a family tradition of party adherence; and it is not, on the whole, an angry or radically questioning one. For this reason the workers' participation in the May revolt, originating outside the established workers' organizations, takes on added significance.

Finally, May 1968 was a people's revolt. The ever-present and ever-opinionated *vedettes* who dominate French intellectual life were notably absent from leadership positions during the actual events, although they rapidly appropriated them afterwards, as May 1968 became the focus for a new wave of literature, analysis, and debate in the early 1970s. The events also spawned a new intellectual faction of their own—the now-prominent but still widely misunderstood *nouveaux philosophes*—who subsequently gave intellectual respectability to the then visceral suspicion of the totalizing and hence inherently authoritarian nature of traditional Marxist thought.

THE LEGACY OF THE MAY EVENTS

DID MAY 1968 'fail?' What was its true legacy? Undeniably, there was a real reaction to the events: massive right-wing demonstrations, an impressive electoral victory for the Gaullists under Pompidou in the legislative elections, a quiet return to work for the workers without significant structural change, and a relative social quiescence since then, fostered by the efforts of the left parties to channel the energies of the protesters into political gains and to avoid the backlash of working-class and petit-bourgeois conservatism. Yet to the extent that one understands the cultural context of the May events, one is also in a position to appreciate that the subsequent dramatic 'return to order' may not have been entirely a feat of political engineering. Intellectually, the French like to think of themselves, whatever their party, as on the left; temperamentally, a good number of them find themselves on the right, whatever their party. From a psychological point of view, May 1968 as a great cultural catharsis calls for an equally strong return to order and thus to normalcy. But it is not the prior historical situation that is restored; the catharsis itself reveals the features of the new social reality struggling to emerge. However hastily denied, this recognition alters the givens of political discourse. It is therefore in the shifting political geography since 1968 that one must look to find the real impact of the events.

Observers sympathetic to Eurocommunism, such as Feenberg, have sought to claim that the PCF is the true heir to the spirit of May 1968, and that it has come out strengthened as a result: granted that the party did not occupy a position of leadership at the time, it has since become more sensitive to the current embodiments of frustration with the capitalist system, i.e., to such issues as bureaucratization and environmental degradation. According to this view, May 1968 also signalled to the party the need to incorporate the concerns of various groups such as students, women, anti-growth activists, etc., which the party is now doing, albeit slowly. Such a view, if not wholly mistaken, is at least disturbingly party-centric. The forces that are urging change on the PCF are those of a globally shifting politico-social context and, in seeking to retain its traditional electoral base, the PCF has demonstrated quite extraordinary rigidities given the pace and direction of change everywhere around it since 1968. The party's approach remains unambiguously productivist: despite widespread questioning of the growth ethic and the spread of ecological awareness amongst party members, the leadership remains committed to the expansion of energy production, industrial development, and growth in consumption as the basis for improving the material conditions of the poor and the working class.

Real change has occurred on the left but it has done so largely through the formation of a strong, heterogeneous, and electorally-oriented Socialist Party on the one hand, and through the proliferation of issue-oriented, and constituency-oriented groups on the other. Each of these developments warrants consideration in its own right.

UNDER GAULLISM, the Socialist Party (the old SFIO) had become a relatively minor political force, seeking to ally itself primarily to parties on the right. The cold war had excluded the PCF from the game of shifting alliances which other parties played; despite repeated Communist overtures, Guy Mollet and his leadership were reluctant to violate this taboo, partly for electoral reasons—they drew much of their support from teachers, technicians, and other middle-class professionals hostile to Communism, including a large Catholic constituency—but also for ideological ones: they supported the NATO alliance, and were openly and traditionally concerned with issues of political democracy. There was a faction drawn to a left alliance, courted assiduously by the PCF as a means of escaping its political ghetto, but under Mollet's leadership this remained impossible. There is a long tradition of humanist socialist thought in France which seeks to transcend partisan divisions, and it remained vital throughout this period, but many socialists tended to gravitate away from the Gaullist-dominated arena of national politics into administration, education, or local politics. A younger generation of more militant Socialists gathered in the PSU *(Parti Socialiste Unifié)* around people like Michel Rocard. It took Francois Mitterrand—a man from a small center-left party with a long political past, yet nonetheless recognized as a man of integrity and a consistent opponent of de Gaulle—to draw together the various strands of the Socialist 'family,' and the Congress of Epinay in 1972 marked the birth of the new Socialist Party.

Yet the new Socialist Party represented more than the coming together of already existing forces under the Socialist banner, for in its willingness to enter into the Union of the Left and its openly governmental aspirations, the party signalled the readiness of French society to embrace institutional change. The party that came together at Epinay was, given the political traditions of France, an extraordinarily heterogeneous one: old Socialist militants, Christian labor union activists, middle-class professionals, Marxist intellectuals (who led the CERES minority group), socially-oriented women's groups, economists and 'progressive' technocrats, and large numbers of people, young and old, who believed in the possibility for change to be achieved through progressive government. For the Socialists, as opposed to the Communists, electoralism is a logical consequence of an active political philosophy; the Socialists wanted state power, and saw an alliance with the PCF as a necessary condition for its attainment. In this respect the rise of the PS directly parallels the emergence of the new center-right coalition under Giscard d'Estaing which, with its openly technocratic orientation and pragmatic political line, has largely displaced the Gaullist faction, reasserting its alliance with it in electoral periods.

Granted that the PS was a Socialist Party, the extensive debate and intellectual activity that it generated showed just how soft a concept 'socialism' is, taking in everything from econometric analyses of the world economy, to theoretical flights on the character of a redefined social democracy, to plans for a national day-care program. In effect, it became an occasion for a continuing discussion of what everyone wanted to see happen. Parallel to this flurry of discussion, however, the 'official' party came to lock itself into an electoral program whose feasibility and real significance remain unclear to this day. The negotiations which were the occasion for the breakdown of the Union of the Left in the fall of 1977 were over the 'actualization' of the Common Program, a subject which the PS had assiduously sought to avoid. The motives and true objectives of the PCF in this alliance were also a source of constant speculation for the PS; the pre-election turn-around of the Communists, which the PS was powerless to prevent, effectively sabotaged the prospects of electoral victory. In retrospect one can well ask whether the PS, and its conception of the 'Union of the Left,' provided the appropriate framework to embody the aspirations of those that it brought together; but there is no doubt that it represented the legitimate, i.e., respectable, heir to the events of May 1968.

May 1968 had another important consequence for French political life: it made intellectually legitimate a whole range of left activity and politics outside the organized left and in particular outside the PCF. Left factionalism has, of course, always existed in France; but it was only with May 1968 that it became clear that the PCF and its 'line' were no longer the exclusive reference point for left politics and radical thought. For a long time the PCF *was* the left in France: it was the organizational vehicle for the workers' struggle, which, by the terms of Marxist analysis, was *the* struggle, and it had links with the international socialist community and with Communist parties everywhere. Its line represented the presumed consensus in terms of theory and practice according to which all pertinent actors were to act. In the hope of retaining effectiveness of action, everyone concerned with radical social change either joined or voted for the party; its journals and policy statements were widely read and minutely scrutinized. This is why otherwise liberal or independent intellectuals continued to put up with the rigors of 'democratic 'centralism'; or, if they chose to remain outside the party, like Sartre, they felt obliged to define their positions with respect to the party's line. It also explains why expulsion from the party was such a serious occurrence.

Yet as the events of May 1968 made plain, the PCF could not comprehend let alone contain the forces of radical change in France. In part this was a function of the longstanding conservatism of its leadership; but more generally it was a reflection of the extensive changes in French society during the postwar period. The modernizing transformation of France distributed certain material benefits to organized industrial labor; it also vastly extended alienation beyond the traditional working class. And the reactions to this 'crisis of overdevelopment' were everywhere apparent in 1968. The non-aligned groups that formed after 1968 were clearly anti-technocratic in outlook, some within an anarchist framework (e.g., the group around *Libération*). Others joined the environmental movement, bringing an explicit political dimension to it. The women's movement, community groups, and regional-autonomy movement such as the Breton separatists found new impetus. For this new generation of political activists the PCF was no longer sacred. At the same time, however, even those activists outside the organized left parties came to see the 1978 legislative elections as significant, as the great symbolic/real event that would finally derail the system from its present course and allow for the possibility of change. The electoral defeat of the Union of the Left was thus not simply a parliamentary setback, allowing the government to continue its policies of economic concentration, industrial development, and nuclear proliferation. It was also an indication of a more profound societal paralysis in the face of an accelerating systemic instability, which threatens to produce an ecological, economic, and political crisis of ever-larger proportions, and not only in France. This paralysis is reflected in the poverty of the political language of the orthodox left, and most notably that of the PCF; but it signifies more generally a crisis of the radical imagination.

RISE OF THE ECOLOGY MOVEMENT

INTELLECTUAL LIFE in France has often been self-consciously faddish. Certain writers, issues, and schools of thought hold center stage for a while and are then discarded in favor of a new intellectual wave. Yet the intellectual debate is invariably serious, and one gets the sense of an intelligent society searching for ways to understand itself. In the 1970s, the major theme has been that of a profound disillusionment with Marxist theory and practice. Solzhenitsyn's work depicting prison camps in Russia has had a marked impact on the intelligentsia, giving the coup de grace to any remaining illusions about the viability of the Soviet model. Psychoanalysis, feminism, pleasure and the body, and 'returning pleasure to politics' have also been important themes, influencing political discussions centered on the 'problem of power,' and leading to a radical redefinition of the political space itself. The state is in question—understandably, given the heavy-handed nature of the French state—not only for its present functions but also as the privileged instrument of social change directed toward an egalitarian ideal. 'Totalitarian frameworks of thought' are suspect in that they invite violence and repression in their actualization.

Most of the left groups that have emerged in the 1970s have exhausted themselves in endless debate and factionalism, yet they have all shared a fundamentally anti-technocratic character and a distrust of old political forms. There was among these groups a sense that 'everything was to be rethought,' and the bitter debates on violence versus non-violence, alliance with the left parties versus independent action, the importance of the workers' struggle versus that of other groups, were all symptomatic of a search for a new political vocabulary and mode of action. The only rallying point was what came to be known as the ecology movement, as first PSU activists and later disillusioned Maoists and others joined and politicized a variety of environmental and other grassroots organizations.

Initially, the environmental movement was not politically oriented. France enjoys a long tradition of 'naturalist' concern with environmental protection which dates from the nineteenth century. The people attracted to the movement tended to be local notables of conservative political inclinations. They would gather around such issues as the preservation of wilderness areas and wildlife, but there was little realization that 'society' was what was really at issue or that their actions had a political dimension. In fact, they belonged to a conservative strain in French society that long resisted industrialization, modernization, and the bureaucratic imperialism of Paris-based government in defense of established ways of life. The *Société Nationale pour la Défense de la Nature* best exemplifies this strain. It was not until the late 1960s that the concept of 'environment' really came to public consciousness; from then on, ecology took on an increasingly political orientation, as a number of local and issue-oriented groups came to identify themselves as part of a new socio-political sensibility.

In its first phase, the ecology movement was mainly concerned with the polluting effects of industrial activity, mass consumption, and a transportation system dominated by the automobile: 1970, designated Environment Year in Europe, was also the year of the major bicycle demonstrations in Paris by the ban-the-automobile movement. Numerous consumer associations were formed, and a group of concerned political journalists got together to promote action on environmental issues (this same group later launched René Dumont's campaign for the presidency on an ecological platform in 1974). President Pompidou announced "100 measures for the protection of the environment," while a number of books started to appear on pollution and global ecology. It was, as one commentator put it, the 'we-are-all-responsible' stage of ecological consciousness. Yet 1970 also saw the emergence of the issue that was to politicize—and polarize—environmentalists in the future: the anti-nuclear issue. In Alsace, a province bordering on Germany, the long struggle of a local population to halt the construction of a nuclear reactor began with a small demonstration.

In 1971, a Ministry of the Environment was created with an antipollution orientation (the minister, Poujade, later resigned admitting that little could be done through moral suasion alone). *Les Amis de la Terre* (Friends of the Earth)—later to become the strongest and most active ecological formation—was formed with a decentralized structure. *Charlie-Hebdo*, a radical post-1968 satirical publication took on the antinuclear struggle while *Gueule Ouverte*, a monthly journal announcing the end of the world started publication. When the Club of Rome report appeared in early 1972 it was severely attacked by both Raymond Barre and George Marchais. At this juncture one starts to see a real politicization of the movement—where adherents become militants—as members of the PSU, the coalition new left socialist party, join ecological associations in large numbers and start animating local groups. That year, 10,000 people demonstrated against a nuclear power station at Fassenheim; 20,000 protested against the building of one at Rodez in the Larzac.

With the appearance of *Le Sauvage* in 1973, the movement gained its first serious intellectual publication: the journal served as a forum for discussions of political ecology by Edgar Morin, Brice Lalonde, Michel Bosquet (André Gorz), Alain Hervé and others. This led the way for the entry of ecologists onto the electoral political scene with the candidacy of Rene Dumont for President in 1974.

Dumont, an agronomist with extensive experience in North Africa and Vietnam, and a lifelong socialist, had written an impassioned book *L'utopie ou la mort* in which he had described "the end of civilization": the last decades of the societies of waste, the inevitable revolt of the poorer nations, and the need for a global "mobilization for survival." Dumont received only 1.4 percent of the vote in a campaign dominated by the confrontation between Giscard d'Estaing and Mitterrand but his candidacy served to sensitize the population, as its supporters had hoped. In its organization the Dumont campaign was really a model of what ecological politics purports to be: over 85 groups and organizations came together at the urging of journalists and PSU activists and ran the campaign in a decentralized, non-bureaucratic way. Although Dumont was a socialist, he situated himself in this campaign "well on the left of the left" and talked of a *"socialism d'austerité"* as a yet to be fully-defined social project that would unite socialist and ecological concerns. Although many groups in the 'naturalist' tradition of the movement refused to support Dumont, those who did clearly identified themselves with a left political orientation.

In the aftermath of the campaign, the membership of various ecological groups increased as many of the 1968 generation claimed that they had finally found 'something worth working for' on the political scene. Given this climate, and considerable resources left over from the campaign, many felt the time was ripe for the formation of a national ecological movement. At the Assises Montargis, 2000 to 3000 people from the Dumont campaign—all delegates from various local organizations—gathered to assess this possibility. At first there was a debate between those who wanted a minimalist organization on a decentralized model and those who argued against any formal organization on the grounds that this would be 'anti-ecological': the syndicalists versus the libertarians. Yet the issue was ultimately beyond resolution, for of the more political members present there were some who obviously yearned for a very militant and well-structured organization, while others were vehemently anarchist in the best post-68 tradition. Montargis ended in a classical gauchiste squabble and René Dumont finally disassociated himself from the whole thing. There were some positive results, however, as the Paris-based *Amis de la Terre* became the central clearing-house for other ecology groups, while the larger movement started to regroup for the anti-nuclear campaigns of 1975-76, concentrated around the Fessen-heim committee in Alsace. Although in its anti-nuclear form the movement was at its strongest and most cohesive, the old divisions rapidly began to appear again: this time between those who conceived of themselves primarily as a pressure group, relying on scientific docu-mentation and making known expert opinions and warnings, and those who saw themselves as fighting for a new society.

The lure of electoral politics also remained strong, no doubt as a result of the Dumont 'success.' In the municipal elections of 1977 the ecologists fielded 1200 candidates and received an impressive 12 percent (2,300,000 votes). Ecological strength was concentrated in Alsace (some candidates there gathered over 65 percent of the vote) but also in the south of France where there is a strong reaction to urban dwellers seeking second homes in the country, exacerbated by the longstanding cultural resentments of the Occitan population toward Parisians. It is natural that the ecologists should be active in local politics; it was in entering the national electoral scene that they found themselves most divided.

As the decisive 1978 legislative election approached there were fierce debates among ecologists as to whether they should field their own candidates and whether having done so, they should urge their suppor-ters to vote for the left on the crucial second round. Since it appeared that Giscard d'Estaing had managed to convince some of his people to run on an ecological platform on the first round, thus hoping to cash in on the public sensitivities around ecological concerns (polls had shown that over 50 percent of the voting population was sympathetic to the ecological stance) the radical ecologists—mostly gathered aound *Les Amis de la Terre* and *Le Sauvage*—felt that they had no choice but to present candidates of their own. They were very concerned to do justice to the ecological position and bring out the full critique of modern industrialized society that it implies, but in the process had to make agonizing decisions about their stance vis-a-vis the Union of the Left. They could not give wholehearted support to the Left: the two were miles apart on such issues as productivism and the future of the industrial system, the role of the state, nuclear energy and defense policy; but neither could they in all conscience refuse support to the left since it represented the one real chance to dislodge the established governing majority. It was clear the election would be close and that it would be decisive. The radical ecologists ended up urging their supporters to go with the candidate most open to ecological themes in his or her position and record but made it amply clear that they themselves were voting 'on the Left.' As election fever mounted, the ecologists became largely invisible, or they tended to be seen as of the marginal left and therefore negligible. In fact, it is clear that many ecologists themselves voted for the Left in the first round since, all told, the ecologists gathered a mere two percent of the vote.

In the general depression that followed the elections, the ecologists have had ample time to reexamine their past performance and activities. One senses that the leadership—i.e. those most heavily drawn to political action and ultimately to electoralism—emerged quite demoralized on the political scene the left squabbles over positions indistinguishable from those of the right, the nuclear program continues unabated, and ecology is no longer so fashionable in Paris intellectual circles. Yet action at the local level is as strong as ever, and membership is swelling, drawn principally from those disillusioned with the PS experience. As Brice Lalonde has often pointed out, the ecology movement can never be a political party; it is not even principally a political movement but a *social* one. It may for various purposes and around various issues engage in political action, but always on a provisional basis, with local groups retaining their autonomy. One may also speak of the constellation of leftish movements and causes that identify themselves globally as "ecological," such as womens' groups, the now quite small PSU, and the *auto-gestionnaires*, but ultimately the movement escapes precise definition. Interestingly enough, a number of the themes that had been downplayed in this last electoral phase of the movement are now re-emerging: the internationalist perspective, the rejection of conventional politics and political rhetoric of all kinds. Many of the radical women who had worked very hard for the movement are now being heard as they criticize the infatuation of their male peers with power politics as part of the problem to be overcome. And many are turning to concerns, such as the organization of food co-ops and citizens' action committees. The Socialists, in their search for a new electoral base, began courting the ecology movement quite assiduously with indefinite results.

THE ECOLOGICAL PERSPECTIVE

IF THE ECOLOGICAL movement is ultimately nebulous and often incoherent, political ecology as an analysis and sensibility offers an increasingly coherent critique of the crisis of modern industrialized societies and suggestive insights on where to go from here. It has been claimed by some that political ecology may be for the twentieth century what political economy was for the nineteenth. Perhaps—it offers, at least, a fresh vision.

It rests, in the first place, on an internationalist perspective: it sees the problems of France in a global context, as tied not only to the emergence of monopoly capitalism in Western industrial nations but as linked more generally to the evolution of the world economic order expressed in state capitalism in socialist countries and underdevelopment in the Third World. Second, it offers a radical critique of the prevalent model of economic development. Serge Moscovici has pointed out that where liberal economics concentrates on the malfunctions of market economics and Marxism on the social contradictions they generate, ecology discloses the paradoxes and dead-ends of the present conception of economic development itself, whether achieved through the market or through state planning. Industrial activity is now meeting the limits of the carrying capacity of the planet and economic systems have evolved to such a level of complexity as to be virtually unmanageable. In social and human terms, we can no longer recognize ourselves in the environments we have created. Political ecology looks to more human-scaled forms of economic and hence social development. Third, it focuses on mass action aimed at halting the development of nuclear energy—the principal symbol of the emerging world technocratic order, and one of its main instruments. Apart from its obvious dangers for human health and environmental integrity, nuclear energy promises to lock societies into patterns of production, consumption, and social organization that are extremely rigid and alienating. Renewable, 'soft' energies are the crucial alternative. Fourth, political ecology proposes action aimed at liberating social creativity, around such concepts as autonomy, decentralization, and self-management. Certainly the class struggle is a reality in a country such as France, but one must also be engaged in a pragmatic form of action that takes into account the complexities of present realities: grass roots organization, the pursuit of different lifestyles, practical action in the energy, environmental, and health fields, new styles of work, the imagining of practical utopias, as part of a vital social experimentation in search of a way out of the present impasse. *Les Amis de la Terre* have in fact come up with a definition of politics along these lines: "the proposal of and experimentation with forms of social organization which do not endanger the ecosystem and respect the species." The project of reconciling this with the vital insights of Marxism remains to be achieved.

THE 1978 ELECTION: DEFEAT AND REASSESSMENT

IN THE WAKE of the defeat of the Union of the Left in the March 1978 legislative elections, the French Left finds itself demoralized and disoriented. As Althusser said, it has "confused the masses" and filled many ordinary militants in both of the major left parties with disquiet. Not only do they feel that prospects for significant social change in the foreseeabale future have been eradicated, but that the very meaning and causes of the defeat elude them still. As accusations and recriminations fly, both within parties and between them, one senses a deep mood of frustration and despair. Even among those of the radical and ecological left outside of established parties, the defeat of the Common Program appears somehow decisive.

Much of this despair arises from the suspicion that the PCF deliberately sabotaged the Union of the Left, by first demanding and then breaking off the negotiations on the implementation of the Common Program six months before the elections. At the time, the PCF claimed that it was forced to do so because of a covert 'shift to the right' by its partners: most importantly, that the PS and the smaller *Radicaux de gauche* were unwilling to carry through the nationalizations called for by the program to their natural conclusions, including all subsidiaries; secondly, that they were unwilling to raise the minimum wage sufficiently; and, unofficially, that they were unwilling to discuss the assignment of ministries to be made to the Communists, and were thus planning to try to minimize their influence in the new government. Yet what do these grievances really amount to? On the matter of nationalizations, the Socialists were arguing that it was not necessary to nationalize all subsidiaries, which were often in a different sector than the primary industries that one wanted to control; and that one could effectively control them anyway, in a less burdensome manner, through the parent companies (which would retain their present holdings), and though heavy state involvement in financial institutions. Moreover, nationalized industry in France is no more enlightened than private industry, and one could question the desirability of wholesale nationalization for its own sake. On the matter of the minimum wage, the disparity between the PCF proposal and that of the existing *Programme Commun* was a mere 200 francs a month, and given the inflationary pressures in the economy, one could see the wisdom of a certain initial restraint. On the matter of the divisions of power in the new government, Mitterand argued that such a discussion before the election would generate a largely paranoid public debate, one that the right could use to its advantage. Even if one agrees with the position of the PCF, did these differences warrant keeping the Left out of power altogether? The electoral opportunism of the PS and the *Radicaux de gauche* was evident from the beginning; why accept it (and undoubtedly partake of it) first, and then reject it?

Althusser, amongst many others, concludes that the PCF secretly changed tactics in mid-course and decided to break off the Union when it became obvious that it was losing electoral strength in favor of the PS, and would come out of the elections as the weaker of the two. This interpretation seems to be borne out by Marchais' mysterious pre-election statement that "25 percent would be good, 21 percent not enough"—implying that the party would rebuild the Union of the Left without further negotiations if it received, say 23 or 24 percent, but not if it received less. In Althusser's view, this change in strategy from collaboration to competition with the Socialists over votes—had to be concealed; for any change involves an admission of error, an examination of the old line.[4] In the end, the PCF retained only its traditional 21 percent, re-entered into hasty negotiations and announced its agreement with the other parties the day after the first round, but without affecting the final outcome.

Appearing on French television the night of the defeat, Marchais was the only left leader who did not look disappointed or dismayed. As one commentator bitterly remarked, "What is a mere electoral setback to a man who has history on his side?" In fact, Marchais did not sound like a man who had suffered a defeat at all; the party had retained its position, and would not now be forced into compromise. Yet this kind of approach no longer seems satisfactory to many within the party itself.

The debate now raging in and around the party thus springs from the profound disappointment of its militants with the defeat, and the leadership is under severe criticism for its maneuvering. Yet neither the substance nor the source of the debate should be misunderstood. The party's leadership has made extensive efforts to curtail the debate; the major dissenting articles have been published in *Le Monde* and not in Communist publications; and much of the debate within the party has been over the question of whether such a debate is possible. Jean Elleinstein, one of the leaders of the present dissident movement within the party, sees the fact that he has not been thrown out as itself a major sign of hope for the future of the PCF, as an instance of its progressive liberalization. More realistically, perhaps, one can see it as a recognition on the part of the PCF leadership that to exclude dissidents now would be politically disastrous.

Both Althusser's and Ellenstein's writings, starting from quite different points of view, reveal the profound nature of the changes necessary. These changes require not merely a recognition of past errors, but also a reform of the party's decision-making processes and its methods of leadership selection; and as these reforms clearly threaten the present leadership, they are not likely to be accepted without a bitter struggle.

Elleinstein has argued that it was a mistake for the PCF to enter into the Union of the Left without having first sufficiently transformed its own strategy and organization: it could, under such circumstances, only come out second to the Socialists. He also argues that it was a substantive error, because, without following through on the liberalization started with the 22nd Congress and rethinking its analysis from the ground up, it could only be an ineffective partner. According to Ellenstein, the party should begin by reexamining and renouncing the errors of its past; it should admit that the intellectuals who sought to pursue de-Stalinization but who resigned or were expelled—including Claude Roy, Roger Vailard, Henri Lefebvre, and Jean Bruliat—were right; it should admit that it was wrong in its failure to support the Algerian revolution; it should admit that it completely missed the boat in 1968 out of a superstitious fear of 'gauchisme'; and finally, it should admit that it was wrong in not fully and consistently condemning the Soviet invasion of Czechoslovakia.

More importantly, according to Ellenstein, the party must now break completely with the notion that the Soviet Union represents in any way a desirable model, and must rethink its analysis afresh in a spirit which recognizes that the socialist project belongs to no particular party. Finally, the party must abandon its 'tribunal' function, i.e., its role as guardian of a sacred truth which it merely asserts without ever putting it to the test of either radical action or the exercise of governmental power, and take on a 'consular' function, i.e., become an active partner in the building of a socialist France.

Both Elleinstein and Althusser converge around the conclusion that the party must 'leave the fortress.' The party must abandon its 'distrust of the masses,' and learn to pay attention to and respond to the needs and initiatives of the people. It must also invent new rules and relationships for its dealings with other parties and other sectors of society: 'democracy,' as Thorez himself once remarked, "is a sustained act of creation." Specifically, Althusser concludes, the conditions for change are (a) a revitalization of Marxist theory, (b) a thorough critique and reform of the party's internal organization and mode of functioning, (c) a concrete analysis of the class situation in France, and (d) a policy of alliance with *all* working-class and popular forces, "at the base as well as at the summit."[5]

But the crisis on the left extends well beyond the PCF. Within the Socialist Party there has been a significant realignment of factions, and the basic division is now between Mitterrand's eclectic but ultimately managerial line and the Rocardist faction, maintaining an *autogestionaire* position close to that of Rocard's old party, the PSU. There is a threat of a leadership struggle which both regard as premature and potentially divisive. Rocard is the obvious heir to the party leadership, but if he is forced by the media to declare himself before his time it will undoubtedly limit his freedom to explore and experiment with various approaches to the *autogestion* concept, and oblige him to play a public politician's game. In terms of intellectual debate, the party's right wing seems intent on establishing that the

Socialist line is of Marxist 'inspiration' rather than 'derivation'; while the left wing is trying to exorcise 'social democracy' from the party's vocabulary. But as a whole the PS retains a fundamentally electoralist, i.e., governmental emphasis and thus a commitment to a renewed Union of the Left, which seems unworkable as long as both the PS and the PCF only want such a union if they can be the dominant party within it.

It has often been remarked that the French political class seems to be involved in an eternal election campaign, and the present behavior of both the PCF and the PS would seem to bear this out. As we have pointed out earlier, the 1978 legislative elections had themselves come to be seen as the decisive event through which the French people were to make a fundamental choice about the nature of the society they wished to live in. Yet a legislative election is, after all, a quite ordinary event, embedded in a given power structure and a given definition of the role of the state. One would expect that the parliamentary system would be one of the last institutions to reflect profound social and economic changes. The almost exclusive reliance on electoralism as the means of realizing the demands of May 1968 may ultimately come to be regarded as the main error of the present period.

Since the elections, the Barre government has been implementing ruthless economic policies aimed at eliminating industries not strong enough to compete in an increasingly ferocious international environment, allowing prices and profits to rise while creating a new climate of austerity. Yet the response of the left (and particularly of the PCF) has been merely to complain about the effects on employment, without providing a credible analysis or an alternative plan to deal with the whole. It is arguable that the left deserved to lose the legislative elections, because the *Programme Commun* purported to be a program of government, but as such could easily be seen by the electorate to be dangerously naive and misguided.

ECOLOGY AND THE CRISIS OF MARXISM

SINCE THE SECOND World War, world history has taken on an apocalyptic character. The arms race and international economic development have created a situation where autonomy within national borders is constrained as never before. National governments are increasingly restricted in their actions, and are increasingly forced to take on a technocratic, managerial mode of functioning. Under these conditions, electoralism becomes a sad farce. Yet it is precisely under such conditions that European Communist parties are seeking to define themselves in a national and parliamentarist framework. It may well be, as the Eurocommunists seek to recognize, that one wants to arrive at a situation of diversity in modes of socialist organization; but the forces to be contended with in order to arrive there demand concerted international effort as never before.

Yet Marxism seems increasingly unreal as a model of political action. Of course one wants to 'overthrow capitalism': but does one really know what that means any more? 'Capitalism' is that web of political, economic, and social institutions which presently trap us, but where are the levers of change? One cannot wipe the slate clean and try again; there are no convincing analyses that do justice to the lived reality. It is not just capitalism but the whole industrial order that must be transcended, and this implies a new vision of people and their interaction with their environment, of an environment with requirements of its own. Moreover, in violating the environment, people have violated hitherto unrecognized psychic aspects of themselves: the "end of history" has arrived, not via the forcible overthrow of the relations which fettered the full development of productive capacities, but by the evolution of these capacities in an alienated, self-destructive mode.

It is for this reason that the ecology movement offers the principal hope for the future. But a new human vison cannot be constituted overnight; political life must go on, underpinned and perhaps gradually undermined by the recognition that what is being sought is more profound, more fundamentally revolutionary than has yet been conceived. Neither the orthodox Marxist understanding of revolution nor a sole reliance on electoral politics is sufficient. Rather, what appears to be needed is a new understanding of what a revolution means, and a sense of what role electoral politics can and cannot play in bringing it about.

As one looks to the future of progressive politics in France, it is clear that both a fresh analysis and a new strategy are called for. This analysis must both comprehend and revitalize the role of the left parties, and indeed of all the forces for change. The European working class, lulled into believing that by adhering to the Socialist and Communist parties it is truly 'living in history,' must transcend the complacency of this self-definition and transform its institutions into the real instruments of liberation. As Roger Garaudy once remarked, "Nothing valid can be done in France without the Communist Party; nothing at all can be done unless that Party radically transforms itself."[6] This transformation is necessary, but not a sufficient, condition of radical change in French society.

In the ecology movement, the divisions created by the 1978 elections have forced many issues into the open, where they must be dealt with at the risk of having the movement as a whole limited to a purely marginal role, fighting what appears to be a losing battle against nuclear technology per se. The alliance between ecologist and 'bourgeois' environmentalists is an inherently unstable one, so long as these issues are concealed. As Vaudrot has remarked: "the situation is, from a historical point of view, of a rare banality: it resembles the ambiguities of an alliance between revolutionary socialists with the traditional liberal bourgeoisie against some commonplace dictatorship. But at first sight there does not appear to be any formula for an ecological social-democracy."[7] It is for this reason that the full spectrum of ecological concerns cannot find its expression in a party such as the PS, with its administrative aspirations, for the Socialists' dominant vision is one of capitalism done right. But the transformation of society required to adapt to ecological constraints is a radical one: either in the direction of the radical left, towards decentralization, scaling down and reorientation of industrial production, *autogestion*, 'soft' energies, appropriate technologies, and a reconstruction of community life; the reduction of work and the development of enduring and endurable lifestyles; a strict control by the society over basic sectors of economic production and the expansion of collective facilities, while at the same time a reduction of bureaucracy and of technocratic planning; or of the radical right, with forced reductions in living standards, vastly increased regulation and surveillance, control over the activity of the population, and continued conflicts with the Third World over resources. There is no middle, reformist path, which leaves in place the structures of capitalist expansion while seeking to moderate their consequences—for these consequences are no longer simply distributive but have become determining of the total societal and economic model.

It is for this reason that the development of an authentic 'Eurocommunism' offers a possible model for European political life, and is not inconsistent with the ecological vision. But it is a Eurocommunism quite different from that which we have examined in this paper.

Notes

1. Georges Lavau, "The PCF, the State, and the Revolution," in Donald Blackmer and Sidney Tarrow, eds., *Communism in France and Italy* (Princeton, N.J.: Princeton University Press, 1975), pp. 89, 132ff.

2. Louis Althusser, "What Must Change in the Party," *New Left Review*, no. 109, May-June 1978, p. 39.

3. Roger Garaudy, *The Crisis of Communism* (New York: Grove Press, 1970), p. 8.

4. Althusser, *op. cit.* p. 25.

5. Althusser, *op. cit.* p. 45.

6. Garaudy, *op. cit.* p. 8.

7. C. M. Vaudrot, *L'Ecologie, histoire d'une subversion* (Paris: Styros, 1978), p. 63.

PART III

THE INTERNATIONAL SETTING

chapter 9

EUROCOMMUNISM AND THE STALEMATE OF EUROPEAN CAPITALISM

Fred Block

THE EMERGENCE OF Eurocommunism is closely tied to the crisis of the post-World War II international order. The developments that are part of this crisis—the end of the cold war, the decline of United States power, the weakness of the international economy, and intensified cultural challenges to capitalist hegemony—have created new opportunities for the Communist parties in Western Europe. The parties have responded by altering their strategies and by modifying long-standing practices and theories. But the breakdown of the old international order has not yet given way to the creation of a new one. Instead, the old decayed order lingers on and its remaining structures frustrate the efforts of the Eurocommunist parties to shape history. The parties are caught in the stalemate created by the crisis of the old order. New opportunities and their own political evolution have not sufficed to bring socialism any closer. If the Eurocommunist parties are to find a way out of the stalemate, their own movement toward internal democratization, theoretical revitalization, and strategic reorientation must progress far beyond the steps taken to date.

THE OLD ORDER

THE IDEA OF "a crisis of the postwar order" has become enough of a cliche to require a more precise definition. The postwar order refers to the political-economic arrangements established in the aftermath of World War II as a consequence of efforts by the United States to stabilize the international environment. But it is more than that, since those arrangements provided both a means of organizing international politics and a context in which world capitalism could experience a dynamic period of growth.[1]

The cornerstone of the postwar order was the United States' economic and political hegemony at the end of World War II. The United States used its hegemony to shape the rebuilding of Western Europe along liberal capitalist lines. This required substantial use of economic resources in Marshall Plan aid and other economic and military aid programs to provide Western Europe with incentives to accept American goals. The coming of the cold war made it possible to persuade Western Europe to opt for a political-military alliance with the United States, and this alliance, in turn, provided another incentive for European acceptance of a liberal world economy. United States-Soviet polarization was, from the start, an integral part of the postwar order because it provided both an ideology and a concrete raison d'etre for the exercise of American political and military power.

United States hegemony was also used to create a stable set of relations between developed and underdeveloped nations, consolidated over time as a system of neo-colonialism. Neo-colonialism contributed to the postwar economic expansion by assuring Western access to raw materials at relatively low prices. In particular, neo-colonialism provided Western Europe with a cheap energy source—Middle Eastern crude oil—that facilitated industrialization and a wave of economic expansion based on widespread use of the automobile.

The most telling indication of the hegemony of the United States was its ability to shape the pattern of economic development in Western Europe in the period of post-World War II reconstruction. Another pattern of development was possible, since there was in Western Europe widespread disillusionment with liberal capitalism and an abundance of social needs that came out of the long years of war and depression. Yet, during the Marshall Plan years, the United States persuaded the Europeans to adopt conservative economic policies that kept wages and social spending to a minimum, in order to maximize productive investment. The Europeans were induced to accept the American model in which labor forgoes immediate gains in exchange for eventual receipt of a constant share of a growing economic pie. In this model, labor gets its eventual reward in the form of consumer durables, while public spending for social needs is kept to a minimum.*

These conservative economic policies would not have succeeded by themselves in creating prosperity in Western Europe, but the United States provided the other key ingredients. First, American aid and investment flows helped to subsidize the European standard of living and provide funds for industrial capital. Second, high levels of foreign and domestic military spending by the United States through the fifties helped to boost global demand for European exports. Finally, the United States encouraged the economic integration of Western Europe, especially the inclusion of West Germany in a European economic bloc. The progress through the fifties and sixties in the reduction of economic barriers within Western Europe played a key role in stimulating economic growth.[2]

The Postwar Order and the Economic Miracles

THE DEGREE TO WHICH the European economic miracles were shaped by the structures of the postwar order can be seen by looking briefly at developments in the three countries with substantial Eurocommunist parties—Italy, France, and Spain.

Italy. The Italian economic miracle of 1950-63 was second only in Europe to West Germany's, but it was even more remarkable in light of the strength of leftist social forces in Italy after the fall of fascism. One would think that the strength and prestige that the left had gained in the Resistance would have allowed it to sabotage an attempted capitalist restoration. But such was not the case—capitalist restoration in Italy was eminently successful. To be sure, the moderate policies of the PCI in the period from 1944 to 1947 made the restoration somewhat easier, but the critical turning point came after the first promises of Marshall Plan aid in 1947.[3]

The Christian Democrats threw the Communists out of the coalition government and began to pursue conservative economic policies with a vengeance. A drastic deflation, designed to squeeze inflation out of the economy and lower real wages, pushed unemployment up dramatically. Marshall Plan aid was used to cushion the blow by supporting consumption levels, and in the mounting cold war climate, the government was

---

*The state, of course, has played a larger role in Western Europe both in planning investment and in direct ownership of certain sectors of the economy. Nevertheless, the state's role has been designed to underwrite a pattern of economic development fueled by private industrial investment and individual consumption.

able to isolate the Communists politically despite the validity of thei protests against anti-labor policies.[4]

The consequence was a period of rapid industrialization as th combination of cheap Italian labor and relatively strong foreign deman led to a high level of industrial investment. The continuing migration o surplus labor from the underdeveloped Italian south kept labor ii abundant supply, so that wage gains trailed productivity advance through 1962. Between 1950 and 1962, Italian national income grew at rate of six percent per year, making possible, as the American mod promised, substantial real-income gains for industrial workers.[5]

Italian economic growth continued after 1963-64, but the reductio in the labor surplus and a changed political environment made it possib] for labor to increase its share of national income. The resulting inflatio led the government to pursue stop-go policies designed to decreas inflation through economic slowdowns. Once the "stop" phase ha succeeded in reducing the rate of inflation, the government would begin "go" phase to expand the economy again. The consequence of suc policies was that economic growth in the period from 1964 to 1970 fell t a rate of 4.8 percent a year.*

Three dimensions of Italy's experience must be stressed. Firs Italian economic growth after 1950 was highly uneven in its geographic effects. The North became highly industrialized while the South tende to become even more depressed. Second, social needs were continuall neglected; social investment in housing, education, and urban service was kept to a minimum.** In fact, the neglect of these public good appeared to be a significant factor in the waves of labor militancy in 196 and 1969. Third, export demand—and investment to produce industria capacity to meet that demand—was the key factor in sustaining Italiar economic growth, particularly after the beginning of the Europear Economic Community (EEC) in 1958. The share of exports in Italy's gross domestic product rose from 9.8 percent in 1953 to 18.9 percent in 1963.[6]

---

*These data and all other data that are not otherwise identified are drawn from the Organization of Economic Cooperation and Development, *Main Economic Indicators.*

**In some respects, services in Italy are more advanced than in the United States. Medical care is free, social security payments are more generous, and Italy spends a far larger percentage of its national income on social services. Nevertheless, the overall picture is one of substantial underdevelopment. For example, hospitals are seriously overcrowded and the quality of care is often low.

France. The trajectory of French growth was different from that of Italy. While France experienced the same turn towards conservative economic policies in the period 1947-48, those policies were less successful in squeezing inflation out of the French economy and facilitating French competitiveness in international markets. Two factors would seem to account for this difference. First, France lacked the enormous pool of surplus labor that allowed both Italy and West Germany to keep wage rates depressed. Second, France was engaged in two wars, first Indochina and then Algeria, that drained resources and contributed to inflationary pressures. Nevertheless, with substantial American aid, French industrial production grew at an annual rate of 4.7 percent between 1951 and 1958.[7]

The major turning point for France was the enactment of economic stabilization measures by de Gaulle in 1958.[8] These measures eliminated many income subsidies, reduced real wages, and prepared the French economy for the higher level of international competitiveness brought by the beginning of the Common Market. Working class resistance to these measures was generally weak as a result of the confused political situation in which de Gaulle came to power. At the same time, France's increased use of immigrant labor and Algerian refugees reduced problems of labor scarcity.[9] Between 1959 and 1966, French industrial production grew at a rate of 4.5 percent a year; during this period, exports grew even faster, indicating that they played a key role in stimulating France's economic growth. But by 1967, the government was again forced to resort to stop-go policies, and in the aftermath of May 1968, continuing economic growth was linked to mounting inflationary pressure.

Spain. Francoism considerably delayed Spain's acceptance of the orthodox economic policies advocated by the United States. Up to 1951, the Spanish economy had been highly autarkic and subject to a wide variety of governmental controls. Under American pressure, and with the promise of American aid, a liberalization was attempted in 1951, designed to restore the free market in both domestic and foreign transactions. But since resistance to economic liberalism within the regime was formidable, the liberalization was only partial and tended to produce both inflation and balance-of-payments deficits.

A far more thorough liberalization was carried out as part of a stabilization plan in 1959. This plan combined a removal of many economic controls with a daily drastic deflation.[10] But the critical factor that made the 1959 stabilization plan successful was Spain's growing ties with the dynamic Western European economy. From 1950 on, increasing revenues from tourism in Spain and remittances from Spanish workers employed elsewhere in Europe provided Spain with the foreign exchange needed to finance imports of capital goods.[11] This laid the basis for rapid industrialization, fueled by low wages, strong foreign demand, and increasing investment by multinationals. Between 1960 and 1966, Spanish industrial production grew at an annual rate of six percent a year. In 1967-68, the growth rate slowed as Spain was forced to resort to stop-go policies to reduce inflationary pressures. But industrial production grew at faster than a ten percent rate in "go" years such as 1969, 1970, and 1973.

However, the Spanish economic miracle was also deeply flawed. Industrial investment was highly concentrated in a few regions, leaving much of rural Spain impoverished. And even more than in Italy, urban services are underdeveloped; there are serious housing shortages and the educational system is woefully inadequate. Furthermore, the entire state apparatus is in need of reorganization and modernization both to eliminate the vestiges of Francoism and to establish the organizational structures needed for an industrial society.

The 1960s and the Decline of the Postwar Order

A NUMBER OF developments in the 1960s tended to undermine the postwar order, beginning a slow process of decay. These developments are interconnected, but three critical factors can be distinguished: the decline of American power, United States-Soviet detente, and the explosion of social needs throughout the developed capitalist world.

The decline of American power first became evident in the form of the United States' balance-of-payments deficit. With the economic reconstruction of Western Europe and Japan, American superiority in international trade was diminished, and the United States could no longer rely on a balance-of-trade surplus large enough to cover the costs of its foreign military and economic investments. At the same time, foreigners became less willing to hold on to the dollars created by the payments deficit. The result, through the sixties, was a continuing crisis around the balance-of-payments position. The problem, in brief, was that the United States faced a choice between effective management of the international economy and its national interests, and chose the latter. The consequence was an increase in tension between the United States and Western Europe (symbolized by American conflicts with de Gaulle) and growing instability in international economic arrangements.[12]

The United States' economic weakness was heightened by the American involvement in Vietnam. The steady escalation of the war worsened the American balance-of-payments position and created problems of domestic inflation. But even more critically, the United States' inability to prevail over the Vietnamese revealed that American power had reached its limits. The failure of United States policy makers to recognize those limits served to weaken American power further. Other nations witnessed the spectacle of American helplessness, and the growing disillusionment of the American population with the war deprived United States leaders of a key resource for the exercise of international power—a citizenry willing to tolerate military interventions elsewhere.

The American decline weakened United States hegemony over its Western European allies, but the same outcome was also a consequence of United States-Soviet detente.* From the late fifties on, the logic pointing towards a Soviet-American understanding became more powerful, but the United States tended to resist a relaxation of tensions for fear that it would weaken the European alliance and the domestic resolve for high levels of military preparedness. In the sixties, however, the United States' hand was forced by European efforts at detente diplomacy. Continued resistance by the United States to detente would have created a dangerous division within the alliance and created the risk that American businesses would lose out in the race for the promising Eastern European and Soviet markets. The irony of the situation was that each concrete step towards Soviet-American understanding served to further undermine the Atlantic Alliance in two ways. First, the reduction in the threat of nuclear war tended to make Western Europe's dependence on the American nuclear umbrella less salient. Second, detente tended to increase Western European fears of a Soviet-American condominium that would reduce Western Europe's freedom of action.

These factors, as well as the difficulties of reconciling Soviet and American ambitions, have place real limits on the depth of detente. Through the seventies, there have been repeated episodes of intensified United States-Soviet conflict. But American policy makers have too much to lose from a return to cold-war levels of Soviet-American conflict. An actual return to cold war could lead to a Soviet-European rapprochement, and the inevitable further escalation of the arms race would have a devastating impact on the American economy.

Even though the present period of detente involves a continuation of conflict, it is still very different from the cold-war era. The passing of

---

*It has been argued that after the OPEC oil price rise, there has been a resurgence of American power. But while the price rise has a more severe immediate impact on Western Europe than on the United States, the thesis that the energy crisis allowed the United States to re-establish its hegemony has not stood the test of time. American weaknesses at the July 1978 summit in Bonn, and the threat by the Common Market nations to move toward monetary union are indications that the American decline has not been reversed.[13]

the cold war ended the hysterical anti-communism of the fifties. This made it far easier for the European Communist parties to play a legitimate role in their national politics. The Socialist-Communist hostility that had been re-created in the 1947-48 period could also give way to common action in a period of reduced international tensions.

THE OTHER IMPORTANT change in the 1960s was the explosion of social needs. The pattern of economic development established in the United States and Western Europe in the forties and fifties was organized around needs that could be satisfied through acts of individual consumption. Social needs were relatively neglected in order to maximize private investment and personal income.* The indictment of American affluence of the fifties—private affluence amidst public squalor—is equally applicable to the Western European countries that experienced rapid economic growth in the fifties and sixties.

But the successes of capitalist development also created new needs that pointed beyond existing forms of social organization. For example, greater affluence generated rising expectations for work that could provide opportunities for learning, just at a time when capitalism was completing its destruction of the craft tradition. Similarly, economic development undermined inherited forms of family life, leading to a new wave of feminism as women expressed a desire for new patterns of social life. The emergence of those new needs, most of which can only be fulfilled through collective goods—more education, more social services, more conscious direction of social life—makes the long neglect of the public sector even more significant. During the sixties, in short, new needs and long-suppressed social needs reinforced each other, creating a broad dissatisfaction with the achievements of liberal capitalism.

This dissatisfaction was expressed in a critique of the consumer society that stressed the narrowness of the needs that capitalism had satisfied. Simultaneously, social movements emerged to press for changes in social priorities. The student movement played a critical role both in advancing the critique of the consumer society and in demanding that universities and other institutions no longer be shaped by the logic of capitalist accumulation. At the same time, advanced sectors of the labor movement in Western Europe sought to break the pattern that made wage rates the principal issue in labor-management negotiations; collec-

---

*To be sure, state spending in Western Europe has been substantial, including large expenditures for investment in state-owned industries and for economic infrastructure. However, spending for such social needs as housing, medical care, and urban services was kept to a minimum during the period of postward reconstruction.

tive needs were introduced through demands for workers' control and for improved access to collective goods such as education, transportation, and housing.[14]

By the late sixties and early seventies, the critique of consumer capitalism was being advanced by still other movements. Feminism expressed the collective needs of women for equality and for alternatives both to the oppressive family form that had developed with the consumer society and to more traditional forms of female oppression. The environmental movement focused on capitalism's neglect of such collective needs as clean air, clean water, and high standards of public health. Movements for regional autonomy and community control expressed the collective need to exercise some control in a society where the most important decisions remained in the hands of private firms.

The explosion of social needs and the growth and revitalization of diverse social movements had a number of important consequences. In a relatively brief period of time, the ideological hegemony of liberal capitalism was fundamentally weakened, making possible a leftward shift of substantial segments of the middle strata in countries such as France, Italy, and Spain. One indication of this shift has been the career of the idea of self-management ("autogestion") in French politics. Before 1968, the demand for self-management in all areas of French life was being put forward only by a few extreme left groups. By 1978, self-management was part of the official platform of the Socialist Party, a platform that won the votes of a quarter of the French electorate. And even that underestimates the idea's popularity, since the PCF, long hostile to the concept, also advanced the slogan in the 1978 election for fear of being out of step with the cultural mood.

Another important consequence of the explosion of social needs has been a tendency towards fiscal crisis. Liberal capitalism in the 1960s tended to respond to new social demands by ignoring the qualitative issues and responding to those issues that could be settled with more money. Hence, through much of the capitalist world in the sixties, provisions for welfare, unemployment insurance, and pensions were made substantially more generous than they had been earlier.[15] This seemed like a small price to pay to contain and limit social dissatisfaction, since such generosity could be easily afforded if rapid economic growth continued. However, rapid economic growth did not continue, and these types of social spending contributed to a squeeze on the state's budget.

The 1970s and Deepening Economic Crisis

WHILE THE WEAKENING of the old order resulting from the

politics of detente and the expansion of social needs has been relatively continuous from the sixties to the seventies, there has been a qualitative change in the seriousness of the old order's economic crisis. There is mounting evidence that the pattern of accumulation that provided for dramatic and relatively smooth economic growth from the forties through the sixties no longer works. Either economies remain relatively stagnant or economic growth is accompanied by costly levels of inflation, unemployment, or the two together. At the same time, the continuing decline of American hegemony creates serious instablities at the level of international economic management. There are few remaining international "rules of the game" within which to manage deteriorating economies, and the United States has been unable to protect the world economy from shocks such as the OPEC oil price rise.

It was earlier noted that despite their different economic histories, from about the mid-sixties France, Italy and Spain were forced to resort to stop-go economic policies. Periods of economic expansion would quickly lead to mounting inflationary pressures, which the government would handle by deflating the economy. In many instances, the inflationary pressures would lead to a weakening in the balance of payments, increasing the need for compensating deflationary action. While the sources of the inflationary pressures are complex, a significant factor has been increased labor militancy in the context of tighter labor markets. Even in Spain, under conditions of semi-illegality, increasing labor militancy led in the sixties to substantial wage gains.[16] Again, it must be stressed that one of the key factors lying behind the heightened militancy has been dissatisfaction with the collective goods provided to the working class; but the militancy was usually more successful in raising wages than in affecting the quantity or quality of collective goods.* Employers knew after all that they could neutralize the impact of higher wages through price increases, but that the same tactic was less effective in reducing the cost of collective goods.

Over time, stop-go policies have become progressively less effective in purging these economies of inflationary pressures. The trend has been for the average rate of inflation to rise with each subsequent stop-go cycle. Governments have been reluctant to continue a contraction long enough to make a major dent in inflation, and the expansion phase of the cycle always sees a sharp rise in the inflation rate, as labor and other groups attempt to win back what was lost during the contraction.

This was the situation when the oil price rise occurred in 1974.

---

*With, of course, the principal exception of government transfer payments for social security, pensions, and unemployment insurance.

France, Italy, and Spain had all been confronting increasing inflationary pressures and greater difficulty in generating non-inflationary economic growth. The dramatic increase in the price of oil magnified these problems enormously. The high cost of oil intensified inflationary pressures, and caused severe balance-of-payments difficulties. It led quickly to a major world recession as the increase in the price of oil served as a kind of excise tax—reducing consumer purchasing power in the developed capitalist countries.

In the aftermath of the oil price rise, these countries had to find ways to finance the huge balance-of-payments deficits created by the rise in their oil import bills. They did this by dramatically increasing their foreign borrowing. Italy, the most severely hit of these countries, increased its public and semi-public foreign debt by $20 billion between 1974 and 1977.[17] But such increased foreign borrowing could not be continued indefinitely. Over time, these countries had to figure out a way to adjust their economies so that they could pay for their oil without resort to increased borrowing. The magnitude of the problem is indicated by the fact that the oil price rise implied a transfer of real wealth equal to two to four percent of GNP from each of these countries to OPEC.[18] In a market economy particularly, it is not easy to accomplish the reduction in real income involved in such a resource transfer.

The strategy that these governments pursued was to reduce sharply the level of economic activity. The logic was that deflation would reduce imports as a by-product of reduced economic activity, and that would solve the immediate balance-of-payments problem. The hope was also that eventually deflation could bring about a reduction in real wages large enough that when the rate of economic activity picked up again, the payments deficit would be substantially reduced by both a long-term decrease in imports and an expansion of exports made more competitive by lower wage rates.

Italy and France began to deflate their economies in 1974, while Spain waited until later to initiate austerity policies because the precarious Franco regime lacked the political strength to risk a severe economic downturn. But in all cases, prolonged deflation was required to neutralize the balance-of-payments impact of the oil price rise. It took Italy until 1978 before its balance of payments moved into surplus, and Spain faces several more years of austerity to adjust its balance of payments.

But the strategy of prolonged deflation has failed to create the conditions for renewed economic expansion. The working classes have been successful, thus far, in resisting a sharp reduction in real wages. So the only way these economies can expand again without suffering serious balance-of-payments difficulties is if they can sharply raise their level of exports. However, such an export boom has not occurred thus far and is unlikely to occur soon for two reasons. First, much of the rest of the world economy has been stagnant and that means reduced demand for French, Italian, and Spanish exports. In particular, the West German economy, the mainspring of Western European economic growth, has remained slack, as the West German authorities wait for demand elsewhere to get their economy moving again. But while they wait, the weakness of the West German economy lowers demand throughout Western Europe, making any expansion in exports difficult to achieve.

The second factor is that these economies are now facing intensified export competition from less developed countries. Third world nations (and some socialist bloc states) are pursuing the same strategy of export-led growth based on cheap labor that made possible Italian and Spanish industrialization. Third world exports of textiles already dominate the American market and their penetration of European markets is increasing rapidly. It is estimated that at present rates of growth, Europe will lose some 1.6 million textile jobs between 1976 and 1982 because of third world exports.[19] While the competition is strongest in textiles, the threat is growing in such other industries as steel, shipbuilding, and ethylene (a basic petro-chemical). In a number of cases, third world industrial export capacity is just now developing, but the danger for France, Italy, and Spain is that when global demand picks up again, their share of certain export markets will be substantially eroded by third world competition. The threat is especially severe for Italy and Spain because they have relied heavily on exports of low-technology goods.

The Role of West Germany

WHILE THE PROBLEM of third world competition is becoming increasingly important, the weakness of the German economy is the immediate factor preventing economic recovery in France, Italy, and Spain. As long as the West German economy remains stagnant, other countries in Western Europe cannot risk stimulating their economies, since without German demand, their imports would rise much faster than their exports. But the weakness of the German economy cannot be traced to the same balance-of-payments constraints that discourage Italian and French growth, since Germany has been able to adjust relatively quickly to the higher oil import bill. Germany, however, has also been dependent through the postwar period on export-led growth; but by the mid-seventies, it became apparent that even strong foreign

demand for German goods would not suffice to stimulate rapid economic growth in Germany. Germany, in short, has exhausted the potential for rapid growth in the pattern of development built around industrial exports, and German policy makers are unable or unwilling to
pursue alternative paths to economic recovery.[20]

At the root of Germany's problem is the displacement of labor
from industry. During most of the postwar period, employment in
German industry has risen steadily as Germany first absorbed millions
of workers from the East and then recruited many "guest workers" from
poorer parts of Europe and from Turkey. The steady growth in the
industrial labor force contributed to increasing consumer demand. The
result was a kind of virtuous cycle where strong demand for German
exports created new industrial jobs, and the increased industrial employment, in turn, expanded domestic demand. But starting in the early
sixties, technological advances reduced the number of person-hours
required by German industry. At first, more generous vacations made it
possible for the number of industrial employees to rise despite the
decline in total industrial person-hours. By 1970, however, the decline in
person-hours began to accelerate and the absolute number of industrial
employees began to decline. From 1970 to 1973, while industrial production rose by 13 percent, person-hours of labor fell by 9 percent; from
1973 to 1977, while the level of industrial production remained fairly
constant, total hours fell by another 17 percent. As a result, between
1970 and 1977, total manufacturing employment fell by 15 percent.[21]

A number of factors help to explain the speed of this change. First,
high domestic labor costs have led to a rapid increase in foreign branch
planting by West German corporations, slowing the rate of industrial
investment and job creation within Germany.[22] Second, the investment that is taking place tends to be highly capital intensive, as, for
example, in the chemical industry where massive investments produce
relatively few jobs. Third, increased competition from Japan and third
world producers, particularly in textiles, has led to the loss of jobs in
more labor-intensive sectors.[23] Finally German capitalists caught in a
profit squeeze since the early 1970s between high wages and the appre-
ciating currency, have been more zealous in efforts to get more work out
of fewer employees.[24]

Germany's large population of guest workers has served to minimize the impact of this transformation on German society; guest workers
and their families have been sent home in large numbers.[25] This has made
it possible to keep the official unemployment level at about five percent,
a rate which has not yet led to substantial political protest. But while the
social impact of the displacement of labor from industry has been
managed relatively well, the economic impact is another story. A reduc-

tion in the industrial labor force breaks the cycle by which expanding foreign demand also stimulates internal demand. In other words, Germany can produce an expanding volume of exports while simultaneously displacing workers and losing their purchasing power. This means that even a substantial jump in demand for German exports would not suffice to return the German economy to full employment.

The problem, in essence, is that Germany needs to restructure its economy in order to absorb the labor being displaced from industry. This requires abandoning the pattern of export-led growth and opting for an alternative that involves dramatic increases in employment in government and services. But this type of restructuring requires fundamental institutional changes that are bound to be resisted by the economic groups that have prospered under the earlier pattern of economic growth. Most importantly, an alternative pattern of growth would require a significant increase in government's share of national income, but the business community in Germany, as elsewhere, insists that it is precisely big government that is responsible for the economy's problems. A government that attempted to shift to a new pattern of development would confront enormous resistance from business, which retains the capacity to make self-fulfilling prophecies. If the business community warns that more government spending will create inflation and a fall in investment, then that is what is likely to happen.

Schmidt's Social Democratic government has succumbed to this kind of pressure and has concentrated its efforts on making the old pattern of growth work once again. Schmidt recognizes that the problems of the German economy are structural and deep-rooted, which is why he has steadfastly resisted the American insistence that a little more Keynesian stimulus would solve Germany's problems. Yet his alternative policy has focused on stimulating export markets and reducing labor's share of national income. His hope is that the combination of expanding foreign markets and higher domestic profit levels will lead to a new wave of business investment. While these policies seem quite unlikely to solve Germany's problems, their great virtue is that they are unlikely to generate opposition within the business community.[26]

The paralysis that prevents Germany from pursuing a real solution to its economic problems is symptomatic of the general problems that faces the entire developed capitalist world. The pattern of accumulation associated with the postwar order appears to be exhausted: capitalists have once again run out of enough attractive investment outlets, while efforts at Keynesian stimulus by governments are likely to lead to unacceptably high levels of inflation. Yet the power of capital prevents governments from initiating the type of institutional restructuring that is necessary for a new period of economic expansion. And, even worse, capital has been able to put governments and the labor movement on the defensive by insisting that the real cause of the economic crisis is insufficient profits and excess state spending. Capital's claim is clearly ideological, since it takes *both* reasonable profits and a promising structure of demand to stimulate investment, and a shift of income toward profits would simply further weaken already inadequate demand. But ideological or not, governments that refuse to accept capital's version of reality risk an even worse economic situation, since firms can shift their remaining new investments to more cooperative countries.

THE CONSEQUENCES of this blackmail by capital are poignant in affluent countries such as Germany, France, and the United States, but they are positively tragic in countries like Italy and Spain, where the grossly underdeveloped public sector still represents the main hope for future economic development. Capital's resistance to an expansion in the state's share of resources in these countries not only perpetuates the present stagnation but promises to undercut future opportunities for economic growth. Without increasing social investment in these countries, the labor force will prove inadequate for whatever advanced sectors are likely to develop in the future.

This is the peculiar conjuncture in which the Eurocommunist parties must now operate. It has been the case for years that the coming to power of governments that included parties committed to socialism tends to produce a crisis of business confidence. Fearing the intentions of the new government, the business community cuts back on its investment, pushing the economy into recession. The new government must quickly choose between the pursuit of pro-business policies to restore investment or the adoption of more resolutely anti-capitalist policies. Yet the latter choice is likely to generate an even greater crisis as capital, and its allies, use every available means to disrupt the economy and undermine the legitimacy of the leftist administration. Such capitalist counteroffensives have been remarkably successful in blocking the electoral road to socialism by driving such governments from power through electoral or military means.[27]

The peculiarity of the present situation is that even thoroughly bourgeois governments face a crisis of business confidence if they threaten to depart from orthodox economic policies. Throughout the developed capitalist world, the business community has little patience for efforts to save capitalism through reforms that would further increase the state's control over economic resources. In short, there is little margin even for the implementation of pro-capitalist reforms. This peculiarity means that no matter how clearly any of the Eurocommunist parties might insist that their short-term program centers on reforms to stabilize capitalism, their claims are likely to fall on deaf ears. In fact, cynical capitalists are likely to seize on anti-communism as an added excuse to defeat the reformist intentions of any government that includes Communists or rests on Communist support.

Hence, the Eurocommunist parties face a paradoxical situation. The breakdown of the postwar order—the economic crisis, the coming of detente, and the explosion of collective needs—has created new opportunities for these parties to play a more central role in their societies. But the political paralysis created by capitalist blackmail makes it extremely difficult for these parties to find an effective way to use their new influence and power. In the next section, this paradox will be explored further by analyzing the strategies of the Eurocommunist parties.

In examining these strategies, the focus will be on their potential effectiveness in beginning a transition to socialism. Yet such a focus sidesteps a number of important questions. It cannot be assumed that the leaderships of these parties are actually oriented to such a transition. They might well be more interested in organizational survival than in socialism.[28] Furthermore, concentrating on the external effectiveness of a particular strategy neglects those ways in which strategies are shaped by internal organizational considerations. A particular strategic conception might be chosen not for its external effectiveness but because it is optimal for maintaining the leadership's power or for holding together divergent wings of the party.

In sum, political strategies, even of Marxist parties, are ideological products in which appearances and reality are not necessarily the same. Nevertheless, for purposes of this essay, my discussion of strategy will remain on the level of appearances. I want to show that even if these parties' present strategies are treated as though chosen only for their efficacy in achieving socialism, it can still be shown that the parties are unable to find a way out of the current stalemate of European capitalism.

Finally, there is one additional complexity in discussing the strategies of these parties. Beyond their explicit programs lies the hope that a breakthrough elsewhere in Western Europe would create new conditions that will bring the possibility of socialism closer. For example, the Italian and Spanish parties have hoped that an electoral victory by left forces in France would set in motion a chain of events that would allow them to pursue more forward strategies in Italy and Spain. While this kind of thinking is in the best tradition of socialist internationalism, it becomes wishful thinking if there is little chance of such a breakthrough elsewhere. In sum, even though these parties' strategies incorporate implicitly these internationalist considerations, a close examination of the prospects for socialist advance on a country-by-country basis will still provide the best test of the adequacy of the Eurocommunist strategies.

ECONOMIC STRATEGIES

France: The Problem of Alliances. The French Communist Party has been committed in its Common Program with the Socialist Party to a series of major reforms that are seen as paving the way for a later transition to socialism. The Common Program envisioned, for example, a significant expansion in public-sector spending, nationalizations in a number of industries, income redistribution, and a broad range of measures designed to democratize French life.[29] The PCF's theory is that achieving these reforms would broaden the forces in favor of socialism and would seriously weaken French capitalism, making possible a subsequent transition to socialism. This is essentially a two-stage strategy: the completion of the reforms of the first stage will create an "advanced democracy" from which the transition to the second stage— socialism—can then be achieved. The difficulty with such a model is that the attempt to implement the reforms of the first stage is bound to lead to a major capitalist counteroffensive.

Such a capitalist counteroffensive is likely to involve investment strikes that increase unemployment and create artificial shortages, capital flight that creates balance-of-payments crises, and inflationary price rises. Economically, the most effective response to such a counteroffensive is to begin the transition to socialism, since depriving capitalists of control over the means of production removes their most effective means of economic sabotage. But beginning the transition to socialism does not make political sense, since the left government needs a transitional period to broaden its political base. The only real alternative is a second-best strategy of responding to the capitalist counteroffensive with a variety of economic controls and policy initiatives designed to create a period of relative economic stability despite continuing capitalist resistance. For example, strict controls would be placed on foreign exchange transactions to minimize balance-of-payments problems, and penalties would be imposed on capitalists who deliberately left production facilities idle. If such measures succeeded in restoring a reasonable degree of economic stability, then the two-stage strategy could work.

There are a number of features of the French political economy that give the PCF reason to believe that this economic stabilization could be achieved. First, France has a tradition of *dirigisme*—extensive governmental intervention in the economy. This means that there are precedents for the economic controls that would be needed to weaken the capitalist counteroffensive. Government ministries have experience in carrying out these kinds of measures. Second, substantial parts of the French economy are controlled by the state and can be prevented from cooperating with private capital. Continued and expanded investment by state-controlled firms would help keep investment levels from slipping too low, and exports by state-owned firms would provide valuable foreign exchange. Third, France is relatively self-sufficient in foodstuffs, so that supplies of food would be relatively unaffected by an international payments crisis. With little need to import food, available foreign exchange resources could be used to assure continued flows of vital raw materials, including oil.

But there are also a number of factors in the French situation that militate against the prospects of successful stabilization in this transitional period. Twenty years of integration into the European Economic Community has created a high level of economic interdependence between France and its Common Market partners, particularly West Germany.[30] In light of West Germany's enormous stake in averting a successful shift to the left in France, it is to be expected that West German capital and the West German state would take advantage of that interdependence to disrupt the French economy. While West Germany might well be constrained from more blatant forms of intervention, less visible types of pressure such as German disinvestment and interference with trade flows could be extremely disruptive. Furthermore, the distribution sector of the French economy is almost entirely in the hands of small capitalists who have been increasingly organized and militant in recent years.[31] It is difficult to imagine the left pursuing the Common Program and maintaining good relations with this stratum. Yet this stratum has enormous power of economic disruption by virtue of its control over the means of distribution. The Chilean experience highlights the economic damage that can be done by truckers, shopkeepers, and certain independent professionals. Finally, the French middle class has a long tradition of responding to crises by hoarding wealth or by sending it abroad. Even with the most severe economic controls, the ingenuity with which these practices are pursued is likely to lead to serious economic disruption.

While it is difficult to weigh the relative importance of all of these factors, it can be said with confidence that the success of the two-stage strategy is extremely problematic. The slim chances of success depend greatly on the political skill with which the initial reforms and the responses to the capitalist counteroffensive are managed. Political skill is critical because of the subtlety of a situation in which the left government must convince the public that it can control the situation without resort to authoritarian tactics, while persuading its more radical supporters that they should fall in line with the government's gradualist strategy. Political skill is also essential for neutralizing sectors of the traditional middle class, including farmers, in order to limit their potential disruptiveness.

IT IS PRECISELY the importance of political skill—subjective political judgments—in this strategy that has made cooperation between the PCF and its coalition partner, the Socialist Party, so difficult. The parties have different histories, different priorities, and there are real grounds for distrust between them, particularly in terms of how each of them might respond to a crisis situation. One can imagine certain circumstances in which the leaders of the PCF might recognize a crisis situation as an invitation to push on more resolutely, while the PS's leadership might counsel compromise or retreat. Under other circumstances, however, it is possible to imagine the roles reversed. Parts of the Socialist Party might respond to a capitalist counteroffensive by attempting a replay of May 1968—a popular uprising—at a moment when the PCF favored a strategic retreat and considered mobilization of the masses to be highly adventuristic.

In light of the difficult politics of the two-stage strategy, the distrust between the two parties helps to explain the behavior of the PCF before the April 1978 elections. The PCF's leadership was well aware that coming to power in the context of a depressed European economy would make a difficult strategy even more problematic. The weakness of the other Western European economies reduces even further the small margin that a leftist government would have to work with, since even limited inflation could lead to massive balance-of-payments problems. Furthermore, PCF leaders had good reason to fear participation in a government that simply presided over a further deterioration of the French economy. The PCF had waited so long for a share of power that to squander its first opportunity in thirty years would be disastrous. PCF leaders had reason to fear that the failure of a Socialist-Communist coalition government would lead to a restructuring of French politics in which the Socialists rejoined a center-left alliance, leaving the PCF in the political wilderness once again.

Since all of these possible negative outcomes were more likely if the PCF entered a coalition government in a weak position relative to the Socialists, the PCF attempted to strengthen its position. It did this first by trying to impose its perspective on the alliance through a renegotiation of the Common Program. When this failed, the PCF launched an attack on the Socialists designed to improve the PCF's electoral position at the expense of its allies. While this tactic failed, it did lead to the loss of the elections, saving the PCF from having to implement the two-stage strategy from a postition of weakness.[32]

Whether or not, as some commentators have argued, the PCF leadership chose deliberately to lose the elections, the decision first to attack the Socialists and then continue the electoral alliance was probably the least unattractive of the available options. For the reasons already noted, embarking on the two-stage strategy as junior partners to the Socialists in the midst of an economic downturn was hardly appealing. But the alternative of definitively breaking the alliance with the Socialists would have returned the PCF to the margins of French political life with no prospects for greater political leverage. And the leadership might even have persuaded itself that attacking the Socialists while continuing the electoral agreement could have shifted the electoral balance of power between the two parties. Since the PCF has routinely been winning twenty percent of the vote to the Socialists' twenty-five, a relatively small shift in favor of the Communists would have made them equal partners. It might have been argued that the party's recent criticism of the Soviet Union and abandonment of the "dictatorship of the proletariat," joined with its tradition of militancy, could win over some Socialist voters who were strongly anti-Stalinist but suspicious of the PS's commitment to socialism.

This was fantasy. The PCF cannot realistically compete with the PS because of widespread suspicions of its lack of internal democracy and its statist inclinations. In the foreseeable future, the PCF's capacity to begin a transition to socialism depends not on its own electoral gains, but on efforts to strengthen its alliance with the Socialists. This means, above all, that the two parties must develop a common strategy for the transition.

But there are no real prospects for deepening the alliance in this way unless the PCF makes real progress towards internal democratization. Developing a common strategy requires extensive open debate both within and between the parties, but such open debate cannot presently take place within the PCF. And without extensive democratization of the PCF, there is no way to allay Socialist suspicions that the PCF's leadership clings to a vision of an Eastern European-style regime for France. These suspicions serve to strengthen the right wing of the PS; and they diminish the entire party's enthusiasm for the resolute steps required for a transition to socialism. In sum, for the PCF to succeed in bringing France closer to socialism, it is necessary (although hardly sufficient) that the PS be strongly committed to a socialist transition. Yet the Socialists cannot become the dependable and reliable ally that the PCF needs unless the PCF increases its own reliability. The only guarantee of Communist reliability, however, is a thoroughgoing democratization of the PCF. Thus far, the PCF's leadership has made only small steps toward such democratization, and France is very far from socialism.

Italy and Austerity. The strategy of the Italian Communist Party is far more defensive than that of the PCF. It is based on the argument that the impact of the global economic crisis on Italy has been devastating, and that further shocks can be expected as third world nations claim their legitimate share of global wealth. The impact of the international crisis will force Italy to restructure its economy, undergoing a prolonged period of austerity. The great danger is that Christian Democratic governments will avoid coming to terms with the seriousness of the crisis, leading to an accelerated deterioration of the economic and political situation. Further deterioration increases the likelihood that a government of the far right would come to power, committed to drastic reductions in working-class living standards and the reversal of all the democratic gains won since the end of Fascism.

While left politicians have often exaggerated the threat from the far right in order to justify moderate policies, there is a realistic component to the PCI's fears. Though the far right in Italy is at present organizationally weak and lacks strong institutional support, there are features of the Italian situation that are ominously reminiscent of Europe in the period of fascism's rise. First, the economic situation is already bad and there are a number of imaginable ways in which it could become far worse. Second, the Christian Democrats—the political center—show clear indications of political paralysis and it is unlikely that they would be able to respond effectively to a deeper economic crisis. Finally, in this context, the rise of terrorism appears to be a serious indication of social disintegration. When these elements are put together, the result is a scenario in which the failure of the center and of the left to respond effectively to economic deterioration makes a rightist solution, that would combine drastic economic measures with political repression, seem to be the only way out. When a previously tiny right-wing movement appears to be the only viable alternative it can suddenly become a formidable mass phenomenon.

The PCI's alternative to this scenario is a period of creative and egalitarian austerity that extends rather than limits Italian democracy.[33] The PCI, and some groups to its left,[34] recognize that a period of austerity is inevitable in order to shift resources from personal consumption to investment. But they want to avoid a typical capitalist austerity that primarily reduces working-class wages while placing no restrictions on how capitalists use their increased profits. The PCI's conception of creative austerity, therefore, has four elements. The first is that all social classes share in the loss of income with the most prosperous losing the most. The second is that the resources made available by the reduction in individual consumption be used both for the production of collective goods and for employment-generating investment. The third is that this shift of resources be carefully planned with a high level of popular participation. The fourth is that in this period of economic reorganization, there be extensive reform of the corrupt and unwieldly state apparatus. This reform is necessary both to eliminate waste in the state apparatus and to make the state an effective instrument in organizing democratic change.

For the PCI, the political means to achieve creative austerity is common action by the three largest political parties in Italy—the PCI, the Christian Democrats, and the Socialists, representing some ninety percent of the Italian electorate. The PCI's goal has been to persuade the Christian Democrats that they have no alternative to common action in pursuing austerity policies. The PCI's offer of working-class cooperation creates for the government the possibility of actually adjusting the economy to the oil price rise and eliminating the inflationary pressures, so as to restore conditions for profitable investment. In the short term, this cooperation could save the Christian Democrats from the possibility of being outflanked on the right or on their left. Successful economic stabilization would weaken the threat from the right, and Communist cooperation in the imposition of austerity policies would minimize the danger of a left-wing challenge to such policies. In the long term, the Christian Democrats can hope that the austerity will lead to a revival of a stable Italian capitalism in which their position as the sole governing party would be restored.

For the PCI, the long-term strategy involves two elements. First, avoiding a return to authoritarian government protects the working class's gains and makes possible further advances. Second, if the program of creative austerity succeeds, it will eventually place the issue of a transition to socialism on the agenda. The experience of dealing collectively and consciously with an economic crisis will persuade previously unconvinced sectors of the population of the power of the socialist idea—a society in which economic processes are controlled through collective social decision-making. Furthermore, the extension of democracy and the reform of the state apparatus during the period of creative austerity will create more effective instruments for bringing about a transition to socialism. Finally, the enhanced prestige of the PCI—its identification with the needs of the Italian nation—will enable it to exercise far more effective political leadership in the period of the transition to socialism. Just as its critical role in the Resistance enhanced the party's political position in the immediate post-World War II period, so its central role in the period of creative austerity is expected to provide the party with the political capital needed to lead Italy to socialism.

This is, however, a long-term strategy for the socialist transformation of Italy. The party envisions an extended period in which Italy will continue to be a capitalist nation. The relative caution and gradualism of the Italian party's strategy is rooted in an assessment of the vulnerability of the Italian economy and the almost certain failure in the

Italian context of the strategy envisioned by the French Communists. If the Italian Communists in coalition with the Socialists were able to gain an electoral majority and form a government of the left, they would find that the long-term weakness of the economy would make it impossible to resist the capitalist counteroffensive. The $20 billion of international debt accumulated by the government and semi-public agencies would prove an overwhelming problem to a left government that would inevitably find itself cut off from additional international credits. The likely resort to a moratorium on interest payments on this debt would lead to international retaliation, endangering particularly the close to twenty percent of Italian exports that normally go to West Germany. A sharp reduction in exports would be particularly serious, since export earnings are necessary to finance both oil imports and substantial food imports. In short, a left Italian government would find it difficult to create enough economic stability even to feed its population, much less expand its hold over political power.

THE DIFFERING SITUATIONS of the French and Italian parties go far to explain their differences on a number of issues of international policy. The Italian party has been strongly committed to strengthening and democratizing the European Economic Community, and since 1975, the PCI favors continued Italian participation in NATO.[35] In contrast, the PCF has been relatively hostile to the EEC and further steps toward European integration, and it has strongly criticized continued French participation in the Atlantic Alliance. The PCF positions are rooted in a fear that these transnational institutions—the EEC and NATO—might impede French freedom of action, and particularly French freedom to pursue a socialist path. The contrasting PCI positions arise from an assessment of Italian national interests; the EEC is seen as critical for Italy's economic growth and doubts about Italy's commitment to the Atlantic Alliance might undermine investors' confidence in the Italian economy. Consistent with its long-term strategy, the PCI is seeking to build an alliance of left forces within the EEC.* Such an alliance could reform the EEC along lines that would make it easier to reconcile a gradual Italian transition to socialism with continued participation in the Common Market.

It is difficult to assess the PCI's long-range strategy intelligently, since so much can change over a ten or fifteen-year period. But there is

---

*Building such an alliance also has short-term objectives. Developing ties to Socialist parties in Western Europe is seen as a way to overcome the opposition of the German Social Democratic government to PCI participation in the Italian cabinet.

much that can be said about the short-term strategy of creative austerity, since the PCI has already begun implementing it, and the strategy involves a number of serious risks. Over the course of the last few years, the Christian Democrats have been forced into increasing reliance on the PCI. The two parties have agreed on the general outline of an austerity program, and the Christian Democrats consult the PCI on all major issues of policy. The PCI, in turn, has supported austerity and other measures that it would certainly have opposed under other circumstances. The present arrangement between the two parties leaves much room for conflict, since the Christian Democratic government tends to move slowly or not at all on the reforms that it has agreed to as a condition for PCI support. In that sense, the limited actual power of the PCI means that the present arrangement falls short of the "historic compromise" in which the PCI would exercise a share of ministerial power. Nevertheless, the present arrangement is perceived as a transitional step towards the eventual entrance of the PCI into the government.

The risks in this strategy can be analyzed in two categories: those that follow from success in stabilizing the Italian economy and those that follow from failure. The scenario of successful stabilization works as follows: a three-to-five-year period of creative austerity would eliminate inflation, modernize the public sector, and create optimal conditions for new private investment. When world demand began to expand again, Italian exports would boom, and massive new investments would be attracted by Italy's labor peace and highly effective public sector. The risk in this scenario for the PCI is that in the resulting economic expansion, the PCI would quickly lose electoral support since Italian capitalism was working once again. Faced with such a situation, the PCI would likely be reduced to making its electoral appeals on the standard social-democratic grounds—that it could make Italian capitalism work more effectively.

Actually, one of the clearest indicators that the PCI is still far from being a social-democratic party is that the party rejects this scenario as implausible. The PCI tends to recognize that the world economic crisis is structural, so that it is mistaken to expect that a sustained international economic upturn will pull Italy into a new period of capitalist prosperity. Instead, the PCI foresees that even after a period of creative austerity, the Italian economy would remain in crisis within a still-faltering world economy. The period of creative austerity would simply eliminate the more pressing problems of the current situations, such as Italy's enormous international debt, its balance-of-payments weakness, and its dependence on imported food. But the period of creative austerity would have to be followed by a deeper period of structural transformation in order for Italy to establish a new pattern of economic development.

THE MORE SERIOUS RISK is that creative austerity will fail to prevent a further deterioration in the political and economic environment. If, during the period of creative austerity, the working class felt that its sacrifices were too great, then popular disaffection with the PCI could spread. This is most likely around the issues of unemployment and working-class restraint on wages. Austerity measures, supported by the PCI had already pushed official Italian unemployment up 7.2 percent in 1977, and there is little chance of immediate relief. If anything, unemployment might rise further, since government subsidies are keeping a large number of people at work in money-losing enterprises in both the public and private sectors. Working-class restraint on wages has widely been seen as a quid pro quo for reforms of the state apparatus that would bring about a gradual improvement in the collective goods available to the working class. Since even under the best of circumstances there is bound to be some time lag between reforms of the state sector and visible improvement in public services, even a low level of Christian Democratic foot-dragging could suffice to convince workers that they are getting nothing to compensate for stable or declining real incomes.

High unemployment (particularly among young people) has already contributed to disaffection with the PCI. Should this sentiment spread to the point that groups to the left of the PCI are able to mobilize large numbers of Italian workers in protests against unemployment and restraint in labor relations, the PCI's strategy would be in serious trouble.[36] The PCI would be of less use to the Christian Democrats if the party could no longer guarantee labor peace, and as support for the PCI diminished, the dangers of sharp and violent political polarization could increase. But before matters reached the point of widespread defection from the PCI, its leadership would probably have to return the party to a stance of active opposition.

This probability is related as well to another danger—that creative austerity will fail to stabilize the economic environment because of resistance by capitalists and the changes in the world economy. Italian capitalists have been insisting that not only wage restraints, but a dramatic reduction in the state's deficit is necessary to restore business confidence and conditions for new investment. But reducing the state's deficit could well jeopardize any prospect of an expansion in social investment and would mean a major increase in unemployment as unprofitable state-run industries are closed down. The problem, in short, is that reaching agreement with the Christian Democratic Party and reaching agreement with Italian capital are two different things. While the Christian Democrats have been willing to expand state spending as a way of consolidating their political base, Italian capitalists attribute much of the blame for Italy's economic predicament to the overgrown state apparatus.[37]

The danger in this situation is that the PCI will be in the position of having to accept more and more severe austerity measures as Italian and international capital pressure the Christian Democrats into more and more conservative policies with the threat of even further reductions in new investment. At the same time, these pressures would mean that the plans for reorganizing the state sector would fall victim to a reduction in state spending. In this scenario, the PCI's acquiescence in austerity policies is seized on by Italian capitalists as a sign of weakness—encouraging the capitalists to push for even greater gains at the expense of the working class.

If this kind of capitalist resistance occurs while the PCI maintains its cooperation with the Christian Democrats, the threat of dissatisfaction with the PCI increases. Hence, obvious capitalist intransigence is likely to push the PCI back into opposition, since there would be nothing to gain from continued cooperation with the Christian Democrats. The strategy of creative austerity depends therefore on both the continued support of the PCI's working-class base and a reasonable level of cooperation by Italian capital. In the absence of one or both of these, the PCI will be forced to find a different strategy.

Yet a strategy of opposition in which the PCI simply attempts to oppose unemployment and attacks on working-class standards of living also has its risks. Since the PCI is so large, its opposition can effectively paralyze Italian society—preventing the government from pursuing any policy. And it is precisely that kind of paralysis on which the far right thrives, since it is then the only organized social force that can propose a way out of political and social stalemate. Furthermore, a strategy of opposition tends to be defensive and provides little ground for gaining or holding electoral support outside the party's recent successes in gaining the support of middle strata, successes that were based on a positive program for the transformation of Italian life. In short, while returning to opposition might allow the PCI to defend the working class better in the short term, it could well mean abandoning any plausible long-term strategy for expanding working class influence on Italian political life.

Spain and Democratization: The PCE's strategy and outlook are very close to that of the PCI, despite its much smaller size and Spain's very different history. The PCE has participated in a Spanish equivalent of the understanding between the PCI and the Christian Democrats—the Moncloa Pact. The pact, subscribed to by all of the major Spanish political parties, calls for wage restraints, a period of economic austerity, and systematic efforts to modernize and expand the Spanish public sector. The pact grew out of the special circumstances of the transition from Francoism. In the last years of the Franco regime, the Spanish government's main response to the oil price rise was to increase foreign borrowing. As a consequence, Spain faced mounting inflation, increased international deficits, and growing foreign indebtedness. It was clear to the post-Franco government that Spain could not continue to live beyond its means and that drastic action would be necessary to reduce imports, reduce inflation, and pay back some of the international debt. The Moncloa Pact was designed for this end with an expansion of public-sector services as a quid pro quo for working class restraint.[38]

The PCE's participation in the pact grows out of its perspective that the critical task in Spain is to protect and continue the process of democratization. As in Italy, the fear is that a worsening of the economic situation could serve as an excuse for the far right to seize power. But unlike Italy's, Spain's far right is not a memory; Francoist officers continue to run the army and much of the police apparatus. The PCE foresees a five-to-ten-year transition period during which Francoist officials are gradually replaced and a democratic political tradition is firmly established. Only after this transition is completed will it become appropriate to confront the problem of a Spanish road to socialism.

In the meantime, a Spanish program of austerity faces many of the same problems as in Italy. Again, a new period of Spanish prosperity depends on an upturn in the rest of the world economy, so a successful austerity program could leave Spain with still massive unemployment. And unemployment is likely to rise further, as Spanish women attempt to enter the paid labor force in rising numbers. Also, both Spanish and multinational business can be expected to resist the expansion in state spending necessary for increased social investment. The results—high unemployment with little improvement in the provision of public goods— could convince Spanish workers to abandon parties that favored moderation.

The Spanish picture is further complicated by the possibility that a government dominated by the Socialist Workers Party (PSOE)—the Spanish Socialists—will come to power in the near future. The PCE would support such a government since the PSOE shares much of the PCE's analysis of the need for moderation, although it is unlikely that the PCE would be given any share of power. But a Socialist Spanish government would be particularly vulnerable to business blackmail and might well be faced with the choice of imposing even more serious austerity measures or of presiding over a further deterioration of the economic situation. If the PCE continued to support such a government, it would run the risk of losing its trade union base to forces on its left who were willing to mobilize workers against continued austerity. In light of the

PCE's small size, the danger might force it back into opposition. But, as in Italy, a strategy of simple opposition provides few possibilities for influencing the course of events in Spain.

ALTERNATIVES

MOST DISCUSSIONS of possible alternatives to the Eurocommunist strategies have focused on more aggressive strategies that combine electoral victories with high levels of popular mobilization.* The idea, in essence, is to thwart the capitalist counteroffensive by beginning a transition to socialism that is coordinated between sections of the state apparatus controlled by socialists and new institutions of popular democracy in workplaces and communities. The obvious difficulty with this strategy is the immense problem of effectively coordinating actions at the center with actions at the base, especially when there are likely to be sharp divergences between the two in their political timetables. But there is a less obvious difficulty as well; such conceptions have in common with the strategies of the Eurocommunist parties an abstract quality. They do not sufficiently respond to the specific contradictions of this moment of capitalist development.

A satisfactory strategy for a transition to socialism must incorporate a conception of how the development of the productive forces will take place in the transition period and under socialism. It is not sufficient to argue that the coming of socialism will automatically eliminate the fetters on the development of productive forces imposed by capitalism. The present sorry state of the Soviet and Eastern European economies provides ample evidence that private ownership of the means of production is not the only fetter. A conception of the development of the productive forces must grow out of a concrete analysis of the state of productive forces under capitalism.

In the present period, this means coming to terms with the exhaustion of the pattern of economic growth that has been part of the postwar order. The pattern that combined export-led growth with individual

---

*See, for example, Nicos Poulantzas, "The State and the Transition to Socialism," *Socialist Review* 38 (March-April 1978). Other alternatives are strategies that involve waiting for a more drastic economic crisis. However, both the recurrence of a 1930s-style depression and the capacity of the left to benefit from it are quite problematic. Even if there were an international financial collapse, governments now have the capacity to restore some semblance of full employment relatively quickly. Hence, strategies built on capitalist collapse are even less appropriate today than they were in earlier periods.

commodity consumption is no longer effective in stimulating investment or in producing full employment. Rather than attempting to refurbish the pattern of export-led growth through support for austerity policies, socialists need to push for a different pattern of development. The alternative is service-led economic growth, where high levels of investment in social services create new types of employment, while simultaneously upgrading the human input into production in other sectors. The expanded productivity of a healthier, more educated, more self-conscious work force in the goods-producing sector would provide the resources needed to finance a dramatic increase in service-sector employment.

The theory behind service-led growth has been developed by Larry Hirschhorn in a number of essays.[39] His argument is that in contemporary advanced capitalism, advances in productivity in the goods-producing sector increasingly rely on such "background" social factors as organization, communication, information, and coordination. The service sector, broadly conceived, is the locus in which these background factors develop. However, as they have emerged historically, the services are not organized to maximize their developmental function. For example, the educational system is prevented from making a greater contribution to the society's ability to coordinate and organize information because of its social-control functions. It takes, therefore, self-conscious social policy to reorganize services to maximize their developmental role.

The argument can be restated in terms of Marx's schema of productive forces and social relations.[40] Advanced capitalism sees the development of new productive forces that are radically different from the productive forces of industrial capitalism. These new productive forces revolve around maximizing the capacity of people to learn, since science, information, and coordination become the keys to economic growth. But the social relations of capitalism constrain and restrict the development of these new productive forces, since those social relations grew up with the old productive forces that were based on the exploitation of measured labor time. In particular, capitalism finds it difficult to expand and reorganize the service sector in order to increase its appropriation of the new productive forces.

Any strategy designed to shift capitalist economies towards service-led growth will, therefore, encounter enormous obstacles. In particular, capital's intense resistance at this historical moment to further growth of state spending would hamper any effort to utilize the state to bring about a shift towards service-led growth. However, the emergence of new productive forces also tends to reorganize patterns of social life, breaking down the family forms and other social relations that developed with the productive forces of industrial capitalism. Out of this crisis of social life, new movements emerge that prefigure the new patterns of social relations that correspond to the new productive forces. Such new movements as feminism, self-management, and ecology anticipate and prefigure the new pattern of service-led growth that could fully develop the new productive forces.

While the connections between these movements and the new productive forces are not obvious, they are compelling.

Two critical feminist issues are central to any model of a service-dominated economy. First, feminism demands that the reproduction of labor power—the production of human beings—not rest on the exploitation of women, but be reorganized in a rational and conscious way. In a service-based economy, those previously neglected areas of social reproduction become crucial and have to be reorganized. Second, feminism demands a flexible life course in which it is possible for women and men to combine child-rearing with meaningful work without the stress presently involved in juggling demands of work and private life. This flexibility seems essential in a service-based economy, where learning is more critical to the production process, and the lifetime job gives way to much more fluid patterns of involvement in the labor force.

Self-management points to the new forms of work organization that could characterize a service-based economy. The expanded role of learning within production would be facilitated through the development of institutions of democratic control. Finally, the ecology movement points to the resource-conserving and planned nature of economic growth in a service-based economy. The present forms of resource waste would have to be eliminated in order to increase resources available for service growth, and a service economy would require a high degree of planning of both the social and physical environment.

These connections suggest a strategy that attempts to link the concrete struggles of these growing movements with efforts in the political arena to organize a shift toward a service-based economy. Such a strategy would ultimately confront the same problems of bringing about the transition to socialism that have thus far frustrated both reformist and revolutionary socialists, but it has distinct advantages. It can provide a way out of the present stalemate by organizing mass support for reforms that can be won within capitalism, since increased appropriation of the new productive forces could actually improve the health of the economy. More critically, a new productive forces strategy would give the socialist movement a number of distinct positional advantages at that time when the transition to socialism would be confronted. First, this strategy points the way toward a significant expansion in the base of support for the socialist movement, since this strategy makes possible the creation of a cohesive historic bloc that includes women and men from the working class and large sections of the middle strata. Second, a service-based economy, built around the new productive forces, provides the socialist movement with a concrete vision of social transformation, rather than the vague and unrealistic promises of documents like the French Common Program. With such a vision, people are more likely to risk the inevitable chaos of a transitional period.*

Finally, this strategy promotes the high levels of self-organization at the base of society that are a strategic necessity in the transition period. A movement that is centrally concerned with expanding the capacity of people to learn can create a mass constituency that understands what needs to be done in the transition period. Each step in the capitalist counteroffensive to disrupt and disorganize the economy can then be met by coordinated actions designed to reorganize society, including the creation of alternative channels for distributing goods and services. In this way, the capitalist counteroffensive can be effectively blunted and the basis laid for a genuinely emancipatory form of socialism that decentralizes political power.

Thus far, however, the Eurocommunist parties have shown little use for such a strategy. Their relationship to movements around feminism, self-management, and ecology has been ambivalent and sometimes hostile. In recent years, each of the parties has shifted toward a more accommodating stance toward these new movements, with the Spanish party, having the least to lose electorally, shifting the most. Still the ambivalence remains—for understandable reasons, since these movements create some tensions with the CP's traditional working class base. The environmental movement, for example, poses a threat to the creation of already scarce industrial and construction jobs. Certain feminist demands threaten the sexual privileges of working class men, and self-management strategies can conflict with the interests and outlook of the established Communist-dominated union bureaucracies. Furthermore, some of the movements are difficult to reconcile with the patterns of organization within these parties. A deeper commitment to feminism would necessitate a complete overhaul of the existing party leadership, since women hold few high-ranking positions. And it would be difficult

---

*Opting for service-led growth also provides a more promising basis for reconciling the interests of European workers with those of the third world than does a strategy of attempting to preserve European industrial jobs. But the danger remains that the gap between developed and less developed nations will widen as developed countries move into service-led growth. To avoid this, any socialist strategy of service-led growth must be linked to a conception of global development.

for the parties to embrace fully the principle of self-management without carrying out extensive internal democratizations.

Whatever the explanation for these parties' ambivalence toward the new movements, continued ambivalence or hostility is likely to condemn the Eurocommunist parties to political marginality. The industrial working class is bound to shrink as a percentage of total population in all of these countries,* and a socialist politics defined primarily by the historical interests of that section of the population will appear increasingly sectarian. The alternative is not to abandon industrial workers, but to engage them, along with other social groups, in a struggle for a society that is no longer dominated by the factory and the alienation of industrial labor.

If they are to move in this different direction, then the Eurocommunists have only begun the process of internal political change. To pursue an alternative direction that links the working class base to the new movements, the Eurocommunist parties must establish a high level of internal democracy and sexual equality. They must redefine the meaning of socialism and develop a penetrating critique of the Soviet model; this requires a creative Marxism that systematically reexamines all of the classical concepts. Without these changes, the Eurocommunists will remain caught in a historical stalemate.

---

*From 1964 to 1973, manufacturing employment as a percentage of all civilian, non-agricultural employment declined in France from 34.4 to 32.0 and in Spain from 39.1 to 33.8, while in Italy there was a slight increase, from 38.7 to 39.0 (OBCD, *Labor Force Statistics*, 1964-1974 [Paris, 1977]). While these data exclude a variety of traditional working class occupations that are outside of manufacturing, they do indicate that even during this period of major industrial growth, manufacturing employment has either stagnated (Italy) or dropped as a percentage of all non-agricultural employment. Even as a percentage of the entire labor force, manufacturing employment either stagnated or increased only slightly in the same period. In France, the figures were 26.5 and 26.8 for 1960 and 1973; in Italy, 25.3 and 30.7 for the same years; and in Spain, 22.1 and 26.9 for 1960 and 1972 (*Handbook of Labor Statistics*, 1975; U.S. Department of Labor, Bureau of Labor Statistics, "Population and Labor Force, Selected Countries, 1950-74). One would expect that with anticipated slower rates of industrial growth, the decline of manufacturing employment will become more dramatic.

Notes

1. This argument is developed at length in Fred Block, *The Origins of International Economic Disorder* (Berkeley: University of California Press, 1977), chs. 3-5. See also Gabriel Kolko, *The Politics of War* (New York: Random House, 1968), and Gabriel and Joyce Kolko, *The Limits of Power* (New York: Harper and Row, 1972).
2. For a discussion of the limits of capitalist planning, see Stephen S. Cohen, *Modern Capitalist Planning: The French Model* (Cambridge, Mass.: Harvard University Press, 1969).
3. Fernando Claudin, *The Communist Movement: From Comintern to Cominform* (New York: Monthly Review Press, 1975), Part 2, pp. 344-369.
4. See Bruno Foa, *Monetary Reconstruction in Italy* (New York: King's Crown Press, 1949).
5. Charles Kindleberger, *Europe's Postwar Growth* (Cambridge, Mass.: Harvard University Press, 1967), pp. 36-41. See also Kevin Allen and Andrew Stevenson, *An Introduction to the Italian Economy* (New York: Harper & Row, 1975), pp 48-64.
6. Allen and Stevenson, *OP. Cit.* p. 59.
7. Vera Lutz, "The French Miracle," in Josselyn Hennessy, et. al., *Economic 'Miracles'* (London: Andre Deutsch, 1964), pp. 84-85. Note that the data for the early fifties is somewhat unreliable and that much of the apparent industrial growth in that early period resulted from returning existing facilities to use, rather than new investment.

8. Maurice Flamant and Jeanne Singer Kerel, *Modern Economic Crises and Recessions* (New York: Harper & Row, 1970), pp. 102-103; Lutz, *op. cit.*, pp. 88-101.

9. Kindleberger, *op. cit.* pp. 64-65.

10. This discussion relies on Juan Estaban, "The Economic Policy of Francoism: An Interpretation," in Paul Preston, ed., *Spain in Crisis* (Sussex: Harvester Press, 1976), pp. 82-100.

11. Manuel Roman, *The Limits of Economic Growth in Spain* (New York: Praeger, 1971), pp. 44-45, 62.

12. Block, *op. cit.* chs. 6-8.

13. See James Petras and Robert Rhodes, "The Reconsolidation of US Hegemony," *New Left Review* 97, May-June, 1976, and Fred Block, "U.S. Imperialism," *New Left Review* 99, Sept.-Oct., 1976.

14. This shift of labor strategy is both reflected and advocated in Andre Gorz, *Strategy for Labor* (Boston: Beacon Press, 1967), first published in France in 1964.

15. For some data on the increases in government transfer expenditures in the 1960s, see Ian Gough, "State Expenditures in Advanced Capitalism," *New Left Review* 92, July-Aug. 1975.

16. The link between increased labor militance and inflation is made in Andrew Glyn and Bob Sutcliffe, *Capitalism and Crisis* (New York: Pantheon, 1972). On Spanish working class activity, see Sheelagh Ellwood, "The Working Class Under the Franco Regime," in Preston, ed., *Spain in Crisis*, especially pp. 169-182.

17. Robert D. Putnam, "Interdependence and the Italian Communists," *International Organization*, vol. 32, no. 2, Spring 1978, p. 314.

18. Putnam, *op. cit.* p. 311.

19. The data and much of this discussion draws on Susan Strange, "The Management of Surplus Capacity: or, How Does a Theory Stand Up To Protectionism 1970s Style," a paper delivered at the Institute of International Studies, U.S. Berkeley, Spring 1976.

20. On the debate over the restructuring of the West German economy, see Michael Kreile, "West Germany: The Dynamics of Expansion," in Peter J. Katzenstein, ed., *Between Power and Plenty* (Madison: University of Wisconsin Press, 1978), pp. 217-222.

21. OECD, *Main Economic Indicators*. See also, Ernest Mandel, *Late Capitalism* (London: New Left Books, 1975), pp. 210-212.

22. Kriele, "West Germany," pp. 217-220; Vassilis Droucopolous, "West German Expansionism," *New Left Review* 105, Sept.-Oct. 1977.

23. Between 1964-74, West Germany lost some 383,000 jobs in textiles, while substantial new investment produced only 114,000 new jobs in the highly capital intensive chemical industry. Organization for Economic Cooperation and Development, *Labor Force Statistics, 1964-1975*.

24. *Business Week,* June 19, 1978.

25. The number of foreign workers in Germany dropped from 2.6 million in the fall of 1973 to 2.1 million in early 1976. Ursala Engelen-Kefer, "Alternatives to Unemployment," in *Reexamining European Manpower Policies*, Special Report No. 10, National Commission for Manpower Policy. If these workers had been added to the official unemployment roles, rather than sent home, German unemployment would have been almost 50% higher than reported in early 1976.

26. For Schmidt's views, see "Interview with Helmut Schmidt," *Business Week*, June 26, 1978.

27. These arguements are developed at greater length in Fred Block, "The Ruling Class Does Not Rule," *Socialist Revolution* 33, May-June 1977, and "Class Consciousness and Capitalist Rationalization: A Reply to Critics," *Socialist Review* 40-41, July-Sept., 1978.

28. This is not so much a question of personal inclination as institutional imperatives. These institutional imperatives have been usefully analyzed for an earlier historical case in Guenther Roth, *The Social Democrats in Imperial Germany* (Totowa, N.J.: Beominster Press, 1963), and J.P. Nettl, "The German Social Democratic Party, 1890-1914, as a Political Model," *Past and Present*, April, 1965.

29. See Andrew Feenberg, "From the May Events to Eurocommunism," *Socialist Review* 37, Jan.-Feb. 1978.

30. In 1975-76 about 17% of French exports went to West Germany. Organization for Economic Cooperation and Development, *Statistics of Foreign Trade*, July 1977.

31. Suzanne Berger, "D' une boutique a l'autre: Changes in the Organization of the Traditional Middle Classes from the Fourth to the Fifth Republics," *Comparative Politics*, Oct. 1977.

32. For an analysis that anticipated the electoral defeat, see Diana Johnstone, "Behind the Split in the French Left," *In These Times*, Nov. 2-8, 1978.

33. The phrase "creative austerity" and much of this analysis is drawn from Enrico Berlinguer, "A Serious Policy of Austerity as a Means to Transform the Country," *The Italian Communists*, Jan.-March, 1977.

34. See, for example, "Italy, Social Democracy and Revolution in the West: An Interview with Lucio Magri," *Socialist Revolution* 36, Nov.-Dec., 1977.

35. R.E.M. Irving, "The European Policy of the French and Italian Communists," *International Affairs*, vol. 53, no. 3, July 1977.

36. But even if groups to the left of the PCI have some successes in mobilizing dissatisfaction, it is unlikely that they will make substantial organizational gains. For a pessimistic assessment of the Italian far left, see Paolo Flores d'Arcais and Franco Moretti, "Paradoxes of the Italian Political Crisis," *New Left Review* 96, March-April, 1976.

37. The problem of excessive Italian budget deficits is analyzed in *Business Week*, Sept. 18, 1978.

38. See *The Economist*, Oct. 29, 1977, and Feb. 25, 1978.

39. See Larry Hirschorn, "Toward a Political Economy of the Service Society," Working Paper no. 229, Institute for Urban and Regional Development, University of California, Berkeley; "Social Services and Disaccumulationist Capitalism," *International Journal of Health Services*, forthcoming; "The Political Economy of Health Service Rationalization," *Contemporary Crisis*, Winter 1978.

40. For an elaboration of these arguments, see Fred Block and Larry Hirschhorn, "New Productive Forces and the Contradictions of Contemporary Capitalism," *Theory and Society*, summer, 1979.

chapter 10

EUROCOMMUNISM AND THE USSR: END OF THE BOLSHEVIK TRADITION IN THE WEST?

Louis Menashe

NOVELTIES

THE LANGUAGE of contemporary politics provides some good clues regarding the fate of communist movements in the twentieth century. The terms "communism" and "socialism" make no sense anymore if they are unadorned; qualifiers have to be introduced. The Czech Communists under Dubcek were compelled to speak of *socialism with a human face*. The Sino-Soviet split accented the existence of *Maoism*. The Maoist groupings pulling away from the main Communist formations underlined their position by putting *Marxist-Leninist* after their names. Earlier, *Titoism* had appeared in the Communist world. Earlier still there was *Trotskyism*. And now we have *Eurocommunism.**

---

* The Soviets, too, are now using a qualifier. As if to sweep away all the false, revisionist, and utopian versions that are appearing of late, Soviet officials and ideologists now customarily speak of "existing socialism"—the genuine article that has been built in the USSR. So there!

Having to resort to qualifiers is a consequence of the historic identification of socialism and communism with the USSR. Behind the splits, qualifiers, neologisms, and new political alignments we find one major motif: a critical attitude towards the policies of the USSR and doubt about the quality of its socialism. The Eurocommunist movement amplifies this theme in potentially novel and dramatic ways. *Novel* because the emerging critique is unlike prior re-evaluations of the USSR within the Communist movement. *Dramatic* because a new breach with Moscow may be in the offing, and because nothing less is at stake than the renewal of communism in societies of advanced capitalism. Eurocommunism can be a historic second wind leading either to political triumphs or exhaustion and demise. Yet the situation is far from stable. Eurocommunist leaders are still groping for a new language amidst tremendous ideological and organizational ferment. Opponents of the Eurocommunist program within the parties may even be able to neutralize or reverse current trends. On the other side, the Soviet party seems not to have made up its mind as to how to handle the new phenomenon. Regular criticism from fraternal parties in Europe with long and solid credentials of reverential friendship with the USSR—not to speak of many years of silent obedience to Moscow's baton—is new for Soviet leaders as well. This is not only disorienting. The issues are so various and complex, and the political consequences so serious that Soviet leaders cannot afford snap judgments.

BEFORE EXAMINING the emerging Eurocommunist critique together with the Soviet response, it is necessary to bring the new position into relief against the background of earlier breaks from Moscow. The first major split in the Communist movement grew out of political struggles inside the Soviet party in the 1920s. Originally, "Trotskyism" was an invention of the post-Lenin leadership of Stalin, Kamenev, and Zinoviev designed to stigmatize opposition currents led by Trotsky and others. By the end of the 1920s, such themes as inner-party democracy, quickening the tempo of industrialization, combatting bureaucracy, and denying the feasability of "socialism in one country" as formulated by Stalin came to be accepted as "Trotskyism" by Trotsky and his followers.

With the consolidation of Stalin's power and Trotsky's expulsion from the USSR, the grounds were set for globalizing the schism. Trotsky in exile assumed leadership over an anti-Stalinist movement based on a core of Trotskyist factions expelled from the Communist parties. The formation of the Fourth Trotskyist International in 1938 gave final organizational form to the schism. The break has never healed. The Trotskyist movement still considers the Soviet party and all Communist parties to be Stalinist, and defines the USSR as a socialist or workers' state with bureaucratic deformations.

The Titoist rupture belongs to the aftermath of World War II, when socialist states or peoples' democracies rose out of the rubble of a vanquished fascism across Eastern Europe and the Balkan peninsula. These new states naturally had their own national inclinations, but the needs of Soviet power imposed internal uniformities on them and made them entirely subordinate to Moscow's diplomacy. Tito's break with Moscow (or his excommunication by Moscow) was not the culmination of long-lasting or substantive philosophical differences. Rather, clashes took place between a powerful state and a small one over matters of sovereignty. Frictions developed between Stalin and Tito around such issues as the character of Soviet-Yugoslav economic activity and relations among the Balkan countries. Although the Yugoslavs went on to develop internal structures different from Soviet forms (greater use of the market, workers' committees, a relative tolerance of certain kinds of Marxist dissent), they have never stood for a socialist vision or a politics broad enough either to differ from the Soviet version or to appeal to the workers' movement as a whole. Titoism was a "nationalist deviation" within the Communist movement, fiercely guarding Yugoslav national sovereignty and the independence of its ruling party vis-a-vis the Soviet party. That granted, the barriers between Moscow and Belgrade came down. The post-Stalin leadership under Khrushchev welcomed Tito back into the Communist fold and even tolerated his "neutralism" in the waning years of the Cold War.

It would not be difficult in the case of the Sino-Soviet rupture as well to trace the basic causes to a conflict of national sovereignties, including the humiliations to which the Soviets subjected the Chinese at state-to-state and party-to-party encounters after Mao's victory in 1949. But serious differences of another kind soon crystallized. The once global appeal fo the Chinese and Maoism stemmed from the character of the revolution itself, from what seemed to be a new and coherent socialist practice with a vitality not to be found in the Soviet model. The Chinese spearheaded the modern critique of the USSR all along a broad front of political, economic, ideological, and international issues. In Chinese eyes, the USSR has become a counter-revolutionary, hegemonic great power with imperial ambitions, where the state is in the grip of a new capitalist ruling class sometimes likened to fascists or "new tsars."

WHAT DO these three schismatic currents in the Communist movement have in common, and what sets them apart from the Eurocommunists? Obviously, by definition, they are all outside Moscow's direct control. Another characteristic is striking: these currents have remained marginal in the workers' movements of the Western world. They have posed no serious challenges to the established Communist (or Socialist) parties. The Soviet-Yugoslav split never generated "Titoist" breaks within other parties. Belgrade's pioneering efforts certainly facilitated the pattern of economic reforms and growing independence from Moscow, in foreign policy matters especially, typical of Eastern Europe today. Yet "Titoism" never was a distinct organizational form with an indentifiable ideological content.

Trotskyism was easily contained by Moscow in the early years through a characteristically Stalinist campaign of abuse and organizational pressure. For most Western Communists the mystique of Bolshevism stayed in Moscow, with Stalin. Trotsky became the hated renegade and his movement became "objectively" anti-socialist and even fascist. The Comintern became the arena for Soviet efforts to stamp out Trotskyism on an international scale, doing abroad what the NKVD and the Moscow trials were doing in the USSR—and the Western parties applauded and assisted in the business. Reduced to a fringe movement by the 1950s, Trotskyism enjoyed some growth in the West during the 1960s and a revived interest in Trotskyist ideas was evident in the wave of New Left thought. Still, the Trotskyist groups affiliated with the Fourth International have not been able to put a serious dent in Communist ranks, nor create mass movements of their own.

It seemed at one time that Maoism would make this breakthrough. Splits did take place, and Maoism had a romantic appeal to student groups and sections of the Communist intelligentsia, especially during the Great Proletarian Cultural Revolution with its anti-bureaucratic emphasis and radical egalitarianism. Moreover, Moscow could do little via international mechanisms in the Communist movement to arrest this tide—the Western Communist parties no longer engaged in excommunications at Soviet behest. But Moscow did not have to do much; the Maoist tide took peculiar turns in China itself and then ran its course in the West, leaving behind only small lagoons of opposition.

THE THREE GREAT schisms thus did not transform mainstream Communism in Western Europe, where the present reevaluation of Soviet socialism and a reconsideration of political philosophy and strategy is taking place *inside* the established parties. It is no doubt true that Titoism, Trotskyism, and Maoism, together with the wider ideological and theoretical explorations of the non-Communist left in the 1960s, some of which echoed earlier traditions of left opposition to Bolshevism, all helped erode entrenched Communist attitudes. It is also true, however, that the ground was particularly cleared for these influences by another force activated by Moscow itself, Khrushchev's de-

Stalinization campaign and especially the secret address to the 20th Congress of the Soviet Communist Party, outlining the crimes of the Stalin era. The impact of Khrushchev's de-Stalinization on the Communist left was enormous. A leading Eurocommunist, Santiago Carrillo, recalls, for example, how his party and others "followed like a flock of sheep" when the Comintern ordered them to condemn Tito in 1948. When Khrushchev went on to "dismantle the whole edifice," writes Carrillo, "we felt that we had been so cruelly deceived and so vilely manipulated that this completed the demolition of what remained of the mystical and almost religious element in our attitude towards the Communist Party of the Soviet Union."[1]

In one sense, then, the Eurocommunist critique of the USSR is part of an unraveling initiated by the Soviets themselves. The Eurocommunists are taking the process further, to extremes Moscow could not possibly consider. For Moscow it was one thing to begin to unravel Stalin's mystique; it was quite another to introduce historical and political questions about a whole ruling stratum governing in the name of socialism and the working class. For the Eurocommunists, this further unwinding would seem to be a vital practical necessity, a philosophical and psychological precondition for defining themselves and their politics anew. And this time, unlike 1956, they would have to come to the project themselves, untutored by Moscow; indeed, in opposition to Moscow.

"Let's face it, we *are* revisionists," an Italian Communist confided to a visiting American.[2] The term has had heretical connotations in the Marxist tradition ever since the late 19th century when Eduard Bernstein reinterpreted the meaning of class struggle and revolution in the mature bourgeois-liberal societies of the time. If they mean to challenge the orthodoxies enshrined by the Bolshevik Revolution, the Eurocommunists would certainly be revisionist. Eurocommunist leaders are emphasizing parliamentary politics, and peaceful democratic roads to socialism. They are questioning the single-party state model.* They are re-defining prole-

---

* The parties are different of course, and it might be best to speak of Eurocommunisms in the plural, but I think it is valid to generalize a clear Eurocommunist outlook based on common features of the three main parties, the Italian, the French, and the Spanish and shared by smaller groups like the British, Swedish, and Belgian. McInnes devises a clever way to look at the problem of definition: how far have the parties changed from the original twenty-one conditions demanded for Comintern admittance? "A western party that ceased to meet any one of those conditions (or groups of conditions) must be held to have evolved significantly" to a position, I would add, now commonly known as Eurocommunism. See Neil McInnes, *Euro-Communism*, The Washington Papers, Vol. IV, No. 37 (Beverly Hills: Sage Publications, 1976), pp. 5-8.

tarian internationalism. They are chipping away at the dogmas of Marxism-Leninism. By contrast, Moscow, Peking, and the Trotskyists all claim to be guardians of these orthodoxies; their primary point of reference is the Bolshevik Revolution. The Soviet party sees itself as the supervisor of an orthodox tradition that has been unbroken from 1917 to the present. Maoists and Trotskyists seek to restore the orthodoxy they claim was subverted by the Soviet party. The Trotskyists date the subversion to the period immediately before and after Lenin's death when the foundations for Stalin's tyranny were established. The Maoists honor Stalin and trace the subversion to the period after his death. Far from seeking the continuity or restoration of this orthodox tradition, with its special codes, myths, language, and mechanisms, Eurocommunist leaders are cautiously exploring a new beginning, a different way of looking at themselves in relation to the Bolshevik Revolution and its aftermath. Implicit here is the recognition (at long last) that their own societies and possibilities unfold as a separate and distinct history that is not derivative from Russia in the epoch of 1917.

In addition, what many have adduced as the "precedents" for Eurocommunism were really quite different. The popular fronts of the mid-1930s as well as political developments after World War II saw many of the Western Communist parties take on reformist colors, cooperate with other left and liberal groups, and even participate in governing coalitions. But these experiments still operated within the tradition of Bolshevik orthodoxy. They were tactical shifts to accommodate acute situations—the threat of fascism, the Franco rebellion against the Spanish republic, the economic and social reconstruction of postwar Europe. The Communist parties participating in these programs never altered their historic identities or the dogmas they lived by. Their organizational forms still came from the Soviet party, their revolutionary model still derived from Petrograd, 1917, and they still equated socialism with what existed in the USSR. Moreover, they still saw the Communist movement as a united phalanx headed by Moscow.

Given this disposition, it was easy enough for Moscow to insert its state interests into the Communist movement, shifting goals and programs among the national parties into line with Soviet objectives of the moment as if the parties were agents of the Peoples' Commissariat of Foreign Affairs. As Togliatti told the Seventh Comintern Congress in 1935: "For us it is absolutely indisputable that there is complete identity of aim between the peace policy of the Soviet Union and the policy of the working class and the Communist Parties of the capitalist countries. There is not, and cannot be, any doubt on this score. We not only defend the Soviet Union in general, we defend concretely its whole policy and each of its acts."[3] Flushed with its battleground triumphs against the

Nazis, and now dealing with the Western great powers on an equal footing, Moscow abruptly closed down the Comintern in 1943. Not long after, Cold War hostilities disrupted the Grand Alliance between the USSR and the Western powers; Moscow again needed the national parties as "border patrols" to protect and defend the USSR. Out of the Comintern's ashes the Stalin leadership kindled the Cominform into being, this time as an agency of the main European parties, east and west.

Ten years later the Cominform, too, was shelved under the influence of the de-Stalinization taking place in the USSR. The same Togliatti was to proclaim the conception of "polycentrism" or independent and equal national centers for the Communist movement. The Sino-Soviet split accelerated the process by which the parties travelled their own national roads. Less and less was the USSR the fulcrum for the movement. The Western European parties are mass organizations with bureaucratic cores. Real changes inside the organizations—as distinguished from externally imposed tacking and 180 degree turns—could only come gradually and organically, when new cadres bearing new attitudes came into leadership positions, reflecting a younger mass constituency no longer mesmerized by the USSR and the mirage of Soviet socialism. By the 1970s the changes started coming in a rush.[4]

Eurocommunism in the 1970s, then, more intensely than prior schisms and parallels, is the deepest symptom of the Soviet party's decline as acknowledged boss of the world Communist movement. But this is only one of several new elements, and it is the least of Moscow's problems. Such a state of affairs is willy-nilly acceptable to Moscow; the world has changed enough and Moscow has changed enough to compel acceptance. More significant and less acceptable to the Soviet party is another symptom represented by the Eurocommunists—the decay of the Soviet myth and a possible rupturing of the Bolshevik tradition in the West.

EUROCOMMUNISM AND THE "SOVIET QUESTION"

THE GENIE of doubt is out of the bottle and is starting to poke into many corners. Subject matters once considered taboo are now taken up in the Communist press. Critical reinvestigations of the USSR are now regularly a part of the party forums, discussions, and publications. Critical analysis is beginning to replace received dogma. The Eurocommunists are condemning the human rights violations that systematically appear in the USSR. Some are daring to suggest that perhaps after all the USSR is not socialist. They are rewriting their party programs minus the shibboleths and ritualistic incantations derived from Soviet customs.

They are re-aligning socialism with democracy. A detailed investigation of these gestures belongs to an analysis of each party, for each is proceeding in different ways and at a different pace. This cannot be attempted here; what follows is intended to convey a sense of the issues involved as the Eurocommunists reconsider "the Soviet question."

One does not have to look very far. Every subject—theoretical, historical, organizational—seems to contain a seed of controversy and an implied or overt rebuke for the USSR. Grievances about Soviet behavior are not new, nor are public criticisms. In the twenty-three years since Khrushchev's secret speech there has been plenty to feel uncomfortable about—the Hungarian invasion, the handling of the Chinese issue, the manner of Khrushchev's dismissal, the halt to de-Stalinization, the Czech invasion, political repression in general, the crackdown on the dissidents in particular, to name some of the more vivid subjects—and many of the European parties have voiced concern through the years over some or all of these matters. Sometimes, as most recently in reaction to the crushing of the Czech experiment, there was enough heat to produce resignations and expulsions. Since the mid-1970s, however, the discomfort and criticisms exhibited by the Eurocommunist parties have entered a qualitatively new phase. Public rebukes of the USSR by the parties officially or by their members individually are now regular and normal. Criticism of this or that Soviet policy now sometimes crosses over to generalized critiques of the structure of Soviet society itself, of some of its founding myths and history, and especially of its service as a socialist model. A dissociation of identities is taking place between the USSR and the Eurocommunists. So long as the Western parties accepted what their enemies charged, that the model for their socialism existed in the USSR, the parties could never be politically appealing to massive sections of the Western public. Giorgio Napolitano of the Italian Communist Party explained this as follows: "We must say that our choice of total solidarity with the socialist world resulted in casting a shadow on our prospects for the advance of socialism in Italy. It gave rise to the suspicion that those prospects were substantially similar to the type of socialist society and administration of power existing in the Soviet Union and the popular democracies. For a long time, this suspicion was costly; it slowed and limited the development of our influence and our policy of alliances.[5]"

For years the Communist movement operated according to an idealized portrait of Soviet socialism based on faith, propaganda, and a misguided sense of political necessity. Communists wanted to believe or forced themselves to accept the official pictures printed in Moscow of a harmonious peasants' and workers' socialist democracy. If they weren't simply denying that Gulag existed or that workers and peasants didn't exercise political power, they contrived contorted apologetics to explain away the "shortcomings." (The capitalist encirclement, the need for vigilance, the need for rapid economic modernization at the temporary expense of full democracy, and so on.) When de-Stalinization faced them with a part of the historical reality, some took comfort in the seeming ability of the Soviet system to correct itself; continuing "deficiencies" could be swept under the rug as unfortunate legacies from the past.

Western Communism can no longer thrive on the self-deceptions and evasions of the past. The new movement must make clear its adherence to freedoms as commonly understood in the West. And stating the obvious and elementary—the connection between socialism and democracy—is in itself an automatic implied criticism of the Soviet system. Frequently now the Eurocommunists tell this directly to the Russians, as did Berlinguer recently at celebrations of the 60th Anniversary of the Bolshevik Revolution in Moscow. Berlinguer put the matter in the tactful, understated style common to the Italian leadership; after honoring the Revolution, he went on to suggest the parting of ways:

> The experience we have gained has led us to the conclusion—as has happened in other Communist parties of capitalist Europe— that democracy today is not only the ground on which the class adversary is compelled to retreat but also represents a historically universal value on which the distinctively socialist society is based. That is why our unitary struggle, in the course of which we are constantly working for agreement with other forces of a Socialist and Christian character in Italy and Western Europe, is aimed at the creation of a new, socialist society that would guarantee all personal, collective, civil and religious liberties, the non-ideological nature of the state, the possibility of various parties to exist, and pluralism in social, cultural, and ideological life...[6]

In short, Berlinguer might have added, all the things that do not exist in the USSR. The Belgian party stated the case more forcefully in a report to its Central Committee in January, 1978: "To put an opponent of the regime in a mental hospital is not a limitation of democracy, it is an unforgiveable act. In any case, we could not be convincing in our international policy—or in our political activity in general—without informing the working class of our opinion about the impasse of democracy in the Soviet Union and the other socialist countries."[7]

Not very much more than asserting such simple truths, it seems to me, is necessary to dissipate the smokescreen of political-ideological mystifications that Soviet socialism hides behind. And without the language of mystification—such language is the lifeblood of sectarianism—socialism can become a vital public issue. The Eurocommunists are beginning to speak in secular tongues and to reach wider audiences through television, the pages of the non-Communist press, and by publishing books that air out the old formulas—Carrillo's *"Eurocommunism" and the State* is so far the best known. In all of this, the image of Soviet socialism acquires a new function, that of a *negative* model. "For the first time in the Communist movement," writes Manuel Azcárate, in the Spanish party's theoretical organ:

> Eurocommunism poses, in a clear and open way, the need for a socialist transformation that is different from those that have taken place up to the present. And not only different in certain aspects...[but] different because...in societies where capitalism has been defeated, in the Soviet Union, in China, even though there is no capitalist property, they do not display some of the basic traits of socialism. That is to say, Eurocommunism wishes to move to socialism, it does not want to head toward a society in which certain basic features of socialism do not exist.[8]

SUCH ATTITUDES might have been expected from the innovative Italians or the flexible Spaniards, but when they pop up in a traditionalist-minded party such as the French, we can be sure something very serious is afoot. A recent work by five members of the French party, *L'URSS et Nous*, published with the blessing of the party's political bureau, is illustrative. Introducing the work to readers of *L'Humanité*, party leaders emphasized that its authors "have attempted to renovate the very manner of studying and evaluating the Soviet Union." One of the authors, Francis Cohen, writes in his introductory essay that "French Communists have need of a true perception of the Soviet Union," and allows that "Soviet reality seems less and less a model to follow for the French masses."[9]

Together with this laudable attempt to look plainly at present-day USSR is the related endeavor of looking with new eyes on the Soviet past, of abandoning the triumphal mode of history, of rediscovering, for example, some of the suppressed traditions in Bolshevism represented by Trotsky and Bukharin. Cohen writes of this need in *L'URSS et Nous*. The British party formed a study group on Trotskyism and produced a pamphlet on the subject, while its new journal, *Socialist Europe*, considers some of Trotsky's ideas— critically, but without the malicious prejudices and absurdities still prevailing in Soviet treatments. Carrillo alludes to the subject by confessing that he, like other "youngsters of the period" swallowed all the nonsense about Trotsky popularized by Moscow in the 1930s. He chides official Soviet texts for their "biased manipulation of facts, which does not accord with the historical reality." Carrillo continues:

This has contributed towards a situation in which the October Revolution and its problems continue to be presented in the form of a sickly sweet fairy-tale, hindering those who study the working class and revolutionary movements from getting to know its rich and contradictory history, disarming them, instead of arming them politically and ideologically. It is high time that Trotsky's role in the Revolution was presented in an objective way...the truth would help in understanding the complexity of the class struggle and in giving the younger generation a clearer picture of that complexity.[10]

HESITATIONS, AMBIGUITIES, AND CONFLICTS

CLEARING UP the record of the Soviet party, especially in the decade of the 1930s, with its collectivization of peasant farming, wholesale arrests, Moscow show trials, and the terrorization of the party by state security organs, is still a very touchy problem for Soviet leaders today. To admit the full picture and to admit that the opposition of figures like Trotsky and Bukharin was justified is politically threatening. Present leaders were the enthusiastic cadres of that period and the chief beneficiaries of its crimes. And if the opposition was correct then, why can't an opposition be justified now? Khrushchev handled the dilemma with the simple expedient of rehabilitation—absolving, often posthumously—thousands of Communists of the lurid charges (wrecking, agents of fascism and imperialism, and the like) for which they were condemned to death or concentration camps. Soviet leaders forestall further investigation by affirming that, aside from the unjust violence and other "excesses," Stalin's regime was essentially on the correct course in all matters of foreign and domestic policy. This process stops short of rehabilitating Trotsky and Bukharin; they are spectres, as it were, of alternative regimes and policies, and of the principle of opposition itself. For the Eurocommunists, whose Stalinist lineage doesn't exactly leave them with clean hands either, a reconsideration of Trotsky and Bukharin is important for their new identities. As L'Unità, the Italian party's daily, suggested recently in an article on Bukharin: "The need to do justice to the eminent representative of the international Communist movement, as well as to the other victims of the trials of the 1930s, is not merely a problem concerning their historical merit, but a moral and political necessity."[11]

The Bukharin case has particular relevance since his son has addressed a personal appeal to Berlinguer, asking for help in securing his father's rehabilitation. In taking up this cause the Eurocommunists accomplish several things: they equip themselves for an auto-critique (of *their* role in Stalinism); they open themselves up to the richness of

Bukharin's thought (or Trotsky's) and take another step away from the monolithic-cum-religious ideological style of Soviet Marxism-Leninism with its taboos, imprecations at heresy, and index of forbidden books; and they deliver an open slap at present Soviet leaders. Thus far, Berlinguer has not responded to the appeal personally (more tact by the Italian party?), but the party press has systematically raised the issue in its pages, as have the organs of the British, Spanish, Swedish, and Belgian parties. Leading members of these parties have also signed a petition on Bukharin's behalf circulating among the European left.*

THE EUROCOMMUNISTS have entered the fray for justice for the historical Soviet opposition; even more forcibly they are defending the contemporary form of Soviet opposition—the dissident movement and the campaign for human rights inside the USSR and the Soviet bloc. The post-Khrushchev leadership signalled its attitude towards dissent by putting the unorthodox writers Sinyavsky and Daniel on trial in 1966; The represseive policies of the Soviet government since then have offered the Western parties a fat target. The Breshnev regime has launched an offensive against dissidence, replete with arrests, expulsions, psychiatric detention, harassment and intimidation of thousands of individuals associated with struggles for civil liberties, the rights of national minorities, religious toleration, free emigration, and (occasionally) democratic socialism. Still, it was not until the 1970s that defense of the dissidents by the Western parties became forthright, frequent, and less selective. An unusually severe wave of criticism by the Eurocommunists greeted a cluster of trials in the USSR in the summer of 1978, especially those of the veteran dissident-activist Alexander Ginzburg, and the Jewish "refusednik" Anatoly Shcharansky, the latter on trial for his life for purported espionage. The Spanish party called the trials "incompatible with social-

---

* A curious sidelight has turned up regarding the role of the French party in quashing a possible rehabilitation of Bukharin during the Khrushchev years. According to Zhores Medvedev, the Soviet dissident biochemist now living in London, Maurice Thorez flew to Moscow in 1958 to urge Khrushchev to postpone Bukharin's (and others') impending rehabilitation on the grounds that "After the XXth Congress and the Hungarian events we lost almost half of our Party. If you were formally to rehabilitate those who were tried in the open trials, we could lose the rest...You can rehabilitate them later, not all at the same time, but one after another, slowly." Khrushchev is reported to have said later, "We should have rehabilitated them, and we should certainly have done so, if not for the interference from Thorez." See Ken Coates, *The Case of Nikolai Bukharin* (Nottingham: Spokesman, 1978), pp. 102-103. So far as I know, the French party has not taken up this question, although some critical retrospection regarding Thorez and the Stalinism of the party is now going on. (See note 15 below.)

ist ideals." In a similar vein, the Italian party said the trials aroused "profound anxiety and reproach," and took the opportunity to remind Soviet leaders and the Western public that democracy and liberty are "inseparable from our concept of socialism."

The biggest surprise was the blunt criticism that came from the French party. In recent years French party representatives have appeared at rallies of the left (Trotskyists included) on behalf of Soviet political prisoners. Marchais has even turned up on French television for a discussion with exiled dissident Andrei Amalrik. In 1978, the French party sent a delegation to the Soviet embassy demanding the release of Ginzburg and Shcharansky, and calling for an end to all persecutions and repression. And in an act breaking with all precedent, party leaders and representatives of the Communist-dominated union federation, the CGT, participated in a demonstration denouncing the Soviet Union for the first time since the founding of the party in 1920. The demonstrators cried "KGB/GESTAPO" and "Socialism Yes, Gulag No!" Azcárate, of the Spanish party, has best summed up the case for toleration, and the need for Eurocommunists to stand up for it:

> Repression of dissidents is a political and juridical monstrosity. To have ideas other than the official ideas of the government, or to oppose the ruling system, is absolutely normal in a socialist society...Communist parties that take a stand for a socialism in freedom must adopt positions of unambiguous solidarity with the dissidents (whether or not they agree with their ideas) and condemn the Soviet Union's repressive measures against them. If this repression continues or gets sharper, the break between the CPSU and the other Communist parties will widen even more. Therefore, Communists must avoid ambivalent positions.[12]

All of the above illuminates the changes shaping up in Western European Communism. The political strategy is different, the criticisms of the USSR are pointed and regular, and the whole tone of ideological and theoretical discourse is undergoing alterations. Can the spots be changed so easily and does changing the spots also require a clean rupture with the Soviet party *a la Chinoise*? Since I believe the transformation process is real and not fraudulent, then hesitations, ambiguities, and conflicts are bound to show up. Already, these powerful issues have caused intra-party splits. In Greece, Sweden, and Britain "Eurocommunist" formations exist alongside Soviet-oriented groupings. Their contrasting attitudes may be glimpsed from the statements made by the heads of the rival Swedish parties in Moscow for 60th anniversary celebrations. Rolf Hagel, Secretary of the Workers Party-Communist expressed solidarity in the conventional idiom: "We will never make the slightest concession to the new anti-Sovietism, whose advocates find one or another so-called dissident in the Soviet Union and organize noisy campaigns about so-called violations of the rights of these 'dissidents'... These campaigns are designed to split and weaken the mighty international movement against the arms race and for peace and detente."

Lars Werner, Chairman of the Swedish Left Party of Communists, asserted the Eurocommunist theme: "We are fighting for a socialism that will strengthen and extend democratic rights and freedoms...We are fighting against any limitation of the peoples' democratic rights and for the extension of these rights in all spheres."

A "Democratic Manifesto" scheduled for discussion at the Swedish party congress (the Eurocommunists) in January 1978 said of the socialist countries:

> There have been abuses and restrictions of fundamental democratic freedoms and rights. This has been true in particular of the rights of opinion and expression...The congress therefore declares that dangerous and prolonged limitations of democratic rights and freedoms such as have occurred and still occur in some of the developed socialist countries do *not* represent a realization of the potentialities of socialism, do *not* help to strengthen socialism, and do *not* promote the development of socialism nationally or internationally.

Unfortunately, the manifesto never reached the floor of the congress, reportedly because the Soviet delegation in attendance threatened to break relations with the Swedish party.[13] This incident suggests one of the limits to developing a comprehensive, unambiguous critique of the USSR: the fear of a total break with Moscow.

THE TIES TO Moscow are exceedingly hard to sever for the Western Communists. They are encased in sentiment and tradition. "We cannot ignore," observes Giorgio Napolitano, "the ideological bonds and the feelings of solidarity with the socialist world—with the peoples of the Soviet Union above all—that are so deeply rooted in great masses of our militants and workers."[14] The heroic image of the USSR still retains the power among many Communists, particularly among the old guard, to overcome misgivings about Soviet reality. Sometimes there are no misgivings. Jeanette Vermeersch, long active in the leadership of the French party (she is the widow of the late party chief, Maurice Thorez), appeared on television in 1978 to defend the USSR in areas from "normalization" in Czechoslovakia to the treatment of dissidents, and argued that to stray from solidarity with the USSR is to weaken the workers' movement. Further signs of the identity crisis in the French party concern clearing up the historical record—facing up to its own past under Moscow's shadow. A leading critic of the USSR in the French party, the historian Jean Elleinstein, chastised his comrades for dragging their feet on this question:

> [The party] will have to own up to its past mistakes more openly and recognize that it is having problems doing this. For example, why doesn't it—26 years after the expulsion of Andre Marty and Charles Tillon—recognize that the PCF leadership made a mistake in 1952 and render justice to the expelled men (without approving all their ideas)? Why was Roger Garaudy expelled? Why hasn't it clearly admitted the influence of Stalinism in the PCF's history, the consequences of the unconditional defense of the Soviet Union and the membership of the Comintern...?

Elleinstein admits that "steps have been taken in this direction" but complains that the party always stops "halfway" and fails to win back ex-members because of this position "mid-stream."[15]

The Eurocommunists are mid-stream in many other matters. One sticky point is the extent of their "Leninism" or "Marxism-Leninism." A good case could be made that the major Western parties long ceased being Leninist, if by that term we mean a narrow organization of revolutionaries preparing an armed insurrection to establish a proletarian dictatorship. Any other definition suggests that the term is broad enough to mean whatever "Leninists" want it to mean, which is to say it means everything or nothing at all. But as often happens in the Communist culture shaped by Moscow, form and language are as important as substance. Western Communists were "Leninists" not only because they had some aspiration for a future Petrograd in their own countries, but because the term symbolized their origins and their continuing identification with Moscow and its official ideology. Now that the parties are "secularizing" their relationship to Moscow, there seems no reason to keep the term; their politics, as George Ross (elsewhere in this volume) describes in relation to the French party, have been "radical reformist" and it is time to bring nomenclature in line with practice.* The Spanish

---

* Francois Hincker of the French party puts it as follows, somewhat self-servingly: "...until the 1970s socialism was not the order of the day in France. The PCF, however much it had elaborated and followed a hightly original policy on many features of the anticapitalist struggle, still held essentially to the Soviet model of revolution and socialist development when it imagined socialism for France. There existed a contradiction between a thoroughly "French" practice

party since the spring of 1978 calls itself "Marxist, democratic, and revolutionary," while the Italian party is reported likely to eliminate from its statutes the need to study and apply "Marxism-Leninism."

The discussion has not reached the level of systematic critique of Lenin's political role and thought, something that most certainly would trigger polemics with Moscow, if not provide the ground for an actual break. Clearly, the Eurocommunists have not gone as far as other socialists of varying persuasions who deny the necessity of the original Bolshevik dictatorship, who see Lenin as having introduced elitist and authoritarian influences into Marxist politics, and who reject the organizational arrogance and rigidity associated with Leninist parties. The mood of the Eurocommunists toward the Bolshevik leader and founder of the Soviet state—and consequently their own political father-figure—is one of increasingly taking a certain distance. Lenin, they say, is to be honored as a great, bold and resourceful Marxist revolutionary, but his terrain was different from ours. As for Marxism-Leninism, Berlinguer, for example, has suggested that to leave the formula in statutes of the Italian party could "give the impression of the existence of...an immutable and closed body of doctrine" and "should be replaced by different phrasing recalling in a more accurate and up-to-date manner our whole heritage of ideas," which, Berlinguer pointed out, has been influenced by not only Marx, Engels, and Lenin, but by Machiavelli, Vico, Cavour, Labriola, and "above all by the attentive study of the forces that move and confront each other in Italian society and the whole world." All true, of course, but a nice way to fudge many issues. In a more substantively critical direction, Berlinguer added that Lenin undervalued democracy: "For us...democracy (including the freedoms called 'formal' that were initially conquered by the bourgeoisie) is a value that historical experience shows to be universal and lasting, and that the working class and Communist parties should thus also take up and assert in the construction of socialist society."*

and a theory of revolution and of socialism that remained either bookish or borrowed from prestigious examples..." See "The Perspectives of the French Communist Party," *Marxist Perspectives*, Vol. 1, No. 2, Summer 1978, p. 132.

*Berlinguer was replying to the editor of *La Reppublica*, August 2, 1978. See Diana Johnstone, "Socialists Compel Communist Leader to Define Leninism," *In These Times*, October 11-17, 1978. That Lenin bears responsibility for failing to guarantee freedoms in the young Soviet Republic—and for the tradition associated with Soviet Marxism-Leninism that has contempt for "bourgeois" (or "sham" or "formal") freedoms—seems to be the most frequent criticism coming from the Eurocommunists.

ATTACKING THE MYTHOLOGY: HOW FAR TO GO?

HOWEVER CAUTIOUS such criticisms are, they do suggest a groping to transcend Lenin and the historical tradition bearing his name. We find more groping when it comes to another acute problem: Is the USSR socialist? Certain principles would seem to point to a straightforward answer. If there is an inalienable connection between socialism and democracy, and if democracy is absent in the USSR, then...? According to a poll in late 1977, only (as many as?) 38% of Italian Communists thought the Soviet Union had attained socialism. Yet prominent members of the Italian party, in common with other Eurocommunist leaders, are reluctant to deny the socialism of the USSR. Napolitano argues "that it is absurd to deny the socialist nature of the processes of transformation completed over the past half century" in the Communist countries. Carrillo, who of the major leaders has been the most critical, thinks "the Soviet state is a transitional state. It is no longer a capitalist state and it is not yet a workers' democracy. It is a transitional state in which a stratum of leaders has the power." The recently adopted program of the Spanish party speaks of a "primitive socialism" existing in the USSR. The authors of the new French study of the USSR conclude their discussion, after a good deal of beating about the bush, with some compromise formulas. The USSR is socialist, they argue, if by the term we mean "a transition to communism traversing a series of stages corresponding to consecutive resolutions of the contradictions that this movement engenders." In plainer words, the USSR has not, as Communists used to assert, attained a fixed state of grace known as socialism simply because private property no longer exists and there is no bourgeoisie holding state power. Instead, the authors see an evolution to economic democracy (since the preconditions have been achieved), and an evolution to political democracy (since state power is "oriented" to the working class). "These evolutions," they write, "are difficult, experiencing high and low points, but they are tendencies oriented more and more towards socialism."[16]

It is easy enough to punch holes in such temporizing arguments. Yet I don't think the Eurocommunists are to be scolded for still cleaving to the myth of Soviet socialism just when they are in the process of questioning the myth for the first time. It is too much to expect a total, instantaneous, and resounding denial of the myth—a denial, moreover, that would crash down upon their own origins and history. If socialism has not existed in the USSR, then Western Communism has been in devoted service to a myth, engaged in a grotesque political charade. It is not an easy denial. An additional consideration is that analytically, the problem of definition is difficult; the non-Communist left has been debating this for decades with no satisfactory answer. That the Eurocommunists are now discussing the question openly—never mind posing the question at all—in the analytic language long used by diverse left critics of the USSR, is reason for encouragement, not ridicule.

Whether socialism exists in the USSR is one problem; the importance of the answer for the direction of the Eurocommunist movement is another. There are several opinions here. One argument is that answering the question goes to the heart of rennovating the Western parties. Elleinstein, who still represents a minority in the French party, is a prominent partisan of this view: "One must have the courage to recognize that socialism exists only in very imperfect form in the USSR...The fact that our party bears the same name as the state parties running the USSR and other countries of this type is a heavy handicap where French public opinion is concerned...It is in fact through a priori criticism of the USSR that the fundamental issue of French Communist identity can be faced."[17]

Another view may be summarized as follows: Whether the USSR is or is not socialist is ultimately an academic and terminological matter, and should not bog us down. We stand for democracy and the Soviets do not; hence our socialism is different from their socialism, which was conditioned by a special set of difficult circumstances.* The Italian party leadership's draft "Declaration of Principles," proposed for adoption by the March 1979 Congress, handles the issue by backing a "process of socialist transformation different from [that of] the Soviet Union." Whatever the view, there always seems to exist a lingering respect for the enormity of Soviet achievements and sufferings, particularly in the antifascist war. Even Elleinstein, who is calling for a more aggressive critique of the USSR, cautions that this should be broached "without becoming anti-Soviet (what Communist can forget the sacrifice made by 20 million Soviet citizens during the Second World War?)..."[18]

For all their newly-found critical voices, Eurocommunist leaders seem determined to avoid a real split with the USSR. In March 1977 when heads of the French, Italian, and Spanish parties met in Madrid to support the Spanish party's legalization, it was fully expected, reportedly under Carrillo's prodding, that they would categorically condemn Soviet and Soviet-bloc repression of the dissidents. Instead, they called for the "full application" of the Helsinki accords of 1975, which pledge the signers to guarantee human rights, and failed to mention their specific violation in the USSR and Eastern Europe. In official declarations and written statements at the end of their meeting, the three leaders offered slightly

---

* Azcárate expressed this view at a private meeting in New York on October 4, 1978. Azcárate is a member of the executive of the Spanish party's Central Committee and editor of its journal *Nuestra Bandera*.

differing estimates of the Soviet bloc. Carrillo specified that "what is missing is democracy." Marchais saw a "positive balance" but hoped they would "perfect socialist democracy," while Berlinguer spoke of "great conquests in the social domain" marred by "authoritarian traits."[19] Carrillo's greater willingness to sharpen the attack on the USSR may be partially explained by the position of his party in the rapidly evolving internal political situation of Spain. Small, struggling for legality (now attained), putting parliamentary democracy and a constitutional monarchy on the agenda as the major short-term goals for post-Franco Spain, the Spanish party has a great deal to gain by taking forthright stands on the Soviet question. The Italian party, by contrast, already operates in a parliamentary democracy, enjoys a mass constituency with broad public confidence, and is quite close to participation in a ruling coalition: the Italians need not be so demonstratively aggressive on the same question. Moreover, the Italian party probably looks forward to the day when as a governing group it must relate to the USSR on a state-to-state level, with all the attention to tact and diplomacy that implies. (The French party falls somewhere between these two situations.)

Perhaps Eurocommunist leaders—and especially the Italians, because of their traditionally correct relations with the Soviet party—no longer view the USSR as socialist but can't say so. The issue has to be confronted, if this is true, less in ideological than in political terms, as a *Rinascita* editorial suggested: "To those who ask that the PCI denounce the non-socialist character of the USSR and make political democracy the axis of a new international organization, we answer, once again, No. The basic problem remains the political one of the reality of the socialist countries in the world, in the concrete equilibrium of the world these days." Even Azcarate, the arch-critic of the USSR among Eurocommunist leaders, still looks upon the Soviets as a great force in the struggle against imperialism and neo-colonialism.[20]

Alongside some lingering affection for the USSR and real ideological ambiguity about calling its socialism openly into question, Eurocommunist leaders have to consider some serious internal implications of any full-throated condemnation of the USSR: it might lead to a split, which might trigger the loss of large numbers of members. How large such a group might be is impossible to tell and would depend on the immediate circumstances. It is probably fair to say that the largest pro-Soviet mass among the Eurocommunists exists in the French party. (Another recent symptom of continuing pro-Soviet drags on a Eurocommunist direction in the French party: at a party exposition in Marseilles late in 1978, a book critical of daily life in the USSR (*Rue du proletaire rouge* by PCF members Jean and Nina Kehayan) was banned by the local branch and led to a debate about the issue that the local party organ even refused to announce to its readers.) The rank and file of the Spanish party, after the failed Soviet-inspired effort to put together a new group warmer to Moscow in the late 1960s, is probably more uniformly critical of the USSR than the memberships of the other major parties. But in Greece, where two opposing factions have emerged, the pro-Soviet ("external") wing is now the larger. Eurocommunist leaders have to weigh the extent of a membership loss against the possible attractiveness that a more substantive and spirited criticism of the USSR would bring. For the present they prefer not to take any great and risky leaps. Organizationally, it is also very difficult to surrender totally the Leninist legacy, with its traditions of discipline and centralism. The Italian and French parties contain large and impressively functioning bureaucracies that conduct enormous amounts of day-to-day business and are capable of rapid mass mobilizations. The Leninist spirit has always been the tonic for such functioning.

In any event, there are two sides to the dynamic. The future of the Eurocommunist challenge to the USSR may depend in part on the Soviet response to it, a subject to which we now turn.

THE SOVIET RESPONSE

SOVIET REACTIONS to the Eurocommunist challenge have not been very consistent. Moscow has not been silent, but neither has it been stridently polemical. There has been, as we shall see, an ideological counter-offensive, but not a very loud one. Once or twice, as when the Soviet weekly *New Times* attacked Carrillo and Azcárate, Moscow dipped a toe into polemical waters only to shrink back and extend a hand of reconciliation.* All in all, there has been on the Soviet side a very modulated response—less, one suspects, out of calculation than from uncertainty and indecision as to how to handle the challenge.

The Soviet leadership cannot be very happy with a situation in which criticism of the USSR is integral to the new identities of the Western parties. Yet there are numerous constraints on Moscow's course of action. For one thing, Moscow has neither the moral authority nor an international instrument at its disposal for disciplining the dissident

---

* Viktor Afanasiev, editor of *Pravda*, headed the Soviet delegation to the Spanish party congress at which the Leninist designation was dropped and declared, "We have supported you in the past and will support you in the future. Yours is a party of a great tradition." As a rare example of Soviet levity—or a typical example of Soviet heavy-handedness—Afanasiev presented Carrillo with a portrait of Lenin. See *Viewpoint*, Vol. 2, No. 2, April/June 1978.

parties or tendencies. Besides, the Western parties are determined to resist any such thing; their independent platforms are firm enough. On this score, they have some support in Eastern Europe. The Yugoslavs, Rumanians, and, less prominently, the Hungarians, have for different reasons backed the ideal of autonomy for all parties in the movement. Faced with an implacable Chinese hostility on their Eastern flank, the Soviets are likely to be wary of provoking further enmity and discord in Europe.

A full polemic with the Western parties would, in any event, run greater dangers than any of the violent exchanges with the Chinese. From the Soviet point of view—perhaps we can understand this only in retrospect—the Chinese were really ideological pushovers. Though they momentarily put the Soviets on the defensive with their accusations of revolutionary timidity and big-power chauvinism, the Chinese threw it all away by adulating Stalin, by making a virtue of economic backwardness, by their Mao cult and the peculiarities of the Cultural Revolution, not to mention its confused aftermath which has seen a succession of arcane power struggles leading to working alliances with Washington and other forces of reaction. The Chinese badly misread the climate of opinion in the USSR, Eastern Europe, and among the Western parties. By contrast, if Moscow were to enter the lists against the Eurocommunist parties, ideological currents very difficult to control might be unleashed. Unquestionably, the Western parties would get deep sympathetic responses in Eastern Europe and, not impossibly, in the USSR itself. (At least one *samizdat* publication has emerged in the USSR that identifies itself as sympathetic to Eurocommunism.) The process of de-Stalinization in the entire bloc, which periodically takes explosive forms—the Khrushchev secret speech and its consequences, the Hungarian rebellion, the Czech Spring, the Polish worker insurrections, the multiform dissident movement—might be enormously abetted and accelerated. Directly or indirectly, the force of the Eurocommunist critique is levelled at the primary contradiction in the USSR and Eastern Europe—the tension of popular strivings up against the bureaucratic domination of a privileged stratum. It is hard to see Soviet leaders running the risk of subjecting the contradiction to a full-scale debate. Instead, they prefer to deflect or cloud the issues with numerous ideological and rhetorical devices. At the same time, they are careful to remain friendly with the Western parties, one or two of which might soon turn up in governing coalitions.

THE CONFERENCE of Communist and Workers' Parties of Europe, held in Berlin, June 29-30, 1976, brought to a close the first phase of the simmering conflict between the Soviet party and a body of opinion dubbed by the Western press not long before as "Eurocommunist." In the two and a half years following the meeting of the French, Italian, and Spanish parties in January 1974, there were many bilateral meetings and declarations involving these three and other parties that provoked sniping from the Soviet side. The idea for a world congress, the first since 1969, was pushed by Soviet leaders but resisted by the main Western parties. Ultimately, Moscow agreed to a strictly European conference. Moscow sees such events not as forums for the exchange and confrontation of different opinions, but as demonstrations of the power and unity of the Communist movement, as well as tacit confirmations of the Soviet party's leading role in the movement and the authority of the dogmas it stands for. Preparations for such events are designed to eliminate possible divergences in views so as to maintain the facade of unity at the meeting, symbolized by a unanimous "final declaration."

On the face of it, the Berlin conference conformed to this pattern; there were no oratorical clashes, no splits, no walkouts, and there was a unanimously adopted final document. But the tranquility did not conceal the deep rifts that rose to the surface. Berlinguer, in his—as usual, politely worded—address hit at the very idea of ritualized meetings and the monolithism they imply: "This meeting of ours is not the meeting of an international Communist body, which does not exist and could not exist in any form, on either the world or the European level. Ours is a free meeting among autonomous and equal parties, which does not seek to lay down guidelines for, or bind, any of our parties. And it is important that this debate is open and public. In the course of it, each party expresses its own points of view, since we are all aware that on various questions, including some important ones, our positions are different, and not only because of the diversity of the objective conditions in which each party works." Berlinguer also acknowledged what the Soviets sought to deny— that the conference had problems in getting off the ground, that it would be better to hold these events without aiming for a final document, and that discussions and mutual criticisms in the Communist movement should develop "more freely and frankly." His address contained a short summary of the Eurocommunist position (he used the term in quotation marks) as conforming to conditions of advanced capitalism, where the fight "for a socialist society...has at its foundation the affirmation of the value of the individual and collective freedoms and their guarantee, the principles of the secular, non-ideological nature of the State and its democratic organization, the plurality of political parties and the possibility of alternation of government majorities, the autonomy of the trade unions, religious freedom, freedom of expression, of culture and the arts and sciences."[21]

Similar sentiments were expressed by the Spanish, French, British, and Swedish parties, with Tito and Ceausescu echoing the ideas of complete equality and mutual respect among the parties. On the Soviet side, much attention at the conference and in later official statements centered not on the substance of the Eurocommunist conceptions, but on the matter of "proletarian internationalism." The charge that this term is a cover for Soviet hegemony was easily deflected by Brezhnev at the conference, citing the "fear that behind calls to strengthen internationalist ties uniting Communists, there is a desire to recreate some kind of an organizational center. These apprehensions are strange indeed. As far as it is known, nobody is proposing the idea of establishing such a center." It was left to other parties to proclaim the orthodoxies, reassert the centrality of the Soviet connection, and rail against "anti-Sovietism." "As we see it," explained Herbert Mies, chairman of the (West) German Communist Party, "a national policy means overcoming anti-communism, especially anti-Sovietism...We are deeply convinced that we serve the interests of our people best of all by actively opposing anti-Sovietism with our dedication to proletarian internationalism and, in particular, with our friendly alliance with the Communist Party of the Soviet Union and the fraternal parties of other socialist states."

In the absence of direct polemical exchanges, one must look for the lines of division according to the use or non-use of some of the totem terms. From this angle, the conference was a victory for the Eurocommunist position. The final document records no rallying to "proletarian internationalism" (instead: "internationalist, comradely and voluntary co-operation and solidarity"); no "Marxism-Leninism" (instead: "the great ideas of Marx, Engels, and Lenin); and no call to combat "anti-Sovietism" (instead: warning about the imperialist uses of "anti-communism"). Withal, however, the conference has to be judged a polite standoff. The Soviets got their meeting, a final, unanimously approved document, and approval for the main lines of their foreign policy, including détente, the Helsinki accords, and so on. Above all, they got a ceremonial show of unity and avoided a full-scale debate.[22]

"The Plekhanovs of Today"

A NEW PHASE began after the Berlin conference. The Eurocommunists deepened their criticisms of the USSR, while Moscow's return fire alternated from occasional sniping to muffled ideological barrages. So far it is still a battle of cautious maneuvering, with each side concerned to avoid full and open confrontations. Moscow, on the defensive, has used a variety of forms in this campaign, picking diverse opportunities to wage it. When the French party sent members to a protest meeting on behalf of Soviet political prisoners in October 1976, the influential Soviet weekly *Literaturnaya Gazeta* fretted: "It is difficult to understand why representatives of the French Communist Party turned up among the participants at the meeting...It is perfectly clear that, whatever the motivating considerations were, the speech delivered by a PCF representative...did a service for the reactionary forces that are organically inimical to the ideals of freedom, democracy, international detente and socialism, for the implementation of which the French working class has always fought."[23]

The theme that the human rights issue is anti-socialist bait crops up repeatedly on the Soviet side. A long editorial in *Pravda*, February 12, 1977, argued that: "all this fuss over human rights is designed to disorient and split the progressive social and political forces in the capitalist countries and to discredit, by attacking real socialism, the ideas of scientific communism and the political platforms of the Communist and Workers' Parties and of all revolutionary movements, in order to bring about a clash between the Western Communist Parties and the ruling parties of the socialist countries." *Pravda* went on to reassure everyone that, as the Berlin Conference showed unanimously, "the world's Communists have tested weapons against the subversive actions of capital— the truth about our noble and just system and internationalist solidarity." As evidence that "these days many fraternal Western parties...are giving a severe rebuff to the organizers of ideological sabotage against socialism," *Pravda* could produce only two statements—from the Dutch and Finnish parties.[24]

Moscow frequently prefers to state its case through other voices. Thus when Michael O'Riordian, General Secretary of the Irish Communist Party (staunchly pro-Moscow), paid tribute to the 60th anniversary of the Bolshevik Revolution—"No other party, no other government has followed the principles of proletarian internationalism as selflessly as the peoples, the party, and the government of the fatherland of Great October"—*Pravda* reciprocated. O'Riordan has, wrote the Soviet party organ, "consistently stressed that...it is the duty of every Communist to expose the slanders of the bourgeoisie aimed at blackening the magnificent achievements of the Soviet Union and to firmly oppose anti-Sovietism and anti-Communism. He has stressed that it is the duty of every Communist to show the falseness of those 'theories' designed to divert the peoples from the path marked out by the party of Lenin 60 years ago."[25]

The Czechs, whose relations with the Eurocommunist parties reached a low point, occupy a prominent position in the ideological battleground. It was the Czech experiment and the Soviet-bloc invasion that stimulated many of the trends emerging as Eurocommunism. "Normalization" in Czechoslovakia, with its broad purges and ongoing repression of a dissident socialist movement that refuses to die, is a natural matter of attention for the Eurocommunists. On the eve of the 10th anniversary of the invasion, *Pravda* cited remarks in *Rude Pravo*, the Czech party organ, castigating certain (unnamed) Communist critics in the West for an analysis only somewhat different from bourgeois propaganda, and for "joining in attacks on our party and disorienting the toiling masses in their own countries."[26]

For its own direct assaults, the Soviet party has singled out the prominant Eurocommunists who most directly criticize the USSR—Santiago Carrillo, Manuel Azcarate, and Jean Elleinstein. Elleinstein in particular, has become a regular target for the columns of *New Times*. Marking the 75th anniversary of the 2nd congress of the Russian Social-Democratic Party in 1903, where the party split into Menshevik and Bolshevik factions, Vadim Zagladin railed at contemporary "revisionists" and "mensheviks." The Plekhanovs of today, wrote Zagladin, would side "not with the Communist parties resisting the pressure of the monopoly-backed reactionaries wearing the kid gloves of votaries of 'Eurocommunism', but with the enemies of the cause of the revolution." (The direct reference to Eurocommunism is as unusual as it is dishonest.) Then comes a shot at Elleinstein: "Some 'revolutionaries' of the type of Jean Elleinstein in France, who is already known to our readers, professing of course to be renewing contemporary Marxism, again seize upon the threadbare stock-in-trade of the opportunists of the beginning of the century to the accompaniment of a clamour about the 'dogmatism' of the Soviet Communists...All that they are trying to pass off as 'new' is nothing but echoes of Bernstein's shopworn sophistry covering up a gravitation to class collaboration."[27]

Anti-Sovietism and revisionism are the twin themes running through many of the Soviet and third-party ripostes at the Eurocommunists. These charges frequently consist of sterile name-calling and hollering boo-words, as in the attack on Elleinsten just cited. But there is a content to the charges as well. When the PCI weekly organ, *Rinacita*, declared that "the struggle against anti-Sovietism is not the touchstone of proletarian internationalism," it was an open disavowal of that scarcely-questioned tradition discussed above: the duty of all Communists to protect and defend the USSR, even if it meant repressing their better critical judgment. There was a certain logic to this position for much of the last six decades, a logic that suited the USSR because it produced approval for all its policies. If the USSR was under imperialist siege from the Civil War through the Cold War, it seemed the correct political course was to take sides and stick up for the USSR, with all the imperfections in its socialism. But for the Western parties it turned out to be a bizarre and almost suicidal logic that reduced many of them to the borderlands of political sectarianism. In defending one Soviet "imperfection" after another, and by going along with the mummery of equating socialism with what existed in the USSR, they sacrificed their potentially great anti-capitalist appeal and compromised their credibility as fighters for freedom and equality.

That logic has begun to evaporate. Many forces have converged in recent years to account for the change. Among them is the growth of Soviet power. Détente is a tacit recognition of an international balance of power in which existing alignments and borders are respected in Europe. The relaxation of international tensions has made it harder for both imperialism and the Soviet bloc to appeal to the dangers of an external menace. Communist parties in the West are now free to address the main domestic issues without having to take the endless sidetracks of disavowing the "Soviet threat" and the "international communist conspiracy," or drumming up the USSR's "peace policy." Moreover, the Western public is much more receptive to socialist ideas and solutions—provided they don't carry Soviet trademarks.*

The Soviets want all the benefits of detente (trade, technology, de facto recognition of the division of Europe, relief from a burdensome arms budget), but one of its side effects—the increasingly critical posture of the Western parties—is not acceptable. Moscow can no longer call the faithful into line with scare-talk about imperialism, but it goes on trying anyway. Warning the Western parties of the perils of "anti-Sovietism" is one way. As might be imagined, "anti-Sovietism" is a very elastic category for the hyper-sensitive Soviet party, which cannot tolerate criticism whatever the source. Accordingly, most criticism of the USSR is by definition "anti-Soviet." Still, that is not the point. It may be that in some sense the Eurocommunists *are* moving to anti-Soviet postitions, based on a fresh examination of many issues. The accusation of "anti-Sovietism" then becomes Moscow's handy way of *deflecting* the issues, and attempting to arouse the old logic and the old sentiments.

THE SAME ZAGLADIN cited above defines the USSR's main global contribution to the socialist cause: "Our party has done and continues

---

* "The Communist Party of Spain has maintained that if it confined itself merely to defending the foreign policy of the socialist countries and the Soviet Union, regarding this as its fundamental task, it would now be no more than a small group of propagandists capable only of making high-sounding statements and manifestos, but with no real strength. It would have been unable to promote a broad mass movement of the most diverse forces ranging from Communists to Christian Democrats." Damian Pretel, member of the Spanish party's Central Committee, speaking at an international theoretical conference of representatives of Communist and workers' parties in Tihany, Hungary, May 1976. *World Marxist Review*, Vol. 19, No. 9, September 1976, 95.

to do everything that as fully and as quickly as possible fulfills its main international duty—the construction of a communist society."[29] Zagladin here expressed an old Bolshevik dream, that Soviet society would be a powerful magnet attracting the sympathies of toilers the world over. This dream has considerably waned in the West. Soviet leaders and ideologists like Zagladin, however, still believe in it (or at least say they do). They begin with the premise that as a socialist society in full bloom the USSR would easily attract masses to its side, if only the world were not rent by acute class struggles in which the workers are constantly misled and "disoriented" by the slander of the bourgeoisie and its unwitting accomplices.

This argument is now supplemented by another explanation: Communist criticism of the USSR also assists those who are bent on sabotaging détente and restoring the Cold War. A leading Soviet ideologist, Boris Ponomarëv, candidate member of the Politburo, developed this whole line of reasoning in an address late in 1977. Opponents of détente, he said, were now using a "slanderous propaganda campaign conducted under the false slogan of defense of human liberties and rights," while "bourgeois ideologists frequently make attacks against socialism under the flag of defending the ideas of 'humanistic' and 'democratic' socialism! Things must indeed be in a bad way when the apologists for capitalism place themselves in the ridiculous position of defenders of a 'better socialism" than the one that actually exists." Ponomarëv then draws the Eurocommunists into the argument: "To butt into the debates on these questions, to try to turn differences into disagreements and disagreements into division—this is the main goal of the current anti-Communist campaigns, and in particular of the propaganda furor over 'Eurocommunism,' a concept invented by the bourgeoisie...Besmirching the glorious historical path of the Soviet Union and the other socialist countries and scorning their experience and services to the revolutionary movement—whatever considerations may motivate such an approach—in the long run backfire against those who build their hopes on such tactics. After all, resorting to such methods means shaking and undermining the peoples' faith in the socialist reorganization of the world and disparaging the prestige of socialism..."[30]

A similar argument—and a similar set of deflections—greeted the publication of Carrillo's book. The now-famous review of the book in *New Times*, which set off a short mini-crisis between Moscow and the Western parties, clumsily sidestepped the questions of substance raised by Carrillo. Significantly, the review was titled, "Contrary to the Interests of Peace and Socialism in Europe." In other words, Carrillo's book was not judged on its merits as a reconsideration of some old problems (the state, revolution, popular power, political parties) in light of present conditions in Western Europe, with some critical evaluations of the Soviet experience along the way. Instead the book was diagnosed as manifesting the syndrome of anti-Sovietism, splitting the movement, assisting the class enemy, and harming detente.

The Spanish party promptly backed Carrillo, suggesting that the real target comprised "the leaders who today give political direction to all the Communist parties that follow an orientation of a democratic road to socialism and socialism in democracy." Meanwhile, a high-level delegation of the Italian party went to Moscow to meet with Politburo members. One of the delegates, Emmanuele Macaluso, revealed what was bothering Soviet leaders, and countered with the Italian position. To Soviet charges that the human rights issue was "artificial" and designed to injure detente, the Italians replied that "this problem does exist and is a result of the fact that the problems of developing democracy remain unsolved in the USSR." When the Soviets noted that the *New Times* article was directed only at Carrillo's criticisms of the USSR, the Italian delegation replied that "they had an indisputable right to answer, but that it was not a response to this part of the book when they characterized Carrillo as an 'enemy of socialism' and when they wrote that the 'interpretation he gives to Eurocommunism corresponds entirely to the interests of imperialism.' This was an unacceptable condemnation." Macaluso also reported that the Soviet side gave its assurance that it "had no intention of sharpening the polemics with the Spanish CP, or of turning against the other Western European parties." In fact, the meeting ended with a joint communique stressing mutual support of detente and a reaffirming of party autonomies: "The opinion was expressed that each party's contribution to the common international cause is inseparably linked with its independent searchings and the elaboration of its own policy."[31]

In short, another stand-off. Moscow continued to direct little barbs at Carrillo, frequently using statements by the pro-Soviet parties (including the American party) to get across its views. But Carrillo was in Moscow for anniversary celebrations of the Bolshevik Revolution, although he was denied the floor at one meeting. The matter went no further. The Spanish party relished the opportunitiy to affirm its critical independence from Moscow while proclaiming its democratic commitments. The USSR was compelled to confirm its support of the principle of independence among the parties, but showed that it was nettled by Communist criticism, particularly of a public character outside party channels.

THE SOVIETS SEEM RECONCILED to the national roads taken by the Western parties so long as these parties respect some of the outward forms or rituals that have united the movement in the past, but especially so long as they do not make a practice of overt criticism of internal Soviet structures. It is almost as if Moscow were concerned with demonstrations of piety even as impious activity is going on. Yet as a condition of their new identity and potential new appeal, the Western parties must, if not quit the church entirely, at least follow through on their critique of Soviet socialism, then Moscow has to respond. So far, the Soviet side has tried to circumnavigate the issues with *ad hominem* attacks, cries of helping the imperialists, jeopardizing detente, and the like. These are lame devices; there is little way Moscow can defend its authoritarian socialism before Western constituencies in the present epoch. There is, on the other hand, one important area where Moscow feels it can stand on stronger terrain, appealing to many militants inside the Western parties—the matter of strategy and tactics of socialist revolution.

THE SOVIET ATTACK FROM THE "LEFT"

NOT SURPRISINGLY, albeit somewhat hypocritically since Moscow had always blessed the reformist politics of the Western parties, Soviet ideologists are attacking from the left. They now warn of the perils of revisionism and opportunism, and stress the militant example of Bolshevism in 1917 or the negative example of Chile in 1973. From the mid-1960s to the end of the decade, the main targets of Soviet ideological writing were the varieties of ultra-leftism lively at the time—Maoism, anarchism, Guevarerism, and, of course, Trostskyism, which were all dismissed as adventurist and disruptive of the workers' movement. Since 1968, new targets have been added. Partly in defense of the Soviet invasion of Czechoslovakia, partly to counter the obvious appeals the Czech experiment exerted within Western Communist ranks, books and articles have been pouring off Soviet presses to repudiate the calls for an open Marxism and new, democratic roads to socialism.[32] Earlier, Soviet critiques singled out such figures as Roger Garaudy, Franz Marek, and Ernst Fischer, who were expelled from the French and Austrian parties for their heretical views. The Yugoslav journal *Praxis* also came under attack, as did the leaders of the Czech Spring. Of late, the Western parties themselves are clearly the objects of the campaign.

Sometimes the writings are tiresomely repetitious morality tales illustrating how Lenin and the Bolsheviks snatched revolutionary scientific Marxism from the jaws of Menshevism, and how only genuinely Marxist-Leninist parties, bound in proletarian internationalist solidarity with the USSR, can ever hope to combat the contemporary descendents of the revisionists. Here is an excerpt from a good example of this genre:

> The revisionist slander of socialism is harmonized with the general chorus of the ideologists of bourgeois and reformist anti-communism, who deny the socialist nature of the social system in the Soviet Union and the other socialist countries...The main elements of the so-called "new" models of socialism are: revision of the Marxist-Leninist theory of the party; substitution of the bourgeois conception of "pluralistic democracy" for the theory of proletarian dictatorship and socialist democracy; and substitution of the "market socialism" concept for socialist economic principles.[33]

In contrast to such canned arguments, which are bound to stir only yawns in the West, some Soviet studies are notable for their thoughtfulness and sophistication. Such studies elaborate standard left arguments concerning transitions to socialism, but they take stock of the economic transformation of capitalist societies in the West, their complex class formations, the role of political superstructures, and how Marxist revolutionaries can go beyond sectarianism to mass politics. A 1977 article in *Pravda* signed by A. Viktorov—almost certainly a pseudonym and consequently denoting the significance of the statement—addressed the transition problem in light of new alignments in class forces and the degree of resistance by the bourgeoisie. The author scorns social democracy for its unfulfilled promises of a socialism through the parliamentary road, but concedes that the new struggles uniting all the democratic forces opposed to the "state-monopoly system"—"peasants, urban middle strata, the working intelligentsia, students, women"—can bring about working-class majorities in parliaments of several capitalist countries. In such cases, parliaments could be converted into weapons for overcoming the resistance of the exploiting classes and safeguarding the transition to socialism. The author adds: "It would be, however, naive to think that with a victory in elections the working class and the toilers would obtain a state that would faithfully and justly serve their interests. The real powers in society belong to those who hold the economic heights, the state apparatus, and the army. And those powers belong to the bourgeoisie. To tear away real power from the bourgeoisie is a matter of extraordinary difficulty."

Noting that a number of European Communist parties are putting forward transitional programs for socialism based on a "state of democratic union, a bloc of the left, or anti-monopoly democracy," Viktorov sounds this warning: "Historical experience has shown that it is impossible to arrive at socialism within the framework of the bourgeois state and bourgeois democracy."[34] Minus some bows to Soviet ideological convention (the need for "unity, unwavering loyalty to the principles of Marxism-Leninism, and internationalist solidarity"), Viktorov's article amounts to a level-headed warning that any sympathetic critic on the left might contribute to an assessment of the Eurocommunist strategy. The Chile theme crops up repeatedly in this "higher" type of Soviet analysis, for understandable reasons. Timur Timofeev, associated with the prestigious Institute for the Study of the World Working-Class Movement, attached to the Soviet Academy of Sciences, writes that the "fraternal Communist parties of Western European and other capitalist countries continue to study deeply...the lessons of the struggle of the forces of revolution and counter-revolution in Chile. One of the main conclusions they are drawing is the need to strengthen the alliance of the working class with the middle strata, and to develop contacts with the Catholic masses and Christian organizations."[35]

An extended discussion of the lessons of Chile also appears in an unusually incisive essay in which the Comintern scholar, A.I. Sobolev, surveys the problematic of peaceful transition in the advanced capitalist countries, with numerous allusions to show that he is aware of what the Eurocommunists are proposing. Sobolev rejects the idea that what was missing in Chile was a parliamentary majority for the left, and turns his attention to failures in the mass, extra-parliamentary arena where mechanisms for class alliances, bridges to the democratic sections of the army, and approaches to the small bourgeoisie never materialized. Successful revolutions and the failure in Chile, he concludes, show that "The most important strategic task of the political vanguard of the working class is the creation of a powerful, active, and firm union of all popular forces" that would constitute "an organized and active *social, political, and arithmetical majority*." Interestingly, Sobolev writes that Lenin "did not absolutize" armed or peaceful forms in 1917, and he admits that in principle a parliamentary, peaceful transition is possible. Such a situation might develop provided a parliamentary majority of a united left bloc, with or without Communists in government, is supplemented by widespread social and economic democratization via mass organizations—a scenario that includes parliamentary victory in tandem with forms of popular power.[36]

Sobolev is here speaking the same language as Carrillo or Sobolev and other Soviet political analysts still frame their discussions according to the revolutionary archetype: a complete and permanent assumption of state power by the working-class party must take place in the course of transitional forms; democratic forms become only means to reach this act. The Eurocommunists, however, seem to be drifting away from that revolutionary ideal altogether, at least in this "classic" form (which of course opens them up to vulgar charges of revisionism). They accept the possibility of getting voted out of power, and take political democracy as substance rather than as a vehicle of power. A consideration of this question, though it cannot be far beneath the surface of expositions such as Sobolev's, has, so far as I can tell, not appeared in Soviet analysis. It is too hot to handle. From a theoretical standpoint, it falls into the realm of the unprecedented and hypothetical. From the official Soviet point of view, it comes close to trespassing into heresy: a workers' government coming to power democratically or getting voted out democratically would dramatize the difference between Western Communism and the Soviet model. For perhaps both reasons Sobolev winds up his first-rate discussion with some hackneyed formulas about how Marxist-Leninist theory reveals no other content for political power in a socialist revolution than the dictatorship of the proletariat, how world history demands proletarian internationalism, and so forth.

Sobolev's perfunctory and ritualistic conclusion is therefore among the most interesting though unintended comments in his article on the overall problem of Soviet attitudes toward Eurocommunism. It suggests that some section of the Soviet intellectual establishment is perhaps not unfriendly to the main Eurocommunist ideas. It is impossible to determine how large this group is or their policy influence. It cannot be much, judging from what official statements convey or what gets into print. But surely the Eurocommunists are stirring things up ideologically, if only a bit at present, in the heart of orthodoxy itself, and we may look for divisions to appear beneath the crust. The widest possible estimate of the implications of Eurocommunism in the long run should include the probability of ferment in Moscow as well. In the short-run, however, different political criteria govern Moscow's behavior. At great cost, the Soviet Union has achieved a rough, all-sided parity with the West. The accommodation with the USA, West Germany, and Giscardian France might be seriously disrupted by growing Eurocommunist strength or, especially, electoral victories. Moscow, we may speculate, would prefer the known, existing stabilities of detente and the bifurcation of Europe into equal military blocs than the unknown, conceivably anti-Soviet adventures of a Eurocommunist Italy or France governed by a left coalition.

EUROCOMMUNISM FROM WEST TO EAST

THE LAST PARAGRAPH of Carrillo's book weaves together three parts of an important political drama of our time—Western Communism, the USSR, and Eastern Europe. Optimistically, Carrillo sketches a successful resolution to the script; it is even an esthetic resolution, for earlier he had told us that the events in Czechoslovakia were instrumental in bringing him and his party out of their slumber. Now the currents may run in the other direction. It is Eurocommunism that will arouse the East, and in so doing renew socialism on a world scale: "The progress of the socialist movement in the developed capitalist countries may help Soviet society and the Soviet Communists to go beyond that (coercive) State and make progress in transforming it into a real working people's democracy. This is a historical necessity which would do a great deal of good for the cause of socialism throughout the world and would uproot and destroy a great deal of bourgeois propaganda. For that reason it is all the more lamentable that the Czech comrades were not allowed to carry on with their experiment in 1968."

How does this hope conform to existing political interactions? In Eastern Europe, at least three major forces are active that have no full parallel in the USSR, and each dovetails with the Eurocommunist program: reformism, a Marxist opposition, and nationalism. All are evident in the Eastern European countries in varying degrees, with Bulgaria the exception for the moment. Two of them, nationalism and reformism, even exist as moods or tendencies within some state and party structures as well as among the public; the third, in favor of an alternative to bureaucratic, Soviet-modelled socialism, exists primarily as a movement of sections of the intelligentsia, although as Czechoslavakia showed in 1968, such a trend can emerge within the ruling parties themselves. By emphasizing national roads to socialism the Eurocommunists are natural allies of the Eastern Europeans in their slow but irresistible journey to emancipate themselves from the Soviet presence imposed 30 years ago. Some of the most tolerant public statements about the Eurocommunists by Soviet bloc leaders have come from the Hungarians. In December, 1976. Kadar told reporters in Vienna that "Eurocommunism is not a new form of anti-Communism," rebutting one of the favorite charges levelled by Moscow and its followers. In Rome in June of the following year, discussing the Eurocommunists' right to differ, Kadar commented, "This is not only their right, but also their duty. With or without the dictatorship of the proletariat, with a pluralistic or some other socialism, all I wish is that they open their people's road to socialism as quickly as possible." Later, during the controversy over the attack on Carrillo, a "senior official" was quoted in the Hungarian party daily as defending the obligation of the European parties "to select independently a path for the democratic transformation of the countries and for building a socialist society" on the basis of different conditions in each country. These sentiments were countered by others: the same Hungarian daily was also cited by TASS for condemning Carrillo's anti-Sovietism.[37] (The Hungarians have come a long way since 1956, owing to the Kadar leadership's adroitness on the tightrope in the shadow of Soviet power.)

The strongest proponents of an independent position in Eastern Europe are of course the Yugoslavs and the Rumanians, who both assert foreign policy lines that make Moscow quite uneasy. Belgrade and Bucharest, it will be remembered, both welcomed Hua Kuo-fend in the summer of 1978 as a pointed demonstration of their distance from Moscow. Both, therefore, are also strong supporters of Eurocommunist nationalism. For both, however, support stops at reforming internal structures, particularly the apparatus of suppressing dissent. At one point, the Yugoslavs even permitted themselves a sally at the Western parties when dissidence and repression were common news stories about the Soviet bloc early in 1977. They condemned "all those who would force any system on another country, including some so-called Eurocommunists who would like to change the Soviet Union."[38] Clearly, only political expediency united the Eurocommunists and a party like the Rumanian—their common challenge to the "proletarian internationalism" minted in Moscow. But their visions of socialism are hardly compatible; the emerging Eurocommunist critique of the USSR could just as easily apply to Rumania. In July, 1977, the Rumanian party stood up for Carrillo indirectly by lauding the independent spirit of the Western parties. The following February, Ceausescu was denouncing Rumanian dissidents as "traitors" while his security forces were arresting human rights campaigners.

THE PLACE IN Eastern Europe where the three elements of nationalism, reformism, and socialist dissidence converge most powerfully is Poland. There the historical nationalism, with its anti-Russian overtones, is pervasive. There too, reformist tendencies ranging from accommodation with the Catholic Church and the property-owning peasantry to a broad tolerance of diverse trends in matters of culture have gradually softened the Stalinism of the regime. And the strength of a critical public opinion confronting the regime is periodically stiffened by the most striking symptom of all—the frequent eruptions of the Polish working class, as in 1956, 1970, and also the summer of 1976. From within the Polish party itself came a plea addressed to the leaders late in 1977 for "a clear-cut program of political and economic reforms" requiring a "frank confrontation of views of members of other political parties and of the non-aligned people."[39] Following the 1976 worker rebellions and the arrest of many accused leaders, a group of Polish intellectuals formed a "Committee to Support Worker Victims of the Repression" and sought amnesty for the imprisoned protesters. The Polish Supreme Court subsequently reduced many of the jail sentences and early in 1978 Gierek announced conditional pardons.

The link between rebellious workers and protesting intellectuals in Poland, and their ability to bring pressure on the regime with a certain measure of success, is unique in Eastern Europe and positively unheard of in the USSR. But it may be a portent of things to come in the entire bloc, with its chronic economic shortcomings and cultural and ideological restlessness. Since 1968, the most visible prolonged signs of unrest have consisted of waves of intellectual protest. One such wave crested in 1976-1977. In the USSR various civil libertarian groups were formed. In Czechoslovakia, Charter 77 apppeared, drawing hundreds of signatures. In East Germany, the Communist poet-singer Wolf Biermann, and Rudolf Bahro, an industrial manager and theorist, angered the regime with their critiques. When the regime cracked down, a dissident group was formed calling itself "The German Committee for the Defense of Freedom and Socialism." Even in Rumania dissident intellectuals announced the first human rights appeal made in that country.

There were many immediate reasons for this wave of protest, apart from the chronic ones. Most prominent was the formal commitment to human rights by the Soviet bloc as embodied in the Helsinki accords of 1975, which also provided for periodic meetings between East and West to review compliance. The dissidents used the accords as a wedge to open up the human rights question in their own countries. This was also the period when Eurocommunist ideas, with their strong emphasis on democratic freedoms, were generating a great deal of interest throughout Europe. The opposition in Eastern Europe—a socialist opposition, unlike the Soviet kind—identified with the Eurocommunists and welcomed their support. Eduard Lipinski, dean of Polish economists and a prominent voice calling for deep reforms in Polish socialism, declared: "I am a Marxist. I am like the Italian Communists. So why should I be considered a dissident?" Jiri Hajek, former Foreign Minister under Dubcek, and now a Charter 77 spokesman, reportedly told the state prosecutor that pleas for civil liberties were entirely in keeping with Marxism-Leninism and identified himself as a Marxist "ideologically close to the West European parties." Friends also reported that Dubcek himself sees a kinship with the parties of Italy, Spain, and France and is known to be corresponding with them about the situation in Czechoslovakia.[40] Addressing themselves to the Eurocommunist parties about the repressions following Charter 77, eleven former members of the Central Committee of the Czechoslavak Communist Party emphasized that such methods "heap discredit on socialism not only in Czechoslovakia, but throughout Europe. These practices damage the interests of your own parties and cannot be considered merely internal affairs of the CCP."[41] This is certainly a new twist to proletarian internationalism.

A new kind of solidarity might be in the making. The Eurocommunists are embarrassed by repression in the Soviet bloc. They are anxious to show that this is not a part of their vision. The socialist dissidents understand this and look for support from the Eurocommunists. They also understand that such support is difficult for the Soviet bloc to dismiss. Finally, there is a comradeship of ideas; many of the reform proposals coming from the dissidents tally with Eurocommunist conceptions. At the core of such ideas is emancipation from the Soviet model, to infuse socialist practice with democratic, mass participation in political rule and production systems. Lipinski's "Open Letter to Comrade Gierek" composed in April, 1976, expressed these themes with clarity and eloquence—and incidentally shows how important the Eurocommunists have been in stimulating this kind of thinking. Lipinsky writes:

> I have been watching carefully for a long time the development of socialist thought in the West (because in the Soviet Union and here this thought has undergone a total calcification), especially in Italy...and I have arrived at the conclusion that the Soviet way has grown out of the ground laid by the despotic traditions of Russian statehood, that it is also hindering the present development of the Soviet Union, and that it is not the way which should be followed by socialist practice in Poland...Throughout the entire world, even among Communists, there is a growing negative attitude towards the Soviet Union's policy, there is increasing understanding of political democracy in the primeval meaning of the word, and the slogans of proletarian and one-party dictatorship are being abandoned.[42]

This cross-fertilization of ideas and experiences between West and East is also evident in the work of Rudolf Bahro. Discussing new Marxist approaches to contemporary problems of emancipation, Bahro draws on the theoretical and political contributions of the Eurocommunists:

> though the proletarian liberation struggle in capitalist society removes certain barriers, they could not be anywhere near the last ones...Man in the complex industrial societies...runs up against more general obstacles that are not bound to a specific class structure: a structure of hierarchic relationships that does not by any means vanish with the elimination of Capital. Since the movement of the working class...is, under these circumstances, a much too narrow base upon which to transform society as a whole (don't the specific workers' interests ever more often play a fundamentally conservative role?), the Western European and Japanese Communists are working at

adapting themselves to the need for changing the world felt by practically *all* the progressive elements, no matter what traditional class, stratum, or section they belong to. Evidently completely different interest fronts are taking shape, and these are already pointing to an order beyond the economies the world has known hitherto.

Especially in the case of Italy, where it is finding its most clear expression...the Communists are successfully proselytizing in all circles of the population...Behind the formula of the Historic Compromise which has de facto replaced the "Dictatorship of the Proletariat" in its superficial aspect, stands the substantial idea (substantial not because it is new but because it now has a practical chance of success) of a comprehensive social regeneration which is to be based on *all the productive forces* of society.[43]

Bahro's treatise also contains a definite political challenge: a call for the formation of a genuine, organized opposition to struggle for an alternative socialism in the Socialist bloc. This is a bold, even a foolhardy proposal; it goes beyond the position of other Marxist dissidents such as Lipinski or the Russian Roy Medvedev, whose individual appeals are directed at what they consider to be those sections of the party and state bureaucracies receptive to reforms. Bahro feels the time for organized opposition is not far off, in part exactly because of the appearance of Eurocommunism. "The truth is," he writes, "that so-called Eurocommunism introduces the spirit of a split into the East European parties, and into the personnel of their apparatuses—right up to the Politburo level...The Eastern European peoples certainly want political institutions in the spirit of the views of Berlinguer, Marchais, Carrillo..." Bahro wants the new opposition to "compel the bureaucracy to adopt a perspective of open intellectual and political combat," but this requires tremendous courage on the part of small groups; there is no question of a mass movement at the present time. Yet, "A start must be made."[44]

THE STRUGGLE FOR ALTERNATIVES

HOW WILLING ARE the Eurocommunists to assist in this start? The record is spotty so far. The Western parties have finally gotten over their reluctance to defend dissidents whose positions are ideologically repugnant. The defense of free opinion must be wholehearted and unqualified; it must be extended to a Solzhenitsyn as well as a Medvedev. (Certainly the dissidents have always understood this.) The consequence of silence on the left is that the moral initiative passes to Carter and

Brzezinski. Now it seems an easy matter to open the protective umbrella over socialist dissidents. Yet it is socialist dissidence that the Soviet-bloc leaderships probably fear most. Will the Eurocommunists intensify what amounts to a *political intervention* in the germinating struggle between a socialist opposition and the bureaucracies? What I have in mind here is not just a communique by this or that Western party defending, say, Bahro's right to publish a book, but material assistance in the struggle— establishing contacts with the dissidents, publishing their books and distributing them inside and outside of the Soviet bloc, giving them a voice at international conferences, demanding that they be allowed to travel and return, and similar steps.

Given the Western parties' determination to avoid a split with the Soviet-bloc regimes, with Moscow above all, it is exceedingly difficult to gauge how far this kind of support might be extended. Conversely, the problem also exists for the Soviet-bloc parties. How far can they tolerate the intervention of the Western parties without feeling politically threatened by it? What measures can they take, when threatened, short of provoking a split with the Western parties? From their side the record is spotty as well. When an Italian party delegation visited Moscow late in 1976 to present Roy Medvedev with an Italian edition of his *Was the October Revolution Inevitable?* published by the PCI press Riuniti, Soviet authorities did not interfere. But the following September, Vittorio Strada—a 30-year member of the Italian party—was denied a visa to attend the Moscow International Book Fair, reportedly because he was suspected of contacts with Soviet dissident writers.[45]

In any event, sections of the non-Communist left are trying to build a new dialogue and a new kind of international solidarity. Slowly, the European parties are joining the effort, allowing others to take the initiative for the present. Dissident Communist exiles from Eastern Europe and the USSR, ex-Communists from Western Europe, independent socialists, Trotskyists, and others are together taking the first steps. In 1976 a suggestion by Roy Medvedev for an international left dialogue on civil liberties inside the Soviet bloc in the era of détente was taken up by the Bertrand Russell Peace Foundation. The result was the publication of a collection of essays entitled, *Détente and Socialist Democracy*. In the first instance, such efforts nourish and encourage the few and isolated socialist dissidents in the USSR itself. Medvedev writes that "It was extremely useful for me to read all these essays and I made them known also to many of my friends and other like-minded people," and mentions how much such people have been cut off from information and from "the general development of socialist thought."[46]

Jiri Pelikan, another contributor to this volume, draws the conclusion that "The Western left's struggle for a socialist alternative and the struggle of the socialist opposition for democratization of the prevailing system are two sides of the same coin." Pelikan, active in the Prague Spring and once head of Czechoslovak television, also made some practical proposals for advancing the struggle, ranging from coordinating Marxist theoretical work and study of the USSR undertaken by Western socialists and the East European dissidents to organizing a solidarity network to protest instances of repression against socialist opposition in the Soviet bloc.

In this spirit, the Manifesto group of the Italian left organized the first of a series of international forums in Venice, in 1977, on "Power and Opposition in the Post-Revolutionary Societies." The forum included members of the Italian, French, and Spanish Communist Parties, and concluded with several resolutions, including one demanding the release of Rudolf Bahro. (Bahro was released and expelled from East Germany in 1979.)

By assisting such efforts, the Eurocommunists not only help their own images, they can strengthen socialist ideas in the entire Soviet bloc. The pressures will be felt most of all by the Eastern European regimes, which are constantly trapped amidst opposing impulses. They recognize the need for reforms, but fear the consequences for their authority. They chafe under Soviet power, but they are also dependent on it. Since so much in Eastern Europe hinges on Soviet permission, the long-range resolution to these dilemmas lies in Moscow itself. A vigorous Eurocommunism might fortify reform currents in the USSR, or at least inhibit the coarser features of its Stalinism. But first, the Eurocommunists must settle matters in their own houses.

The Western parties once defined themselves through their identification *with* the USSR. Now they are in the uncertain process of identifying themselves *against* the USSR. Is it too late for that—has the historical association with the USSR tainted the Western parties beyond political redemption? If there is a revival of democratic socialism in the West, it is the non-Communist socialist groups that may gain most, leaving the Communist parties wallowing in their pasts, caught between Stalinism and their struggle to overcome it. The break-up of the French Union of the Left and the Giscardian victory in the spring of 1978, the strong showing of the Spanish socialists in elections of the same year, the continuing failure of the historic compromise in Italy to live up to expectations are all perhaps suggestive of this outcome. Breaking with the Soviet myth removes an old ideological and emotional center of gravity which could leave the Communist movement dangerously adrift. But it can also release new energies and open up new possibilities. The internal renovation of the Western parties could be the prelude for the reunion of all elements in a European labor movement based on democratic socialism. The European socialist movement, once split by the Bolshevik Revolution, may yet be united, in part because of the wayward course of that revolution. In a peculiar and complex way, and certainly in a way never envisaged by the Bolsheviks who developed the idea in the first place, the road to socialism in Eastern and Western Europe still runs through Moscow.

Notes

1. Santiago Carrillo, *Eurocommunism and the State* (Westport, Ct.: Lawrence Hill & Co., 1978), p. 112.

2. Ronald Radosh, "Italy Seeks a Coalition," *The Nation*, February 28, 1976, p. 237. David Plotke offers a useful summary of the historical meanings of "revisionism" in "The Problem of Revisionism," *Socialist Revolution*, No. 36, November-December, 1977, pp. 79-93.

3. Quoted in Fernando Claudin, *The Communist Movement: From Comintern to Cominform*, Part One (New York: Monthly Review Press, 1975), p. 187.

4. See R. Neal Tannahill, "Leadership as a Determinant of Diversity in Western European Communism," *Studies in Comparative Communism*, Vol. IX, No. 4, Winter 1976, pp. 346-368.

5. *The Italian Road to Socialism: An Interview by Eric Hobsbawm with Giorgio Napolitano of the Italian Communist Party* (Westport, Ct.: Lawrence Hill & Co., 1977). p. 22.

6. *Pravda*, November 3, 1977. For the English translation see *The Current Digest of the Soviet Press*, XXIX, No. 44, November 30, 1977, pp. 7-8.

7. *Intercontinental Press*, Vol. 16, No. 10, March 13, 1978, p. 299.

8. *Nuestra Bandera*, No. 92, 1978, pp. 17-18.

9. Alexandre Adler, Francis Cohen, Maurice Décaillot, Claude Frioux, Leon Robel, *L'URSS et Nous* (Paris: Editions sociales, 1978), pp. 9-10. *L'Humanité*, September 4, 1978.

10. *Eurocommunism and the State*, pp. 117-118. John Gollan, late general secretary of the British Communist Party, called for the study of Bukharin and Trotsky in an important "revisionist" article, "Problems of Socialist Democracy," for the party's theoretical journal, *Marxism Today*, January 1976.

11. *L'Unita*, June 16, 1978.

12. *Liberation*, July 12, 1978; *Le Monde*, July 12, 1978; *New York Times*, July 13, 1978. Azcarate: "Die UdSSR gegen uns Dissidenten und Eurokommunisten, *Wiener Tagebuch*, Nr. 1, Janner 1979, p. 28.

13. *Pravda*, November 5 and 6, 1977. (In English, see *Intercontinental Press*, Vol. 15, No. 44, November 28, 1977, p. 1302.) For the Swedish "Democratic Manifesto," see *Intercontinental Press*, Vol. 16, No. 12, March 27, 1978, pp. 364-65.

14. *The Italian Road to Socialism*, p. 87.

15. On Vermeersch, see *Le Nouvel Observateur*, July 3, 1978. Party leaders replied by expressing "regrets and indignation" at her attitude, and charged that she wanted to "transform the Party into a small narrow sect." For Elleinstein, see *Le Monde*, April 15, 1978. (In English, see the *Manchester Guardian Weekly*, May 7, 1978.) Elleinstein is Professor of History and Assistant Director of the Center for Marxist Studies at the University of Paris, and the author of *The Stalin Phenomenon* (London: Lawrence and Wishart, 1977). After the defeat of the Left in the elections of the Spring, 1978, Elleinstein and other members of the PCF used the non-party press to complain about continuing rigidity in the French party, including lack of organizational democracy, insufficient support of the dissident movement in the Soviet bloc, and failure to deal honestly with the party's Stalinist past. On the party's timidity and ambivalence toward the dissidents, Elleinstein cited the party's having pulped a pamphlet that showed a photo of exiled Soviet dissident Leonid Plyushch shaking hands with Pierre Juquin of the party's Central Committee. See Thierry Pfister, *Le Monde*, April 21, 1978. (In English, see the *Manchester Guardian Weekly*, April 30, 1978.) Elleinstein replied to Vermeersch in *Le Monde*, July 5, 1978. In his preface to *L'URSS et nous*, Cohen criticizes Thorez's role in suppressing Khrushchev's report to the 20th Party Congress in 1956: "Was it not, in a sense, a lack of confidence in the ability of the party to face up to the situation and in the power of the truth among the masses of the party?"

16. *L'URSS et nous*, p. 216; Lucy Komisar, interview with Carrillo, *New York Times*, November 23, 1977; *The Italian Road to Socialism*, p. 85.

17. *Le Monde*, April 13 and 14, 1978 (in English, *Manchester Guardian Weekly*, April 30, 1978). Claudin, whose "Eurocommunism *avant le mot* caused his expulsion from the Spanish party in 1964, and who is now a trenchant friendly critic of the Western parties, is most emphatic on this point. See his *Eurocommunism and Socialism* (London: NLB, 1978), pp. 60-64.

18. *Le Monde*, April 13, 1978.

19. *New York Times*, March 4, 1977.

20. *Rinascita*, July 1, 1977. Azcarate in *Wiener Tagebuch*, p. 27.

21. *The Italian Communists Speak for Themselves*, ed. Don Sassoon (Nottingham: Spokesman, 1978), pp. 75, 78-79.

22. *Europe and the Communists*, ed. V. Zagladin (Moscow: Progress Publishers, 1977), pp. 161-195. Mies' remarks, *ibid.*, p. 100; Brezhnev's, p. 102.

23. No. 43, October 27, 1976. (In English, *The Current Digest*, Vol. 28, No. 44, December 1, 1976, p. 1.)

24. February 12, 1977. (In English, *Current Digest*, Vol. 29, No. 6, March 10, 1977, p. 4.)

25. *Pravda*, November 12, 1977. (In English, *Intercontinental Press*, Vol. 15, No. 45, December 5, 1977, pp. 1338-1339.)

26. *Pravda*, August 20, 1978.

27. *New Times*, July 29, 1978, pp. 5-7. Zagladin is a candidate member of the Soviet party's Central Committee, responsible for liaison with the Western parties. Azcarate first angered Moscow with his report to the Central Committee of the Spanish party attacking Soviet policies in September 1973. See Claudin, *Eurocommunism and Socialism*, p. 48.

28. In February 1976. Quoted in McInnes, *Euro-Communism*, p. 59.

29. *Probemy mezhdunarodnoi politiki KPSS i mirnogo kommunisticheskogo dvizheniya* ("Problems of the International Policy of the Communist Party of the Soviet Union and the World Communist Movement") (Moskva: Izdatelstvo politicheskoi literatury, 1977), p. 16.

30. *Pravda*, November 11, 1977. (In English, *Current Digest*, Vol. 29, No. 45, December 7, 1977, pp. 1-4.) The Soviet response to *L'URSS et nous*, in the ideological journal *Kommunist*, expresses similar sentiments: "But how can the working people be inspired to join [the socialist] struggle if they are told...that after six decades of revolution and building of a new society, real socialism has entered the blind alley of crisis?" See *Soviet Weekly* (London), January 6, 1979.

31. *New Times*, No. 26, 1977; *Intercontinental Press*, Vol. 15, No. 27, July 18, 1977, pp. 820-822; *Pravda*, July 3, 1977. (In English, *Current Digest*, Vol. 29, No. 27, August 3, 1977, p. 16).

32. Examples of such literature available in English are: M.I. Basmanov and B.M. Leibzon *The Revolutionary Vanguard: Battle of Ideas* (1977); B. Topornin and E. Machulsky, *Socialism and Democracy: A Reply to Opportunists* (1974); *Problems of the Communist Movement* (1975); *Right-Wing Revisionism Today* (a joint Czechoslovak-Soviet publication, 1976). All are published by Progress Press, Moscow.

33. Yelena Modrzhinskaya, *Leninism and the Battle of Ideas* (Moscow: Progress, 1972), pp. 343-347.

34. *Pravda*, March 1, 1977.

35. In *Problemy mezhdunarodnoi politiki KPSS*, cited above, p. 101. But the same Timofeev has also attacked "present-day successors" of Karl Kautsky such as Claudin, Garaudy, and Elleinstein. *New Times*, No. 46, November 1978.

36. *Ibid.*, pp. 179-196.

37. *Intercontinental Press*, Vol. 15, No. 30, August 1977, p. 917; *New York Times*, July 1, 1977; *Pravda*, July 28, 1977.

38. *New York Times*, February 26, 1977.

39. *New York Times*, January 7, 1978.

40. *New York Times*, January 26, 1977; February 16, 1977; February 8, 1977.

41. *Intercontinental Press*, Vol. 15, No. 30, August 8, 1977, p. 916.

42. The letter appeared in *Robotnik*, organ of the Polish Socialist Party, published in London. One would have preferred to see an English translation of Lipinski's letter in some "Eurocommunist" organ in the U.S.; instead, it turned up in a publication of the cold-warrish Freedom House, *Freedom at Issue*, No. 38, November-December 1976, pp. 7-12.

43. *Die Alternative: sur Kritik des realexistierenden Sozialismus* (Frankfurt, 1977), pp. 304-308.

44. *Ibid.*, from the excerpts in *New Left Review*, No. 106, November-December, 1977, pp. 34-36.

45. *New York Times*, January 30, 1977; *Intercontinental Press*, Vol. 15, No. 35, September 26, 1977, p. 1054.

46. *Detente and Socialist Democracy: A Discussion with Roy Medvedev*, edited for the Bertrand Russell Peace Foundation by Ken Coates (New York: Monad Press, 1976); Il Manifesto, *Pouvoir et Opposition Dans Les Societes Postrevolutionnaires* (Paris: Editions du Seuil, 1978). the British party's *Socialist Europe* is offering its pages to socialist dissidents in the Soviet bloc. See, for example, No. 4, 1978, for an interview with Roy Medvedev and an article by Milan Hubl, a leader of the Czech Spring and a Charter 77 activist.

chapter 11

AMERICAN POLICY
AND THE ITALIAN LEFT

Paul Joseph

SOCIALISTS MUST CONFRONT the following dilemma: the contest for political power is waged within the boundaries of the nation-state, yet in every respect, socialist politics are ever the more conditioned by developments in the international arena. Successful socialist movements always contain a national dimension, usually meeting historically specific tasks left unfulfilled by the bourgeoisie. The particularities of the national situation, while often recognized as decisive in the case of national liberation movements in countries dominated by imperialism, are of major influence in the developed capitalist world as well. One problem for socialists is to develop strategies that take account of the national dimension without ignoring international forces. In most cases the choice of domestic strategy contains a reading of the international situation. Is the balance of forces favorable, enabling a more militant posture, or hostile, usually forcing a more cautious course? *

In the case of the Italian Communist Party (PCI), political strategy since World War II has reflected the need to integrate a program for national tasks with an assessment of the possibilities contained in the world balance of power. This has meant continually confronting the

---

* I do not mean to suggest that there is an *automatic and necessary* relationship between the possibilities presented by the international situation and the degree of militancy adopted by a radical party. Nor does this essay's focus on international circumstances imply that political developments in Italy can be reduced to the posture of the United States.

enormous influence—at times even virtual control—of the United States over political developments in Western Europe. In addition, the political stance of the PCI has been affected by the policies of the Soviet Union, relations between the U.S. and the USSR, the development of the European Economic Community (EEC), the international balance of power (including the reality of NATO and nuclear weapons), and the state of the international economy—in short, by elements over which no Italian political force has control. For the PCI, making an accurate political analysis is complicated by the existence of important political disagreements within the policy-making establishment of the United States. All those responsible for the development of U.S. foreign policy share the goal of preventing a socialist government from emerging in Italy. But there have been considerable disagreements over the means to achieve this goal. And the disagreements over means reflect deeper differences about the nature of "Eurocommunism" itself.

This essay examines U.S. policy towards Italy. It attempts to analyze both the overall hostility and opposition of Washington toward the PCI and the important differences between partially opposed policy camps. Part I summarizes the contemporary debates about Eurocommunism within U.S. policy-making circles. Part II briefly outlines the theoretical basis of the policy camps approach. Part III applies the approach to the postwar history of U.S. foreign policy toward Italy. The conclusion discusses future possibilities.

PART I: POLICY CAMPS AND EUROCOMMUNISM

THERE ARE NOW two distinct policy camps in the United States. They differ over such fundamental issues as the nature of Eurocommunism, the relationship between the USSR and Eurocommunist parties, the role of NATO and the EEC, and the strategic options open to Washington. One camp favors an intransigent approach to Eurocommunism and can be called the "hard-line" position; the other favors flexibility, cooptation and can be called the "soft-line" position. Each has representatives within the State Department, the CIA, Defense Department, and among the foreign policy advisors on President Carter's staff. While the details of their deliberations are secret, materials in the public record mirror the essentials of the private debate. The comparison of the two camps that follows merely presents the positions; a more complete analysis is contained in subsequent sections.

Are the Eurocommunist Parties Committed to Democracy?

"NO," ANSWERS THE hardline camp. Party congresses that have jettisoned the concept of the dictatorship of the proletariat have been motivated by an opportunist attempt to capitalize on the Western commitment to democracy. The authoritarianism of the parties' internal deliberations gives the game away. Former Secretary of State Henry Kissinger, a leading member of the hard-liners, has argued that "one need not be a cynic to wonder at the decision of the French Communists, traditionally perhaps the most Stalinist party in Western Europe, to renounce the Soviet concept of the dictatorship of the proletariat without a dissenting vote among 1700 delegates, as they did in their Party Congress in Feb. 1976, when all previous Party Congresses had endorsed the same dictatorship of the proletariat by similar unanimous vote of 1700 to nothing. Why was there not at least one lonely soul willing to adhere to the previous view? Much was made of this change as a gesture of independence. Now it turns out that the new Soviet Constitution, in preparation for years, drops the terms as well."[1]

The hard-liners maintain that there is a contradiction between the goals of socialism and democracy. Basing themselves on a reading of Marxism that stresses those passages that view the transition from capitalism to socialism as inevitable, the hardliners suggest that the commitment to an irreversible process and the professed willingness to leave office following an electoral defeat are in conflict. As a result this group also distrusts pledges of the Spanish, French, and Italian Communist Parties to work within a pluralist structure and to respect individual and collective freedoms. Communists have never shared power with any other party, the argument goes. Any position of leverage will be used to attain their goal of total power. The willingness of the French and Italian parties to leave ruling political coalitions in the immediate postwar period occurred in a different historical situation. That more benign behavior was conditioned by the unity of the West, and its forceful opposition to Communism.

The soft-liners contend that the Eurocommunist parties' experiments with democracy are genuine. They stress the history of the commitment to democracy within the parties (citing statements going back to World War II) and the constraining role of national traditions of Western Europe (especially France) as well. In their view the coalition strategy of the PCF, PCE, and the PCI results in a centrist tendency that reinforces a commitment to democracy. The soft-liners view democratization as a process that can either be encouraged with the proper U.S. foreign policy or repressed. Those democratic tendencies emerging within Eurocommunism are in the overall interests of the U.S.—an intransigent stance will only reverse promising trends.

What is the relationship between the
Eurocommunist parties and the Soviet Union?

THE HARD-LINERS' argument appears to be contradictory. They discount the many Eurocommunist pronouncements of "national roads" to socialism and independence from the Soviet Union. These statements have been advanced for years, they claim, without significant evidence that they signify genuine intent. Events such as the PCI criticism of the Soviet invasion of Czechoslovakia or Carrillo's recent difficulties in Moscow are passed over in silence. Even domestic squabbles involving Eurocommunist parties, such as recent difficulties between the PCF and the French Socialist Party (PSF) are attributed to Moscow's control.[2]

The hard-liners do take note of the polycentric tendencies within the Communist world, but avoid the usual conclusion that these differences work to the benefit of the West. In some respects, they argue, the disputes *within* the Communist world are stronger than *between* East and West. The direct use of Soviet military power in the postwar period has been restricted to other Communist nations (East Germany, Hungary, Czechoslovakia, and along the Sino-Soviet border). The implication is that a Western nation governed by a Communist party would be in *more* danger of a Soviet attack than a government led by political forces from the center.

The soft-liners recognize the polycentric tendencies, stressing the difficulties that the leaders of some Eurocommunist parties have had with Moscow. Some have noted that while the PCI has not officially stated that the Soviet Union is "authoritarian socialism," some prominent individual members have said as much.[3] The possible military threat from the Soviet Union is dismissed as absurd; at any rate the Eurocommunist parties pledge to defend their nations in case of attack.

In some respects the soft-line perspective is at least as aggressive toward Moscow as that of the hard-liners, as in their analysis of how the emergence of polycentric tendencies serves U.S. interests. A more democratic Eurocommunism, critical at least by implication of the Soviet Union, will encourage liberalizing trends in Eastern Europe, weaken the grip of the Soviet Union over the domestic arrangements of those countries, result in some destabilization of those regimes, and create more problems for Moscow.* The two currents offer opposite assessments of the relationship between Moscow and the Eurocommunist parties. Yet underlying each approach is hostility toward the Soviet Union, a shared factor that revisionist interpretations of U.S. foreign policy consistently underemphasize.

* For the hardline current greater democracy within Eastern Europe would pose problems for Moscow, but even greater ones for the West.

What conditions have given rise to Eurocommunism?

THE HARD-LINE CAMP suggests that increased support for Eurocommunism is to be explained by "default," by the "moral decay" of the West, rather than by a self-conscious choice for socialism. The problem is really a failure to provide the requisite firmness, faith in values, and quality in leadership that is part of the Western tradition. There is a worldwide crisis of at least moderate proportions but the turbulence and disillusionment that allegedly characterize Eurocommunism are primarily due to massive bureaucracy, lack of political imagination, and a loss of confidence in already existing values.

The soft-line camp is more appreciative of the depth of the world crisis, stressing such factors as the high cost of energy imports; severe balance of payments problems; a backward, corrupt government machinery (Italy); a failure to initiate democratic reforms fast enough (Spain); and inflation and unemployment.

What are the implications for U.S. interests if a Communist Party participates directly in government?

"DISASTROUS," REPLY THE hard-liners. Within Europe, Eurocommunists would hinder progress toward European unity and gravely weaken the strength and unity of NATO.[4] The PCF and PCI could be expected to use the EEC, especially the European parliament, as a forum for ideological propaganda. And how could Western nations share defense secrets with representatives of Communist parties? At the extreme, NATO might turn into a largely U.S.-German alliance. Any diminution of the role of the Atlantic Defense Community would undermine the strategic balance between U.S. and USSR, undercut detente (which is based on military equilibrium), and pose a threat to world peace. The weakening of NATO would permit the Soviet Union to widen its lead in strategic and conventional weapons, and make the Warsaw Pact hegemonic over the European continent. Eurocommunist expressions of support for European institutions are dismissed.

While acknowledging that Eurocommunists have their disagreements with Moscow on issues within the Communist movement, the hard-liners argue that on matters such as South Africa, arms control, or Angola, Eurocommunists can be expected to side with Moscow and against the interests and foreign policy goals of the U.S. Eurocommunists can also be expected to side with the demands of third world and non-aligned nations for a new international economic order.

The hard-line camp also favors a psychological version of the domino theory, in which Communist participation in government in one country encourages a similar result elsewhere. In Kissinger's words, "there is no doubt that a Communist breakthrough to participate in a share in power in one country will have a major psychological effect on the others, by making Communist parties seem respectable or suggesting that the tide of history in Europe is moving in that direction."[5]

This scenario has the participation in government of any Eurocommunist party producing a U.S. Congress more reluctant to vote aid. The hard-liners believe that Congress will think that by voting Communist the Europeans are saying that they don't want our protection—U.S. policy will then become more "isolationist," and Soviet influence will increase.

The soft-liners downplay the radicalism of Eurocommunism. The fact that Eurocommunists are working in coalition with other political parties and must appeal to voters outside of the workers' movement tempers militant tendencies. Even a ten percent increase in electoral strength—an enormous shift in the context of European politics— would leave Eurocommunist parties with only a slight majority. No Communist party could afford a polarization of political forces. As a result, there is a strong pull toward social democracy. In Italy, the necessity of appealing to the middle classes and avoiding a confrontation with the Church has a substantial conservative effect. Both the PCI and the PCE see a continued role for the private sector. And in France, where much has been made of the PCF's desire to nationalize many more private industries than the Socialist Party, the soft-liners are more likely to see increased state control as an inevitable tendency of modern capitalism. Even DeGaulle nationalized over 2500 companies.

THE FOREIGN POLICY of the PCI would not be all that different from that of the current government. There would be no immediate withdrawal from NATO. Minor changes would include the unavailability of certain bases for use in a Middle East war, and pressure for more weight for European institutions. The PCI along with the rest of the West would oppose any concerted Soviet efforts to gain influence in Yugoslavia.

At any rate, the French and Italian contribution to NATO is probably not crucial. The Spanish air bases are somewhat more valuable, but their use will not be denied to the West if the Spanish Communists participate in government. Both the French and Italian parties *do* want to dismantle NATO (*and* the Warsaw Pact), but will not do so in a precipitous fashion, and certainly not in a way that opens the door for Moscow. In the long-run the PCI desires a European community freed from the dictates of both superpowers.

Finally the soft-liners do not accept the version of the domino theory offered by the more intransigent position. They point to the recent history of Southeast Asia. Communist movements have been successful in Vietnam, Cambodia, and Laos. But Pentagon predictions to the contrary, the Philippines, Indonesia, and Thailand have not "fallen," and Cambodia and Vietnam are at each other's throats. A direct role for the PCI in government would not produce any immediate gain for the PCF; relations between the PCF and PCI have not grown worse since 1968. And in Germany, the PCI's success might add to the retrenchment of the right. Advances in one country do not automatically produce gains for Eurocommunism in other countries.

What should be the U.S. Strategy toward Eurocommunism?

THE MOST IMPORTANT point, argues the hard-line camp, is to avoid treating the governmental participation of Eurocommunist parties as inevitable. This approach would undermine our longstanding allies and serve as a self-fulfilling prophecy. In the words of one commentator, "the impression that Italy's allies have fully resigned themselves to the progress of the PCI must at all costs be avoided. Any sign of support for the PCI would be highly damaging to traditional democratic parties."[6]

This view follows from a long-standing principle held by many leading policy makers: the U.S. is the leading power in the world—but only if it acts like it. From this general premise several particular approaches follow. Washington's efforts to "make our position clear" will stiffen the backs of the "democratic forces"; "firm leadership" will discourage "Soviet initiatives" elsewhere; and official contacts between representatives of the State Department and leaders of Eurocommunist parties should be avoided. Official contacts only further the legitimation process and enhance Communist chances at the polls. In this policy, leading figures of Eurocommunist parties are discouraged from visiting the U.S. even for academic gatherings. Economic aid should be supplied, but timed in order to enhance the position of anti-Communist political forces. Recent adverse publicity surrounding the role of the CIA has forced the hard-line camp reluctantly to reject significant amounts of covert aid as a current option.

The soft-liners think of themselves as realists who recognize the limits of the situation. This is not 1947. It is impossible for the Christian Democrats to work alone or with the Italian Socialist Party (PSI) as a junior partner (as was the case after 1962). Support for Eurocommunism is a significant current in European politics, and cannot be ignored or wished away. There is little that the U.S. can do, barring direct intervention, to prevent the PCI from assuming some role in national government. And anything remotely approaching a Chilean style solution is unthinkable. The critical question is not how should the U.S. prevent Communist participation in government, but how to keep Communist participation in government under control. The U.S. should bring its foreign policy out of the depths of the Cold War. Hard-line statements, refusal to supply economic aid except under limited conditions, and denial of fundamental traveling rights may produce limited short-run benefits. But in the long-run they are counter-productive. Even non-Communist Europeans are irked by rude political blackmail. Strongly worded statements of the type favored by the intransigent current will be taken by currently pro-American popular and elite opinion as unwarranted interference in a nation's domestic affairs. The result of such tactics is sympathy, not hostility toward Eurocommunism. The first thing for Washington to do is to shut up.

The issues surrounding strategic choices produce the most intense debate between the two policy camps, for each side feels that the other's position is counter-productive. For the hard-liners, shifting perceptions of the nature of Eurocommunism and the willingness of some official to see both a democratic mellowing ("social democracy with a Leninist face") are both factually wrong and encourage opposition to U.S. interests. For the soft-line current the clear unambiguous statements of support for the Christian Democrats favored by the hard-liners only identify the U.S. with the most corrupt, clientelistic, and inefficient government machine in the West, creating conditions that in the long-run favor the Communists. The soft-liners do favor the DC over the PCI but only after a thorough reform of its current practice.

An intransigent position on the part of the U.S. would also undermine democratization and deepening polycentrism of the Communist world. The following scenario is projected: Suppose Washington succeeds, in the short-run, in forcing the PCI away from significant government participation. Neither the party, nor the social conditions supporting it, will disappear. Without the involvement of the PCI, the necessary economic transformations would not be carried out. Two or three years of continued failure by the Christian Democrats (DC) to solve Italy's crisis would again bring the PCI to the brink of power. Only this time those groups closer to the Soviet Union, less committed to political freedoms, and more radical on particular issues would be in greater control. The already deepening fragmentation of Italian society would accelerate. In other words, a PCI in opposition is more of a threat than a PCI captured by the contradictions of a governing position.

The soft-line *is* part of the foreign policy establishment and would like to influence the future course of events in Europe. It is not adverse to inflicting political costs on Eurocommunist parties for failing to live up to promises of moderation and democracy. These pressures are to be administered through contacts built up between the PCI or the PCF and the U.S. Washington should not oppose Eurocommunism *per se*, but establish a set of criteria (which reflect U.S. foreign policy interests) to evaluate the performance of any government, with or without the participation of Communist parties.

The relationship of these political disagreements to the overall direction of U.S. foreign policy shall now be addressed on a more systematic and theoretical basis.

PART TWO: THE CONCEPT OF POLICY CURRENTS

THE PRECEDING SURVEY of substantial differences among policy makers raises some important theoretical issues. Two will be addressed in this section. The first concerns the need to link the dominant theme of continuity in U.S. foreign policy, aimed at reducing the influence of socialism in the world, with the sub-theme of substantive and genuine political differences among policy makers. Here the task is to focus on the existence of political differences within the dominant class without losing sight of the overall class bias that characterizes U.S. foreign policy. The second issue concerns how to situate these differences in a larger social setting. The usual tendency among left-wing analysts to "root" political differences within the state in competing fractions of capital or regional differences offers an unacceptable reductionism. Here the task is to thread our way between a collapse of politics to "material" sets of opposing interests and a presentation of policy debates as an elite process occurring in a social vacuum. The concept of policy currents is a step toward confronting these two issues. Policy currents consist of a series of notions of how to grapple with a recurring range of problems that confront the capitalist class in a particular policy area (such as responding to the growth of Eurocommunism). The phrase "series of notions" implies that the tendency to react in relatively consistent ways reflects deep-seated ways of looking at the world. For a variety of reasons, some involving the need to retain legitimacy or ideological control over dominated classes, policy currents are not crystallized into coherent and explicit political manuals. The concrete expression of these diffuse sets of notions generally supportive of the capitalist order is policy.

Policy currents arise from and are sustained by two factors: the *costs, obstacles, or contradictions* that the capitalist class must confront in a particular situation (the "objective" dimension); and the *historical experience* of state managers in confronting recurring types of problems (the "subjective" dimension). U.S. capital is not completely free to impose its will or dictate its terms in world politics; state managers draw their own lessons from confronting these obstacles, which are then applied in other situations that appear to be similar. To take an example from the material presented in the first part of this essay: Some state managers believe that in foreign policy "force should not be exercised until all areas of diplomacy have been exhausted." Others maintain that the United States "is the strongest country in the world if it only acts that way." The first position implies a faith in diplomacy (and a belief that the economic losses associated with military conflict or the loss in business confidence associated with the threat of war are greater than the losses associated with compromise). The second implies a tendency to flex military muscle through both symbolic and actual demonstrations of force (and the belief that political control is at least as important a priority as maintaining business confidence). The first "historical lesson" is part of the basis for the soft-line approach; the second for the hard-line course of action.

Chart One contrasts the hard and soft-line approaches on several important issues. The comparison exaggerates the difference between the currents, as the fluidity of the actual exercise of power as well as the shared project of consolidating the power of capitalism tempers the actual degree of difference. At the same time it is possible to detect roughly the same pattern of differences in other policy areas. The "China hands" in the State Department held some of the same positions toward the Chinese Communist Party and Chiang Kai-Shek during World War II and up to 1949 (for which they were later persecuted by the China Lobby). Some of the same configuration can be found in the current policy debates surrounding the development of U.S. policy toward Southern Africa.

Policy currents are the product of a reaction to changing objective circumstances together with an application of the state managers' reading of the history of foreign policy. Analysis is incomplete without reference to both external political and economic developments and the state managers' own interpretations of these changes. Policy currents, then, contain:

*ECONOMIC ELEMENTS, such as strategies for maintaining domestic capital accumulation, structuring world trade, and organizing international monetary arrangements. In the case of Eurocommunism, the key problem is the impact of socialist forces on the European Economic Community and, in turn, on the economy of the United States.

TABLE ONE: COMPARING THE SOFTLINE AND HARDLINE CURRENTS

ISSUE	SOFTLINE	HARDLINE
Stance Toward the Left	Deradicalize the Left	Isolate the Left
Method of Consolidating Power	Effective Economic, Political and Administrative Reform	Bolster the Position of Existing Power Elites
Favored Tactics	Cooptation	Repression
Role of U.S. Aid	To Encourage Capitalist Development	To Be Used as a Weapon to Achieve Desired Political Results
Relations Between Socialist States	Increasing Tension	Moscow Controls
Significance of Left Victory	No Necessary Domino Effect Leftwing Victories Can Cause Problems, Especially for Moscow	Psychological Version of Domino Theory

*POLITICAL ELEMENTS, such as thwarting the growth of socialist movements, reducing the autonomy of non-socialist forces (including the non-aligned movement) which attempt to reduce the degree of U.S. international control; and limiting domestic opposition. Here the debate focuses on the degree to which Communist government participation encourages socialism and/or reduces capital's control in other countries, including the United States.

*ORGANIZATIONAL ELEMENTS, or ideas of how to structure an administrative apparatus to implement the above programs. An example would be the implicit threat of NATO against the European left as well as the Warsaw Pact.

*TACTICAL ELEMENTS, or predispositions to employ particular maneuvers and react in particular ways in political battles. For example, should Washington issue an unambiguous statement linking the provision of economic aid to the exclusion of the PCI from the Italian Cabinet, when it is possible that these moves will incur opposition as unwarranted interference in the internal affairs of another country.

There are several other features of the policy currents approach relevant for analyzing U.S. foreign policy toward Italy during the postwar period. Policy currents, for example, are in some sense in permanent opposition. But the overall terrain is constantly shifting. That is, relative distance is constantly reproduced even while the particular issues of conflict are in flux. Since World War II, the terrain has moved toward greater accommodation of the left. This shift reflects the gradual, but nonetheless significant decline in U.S. power in the world arena. In the case of Eurocommunism, the ability of Washington to control political developments has diminished over the last thirty years. In Italy, for example, one of the original issues of disagreement was over how to define a political role for Fascist collaborators. Now the issue is participation or exclusion of the PCI.

Policies are usually formulated from the point of view of preserving an entire social order. But the task of providing a secure political umbrella and political climate within which capital accumulation as a whole can develop is complicated by two (sometimes conflicting) priorities. The first is the responsibility of the state for maintaining the hegemonic position of the U.S. and its capitalist class within that system. The second complicating factor is the existence of particularistic interests which are found in the organizations and agencies administering a policy, branches of industry and individual corporations that stand to profit from it, and segments of the armed forces that would benefit. Each group of interests usually finds a set of Congressional allies.

The hegemony of capital is most secure when policies are formulated from the more general levels, that is, without undue regard for the influence of specific or parochial interests. From the point of view of capital, policies can become limited by the intrusion of particular interests. Thus the area of agreement among policy currents tends to increase during periods of relative stability and to widen during periods of political crisis. (The particular interests who see an opportunity to benefit from a change in policy contribute to the general clamor associated with a crisis.)

State managers use crisis situations in a variety of ways. A tension-ridden situation may make it possible to implement a new policy. The ultimate source of the change in policy is not individual state managers but the circumstances to which they respond, especially the strength of oppositional political movements abroad and at home. Policy currents "convey" external conditions into state deliberations and represent different methods of responding to them. Policy currents are also ideological bridges between members of the capitalist class proper and state managers. The critical question is not so much the relationship between the "state and the ruling-class," but the relationship of the policy currents to each other and the particular historical conditions from which they arise. The link between the capitalist class and the state primarily involves shared assumptions regarding the organization of the social order rather than the maximization of immediate self-interest. The individuals who define and promulgate policy currents are not limited to state managers and the corporate elite. The political logic of policy currents is reflected in the writings of academics, journalists, and newspaper editors. The political constituency of policy currents includes academic "think-tanks," trade-unions, business associations and the like.

Policy currents also tend to persist even after the original conditions and appraisals have changed or become outmoded. The presence of these outdated policies, whose continued impact is explained in part by the persistence of supporting particular interests, can complicate the process of developing rational policy.

THE EXERCISE OF political power contains a centripetal tendency which narrows the differences between policy currents as they are expressed within the state itself. For example, since assuming office many members of the Carter administration have moved away from the original support of the soft-line position articulated before the '76 elections. Their current actions are much closer to the positions followed by the previous administration. The expression of policy currents is more explicit and distinct as it develops in such non-governmental planning committees as the Council on Foreign Relations, Committee for Economic Development or even the National Association of Manufacturers, or in periodicals such as *Foreign Policy, Foreign Affairs,* and *National Security.* At the other extreme is the behavior of the top state managers, particularly the president. Jimmy Carter is the perfect example of a president whose decisions are drawn from different policy currents; this mixture reflects the complexity of the political process with its bargaining and trade-offs.

Finally, policy currents are also methods of attempting to maintain control over domestic public opinion (the problem of legitimacy). All state managers share a general interest in restricting the influence of the American public. Foreign policy is "bipartisan," "complex," the "realm of the expert," requiring "sensitive diplomatic skills," and, above all, "beyond politics." While implicit in each policy current is a different method of "handling public opinion," all of the tendencies share a common class interest in maintaining the appearance of a "depoliticized foreign-policy."

The rest of this essay will illustrate the policy currents perspective by examining U.S. foreign policy toward Eurocommunism, especially in Italy. Five periods will be analyzed: the end of World War II, the 1948 elections, the early 1960s, the Nixon Administration, and the Carter Administration to the present.

PART III: U.S. FOREIGN POLICY TOWARD ITALY AND THE PCI, 1943 TO THE PRESENT

WASHINGTON'S PROJECT OF restoring and stabilizing capitalism throughout postwar Europe encountered two interrelated obstacles. The first was the potential influence of the Soviet Union; the second, popular and social forces, especially in regions where the underground fight against fascism had been extremely strong. By the end of the war Soviet troops had established a sufficient military presence to block the U.S. in Eastern Europe. With the possible exception of Greece, the left was probably not strong enough to seize power in the West, yet its influence was sufficient in several countries to create a form of capitalism less favorable to U.S. interests. From Washington's perspective this form of capitalism would, at best, have been limited to a resdistribution of income in favor of the lower classes, greater social services, and policies favoring a larger economic role for the state, over a policy permitting greater economic penetration by the U.S. At worst this more national form of capitalism would serve as a transition stage toward socialism.[7]

The U.S. had essentially two options. The first would have created a multinational political structure favoring easier economic and political access for the U.S. in Eastern Europe (and the Soviet Union in the West). It was embodied in British Foreign Secretary Anthony Eden's proposal, two months before the fall of Mussolini, for a "United Nations Commission for Europe" that would arrange and execute armistice agreements with the European members of the Axis. While minor European allies would enjoy formal participation rights, the Commission would be directed by a steering committee composed of the U.S., the U.S.S.R. and the United Kingdom (and France "if she recovered her greatness").[8] Had subsequent European history developed within this structure, the Soviet Union would have participated in the determination of policies affecting postwar Italy (and the U.S. and Britain would have had substantial influence in Eastern Europe). The danger lay in the possibility that the necessity of participating and consulting with other powers would temper Washington's influence over major developments in the West without compensating influence in the East.

Washington favored a second option, one which gave up partial leverage in the East for virtual hegemony in the West. The great power conferences that followed polarized Europe. The U.S. preferred secure control over opposition forces in the West and isolation of the Soviet Union to a political "open door" in which the relative strengths of political groupings and classes would be permitted free rein. Washington's consolidation of strength within the West did not eliminate the desire of right-wing policy currents to attempt to gain access to the "People's Democracies" of the East.

The analysis that follows is developed on two interrelated levels. One concerns the overarching goal of isolating the Soviet Union from substantial influence over Italy, and limiting the growth of the domestic left. The second concerns differences, within Washington, over constructing a policy to achieve these goals. "Washington" or the "United States" are terms that reflect the first level of analysis; "policy currents" are formulated in the second.

Period I: 1943-1945

AS THE FIRST country to leave the Axis, Italy served as the test for Washington's policy of excluding Soviet influence and limiting the power of the Italian left. The structure of this policy was increasingly bilateral—that is, elaborated directly between the United States and Italy. Not only the Soviet Union but England lost leverage over subsequent events.

The post-Mussolini government that took power in July 1943 wasted no time in contacting the British and Americans about a possible armistice and diplomatic recognition. The emissaries of Marshall Pietro Badoglio informed the Allies that nothing stood between the new government and "rampant Bolshevism."[9] Stalin was told of the Italian overture but remained excluded from the subsequent decision-making process. Stalin eventually accepted an advisory role in a newly created Political-Military Commission, ignorant of the fact that Britain and the U.S. planned to establish a purely Anglo-American Control Commission (ACC) for the occupation of Italy. These maneuvers effectively excluded the Soviet Union from formal participation in Italian affairs.

Britain was the next to go. At first London assumed primary responsibility for Allied interests in Italy. The British intended to preserve the monarchy, institute a punitive peace treaty (perhaps even detaching the islands of Sicily and Sardinia thus opening the door for a continuing major British influence in the Mediterranean), and maintain a weak Italy.[10]

For example, in December of 1943 Allied Force Headquarters (ACF) ordered that relief supplies and food be provided for the civilian population in Italy at only those "standards that would be the absolute minimum necessary to prevent disease and unrest behind the fighting lines."[11] The ACF also imposed a ban on political activity.[12]

Washington's policy toward the British began to change shortly after the use of U.S. troops in the liberation of Italy. The provision of relief funds became the first point of conflict between the two countries. The British had been dragging their feet, providing even less than the minimal standard established by the existing agreement. Undersecretary of State Sumner Wells linked the inability of the ACF to deliver necessary food, raw materials, housing, trucks, and other means of transportation to the growing skepticism among the Italian people that an anti-Fascist, non-Communist regime could provide a higher standard of living.[13] An economic mission to Italy recommended a shift from the provision of relief services to the selective reconstruction of industry and agriculture.[14] Just before the 1944 U.S. elections Washington announced that it would reimburse the Italian government with dollars for the lire issued American troops in Italy.

The British and Americans were also divided over the question of whether the Badoglio government could govern. Both Badoglio and King Victor Emmanuel were identified with the collaborationists of the Mussolini regime; no serious purge of fascists was carried out. The question of breaking decisively with the Italian right also produced divisions *among* U.S. policy-makers. Officers of the Office of Strategic Services, who conducted massive psychological operations designed to convince Italians of the democratic aspirations of the U.S., pushed for a foreign policy more tolerant of the left. The OSS felt that U.S. policy was too conservative in these respects: "(1) the use of local Fascist officials by AMG and ACC; (2) support of the House of Savoy and the Badoglio regime; (3) generally avoiding or ignoring the anti-Fascist political leaders who returned from exile; (4) generally ignoring the liberal elements, particularly labor, which had remained in Italy; (5) rebuffing the partisans, especially those in northern Italy who materially contributed to the success of the Allied campaign."[15]

In their fear of a restoration of quasi-Fascist rule and their optimism about the prospects of de-radicalizing the left, the most liberal elements of the Roosevelt Administration pushed for a more tolerant policy. Secretary of State Cordell Hull recommended that the U.S. remove the King even at the danger of a break with the British. At first Roosevelt attempted to straddle the tension between permitting the center to participate in Italian politics and preserving a role for the British. But the issue of defining a political role for Count Carlo Sforza soon pushed Roosevelt and Churchill to loggerheads. Sforza spent most of the war in the U.S., was popular among Italian Americans, and, along with philosopher Benedetto Croce, represented the Committee of National Liberation within the Badoglio government. More liberal elements in Weahington favored Sforza, for he was untainted with fascist collaboration; the conditions of political and economic crisis, moreover, favored the logic of the "soft" current in Roosevelt's Administration. Churchill, who favored a constitutional monarchy and who had contempt for the opposition, interpreted Sforza's arrival in Italy as a simple power move by Washington.

Some advisors, including Dean Acheson, advocated direct involvement in Italian domestic politics. Yet Roosevelt continued to equivocate, while Churchill's support for the Badoglio government, the reluctance of the Allies to permit Italy to join the war against Germany as an equal, the undemocratic nature of the ban against political activity, and the rapidly deteriorating economic situation all seemed to favor the left.

The independence of the Italian resistance was one of the main U.S. concerns. The Committee for the National Liberation of Northern Italy (CLNAI) created in early 1944 included Communists, Socialists, Christain Democrats, Liberals and the Action and Labor Democratic Parties under the leadership of Ivanoe Bonomi. There was no single resistance ideology. By the summer of 1944 these partisans were tying down fourteen Axis divisions. In late winter between a half a million and a million participated in strikes despite the German presence. Despite a directive that all Italian territory was to be liberated by the Allied Armies, CLNAI forces captured Genoa, Milan, and Turin and played a major role in freeing Val D'Aosta in the northwest and parts of the Venetian plain in the northeast.

In March 1945 the OSS estimated that 182,000 partisans were active in occupied areas (with an additional 500,000 potential recruits). Over 45,000 had been killed in battle. The size of the Communist Party itself rose rapidly, growing from 402,000 in July 1944 to over two million by the end of 1946. The OSS attempted selectively to supply non-Communist elements of the resistance. In November, 1944, Supreme Commander in the Mediterranean General Alexander Kirk broadcast a message to the resistance stating that Allies would be digging in for the winter, that further supplies would not be forthcoming, and that large-scale operations should be suspended. Whether by design or accident, Kirk's broadcast enabled the Germans to turn their attention to the north; a widespread hunt and elimination of many resistance leaders shortly followed.

Moscow's diplomatic activity complicated the situation for the United States and Britain. In March 1944 the Western allies were informed that the Soviet Union and Italy would be exchanging diplomatic representatives (although not full ambassadors).[17] As Harold Macmillan observed, "The whole situation had been largely changed by the Communist move. Under orders from Moscow, they have let it be known that they will enter a goverment *without* raising the question of the King and the monarchy... but this Communist position makes the liberal and moderate parties very uncomfortable. On the one hand, they long to enter the Government and would hate to see the Communists and Socialists collar all the best jobs and all the power; on the other hand, they have made so many speeches and uttered such brave words, that a lot of the latter would have to be eaten if they were to come along and join Badoglio."[18]

PCI leader Palmiro Togliatti returned from Moscow on March 26. His tacit support for the Badoglio government without the prior removal of the King signalled the Communist intention that nothing should impede the war effort against Germany. Togliatti promised a role for the Catholic Church in Italian life, respect for private property, and support for a coalition government. While not as important a factor as the anti-Nazi struggle, his move contributed to the spectacular growth of the Party, as it was no longer perceived as intransigent or sectarian to the same degree.

The Communist Party continued to occupy the center. While the Action and Socialist Party members of the CNL desired a reconstructed social order including a modified form of workers' councils, the PCI refused to endorse the more radical position. In the secret "Protocalls of Rome" in December, 1944, the CLNAI (including the PCI) received financial subsidies, food, clothing, and limited arms in exchange for subordinating itself politically to the Supreme Allied Commander.

THE SITUATION PERMITTED two possible constellations of political forces. The first would have been a polarization between a right-wing unpopular Italian government and a limited but extremely militant left, with the possible conflict assuming the contours of a civil war. Within the PCI this situation would have favored militants supporting a more insurgent strategy. Within Washington the situation would have favored policy currents advocating military intervention and (on economic issues) protectionism. The second possibility was a more regulated disagreement between a broader center government and a larger but less radical left. Conflict in this case would be less likely to assume the question of socialism versus capitalism, while within the PCI it would favor the policy that eventually became part of Togliatti's strategy of "structural reforms." For Washington the situation would favor policy currents desiring the incorporation of the center (although still not the Communists or Socialists) and, on economic issues, a more active stance toward reconstructing the world economy on the basis of free trade. In other words, alternative political outcomes would reflect the balance of forces within Italy, within the U.S., and within the structure of the national states and international agencies that would monitor the postwar capitalist order. British policy seemed likely to create the first situation. Under Roosevelt, American policy increasingly favored the second. The Soviet Union and the PCI also desired the second. In addition to the decision to avoid mobilization for revolution it seemed to guarantee the most effective fight against Germany.

While of course differing in specifics from the present, the situation prefigured the contemporary interplay among political currents within the capitalist and socialist worlds. The end of the war carried, for the U.S., the same strategic options as the present. From the point of view of preserving the long-term stability of capitalism, is it better to isolate and repress the left (and in the process leave it more militant and hostile), or to moderate the leftist presence (in part by trapping it in the "responsibilities of power"). Over the postwar period the U.S. has had less and less power to define the answers on its own terms.

PERIOD II: TRUMAN, THE NEW HARD LINE AND THE 1948 ELECTIONS

ROOSEVELT'S DEATH, THE end of the war, the Potsdam Conference, and the Truman presidency all contributed to an increasingly antagonistic U.S. stance toward the Soviet Union and socialism in general. Disposition of purely Italian issues (such as the extent of reparations, and the status of Trieste and the former colonies) was increasingly linked with broader international affairs such as the division of Germany, drawing up Poland's new borders, and the political composition of the new governments of Eastern Europe. Both private and public rhetoric became more inflated. In a series of briefing papers prepared for Truman before the Potsdam Conference, Acting Secretary of State Joseph Grew developed the logic of the "new totalitarianism." In the paper Grew wrote that the "Communists have the same attitude Goebbels did—that civil liberties in the democracies are convenient instruments for Communists to facilitate their tearing down the structure of the state and therefore abolishing all civil rights."[19] Washington's desire to avoid a harsh peace for Italy was linked to the fear of the spread of Communism. Allied Commissioner Ellery Stone wrote Truman that a fair treaty would "preserve Italy as a democracy and will contribute greatly to peace and security in the Mediterranean."[20]

Some political developments seemed to confirm the thinking of the hard-line current. For example, when Yugoslavian troops moved westward in 1945, the U.S. feared that the capture of Trieste might result in the collapse of the shaky Italian government. Many policy makers interpreted the situation as another Munich, a showdown between East and West. When Tito agreed to Allied occupation of Trieste and Venice (with some Yugoslavian troops remaining in the area) Washington attributed the change in position to its own firm stance, including blunt telegrams to Stalin. For the hard-line current the incident confirmed that Communism would retreat in the face of counter-pressure.

DESPITE THE SUCCESS of various ideological efforts to legitimize U.S. policy, the left continued to grow. In the 1946 elections the combined vote for the Socialist and Communist parties reached forty percent. (See Table Two) The Socialists and Communists were bound by a Unity of Action Pact (Patto d'unita d'Azione) originally concluded in Paris in 1934 but reconfirmed on October 25, 1946. The pact provided for the coordination of joint decisions on all problems and at all levels. The two parties were joined by the Action Party, headed by Ferruccio Parri, in calling for "prompt elimination of the monarchy, immediate land reform of the most far-reaching nature, workers' control, and a socialist republic."[21] In January 1947 the Socialist Party of Proletarian Unity split into two factions over the question of the Unity of Action Pact with the PCI. The right wing of the Party, led by Guiseppe Saragat, received secret U.S. funding in forming what eventually became the Social Democratic Party (PSDI).[22] By December 1947 the Social Democrats had moved sufficiently to the right to join the DeGasperi coalition. The PSI formed an electoral alliance with the Communists which offered a single list of candidates for the 1948 elections.

The postwar economic situation in Italy continued to hold little comfort: the 1947 Gross National Product was only 83% of the prewar level, inflation rose, Finance Minister Luigi Einaudi's response (strict credit policies and a prolonged deflationary period) did not augur well

TABLE THREE
ITALIAN POSTWAR ELECTORAL RESULTS
1946-1963

Parties	1946 Pop. Vote %	Seats	1948 Pop. Vote %	Seats
Christian Democratic	35.2	207	48.5	305
Socialist	20.7	115	31.0	183
Communist	19.0	104		

	1953 Pop. Vote %	Seats	1958 Pop. Vote %	Seats
Christian Democratic	40.6	261	42.4	273
Socialist	12.0	75	14.2	84
Communist	22.7	143	22.7	140

	1963 Pop. Vote %	Seats
Christian Democratic	38.3	260
Socialist	13.8	87
Communist	25.3	166

Source: Italia, Istituto Centrale di Statistica, Platt, "U.S. Policy Toward 'The Opening to the Left' in Italy," pp. 302-03

for government parties in the forthcoming elections, and unemployment hit two million of a working population of only twenty million. Two years after the war, the average Italian was still living on 1900 calories a day, the lowest in Europe. The prewar Italian average was over 2,500 per day.

The U.S. continued to supply aid to Italy during the spring of 1947. Following the logic of the hard-line current, the provision of further aid was increasingly linked to the establishment of a new government without Communist participation. Aid was conceived less as an instrument promoting economic growth in which a de-radicalized left might participate than as a lever designed to exclude socialists from participation in political power.

In 1947 Italian Prime Minister Alcide de Gasperi visited the United States. During his meetings with Truman and Secretary of State Byrnes, De Gasperi stressed Italy's desperate economic plight and the determination of the Italian government to rebuild a stable and democratic country without Communist participation. (At the time the PCI was a member of the ruling coalition.) De Gasperi noted the possibility of future "left-wing totalitarianism" and asserted that greater American aid was essential to maintain favorable political conditions.[23] On May 3, 1947 a telegram from U.S. Ambassador to Italy James Dunn to Secretary of State Marshall linked the resolution of Italian economic problems with the removal of the Communists from participation in government:

> We are convinced that no improvement in condition here can take place under the government as at present composed. [The] Comm. who are rep. in Cab. by [a] second-string team are doing everything possible outside and within the government to bring about inflation and [a] chaotic economic condition...The pity is that there exists all over Italy a real will to work and there could easily be a general confidence in the future were it not for the pol. agit. of the Comm. I doubt that there can be any real effective measures taken to improve the situation as long as the Comm. participate in government. The CP would of course, fight hard against any effort to form a government without its part. But I do not believe it is too late for a government to be formed without their part, and there appears to be a growing realization that the CP is not really trying to bring about the restoration of economic stability.[24]

The 1948 Elections

THE CAMPAIGNS FOR the April 1948 elections in Italy were conducted in a polarized international environment. By April the U.S.

had decided to supply military aid to the Turkish and Greek governments through the Truman Plan, announced a program of economic and military assistance through the Marshall Plan, and witnessed the Communist Party come to power in Czechoslovakia.

The hard-line current typically magnifies the significance of any particular confrontation between oppositional and loyal political forces beyond the immediate issues at hand. Thus Washington stressed the importance of the 1948 elections, painting the events more as a referendum between East and West than a process of selecting national representatives. U.S. efforts to secure a favorable outcome knew virtually no bounds. Italy was viewed as the crucible of the struggle between the capitalist and socialist systems, and a major test of the U.S. postwar political role. The magnitude and diversity of Washington's anti-Communist effort reflected the hard-line tendency to raise the ante over particular arenas of struggle. The particular *form* of the response, including the threat of military force, the tying of aid to particular political developments, and the beginning of massive covert aid, reflected the logic of the hard-line current as well.

(a) Military

THE U.S. PREPARED for nothing less than direct military involvement. Some policy-makers were prepared to intervene directly with U.S. armed forces in the event of a left victory at the polls. All were willing to "demonstrate U.S. resolve and military strength."

The Italian Peace Treaty signed in February 1947 called for the withdrawal of U.S. troops by December 15, 1947. These were pulled out on the last possible day, with Truman's Final Declaration leaving open the possibility of their future use. In violation of the Peace Treaty thousands of machine guns and millions of rounds of ammunition were left by withdrawing American occupation troops.*

(b) Economic Assistance and Relief

In the fluid Washington political environment at the end of the war, the U.S. began to supply aid designed to stimulate economic development. Relief was also provided to ameliorate economic conditions favoring the growth of the left. By 1947 the ascendant hard-line current could link the continuation of aid with a change in overall political conditions, especially the issue of the participation of the PCI in government. In part this shift reflected the power of the protectionist

* The capacity of the U.S. to use American troops in Italy seems to have been limited by domestic public opinion. When asked the question, "Suppose the government of Italy seemed likely to be taken over by the Italian Communists in a revolution—would you be willing to see United States military forces used to prevent this or not?" only 28.3% indicated affirmative answers, 52.2% said no, 5.5% said only through the United Nations, and 14% said don't know or gave no answer. See Mildred Strunck, "The Quarter's Polls," *Public Opinion Quarterly*, no. 2, Summer 1948, p. 365.

lobby in U.S. domestic politics. But the retreat from the starry-eyed idealism that would have transformed radicals of every stripe into progressive elements within capitalism also reflected the removal of representatives of the soft-line current who had secured bureaucratic niches under the Roosevelt Administration. The *short-run* political impact of the aid program was stressed as well. In 1944 foreign aid was intended to foster independent capitalist growth; by 1948 aid had taken on political and propaganda elements as well.

The United States first formally stated its intention of withdrawing aid from Italy following a victory by the Popular Front, in a March speech by Secretary of State Marshall:

> In connection with the electoral campaign now in progress in Italy, the leaders of the Communist Party have given their interpretation to the policy of the United States in connection with the outcome of the elections. They publicly asserted that if their party, the Communist Party, is victorious at the polls, American assistance to Italy will continue without change.
>
> I have only this comment to make regarding that interpretation of the policy of the United States: The European recovery Program has been created on the basis of the voluntary association of sixteen nations.... Every European nation under the influence of the Communists has been prevented from participating in the European Recovery Program. Some have been deprived of the right to participate, clearly against their wishes.
>
> Since the association is entirely voluntary, the people of any nation have a right to change their mind and, in effect, withdraw. If they choose to vote into power a government in which the dominant political force would be a party whose hostility to this program has been frequently, publicly and emphatically proclaimed, this could only be considered as evidence of the desire of that country to dissociate itself from the program. This government would have to conclude that Italy has removed itself from the benefits of the European Recovery Program.[28]

The aid issue illustrates how the policy currents perspective focuses on the interplay between class politics within the United States and political developments within Italy.

THE PCI ATTEMPTED to enlist, through the CGIL, a promise from what they took to be a still progressive CIO, to support American aid to Italy regardless of the outcome of the 1948 elections. According to

Avanti! and *L'Unita,* conversations between CGIL officials and American labor delegates took place at a London conference to discuss the Marshall Plan. The U.S. labor movement would supposedly intervene to guarantee aid to any legal Italian government. But the CIO, in the midst of a swing to the right, disagreed with the Italian left's version of the talks. CIO Secretary-Treasurer James Carey denounced the newspaper accounts as a "gross misrepresentation" of the organization's position:

> The Communists, by opposing the Marshall Plan for political motives, are completely disregarding the needs of the Italian people. The CIO therefore welcomes and supports Secretary Marshall's statement that those who refuse to associate themselves with the Marshall Plan for political reasons can hardly expect to share in the benefits of the European Recovery Plan.[29]

Carey's reply was prominently reported by *Il Popolo.* AFL President William Green later read a similar speech over the Voice of America.

By blocking the ability of the hard-line current to tie economic aid to the exclusion of the PCI from government participation, a more militant labor movement in the U.S. might have been able to create greater freedom of maneuver for the Italian left. The Socialist and Communist Parties, for example, would have been able to campaign without the threat that electoral success would bring economic disaster. The capacity of the progressive and left movements within the United States to force state managers to conduct foreign policy on democratic principles was and remains a critical element in the strategic judgements of revolutionary forces elsewhere in the world.

(c). Propaganda

THE UNITED STATES EMBASSY organized a variety of efforts ranging from the hard sell to more subtle attempts to depict the advantages of the American way of life. Washington tried to play on Catholic sympathy by appointing pro-clerical Ambassadors. James Dunn, for example, tried to define the 1948 elections in terms of "Christ versus Communism."

The U.S. Information Service maintained an operation in Italy and the Voice of America broadcast two hours daily. Italian trains carried signs reading "This train runs thanks to American coal." Postage stamps were cancelled with the insignia "American aid—Bread and Work." Household bills for gas and electricity carried a rubber stamped notice that the energy was produced by free American coal.[30] "American Way of Life" picture displays were presented in numerous cities; documentary films were seen by over 600,000 persons in the month before the elections.

While the anti-Fascist role and the history of emigration were largely responsible, these efforts contributed to the already high opinion of the United States held by most of the Italian public. Polls of emigration preferences during the 1946-1948 years found a full quarter of Italian adults desiring permanent emigration (and an additional 16 to 23 percent temporary emigration). As late as 1952, 59 percent of the *braccianti* (agricultural day laborers) would have emigrated, given the opportunity. Even among the population of a Communist stronghold in Rome, only forty percent of the industrial workers preferred to stay in Italy for the rest of their lives. Twenty-seven percent wished to emigrate to the United States; only two percent to the Soviet Union.

Washington did not shy away from direct pressure tactics. On March 17 for example, the State Department announced that Italians who joined the PCI would never be allowed to emigrate to the United States. Several weeks later this was amended to include all those voting for the PCI.[31]

ON THE DIPLOMATIC front, the U.S. brought Italy up for membership in the United Nations several times. At first the USSR blocked the application for lack of a formal peace treaty establishing Italy as an independent nation; later the opposition was based on the UN's refusal to accept the applications of Hungary, Bulgaria, and Rumania. On the eve of the election, April 3, 1948, the U.S. brought Italy's case to the UN for the third time. The Soviet veto created sympathy for the De Gasperi government; *Il Popolo* ran a headline, "Third Russian Veto in the UN for Our Admission."[32]

(d) Covert Activities

IN FEBRUARY 1975, the State Department published the latest volume of documents in a series entitled *The Foreign Relations of the United States*. While there are many deletions, some references to secret activities aimed at preventing a left victory in the April elections remain. These include:

—"activity combatting communist propaganda in Italy by an effective U.S. information program and by all other practical means (rest of sentence deleted)."

—"efforts by all feasible means (deletion) to detach the Italian leftwing Socialists from the Communists."

—Truman's approval of a secret recommendation that the United States "make full use of its political, economic, and if necessary military power" to prevent a "Communist take-over."[33]

PERIOD III: THE APERTURA A SINISTRE
(OPENING TO THE LEFT)

FOLLOWING THE DEFEAT of the Popular Front in the 1948 elections and the continued polarization of cold war politics, the Italian Socialist Party began to move away from the PCI, especially in the realm of foreign policy toward the Soviet Union. In 1958 the PSI ended its Unity of Action Pact with the PCI; the U.S. started to secretly fund both the party and key political leaders who favored the trend. In April 1953, Clare Booth Luce replaced Ellsworth Bunker as Ambassador to Italy. The appointment signalled the U.S. decision to avoid pressuring the DC to reform its increasingly corrupt political structure (one of Luce's favorite publicity stunts was allowing herself to be photographed handing out crucifixes to peasants during the inauguration of some token land-reform program).

During this period all official contact between members of the U.S. embassy in Rome and representatives of the Communist and Socialist parties was banned. Covert financial support was also forthcoming for the DC and non-CGIL (Confederazione Generale Italian de Lavoro) union leaders. The embassy kept close contact with the leaders of the ultra-right Monarchist Party, and sympathized with the "crackdown" on Communists and Socialists within the Italian bureaucracy. The Embassy dabbled in internal DC politics, arranging a U.S. trip for conservative leader Mario Scelba in March 1955 (thus boosting his prestige) and opposing the installation of left-wing Christian Democrat Giovanni Gronchi as President of the Republic. (Luce considered Gronchi "a pro-Communist who would steer Italy toward a neutralist foreign policy."[34]) Washington also ended military contracts with firms whose labor-force voted more than fifty percent for CGIL candidates. This was no small matter, for these contracts reached more than 400 million dollars a year.[35]

Despite PCI failure to make significant headway during the late fifties, some U.S. decision-makers became increasingly alarmed by the inability of the DC to provide political stability, effective leadership, and overall legitimacy. This current grew strongest under the new Kennedy administration. Kennedy Special Assistant Arthur Schlesinger, roving Ambassador W. Averill Harriman, National Security Council Staffer Robert Komer and Dana Durand of the CIA used the pretext of Premier Fanfani's visit to Washington in June 1961 to lobby for a change in policy. The shift would support elements of the DC that favored close cooperation with the Socialists, or what became known as the *apertura* or "opening to the left." The arguments parallel in important respects those currently employed by the soft-line approach. For Harriman, for example, the *apertura* policy was necessary for the following reasons: necessary reform in Italy was impossible without the inclusion of the

Socialists, the official American position of neutrality toward Italian politics was widely perceived as *de facto* support for the center and center right, and continued U.S intransigence might push the Socialist Party back toward the PCI.[36] For Schlesinger, "the opening to the left"—if successful—could also serve as a model for a Catholic and Socialist alliance in Germany after Adenauer or France after DeGaulle (and serve as a good guarantee against efforts to revive a French alliance between the Socialists and Communists). Both men were confident that the PSI had long been coaxed away from its revolutionary past. For a large part this transformation was based on internal Italian developments, including changes within the PSI toward the right and the emergence of left factions within the DC. But Washington's covert aid to its still official antagonist accelerated the de-radicalization process.

In the meantime, the position of the U.S. Embassy in Rome remained strongly anti-*apertura*.* Deputy Chief of Mission Outerbridge Horsey argued that leftist claims of *immobilismo* (a political and economic stalemate caused by the erosion in political authority of the DC) were greatly exaggerated. Horsey maintained that public U.S. support for the *apertura* would gravely weaken the DC, that the PSI still included "fellow travelers" of the PCI, that the Socialists were still at least partially answerable to the Communists, and that any rash move in Washington might upset the delicate balance of forces sustaining the Fanfani government. As late as November 1961, some members of the U.S. Embassy advocated the direct use of Amerian troops in case of a severe political crisis.[38]

The pro-*apertura* officials marshalled their political supporters. Non-government officials (including James King, a research analyst at the Institute for Defense Analysis) traveled to Italy and circulated reports of the fragile political situation in Italy. King circulated a widely read pro-*apertura* memorandum after an eight-day visit in April 1961 and helped arrange for Socialist leader Pietro Nenni to publish an article outlining the principle differences between the PCI and the PSI in *Foreign Affairs*.[39] Nenni outlined the PSI's acceptance of NATO and the European Community, and guaranteed never to sever all ties with the PCI. Following a trip to Italy, Senator Hubert Humphrey also supported the *apertura*. Kennedy, meanwhile, avoided any public statement supporting

---

* The Embassy might have done well to quote the soothing council of Italian man of letters Gaetano Salvemini: "During the first World War we used to say that the situation in Germany was serious but not desperate, in Austria desperate but not serious, and in Italy desperate but normal. The Italian situation is always desperate but normal."[37]

the *apertura*. But during Fanfani's visit to Washington, the President secretly "formulated a position of sympathy toward the Italian Socialists."[40] Kennedy reportedly told Fanfani that if "the Italian Prime Minister thought that it (the *apertura*) was a good idea, we (the United States) would watch developments with sympathy."[41]

The first official meeting between Nenni and a member of the U.S. Embassy occurred a year later. By the fall of 1962, the last vestiges of official American opposition to PSI participation disappeared. Contact between left-wing members of the DC and PSI officials became regular; covert financial support to the PSI continued and the cabinet formed by Aldo Moro in December 1963 included four Socialist ministers.

WHILE THE BATTLE among the elites in U.S. policy-making circles was significant, the overall context of that debate reflected changing historical and political circumstances over which Washington had only partial control. It could be plausibly argued that by 1961 support for the PSI's participation in government did not signify a dramatic shift to the left. Indeed the Socialists' shift to the right, greased by covert U.S. financial support, left doubt as to whether the former partner of the PCI could be considered revolutionary in any sense of the word. Yet U.S. policy makers did think that the shift in policy was a significant change in posture. There is some continuity in U.S. policy— behind support for the *apertura* lay a firm anti-Communism. And there are differences as well. Here we must also appreciate how the shift in policy was *forced* on Kennedy by the uncertainty of the Italian political situation, the failure to fully consolidate hegemony over the left, and the erosion of effective rule by the DC, in short the influence of popular forces on history. Some political currents grasp the need for change in order to maintain control earlier than others. The conflict among the elites continues, but over changing political terrain molded by the history, direction, and intensity of class struggle.

PERIOD IV: THE NIXON ADMINISTRATION

WASHINGTON'S CAPACITY TO shape Italian politics has been further reduced during the Nixon and Carter administrations. The state managers have been forced to conduct foreign policy with an ever stronger sense of limitations. These constraints have been imposed by a decline in the vitality of the postwar international economy, deepening tensions within the capitalist world, the growing strength of the Eastern European nations and non-aligned movements, and a lack of confidence due to the failure of old solutions and the inability to construct new popular political coalitions. The success of the Vietnamese Revolution played a particularly important role in this process, demonstating that resistance against even a massive U.S. commitment is possible and that the continued loyalty of the American public in supporting the international interests of the capitalist class is no longer a permanent part of the political landscape. It is possible to exaggerate the depth of this imperial dissolution; after all the U.S. remains the strongest global power. But it no longer rules through a system that operates as smoothly as it has for most of the postwar period. This gradual weakening process has produced strategies that are more symbolic and less effective in their direct influence on Italian politics. Washington has been forced to operate more on an immediate or tactical level than through a coordinated system of control.

The methods of support for the Christian Democrats and other non-Communist parties under the Nixon Administration became more and more sordid. In some respects Nixon and Kissinger, and later Ford, reacted to increased Communist influence in much the same way as the Truman Administration. Kissinger, in fact, ordered a review of tactics employed in the postwar period for possible use during the Nixon Administration. At the Puerto Rico economic summit meeting in June 1976, the U.S., West Germany, France, and Great Britain discussed the possibility of cutting off economic aid to Italy, then in dire financial straits, if the PCI participated directly in the cabinet.[42] And the importance of maintaining symbolic steps to isolate the PCI was reasserted. Sergio Segre, head of the foreign section of the PCI, was not permitted to attend a Council of Foreign Relations dinner where Italian politics was to be discussed.[43] Washington delayed plans to remove obsolete nuclear warheads from Italy for fear that it might be construed as a sign that Italy would eventually go Communist and that the U.S. was cutting off military ties.[44] The publication by the *New York Times* of an op-ed article by PCI leader Giancarlo Pajetta was treated as implicit endorsement of the historic compromise. Ford announced that the United States would be "very disturbed" if the PCI were allowed a role in government.[45] And in Italy members of the U.S. Embassy met publicly with Italian Social Movement (MSI) leader Giorgio Amilrante.

The strategy may have been similar but the Italian and international response was quite different. Great Britain and France, for example, were forced to dissociate themselves from the Puerto Rico summit decision to tie economic aid to Italian politics. Within Italy itself not only the PCI but the DC reacted negatively to the news. Some Europeans feared that Kissinger might prefer an Italy in chaos or in the hands of the extreme right to one with Communists in power.[46] The news of contacts between the U.S. Embassy and Amilrante touched off a political storm in Italy, with some members of the DC feeling that the publicity resulted in a political loss for the U.S.

THE PUBLIC SURFACING of the extent of U.S. multinational involvement in what Italians refer to as "the politics of lubrication," also contributed to declining American legitimacy and a loss of leverage for the state managers. The incidents listed below illustrate how specific interests can interfere with the stability of general policies formulated from the point of view of the capitalists class as a whole.

* In testimony before the U.S. Senate Foreign Relations Committee on Multinational Corporations, Gulf Oil Chairman Robert Dorsey admitted that his company may have made illegal political contributions in Italy.

* Chairman of the Board J.K. Jamieson reported that Exxon subsidiaries in Italy contributed to various non-Communist political parties.

* Mobil Oil Chairman Rawleigh Warner Jr. reported illegal contributions to Italian parties totaling more than a half million dollars.

* Between 1970 and 1974, United Brands Company spent more than two million dollars bribing Italian officials in order to increase banana imports.

* Lockheed made payments totaling 1.6 million dollars to Italian politicians to ensure the sale of C-130 transport planes. Named as recipients were President Giovanni Leone, Foreign Minister Mariano Rumor, and Prime Minister Aldo Moro. (Rumor and Moro were later cleared.)

* Between 1969 and 1973, the Shell Oil Company attempted to influence Italian politics with contributions of more than six million dollars.

* ITT gave more than $300,000 to Italian tax agents to "facilitate negotiations" over taxes owed between 1969 and 1972.[47]

Under the Republicans after 1968, covert aid continued in ever greater quantities. A report by the House Select Committee on Intelligence found that between 1947 and 1975 the CIA supplied over seventy-five million dollars to Italian parties and candidates. The DC received three million dollars annually between the late-50s and 1967. The funds were not concentrated in the early and middle period. American Ambassador Graham Martin, during his four-year stint beginning October 1969, gave ten million dollars to the DC and to twenty-one individual candidates for office. Martin, who was replaced by John Volpe in 1973 in order to become the last U.S. Ambassador to South Vietnam, channeled $800,000 to General Vito Miceli, a prominent right-wing general who headed the Defense Information Service, Italy's military intelligence agency. Miceli was eventually arrested in October 1974 on charges of involvement in plots to overthrow the Italian government.

The politics surrounding covert payments deserve a little closer scrutiny. The CIA Chief of Station in Italy *opposed* the payments to Miceli on the grounds that they would aid the extreme right, and that U.S. policy would be more effective if it strengthened the center. The CIA chief cabled his Washington superiors that Martin "has made clear his intention of not asking for too many details from the recipient of the money and not to impose any condition on the use of the money."[48] Whatever alternatives the CIA might have had in mind were blocked by the knowledge that Martin had obtained approval for his actions from Henry Kissinger, then the director of the National Security Council and the Chairman of 40 Committee (established to approve covert actions). The CIA did funnel more than ten million dollars to the PSI and DC, with Nixon's approval,[49] and six million more were approved by Ford in an effort to prevent further Communist gains in national and local elections.[50] The CIA did not oppose "traditional methods" designed to strengthen the center. But their reluctance to support measures bolstering the extreme right was an issue in later bureaucratic battles, culminating in the appointment of top CIA officials whose loyalty was to the White House rather than to the Agency. Many of the leaks associated with the Watergate period (and upon which parts of this essay are based) were made by former CIA members angered by the incursion of the White House into the "independence" of the Agency. What started as secret conflicts over relatively restricted issues (such as the accuracy of intelligence information in Vietnam, or the decision to funnel money to right-wing politicians in Italy) eventually led to public revelations that have handicapped the ability of the CIA to operate as freely as it has in the past.[51] The newspaper accounts on which this analysis is partially based would not have appeared save for the general Watergate atmosphere. The political environment, in other words, has been structured by the relations among the following: U.S. domestic politics; particular bureaucratic interests such as those of the CIA; policy currents; the original goals of restricting the influence of the Italian left; and developments in Italian politics. The result has been to improve the position of the PCI in Italy.

PERIOD V: THE CARTER ADMINISTRATION

IT WAS PRECISELY THE possibility that continued U.S. intransigence (including the identification with the center-right and the implicit endorsement of the corruption and ineptitude of the ruling DC) would backfire into more sympathy for the Communists that led influential Democrats and soon-to-be President Jimmy Carter to consider alternative policies in 1975-76. Former Democratic officials George Ball and Paul Warnke, for example, were joined by then Professor Zbigniew Brzezinski in stating that future Italian governments would probably include Communists and that the U.S. should be prepared to deal with them responsibly.[52] At approximately the same time Brzezinski's Research Institute in International Change issued a study concluding that PCI participation in a coalition government represented no immediate threat to NATO or the European Community. The report went on to argue that the PCI's commitment to political pluralism, European economic integration, and political independence from Moscow was genuine. In the government, the PCI could be counted on to resist calls for nationalization.

In a speech before the Foreign Policy Association in New York before he became president, Carter attributed Italy's difficulties to an "underlying social malaise" and hinted at the need for more thorough reform than then contemplated by Washington. Carter also called for greater foreign assistance to help Italy grapple with its "political problems."

Upon assuming office the Carter Administration was widely regarded as having a different policy toward Eurocommunism than Ford and Kissinger. And the first six months seemed to support this contention. An April 1977 State Department release was concerned less with Eurocommunist "participation" than possible "domination." In a June interview, Secretary of State Cyrus Vance said that the U.S. would "clearly prefer" non-Communist governments in Western Europe, but added that "it is not for us to tell any country whom they should elect in the way of the political leaders."[54] In France two U.S. Embassy officials met with PCF Politburo member Jean Kanapa. In September the PCI newspaper *L'Unita* was permitted to send a correspondent to Washington. In Madrid, American officials met with a middle-level member of the Spanish Communist Party. During a speech at Notre Dame University, shortly after taking office, Carter said the U.S. was free from its "inordinate fear of Communism," and promised a policy of non-interference. Brzezinski, now National Security Adviser, argued that "hectoring the West Europeans about the Communist threat just makes the Communists more popular."[55]

Starting in October 1977, the Carter Administration began to move away from its original position; official statements began to express the hard-line rather than the soft-line current. In an October 20 interview, Carter said that "if Communists should become part of European government there would be concern about NATO defenses." Carter went on to "doubt whether the loyalty of some of the Communist leaders might go to their own nations or to the Soviet Union."[56] When in January 1978 it was faced with the actual prospect of Communist participation in both Italy and France, the Carter Administration recalled U.S. Ambassador to Italy Richard Gardner, already a member of the hard-line current, and issued a public statement "opposing" Communist participation in government. The statement added that the U.S. "would like to see Communist influence in any Western country reduced." In an implicit rejection of earlier statements that Eurocommunist forces respected political pluralism, Carter and the State Department also called on Europeans to "show firmness in resisting the temptation of finding solutions in non-democratic forces."[57]

CONCLUSION

WHAT LIGHT CAN THE policy currents perspective shed on the shift in policy? The PCI's political strategy is based on the recognition that there are limits to the rapid construction of a socialist society. These include the need to build a vast constituency for socialism; the desire to avoid the disastrous consequences of a thorough rupture with capitalist society; and the need to overcome the still strong forces of opposition, including the current foreign policy of the U.S. For example, the PCI would much prefer a Europe freed from the restrictions imposed by NATO and the Warsaw Pact. Yet in a recent speech setting out the foreign policy of the PCI, Enrico Berlinguer argued that "to attain this goal of overcoming the division into opposing blocs, it is necessary not to tackle it immediately or head-on, but rather to realistically take a longer road: the road of international detente."[58] Berlinguer went on to argue that "realism" in this context meant "carefully pondering the existence and deep roots" of the blocs and "not questioning our [Italy's] country's membership in the alliance to which it belongs."

All of which brings us to the theme on which this essay has been based—the difficulty of developing socialist politics within a single country when the conditions affecting such developments are increasingly determined by the influence of international factors.

Does the persistence of U.S. attempts to restrict the PCI contradict the argument that Washington's capacity to exert such influence is on the decline? The answer would be "no." Domestic political developments are increasingly affected by international developments, but in contrast to the relatively secure hegemony exercised by the U.S. in the immediate postwar order, global politics are more uncertain, more in flux, and more likely to reflect the emergence of diverse centers of power. The impact of global politics is both stronger and more contradictory.

Washington's leverage over political development in Europe has declined over the last thirty years for several reasons. The most important is the increasing instability and sense of crisis in the capitalist world as a whole. This is manifested most visibly in the absence of a stable monetary system, deepening inflation and unemployment, and the failure of Trilateralism to produce a policy capable of providing renewed cooperation among the capitalist powers. Elsewhere in the world, centers of opposition of many types have grown, both in number and strength. The U.S. no longer commands the respect that it enjoyed at the close of World War II from its identification with the anti-fascist struggle. Despite its counterinsurgency programs, the U.S. armed forces are still better adapted to nuclear war than to foreign intervention. The weakness of the U.S. domestic economy also hinders the pursuit of foreign policy: military Keynesianism no longer seems to provide an adequate stimulus. There is a growing sense of limits. Another crucial element of postwar strength—the relative absence of class-based political opposition— is undergoing changes. The political coalition supporting foreign policy for most of the postwar period has collapsed and the antiwar movement has left a legacy restricting the use of more militaristic options.

With particular reference to Italy and the PCI, this decline in power can be demonstrated by contrasting the strategies utilized in 1948 with those available in the present. At that time Washington successfully linked the provision of economic aid to the political exclusion of the PCI. A similar, more subtle attempt in 1976 backfired, causing adverse reaction not only within Italy but in the rest of Europe as well. Covert activities directed through the CIA were an important component of the 1948 anti-Communist effort. While probably continuing in some modified form, the full use of "dirty tricks" is now restricted by a widespread process of delegitimation that has deepened both in Italy and within Congress and the intelligence agencies themselves. The U.S. is not as popular among the Italian populace as in the immediate postwar years. And finally, where some policy-makers considered direct military intervention in the event of a left victory in the '48 elections, only a dramatic shift in U.S. politics would sustain such an action today. NATO of course is a continuing constraint for the European left as a whole, but its restrictions are not insurmountable. Further evidence of declining influence can be detected in the Carter Administration's firm statement of January 1978, which merits brief discussion.

U.S. foreign policy is based fundamentally on the attempt to influence the overall political contest between capitalism and socialism, in this case the relative strengths of the PCI and the DC. As Washington's influence declines, there is a greater attempt to shift the relative strengths of political currents that exist *within* each of those parties. To some extent diplomacy has always sought to influence political forces within opposing movements and political parties. But declining leverage at the level of the conflict between the PCI and the DC has led to greater concentration on the narrower effort. Thus the Carter Administration's January 1978 statement reflected both the logic of the hard-line emphasis on a firm anti-Communist stance *and* an attempt to strengthen the position of the right within the DC, against those favoring the "historic compromise." At the national level this has meant supporting Andreotti over Moro (before the latter's death), Fanfani and Minister of Industry Carlo Donat Cattin. At the regional level the statement works to the benefit of Milan "new right" leaders such as Massimo De Carolis.[59]

THE CURRENT U.S. policy is likely to exasperate members of the Italian bourgeoisie who favor reform of the corruption and "spoils system" of the Christian Democrats. Umberto Agnelli (brother of Giovanni Agnelli, head of Fiat) envisions a transformation of the party along more technocratic lines similar to President Valery Giscard d'Estaing's Independent Republican Party in France. U.S. actions may also hinder the desire of some supporters of capital to enlist the support of the PCI in gaining the cooperation of organized labor in modernizing and rationalizing the economic structure. This may also undercut the position of the "moderates" within the PCI as well. The "left" and "technocratic" wings of the DC fear, along with the soft-line currents, that the U.S. may be creating a situation where the possibility of a right-wing coup and subsequent military participation in government is more likely. By strengthening the right, the chances of providing a stable government between the PCI and moderate DC are reduced. Future elections may strengthen the right within the DC, but reduce the chances of providing effective government and the stability necessary for capitalist development.

It is precisely the fear that the relative tranquility of current Italian parliamentary politics will explode into yet another crisis that gives sustenance to the continued conflict of policy currents. The hard-line position that presently dominates the Carter administration would like to deny the PCI the symbolic victory of direct participation while tying the Communists to the responsibilities of managing Italian society. In this respect, the consultative role played by the PCI until January 1979 was ideal. The soft-line counters that U.S. policy has accomplished little toward the goal of overcoming the crisis of Italian society. The PCI is temporarily blocked, but the long-term consequences of unresolved problems are potentially catastrophic—far more damaging than any symbolic loss stemming from the recognition of the PCI as a valid political force in Italian society. The short-term advantages of formal exclusion of the PCI have to be measured against the long-run dangers of a more militant PCI in opposition. In contrast to the postwar years, the choice and outcomes are no longer under complete American control. At bottom, policy currents are a product of obstacles to the rule of capital, among which oppositional movements are the most important. Policy currents are disagreements over how to respond: we can expect conflict between them to continue, for there is little likelihood that the U.S. will be able to permanently undermine the growth of the PCI and other Eurocommunist movements.

Notes

1. "Communist Parties in Western Europe: Challenge to the West," vol. 15, no. 3, Fall 1977, p. 263.

2. See for example, Heinz Timmerman, "Eurocommunism: Moscow's Reaction and the Implications for Eastern Europe," *The World Today*, vol. 33, no. 10, October 1977, p. 5.

3. See Arrigo Levi, "Italy's 'New' Communism," *Foreign Policy*, no. 26, Spring 1977, p. 29.

4. In this view a Eurocommunist "seizure of power" would present NATO with the following difficult options: (a) encouraging the withdrawal of the government under Communist influence or control; (b) quarantining a NATO member if loyalty is in doubt; (c) pursuing an "empty chair" policy (for example, Italy could be a member nation but without active participation); (d) replacing NATO with bilateral treaties. James Dougherty and Diane K. Pfaltzgraff, *Eurocommunism and the Atlantic Alliance*, (Cambridge: Institute for Foreign Policy Analysis, Inc., 1977), p. 64.

5. Kissinger, *op. cit.* p. 262.

6. Levi, *op. cit.*, p. 38.

7. See Fred Block's distinction between "open" forms of capitalism and "national capitalism" in *The Origins of International Economic Disorder*, (Berkeley: University of California Press, 1977), pp. 4-10.

8. S.J. Woolf, *The Rebirth of Italy, 1943-1950*, (London: Longman, 1977), p. 30.

9. Gabriel Kolko, *Politics of War*, (New York: Random House, 1968), p. 45.

10. Norman Kogan, *Italy and the Allies*, (Cambridge: Harvard University Press, 1956), p. 19.

11. *Ibid.*, p. 82.

12. See Gregory Black "The United States and Italy, 1943: The Draft Toward Containment," Doctoral Dissertation, University of Kansas, 1973, p. 111.

13. Sumner Wells, *Where Are We Heading*, (New York: Harper and Row, 1946).

14. Kogan, *op. cit.* p. 82.

15. Robert Holt and Rober van de Velde, *Strategic Psychological Operations and American Foreign Policy*, (Chicago: University of Chicago Press, 1960), p. 154.

16. *Cordell Hull Memoirs*, Vol. II (New York: Macmillan, 1948), p. 140.

17. The United States was first to extend full diplomatic recognition to Italy. In the fall of 1944, just before the presidential election and motivated in part by the desire to win greater support from Italian-Americans, Roosevelt announced recognition, an aid program, immediate credit of $100 million, and partial relaxation of military controls. See A. Platt, "U.S. Policy Toward 'The Opening to the Left' in Italy," Doctoral Dissertation, Columbia University, 1973, p. 51.

18. Harold Macmillan, *The Blast of War*, p. 488. Quoted by Black, *op. cit.* p. 147.

19. Black, *op. cit.*, p. 246.

20. *Ibid.*, p. 302.

21. Kolko, *op. cit.*, p. 55.

22. "Confidential Interview," cited by A. Platt, Columbia University, 1973, p. 51.

23. "Exchange of Views with the Italian Prime Minister on Italy's Needs, January 15, 1947," *U.S. Department of State Bulletin*, vol. XVI, January 26, 1947, p. 165.

24. Incoming telegram from the Embassy in Rome to the Department of State "For the Secretary," Top Secret, no. 1031, May 3, 1947, cited in Platt, *op. cit.*, p. 141.

25. U.S. Senate, Committee on Foreign Relations, *A Decade of American Foreign Policy, Basic Documents 1941-1949,* (Washington: Government Printing Office, 1950), p. 478.

26. Walter Milles, *The Forrestal Diaries*, (New York: Viking Press, 1951), p. 280.

27. The State Department later credited the aid program with affecting the outcome of the election "to a considerable degree," *Department of State Bulletin*, July 25, 1948, p. 101.

In addition to government grants and credits, substantial private aid, much of it prompted by Washington, reached Italy from the United States. The War Relief Services of the National Catholic Welfare Conference sent 54 million pounds of food, clothing and medicine (*New York Times*, April 14, 1948). And Cooperation for American Remittance to Europe (CARE) transmitted 2,856,989 parcels to Italy (*New York Times,* March 22, 1948). Other non-government efforts included progaganda efforts such as a massive letter-writing campaign from Italian-Americans urging their friends and relatives in Italy to vote against the Popular Front.

28. *New York Times*, March 20, 1948.

29. *New York Times*, March 30, 1948.

30. Examples drawn from E. Rossi, "The United States and the 1948 Italian Election," Doctoral Dissertation, University of Pittsburgh, 1968, pp. 230-239.

31. Hadley Cantril, *Politics of Despair*, (New York: Basic Books, 1958), pp. 112-113.

32. Rossi, *op. cit.*, p. 239.

33. *New York Times*, February 12, 1975.

34. Platt, *op. cit.*, p. 85.

35. Kogan, *Political History*, p. 90.

36. Interview with Harriman conducted by Platt, p. 112.

37. Salvemini, *Lettere dali'America,* Vol. II, p. 148; quoted by Woolf, *op. cit.*, p. 243.

38. Platt, *op. cit.*, p. 168.

39. "Where the Socialists Stand," *Foreign Affairs*, vol. 40, January 1962, pp. 213-223.

40. Platt, *op. cit.*, p. 142.

41. Arthur Schlesinger, *A Thousand Days*, (Boston: Houghton Mifflin, 1965), p. 878.

42. *New York Times*, July 17, 1976.

43. *New York Times*, September 14, 1975.

44. *New York Times*, July 24, 1975.

45. *New York Times*, July 11, 1975.

46. Reported by Anthony Lewis in *New York Times*, July 29, 1976.

47. Collected from the following editions of the *New York Times*: May 17, 1975; July 18, 1975; July 20, 1975; July 24, 1975; February 2, 1975; April 14, 1976.

48. *New York Times*, January 30, 1975.

49. *CBS News*, aired December 20, 1975.

50. *New York Times*, January 7, 1976.

51. For a discussion of the Vietnam situation, see my "Politics of 'Good' and 'Bad' Information: The National Security Bureaucracy and the Vietnam War," *Politics and Society*, July 1977, pp. 105-126.

52. *New York Times*, April 14, 1976.

53. *New York Times*, May 9, 1976.

54. Quoted in the *New York Times*, October 30, 1977.

55. *International Bulletin*, vol. 5, no. 2, January 30, 1978, p. 4.

56. *New York Times*, January 13, 1978.

57. The test of the statement can be found in the *New York Times*, January 13, 1978.

58. See Enrico Berlinguer, "An Autonomous Policy of Disarmament, Peace and Cooperation for Western Europe," *The Italian Communists: Foreign Bulletin of the PCI*, no. 3, July-September 1977, p. 16.

59. On divisions within the Christian Democrats, see articles by Diana Johnstone in *In These Times*, February 15-21 and April 19-25, 1978, and Henry Tanner, "Italy's Major Party Has a Major Conflict On Ideology," *New York Times*, February 26, 1978.

chapter 12

INTEGRATING EUROPE
TO DISINTEGRATE THE LEFT

Diana Johnstone

THE ECONOMIC AND political integration of Western Europe, through the European Economic Community (EEC), has been accelerated in the late 1970s as a means of binding countries that might be tempted to move towards socialism—notably France and Italy—more firmly into the capitalist system. Most of the left in those two countries has gone along with European integration, tacitly abandoning the prospect of any serious break with the capitalist system in the foreseeable future. At the same time, the question of what attitude to take towards the EEC, and the campaign for the first direct election of the European Parliament in June 1979, have deepened divisions between Socialist and Communist Parties and caused new rifts among the latter in various countries. European integration threatens to contribute, at least in its initial stages, to the disintegration of the European left.

Around 1976, it appeared possible that left-wing coalition governments with Communist participation might come to power in France or Italy. This could be seen as a threat to the capitalist system—or more precisely, to the revised and more "interdependent" version of the capitalist system emerging in the 1970s along the lines laid down by major international financial institutions and multinational corporations. This threat was not removed by the reformist intentions of the Italian Communist Party (PCI) or of the French left's Common Program. Even if only reformist, a left-wing government in France or Italy could have been led by the country's internal political dynamic and its economic situation to seek trade arrangements with Third World countries, especially around the Mediterranean, without consulting the German and American architects of the "new economic world order." This could be a very serious matter.

One of the main strategies adopted by defenders of the capitalist system to meet this threat was to strengthen the EEC and give its already considerable economic leverage over member countries (especially Italy) more political legitimacy by proceeding to direct election of the European Parliament. In France or Italy, a left influenced by Marxist thinking and linked to a mass movement with revolutionary aspirations might conceivably win a majority. In a supranational Europe composed of the EEC countries, such a majority is quite out of the question. Diluted in Europe, the Marxist left of the Latin countries becomes an apparently eternal minority, which the capitalist planners hope may die out as an anachronism.

THE STRUCTURE OF EUROPEAN INTEGRATION

THROUGHOUT THE 1970s, the main policy-makers of the capitalist world, as exemplified by the Trilateral Commission, have been vigorously promoting a "new world economic order." The advantages of this new order include simplifying the rules and procedures under which multinational corporations and financial institutions do business, and restructuring the international division of labor to plug nations more firmly into the world market by increased specialization, thereby making it practically impossible for any single nation to break out of the system. The development of the EEC into a supranational Europe has been a principal feature of this overall Trilateral policy.

The United States has consistently championed European integration, both for substantial economic and political reasons—advantages to U.S. business interests and the cementing of an anti-Soviet bloc—and superficial or mistaken cultural reasons, based on an ignorant impatience with the deep historical differences between the European countries. West Germany is obviously most favorable to an integrated Europe that it can expect to dominate. The Communist gains in Italy in 1976, along with the anticipated French left victory in 1978, gave the Germans a furthur incentive by provoking a fear of "encirclement" by "communism." As West German foreign minister Hans Dietrich Genscher put it, agreement to elect the members of the European Parliament by direct suffrage would be a "clear and sharp" answer to the "grave problems" facing the European Community and the Atlantic Alliance if Communists took part in a Western government.

The European Parliament was established by the March 25, 1957, Rome Treaties founding the EEC. It began meeting a year later—its members appointed by the national parliaments of the six (later nine) EEC countries,* but caucusing by party, with Socialists and Christian Democrats forming the largest caucuses in a body with a generally conservative cast. It has been meeting sometimes in Strasbourg, its official seat, and sometimes in Luxembourg, where its secretariat is located, but there is pressure to have it meet in Brussels, so that it can be near the European Commission, which is the EEC's executive branch charged with initiating policy and running the administration.

The balance of powers between EEC bodies reflects a concern for preserving national sovereignties that was written into the Rome Treaties. The Parliament is formally designated as a consultative rather than legislative body, although it has the typically parliamentary powers of approving budgets and censuring the Commission. Decision-making power is vested in the Council of Ministers, which directly represents member governments and is therefore the body where national sovereignty can be asserted. The Ministers, with other preoccupations, may give only partial attention to Community matters, which is irritating to the "Eurocrats" of the Commission, as is the ability of a minority (in some cases a single country) to block Council decisions.

The Commission's fourteen members are unanimously appointed by EEC country governments to four-year terms, during which they are answerable not to those governments but to the European Parliament. The Commission naturally finds the Council a dreadful nuisance and would much rather deal simply with the Parliament. Direct election of the Parliament is designed to enhance its authority, making it harder both for national governments and for the Council of Ministers to resist its decisions. Commission and Parliament can be expected to work hand in hand to strengthen their own powers relative to the Council, in turn strengthening the supranational powers of the EEC. Claude Bourdet, a leading French left-wing critic of European integration, predicts that disputes between the Commission and the Parliament on the one side and the Council on the other will be brought before the European Court of Justice (the Community's judicial branch), which has always ruled in favor of supranationality. In this way, without any amendment to the Rome Treaties, the safeguards to national sovereignty written into them will be eroded away, and the Council will be reduced to the role of a relatively powerless upper house, like the British House of Lords.

*France, the German Federal Republic, Italy, the Netherlands, Belgium, and Luxemburg, joined after 1972 by the United Kingdom, Ireland, and Denmark. Norway was admitted, but in a referendum Norwegians chose to stay out.

CERTAINLY, THE QUESTION of sovereignty versus supra-nationality has not always been treated with utmost candor by advocates of direct election of the European Parliament. Hailed as a step towards European integration and supranationality in countries favorable to such a development, the direct elections were described as making no difference in countries nervous about national sovereignty, such as France and Britain.

Opposition in France to supranationality is naturally strongest in those sectors of production most threatened by "restructuring" within the Common Market, such as steel and textiles. After the left lost the 1978 elections, President Valery Giscard d'Estaing's Prime Minister, Raymond Barre, has pushed rapid "restructuring," which takes the visible form of large numbers of factories being shut down and workers being laid off. A new boom is promised in the sectors with a future, such as computers, aerospace and ocean development. But the dismantling of traditional industry, which employed large numbers of workers and was primarily sustained by the domestic market, is initially more evident than the growth of the new industries, which in any case promise to employ fewer and more highly qualified workers and to be dependent on export.

French attitudes toward these developments cut across class lines and are influenced by both sentimental and practical factors. It is not, in fact, the Common Market, but the rising cost of petroleum that has been the decisive and unanswerable argument for gearing the economy to exports, in order to pay for oil imports. Germany is France's main trade partner as well as the strongest economy within the EEC, so that greater emphasis on exports and on the Common Market can be felt as growing dependence on Germany. The Gaullist right expresses an opposition to EEC supranationality based partially on concern for preserving the decision-making mechanisms of the state from foreign (German) control, and partly on fears of business sectors that feel threatened by current economic trends. But capital is more mobile than labor, and despite strong misgivings, the French bourgeoisie can hope for important advantages in the new international restructuring of capitalism. The French ruling class still has an important international role to play, notably in Africa, which can be combined with the export of advanced technology. Moreover, greater integration into international capitalism strengthens the French bourgeoisie in its confrontation with the French working class. Once France no longer produces certain things it cannot do without, and once its economy is firmly inserted into a Europe dominated by anti-Communist Germany, it can elect as many left-wing governments as it wants, but none of them will be able to take the country any closer to socialism than its European partners allow it to go.

French left-wing opponents of European integration recall that forty years ago, most of the French ruling class accepted subservience to Germany and the passive fascism of General Petain's Vichy government after getting a scare from the Popular Front. Some accuse the Giscardian bourgeoisie of being ready to wreck large parts of the French economy to disperse and weaken a working class infected with Marxism.

Restructuring attacks traditional strongholds of the organized working class, reducing its numbers and creating a "generation gap" with young workers who find only precarious, part-time jobs, with none of the protections and benefits of hard-won labor contracts. Such restructuring, identified with a European perspective, thus arouses the strongest opposition within the organized working class. There is also a widespread feeling in the French working class that sectors like steel and textiles are in the long run more solid and essential than the new technologies for which they are supposedly being sacrificed. Industry will always need steel, and people will always need clothes. How quickly will the market for nuclear power plants and communications satellites be saturated, creating a new crisis?

On the other hand, autarky has a bad name, as does "socialism in one country," especially within the intelligentsia. Moreover, the Germany that has promoted European unity in the 1970s is governed by the Social Democratic Party (SPD) of Willy Brandt and Helmut Schmidt, and this situation has certainly contributed to the enthusiasm for the European Parliamentary elections among Socialists.

THE SOCIALIST INTERNATIONAL AND THE COMMUNISTS

MOST SOCIALIST PARTIES are for Europe, if only because the Socialist bloc was already the largest in the old Parliament. Every country has some sort of Socialist party, and Socialists hope to dominate the elected Parliament. Socialists, convinced that they and internationalism are good things that go together, readily see the European Parliament as their natural stage. The revival of the Socialist International (with Willy Brandt as chair) has strengthened this notion. The prospect of caucusing in the directly-elected European Parliament with the powerful SPD and the prestigious French Socialist Party has given the weaker Italian Socialist Party new hopes of increasing its electoral showings even in national elections, as the party best able to represent Italy in Europe. The SPD, which successfully sponsored Mario Soares' Portuguese Socialist Party, is widely believed to subsidize fellow Socialist Parties— or friendly factions within them, especially in Southern Europe—just as the right-wing German Christian Democrats subsidize Christian Democrats (or more rightist groups) in other countries. The prospect of

German favors is naturally encouraging to politicians inclined to express opinions pleasing to German ears.

With the notable exception of the British Labor Party, which takes scant interest in continental politics and has often simply failed to show up at international meetings of Socialist Parties, internationalism is a genuine article of faith to most European Socialists. Internationalism is so obviously a positive force, when perceived as the opposite of old-fashioned nationalism, that it is easy and virtually inevitable for Socialists today to approve European integration as a way of furthering that ideal. But what it means in practice is today still unclear. The parties of the Socialist International have taken "For a Europe of Working People" as their slogan; however sincere this aspiration, the obstacles to its realization appear great.

Within each European country, parties with a working class base must formulate policies that are credible to that base on issues it understands from its own struggles in confrontation with a ruling class whose strengths, weaknesses, and ruses it has learned something about from a long and eventful history. Within each national working class, however, there is relatively little understanding of the class struggle in other countries. This is variable: for historical reasons, there is probably greater awareness within the Italian working class of French and German social history than the other way around. But in general when party leaders make proposals on the European level they will be raising issues that the base cannot so readily grasp and evaluate. This is apt to weaken whatever democratic control the working class can have on the parties representing its interests. Coordination between ruling classes—with their knowledge of foreign languages, facilities for travel and communication, as well as their control of major media—is vastly easier than between the organizations of the working class.

Within the European Parliament, Socialists (like Communists) will promote the extension and standardization of "welfare state" measures. This is what northern European Social Democracy means by "socialism." It is hard to see what other definition of socialism could be explored in the technocratic upper reaches of the EEC. (The standardization of social legislation may offer some advantages to employers as well as to employees and stabilize the system more than threaten it.) The most radical demand that Socialists have taken up for their European campaign is the 35-hour work week. The SPD took up this demand under pressure from its union base. The SPD leaders have the task of persuading German workers that the 35-hour week would be disastrous for the competitive position of German industry and thus can reasonably be advanced only as a European-wide measure.

AN IMMEDIATE result of the European Parliamentary elections has been to deepen splits between Socialist and Communist Parties in France and Italy, as well as between the various Communist Parties—which unlike the Socialists are quite divided over what attitude to take towards Europe.

In France, the Communist Party (PCF) cited the French Socialist Party's alleged readiness to abandon the Union of the Left in favor of rapprochement with the SPD as one of the causes of the breakup of the Union of the Left prior to the March 1978 parliamentary elections. The PCF has pointed to the fact that the Socialist Party agreed with Giscard in favoring direct election of the European Parliament as proof that the Socialists were ready to go along with a "centrist" coalition with the Giscardians. The PCF's sectarian way of apparently promoting the very "betrayals" it predicts by providing the Socialists with no other course has probably contributed to widespread left acceptance (despite the holdout of PCF stalwarts) of the idea that European integration is inevitable. Rather than try to develop a serious debate around the political and economic implications of the European Parliament, the PCF has decided to go along with it while sniping at European integration in secondary ways. The PCF has opposed the entry of Spain, Portugal, and Greece into the EEC by taking up the battle-cry of southern French wine-growers afraid of Spanish competition—thereby enraging Spanish Communists, who see their country's entry into Europe as the best safeguard of its still precarious bourgeois democracy, which they far prefer to fascism. The PCF approach, flagrantly short on "proletarian internationalism," has convinced much of the French left that the only arguments against European integration stem from demagogy or chauvinism.

Electoral competition plays a significant role in all this. The small vegetable farmers and fruit growers of southern France, who traditionally vote Socialist, are in a real panic at the prospect of Spanish competition within the Common Market. The PCF thus hopes to make serious inroads into this Socialist stronghold. It scored an initial success by getting a colorful figure in the leadership of the Languedoc-Roussillon wine growers, Emmanuel Maffre-Bauge (a devout Christian), to run for the European Parliament on the PCF ticket. As part of its general program the PCF promises to champion the besieged family farm against encroaching agribusiness. Thus both in industry and in agriculture, it stands to pick up votes from producers who feel most threatened, at the risk of deepening its identification with the "archaic" and probably declining sectors of the economy.

The PCF has based its public campaign against Spanish, Portugese, and Greek entry mostly on vote-seeking protectionist arguments. A second argument, addressed more to the intellegentsia, is that enlarging the EEC would further weaken arguments to preserve the unanimity rule (veto) with the Council of Ministers and thus strengthen supranationality. It may be that the PCF went farther than it wanted in the direction of European integration to please the Socialists during the Union of the Left, but has since been trying to backtrack.

Things look different on the other side of the Alps. While the PCF (and much of French public opinion) views weakening the Council of Ministers in favor of the Parliament as destroying the French veto power and thus favoring German control, there are Italian leftists who perceive the veto primarily as a German weapon that can be used against Italy. For historical reasons, the population of France (as of England) tends to cherish and believe in the nation's independence from outside powers, while the population of Italy more readily believes that it is already buffeted about by outside powers. This can be partly attributed to the fact that France has the sort of effective state apparatus that is lacking in Italy. Such differences help to account for the contrasting positions of the French and Italian Communists toward the EEC.

In November 1978, PCI leaders came out strongly for the European Parliament as the leading institution of a new plurinational power, and emphasized that they would seek EEC alliances with Socialists and Social Democrats rather than with other Communist parties (in particular the PCF). As on its home ground, the PCI has once again shown great imagination in embracing political adversaries; but the German Social Democrats could prove harder to woo than the Italian Christian Democrats. It was Helmut Schmidt, after all, who disclosed in Washington in July 1976 that the United States, Britain, Germany and France had reached a secret agreement at the Puerto Rico economic summit meeting a couple of weeks earlier not to grant Italy any support loans if Communists entered the Italian government. It is the SPD that initiated repressive policies against "radicals" in teaching and other branches of West German public service which, if applied to Italy, would probably disqualify about half the population. It is hard to imagine how the PCI could use a few seats in the European Parliament to break through the quarantine which the SPD has laboriously set up to protect the German working class from contagion.

The PCI is in a good position to know that Schmidt's threat had teeth in it, and that Italian sovereignty is already limited by the need to make economic policies satisfactory to the German Federal Bank. In 1976, Trilateral Commission policy-makers advised Jimmy Carter to let Italy's European neighbors, especially Germany and the EEC, see to the task of keeping the PCI out of the Italian cabinet. The PCI position seems to be that since Italy is already a prisoner of Europe, it is preferable to make this interdependence official, visible, and subject to democratic decision-making through the European Parliament.

But there are others who fear that the European Parliament will epitomize the most deceptive features of bourgeois parliamentarianism, by making technocratic answers to the problems of capitalism appear as the freely deliberated expression of the people's representatives. In this vein, Riccardo Albione of *Democrazia Proletaria* (an Italian far left group) has called the Europarliament a "phony parliament" whose function, like that of all the European institutions, is "mystification of real political processes" and the transformation of politics into technique, thereby "excluding even the slightest possibility of popular control." Within the European far left as a whole, total indifference to the Common Market seems to be giving way to hostility. While the Italian Communists see the European Parliament as a way to counter the concentration of investment capital in the most developed regions and promote more even development that would benefit backward regions such as Southern Italy, others see it as a potential rubber stamp for projects devised by the Eurocrats or the Commission in Brussels and dictated by the economic logic of the multinational corporations and banks. Jean-Pierre Vigier wrote in the *Monde Diplomatique* (December 1976) that the economic crisis was dividing the developed countries into two categories: economic "winners" such as Germany, and "losers" such as Britain and the southern European countries. "This split obliges Europe's ruling classes to quickly construct an institutional framework enabling the losers...to be kept under control," wrote Vigier. "Thus the project for a European Parliament...is an essential condition for the 'Latin Americanization' of southern Europe."

This is not far from the viewpoint of the Greek Socialist Party (PASOK), which is hostile to Greek entry into the EEC, as is the Greek Communist Party of the Exterior. The Portuguese Communists are also against joining, and the British, Danish, and Irish Parties continue to oppose their countries' membership in the EEC. But PCI foreign policy specialist Giancarlo Pajetta sees the EEC as "rich in positive prospects" and calls the Europarliamentary elections "an important but not exhaustive step" in the direction of the democratization of the EEC. PCI leader Giorgio Amendala, "the most European Communist and the most Communist European," envisages a "new plurinational power capable of dealing with problems that national states can no longer solve, such as those concerning energy, currency, and the environment."

THE NATION-STATE AND POLITICS

THE DISARRAY on the left reflects a real dilemma. Europe's left-wing parties are built for achieving social change at the nation-state level, in coordination with nationwide grassroots movements, especially the labor unions. The whole political organization of the left implicitly assumes that socialism can be created within the nation-state unit. But events of the 1970s, such as the Chilean military coup and the oil crisis, have undermined this assumption. It is hard to escape the conclusion that a Europe designed to block the path to socialism has been accepted so readily because the very parties theoretically committed to that path have in reality no viable strategy for achieving socialism—even if they have any clear idea today of what socialism ought to be. This is something that the leaders of a mass Marxist party cannot say bluntly to their rank-and-file. But actions may speak louder than words.

It is not in fact delegates of working people who are building European unity, but technocrats steeped in the outlook of international finance. Capitalism is currently being rehabilitated ideologically, as well as practically, by enforcement of its "laws"—those economic laws pronounced by its economist-oracles, who may not agree with each other or even with themselves from one year to the next but who speak for "reality." Socialism, whatever it may ultimately mean, starts with non-acceptance of that "reality" and those "laws" as necessarily unalterable and paramount.

In countries where socialist ideals are alive and where the masses of working people, through a tradition of class struggle, have gained some familiarity with the structures and mechanisms of their national economies as well as with the behavior of their ruling classes, appeals to "economic law" voiced by government leaders are readily perceived as expressions of particular class interests. It is somewhat different when the interests of "Europe" or the demands of the "world market" are invoked; suspicion may remain, but the images tend to blur and the arguments grow more uncertain.

In the wake of the 1978 electoral defeat for the left in France, along with the more complicated predicament in Italy, there is widespread disillusionment with traditional politics and political activism. By design or by coincidence, the apparent approach of Communists to national government in Rome and Paris was accompanied by a wave of critiques of the state, which promoted the notion that no good can come of national government. In such a mood of disaffection with national politics and suspicion of the nation-state, it is particularly easy for supranationality to be accepted passively as perhaps offering better prospects. The anti-statism of the late 1970s has also injected a perceptible dose of libertarian commonplaces into political discourse, which may prepare a new acceptance of economic liberalism.

The real issues before the European Parliament are likely to be highly technical and involve many factors outside the realm of even the more educated sector of any one component population. More than in national affairs, the media of the various nations will be able to present the issues as they please, permitting much greater manipulation of public opinion. The campaign will be expensive and thus less open to small parties than national and local elections. It remains to be seen whether the more distant and unfamiliar issues will educate the public or contribute to depoliticization and a growing gap between those whose political culture accords with the dominant framing of international economic issues and those whose political culture is rendered outmoded and marginalized.

THE EUROPARLIAMENTARY elections have tended to favor a new style of discourse in the southern European Socialist parties. At the 1977 French Socialist Party Congress in Nantes, Michel Rocard—one of the most "European" of the French Socialists—distinguished between "two political cultures" on the left. He contrasted the "Jacobin, centralizing, statist, nationalist, and protectionist" culture of the Communists with a "decentralizing" school of thought which prefers grassroots autonomy, social experimentation, and *autogestion* (self-management). Roughly the same distinction was advanced a year later by the young secretary general of the Italian Socialist Party, Bettino Craxi, in an ideological campaign against the "Leninism" of the PCI. The PSI, long overshadowed by the PCI, has pinned its hopes for revival on playing the role of the Italian branch of European Socialism. Craxi gradually replaced the traditional hammer and sickle with the carnation as the PSI symbol, and promoted a cultural offensive implicitly critical of Marxist orthodoxy which had the double advantage of attracting strays from the new left and drawing closer to the position of the German SPD, which officially abandoned Marxism at its Bad Gödesberg Congress in 1959.

The new pragmatic leaders are much farther than their predecessors not only from Marxism, but much more strikingly from the whole traditional cultural style of their particular countries. In the summer of 1978, Rocard complained of the "archaic" approach of certain Socialists, evidently referring to Francois Mitterrand, whose style is as literary as Rocard's is sociological. The pragmatic or sociological style implicitly denies the existence of a totality that could be transformed—in other words, it denies revolution and is "anti-totalitarian." The "archaic" style, with its allusions to presumably shared memories and ideals, creates the impression (illusion?) of an area of potential consensus and synthesis, an area of complicity about the past, the present, and the future, in which the world of the present can be contemplated as a totality and rejected. The "break with capitalism" called for in the 1971 platform of the French Socialist Party is probably an "archaism," and in any case is incompatible with European integration. Perhaps to an even greater extent than

Marxism, the cultural style of the Latin countries has encouraged the belief that revolution is possible.

Rocard is a graduate of France's elite school of administration, ENA, and at least seems capable of understanding the intricacies of European industrial restructuring and monetary policy. Simultaneously heralding the concept of grassroots "self-management," he seems to embody a Socialist trend to separate general economic issues, which are left to the experts (Socialist Party experts, preferably, who have good intentions), from grassroots movements concerned with qualitative or cultural issues. Once the main lines are laid down by "economic realism," as interpreted by specialists, new space is created where a new sensibility influenced by ecology and feminism can attempt to affect the quality of life without touching the basic power structures (which, beginning with the state, are disdained as incapable of doing anything but harm). The CERES left wing of the PSF has polemically stigmatized this school of thought as the "American left," as an abandonment of the notion of political militancy as a continuous effort from the workplace to the dominant economic structures.

A "GERMANIZATION" OF EUROPE?

ASSUMING THAT A "Rocardian" pattern of politics prevails on the left in the coming period, the question of what might be the conflicts, or articulations, among the various levels of economic and political power remains unanswered. The most pessimistic critics of Europe foresee a generalized "Latin Americanization" of southern Europe, in which the nation-state is reduced to its police functions of enforcing a social order determined elsewhere. And in this scenario, police forces themselves come increasingly under the direct technical control of the German police, already experienced in modern methods of population checks and controls. This vision of a "Germanized" Europe, whose working class is largely depoliticized by Social Democratic leaders while radicals are "marginalized" and persecuted, is entertained by sectors of the far left, notably in Italy.

The left will have contributed to an integrated capitalist Europe, at least passively, by offering no credible alternative. As integrated Europe approaches, the left is strikingly short of ideas. Those who are hostile to such a development—and they are extremely diverse—tend to embrace catastrophic visions of technological manipulation of the masses while a German repressive apparatus does its best to wipe out pockets of political or cultural resistance. Such fears reflect certain trends in contemporary society but are more apt to produce interesting literature than any concrete political strategy.

Those more influential sectors of the left which are welcoming European integration offer, instead of precise fears, vague hopes—but no real strategy. The notion that it is possible to conquer power at the nation-state level and thereby replace capitalism with socialism is being abandoned as an illusion. But has such potential power moved from the level of the nation-state to that of a supranational Europe, or is that another illusion? Those who argue for or against expanding the powers of the European Parliament evade the question as to whether or not that Parliament can be the locus of democratic control. The real power of the banks and the multinational corporations continues to be exercised free of democratic involvement or even understanding. Decision-making power is diffused and concealed by the intricacies of post-industrial society; it may interact with elective bodies, but it is not wielded by them. The problem for the left today is apparently not to seize power but to try to find it.

WHATEVER THE POWERS, or powerlessness, of the Euro-parliament, it will of course not necessarily be dominated by the left. Projections in 1978 indicated that Socialists, Social Democrats, and Laborites could expect to win roughly 37 percent of the seats, making them the largest single caucus even if not a majority. The most the Communists could hope for was around 8 percent of the Community vote. Socialists and Communists together would fall short of an absolute majority, even supposing a "union of the left" were possible between such incongruous partners as the German SPD and the French Communist Party.

It is thus particularly unrealistic for the Eurocommunist parties to entertain any hopes of playing more than a very subordinated role in EEC political institutions. Initially at least, the parties have drawn quite opposite conclusions from this state of affairs. The French Communist Party, accepting its isolation in the European context as inevitable, is falling back on its Resistance role as defender of French national interests, and seems determined to use European politics to enhance its position vis a vis the Socialists within France itself—but with little hope of extending its influence to Europe as a whole. This pessimism about Europe is shared by most of the smaller Communist parties, which will not, however, provide real allies to the French, both because of their attachment to national issues and even more because they are unlikely to get enough votes to be represented.

The Italian Communist Party, on the contrary, is convinced that all European parties with strong working-class support, including anti-Communist Social Democrats and Laborites, are obliged by the economic crisis to grapple with the same problems. It hopes that by employing the European forum to offer constructive proposals dealing with these common problems it may begin to break down the barriers that have long divided the European left. Once Spain enters the EEC, the PCI can hope to find allies in this approach among the Spanish Communists.

The attitude of both the Italian and Spanish Communist Parties toward Europe is probably decisively influenced by their desire to build powerful bulwarks against Soviet intervention in their affairs. More than they will say publicly, many Eurocommunist leaders seem convinced that creating a genuine socialism is out of the question in a Europe that remains the field of American-Soviet rivalries.

THE EUROPEAN LEFT as a whole has been caught short of ideas to deal with the economic and ideological counter-offensive of capitalism in the 1970s. European integration is part of that counter-offensive, but it will generate its own contradictions. A new reality may stimulate new creativity. This, at least, is a hope more in keeping with the mood of contemporary Europe than the nostalgia for popular movements of national resistance. It remains to be seen whether European integration will hasten the disintegration of the left, or bring it face to face with real problems it can no longer evade, and thus prepare its revitalization and recomposition.

POSTSCRIPT: AFTER THE ELECTIONS

THE EUROSOCIALIST BUBBLE burst with the June 10 European parliamentary elections. Europe's Socialist and Social Democratic parties raised their hopes high in a rather grandiose and artificial campaign for the first direct election of Europarliamentarians by voters in the nine member countries of the EEC. With red roses clutched bravely in their fists, Willy Brandt, Francois Mitterrand, and their friends sang the "Internationale" together in Paris and tried to drum up enthusiasm for a future "Europe of the working people." The crowds failed to turn out or on, and when the June 10 vote was counted, the Europe of the EEC was overwhelmingly conservative and decidedly capitalist.

In the old Europarliament, whose members were appointed from their national parliaments, the Socialist caucus held one-third of the seats. Instead of advancing as expected, they fell back to about one-fourth, with 112 out of 410 seats. But the Eurocommunist caucus held its own with 44 seats.

The main cause of the Socialist debacle seems to be that many workers in northern Europe expressed their distrust of the EEC by abstaining. With few issues raised, the elections had the look of a plebiscite "for Europe." What difference does it really make to elect the Europarliament directly, which meets now and then in Strasbourg or Luxembourg to approve the highly technical budget prepared by the

"Eurocrats" of the Commission, the Brussels-based EEC executive? Will the Europarliament gain power away from the Council of Ministers, which under Rome treaties is the real decision-making body of the Common Market? And if so, then what? All that was clear was that direct election was aimed at giving the EEC more authority by making it appear more democratic. And that authority can be used by member governments to impose unpopular economic policies on their recalcitrant populations. Internationalism may be a noble ideal of the working class but it is a practical reality of the business community.

The worst blow to the Eurosocialist caucus was the resounding defeat of the British Labour Party, which won only 17 of the 81 seats given each of the four biggest EEC countries. Only a third of British voters bothered to go to the polls. The record low turnout proved what everyone already knew: that Britain's heart is not in Europe. Seen from the continent, the British seem to be in the EEC mainly to grumble that they are victimized by its farm price support policy and to block any measures that might go against American interests.

Continental Socialists blamed the British Labor Party's anti-EEC stance for persuading Labor voters to stay home and give the Conservatives a landslide victory. French Socialist Commission member Claude Cheysson commented that "the English now seem to be making a specialty of missing the boat" and angrily blamed the Labor Party for "finding nothing better to do than choose some of the least-known politicians as their candidates."

But the rudest shock to the European left was the poor showing of the West German Social Democratic Party which got only 40.8 percent of the vote compared to 49.2 for the combined lists of the Christian Democrats (CDU) and Franz Josef Strauss' even more right-wing Bavarian Christian Social Union (CSU). Winning CDU-CSU lists included some of the most openly rightist candidates to emerge in Germany since the war, such as Otto Von Hapsburg, an unabashed reactionary descendent of the old royal family, and Hans Edgard Jahn, who wrote pamphlets against "Judeo-Bolshevik Imperialism" back in his Nazi days.

Germany is clearly the major power in the EEC. Socialists set out eagerly to build a unity dominated by Germany, perhaps, but the Germany of Helmut Schmidt and Socialist International leader Willy Brandt. Instead, they could be getting the Germany of Strauss.

"Europe yes, Socialism no" was the winning CDU slogan. Perhaps some German workers, faced with that choice, voted no for Europe by staying home. Voter turnout was low in German working class districts.

IN FRANCE, MARCHAIS concentrated his attacks on EEC economic policy, which he accused of favoring multinational corporations and promoting massive unemployment in member countries. Critics who accused Marchais of nationalism tended to stick to vague generalities and discuss issues less than he did. And there is a side of the popular French character that gets a kick out of the impertinent style Marchais has perfected in television debates—like the nervy kid who sits in the back row and drives the teacher crazy with impossible questions and rude answers.

Neo-Gaullist Jacques Chirac and Mitterrand had a hard time marking off their own terrain. Chirac, both supporting and opposing Giscard's government, came out looking opportunistic and hypocritical and the mere 16 percent scored by his list probably spells the end of his presidential ambitions. The Socialist score of 23.5 percent was also bad news for Mitterrand. French ecologists just missed getting the 5 percent that would have given them a seat and the Trotskyist ticket headed by Arlette Laguiller and Alain Krivine got over 3 percent of the vote by campaigning for utopia—"A United States of Socialist Europe."

Stressing that French Communists were "encouraged" by their 20.5 percent of the vote, Marchais immediately began talking of reviving the union of the left. "We have begun to reduce the gap that separated us from the Socialist Party," he said. The real object of this most "European" campaign was domestic politics—each party wanted to show strength in preparation for the 1981 presidential election.

Although surrounded by enticing beaches on a hot summer day, Italians won first prize in European citizenship by a top voter turnout of nearly 86 percent (compared to 65 percent in Germany and 60 percent in France). With their habitual self-deprecation, Italians explained this zeal by their sense of being the "poor relation." The high turnout meant that the Italian contingent in the Europarliament will reflect approximately the same political landscape revealed by the national parliamentary elections just one week earlier. The overall strength of the left remained the same, with the Socialists picking up a point lost by the Communists.

Unlike the other big countries, Italy's proportional representation allows small minorities to win seats. Thus Italy will sent not only the largest Communist contingent (24 seats) but also five representatives of the far left: Luciana Castellina of PDUP, former student leader Mario Capanna (Proletarian Democracy-New Left) and three prestigious Radicals: novelist Leonardo Sciascia, ex-Communist journalist Maria Antonietta Macciocchi and Marco Pannella (unless they step aside for other names farther down their lists). The Socialist contingent includes a number of prominent cultural figures, perhaps the most intriguing being dissident Czech Communist Jiri Pelikan, who has acquired Italian citizenship since going into exile after the Soviet suppression of the "Prague Spring."

What are all those interesting Italians going to do in that boring European parliament? Who will know or care? "Italy has something to offer Europe," Radical candidates said during the campaign, "its political vitality, its active minorities." The Europarliament is only a forum, say the Radicals, but they mean to use it to sound the alarm against any sign of the growth of a police-state Europe promoted by the German right—a danger perceived by many leftists in Latin countries as Brandt fades and Strauss looms.

PART IV

THE PROSPECTS OF
EUROCOMMUNISM

chapter 13

EUROCOMMUNISM
AND THE AMERICAN LEFT

David Plotke

THE AMERICAN LEFT'S interest in Eurocommunism has derived in part from a desire to assess what its emergence suggests about the opportunities and problems confronting the left in this country. The following essay is divided into two main parts: the first discusses the recent evolution of the American left, and particularly its treatment of Eurocommunism, while the second presents an analysis of contemporary American politics based on the earlier evaluation.

The main argument linking the two sections is that the emergence of Eurocommunism signifies the exhaustion of the Bolshevik model of political and ideological activity in the West, as it has been conceived within the Communist movement since the early 1920s. This exhaustion is most apparent in the failure of such a model to produce a transition to socialism in any part of Western Europe after the period following World War I. This failure has been tied to several features of advanced capitalist societies that were present from the beginning of the Communist movement, but which gained in importance after WWII and the defeat of fascism in most of Europe: the expansion and internal differentiation of the state apparatus, under pressure from all classes to satisfy diverse demands; the complex relations between liberal democratic institutions and popular democratic impulses; the weight of the Stalinist experience in identifying socialism with authoritarianism and radical centralism; and finally, the recomposition of the class structure and reduction of the relative social and political strength of the industrial working class.

These themes are discussed at length in several essays in this book. So far, what is most novel about Eurocommunism is the political situation; less interesting has been the doctrinal response of the parties in question, whose efforts at renovation are overall still modest. Even as the old orthodoxies are jeopardized and in some cases destroyed, new opportunities for anti-capitalist politics have emerged. Eurocommunism reflects—and deepens—the dissolution of an approach to party organization, class analysis, and socialism itself that guided the project of the Third International, but this process is slow, uneven, and unfinished.* This dissolution of orthodoxy bears complex meanings for the left in the U.S., where such orthodoxy was never really a major political or even intellectual force.

PART ONE: THE AMERICAN LEFT
RESPONDS TO EUROCOMMUNISM

THE LEFT IN THE 1970s — AND 1980s

IF THE OBJECTIVE significance of Eurocommunism is the gradual end of a whole period, this ending does not guarantee renewal. Will Eurocommunism provide a transition to forms of political, social, and cultural activity that can surpass the obstacles that blocked the realization of the old orthodoxy? If not, then a long period of organizational difficulty and perhaps fragmentation may be in store for the Eurocommunist parties. Here a comparison with the American situation is possible. Despite the different history and qualitatively greater scale of the Eurocommunist left, it shares with the American left the problem of transcending its own historical limitations in a period of political and social change, change whose content is not yet clear.

FOR MOST SECTIONS of the American left (particularly socialists), the 1960s promised to initiate a period of political renewal and

---

*This perspective might be rejected on grounds that the Eurocommunist parties are no longer authentic representatives of Bolshevism in the West—that they lost this character in the late 1920s and early 1930s (the Trotskyist view) or in the 1950s (the Maoist view). While such arguments may cast doubt on Eurocommunist claims about their relationship to the Bolshevik heritage, the fact that Maoist and Trotskyist organizations have not come close to playing a leading role in working class and popular movements implies that the "betrayal" of Bolshevism occurred in a context in which this Bolshevism was no longer a real force, given the fate of such "authentic" heirs.

expansion; not since the 1930s had such a wide range of militant social and political movements emerged. For the older organizations that claimed to represent a Leninist tradition—primarily the Communist Party and the Socialist Workers Party—the mass movements among blacks, Chicanos, women, and students seemed to provide an opportunity for enlarging their organizations and creating a more dynamic contact with popular struggles than had been possible for years. For left organizations emerging directly from the new movements, beginning with SDS and SNCC, the 1960s appeared to open a new political era that departed from both the conservatism of the 1950s and the liberalism of the early 1960s.

For all left tendencies, the Vietnam war was central to political life throughout the decade and into the 1970s. Despite very deep divisions within the left about how best to oppose the war, there remained a sense of solidarity with an international opposition to American intervention. For a crucial, though brief, period in the late 1960s, a new global movement seemed to be taking shape. The diverse expressions of Guevarist radicalism in Cuba and Latin America, aspects of the Cultural Revolution in China, efforts to escape from Soviet hegemony in Czechoslovakia, the French May events in 1968, and so forth all merged into a developing movement aimed not only against capitalist power but against all forms of authoritarianism.

It soon became clear that this was essentially a construct imposed upon extremely diverse realities; by the mid-1970s it was no longer possible to point credibly to such a global phenomenon. It is likely that the waves of revolutionary activity of the late 1960s postponed a recognition, within the American left, of the depth of divisions throughout the international left.

IN MANY WESTERN EUROPEAN countries the traditional left organizations made significant gains as a result of the radicalism of the 1960s, even though conflict between the two was often sharp. In the U.S., the situation turned out differently. The established left organizations did make some numerical gains, but none made the sort of gains necessary to transform its relations to American political life, while some experienced no real growth whatsoever.* (In some countries, such growth did occur.

---

*After the 1960s, the SWP remained at around 2,500 members, with the CPUSA in the area of 8,000 to 10,000. These figures are qualitatively smaller than those for similar parties in most other advanced capitalist countries. The Communist Party of Great Britain, for example, has a membership in the range of 15,000 to 20,000: in terms of population, this small party is about eight times as large as the CPUSA.

For example, both the Socialist Party in France and the Communist Party in Mexico gained enough from this radicalization to change their basic political status.) At the same time, those new organizations that emerged from the 1960s either disappeared or managed to stabilize their memberships at levels that only hinted at the mass involvement of the 1960s.

The 1970s closed without any socialist organization becoming more than politically marginal. Two points need emphasis, beyond routine acknowledgment that at certain times—particularly around the war in Vietnam—the left played an important role. The first concerns the extent of the gap between the movements of the 1960s and the existing organized left. This gap cannot be explained fully by referring to the rightward turn in American politics, which was unanticipated by the left. The second concerns sequence: it is one thing to stress the marginal status of the American left in the late 1950s, in the aftermath of McCarthyism and revelations of the horrors of Stalinism in the Soviet Union. It is another to confront a similar situation twenty years later—after a decade of the civil rights, student, antiwar, and feminist movements. Despite the American ideology of endless new starts, such starts aren't necessarily available, even if hopes for them are given a Marxist gloss by pointing to the ever-intensifying contradictions of capitalism.

American leftists have by now grown accustomed to the marginal quality of their organizations and efforts. While it is impossible to imagine an advanced capitalist society without a multitude of social conflicts and popular struggles, this does not rule out a more complete marginalization of the organized socialist left than is now the case. Such an outcome would mean the present socialist left would be as distant from new forms of social and political activity as most of the socialist left was from the emergent radical movements of the 1960s. Repeated failure leads to crises within left organizations, the most immediate consequence being not so much dramatic rupture as a steady departure of members from organizations which seem only to mock their aspirations while making political life even more painful than it need be. This process tends to consolidate groups-as-sects, despite the best intentions of their members. The American left now faces an impasse that if not surpassed will more likely result in further decline than stagnation.

THE SEARCH FOR MODELS

IN A SITUATION of difficulty for the left, one response is to look elsewhere—either for inspiration, or more ambitiously, for models of political strategy. Thus an examination of the reception of Eurocommunism in the U.S. converges on the problem of "models" throughout the history of the left. The weak implantation of radicalism in American political and social life has reinforced a strong attachment to foreign models of socialist political action—and of socialism itself—for decades. This attachment has characterized many sectors of the left, not only the Communist movement; the process of emulation became imitative long ago.

With the left's resurgence in the 1960s came new forms of identification, some of them previously unimaginable. The line between identification with an international movement and copying the particular forms of a movement in other national settings was now blurred past the point of recognition. One visible result has been that as the international left has further fragmented in the last fifteen years, its divisions have been immediately reflected within the American left. In most cases, the identification that once seemed to promise so much led to great disappointment and loss of political credibility.

It is worth describing this process in some detail, as it has shaped the response of the American left to the emergence of Eurocommunism:

1. Confined in the U.S. to a small Communist Party, the pro-Soviet left has been confronted with the crisis of a de-Stalinization process that was halted long before its completion. Having chosen to identify with the existing leadership of the Soviet Party and state—and with the model of social and economic life presented by the Soviet Union—the CPUSA is left with a strikingly unappealing alternative to what exists in North America and Western Europe. In some respects, the behavior of the CPUSA represents the extreme form of a more general process. After conflict within the party over the Soviet invasion of Czechoslovakia, the victory of uncritically pro-Soviet forces meant that there would be no limit to support for the Soviet Party—to the point of vocally endorsing the political trials of dissidents in the late 1970s. In the absence of any popular constraints on CPUSA policy, there is every reason to believe that its pro-Soviet policy can be pursued indefinitely.

2. The pro-Chinese tendencies that emerged from the new left could claim an affinity with the anti-bureaucratic and egalitarian aspects of the Cultural Revolution and, more broadly, with the official Chinese opposition to the Soviet model. As these themes disappeared in Chinese politics (a process underway well before Mao's death), the Maoist left has been saddled with the bureaucratic authoritarianism that was always an element in the Chinese revolution. The apparent character of Chinese politics as a series of struggles at the top of party and state apparatuses—inaccessible even to the great majority of party members—has meant that a "Chinese solution" to the political crises of advanced capitalist societies could not be taken seriously.

Maoist groups are consequently left to debate the character of the Chinese leadership in terms of its conformity with idealized conceptions of Mao's own practice, in an increasingly restricted political space. Within this milieu, serious reflection on the recent history of the Chinese revolution, the meaning of politics in socialist societies, and the nature of "Marxism-Leninism" can be given cursory treatment compared with the problem of defining the forces of good and evil and their respective errors. The most glaring example of this process has been the break-up of Maoist organizations, particularly the Revolutionary Communist Party (formerly the Revolutionary Union), over differences about the character of the existing Chinese leadership. The dependence on foreign models has so diffused this section of the left that the merit of splitting over such a question seems simply to have been assumed. On the theoretical side, one recent example is the work of Charles Bettleheim, who combined a severe critique of the present leadership and occasional criticisms of the "Gang of Four" with a studied avoidance of the socialist model shared by both: a monolithic single party, fused with the state, possessing an ideological monopoly. In the absence of analysis of this model, Bettleheim is left with an uninspired attempt to rescue an imaginary "Marxism-Leninism" from one more episode of betrayal.[1]

3. The social democratic left remains in a protracted crisis of inspiration that hinges on the fate of the ruling social democratic parties in Northern Europe. While this process of identification is usually not so mechanical as in the previous examples, it is very strong nonetheless. Without discounting the presence of left tendencies in some of the major social democratic parties, or the possibility that one or another party might move significantly to the left, it is hard to see how they might become instruments for moving beyond capitalism in the near future—regardless of statements to that effect made periodically by the various parties. For parts of the social democratic left that have abandoned a commitment to any form of socialism, such as the tendencies in and around Social Democrats, USA, this situation presents little difficulty. But for parts of the social democratic left (for example, the Democratic Socialist Organizing Committee and the Socialist Party) that take seriously the problem of transforming capitalism, the problems of the large social democratic parties are more threatening. If these parties are unlikely to be able to move beyond capitalism, why attempt to build such organizations in this country, instead of simply working to strengthen the best aspects of the Democratic Party? If the Democratic Party is hardly a classical social democratic party, in terms of the power of the labor movement within it and its formal ideology, it can nevertheless be pushed in functionally similar directions under the right circumstances. If so, why not abandon a socialist rhetoric that only complicates the task of

realizing advanced liberal reforms?[2] The limitations of northern European social democracy undermine American attempts to outline either an autonomous political project or a compelling vision of socialism.

4. The "anti-imperialist" left that flourished briefly in the late 1960s has been faced with the defeat of many of the organizations abroad with which it identified. Guerrilla movements have generally either stagnated, as in Asia outside Indochina, or have been defeated and sometimes destroyed as in Latin America. Still, there have been some successes— notably in southern Africa—and it is impossible to imagine the contemporary world without national liberation movements strong enough to capture the attention of the American left. Yet forging a movement that could offer real political support to these efforts from within the U.S. has become more complicated since the end of the Vietnam war, while the third worldist left that emerged from the 1960s (most of which went through a period of Maoism or Pan-Africanism) now finds itself without even a means of creating a frame of reference for analyzing American politics.*

5. Finally, the sections of the new left that identified with the Western European students' and workers' struggles of the late 1960s have been forced to confront the failure of such struggles to generate lasting organizational forms that could seriously challenge the traditional left parties. In some cases, popular movements merged with the traditional parties; in other cases, they tried to remain independent. But at present there is no far left in any Western European country sufficiently large and coherent to offer a model to the American left, though of course it is

---

*If this latter statement seems somewhat extreme, it is only necessary to read the *Guardian*—a leading proponent of this viewpoint. In one 1978 issue, when defining their political outlook, the editors wrote: "This movement, of which the *Guardian* is a part, views itself as anti-revisionist, anti-Trotskyist, and anti-dogmatist, committed to developing a genuine Marxist-Leninist party based on the independent application of Marxism-Leninism to the concrete conditions which prevail in the U.S. today. This tendency is based on the principles of scientific socialism as developed principally by Marx, Engels and Lenin, further developed in the modern era by Mao Tsetung, amplified by the contributions of Stalin, Ho Chi Minh, Kim Il Sung, Enver Hoxha, and Amilcar Cabral among others and the concrete experiences of the international working-class movement." (*Guardian*, October 18, 1978, Staff position on "The State of the Party Building Movement").

One wonders what the *Guardian* staff views as Stalin's contributions to solving the problems now faced by the American left. Beyond that, the above list of theorists includes not a single person who lived in any advanced capitalist country for more than a brief period. It would be hard to find a single quotation that could better capture the fantasizing and dreary isolation of this part of the left.

possible to sympathize with the aspirations of one or another tendency in the European far left.* In the United States, the difficulty is compounded by the weakness of the traditional left; what does it mean to be a "far left" when the "near left" is so hard to find?

THIS SURVEY UNDERLINES the fragmentation of the American socialist left. Insofar as fragmentation of the international left is apt to continue, the American left might suffer even further decline, given the explosiveness of current conflicts:

—in the Horn of Africa, where combinations of avowedly socialist and anti-imperialist forces are locked in many-sided battles;

—in Southeast Asia, where a new war and hostility between Vietnam and China dominate the scene;

—and in the continuing conflict between the Soviet Union and China, which has repercussions almost everywhere in the world.

The destruction of capitalism in parts of the world has seen the growth of new social and political forces capable of entering into relationships almost as brutal as those of capitalist domination itself. Meanwhile, protracted economic stagnation in the U.S. has been coupled with a cultural and political drift toward the right. These cirsumstances frame the predicament of the American left today.

THE AMERICAN DISCUSSION

THE AMERICAN DISCUSSION of Eurocommunism began in 1976-77. This was not much later then the term started to gain wide use in Europe. But such immediate recognition concealed a longer inattention to the general political evolution of the Western parties.** In some cases, a "Eurocommunist" direction had actually developed further by 1976 in parties that received little serious attention in the U.S.—for example, the Australian and the Japanese. There are several reasons why the American left responded to Eurocommunism without a widely-shared prior concern for the evolution of the main parties involved. First, many

*If the largest far left groups in Italy or France are small (and fragmented) compared to organizations of the traditional left, they are still in some cases larger than any socialist organizations in the U.S.

**Eurocommunism has been the subject of debate in *Monthly Review, Dissent,* and *Socialist Review,* as well as in *In These Times* and the *Guardian*—the largest socialist journals and newspapers in this country. Yet prior to these recent discussions, there were very few substantial treatments of the Western European CPs in those same journals and papers.

left tendencies looked to the third world for political inspiration, and were not interested in European politics. Second, those parts of the American left for whom European politics was important found their main points of reference outside the major CP's in Western Europe (either to their right or left, or in Eastern Europe).

Once recognition of Eurocommunism occurred, however, little time was lost in making largely critical judgments. These evaluations measured Eurocommunism either against what was understood to be correct socialist doctrine or in terms of its adequacy as a model for the American left. The main questions were posed as: is Eurocommunism heretical; can it function as a new model? These questions—which might have been put aside, or answered quickly (yes and no)—preempted a range of questions that flow out of a recognition of the significance of Eurocommunism for the process of decay of "Marxist-Leninist" orthodoxy, the fragmentation of the international left, and the exhaustion of existing socialist models. Because of the way in which these questions were posed, the effects of Eurocommunism on the American left (particularly at the level of strategic rethinking) have been quite modest.

CRITICAL ASSESSMENTS OF Eurocommunism have taken diverse forms. The general reaction of Maoists in the U.S. has been to condemn the Eurocommunists for their abandonment of an insurrectionary approach to the transition to socialism, and for rejecting the concept of the dictatorship of the proletariat in favor of an emphasis on the continuity between bourgeois and socialist democracy. The tone of these critiques has varied, from strident accusations that these parties amount to nothing but agents for Soviet designs on Western Europe to somewhat more measured denunciations, in which the major defects of Eurocommunism are seen as departures from an orthodoxy that is still presumed to exist.[3]

The CPUSA has persistently attacked the main Eurocommunist parties, especially the PCE, for their criticisms of the Soviet Union. Mild though these latter critiques have generally been, the CPUSA has played a leading role in trying to build an international front of staunchly pro-Soviet Communist parties that could stem the rising tide of "anti-Sovietism." In the course of this effort, the CPUSA has on occasion offered left critiques of the Eurocommunists, but this cannot be taken seriously, given the obvious predominance of pro-Soviet concerns in shaping CPUSA policy.[4]

Third, there has been a Trotskyist critique of the Eurocommunist parties which has rejected the concept of a transition to socialism through existing representative institutions in favor of an emphasis on creating institutions of dual power during a relatively brief revolutionary break.

The Trotskyist argument has also criticized the policy of broad class alliances pursued by the Eurocommunists, on grounds that these policies have generally limited the capacity of the working class to sustain autonomous forms of organization and to act politically. To a certain extent, this critique has been tempered by a positive assessment of the role of Eurocommunism in subverting the international authority of the CPSU within socialist movements.[5] The Trotskyist response can be seen as the most doctrinaire form of a general view shared by many groups and individuals whose point of reference is the new left in both Europe and the U.S. The most valuable and least dogmatic critiques of Eurocommunism have been made from this perspective, generally focusing on the relationship between representative political institutions and popular action in terms of both the concept of the transition to socialism and the vision of socialism that is advanced.*

Finally, the most conservative tendencies of American social democracy have attacked Eurocommunism as a clever effort by Stalinists to conceal their essential purposes in order to sneak into national power. This perspective, shorn of its socialist rhetoric, is typical of parts of the AFL-CIO leadership and has significant political consequences.

BEYOND THESE CRITICAL judgments, more positive evaluations of Eurocommunism have been made by left socialist currents (Democratic Socialist Organizing Committee), sections of groups descended from the new left (such as the New American Movement), and groups that have left the CPUSA during the last two decades over questions similar to those that animate the current debates. For these groups, a number of themes have been important in proving the merits of Eurocommunism. First, the parties have developed through the last two decades as large mass formations with substantial working-class memberships; in the last decade, especially, they have gained in political influence. Second, each of the main parties has marked itself off to a considerable degree from the Soviet Union—at least in terms of presenting a model of socialism for the West. Third, for some of these groups Eurocommunism appears to combine the militancy of the Communist tradition with an allegiance to democratic procedures and institutions.

Yet among groups that have viewed Eurocommunism most favorably, the terms of discussion have not been very different from those of its critics. The desire to see in Eurocommunism a new model for American

---

*Despite its insights, this perspective (like the Trotskyist one) generally founders on the problem of explaining why groups to the left of the CPs have failed to gain a durable mass base.

socialists is at times all too apparent. More or less identical questions are posed: Is it "correct?" Is it a model we can use? (For left social democrats, the operative question has often tended to be: Is it really a break with Stalinism?)* Both questions tend to obscure the historical nature of problems as they are actually posed in Europe and the United States. It makes little sense asking whether Eurocommunism is "correct" without simultaneously inquiring into real alternatives in the societies where it has emerged. Nor is it particularly useful to approach it as a model, when that issue tends to close off inquiry into what Eurocommunism suggests about our own history and political difficulties.

In the complex arguments about Eurocommunism, it is difficult to say which positions are most perceptive; ironically, the most hostile critiques—from the CPUSA, Maoists, and Trotskyists—are the best signal of its meaning. Those parts of the left that perceive it as a threat, as the liquidation of a particular heritage, are accurate in crucial ways, and the intensity of their criticism reflects the urgency of the matter. That is, if Eurocommunism really marks the eclipse of the Bolshevik tradition in the West, then efforts to capture a "Marxist-Leninist" heritage from its "betrayers" must be seen as pathetically too late.

Those groups more positively oriented toward Eurocommunism have generally been more perceptive of the political realities in both Western Europe and the U.S.[6] Once again, however, the temptation to create new models has been hard to avoid. Such an approach not only sidesteps the problem of analyzing American politics but confuses the objective historical meaning of Eurocommunism with the self-presentation of its protagonists.**

---

*This question is one that concerns all socialists, and is a legitimate topic for discussion, but should not completely replace strategic discussion of Euro-communism. A symposium in *Dissent* (Winter, 1978) focused almost exclusively on whether or not the Eurocommunist parties could be regarded as having moved significantly away from Stalinism. Only Bogdan Denitch's contribution to the symposium managed to move beyond this question in any serious way.

**This survey of left responses to Eurocommunism—which is not intended as a survey of the state of the American left—has not referred to the attitudes of the black or feminist movements. The fact is that there is little to refer to, because of a complicated history (which stamped the left of both movements with a third worldism that was strong within the left as a whole in the 1960s) and an even more complicated process of political marginalization. These movements have devoted little attention to Eurocommunism. Individual black or feminist activists and intellectuals have expressed opinions, but not in the main left journals such as *Black Scholar, Quest,* or *Feminist Studies.*

THE PROBLEM OF MODELS AND
THE "LESSONS" OF EUROCOMMUNISM

THE TENDENCY TO RELY on foreign models in formulating a socialist politics has a number of dimensions. One involves a methodological difficulty—that of trying to determine how to compare political experiences across national boundaries. What criteria are appropriate to the task of arriving at comparative generalizations? Analysis concerned with the strategic questions of political change, particularly those related to the state, must employ units of analysis much more specific than either the general notion of class society or the typology of social formations characterized by a dominant mode of production (feudal, capitalist, etc.). Neither framework is capable of directly yielding substantial strategic insights, nor are the general theories established at these levels properly understood as inclusive (with specific groups of societies viewed only as subcasts).

Thus political analysis cannot be based either on the shared features of all societies that have states, or on the shared features of societies that have capitalist states. The broadest level of comparison possible associates particular types of states with particular social formations. The crucial questions here include:

—To what extent does the state play the role of ensuring the dominance of capitalist relations of production over subordinate forms?
—To what extent does the state find itself autonomous from other national states?
—What are the characteristic governmental forms of the state, the weight of representative elements within it, etc.?
—To what extent is the state involved directly in guiding the economy, rather than in simply ensuring the conditions for economic activity?

Within the framework established by these criteria, it is possible to specify the concept of *advanced capitalist societies*, as a basis for comparative political discussion. Such societies are characterized by the *relative* insignificance of noncapitalist relations of production, and the involvement of the majority of the labor force in wage labor; by the autonomy of the national state, through membership in a community of advanced capitalist systems—if not through the self-sufficient power of individual states; by the predominance of representative political forms, with more or less durable liberal democratic traditions; and by the extensive and growing involvement of the state in directing economic activity.

Within this type of society enormous variations are sufficient to make problematic many kinds of immediate political and strategic generalizations. The category provides "only" a basis for marking these societies off from others—from underdeveloped and intermediate capitalist social formations, from nations where capitalism has been eliminated, and from earlier periods of capitalist development. For example, while it may seem obvious that the U.S. today is a different type of country than Russia in 1917 (or contemporary Mozambique), this point is too rarely incorporated into strategic discussions that take place among socialists.

Without using a concept as specific as that of advanced capitalist society, the way is left open for modes of political argument that—even when perceptive—are basically arbitrary. Drawing "conclusions" about politics in capitalist societies then becomes a matter of skill at selecting appropriate examples from different types of societies and states. There is no barrier to claiming, for instance, that what occurred in Russia in 1917, Spain in the late 1930s, or China in the 1930s and 1940s proves the validity of one or another judgment about strategic choices in the contemporary U.S. Given the multitude of possible examples, most comparative arguments usually yield only a predictable confirmation of their proponents' initial views.

If some left critics of Eurocommunism have adopted an eclectic form of argument, rejecting the strategy because it contravenes the "lessons" of Russia in 1917, Spain in the 1930s, or Germany in the early twentieth century, its supporters have tended to identify the general imperatives of political activity in advanced capitalism with the specific strategic and even tactical choices of the main Eurocommunist parties. In this respect, the supporters mirror the more sectarian aspects of the ways in which those parties present their strategies. At the level of abstraction involved in the concept of advanced capitalist societies, the "lessons" of Eurocommunism can't be identified with positive (or negative) assessments of the immediate strategic course of various parties (for or against the historic compromise in Italy, for or against the PCF's attitude toward the French Socialists, and so forth.)*

CERTAIN GENERAL FEATURES of political organization and perspective can be linked to the forms of the advanced capitalist state; such features will have a crucial bearing on political activity that has any serious prospects of success. These features are to varying degrees characteristic of the Eurocommunist parties, and are often shared by

---

*One example: it is not certain that the PCI will continue its "historic compromise" in the forms so far employed should the costs threaten to become irreparable for relations with parts of the PCI's base. The Party might, within the framework of its Eurocommunist orientation, pursue a number of alternative policies.

other political tendendies. Consequently, they can be understood as "lessons" of Eurocommunism only in a specific sense: that the new strategic directions have underlined their importance, and contributed significantly to establishing them as a terrain on which political struggle can occur.

At this level, three themes are relevant: the concept of a democratic transition to socialism, in which the transformation of capitalism is a thoroughly majoritarian process; the view of the transition as a national, multi-class process; and a vision of socialism in which society is not consumed by the state, where autonomous forms of political, social and cultural life flourish.

With regard to the first theme, the emphasis on a sustained democratic transition goes beyond parliamentary and extra-parliamentary forms. There is obviously no guarantee that formally democratic procedures will produce a transition to socialism. But it is by now cynical to assert that there is no such thing as democracy above classes and consider that the discussion has been settled.

The second point requires new emphasis in the context of the growing demographic and social role of the working class, and the accompanying stagnation or even decline of the industrial proletariat. Images of a transition to socialism in which classes assign themselves political labels and then act homogeneously in accord with the motives imputed by these labels can only inspire sectarian impulses. Political divisions in advanced capitalism cut across all class lines; the complexity of political struggles, along with the role of cultural and social factors, ensures that this will continue to be the case. The consequence is that a majoritarian transition could only be multi-class in nature.

Finally, the representative character of the advanced capitalist state—and the provisions made by it for the autonomous expression of political and social impulses—can only be surpassed from the left by a political practice based upon the concept of a socialist polity in which existing elements of autonomy and freedom are expanded. This point requires elaboration, since even more is at stake than the question of what sort of socialism is desirable; the question is whether any socialism can develop as an alternative to liberal democratic capitalism.

The experience of various socialist revolutions has made clear the possibility of a range of outcomes, rooted in the character of pre-revolutionary circumstances, but never reducible to them. The autonomous role of political organizations is clear, as is their contribution to the shaping of political institutions. Ideological struggle in advanced capitalist countries is thus bound up with an assessment of existing socialist societies. Since many parties and states in the world make socialist claims, socialists must avoid reducing this diversity to differential historical development. The task is to outline the aims of political practice in the context of existing tendencies in socialist societies, providing a serious analysis of what exists as part of framing programmatic and strategic conceptions.*

Within advanced capitalism, the forces potentially favoring socialism are much broader than either the industrial proletariat or the working class as a whole, and the political forces potentially favoring socialism are broader than existing socialist organizations. The forging of alliances—within and among social classes and political organizations, across diverse cultural traditions within the same nation—cannot be achieved through a conception that views political forms within socialism as having little intrinsic importance, as being subordinated entirely to the long-term requirements of the transition to communism. Neither political organizations in capitalist societies, nor political institutions in socialist societies, can be treated merely as instruments through which other goals are to be reached.

THE ABOVE POINTS, taken together, mark a definite break with the main lines of orthodoxy as developed in the Communist tradition, in both its pro-Soviet and Maoist forms. What comes after this break remains to be seen. The Eurocommunist parties are both the expression and protagonists of a complex historical process. Part of the reason they cannot be adopted as models is that they are caught up in a process whose outcome is uncertain—one can welcome the process without trying to freeze any of its moments as a model.

The decay of orthodoxy also signals the exhaustion of several other socialist traditions that have come to define themselves largely in opposition to it. A social democratic tradition unable to spell out its aims beyond a desire for social justice and a thoroughly reformed capitalism could always refer to the negative model of Stalinism to legitimate its timidity and lack of strategic thought. Without this negative image, at least as a coherent point of reference in the West, the social democratic

---

*This suggests that the question of Stalinism cannot be avoided by arguing that it mainly concerns the experience of societies emerging from economic underdevelopment. It is true that an authoritarian socialism in the West would not look like the Soviet type of the 1930s; but there is good reason to think that the seeds of an authoritarian centralization are present in advanced capitalism, given the centralizing forces in economic and political life. Since the authoritarianism of existing socialist societies is not reducible to levels of development—compare Czechoslavakia and Cuba, for example—the elaboration of a non-statist model of socialism remains an urgent task. Efforts in this direction among the Eurocommunist parties are conditioned by immediate political concerns, including the desire to avoid a complete break with the CPSU.

parties find themselves faced with a political choice that they could previously delay by pointing to the dangers of Stalinism: either transform themselves completely into parties of order, or undertake a major strategic rethinking and shift to the left. For the Trotskyist tradition, the dissolution of orthodoxy is even more disorienting, since its groups have little base in the working class or other popular sectors and are often constituted almost completely on the basis of anti-Stalinism. They tend to respond to the situation by combining their traditional triumphalism with a version of Leninist orthodoxy, in order to condemn the CPs once more for their betrayals. Trotskyism remains unable to reflect seriously upon that orthodoxy—beyond occasional statements that Lenin may not have written the last word on representative and popular democracy.[7]

PART TWO
A NEW POLITICAL TERRAIN

"PREVIEWS" OF EUROCOMMUNISM

MUCH OF THE American left now remains outside the premises sketched above, hoping to install one or another orthodoxy within a recalcitrant social and political setting. Yet during each of the three main periods of left opposition in this century, dominated in succession by the pre-World War I Socialists, the Communist Party in the 1930s and 1940s, and the new left of the 1960s, tendencies emerged that appear to have shared the now general perspective identified as Eurocommunist. As reference to these experiences has figured in assessments of Eurocommunism, some discussion of these periods is appropriate.

For the Socialists, the building of a diverse mass movement for socialism was not systematically connected either to an analysis of the state or to an understanding of the U.S. emergence as a leading imperialist power. Despite its success in establishing a base in parts of the American working class, it remained small and vulnerable to repression during and after World War I. Its decline, however, cannot be attributed to this repression, nor to the sectarianism that spread throughout the socialist movement after the war.[8] Such explanations beg the question of why the party was unable to withstand the repression, and why little could be done to surmount the sectarianism. The decline of the SP was largely the result of its inability to conceptualize a strategic relationship to the politics of an imperial America that had experienced a major social and political shift during the Progressive period. The transposition of a Bolshevik model in the early 1920s was hardly appropriate to deal with the problems raised by the changing structure of the state and its expansion into new areas of social life; the steady recomposition of the working class through the development of Fordist mass production; and the extensive reorganization of culture and family life. But pointing out the defects of the early Communist movement should not obscure the extent to which Socialists had been lost amidst these transformations and could offer little beyond a left-Progressivism tied awkwardly to a socialist vision.

The CPUSA in the late 1930s and 1940s took up some themes similar to those of contemporary Eurocommunism, such as an emphasis on broad class coalitions and the expansion of democracy as crucial for the transition to socialism. Yet several features of this experience distinguish it from those now underway in Europe: the predominance of anti-fascist concerns, the relatively small size of the CPUSA, and most important, the more intimate relations between the Popular Front CPUSA and the Soviet Union. The democratic themes of Communist discourse, so far as they went beyond anti-fascism, were delegitimated by identification with the Soviet Union—not only as a point of reference for the international movement, but as a model of socialism and source of strategic and tactical direction. To the extent that present developments are shaped by a gradual break with the CPSU, and by declining Soviet power in the world left, the two experiences are not comparable.*

A subsequent period in the history of the CPUSA, 1956-58, also gave rise to themes similar to those now expressed by the Eurocommunist parties. Recent interpretations have portrayed this period as an anticipation of current developments. While on a formal doctrinal level this is partly correct, it leaves aside the crucial fact that years of McCarthyism and Communist sectarianism had already taken their toll, and that the party by 1956 was only a fraction of what it had been ten years earlier, in no sense a major pole of political attraction during those few turbulent years of its internal life.[9]

In the early and mid-1960s, parts of the new left advanced themes somewhat similar to those sketched above. This period is generally viewed as one that stressed direct political action and the role of immediate personal experience as the basis for social change. (It was also a period in which reliance on foreign models was limited.) While this was true in the context of the political passivity of the preceding decade, in

---

*This decline has gone further in terms of the Soviet model of socialism than in terms of the actual power of the CPSU, which, given the present relations among the U.S., China, and the USSR gains allies from forces unable to get sources elsewhere.

more general terms—for example the relationship between institutional and extra-parliamentary struggles—it was certainly within the range of currents associated with Eurocommunism. But given the splitting up of the early new left (both black and white) further elaboration of these themes was never possible.

WHILE THERE IS much to be learned from each of these experiences, they do not provde any real test of the general themes noted above with reference to the political opportunities for the contemporary American left. In the first case, factors related to the war, an emergent imperialism, and the restructuring of American capitalism were crucial; in the second case, deep attachment to the Soviet Union largely vitiated the idea of an autonomous road to socialism; and in the third case, the fragility of left politics was such that no comprehensive analysis is possible.

This third point is crucial for an analysis of the political differences between the American and European experiences. Up to the present, the central task in the U.S. has been building a left that incorporates a wide range of cultural, social, and political dimensions. It is this condition which determines the historical appearance of "Eurocommunist" tendencies as "rightist"—as emerging within the Socialist Party rather than the syndicalist left; within the Communist Party, in comparison with the various orthodoxies prevalent after the Browder period; and within the new left, as distinct from the anti-imperialist militancy of the late 1960s. In none of these cases can it be argued that the "left" tendencies were better suited to build a coherent left movement. But the direct transposition of a strategy forged during the attempt of a mass party to move toward power—a situation shared by the PCI, PCF and PCE—to a context where there are no such parties almost inevitably occludes those problems concerned with building and sustaining a movement. In particular, any effort at direct translation overlooks the complex processes through which the Eurocommunist parties became *mass* parties—processes that involved, among other things, an enormously difficult and turbulent period in which the left led national struggles against a combination of foreign and domestic enemies.* In other words,

---

*Currents that emphasize mass involvement and direct participation are still present in the contemporary Eurocommunist parties. A common criticism by the American left of the Eurocommunist parties has been that they are disinterested in mass struggles and do not see them as playing a major role. This criticism grossly oversimplifies the political history and reality of these parties, which is one of immersion in and leadership of diverse popular struggles. It thus fails to provide the basis for a serious critique of the extent to which mass struggles are instrumentalized in specific periods for partisan aims, and of the extent to which the limiting of goals and demands of particular struggles has or has not been necessary.

none of these parties attained its present strength only through long and sustained periods of growth. What this means is that the task of constructing a left in the U.S. cannot be accomplished strictly by referring to the Eurocommunist context, because (a) no such "national" experience has recently occurred or is likely to occur soon in the U.S., and (b) social and political conditions in which the Eurocommunist parties waged their founding struggles were quite different from those in the contemporary U.S.

STRATEGIC PERSPECTIVES

THE WEAKNESS OF socialist political forces in the U.S. thus remains the necessary starting point. Here it is possible to identify three main lines of historical explanation. The first emphasizes the importance of ethnic, racial, and national divisions in the working class, particularly in the period from the mid-nineteenth through the early twentieth century. In this view, waves of immigration (and departure) produced a working class so culturally and socially fragmented that political action was impeded; divisions emerged not only within the working class, but between various subordinate classes and strata, so that alliances with radical movements based outside the working class (e.g. populism) were hindered. The key difference between the U.S. and most other advanced capitalist societies has been the intersection of ethnic and national categories with racial categories along a rigid white/nonwhite division. This division exacerbated other social cleavages within the subordinate classes. The development of monopoly capitalism deepened previously formed divisions (including those between community and work.) The resulting fragmentation has impeded the formation of a socialist politics rooted within the working class and other subordinate groups that would be more than a cultural expression of the impulses for protection and advancement of various groups.[10]

A second line of argument concerns the position of the U.S. in the world capitalist system. In this view, the crucial periods were the late nineteenth and early twentieth centuries—with the emergence of monopoly capitalism and a growing American economic expansionism—and after World War II, when the U.S. appeared as the leading imperialist power. This approach stresses that U.S. expansion has provided the basis for sufficient internal political and social flexibility to incorporate enough demands of subordinate groups to undercut left opposition, while also creating a powerful repressive state ready to thwart serious challenges. It further emphasizes the role of a distinctively American prosperity in shaping political and ideological struggles, with decisive effects for the entire society.[11]

The third line of argument—to which Marxists devote insufficient attention—stresses the vitality of the American bourgeoisie in the nineteenth and early twentieth centuries, along with the prosperity and vitality of a massive (urban and rural) petty bourgeoisie. The welding of stable bonds between those classes, whatever the obstacles, provided a more secure basis for bourgeois rule than existed in most European countries. These class alliances are often viewed as a natural, inevitable condition of American development, starting from the absence of feudalism in most of the early colonies.[12] In other formulations, critical phases are identified—for example, the formation of a bourgeois-radical alliance in the Civil War period, or the defeat of the radical petty bourgeois impulses expressed through populism, or the transition from Progressivism to the New Deal. In any case, the pattern of class alliances that emerged depended on both the containment of petty bourgeois radicalism and the marginalization of anti-industrial elitist conservatism. The result of this arrangement was (and is) a political system and ideological universe strongly bourgeois-democratic and fiercely anti-socialist.

EACH PERSPECTIVE, if made the exclusive basis for a general interpretation of American history, is inadequate; the political viewpoints that flow from looking strictly at any one of them are simplistic. The goal is to weave them together into a coherent account; the value of such an approach is that it can identify the ways in which new political situations are emergent.

What was distinctive about the postwar period, at least until the 1960s, was the convergence of all three sets of forces to create political quiescence. Yet central elements of these forces have changed in ways that may make possible a new growth of the American left. The relative decline of national and ethnic divisions—even across racial lines—is a significant recent development. It has permeated most institutions and has been felt in an egalitarianism among whites more pronounced than at any time before World War II. There is no reason to think that any automatic processes will eradicate the divisions that still exist. In fact, the economic stagnation and cultural conservatism of the 1970s have slowed (and on occasion partially reversed) the decline of racial and ethnic divisions. The evolution of a modern mass culture has eroded some conventional social divisions, but not in terms that point to classes as much more than descriptive occupational or income categories. The decline of American international power is clear, but the U.S. remains by far the strongest capitalist country, in ways that continue to shape domestic political life. The destruction of large sections of the urban and especially rural petty bourgeoisie in this century has undermined the basis of the dynamic class alliances that pushed forward earlier periods of expansion. And obstacles to rebuilding a system of class alliances between the corporate bourgeoisie and the new middle strata, whose position approaches that of the working class, are quite serious. Still, the political and ideological forms that grew out of earlier periods are not likely to disappear soon.

In sum, the political landscape is shaped by a slow and complex evolution of forces rooted in decades—and in some instances centuries—of American history. A new alignment of political forces might develop, but not in a sudden and complete transformation. There is a dual political meaning to this process. On the one hand, it provides an opportunity for the left to play a larger role in social and political life than it has in the 1970s and probably even in the 1960s. On the other hand, there is little likelihood of a "return" to "normal" patterns of capitalist development (especially patterns that would confirm a political outlook rooted in expectations of cataclysm). That is, the rather gradual erosion of the forces that undermined the development of a socialist left in most of the twentieth century is by no means sufficient to produce the emergence of a left; new barriers might well emerge out of the new patterns of economic and social life taking shape in the late twentieth century.

CLASS ALLIANCES AND POPULISM

AT THIS POINT it is possible to address several questions tied to the general themes discussed above—the problem of class alliances; the question of democracy and "social democratization;" and the issue of political pluralism. In each case, I will try to link the current situation to long-term processes in American society and to the broader discussion of political strategy for the advanced capitalist societies.

EUROCOMMUNISM HAS OFTEN been understood as aban-doning a focus on the industrial working class as the main agent of social transformation, in favor of a broader concept of blocs of classes and strata within which workers remain the leading force. For some Eurocommunist theorists, the strategic task (following Gramsci) is to weld together a cohesive "social bloc"—a formation of classes and strata with more than tactical or defensive bonds, a bloc that would provide the basis of a majoritarian social transformation.*

Critics and supporters of this apparent shift away from the indus-

*This approach is most characteristic of theorists and leaders within the Italian party, such as Luciano Gruppi and Pietro Ingrao.

trial working class have often failed to notice the extent to which even orthodox Communist strategies in the West have emphasized the building of class alliances for several decades. What has changed is the recognition that a broad social bloc is capable of furthering the struggle not only against the right, or for an "advanced democracy," but *for socialism*. The notion that advanced capitalism contains new strata whose "interests" are opposed to the established economy and state *does* mark a point of transition.

In Western Europe, this doctrinal change is a response to growing working-class political strength (making it possible to pose the question of long-term stable alliances in new ways) and at the same time to a shifting class structure in which the industrial working class is stagnant or declining as a proportion of the labor force and population. In terms of class alliances, the situation for the European left hence differs considerably from that of the American left. The outward (and upward) initiative of Eurocommunist strategies is not directly relevant where the basis for them—a "traditional" working class movement dominated by Socialist and Communist politics—does not exist. Consequently, American leftists must confront a shifting class structure without benefit of experiences resembling those in much of Western Europe. The result is that most American Marxist discussions of class tend to be very abstract; in their search for political potential in one or another social class or stratum, they implicitly express the desire for another history, for a working class and political left that ought to have existed.

Many efforts to build a Marxist political sociology have been marked by categories derived immediately from interpretations of the history of European working-class movements in the nineteenth and twentieth centuries; this is especially so with regard to establishing relationships between economic or social location and political action. But such relationships were never carefully theorized past a crudely utilitarian and empiricist social psychology.

The American left, which remains essentially outside the industrial working class, is forced to confront a general theoretical and political crisis, given the impossibility of making intelligible statements about American political reality that rely upon the industrial working class as presently the main site of revolutionary impulses. For example, the debates within the French left around building alliances between the working class and the middle strata become politically meaningless if applied directly to American experience.

What then is left to replace an orthodoxy whose limits have been reached even in those societies where it has made a certain amount of political sense? One option is a schematism that conceals the absence of any serious account of relations between class positions and political practices by demanding that American history conform to given expectations of capitalist development. But the petulance of this approach usually produces bursts of sectarianism.

Another possibility is a "neo-populism" that simply avoids the whole murky discussion of class in favor of analysis based on a general opposition of "the people" to the corporations (and/or the state). Despite its theoretical defects, this approach is intuitively more perceptive than the former. A neo-populist approach to American politics grasps two points that are essential for any leftist movement. First, the main tendency of modern capitalism is toward the expansion of the working class and decline of the traditional petty bourgeoisie. This working class is no longer centered in one or two sectors; to the extent that any such centers exist, they are conjunctural rather than structural. In the United States, to imagine such a centering around the industrial proletariat captures neither the historical logic of political militancy nor the direction of class recomposition (with the dramatic expansion both of "deskilled" and highly-educated service labor, the internal transformation of much industrial labor, etc.) The most immediate forms of class-based political and social opposition—beyond wage struggles—usually revolve less around the "working class" than around disparate working-class and lower middle-strata groups bound together as "the people." The theory that would account for these aspects of contemporary social struggle—as in urban politics or tax conflicts—does not yet exist. While such a theory is not contained in populist statements that simply repeat themselves within a self-enclosed set of references to "the people," these statements do point toward the crucial theoretical and practical problems, rather than submerging them.

Second, a "populist" language is not in itself indicative of political backwardness—neither in left analyses nor at the mass level. Populism typically proposes a set of conflicts between the people and the state, the people and the rich, and so forth, simplifying complex relations into binary formulations and calling for a unified "popular" struggle against the oppressors.

Marxism characteristically views populism as a stage ultimately to be surpassed by a "genuine" working-class and socialist movement. Yet populism, as a deep ideological impulse and as a political rhetoric, is a thematic element of both immature and mature oppositional movements; the most "mature" moments of political development are strongly populist (and not simply "popular") in character, as when a revolutionary movement represents the masses of the population against clearly-defined adversaries and obstacles. Instead of being treated as a primitive stage that will disappear when the real history of the left finally begins, populist discourse should be understood as a more or less permanent feature of political conflict in advanced capitalism.

IN THE UNITED STATES, this conceptualization of populism is all the more appropriate given the vital historical role of self-defined populist movements.[13] The question here concerns the articulation of socialist ideologies that contain populist themes. Whatever new ideologies emerge, the only way that the linkage populism/socialism might be dissolved in favor of a supposedly homogeneous socialist ideology would be through the building of new sects with a limited popular appeal. The heritage of American populism needs to be taken more seriously than has usually been the case within the left, in efforts to point out how populism in the late nineteenth century was linked with the declining position of its social base. It is important to understand the ways in which populism was an assertion of a notion of democracy against what was perceived as statism and corporate centralization.

Despite the insights of contemporary neo-populism, its limits are clear. While it poses the question of broad social alliances, it has no means of understanding the dynamics of such alliances. And American populism is full of elements that are not just anti-statist, but anti-socialist, so that it is hard to imagine a simple fusion of populist and socialist themes. But perhaps the main problem is that while neo-populism is more politically astute in most cases than orthodox Marxism, it does not really provide an understanding of the emergent forces in American social and economic life: the vast expansion of the service and state sectors, the crisis of the labor movement, and the restructuring of the domestic economy in the context of changes in the international division of labor.

THE PROBLEM OF SOCIAL DEMOCRACY

LEFT CRITIQUES OF contemporary non-socialist progressive movements in the U.S. frequently make pejorative reference to "populism" and "social democracy," the second as a warning against strategies aimed at reforming the state and other instituions. The same language is often used in critical assessments of Eurocommunism; for example, the dangers of "social democratization" are stressed by a number of left observers. Here again it is necessary to return to a basic theme: the emergence of Eurocommunism signifies nothing so much as the exhaustion of insurrectionary perspectives linked to the heritage of Bolshevism in the West. Eurocommunism rejects those instrumental conceptions according to which the state is shattered from the outside and then completely replaced to pave the way to socialism. There is, moreover, a wide range of political perspectives within the Eurocommunist parties— and no single perspective, within or outside the parties, has begun to resolve the major theoretical and political questions at stake.

This situation ought to refocus attention on the distinctive features of American politics. Some interpretations have viewed relations between the Democratic Party and the AFL-CIO as amounting to a social democratic political grouping, but it is more correct to note the weakness of social democracy in the U.S., a weakness that is a crucial feature of American politics. While the postwar period witnessed the implementation of some reforms characteristic of social democratic experiences, such reforms were limited; in addition, the power of the organized working class in winning reforms was also limited. The basic gains of social democracy in Northern and Western Europe (such as national health insurance) are barely on the political agenda in the U.S.

In strategic terms, the problem in the U.S. is whether a transition to socialism is possible without a "social democratic" experience—not whether an already-established revolutionary movement can survive the dangers of impending social democratization. When this question is posed, the idea of an intermediate social democratic phase is often dismissed, based on two arguments. It is claimed that a sustained process of social democratic development can only occur in a period of economic expansion, and that in any case the U.S. already underwent something like a social democratic experience after World War II, the failures of which are before us today. The second argument overstates the extent of "social democratization" that has taken place in the U.S. A period of seriously expanded state intervention in the economy for the purpose of modifying the cycle, especially with respect to directing investment, has not yet occurred. Nor has there been sustained implementation of extensive social welfare measures. Perhaps most important, the role of trade unions and other working-class organizations within the party system is often confined to a veto power over (some) party policies. At best, the postwar reforms helped to create a conservative and limited welfare state which remains relatively insecure.

The first objection to the notion of a social democratic phase needs further discussion. It is correct insofar as it points out one difference between what a social democratic experience might be in the present period, and what it could have been after World War II. But it oversimplifies the relations between economic and political phenomena. The fact that the economic predicament imposes severe constraints on reformist social measures does not by itself negate such efforts; nor does it mean that the ideological perspective underlying these efforts cannot become popular.* In a phase of economic stagnation and intermittent

---

*There is a crucial difference between a political movement that only succeeds in gaining a mass following and even governmental power, and one that both

recession, pressures toward some type of social democratic experiment will likely mount. Signs of this have emerged within the last few years: in the willingness of some influential figures in the left of the Democratic Party to use an anti-corporate and even socialist rhetoric; in the efforts of some leadership elements of organized labor to build alliances with community and electoral forces; and in the growth of socialist sentiment among left-liberal intellectuals.

It remains to be seen whether the constraints imposed on social democratic efforts by economic and social forces will be as important as some have predicted. Of course the political problems could prove insuperable, especially in blocking any attempt to expand the state (to furnish social services and regulate the economy) while simultaneously responding to the anti-statist initiatives of the right.

But looking beyond the immediate future, some type of social democratic phase would seem to be necessary for the long-term development of a left political movement in the U.S. This phase would not mirror social democratic politics elsewhere, because neither the economic situation nor the political and ideological milieus are the same. The distinctive forms of an American social democracy might include: (a) less explicit socialist ideology than elsewhere; (b) somewhat less power exercised by the trade unions, with more diffuse control from various working-class and popular organizations; and (c) a less statist outlook than in Europe, particularly concerning investment and ownership.*

It is hard to imagine a complete bypassing of a social democratic period, moving directly from the present to a highly polarized situation

---

accomplishes those goals and realizes its explicit objectives. There is no structural logic that automatically negates the first type of movement, because the meaning of success can be redefined circumstantially. The fact that there are serious obstacles to achieving reforms commonly identified with social democracy does not mean that a political movement aimed at such reforms (among others) is incapable of sustaining its mass character.

*There are a number of possible components of such a process: a recomposition and/or splitting of the Democratic Party under pressures from within and outside it, leading to the emergence of a new major party; the defeat of the postwar AFL-CIO trade union leadership, and the formation of new labor coalitions; the consolidation of community and neighborhood movements into state-wide and regional organizations; and the rebuilding of organizations like the National Black Political Assembly among racial and national minorities. The notion of a social democratic phase can be concretized by examining the range of above alternatives. In the Democratic Party, for example, a recomposition of forces within and outside it would at best produce a new formation that included many of the individuals and forces currently on the left of that party (whether or not a new organization were called the Democratic Party).

that would unleash prospects for a more or less immediate socialist transformation. Thus if a social democratic experience is not necessary to reach the "objective" limits of capitalist reform—those limits are not clear, even in periods of economic downturn—it is no doubt a political necessity that would indicate the limits of political possibilities within the framework of American capitalism.

What the development of Eurocommunism (as well as some new developments within the Socialist parties) indicates, however, is that reaching such political limits is not apt to mean an absolute inability to gain redress that would be followed by an equally absolute mass opposition to the existing state. Whatever the ultimate nature of an open political conflict, it will surely be preceded by long periods of many-sided conflict within and around the state. Given this long-term perspective, it will be difficult to make a rigid distinction between "socialist" and "social democratic" efforts at a particular point, as these terms do not designate unambiguously distinct positions vis-a-vis the state.

Since an instrumentalist view of the state cannot be the basis of a socialist politics, it is impossible to produce a set of doctrines that would distinguish efforts to challenge and transform the state from efforts to administer and consolidate it, irrespective of time and place. The line between these two projects is not smooth or unbroken, and constantly needs redrawing.

A SOCIAL DEMOCRATIC phase might provide part of the foundation for a later transition to socialism, through the medium of mass political experiences. It is not a matter of socialists waiting until such experiences "fail" in order for them to "gain leadership" over existing mass movements, but of starting to create a political dynamic that is not restricted to social democratic conceptions in either its ideology or its structure. In the U.S., such a dynamic is unlikely to be developed in the absence of a social democratic phase—much less in opposition to nascent social democratic efforts.

Critiques of social democracy that emphasize only the integration of subordinate groups within existing political and economic relations wind up missing the point. At best they only touch upon part of the problem. What needs to be determined is whether this "integration" strengthens or weakens the power of various social groups in particular circumstances, and whether it produces conditions for a break with the logic of the system as a whole. It is one thing to stress conservative elements of the integrative strategy of large social democratic parties, or of social democratic tendencies in formation, but quite another to suggest that this critique amounts to a practical alternative that strengthens the power of subordinate groups and is not integrative.

IN THE U.S., there is little reason to assume that a major social democratic experience will occur. Precisely because of new elements in the economic and social situation, not to mention political opposition to even a mild social liberalism, there is less room for modestly redistributive policies and less room for capital to suffer the encroachments of state planning. The chances are therefore great that such efforts will lead toward political polarization rather than a smooth harmonization of interests. In this setting, it would be difficult for even the most self-consciously social democratic parts of the labor movement to articulate a comprehensive program that could integrate the diverse and often conflicting interests within the working class and other strata. The problem is deepened, in that the traditional approaches of social democracy are scarcely more relevant to issues concerning the recomposition of the working class and restructuring of social life than the analyses of orthodox Marxism or conventional social liberalism.

The medium-term political choices for the U.S. are an American social democracy, a continued conservative social liberalism, and an authoritarian neo-conservatism. The present choice is not between the "social democratization" of a revolutionary socialist movement and a genuine social transformation, but between some version of social democracy and worse alternatives. The strategic implications of arguments which urge that social democracy be avoided, or which suggest that it is inevitable and therefore not the concern of socialists, are in effect an abstention from politics in favor of the creation of a socialist subculture, or sectarian attacks on the development of reformist movements and organizations.*

The situation confronts socialists with a dual task: that of building a "populist"/popular social democratic movement, while at the same time advancing a socialist movement within, alongside, and at certain points in opposition to it. The problems of stressing only the former—either with the hope that it will automatically become socialist or under the illusion that is *is* socialist insofar as it represents an impulse toward social control—are clear enough. And attempts that focus strictly on the latter are not likely to bring more success than similar efforts in the late 1960s and early 1970s. The problems are compounded by the appearance of this

---

*The sectarian element does not logically derive from the criticism of the limits of reform, but is contained in the assumption—spelled out only in the most extreme cases—that were it not for the leadership and/or organization of particular reform efforts, the "base" would have made its way much further leftward. Obviously there are cases when this is true; but as a basic stance toward American politics, such a view exaggerates the degree of openness to socialist perspectives in a way that gives rise to impatiently elitist views of existing popular organizations.

complex strategic agenda alongside new crises in the global development of Marxist theory and socialist politics, so that the socialism to be attained, beyond social democracy, requires new elaboration. An American social democracy—a chaotic assortment of populist, radical, and social democratic themes that is anti-statist even as it expands the role of the state—is possible in the relatively near future. What could come after it?

POLITICAL PLURALISM AND THE STATE

THE EMERGENCE OF Eurocommunism has called attention to the form of political parties during and after a transition to socialism. In the long run, it is not possible to break with the conception of socialism as a society dominated by a single leading party while retaining the other main concepts that have come to define "Marxist-Leninist" orthodoxy in the West. This process has been slow and uneven for the Eurocommunist parties; the questions that it raises for socialists in the U.S. have for the most part been obscured by the predominant critique of Eurocommunism as reformism. Abandoning a view of socialist politics that is centered on a single dominant party, fused with the state, which exerts monopolistic control over an official ideology, opens the way to many positive political and theoretical innovations (whatever the intentions of those active in revising previous doctrines).

In the U.S., various types of "Leninist" orthodoxy have served to misdirect discussion within the socialist left. More important, perhaps, has been the absence of a major socialist or communist party. In its absence, it is easy to *imagine* a party that would encompass all political and social struggles, incorporate the demands of all subordinate groups, and so forth. "The Party" from this standpoint amounts as much to a projection of desires for resolving difficult political problems as a political organization that actually could be constructed. (And even at the level of fantasy, it contains an apparent authoritarian moment.)

THE NOTION OF a single leading party has often been linked to a general critique of representative "bourgeois" democracy, though the two positions are logically separable. In the present period for the U.S., a general critique of representative democracy or of electoral politics tends to be politically powerless. It is either crippled by association with various forms of authoritarian rule that is held up as a model; or it is rendered meaningless by its failure to pose a developmental connection between existing politics and a fully democratic society. The extent to which this failure typifies particular organizations of the European far left is open to debate. The problem arises in the most extreme ways, however, when the views of one or another part of the European far left are mapped directly onto the American political terrain, creating insuperable difficulties in relating to actual political formations and social struggles.

For socialists in the U.S., the strategic tasks involve elaborating an approach that gives full weight to the historical advances made within representative institutions, while pointing to their limits; indicating the prospects of a socialism not confined to parliamentary forms, while making a commitment not only to defense of the rights won under capitalism but to the retention and expansion of those gains in a socialist society. The general critique of parliamentary forms now has limited political potential—and will have none if it suggests the desirability of suppressing parliamentary forms—and can have meaning only when mass political forces experience the limits of such forms as boundaries to be surpassed. Political tendencies that center around a critique of parliamentary institutions will otherwise probably not achieve significant results either within or outside them.

The process of reaching the limits of parliamentary institutions—as the basis of transforming them—contains the dangers of bureaucratization and institutionalization that radical critics of parliamentarism have so often stressed. But these dangers are not located exclusively in political as opposed to economic or social institutions; nor are they solely present in large-scale rather than small and decentralized organizations. In the current American context, there is no way to avoid facing these dangers in whatever arena, and claims that they can be overcome somewhere outside politics are wishful.

Among contemporary American leftist critics of parliamentarism there is often a deep hostility toward politics. This hostility can find theoretical justification in Marx, though not unambiguously. In Marxist (and Leninist) theory there are diverse contradictory attitudes toward politics. For example there is a vision of eliminating politics as a separate realm of social life, alongside an emphasis on the political as the decisive part of efforts aimed toward realizing that vision. Even the ultimate vision is mixed, sometimes suggesting a society without politics, other times indicating a society in which all institutions are politicized and all people are active political agents. In fact, no society that has experienced a social revolution has been able to dispense with some system of national representative institutions. Though the forms of these institutions vary, the real question is the extent to which a genuine political dynamic occurs within them.

Hostility toward politics takes several forms within the left. In its crudest form, it simply denounces elections as a sham; and what is true about that statement does not conceal the inability of those same elements of the left to influence the course of events. In a more positive way, similar viewpoints are employed to criticize the narrowness of traditional conceptions of politics. This critique is correct insofar as it focuses on the ways in which the left has traditionally ignored large areas of social life. But when this critique redefines politics as nothing more than power—expressed and reproduced constantly in all social institutions—there can be no serious discussion of political strategy. The way is then opened for arguments claiming that one or another location is the site of the most immediate needs and concerns of various groups—the family, workplace, community, etc.—and must be the focal point of political strategy, defined in terms of amplifying the struggles that arise there.

IN THE TRADITIONAL language of the socialist movement, this approach has been called economism, as it was perceived to center around immediate economic demands at the workplace. But the complexity of advanced capitalist societies encourages new approaches that privilege one or another social sphere as the site of genuine experience, real needs, etc. It usually turns out that claims for the primacy of a single sphere only duplicate the initial preferences of their advocates—without indicating how such choices bear on the global organization of political power. In fact, the fragmentation of social life that has accompanied the growing role of the state means that, in addition to giving organized expression to political power, the state becomes the object of immediate social needs in new ways. The language of "needs" and "experience," when used to assert the priority of social or economic struggles vis-a-vis contests over state policies only suppresses the strategic discussion of relations among different components of society. Approaches that stress immediate concerns tend to avoid critical examination of the formation and content of the immediate concerns of various groups, and how those concerns are linked to other issues. As a result, the whole language of needs, experience, personal life, immediacy, etc. has deteriorated in contemporary American leftist discussion to the point that it often becomes simply a fashionable way of expressing strategic preferences without any careful examination of the processes that shape various needs and experiences.

All this is to say that parochical, narrow perspectives are by no means the sole property of reformist labor parties—or of European Communist parties. There are many ways in which the framework (and language) of needs and concrete experience can be structured to meet political purposes quite different from those of the anti-authoritarian tendencies in the American left. Yet the emphasis on immediate experience often does express a justifiable hostility toward the abstracted authoritarianism found in much socialist political theory. Generally implicit here is rejection of the idea that an omniscient party could substitute its knowledge for direct experience of a multi-textured social reality; in this respect, the decay of orthodoxy could open up new possibilities for political activity and analysis, since the need to establish oneself for or against the model of a single leading party no longer exists. Still, the anti-political stance of some of the most democratic currents in the American left has strong negative features insofar as it freezes discussion and abandons the actual political world.

ARGUMENTS EMPHASIZING THE struggle for social and economic control by those directly involved are no substitute for confronting the forms and nature of the exercise of political power. Whatever the extent of workplace and community forms of power, the task of resolving global questions about the broadest developmental choices inevitably persists. These global concerns remain the focus of political struggle, which can be conducted more or less democratically, but never suppressed or avoided.

In France and Italy, the limits of the concept of a single leading party have been reached by the only parties with a chance of implementing them. Those notions, along with their organizational accompaniments, are in decay even if they have not fully disappeared. In the U.S., the question of pluralism is already closed: a socialist politics framed in terms of aspirations toward a monolithic party-state fusion will probably never gain any significant legitimacy or major organizational expression. Socialist organizations that present themselves as parties that, once expanded, could provide a comprehensive basis of political life are routinely defeated by any competent defense of existing institutions. The pretensions of such groups can easily be made to seem ridiculous, grotesquely out of proportion to their political attributes and potential.

A long-term conception of political pluralism in the U.S. is also rooted in analysis of class relations. There is a *possibility* of a socialist movement that is majoritarian. Yet the expansion of the working class and intermediate groups, along with the growth of new social groupings, creates a situation of extraordinary social and political complexity. There is no automatic process leading to homogeneity within the working class, much less of all the forces that are potentially anti-capitalist. In this setting, a Marxist analysis claiming that parties express the interests of a single class—with the corollary that the working class "needs" only a single party—reduces political struggle to a vision of final upheaval which can only be resolved by a unified subject (the party).

The development of a socialist movement in the U.S. will have to involve the unification of diverse emergent anti-capitalist formations. This can never be achieved if socialist forces pose their goal as a society in which only a single party is an effective political agent. Political pluralism is consequently not just a preference for a multi-party system (a judgment which can be defended theoretically) but the precondition for any effective socialist politics. While it is crucial to build socialist political organizations and encourage their unity, this process can only be retarded by conceptions that view the end to be attained through alliances and conflicts as the formation of a single leading party.

To take one example of how these themes bear on the recent history of the left: one recurring question involves the relationship between organizations composed of both women and men, and those composed exclusively of women. This question is frequently posed in terms of defining "autonomy." The problem with this approach is that it assumes the presence of a "center" that does not exist, in relation to which certain organizations are "autonomous." Thus most "mixed" socialist groups (at least implicitly) see the problem as one of surpassing this autonomy through one means or another. This approach does grasp the need for *strategic* unity, but misses the essential dynamic underlying autonomous organizations. "Autonomy" is based not only on a recognition of inequality within the left, but on a more profound recognition of the persistence of the sexual division of labor in socialist societies. This recognition suggests a view of socialist society as one in transition— where traditional forms of domination persist, and where new forms can develop. It also points to a genuinely pluralistic and open conception of politics within this transitional society. To the extent that "mixed" socialist organizations present themselves as exclusive political centers, the task of building viable political formations will be all the more difficult. The "autonomous" organizations are also undermined in situations where they constantly have to defend their existence and protect their identity from hostile left criticism. This complicates their problems in framing general political objectives and establishing alliances. In the recent history of the feminist movement, this difficulty has merged with the anti-political tendencies already noted; among left feminists this has at times produced an inclination to abandon politics, which in effect cedes that terrain to other parts of the feminist movement (or to the non-feminist and even anti-feminist left).

IT IS NECESSARY to emphasize that political pluralism is fully relevant during and after a transition to socialism in the U.S. A socialist society—one that still contains classes, as well as the tendency toward the formation of new classes—contains no predetermined subject, no inevitable outcome. The emergence of new class formations is possible— formations that will not necessarily resemble those of capitalism. Diverse problems involve the nature of working class domination, the relationship between the working class and other social strata, and the development of a political process within which new historical questions can be effectively posed. The capacity to resolve these questions, and to establish new forms of working-class rule, requires a broad democratic state, one that permits and encourages freedom of political organization, both as the *means* toward the abolition of classes and the *content* of a socialist society that is dynamic and open.

PROSPECTS

FOR THE NEAR FUTURE, the problem is not so much to ensure a pluralistic political dynamic as to create some minimal commonality of purpose among a mass of competing and often conflicting social forces. The process that gives expression to this commonality is not likely to be unilinear, in the sense of producing a greater uniformity of vision and purpose over time. Such political homogenization (of social strata, racial and ethnic groups, etc.) is neither probable nor desirable, given the rich diversity of political and social organizations that already exist in the U.S.

The vision of a pluralistic socialist polity is not the invention of the Eurocommunist parties. It has existed for decades, was most often either on the margins of the left, or a matter of principle among social democratic parties whose very commitment to socialism was in question. Thus Eurocommunism does not represent a new orthodoxy, so much as a signal that a new conception of socialism is possible on a mass scale in the West. In the U.S., what this means is that it is now easier to start from assumptions that ought to have been common long ago.

THIS ESSAY HAS not explored the implications of Eurocommunism for a theory of the transition to socialism in the U.S. This absence has been deliberate, in order to focus attention on questions raised by Eurocommunism for the American left in its current state of political development—in other words, to clarify elements of the new political and ideological terrain that Eurocommunism has helped to create. What remains is to elaborate a socialist politics without doctrinal preconceptions and frustrated desires for another history.

Notes

1. In assessing why the current "revisionist" leadership ws able to defeat its opponents, Bettelheim does acknowledge that the sectarian style, rhetorical excesses, and failure to conduct detailed studies of Chinese social reality were flaws that cost them politically. He asserts the importance of free debate within the party, and of methods of leadership that can encourage the development of mass democracy. These points are the limit of his critique of political relations in China after the Cultural Revolution. See Charles Bettelheim, "The Great Leap Backward," in Charles Bettelheim and Neil Burton, *China Since Mao,* (New York: Monthly Review Press, 1978).

2. A good example of this critique was made by James Loeb in *Dissent* (Winter, 1978), where he suggests that the differences between social democrats and social liberals are rhetorical, and that while socialist rhetoric may play a positive function in Europe, it only isolates progressives in the U.S. The two editors of *Dissent* who responded had problems finding substantive political grounds for disagreement with Loeb, and thus ended up arguing that the basis for retaining socialist terminology was to maintain an ideological basis for their rejection of greed and desire for social justice. This sort of collapse is not the only development within Amerian social democracy; subsequent issues of *Dissent* featured a symposium entitled "Beyond the Welfare State," which mixed together routine statements advocating more public regulation of social and economic life with efforts to outline a vision of socialism that would go beyond what has been accomplished by social democratic governments in power. ("Beyond the Welfare State," Summer and Fall 1978 *Dissent*).

3. For the latter, see Irwin Silber's series on Eurocommunism in the *Guardian*, in March and April, 1977, and the editors' critique of Eurocommunism in *Monthly Review* ("The New Reformism," vol. 28, no. 2, June 1976).

4. See most issues of *Political Affairs*, the journal of the CPUSA, in 1977 or 1978.

5. Henri Weber's "Eurocommunism, Socialism, and Democracy" (*New Left Review*, July-August 1978, no. 110, pp. 3-14) lucidly expresses this perspective.

6. For one such positive assessment, see Max Gordon, "The Theoretical Outlook of the Italian Communists," *Socialist Revolution*, no. 33, vol. 7, May-June 1977.

7. Henri Weber, *op. cit.* acknowledges superficially the idea that grounds might exist for criticizing the original Leninist conception of democracy—and not only of its Stalinist degeneration. Then, having dispensed with the formalities, he states: "Against those pioneers of the democratic transition to socialism, Lenin registered a number of common-sense points that fully apply to the Euro-communist theorizations of today. Whoever speaks of 'democracy' in general, as if it were an ahistorical essence defined by its attributes, is speaking as a liberal, not as a Marxist. In class societies, 'we cannot speak of pure democracy...we can only speak of class democracy.'" (The quote is from Lenin's *The Proletarian Revolution and the Renegade Kautsky.*)

For all his anti-Stalinism, Weber here closes off discussion of the problem of democratic power; if it is not legitimate as a general theoretical problem, how can it be grounded theoretically with respect to specific social formations? Weber provides no means of distinguishing his basic conception from the potentially authoritarian relativism—democracy being viewed as a set of practices ensuring proletarian rule—which he criticizes.

8. This view characterizes James Weinstein's treatment of this problem, though it should be noted that his analysis was a polemic against those who argued that the Socialists failed because socialist politics must necessarily fail in this country. James Weinstein, *The Decline of Socialism in America, 1912-1925* (New York: Vintage, 1969), chaps. 4 and 9.

9. For the first approach, see Peggy Dennis' *Autobiography of an American Communist* (Lawrence Hill, 1978). For the second, more pessimistic evaluation, see Joseph R. Starobin *American Communism in Crisis, 1943-57* (Berkeley: University of California Press, 1975).

10. See Herbert Gutman, "Work, Culture, and Society in Industrializing America, 1815-1919," in *Work, Culture, and Society in Industrializing America* (New York: Alfred Knopf, 1976); and Stanley Aronowitz, *False Promises* (New York: McGraw Hill, 1973).

11. This is the basic position of the journal *Monthly Review*, expressed by its main editors over the years.

12. See Louis Hartz, *The Liberal Tradition in America* (New York: Harcourt, Brace & World, 1955).

13. For an excellent discussion of these issues, see Ernesto Laclau's essay, "Towards a Theory of Populism," in his *Politics and Ideology in Marxist Theory* (London: New Left Books, 1977). The best recent account of American populism is Lawrence Goodwyn's *Democratic Promise* (New York: Oxford, 1976).

chapter 14

THE DEMOCRATIC ROAD: NEW DEPARTURES AND OLD PROBLEMS

Carl Boggs

WHATEVER THEIR DIFFERENCES, Eurocommunist parties are all committed to a "democratic" transition to socialism engineered through the political institutions of advanced capitalism. For its architects in the Italian, Spanish, and French Communist parties, the democratic road assumes that the traditional Marxist goals of expanded production and social equality can (and *must*) be realized through a progressively democratized bourgeois state.

The idea of merging the struggles for socialism and democracy is hardly new within Marxism; it was a vision of Marx himself and was later embraced by theorists as diverse as Lenin, Kautsky, and Luxemburg. But Marx (and Engels) never specified the political character of the transition to the extent of spelling out the forms that socialist democracy might assume once the working class wrested power from the bourgeoisie. Lenin and Luxemburg were both hostile to bourgeois democracy, agreeing that revolutionary mobilization must be directed primarily *outside* and *against* liberal structures, rooted in new proletarian institutions capable of replacing the old state apparatus. As for Kautsky, his strategy of democratic transformation (which guided the Second International) is perhaps closest to the Eurocommunist model—in its emphasis, for example, on utilizing elections and extending parliamentary institutions, civil liberties, freedom of political opposition, and ideological diversity, and creating a favorable balance of forces as the precondition for conquering state power. Eurocommunism departs from classical social democracy, however, in its rejection of the orthodox crisis theory that foresaw a transition spurred by economic collapse and cataclysmic upheavals. In contrast, it anticipates a prolonged contestation for hegemony: "democratization of the state" occurs systemically but as organically and peacefully as possible, with no sudden or qualitative rupture, under conditions of relative institutional stability.* It envisages no dramatic sweeping away of the old order, no frontal assault on the bourgeois state apparatus. Whereas the Kautskian concept of the democratic road was ambiguous and confined to the mechanistic premises of traditional Marxism, the Eurocommunist version—having presumably shed past illusions—establishes hope for a more coherent strategy of socialist transformation.

This reconstituted theory of the democratic road goes back to the immediate postwar years when a few innovative Communist Parties (notably the Yugoslav and the Italian) already began to reassess the Stalinist legacy. While the phenomenon of Eurocommunism is in many respects novel, its guiding concepts are not. The PCI's theory of "structural reforms" can be traced to the 1944-47 period, when Palmiro Togliatti first outlined the *via Italiana* based on strategic protection of Republican institutions. Only crudely sketched at first as a response to fascism and then muted by the cold war, this model was followed rather consistently in practice and, in the period after 1956, refined by Togliatti and his successors, who in the early 1970s introduced the "historic compromise." The PCE, though struggling as an underground party to survive Franco's authoritarian rule, endorsed the democratic road as early as the late 1960s even in the absence of electoral possibilities before mid-1977. Santiago Carrillo's increasingly harsh critique of the Soviet model, the publication of his *Eurocommunism and the State* in 1977, and the PCE's jettisoning of "Leninism" in favor of identification as a "revolutionary, democratic, and Marxist" party at its Ninth Congress in April 1978 marked the culmination of a long process of ideological transformation. The PCF's decision to abandon the "dictatorship of the proletariat" at its 22nd Congress in February 1976 was, likewise, really a theoretical codification of the party's actual political practice since World War II. In each case, continued adherance to Leninist theory and

---

*One variant or another of crisis theory was generally accepted within Marxism before World War I. In this respect, the classical tendency most resembling Eurocommunism was that represented by Bernstein, for whom long-term economic and political stability was necessary for democratization.

to the Soviet mystique served more as a fiction to reinforce party identity than as a strategic guide to action. The appearance of "Eurocommunism" in the mid-1970s thus signifies above all a final and irrevocable shift of identity from a Soviet defined international movement to a national or regional one where local factors play the overwhelming role; only to a lesser extent does it reflect the sudden emergence of new democratizing impulses within the parties.

What is new, however, includes the following: the exacerbation of the global and European crisis of capitalism, which is especially acute in the Mediterranean countries owing to their subordinate position in the international division of labor; the recent electoral successes of the PCI, legalization of the PCE, and the PCF's formation of an alliance with the Socialists, conferring on these parties an image of respectability and (for the PCI) bringing governmental power closer; and a more self-conscious theoretical and political assertion of the democratic road strategy, thus widening the breach with the CPSU.

FASCINATING AS THESE developments are, a familiar question presents itself: given the general premises of the Eurocommunist parties and the conditions they face, how far in political reality can they advance along the democratic road? Here we come to the dilemma of how to achieve instrumental (effectiveness and power-oriented) goals without undermining revolutionary (democratic and egalitarian) ones. Looking at Eurocommunist strategies and programs, it is clear that alongside the commitment to democratization is the long-range project of rational-ization—the augmenting of economic productivity and institutional cohesiveness by means of stripping away pre-capitalist residues (tradi-tionalism, outmoded techniques, parasitism, social fragmentation), developing science and technology, building new planning infrastruc-tures, expanding and professionalizing the public sector, and stabilizing the political system. To some degree, this project has always been central to Marxism, especially where movements have come to power (usually in pre-industrial countries) and set in motion a modernizing process of "socialist construction." This secularizing, rationalizing side of Marxism has usually coexisted in some fashion with its democratizing, emanci-patory side. The difficulty is that in the historical development of Marxist party-states, rationalization has often prevailed in a way that generates profoundly *anti*-democratic consequences: bureaucratic centralism, rou-tinized and alienated labor, mass depoliticization.

But if such movements have yielded to certain imperatives of rationalization, then the Eurocommunist parties—situated in econom-ically developed countries with (except for Spain) substantial bourgeois democratic traditions—could surely hope to escape its authoritarian logic. Clearly, the strategic potential for a democratic transition to socialism is greater in France or Italy today than it was, for example, in Russia at the time of the Bolshevik Revolution. Yet most of the old obstacles and limitations remain, though in new form. In the first place, Mediterranean capitalism is today characterized by growing production and legitimation crises that expand the terrain for rationalization within a bourgeois framework. Secondly, where the Eurocommunist parties are able to win hegemony—and the PCI has already been doing so in many areas of local Italian politics—one outcome might be the gradual displacement of traditional capitalist domination rooted in private property by a bureaucratic system of authority linked to a more encompassing state apparatus. Thirdly, bureaucratic obstacles to the democratic road are strengthened by the Eurocommunist attempt to chart a path primarily through the existing state and, conversely by the absence of a fully-developed theory of *socialist* democracy grounded in new popular forms of state power. Hence the possibility emerges that the democratic road, lacking a revolutionary conception of the state, will be rendered abstract when thrown up against the forces of rationalization, paving the way to a bureaucratic and statist mode of development even within a pluralist system.

Expressed in these terms, the conflict between democratization and rationalization includes several pitfalls that Marxist parties have never managed to avoid. Revolutionary change in the developed countries will surely be unpredictable, open-ended, conflictual, at moments even chaotic. It follows that a major predicament for such parties—especially those largely restricting their activity to the dominant political and institutional sphere—is that of trying to expand the democratic and liberating potential of capitalist development within a framework that in many ways protects hierarchical and exploitative relations. For Eurocommunism, the strategic assault on bourgeois power revolves around the themes of legitimacy and bureaucratic domination. How is the diffusion of technocratic rationality compatible with the emergence of a democratic socialist hegemony? How can state planning and social investment be increased without risking further bureaucratization? How is it possible to broaden and democratize the "participatory" side of the state while curtailing and streamlining its "administrative" side?* Finally, to what extent can a rather stable institutional order—required for the Eurocommunist strategy of democratization—be maintained in the

---

*The "participatory" sphere of state activity includes parliament, elections, the party system, local representative assemblies, and certain aspects of interest group (e.g. trade union) politics; the "administrative" sphere includes national and local public bureaucracies, the military, police and court system.

midst of an intensifying economic and political crisis?

Although the time for conclusive judgments is still far off, I wish to argue that these contradictory forces are already producing a serious impasse for Eurocommunism—an impasse that stems from the very logic of its concept of socialist transformation. Fundamental to this logic is a vision of democracy that for the most part does not go beyond the bourgeois political-institutional realm or a hierarchical concept of authority relations. Beneath this lies the problem of rationalization: the Eurocommunist parties are committed to a transformative process that bolsters the growth of productive forces in a way that is at odds with the potential for comprehensive democratization.*

THE DEMOCRATIC ROAD: TOWARD A PLURALISTIC COMMUNISM?

IN THEIR FORMATIVE years—from the early 1920s to the mid-1930s—the French, Italian, and Spanish Communist Parties were, as disciplined Comintern members, attached to the Leninist world-view. Their leaderships, having left the Second International out of frustration with the fatalism and paralysis of social democracy, embraced the "21 principles" that committed them to the vanguard party, democratic centralism, the "dictatorship of the proletariat," and the demands of Soviet foreign policy. The guiding principle of Leninism was insurrectionary conquest of power by the party: bourgeois democratic institutions might be used for tactical purposes, but never for *strategic* objectives. The Leninist attitude toward the liberal tradition was one of total contempt. Hence the vastly different social and political conditions in Western Europe were granted little strategic importance in the early days.

Roughly a half-century later, these parties have evolved full-circle. They now ardently celebrate the positive features of pluralist democracy. In a March 1977 meeting in Madrid, the three general secretaries

---

*I do not intend to make a case for any singular logic of rationalization, much less for any irreversible trend toward state capitalism. Economic development, or "modernization," can assume different forms. For example, it is possible to distinguish a socialist from a capitalist (or state capitalist) mode of economic transformation, in that the former attacks the social division of labor by carrying out a struggle for non-bureaucratic authority relations. John Gurley differentiates these models in his "Maoist and Capitalist Economic Development," *Monthly Review*, February, 1971. The significant point is that Eurocommunism has not really elaborated socialist alternatives to bourgeois (and neo-Weberian) forms of industrialization and rationalization.

(Georges Marchais of the PCF, Enrico Berlinguer of the PCI, and Santiago Carrillo of the PCE) issued a joint statement declaring: "The Communists of Spain, France, and Italy intend to work for the construction of a new society, respecting the pluralism of political and social forces and the guarantee and development of all individual and collective freedoms: freedom of thought and expression, of the press, of association, assembly and demonstration, of the free circulation of people inside their country and abroad, trade union freedom, autonomy of the trade unions and the right to strike, the inviolability of private life, respect for universal suffrage and the possibility of the democratic alternation of majorities, religious freedom, freedom of culture, freedom of expression of the various philosophical, cultural and artistic currents and opinions. This determination to build socialism in democracy and freedom inspires the conceptions elaborated in full autonomy by each of these parties."[1]

Hardly a trace of Leninism here—though the party leaderships do insist upon retaining the "spirit of Lenin." This transformation took place gradually and unevenly, over a long period. In the case of the PCF and the PCI, the democratic road has origins in the anti-fascist struggles of the Popular Front and Resistance years in the late 1930s and early 1940s, from which the parties emerged as patriotic mass organizations committed to electoral politics and postwar "democratic reconstruction" leading, in 1947, to short-lived participation in the French and Italian governments.

What began as essentially a defensive maneuver evolved into an institutional strategy of "structural reforms," once the parties adapted to relatively stable parliamentary systems. For a while they were trapped in a politics of "duplicity," suspended between a Leninist ideological identity and an everyday parliamentarism. In the PCI, this strategic ambivalence was resolved by 1953 in favor of Togliatti's model of structural reforms, which was later openly championed in the wake of the 1956 events: the beginnings of de-Stalinization in the USSR, (including tentative approval of "different paths" to socialism); the Hungarian Revolution; and the first appearances of "polycentrism" in the world Communist movement, which Togliatti outlined at the Eighth PCI Congress in 1956. In the PCF under Maurice Thorez, dual politics continued well into the 1960s, its contradictions mystified and repressed by a residual Jacobin ideology, a heavy-handed organizational centralism, and a sense of embattled political isolation (explained by the party's failure to sustain its popular support at its postwar peak level). While involved in frontist and electoral politics since the mid-1930s, only after 1964 did the PCF begin to present a strategic self-conception in tune with this history and critical of the Leninist insurrectionary model. Even so, it took the leadership a decade to abandon the pretense that Leninism and the democratic road were somehow compatible.

Once the PCI and PCF started to reassess their identities openly and systematically, once their indigenous political entanglements began to take precedence over Soviet "internationalism," then their structural reformism became more uncompromising. The strategy of democratization was now less a matter of choice than a requirement of political success, or even survival; it was, above all, geared to a phase of capitalist development in which monopolistic rule of a single party seemed no longer defensible or plausible. Events of the late 1960s and early 1970s added to this momentum: the decline of Gaullism in France and the immobilism of the Center-Left coalition in Italy; the Soviet invasion of Czechoslovakia, which the PCI and the PCF vigorously protested and which illuminated the issues of pluralism and national autonomy; the challenge of the new left and feminism (dating from the May 1968 events in France and the "hot autumn" of 1969 in Italy), which dramatized the authoritarianism of the parties and softened them to new ideological currents; the leftist defeats in Chile and Portugal, which revealed the importance of parliamentary democracy and the need for broad popular alliances; a mellowing of the postwar Socialist antagonism toward the CPs, clearing the way for leftist electoral coalitions; and the consistent electoral gains of the PCI, which for the first time won more than one-third of the vote in the 1975 (regional) and 1976 (national) elections, carrying it to the doorstep of national power. Beneath this were three significant long-term factors—the gradual erosion of bourgeois hegemony in Italy and France, detente between the U.S. and the USSR, and, more importantly, the stable institutionalized involvement of the two parties in parliamentary politics.

The PCE's transformation, on the other hand, occurred later but more rapidly. After nearly four decades of clandestine activity under the Francoist dictatorship, the PCE leadership was anxious to shed its "outlaw" status. Underground politics took its toll, not only physically but ideologically: the PCE became more and more insulated, detached from social reality, during the harsh and repressive generation following the Civil War. Particularly in the pre-1956 period, the PCE's Leninism meant rigid attachment to Bolshevik strategy and passive subservience to the CPSU line and to Soviet foreign policy. Its centralized apparatus remained intact. The first signs of change appeared in the mid-1960s, with the Franco regime's slippage and the PCE's growing presence in the newly-emergent worker's commissions, which in many areas (especially in Catalonia) had established bargaining relationships with management. Then, in 1968, Carrillo stepped forward as a vocal critic of the Soviet intervention in Czechoslovakia, seizing upon this moment to attack Soviet bureaucratic centralism and, by extension, the concept of the dictatorship of the proletariat, which Carrillo now argued was outmoded and incompatible with revolutionary goals. From this standpoint, and with the expectation that the decaying Franco dictatorship would soon give way to bourgeois democracy, the PCE embraced the democratic road. It took until 1977, however—after Franco's death, the legalization of the PCE, and the holding of Spain's first national elections since 1936—before the party could implement this strategy in practice.

What distinguishes the situation of the PCE from that of the PCI and PCF, of course, is that bourgeois democratic institutions have not yet fully appeared in Spain. The requirements of anti-fascist struggle still weigh heavily on the Spanish left. This reality permeates every aspect of the PCE's program and strategy, and is also reflected in Carrillo's books, interviews, and statements.[2] It further shapes the two-stage conception of the transition advanced by Carrillo: first destroy the remnants of fascism and secure liberal democracy, then begin the struggle for socialist transformation. In Carrillo's words: "The great thing today is to smash the forced integration constituted by fascism. In order to do this, what is needed is a coalition government which will restore liberties. Tomorrow the advance to socialism will be posed."[3] The PCI and PCF have also been preoccupied with the threat of reaction, but Spain today is at a different level of *political* development than either Italy or France. Hence the likelihood that the PCE will play an integral role in a pluralist transformation of Spanish society, helping to resolve the imbalance between productive forces and political institutions while staking out its own claim to legal opposition.

THE STRUGGLE FOR A NON-LENINIST IDENTITY

WITH THE STRATEGIC outlook of the three parties changing drastically, new theoretical formulations (e.g., on the state, concept of the party, nature of the transition) were bound to follow. Interestingly enough, it was the theoretical codification of already established organizational practices—a step that coincided with the *political* birth of Eurocommunism—that triggered the initial Soviet counter-response. In this case, as in others, the conflict focused around Lenin or at least what passed for "Leninism" within the Communist tradition.

What the Eurocommunist parties ultimately had to confront, and reject, was the sacred notion of the dictatorship of the proletariat. While the official break did not occur until the 1975-78 period,[4] such a departure was already suggested in Togliatti's postwar writings on the *via*

Italiana, where he tried to honor tradition by employing the term "democratic dictatorship of the proletariat."[5] Togliatti's concept of "progressive democracy" outlined in 1944-46 necessarily relied upon a non-vanguardist party—a mass organization that represented the working class and allied forces within the conditions of pluralist competition. The Communist Party was seen as *one* part of the state and society alongside other parties and forces; no single party had exclusive moral claim to rule, no Marxism possessed absolute scientific authority. For Togliatti, a democratic transition would require the PCI's continuous institutional presence in a "secular, non-ideological, and pluralistic" state. He noted, accurately, that the dictatorship of the proletariat was always vague in classical Marxism and that its only historical embodiment (in the Soviet Union) was not something that most Italians, with the memory of Mussolini still fresh, wanted to duplicate. Yet, despite the obvious contraditions between the *via Italiana* and Bolshevik strategy, Togliatti—owing to his long and deep attachment to the USSR—could never break with the party's official Leninism.

Still, Togliatti was the first within international Communism to argue that Stalinism was a *systemic* feature not reducible to the personal machinations of any single leader; implicit here was a more general critique of the Soviet model and of Leninism. More explicit was a whole series of related issues that the theory of the dictatorship of the proletariat had obscured: the political "uniqueness" of Italy, the role of parliamentary institutions in the transition, the nature of popular alliances and the task of maximizing participation at the base; the debate around internal party democracy, etc. Ferment within the PCI spread until the 10th Congress in 1962, when Leninism (in its Soviet-defined form) finally came under siege. Togliatti conceded that Lenin no longer provided a guide to action for Marxist parties in the advanced countries. To fill this void, the PCI looked to Gramsci, whose notion of a gradual transformation of civil society as the prelude to conquest of state power now became the theoretical rationale for the *via Italiana*. Filtered through Togliatti, the PCI's "Gramscian Marxism" allowed the party to occupy a new (parliamentary) strategic terrain while retaining its nominal Leninism. Despite pressure from the most committed electoralist faction (led by Giorgio Amendola), however, the Longo leadership feebly clung to its Leninism throughout the 1960s. These pretensions were abandoned only in the aftermath of the 13th Congress in 1972, when Berlinguer introduced the "historic compromise." Fueled by electoral successes and the decline of the Christian Democratic hegemony, the PCI focused its sights on national power. Under such conditions, the authoritarian connotations of Leninism would constitute a severe handicap by enabling opponents to raise the bogey of Soviet dictatorship. In any case, the theoretical innovations that grew out of the 13th Congress hastened the PCI's liberation from past myths, legitimating in unambiguous terms its *strategic* adaptation to representative democracy and prefiguring the rise of Eurocommunism.[6]

BOTH THE PCE AND PCF, on the other hand, experienced a later and much briefer process of internal debate around Leninism. Once the process started (in the early 1970s), the orthodox symbols were resolutely swept aside by leaderships ready to demonstrate their Eurocommunist credentials.* Carrillo argued that in advanced capitalism the complexity of political structures ruled out armed insurrection as the route to socialism and made the single-party state obsolete. By 1976, he rejected bureaucratic centralism of the Soviet type in principle. Carrillo could "easily imagine a socialist regime governed jointly or even alternatively by Communists, Socialists, and Christians who are in favor of Socialism: a socialist state with a plurality of parties."[7] The positions staked out by the PCE at the Ninth Congress in 1978 demonstrate the most extensive commitment to pluralist democracy of any Communist party in history.

The PCF has been neither so critical of the CPSU nor so devoted to pluralist forms as the PCE. At the 22nd Congress in 1976, Marchais concluded that the terms "dictatorship" and "proletariat" were negative symbols that isolated the PCF—the former conjuring images of Hitler, Mussolini, and Franco (and presumably also Stalin), the latter suggesting a restricted working-class rather than "mass" base. In the new phase of struggle, characterized by crisis of monopoly capital, radicalization of the middle strata, and "peaceful coexistence," socialism can be attained without civil war or an overturning of bourgeois state power— assuming the PCF can mobilize a broad anti-monopoly social bloc.[8] However, the PCF leadership has been less willing to question its vanguardism (the idea that the PCF alone is the judge of Marxist theory and strategy, that mass organizations must be controlled by the party, that it is the sole representative of the working class) and democratic centralism. Here, to a greater degree than in either the PCI or PCE, the residues of Leninism survive.

This stripping away of Leninist *strategic* imagery, even where old organizational principles linger, is the hallmark of Eurocommunism. It would be easy to analyze the transformation as merely symbolic, the delayed theoretical recognition of routinized political practices. But that

---

*For a sampling of post-Congress debate, see Etienne Balibar, *On the Dictatorship of the Proletariat* (London: *New Left Books,* 1977).

would be only half-true, since the break with Leninism has also cleared away obstacles to change within the parties, permitting them to glimpse a more comprehensive democratic theory of transition. Contradictions remain, but the foundations of a contemporary structural reformism are more solidly established.

The view of a non-Leninist transition developed within Eurocommunism can be summarized as follows, taking into account varying emphases among the parties:

1) Utilization of the forms and practices of bourgeois democracy—elections, parliament, local government, interest groups—as the fundamental means of achieving a power transfer. Whereas Lenin emphasized the *tactical* importance of these forms, arguing that they could help realize limited objectives, the Eurocommunists view them as the locus of a long-range strategy for dismantling bourgeois power and moving toward socialism. Insofar as the objective conditions exist within capitalism for democratization of the state apparatus, no forcible destruction of existing institutions is necessary.

2) The dynamic basis for this transfer is structural reformism—gradual democratization of representative structures that brings new content to old forms in which the working class and other popular strata achieve a steadily more powerful voice, sense of citizenship, and political strength. With each electoral advance, with each institutional gain, with each capture of new positions within the state, the left is better able to subvert bourgeois hegemony and assert control over the main sectors of the economy and society. The PCI, and to a lesser extent the PCE, advertises this strategy as an institutional Gramscian "war of position" capable of producing an authentic mass party and new levels of collective participation.[9] For the PCF, this approach is more narrowly defined as a "transition from a state of the monopolies to the state of the working people"[10] in which "advanced democracy is a stage toward socialism."

3) Alliance politics that attaches new significance to an expanding "middle strata" (civil servants, professionals, technicians, etc.), broadens the "social bloc" to include all social forces (potentially) opposed to the monopolies and multi-nationals, and encourages coalitions with non-socialist parties. Resembling the surface features of the Popular Front, Eurocommunist strategy differs from frontism to the degree that it is primarily anti-capitalist rather than anti-fascist, and ostensibly strives for mobilization toward socialism instead of being preoccupied with temporary defensive maneuvers. The PCI's skillful use of alliance strategy has helped it develop a large, heterogeneous popular base and a vast local power network throughout Italy. The PCF and PCE share the PCI's goal of an ever-broadening social bloc tied to electoral successes, and both stress the role of the new middle strata. But they are more

skeptical of party coalitions than the PCI, in part because they lack the PCI's strength and hence risk being dominated by larger Socialist parties.

4) The preservation of constitutional rights and liberties—including those of political opposition—beyond the transitional period and into socialism itself. Though still formal and abstract in their bourgeois applications, such rights and liberties develop new social content as power relations begin to favor anti-capitalist forces. Pluralist institutions are more compatible with egalitarian social development than is Soviet-style bureaucratic centralism, whatever the economic arguments on behalf of the latter. (The Second International parties also supported legal-constitutional principles, but their schema of *post-capitalist* politics remained hazy, bound as it was to such incompatible concepts as the "withering away of the state" and the "dictatorship of the proletariat.")

5) As a corollary to the acceptance of ideological and cultural diversity, a jettisoning of the vanguard theory of organization—though except for some of Carrillo's statements this cornerstone of Leninism has not yet been systematically overturned. Carrillo's position, adopted at the Ninth PCE Congress, is that genuine pluralism compels the party to abandon its "scientific" claim to be sole bearer of working-class interests; he sees the PCE as part of an unfolding "new political formation" in which other parties and mass organizations play equal roles, in which the party and state are not identical.[11] Carrillo's model also abolishes the Leninist "transmission belt" concept of party control over popular movements such as the workers' commissions and trade unions. The PCI too has long endorsed ideological and religious pluralism, necessary for survival in a largely Catholic setting, and more recently accepted the principle of trade union autonomy. Yet the PCI holds to its last vestiges of vanguardism, as reflected in the tenacity of its "scientific" Marxism and in its drive to control mass organizations.* The PCF, meanwhile, has departed very little from its entrenched vanguardism and centralism, but it is unlikely that it can long reconcile this rigidity with its general strategic reformulations.[12]

6) Commitment to a process of institutional "renewal": professionalizing the civil service by eliminating huge patronage networks, nepotism, and corruption; simplifying the system of state ministries and agencies; making the public sector more accountable to the masses by undermining monopoly and "parasitic" influences while bolstering parliamentary control; decentralizing state power by turning over more

---

*Strong forces within the PCI, led by Giorgio Amendola, moved to discard this vanguardist ideology in the 1960s but were repelled at the 12th congress in 1969. At one point Amendola argued for junking the label "Communist" and adopting in its place "Party of the Working Class."

decision-making authority to local and regional governments and (in the case of the PCE) encouraging the growth of popular democratic structures such as factory and neighborhood councils; and democratization of the police, the military, and the court systems. The PCE and PCI have both established a material basis for this strategy—the PCE in the workers' commissions and mass organizations, the PCI in municipal and provincial governments. The PCF agrees with all this in theory, but has a relatively weaker local base from which to pursue it and thus its centralism tends to prevail, by default.

7) The beginnings of an internal party democratization, typified by groping moves away from hierarchical, disciplined, cell-based structures toward broader participatory organizations that allow a freer exchange of ideas. If none of the Eurocommunist parties has disavowed the concept of democratic centralism (although the PCE did entertain this notion at the Ninth Congress), each finds it more and more difficult to resolve the contradictions of pursuing a non-Leninist strategy while retaining a Leninist structure. First, the impact of the new left and mass movements since the late 1960s has forced the parties to confront new issues and adapt to a more participatory style. Second, during recent years internal debates have been raging around the many issues posed by Eurocommunism—for example, in the PCF and PCE over the break with Leninism, in the PCF following the dissolution of the Common Program and the left's electoral setback in March 1978, in the PCI around whether and how to pursue the "historic compromise." Since the party leadership can no longer prevent those struggles from moving into the open and taking a mass character, internal secrecy—and perhaps some other norms—are rapidly losing their hold.

TRANSFORMING THE BOURGEOIS STATE

WHAT UNDERLIES THESE strategic changes is a reconstituted Marxist theory of the state and the role of the party.* A major premise of Leninism is that the bourgeois state rests above all upon its coercive apparatus, that it functions essentially as an agency of class domination, and that even the most liberal states are but thinly-veiled repressive organs immune to real democratic transformation. The Eurocommunists reject this theory, arguing that the political institutions of advanced

---

*In this respect it is misleading to argue, as the editors of *Monthly Review* have done, that Eurocommunist strategy is nothing but a recylcing of Kautskian Social Democracy. See "The Age of Reform," *Monthly Review*, June 1976.

capitalism are quite complex and contradictory, their strength resting not so much upon force as ideological consensus, or "hegemony" in Gramscian terms.[13] Bourgeois democracy, moreover, cannot be reduced to a simple mechanism of class domination; it is *in part* an outgrowth of mass struggles that won social and political reforms opposed by the bourgeoisie. There is no monolithic political system controlled by a single class. Instead of overturning or "smashing" bourgeois democracy, as Leninist strategy indicates, the Eurocommunist parties strive for an *internal* process of democratization on the assumption that representative *forms* of state power can be gradually infused with socialist *content*. Since the bourgeois state is a vital, if not decisive, arena of class conflict it becomes an autonomous mechanism that can be utilized by leftist opposition as well as by the ruling class.

Following their interpretations of Gramsci, Eurocommunist theorists point to a shifting of ideological and social blocs within the state—a changing equilibrium of class forces rooted in an expanding socialist consensus and leading to a "gradual modification of structures" that PCI theorist Pietro Ingrao calls a new "hegemony in pluralism."[14] The transition is viewed as an infinite series of steps toward democratization, in which the Marxist party does not prefigure the socialist state but functions as a mediator between the state and the masses.[15] As Carrillo notes, a breakdown in the old postwar class equilibrium in Europe is already occurring, as shown by the demise of Francoism in Spain, the erosion of Gaullism in France, and the crisis of Christian Democracy and Catholicism in Italy. This enables the left to insert itself into the political arena, for it can now more easily "turn around the ideological apparatus" and employ it against monopoly capital.[16] With each stage of democratization, with each advance of the left *within* bourgeois democracy, the crisis of legitimacy and of the state mounts. Carrillo adds that not only the state, but also the Church, education, the family, and other institutions of civil society must be democratized as part of the attack on bourgeois hegemony.

This theoretical-strategic framework, while not yet systematically worked out by the Eurocommunist parties, is already more coherent and visionary than the rationalist schemes of classical social democracy. For one thing, even though it shares the same commitment to electoral politics, it does not accept a scenario of *catastrophic* crisis leading to socialism and thereby rejects a crude two-stage theory of transition—a pre-cataclysmic (adaptive, fatalistic) period followed by a post-crisis (utopian, indeterminate) phase of revolutionary development. In contrast to the orthodox "before" and "after" model, it presupposes an organic, evolutionary transformation in which bourgeois democracy shades gradually into *socialist* democracy. There is to be no epochal crisis, no precipitous collapse of capitalism, no insurrectionary upheaval.

The Eurocommunist sketch of a new model of transition depends upon a number of crucial interrelated assumptions. First, it asserts that advanced capitalist societies will experience prolonged periods of relative economic and institutional stability even where chronic production and legitimation crises persist. Carrillo suggests, for example, that "economic and political catastrophe" are difficult to imagine today in the developed countries.[17] Secondly, it assumes that a period of ideological and political coexistence between rival social forces is possible during the transition, allowing socialist forces to flourish in a generally non-repressive atmosphere. Thirdly, that the material and political basis of capitalism can be overturned without recourse to large-scale violence or civil war. Fourthly, that the "participatory" side of the state can be democratized and strengthened against its "administrative" side, which has become increasingly bureaucratized with the growth of the public sector. And finally, it assumes that socialist hegemony can be established within a give-and-take framework of multi-party politics, and that institutionalization can be resisted after long years of adaptation and compromise. These assumptions cannot be conclusively tested until the Eurocommunist parties have been able to sustain electoral successes over a lengthy period—something accomplished so far by only the PCI. But even granting the prospects of further gains, an even more problematic assumption remains—namely, that the historic Marxist goals of rationalization can be achieved without subverting the Eurocommunist principles of democratization.

RATIONALIZATION OR DEMOCRATIZATION?

ONE OF THE driving forces of industrial development, as both Marx and Weber understood, is the process of rationalization—the expansion of productive efficiency and administrative control through the progressive adoption of new scientific, technological, and organizational methods. Rationalization, whether introduced by the bourgeoisie, social democracy, or Soviet-type Communist regimes, generally fulfills three basic economic and political purposes: accumulation, domination, and legitimation. Bureaucracy, and increasingly *state* bureaucracy, is the catalyst for reproducing the material and social bases of rationalization, while the ideologies it generates—secularism, technological and bureaucratic rationality—constitute the dominant belief-systems of advanced capitalism, serving to enforce the social division of labor. As Marcuse, Gorz, and Habermas have argued, this form of hegemony generates an instrumentalized world-view (extreme pragmatism, rigid adherence to established rules, worship of expertise, etc.) that can lead to mass depoliticization. To the extent that it perpetuates hierarchical social relations, rationalization conflicts with the goals of democratization—in both its Marxist and liberal forms.

Although Marx himself never associated rationalization with socialist transformation, the 20th century Marxist tradition has for the most part adapted to it. Marx in fact had a two-sided approach to this question: on the one hand, he assumed that capitalist production techniques would themselves create the material foundations of a mature communist society, while on the other hand he understood that these same techniques were the source of an alienated work process and would ultimately have to be transcended through entirely new forms of culture and social organization. Under conditions of social equality and workers' self-management, there would be no contradiction between the needs of economic efficiency and those of democratic participation. But the transition to socialism, as Marx apparently viewed it, is a lengthy process that necessarily *combines* capitalist and revolutionary elements in a tense equilibrium shifting gradually toward the latter, in which bourgeois productive forces must be destroyed before the last obstacles to democratization are removed. However vague this conceptualization, Marx did at least develop the kernel of a *critique* of capitalist rationalization. But this critique, and with it the emancipatory side of the transition he envisaged, has been distorted and repressed in the actual history of Marxist parties and regimes—social democracy, Leninism, the Soviet and Eastern European systems, most Communist movements in Africa, Asia, and Latin America.[18] Since Marxist politics has generally stressed economic modernization as the "main lever" of development, it could hardly escape the logic of productivism and statism which also underlies bourgeois rationalization. In the Soviet Union, this meant full-scale mobilization of resources behind a "scientific-technological revolution," centralized planning, hierarchical organization of production and administration, streamlined "one-man management," and labor discipline. The result was bureaucratic centralism.

Eurocommunism, however, appears to offer a way out of this authoritarian impasse—the democratic road. It claims to restore the participatory, anti-bureaucratic side of the transition that disappeared after Marx. It articulates a comprehensive vision of pluralist socialism that emerges with the cultural and political traditions of bourgeois society at the very moment it seeks to transform them. And, in moving some distance along the "new course" charted by Togliatti, it has won the support of large sectors of the working class, established new positions of institutional power, and attained a broad popular legitimacy. Yet, even as these strategic advances mount, Eurocommunism seems unable to transcend the old impasse, in great measure because its concept of socialist transformation (and also of democracy) is in the final analysis limited to bourgeois categories of economic and political development. The "new course," however successful it might be on its own terms, contains no revolutionary project for overcoming the division of labor.[19]

The dynamics of rationalization, as Weberian theory stresses, involve not only the capitalist obsession with productivity but also the impetus toward social control (especially labor discipline) and political legitimation. In extending the division of labor, it stabilizes new forms of domination that increasingly rely upon subtle ideological manipulation—technocratic rationality, the culture industry, consumerism. Rationalization thus encompasses much more than the physical appropriation of science and technology. At the most general level, it underpins new bureaucratic organization and social relations—in the process laying the basis of a new administered popular consciousness—that reshape politics and class struggle.

For purposes of this essay, the most far-reaching implications of rationalization can be singled out as follows: (1) The state, as the main locus of rationalization, assumes qualitatively new functions within society as a whole. With the collapse of traditional capitalism and the rise of social democracy, fascism, and Soviet bureaucratic centralism, the state began to act upon and transform civil society through its enlarged role in the economy, planning, education, and social relations. In advanced capitalism, the state no longer merely expresses class interests but also a bureaucratic logic that merges with the class principle or property relations while shifting the old contradictions to the political-administrative arena. (2) With advancing rationalization, the norms of bureaucratic culture are more widely internalized; technique, hierarchy, and routine, insofar as they require submission and passivity, reinforce the depoliticizing trends toward what Habermas calls "civil privatism."[20] Where technocratic rationality displaces pre-industrial and "archaic" forms of traditionalism and religion, it often supports bureaucratic systems of authority that are more pervasive. (3) To carry out the tasks of capital accumulation and legitimation, a new technocratic intelligentsia appears within the state apparatus, military and corporate sectors, and universities as well as the political parties and trade unions. Though not a "ruling class" as such, this stratum operates within the orbit of bourgeois domination through control of bureaucratic roles and manipulation of knowledge, and under some conditions (e.g., seizure of power by the military) elements of this intelligentsia might constitute a technocratic political class. (4) To the extent that the "rational-legal" aspect of bureaucratization encourages formal rules, contractual bargaining, and pragmatic ideology, it produces the conditions that institutionalize leftist oppositions, transforming them from subversive, combative instruments into stable participants within the legitimate political system. In this situation, a Marxist party may be forced either to abandon its identity or resort to desperately utopian and adventuristic attacks against the system. (5) In repressing democratizing impulses, rationalization generates new contradictions which give birth to new struggles—for example, around the shortage of material and political resources to meet expanding social demands upon the state, around the narrowing cultural basis of legitimation, around the *claims* of technocratic rationality (to deliver better health care, a more livable urban environment, etc.) and the capacity of a system that honors profit and bureaucratic criteria to satisfy such claims.

THE IMPACT OF rationalization depends upon how widely the cultural norms of bureaucracy are diffused. A pervasive bourgeois consensus is realized where the obstacles to capitalist development are minimized—in the first phase, by breaking down the residues of feudal or pre-capitalist formations, in the second phase by organizing a state-directed capitalism that can manage crises. The key to both phases, but particularly the latter, is the enforcement of labor discipline. A century ago Marx was able to analyze the debilitating consequences of machine technology for proletarian social relations and consciousness. So too at a later point did Gramsci, who saw in "Fordism"—the drive toward comprehensively-administered production—a process in which "subaltern forces are manipulated and managed to meet new ends."[21] With the submission and routine demanded by rationalization appeared a new working-class personality whose "regulated social life" necessitated repression of desire, passion, self-activity.[22] Gramsci was describing a transitional stage of capitalist development in which modernizing forces (led by the big bourgeoisie) were struggling to prevail over traditional forces (the Church, large landholders, petty bourgeoisie) who stubbornly clung to the "great traditions" of the past.

Since the "past sedimentations" of feudalism were still strong in Italy even after World War I, the bourgeoisie could never secure firm hegemony. In seeking to fill this void, fascism set out to destroy traditional obstacles to economic modernization (while initially relying upon anti-capitalist romanticism as a springboard to power) by a forced integration from above, including a harsh labor discipline imposed by Mussolini's corporate state. But fascism—itself in many ways tied to the past—failed to achieve most of its rationalizing objectives, in Italy as elsewhere in Europe. In the United States, the collapse of market capitalism was remedied first by the New Deal and then, more effectively by wartime mobilization, which was the stimulus of postwar monopoly development. More successful yet was the "progressive" model of European social democracy, which tackled the old contradictions by enlarging the public sector through nationalizations, state planning, and augmented social expenditures, making possible a new dynamic of capital accumulation and legitimation under the political aegis of working-class organizations. Only in the U.S. did primary initiative for rationalization come from the bourgeoisie; elsewhere, working-class struggles for social reform played a more important role, since the ruling class was generally too weak to carry it out. At the same time, the growth of technology and social investment helped to legitimate bourgeois institutions by creating a new infrastructure for capitalist development,[23] organizing new forms of consumption, and generating new consensual ideologies.[24] One result of this was an ever-greater domination of the state over civil society.[25]

THE MEDITERRANEAN:
A PRECARIOUS BOURGEOIS HEGEMONY

IN THE MEDITERRANEAN countries, however, rationalization has taken place at an uneven and retarded pace in comparison with Northern Europe, Japan, and North America. What typifies Italy and Spain in particular is the survival of traditionalism: the Catholic Church, a strong patriarchal and family structure, a deeply-rooted peasant culture, a fragmentary system of agricultural production, the predominance of medium and small-sized family-owned enterprises, patronage-ridden public bureaucracies. While industrialization has undermined much of this—reflected, for example, by the erosion of Catholicism—the distinctive character of Mediterranean capitalism remains an uneasy mixture of industrialism and tradition, rationalizing impulses and pre-industrial *"ressentiments."* An outgrowth of this is recurrent legitimation crises, expressed on the one hand by a precarious bourgeois hegemony and on the other by combative working-class movements and strong left oppositions. Moreover, the Mediterranean systems suffer because of their weakened and dependent economic position vis-a-vis the developed countries.[26] Long-term structural crisis generates a vicious cycle of declining productivity and strengthened international dependency, which further erodes bourgeois domination. It is this logic that shapes the rise and development of Eurocommunism.

The immediate economic and social impact of the crisis is thus particularly acute in southern Europe. Inflation rates have exceeded 20 percent; unemployment levels have approached 10 percent and have been the focus of European-wide demonstrations; currencies have been extremely unstable; balance-of-payments deficits have soared, creating a precarious reliance on both the oil-producing nations and the International Monetary Fund; and municipalities are experiencing severe fiscal crisis—to identify just the most visible signs of paralysis. This decline has intensified since the early 1970s, partly because of the reversal of Europe's long period of postwar industrial expansion and partly because of trade union gains.

The crisis has been met, on the political side, by an immobilism typical of fragile bourgeois states. In Italy, the Christian Democrats have yielded their once-commanding position, giving way first to a series of patchwork, futile Center-Left coalitions and then to an "imperfect bipartism" that put the DC face-to-face with the resurgent Communists. Grand promises never fulfilled, the constant shuffling of cabinet posts and leadership roles, and the massive extension of patronage networks have substituted for a viable rationalizing force that could implement effective social reforms and overcome the crisis of legitimacy. By the mid-1970s, the decline of bourgeois hegemony in Italy compelled the DC to choose between a shaky *monocolore* (single-party) rule or join the historic compromise with the PCI, neither of which could be durable solutions.

The political situation in Spain is even more tenuous. On one level, the "Prussian" model of industrialization adopted by Franco produced an entirely new economic infrastructure and an expanded urban culture that can no longer be contained by the old authoritarian forms. As the Spanish bourgeoisie looks for new space to maneuver, important traditional groups (the Falange, landholders, the Church) that propped up Francoism have lost popular support; the Prussian model has generated social forces that will inevitably lead to its own unravelling, while the modernizing capitalists can find little political terrain for advancing their interests. This is partly because popular movements have grown remarkably in the last several years, challenging not only Juan Carlos' "liberal" monarchy but threatening bourgeois efforts to establish a rationalizing legitimacy. Today, with electoral reforms, legalized opposition, and a new constitution, Spain is moving through the liberal democratic stage of its bourgeois transformation, but the social forces representing it are squeezed into a narrow space between traditionalism and left opposition.

The French case differs somewhat from the Italian and Spanish, since France has both a more developed capitalism and a weaker legacy of traditionalism and fascism. The French bourgeoisie has thus been able to achieve a rationalization of the state and economy (in certain areas of planning, for example) far surpassing that of other Mediterranean countries. But in the absence of any real social democratic formation, the consensus behind capitalist-directed rationalization has always been weak, marked by widespread working class disaffection. This helps to explain the French bourgeois postwar "Jacobin" embrace of Gaullist authoritarianism. In the wake of the May 1968 events Gaullism waned while the left (Communists and Socialists) grew to nearly half of the electorate. As in Italy and Spain, the crisis of legitimacy narrowed the options of a bourgeoisie striving toward consolidation of power in a period of crisis.

HOW DO THE Eurocommunist parties fit into this picture, and what is their ideological stance toward the crises? In general, allowing once again for differences in emphases and political context, their strategy entails rationalization—though from a perspective that stresses social and welfare reforms, decentralization, and equal working-class participation within the political system. The Eurocommunist model of rationalization is shaped first by a faith in science and technology as the material basis of the transition, which takes on added meaning given the peculiar crisis of bourgeois hegemony in Southern Europe. In principle, the model proposes an intermediate "solution" that would in time produce a more far-reaching socialist transformation. The stabilization of capitalism (on a new footing) would be a necessary step, since in sweeping away the parasitism, inefficiency, corruption, and waste associated with tradition it would dispose of barriers to further social development. In political actuality, however—assuming that the parties achieve their power objectives—no such rupture between stages is likely to occur, nor has one been theoretically stated by any of the party leaderships. The probability is that the strategic premises of the "first stage" cannot be arbitrarily overturned at some future moment in the transitional process; on the contrary, the initial logic of development can be expected to permeate every phase of transformation, as the Soviet experience shows. Hence where the schema of rationalization is built into present social reality it is bound to shape the future.

THE PCI AND THE "CRISIS OF INSTITUTIONS"

HOW DOES THIS general conception translate into specific programmatic goals for the Eurocommunist parties? Setting aside temporarily the question of whether such a rationalizing project can *succeed* under present conditions, the main features include: stimulating industrial productivity through scientific and technological progress as the first step toward improving the position of the Mediterranean countries within the world capitalist division of labor; expanding public involvement in the economy by means of consolidating state ownership of large enterprises, strengthening "democratic" planning and coordination, and adopting new forms of public investment to reverse uneven development; modernizing state and corporate structures through professionalizing the civil service and industrial management, ending patronage, and simplifying the ministerial system; enforcing labor discipline to encourage routine contractual bargaining, channel struggles at the base into legitimate arenas, and impose austerity measures that set limits to working-class claims; and developing the countryside through state investment programs, stimulated agricultural productivity based on more effective use of technology, and reclamation of abandoned lands.

IT WILL HELP to look more closely at the Italian situation, where the crisis seems most aggravated. On the one hand, past rationalizing initiatives in Italy came primarily from the northern bourgeoisie along lines of the "Fiat model" that led to economic chaos, privatized styles of consumerism, and uneven development. Although highly-advanced in some areas, rationalization was never *systematic* or planned in a global sense; it therefore only exacerbated the contradictions of Italian capitalism. On the other hand, the PCI—its local power base long-established—has had more time to refine its strategy than the PCF and PCE. In trying to steer a course somewhere between classical social democracy and Leninism, the PCI nonetheless looks to the state, or more accurately to the *public sector*, as the main lever of rationalization.

The PCI's schema rests upon a compelling logic. Not that the Center-Left governments failed to build a sizeable public sector; they succeeded in this during the 1960s, but their efforts wound up mired in political quicksand. From the standpoint of rationalization, the most capital-intensive, technologically-sound, and productive sector in Italy is that of the export-oriented monopolies in the north, but it is this sector over which the state has least control. The central plan has no real sanctions, regulatory policies are practically non-existent, the taxation system works erratically, and no effective fiscal policy has been instituted. On the other side, the proliferation of small, technologically-backward enterprises with fragmented, non-unionized workforces and lagging productivity poses obstacles to planned development and social reform. For similar reasons, the agricultural economy remains a bastion of opposition to rationalization. Italy is locked into a system of small, unproductive farms that do not have the necessary capital for mechanization, requiring the import of vast amounts of foodstuffs and raw materials. In the south, social fragmentation and economic backwardness are even more pronounced. And with the postwar collapse of pre-capitalist production and social relations, large farming areas have been abandoned while most young people go north in search of jobs. Meanwhile, the patronage and clientele networks remain—the fiefdoms of landed and commercial interests, and in some cases of party machines—

as formations hostile to social transformation. Efforts through the public sector to "modernize" the south, for example by setting up the *Cassa per il mezzogiorno* and a few state corporations like Alfa Sud, have generated only small pockets of growth and just the first signs of a modern labor force.

The situation is hardly better within the public sector itself. First, the state-holding companies (including steel, shipbuilding, telephone, banking, oil and chemicals, electronics, computers, and nuclear engineering) have suffered enormous losses in recent years. This is less a technological than an administrative problem: many of the holding firms have become bureaucratic empires controlled by corporate magnates, thriving on patronage, corruption, and waste that is subsidized by the mass of taxpayers. Moreover, while the holding companies are nominally subject to ministerial control, in practice they are governed by joint private-public investment structures resulting in bureaucratic rivalries and muddled systems of authority.[27] Secondly, the planning structure established by the Center-Left is one in name only. Many national targets are set, but they cannot be reached because of insufficient administrative control over private enterprises, because the public bureaucracy obstructs their implementation, or because political consensus is lacking. Not surprisingly, social and welfare services fall woefully short of even limited objectives. Another consequence is that postwar urban growth has been chaotic and ecologically disruptive. Finally, the state apparatus in general is poorly-organized, patronage ridden, colonized by corporate interests, and remote from the scrutiny of representative assemblies. Under DC hegemony the practice of *clientela* has resulted in an institutionalized tripartite relationship between government agencies, private interests (e.g. Confindustria, Catholic Action). and the party machine. The DC has also recruited from traditional strata to fill leading civil service posts rather than from the ranks of the technocratic intelligentsia. The entire public sector, then, expresses the contradictions of Italian capitalism as a whole, diminishing the prospects of rationalization under existing conditions.

The PCI's strategy, however, anticipates a set of political institutions that would liberate the rationalizing potential contained by a faltering bourgeois regime. If the Communist program lacks political specificity, it is still more coherent than the programs of other Italian parties. For the immediate future, the PCI is preoccupied with the crisis—above all with overcoming the "marginalization" of the Italian economy within global capitalism. Initial measures are viewed as organically linked to socialist objectives in that they would lay the groundwork for the transition. The dynamic element throughout is the state, beginning with the bourgeois democratic state through which the PCI strives to introduce "elements of socialism"[28] within a gradually expanding public sector. At the same time, this reconstituted political sphere would combine centralized direction with local initiative, decentralization, and a "mixed" economy involving small-scale private enterprise as a way of avoiding *"dirigismo"* (bureaucratic centralism) of the Soviet model.[29]

Since the existing capitalist state is too fragmented and immobile, too plagued with "sectoralism" and inefficiency to promote rationalization, the only solution would be a transitional state that could introduce "global" planning and coordination. A PCI-dominated state would stimulate institutional "renewal" and begin to constitute what Ingrao calls the "protagonist of the masses."[30] It would possesss authority to break down obstacles to social transformation (parochialism, monopoly power, the bureaucracy, interest-group politics[31]) and counter the "anarchic character of capitalism."[32]

The first priority for resolving what the PCI refers to as the "crisis of institutions" is the dismantling of DC control over the public sphere—starting with the complete revamping of the civil service and public management. The second priority is a system of "democratic planning" that would mobilize Italy's economic resources through a coordinated program, with the state initiating "a series of industry-wide plans that give a new orientation to investment and at the same time prepare new market outlets" and social priorities.[33] How such a plan would operate has yet to be specified in PCI programs. Clearly, however, democratic planning would require more state-directed scientific and technological research—and hence educational modernization—than now exists; for example, the PCI has been calling for new research centers and for a more standardized and production-related university curriculum. It would also require firm ministerial control over the state-holding sector and complete reorganization of the state apparatus in order to streamline decision-making. What makes this more democratic than, say, traditionat capitalist or Soviet planning is greater working-class participation (through trade-union "co-management" within the state), accountability to parliament, and stronger local and regional bodies.* For the model to succeed, however, monopoly power—and class domination of the state in general—must be broken, but the PCI leadership remains vague about how this will be accomplished.

PCI-directed rationalization would also engineer the transition from private to social modes of consumption. Whereas the "Fiat model"

---

*Berlinguer and other PCI leaders also distinguish their approach to planning from the social democratic one, but on the basis of criteria outlined here the contrast seems negligible. See Berlinguer, *La grande avanzata communista* (Roma: Sarini, 1976), pp. 21-23 and 96-97.

produces for both exports and personal commodities, the PCI model would utilize the state to fulfill social needs like health care, public transportation, agriculture, low-cost subsidized housing, education, and energy development. This would be no mere recycling of the "welfare state" which depends mainly upon capital transfers from one sector to another; it means creating an entirely new *infrastructure* of investment and consumption that goes beyond the simple reallocation of resources. The shift to social consumption, moreover, demands a complete redefinition of working-class politics, away from pitting the claims of one sector against the total economy and society. For the long run, this means abandoning "corporative-economistic tendencies" and the wage demand-consumerism syndrome that feeds inflation, dissipates resources, and encourages privatized social relations.[34] For the short run, it means a "politics of austerity" that requires workers to restrict their demands to help restabilize the Italian economy.[35]

The PCI's "austerity with a socialist face" would presumably differ from the capitalist stratagem of imposing labor restraints on behalf of a fictitious "common good." First, it would be tied to a general program of economic planning and social investment that looks to the future interests of the working class. Second, in return for supporting austerity measures, the major leftist trade union organization—the Italian General Confederation of Labor (CGIL)—can expect greater managerial representation within state-operated industries. Third, austerity is seen as part of the PCI's overall attack on privatized consumerism as an impediment to social transformation.[36]

Perhaps the most urgent priority of rationalized state intervention is reversing Italy's chronic uneven development, starting with agricultural modernization. The PCI plan would break the extreme subordination of the countryside to urban centers; through new "public instruments" and "combined technologies," the agricultural and industrial sectors could be integrated for the first time, within a system of "agro-industrial production" designed to increase farming efficiency and transform social relations in the less-developed regions.[37] This would involve a massive program of capital investment in the *mezzogiorno* (with possible assistance from the European Investment Bank) that, among other things, could generate a proletarianized work force. Traditional patterns—for example the fragmented, labor-intensive system of land tenure typical of what the PCI calls the "anarchism of rural markets"—would gradually give way to larger, more mechanized operations. The PCI's strategy of democratization would logically flow out of this process.[38]

THE UNIQUENESS OF PCI strategy has not discouraged other Eurocommunist parties from looking to it as a model. On the contrary, it is sometimes viewed as an "advanced" perspective that maturing Communist parties are expected to adopt sooner or later. What is interesting about the Eurocommunist vision is its attempt to rally the best traditions of bourgeois democracy against the authoritarian features of rationalization. It is a strategy suitable to a relatively stable pluralist democracy where revolutionary goals seem remote. When viewed as a methodology of socialist transformation, however, its limitations and contradictions become apparent.

An initial problem is that, whatever its contrasts with Leninism and social democracy, Eurocommunism relies on many of the same statist premises: the state becomes the primary locus of political initiative, legitimation, and economic development. Of course its statism is moderated by strong democratizating impulses, but not enough to counteract the logic of bureaucratization. Statism is one outgrowth of rationalization, in both production and state authority. Beneath their ideologies, the Eurocommunist parties embrace programs that are in some ways compatible with the development of a progressive state capitalism. This is no incidental phenomenon, but rather the function of deeper theoretical and strategic postulates (that will be spelled out later).

The triumph of rationalization under Eurocommunist hegemony, if it is not aborted by a Chilean-style coup, economic collapse, or foreign intervention, would thus impede rèvolutionary goals at the very moment "Marxist" governments were coming to power. To the extent that Eurocommunist parties fail to utilize their newly-won legitimacy to at least begin the assault against the social division of labor, the struggle for revolutionary alternatives can more credibly be undermined as disruptive and utopian.[39] Under these conditions, Eurocommunism eventually creates a new basis of legitimation and accumulation as it sweeps away the "archaic" features of Mediterranean capitalism.

A NEW SYSTEM OF LEGITIMATION?

FUTURE EUROCOMMUNIST advances will probably raise the conflict between democratization and rationalization to new levels. In situating the analysis within this conflict, the narrowing of the critique to one of two extremes—leadership motives or determination of social forces—is avoided. There exists in Eurocommunism a dialectical rellationship between ideological and material factors: theory and strategy shape political involvements, while social conditions and organizational commitments in turn influence strategic choices. The process of rationalization, once set in motion, has anti-democratic consequences not fully anticipated in Eurocommunist theory. Yet the theory itself, which accepts an instrumentalist concept of the transition at the outset, ends up restricting the content of democracy. It is a fallacy, therefore, to explain the moderating tendencies of Eurocommunism as simply the opportunist betrayal by "revisionist" leaderships or, conversely, as a shrewd tactical ploy to deceive class enemies before the late unveiling of a full-blown revolutionary essence. Equally short-sighted is the analysis which sees modernization as a process that universally engulfs Marxist parties in late capitalism.

Eurocommunist politics reflects a very mixed and quite volatile situation. On the positive side, the electoral gains of leftist parties stem from a popular radicalization that has deep roots in the present structural crisis. In the context of a decaying and partially-delegitimized capitalism, Eurocommunism is today posing new challenges, pressing for extensive social reforms, and mobilizing new sectors of the working class into the political arena. Future leftist governments in the Mediterranean will no doubt accelerate this process; under some conditions, they might even help to intensify class conflict as new contradictions unfold. On the negative side, insofar as revolutionary change means ongoing mass struggles against the bourgeois social division of labor—i.e., against *all* forms of domination (including bureaucracy and patriarchy), against the exploitative and alienating features of the entire production apparatus— then the Eurocommunist parties clearly have no revolutionary strategy or program. They appear (potentially) as twofold phenomena—first, as rationalizing agencies that legitimate a rebuilt state bureaucracy on "socialist" foundations and, secondly, as institutionalized oppositions that expand political inputs while at the same time *reducing* the public sphere by narrowing the content of those inputs.

The legitimation crisis of Mediterranean capitalism is the outgrowth of severe strains in the international capitalist economy; yet the *specific* features of this crisis are deeply embedded in the particular traditions of France, Italy, and Spain. These features include the absence of any *efficient* directive or planning mechanism for mobilizing resources and managing economic crises, the failure of public services to meet popular needs and demands, and the void left by the erosion of traditional social relations and belief systems, whih has not been filled by any new ideological system. In short, these are societies that have not completed the transition from liberal to organized state capitalism.

Given this situation, Eurocommunist strategies could produce the sort of structural and ideological transformations that might facilitate the transition to a more rationalized bourgeois order. A bureaucratized state, grounded in a more refined division of labor, would in such a case supersede the most "inefficient" elements of both commodity production and pluralist democracy (overcoming the "anarchy" of both the market and the political arena).

Functioning as a "collective capitalist," it would also require new legitimating ideologies,[40] since traditional supports are less and less binding. Moreover, since the authoritarian tendencies of the modern bourgeoisie belie its claim to "democracy," mostly what remains of liberalism is the sanctity of private property; but this is an impossibly narrow base on which to build ideological consensus, the more so in a period of mass radicalization. Here too Eurocommunist parties, with their working-class strength, might well become the center of a revitalized system of hegemony. If so, it would probably take two forms. One would be technological rationality, with its appeal to what is progressive and "rational": scientific and technological progress, the power of knowledge and expertise, administrative efficiency, economic growth. The other would be the democratic mystique of "Marxism" or "socialism," which promises to infuse pluralist forms with radical social content and would legitimate rationalization in terms of the common good. The clash between rationalization and democratization in social reality does not *necessarily* undermine this complementary dualism, since the Eurocommunist ideology of democratic transformation is sufficiently ambiguous and future-oriented.*

Technological rationality expresses the interlocking development of industrialization, science, bureaucracy, and the state in advanced capitalism. Its legitimating virtue derives from the fact that it "represents" progress through expertise and innovative methods; to oppose it is to resist the logic of growth and productivity, which presumably confers benefits on society as a whole. It also embodies an anonymous power of technique, which infuses social and political processes with a transcedent "classless" character—a requisite component in the hegemony of organized capitalist state, as Poulantzas notes.[41] For Marxist parties and regimes, it has historically reinforced the positivist assumption that socialism can simply inherit the material achievements of capitalism.[42]

Beneath this "neutrality" of science and technology, however, are sophisticated social control dynamics through which the division of labor is reproduced. This occurs by justifying the privileged role of a technocratic intelligentsia and a professionalized political-bureaucratic elite, whose power in crucial spheres—economic planning, social services, the military, education, health care—relies on the claim to specialized, "non-partisan" knowledge; by failing to challenge the hierarchical and fragmented ensemble of production relations that, insofar as it appears natural, subjects the working class to an ideology of managerial

---

*At present, of all the Eurocommunist parties only the PCI has succeeded in legitimating itself among broad social groups (notably the middle strata) outside of the industrial proletariat. The PCI's firm commitment to rationalization helps to explain this success.

domination that makes rational the conditions of alienated labor; and by accepting the rational-legal ethos in both its formal democratic and bureaucratic manifestations, thereby encouraging a narrow institutional politics that blurs class and power divisions and favors depoliticization. What this could mean, given Eurocommunist hegemony, is a shrinking of the public sphere—i.e., a narrowing of the ideological framework within which class conflict is carried out[43]—precisely the opposite of what structural reformism presents as the basis of its strategy. This is not to argue that technological rationality under such conditions will lead to Soviet-style bureaucratic centralism or that the democratic road contains no participatory thrust whatsoever. What in fact distinguishes the Eurocommunist from the Soviet model, as I have suggested, is the actuality of *conflict* between the process of rationalization and the aim of democratization—a conflict that in the USSR was long ago "resolved" by the party-state. But so long as the Eurocommunist parties do not systematically confront the social division of labor, this conflict will be restricted mainly to the boundaries of parliamentary democracy.*

RATIONALIZATION AND THE NEW MIDDLE STRATA

IF EUROCOMMUNIST theory is understood as a radicalization of bourgeois ideology, its strong reliance upon the state can be viewed as the logical extension of industrial development. For an expanded and organized state has already taken on qualitatively new tasks: nationalization of large enterprises, planning, fiscal and monetary management, public services, research and development on the *accumulation* side; and social welfare, influence over education and culture, institutionalization of class conflict, and "patriotic" mobilization on the *legitimation* side. Since the Mediterranean bourgeoisie (the French partially excepted) has not effectively pursued these tasks, the Eurocommunists—in alliance with Socialists or other left-center parties—would be in a favorable position to implement their own modernizing strategies in a context of uneven development. As the imperatives of accumulation and legitimation merge within the directive state, technological rationality emerges as a binding ideology that unifies the two realms and supplies a "global"

---

*This argument stops short of Marcuse's more extreme formulation, which holds that technological rationality inevitably narrows politics to questions of technique, empties the democratic process of all content, and renders oppositional tendencies powerless. See *One Dimensional Man*, pp. 156-65.

dimension.* The state becomes the guiding cohesive structure, the repository of ideological hegemony, penetrating and transforming the larger society in new ways.** As such, it constitutes the terrain on which new universalizing objectives (socialism, democratization, rational planning) are advanced.

Eurocommunism accordingly assigns a critical strategic role to the new middle strata of technicians, professionals, intellectuals, service and public sector workers. With varying emphases and degrees of success, the PCI, PCF and PCE are trying to incorporate these strata into a "social bloc" that, in a new system of governance, would perform both technical and ideological tasks. This shift from an essentially proletarian outlook involves a twofold logic. First, the growing numerical and institutional strength of the new middle strata—owing to the importance of mental labor in a rationalizing capitalism—alters the conditions of electoral mobilization. As the traditional working class-peasantry alliance fades with advanced industrialization, Marxist parties that ignore the middle strata consign themselves to isolation. Secondly, because the state takes on a more complex, specialized, and ideological character, efforts to transform capitalism will require the contributions of social groups with special knowledge and skills. Here the new middle strata emerges as the vital social link between the existing state apparatus and the Euro-communist commitment to new modes of legitimation. And this constituency represents a larger proportion of the membership and mass base of the parties with each passing year.***

*This amends the thesis of Claus Offe, Habermas, and others, who contend that in late capitalism the imperatives of accumulation and legitimation are in conflict, generating new contradictions. Such conflict exists only where the "technical" needs of accumulation oppose the "democratic" norms of legitimation; but to the extent that technological rationality supplies the legitimacy requirements of a rationalized industrial order, the antagonism tends to disappear. Of course whether it would disappear entirely in a Eurocommunist-dominated system is problematic, given a deeper commitment to democratization than in the advanced capitalist and Soviet-type bureaucratic centralist systems.

**In this respect Weber's theory of legitimacy as rooted in the bureaucratic structures of modern "rational-legal" states is more helpful than Gramsci's concept of hegemony based upon pre-industrial "survivals" typical of the transitional period between early and late capitalism. Hence most of Gramsci's attention focused on the role of Catholicism, liberalism, and unique cultural traditions in Italy and elsewhere; one exception was his essay "Americanism and Fordism," although even it does not analyze the state directly.

***This increase has been most dramatic in the PCI, where the percentage of middle strata membership (defined as white collar workers, teachers, and professionals) in the party has grown from less than 10% in 1950 to nearly 25% in 1978.

Togliatti recognized the strategic importance of the *ceti medi* as part of a potential anti-monopoly alliance as early as the mid-1930s, and the PCI integrated this into its theory of structural reforms by the late 1940s. While the PCI conceded that the middle strata had developed little socialist consciousness, the party's viewpoint was that their location between the bourgeoisie and the working class made them amenable to radicalizing swings, especially during crises, when their demand for social reforms and job autonomy would ally them with the working class. This sensitivity—linked to Togliatti's fascination with the problem of ideological hegemony—is one reason for the PCI's postwar electoral successes and its durable local coalitions with the Socialists.[44] Meanwhile, only with their departure from Leninism did the French and Spanish parties seriously look toward the middle strata—the PCF after a long period of orthodox attachment to the industrial proletariat, the PCE after four decades of underground confrontation with fascism. In the case of the PCF, this reorientation was facilitated by the May Events of 1968, which revealed the explosive radicalizing force of professionals, technicians, intellectuals, and students.[45] In the case of the PCE, it reflected the party's greater isolation and desperate need for new allies in the struggle to establish pluralist democracy.* For Eurocommunism in general, appeals to the new middle strata are logically bound up with the goals of rationalization. Change within the PCF, however, is taking place slowly and ambivalently because of strong workerist tendencies in its ranks; the PCI and PCE, in contrast, have actually broadened their definition of "social bloc" to include certain "progressive" sectors of the bourgeoisie.[46]

To the extent that the new middle strata are pivotal, their contribution to a modernizing and socially-directed Eurocommunism would be to form an expanded technocratic intelligentsia that would carry out technical (accumulation) and ideological (legitimating) functions during the transition to a new system of rule. A growing force within the party itself, they could provide organizational cohesion, facilitate relations between the party and the state, and articulate the normative rationale for modernization.[47] While no longer dependent upon monopoly capital, the middle strata would thus help to extend the social division

---

*The PCE now receives roughly 15% of the vote in national elections. Carrillo's strategy is to construct a broad "social bloc" around a general democratic platform that could crystallize leftist opposition and transform it from an anti-fascist into an anti-capitalist formation. Yet the alliance Carrillo has in mind is, for good tactical reasons, quite amorphous and all-inclusive, with the middle strata assigned no theoretically specific role in socialist transformation.

of labor by putting their imprint on authority and social relations, work patterns, culture, and lifestyles. There is little in either the theory or the programs of Eurocommunist parties that explicitly challenges this division of labor.

The conflict between this and the aims of democratization is obvious enough. The institutionalization of the separation between mental and physical work in both production and administration would simply extend the realm of technocratic domination over the working class and others subjected to bureaucratic regimen.[48] To what extent any Eurocommunist party could impose such organizational control is unclear, particularly where governing coalitions are involved. In any case, the possibility that a broad leftist formation will emerge as the locus of technocratic hegemony and bureaucratic control of production cannot be dismissed.[49] Some critics of the PCI have suggested that the party is well along the road to becoming a "new bourgeoisie."[50] For this to occur, however, the Eurocommunists will have to resolve how—within the matrix of rationalization—*both* the middle strata and working class can be effectively represented within the same party. In the PCI, where the middle strata presence is strongest, disruptive internal strains have already surfaced—for example, in the widespread demonstrations against "austerity" and the "historic compromise."* The chronic antagonism between middle strata and industrial workers, exacerbated by economic crisis, produces tensions paralleling those of the often ill-fated peasantry-proletariat alliances in the past. If the middle strata have been moving leftward in recent years, their radicalization is both contradictory and limited. On the one hand, large sectors of intellectuals, professionals, and students have been mobilized or at least touched by the social and cultural struggles of the new left; on the other hand, many technicians, scientists, and civil servants—the more narrowly technocratic groups—have come to oppose capitalism, but their "socialist" leanings are motivated by the desire for job or professional autonomy, social reform, and rational planning within a bureaucratic framework. This latter sector is the one most closely identified with Eurocommunist politics, and it is also most concerned with expanding social production and democratizing the state under an umbrella of institutional stability. A clash between the interests of this stratum and sectoral working-class demands

---

*The weakness of the Italian Socialists relative to the PCI helps to account for the latter's strong presence within the middle strata, since in postwar Western Europe the Socialists have been the party most closely linked to this constituency. In France, where the political balance is more even, and in Spain, where at the moment the PCE is overwhelmed by a much larger "catch-all" Socialist party (the PSOE), the dilemmas of building middle strata support are obvious. In these cases, alliance strategy might assume an even more "frontist" character if Eurocommunist strategy is to succeed.

for higher wages and better workplace conditions, especially if the economic crisis intensifies, would seem hard to avoid. Yet the Euro-communist program for a revitalized public infrastructure, new social services, and strengthened trade unionism might offset this antagonism and allow for a political merging of new middle strata and industrial workers.

Such a merging, however, would not change the subordinate position of the working class in the social division of labor; on the contrary, it would simply legitimate it in an even more rationalized form. For the effects of rationalization, as Gramsci foresaw, would be an increasingly administered and disciplined production apparatus that would impose new obstacles to working-class solidarity and self-activity, while reinforcing managerial-technocratic hegemony within a more comprehensive network of planning and control—whatever the advances in the material standard of living.

The Eurocommunist parties to date have not really taken up this problem or confronted its depoliticizing effects. Worker militancy is widespread, but often it is directed *against* the parties and unions. In France and Italy, a long period of electoral politics has set in motion forces dividing parties and unions, politics and economics, and elections and contract struggles around the themes of labor "autonomy" and "incompatibility" between party and union leadership roles. The task of achieving general reforms in the political sphere is viewed as the responsibility of the PCF and the PCI, while the major leftist unions (the CGT in France, the CGIL in Italy) utilize their growing independence to push for contractual bargaining at both plant and industry-wide levels premised upon securing wage increases tied to maximizing output and efficiency.[51] This separation, while clearly more appropriate to a modernizing strategy than the old Leninist "trans-mission belt" concept, nonetheless tends to distance the party from the workers. On the one side, the parties have a more limited presence at the workplace; they approach the workers primarily as *voters*, supplying legislative reforms, some local social services, and the promise of fundamental "renewal" in exchange for electoral support. On the other side, the unions have built solid ties with workers at the workplace but the union leadership is generally bureaucratic and economistic. What the unions offer is a structure that can defend workers' interests, negotiate better contracts (at least in stable times), and, more recently, secure limited managerial power through "co-management" within the public sector. What it expects from the workers in return, however, is containment of militancy and compliance with norms of productivity and discipline—the stance most compatible with an emerging tripartite bargaining relationship among the state, large industry, and trade unions. In periods of economic downturn, austerity measures are also emphasized purportedly to control inflation, stimulate private investment, and encourage public investment. Whether the Eurocommunists in power could impose austerity on whatever basis, given the history of combative working-class movements in the Mediterranean, remains to be seen.[52] For the present, however, neither the parties nor the trade unions envisage a democratization of the workplace or a struggle for workers' self-management.

THE LIMITS OF DEMOCRATIC TRANSFORMATION

THIS BRINGS US TO the role of electoral politics—and the process of institutionalization—in limiting and distorting the Eurocommunist pursuit of democratization. The strategy of the Italian and French parties has largely centered around parliament, local government, and trade unions. In these arenas some notable successes have been achieved, but not without encountering many of the same difficulties experienced by classical social democracy. After more than four decades of parliamentarism, in fact, it would be miraculous if the parties had avoided stable attachments to the dominant political structures—and indeed the party programs and leadership styles more and more reflect this attachment, in varying degrees. With institutionalization, the affirmation of a Marxist identity by the party leaderships becomes increasingly abstract as the narrowing of the public sphere tends to close off revolutionary alternatives (at least for the parties involved).

This predicament can be partly traced back to the statist viewpoint that the existing apparatus of power, once purged of bourgeois control by working-class parties, constitutes the primary framework of political struggle. The Eurocommunist version of democratization thus comes down to a progressive reconstitution of the state, where the established political instruments are in effect turned around at the summit and given new social priorities and new ideological content. It would be unfair to criticize Eurocommunism, as some have done, for simply wanting to take over the leading positions of state bureaucracy;[53] its objective is to *restructure* the bourgeois state. A more telling critique is its virtual muteness concerning new forms of political life (e.g., workplace and neighborhood councils) that could lay the basis of a non-authoritarian revolutionary state. The result is that while the scope of mass participation broadens within "advanced" pluralist democracy, statism intercepts this transformation short of *socialist* democracy. This is hardly surprising, since the latter requires a gradual *disintegration* of the bourgeois state, whereas the Eurocommunist model stresses internal democratization. The parties no doubt fear that proliferation of grassroots structures would lead to chaos and erode the infrastructure necessary for rationalization, perceiving that centralized authority is more compatible with planning, labor discipline, and routinized decision making.* The logic here once again favors the persistence of bourgeois authority relations and institutional politics over dual power struggles that would lead to fundamentally shifting class and social relations.

Here it is necessary to confront what Lenin called the "illusion of bourgeois democracy." The Eurocommunist conception of democracy— universal suffrage, civil and political freedoms, a multi-party system, broadened mass representation, etc.—is, despite its "advanced" character, still confined to pluralist boundaries; having rejected Leninist centralism, it so far has failed to elaborate a socialist democracy. Aside from isolated attempts within the PCI and PCE,[54] party theorists have produced few critiques of representative democracy (or of bureaucracy) and even fewer efforts to develop revolutionary principles of collective participation. To the extent that democratization does not transcend pluralism and establish a basis in grassroots structures and popular movements, it is bound to fall back on the most indirect and corporativist types of representation. In this case, political action is likely to become increasingly divorced from its social context, thus yielding to what Claudin describes as "fatalistic gradualism."[55]

Since parliaments are arenas in which decisions are often distorted by the extraparliamentary power of capital, the state bureaucracy, and the military, leftist parties will find it difficult to achieve enough hegemony through electoralism to enforce social programs that could facilitate socialist transformation.[56] Of course pluralist structures cannot be dismissed as *strictly* mechanisms of bourgeois domination; their history is too complex, especially in countries like Italy and Spain where mass intervention against fascism revived them and where they remain important spheres of contestation. Still, formal democracy is a complex system of rules and procedures that generally works against rapid or fundamental change and enforces ruling class interests by obscuring power relations beneath the myth of popular sovereignty and "balancing of interests." It is compatible with mass participation and social reform (up to a certain point) but it simultaneously creates a fragmented and

---

*The PCF is usually viewed as more centralist and statist than the PCI or PCE— and this is true, especially where internal party structure is concerned. Still, the generalizations insofar as they concern the role of the state in the transition remain applicable. Where the PCI is willing, for example, to encourage private and local initiatives in various areas of the economy, it does not look upon this initiative as a catalyst of socialist transformation.

depoliticized public sphere that encourages class collaboration. As Offe notes: "The pluralistic system of organized interests excludes from the process concerned with consensus formation all articulations of demands that are *general* in nature and not associated with any status group."[57] Pluralist fragmentation thus impedes class-based movements and programs concerned with systemic transformation, forcing Marxist parties in parliament to accept a diffuse, minimalist politics.

While in principle electoral politics can be combined with workplace and community forms of popular struggle, the tension between the two poles has historically been resolved in favor of one or the other— electoralism or councillism. When strategies are built almost primarily around the former, as in the case of Eurocommunism, that is where the bulk of organizational energies inevitably goes; in time, institutionalization strengthens this commitment and limits the scope of popular mobilization.[58] This partial and one-sided emphasis favors an alliance politics concerned mainly with elite agreements and party coalitions. For the PCI, which has recently reformulated the "social bloc" in essentially frontist terms, this has opened up new power opportunities that, however, can only be actualized through a merging of leaderships (the PCI, Christian Democrats, and Socialists) suggested by the "historic compromise."* The realization of Eurocommunist power objectives would in some way perhaps further detach politics from social life—a dynamic that seems to grow out of electoralism.[59]

There remains the Eurocommunist vision of "decentralization"— the dispersing of power to local and regional governments as a means of revitalizing mass participation. So far, only the PCI has really been able to establish a strong presence in grassroots administrative politics; its foothold in municipal, provincial, communal and regional governments throughout Italy is vast. Yet PCI development in this sphere too has been shaped by institutionalization, with all the flourishes of local machine politics. On the one hand are the symbiotic ties with established interests (industrial firms, banks, the Church) that build smooth administration; on the other, there are the clientele networks that in some areas are regarded with envy by even the Christian Democrats. The PCI's clientelism operates according to conventional machine principles: the

---

*The convergence of the PCI and DC is particularly significant, since the last attempt to construct a frontist government collapsed in 1947 with the onset of the cold war and was followed by 30 years of mutual hostility. For Italy, this could signal the return to a politics of *trasformismo*, where elite coalitions strive for a centrist solution to general societal crisis and polarization. See Giuseppe Di Palma. *Surviving Without Governing: Italian Parties in Parliament* (Berkeley: University of California Press, 1977), conclusion.

exchange of jobs, services, and favors for votes and organizational support.[60] While in this sense close to the masses, the PCI's political activity tends to follow a limited give-and-take of interests that is justified by abstract ideological symbols, in such a context, the local party leadership rarely acts to stimulate popular mobilization.[61] Local power conquests alone, while they might give the appearance of grassroots political initiative, cannot within the present Eurocommunist strategy be expected to fundamentally alter the nature of authority relations.

The potential role of Eurocommunist parties as institutionalized forces that could legitimate new systems of domination suggests a basic theoretical flaw in the democratic road: the very *concept* of democratization is formulated in pluralist terms.* Above all, it downplays or ignores the place of collective organs of struggle—workers' and neighborhood councils, action committees, grassroots movements of feminists, students, unemployed, etc.—in shaping democratic transformation. As popular forms of contestation, they could more effectively subvert the logic of statism insofar as they can prefigure a socialist democracy that requires more than the internal reconstruction of the bourgeois state. The task here is one of developing a synthesis of dual power structures and the most advanced features of parliamentary democracy, rather than simply jettisoning the latter in favor of an unmediated direct democracy However this is resolved, democratization will ultimately depend upon the growth of new centers of state life, upon a qualitatively different relationship between political structures and mass activity. Since the Eurocommunist approach has not really confronted this problem directly, it runs the risk of divorcing politics from the totality of bourgeois authority and social relations and thus sidestepping the major bureaucratic impediments to democratization.

The two most turbulent waves of revolutionary upheaval in postwar Western Europe—the anti-fascist struggles between 1943 and 1947, the peak years of the new left between 1968 and 1971—gave birth to vigorous dual power movements (notably in France and Italy) in workplaces, schools, the military, and the communities. The attitude of the Communist parties toward these movements has varied from ambivalence to contempt. In the end, the parties' commitment to electoralism and rationalization has never been reconciled with struggles for workers'

*This critique is close to Althusser's attack on the PCF's turn from Leninism at the 22nd Congress, except that in posing the choice between the dictatorship of the proletariat and pluralist democracy Althusser never really addresses the issue in terms of the social division of labor. See "The Historic Significance of the 22nd Congress," in Balibar, *Dictatorship*, pp. 204-207. Mandel's critique, in *From Stalinism to Eurocommunism* (pp. 164-177), is more attuned to this problem but his analysis is flawed by a mechanistic view of power.

control and self-management. Even where a merger of party and local forms did evolve (as with the PCI's presence in the *Consigli di Gestione,* or management councils, that grew out of the Committees of National Liberation during the Resistance), it dissolved once the party leadership turned its energies toward electoral and trade union politics. The local forms either disintegrated or were eventually absorbed by bureaucratic structures. Since the late 1960s, when the May Events in France triggered a crisis within the Communist parties, the PCF and PCI have mounted offensives against the extraparliamentary left. Today, they dismiss the organized revolutionary left as "adventurist" and "Stalinist" and characterize the popular or "emergent" movements of unemployed, students, women, and workers as "spontaneist" and "utopian." The latter groups, which are particularly strong in both Italy and Spain and reflect one dimension of the crisis, produce ambivalence within the party leaderships, which strive to mobilize this political energy behind their own strategic priorities.* The PCE, on the other hand, is a partial exception to this tendency; it has approached popular struggles in Spain, where issues of workers' control and organizational autonomy are salient, with flexibility and in some cases critical support. This is so for several reasons: the PCE's smaller size and relative lack of institutionalization; the strength of the anarchist and syndicalist traditions in Spain; the role of regional movements for national autonomy; and the continuing importance of broad anti-fascist politics. The PCE also has less political attachment to the middle strata at least for the time-being than either the PCI or PCF. Since the membership and electoral support of the latter parties includes substantial middle strata representation, any alliance that would incorporate the goals and styles of the emergent groups is unthinkable—the political methods are too contrasting, the approaches to bureaucracy, technology, and culture too conflicting.

The outer limits of democratization are, finally, imposed by bureaucratic processes *within* the parties and their supporting organizations. Insensitivity to the themes of socialist democracy is conditioned as much by survivals of Leninist democratic centralism as by general strategic priorities and institutional commitments. The question is: how can a political organization that is internally authoritarian struggle effectively for democracy in the society as a whole? Interestingly enough,

---

*Thus while Eurocommunism does actually identify with many objectives advanced by these movements (e.g., feminism, ecological and educational reform, even "self-management"), such identification is generally accompanied by rejection of the groups themselves. Party claims must therefore be viewed with skepticism.

recent Eurocommunist declarations concerning the democratic road say little about abandoning the hierarchical premises of democratic centralism: while a certain amount of open discussion is permitted, especially in the PCI, real diversity in the form of competing tendencies and factions is still not tolerated and rigid discipline continues to be enforced within the party organizations. At the same time, the days of monolithic party "unity" are probably numbered, since internal debates at all levels over the question of democratic centralism have been increasingly explosive and overt, notably in the PCE and PCF. A major factor in the decline of Leninist norms is that they clash with the logic of electoral politics and above all with the needs of pluralistic legitimation.

Despite the recent dramatic breaks with Marxist and Leninist orthodoxy, the Eurocommunist parties have in fact inspired relatively little movement toward innovative conceptions of democracy, even if—from time to time—they have chosen to employ a certain rhetoric of "self-management" and "workers' control" borrowed from popular movements that grew out of the 1960s. Given such limits of democratic vision, they may find it more and more difficult to carry out mass mobilization for socialist objectives—although the possibility that such mobilization will be a by-product of mass struggles around party-inspired reforms should not be discounted. Clearly, Eurocommunist successes would improve the living standards of the masses, assuming stable conditions of governance; they would also generate a new system of power in which the state encompasses as much if not more of civil society than it now does. Where the state enhances its domination over the social order, even with an "advanced" pluralist democracy, the transformation of everyday life (including the struggle for new organs of state authority) cannot be carried out. The Eurocommunist strategy of democratization is centered largely in the political/institutional realm, which tends to engulf and distort vital elements of the transition: ideological hegemony, social bloc, self-government.* The content of this process is actually more appropriate to the transition from liberal capitalism to organized state

---

*These Gramscian concepts, along with the whole mystique of Gramsci's Marxism, have been misappropriated by Eurocommunist theorists, beginning with Togliatti. Ideas have been translated into a strategic framework in a way that has destroyed their revolutionary content. For example, Gramsci never saw the formation of social blocs or the struggle for ideologicl hegemony as a process that would be advanced primarily through the structures of bourgeois democracy. On the contrary, he was always emphatically critical of electoralism and trade unionism. His theory of hegemony and counter-hegemonic politics, incorporating as it did a broad attack on the social division of labor within the "war of position," does not appear to be taken seriously by Eurocommunist strategists.

capitalism in which leftist political formations achieve hegemony. Though more rationalized and socially egalitarian, it would nonetheless be a system where class oppression, bureaucracy, and commodity production are perpetuated.

In the final analysis, the Eurocommunist version of the democratic road fails to point toward a radical transformation of social and political life not because it is committed to preserving pluralist democracy, but because it views the transition as a process that passes more or less exclusively through the existing state machinery. If the complex task of building a new ensemble of political forces and social relations is obscured by Leninism, with its scenario of frontal maneuvers *against* the state, it is also distorted by Eurocommunism in its nearly singular preoccupation with an *internal* modification of structures. For contemporary capitalist societies, the main strategic question is not whether to retain or destroy representative institutions but how to broaden the concept of democracy and social transformation to incorporate autonomous centers of dual power so that an overturning of the social division of labor can begin. As Poulantzas has argued, only a synthesis of two levels—a combining of the "transformation of representative democracy with the development of forms of direct, rank-and-file democracy or the movement for self-management"—can counter the authoritarian statism and depoliticization that develop from either extreme.[62]

CONCLUSION: TRANSITION AND CRISIS

REALIZATION OF THE Eurocommunist program in the Mediterranean countries, at least for the immediate future, seems unlikely. For one thing, the balance of political forces is still highly unfavorable; only the PCI has built the necessary momentum to make a serious bid for national power. If the parties hope to achieve political hegemony in the future, they must further legitimate themselves electorally in order to destroy the remaining ideological barriers to political growth and they must extend their organizational presence, parliamentary strength, and clientele networks far beyond what now exists. To accomplish this, however, is also to encourage the logic of institutionalization. In addition, such advances would require an extended period of economic and political stability not only in the Mediterranean, but for European and global capitalism as a whole. The Eurocommunist theory of transition is premised on the concept that socialism must develop out of the very *enlargement* of bourgeois forms of social and political organization. Its prospects rest upon a growing public sector, entrenched liberal traditions, the rise in educational levels and political consciousness of the working class, and the progressive role of the new middle strata.

Structural crisis is still viewed as an inevitable feature of capitalist development, but systemic collapse is more or less ruled out.

The possibility of launching socialist transformation from such a developmental schema at the present time, however, seems no less remote than it was for Bernstein's ill-fated "evolutionary socialism" more than a half-century ago. To the extent that the Eurocommunist model depends upon accelerated economic and technological growth, large increases in public spending, and the capacity of the state to manage crises, it will encounter new obstacles as the contradictions of Mediterranean capitalism intensify.[63] That the crisis might become unmanageable, especially if developed countries like West Germany and the U.S. are immobilized by internal challenges, is easy to imagine. One possible scenario, the European countries, having exhausted most of their natural resources, experience a massive energy crisis that is aggravated by the decision of the OPEC countries to increase oil prices or by a rapid decrease in supplies. The balance of payments deficits in countries like Italy and Spain would dramatically worsen, generating severe inflation and overall economic paralysis that would lead to a sharp decline in investments as well as renewed demands for austerity. The twin outcomes would almost certainly be accentuated political disorder within the ruling class and rising militancy among the masses, with the bourgeoisie moving desperately to recover its increasingly fragile domination. Whether in power or in opposition, the Eurocommunist parties would find their vision of an orderly ascent to power shattered by such a scenario. In government, they would find it impossible to rule effectively (let alone advance socialism) and would be vulnerable to a Chilean-style capitalist counteroffensive; in opposition, they would probably be outflanked on the left and (barring a drastic shift in their strategy) undermined as a credible revolutionary force. In this respect, Rosa Luxemburg's critique of Bernstein is still valid—namely, that far from being more "realistic," the idea of a stable, non-confrontational path to socialism is in actuality quite utopian.[64]

Notes

1. This declaration appeared in *l'Unita*, March 4, 1977 and was reprinted in *The Italian Communists*, January-March 1977.
2. See, for example, *Dialogue on Spain* (London: Lawrence and Wishart, 1976), based on interviews with Regis Debray and Max Gallo, and *Eurocommunism and the State* (London: Lawrence and Wishart, 1977).
3. *Dialogue on Spain*, p. 15. Whether, in terms of the conflict between democratization and rationalization, such a two-stage theory of transition is viable will be discussed later.
4. The first of these pronouncements was the joint PCI-PCF statement in November 1975, an English translation of which appeared in *Socialist Revolution*, No. 29.
5. The most strategically important of Togliatti's essays have been assembled by Luciano Gruppi in the volume *Il Compromesso storico* (Roma: Editori Riuniti, 1977).
6. This post-13th Congress theoretical gestation took place mainly in the pages of the PCI weekly *Rinascita*, where party leaders contributed to a long series of articles, many of which were assembled by various authors and published in book form. The most comprehensive of these volumes, and the one containing Berlinguer's important essays on the "historic compromise," is *Il Compromesso storico*. Others include Luciano Gruppi, *Togliatti e la via italiana al socialismo* (Roma: Editori Riuniti, 1975) and, from a more left position, Pietro Ingrao, *Potere e masse* (Roma: Editori Riuniti, 1977). A brief but illuminating sketch of the historical experiences underlying the PCI's democratic road is Giorgio Napolitano, *Intervista sul PCI* (Bari: Laterza, 1976)—an interview by E.J. Hobsbawm that has been published in English as *The Italian Road to Socialism* (Westport Conn.: Lawrence Hill, 1977).
7. *Dialogue on Spain*, p. 198. In a 1976 interview, Carrillo was even more explicit on this point: "We are ready to get out if we lose elections—just like any other party. When I speak of democracy I mean Western democracy. I consider universal suffrage to be the criterion. I said this in front of Brezhnev. We

want power by force. I am a Spaniard, not a Russian. I certainly don't want to be another Franco but it would be impossible for me to be a Lenin. I believe in the ultimate goal of convergence in ideologies. The West must become more socialist but the East must become more democratic." *New York Times*, August 6, 1976.

8. See Georges Marchais, "Liberty and Socialism" and "In Order to Take Democracy Forward to Socialism, Two Problems are Decisive," in Balibar, *Dictatorship,* especially pp. 161-64 and 184-86. Balibar's defense of traditional Leninism is spelled out in the same volume, in "On the Dictatorship of the Proletariat."

9. An excellent recent PCI elaboration of this is Ingrao's inroduction to *Masse e potere*. See also Ingrao's "Democrazia borghese o stalinismo? No: democrazia di mass," *Rinascita,* February 6, 1976. For the PCE, see Carrillo, *Eurocommunism and the State,* pp. 89-91.

10. Guy Besse, "Reply to Balibar," in Balibar, *Dictatorship,* p. 177.

11. *Eurocommunism and the State,* pp. 101-102. Carrillo defines the "new political formation" as a "confederation of political parties and other forces" that would expand on the basis of growing socialist consensus. *Ibid.,* p. 102.

12. Fernando Claudin's critique of Eurocommunism on this score is valid for the PCF but much less accurate in the more ambiguous and complex cases of the PCE and PCI. See *Eurocommunism and Socialism* (London: New Left Books, 1978) pp. 131-132.

13. The emphasis on ideological hegemony—and the looming presence of Gramsci—is clearly evident throughout Napolitano's *Intervista sul PCI* and in Carrillo's *Eurocommunism and the State,* ch. 3. See also Ingrao, *Masse e potere,* pp. 240-253.

14. Ingrao, *op. cit.* pp. 240-41.

15. *Ibid.* pp. 250-53. This takes up a familiar Togliattian theme—the gradual modification of structures—and carries it one step further by arguing that the party itself should never be an exclusive agency of hegemony. Of all PCI theorists, Ingrao's views on the transition are probably the most carefully developed.

16. Carrillo, *Eurocommunism,* pp. 27-28. Carrillo stresses that as the bourgeois state expands in scope and functions it becomes a major locus of contradictions in late capitalism. However, he never really develops this point.

17. *Ibid.* p. 28. It is necessary to distinguish here between *chronic,* ongoing crises that are endemic to capitalism—basic contradictions—and *catastrophic* crises of the sort that might lead to systemic collapse. The Eurocommunists recognize the first—indeed premise their strategy on it—but insist that global capitalism (in the absence of war) is strong enough to contain the latter. The theoretical outlook of orthodox Marxism and traditional social democracy was that normal crises, manifest in the falling rate of profit, immiseration of the proletariat, conflict between the forces and social relations of production, would gradually build toward cataclysmic crises and immobilize the capitalist economy.

18. The "modernizing" compulsion of Leninism, and its impact on Soviet development, is insightfully analyzed by Fred and Lou Jean Fleron, "Administrative Theory as Repressive Political Theory: the Communist Ecperience," *Telos,* Summer 1972. This is not to argue that *every* Marxist current is oblivious to this critique or has failed to emphasize the anti-authoritarian, anti-statist side of the transition. Two notable exceptions were the European council movements and Chinese Communism; however, the council legacy never outgrew its marginal status within the left while Maoism, at least since the early 1970s, has increasingly yielded to the pressures of bureaucratic centralism.

19. For a critique of Marxist (and especially Communist) approaches to science and technology, see Fred Fleron, ed., *Technology and Communist Culture* (New York: Praeger, 1977).

20. Jurgen Habermas, *Legitimation Crisis* (Boston: 1973), pp. 37 and 75-78.

21. Antonio Gramsci, "Fordism and Americanism," in Quintin Hoare and Geoffrey Nowell-Smith, eds. *Selections from the Prison Notebooks* (London: Lawrence and Wishart, 1971), p. 279.

22. *Ibid.* p. 312.

23. The systemic necessity of social investment for capitalist accumulation *and* legitimation, within the framework of rationalization, needs to be more extensively analyzed. For a general treatment of this problem, see Larry Hirschhorn, "The Political Economy of Social Service Rationalization," *Contemporary Crises* 2, 1978.

24. On the hegemonic role of technological rationality in late capitalism, the most comprehensive analysis is still Herbert Marcuse's *One Dimensional Man* (Boston: Beacon Press, 1964). For a comparative perspective, see William Leiss, "Technology and Instrumental Rationality in Capitalism and Socialism," in Fleron, *Technology and Communist Culture.*

25. The statist component of rationalization is not the function of any internal or autonomous logic of technique, as theorists like Ellul have argued. It is rather one aspect of the capitalist imperatives of accumulation, legitimation, and domination—technique itself being only one part of the totality. For Ellul's perspective, see *The Technological Society* (New York: Vintage, 1964), pp. 133-34; 194; 207-09; 280-88. An antidote to this outlook, and one that avoids the other extreme of reducing the problem of rationalization to its class dimension, is Henry Jacoby, *The Bureaucratization of the World* (Berkeley: University of California Press, 1973), pp. 61-110 and 147-168.

26. Samir Amin stresses this point in "Toward a Structural Crisis of World Capitalism," *Socialist Revolution* No. 23, pp. 33-37. Amin notes that "The failure of social democratic integration makes southern Europe a weak link in the present crisis. Its class alliances limit the competitiveness of its capital with respect to the northern countries, and an attempt to make the working class bear the burden of crisis risks creating an explosive situation in those countries with a revolutionary tradition." (p. 35)

27. Kevin Allen and Andrew Stevenson, *An Introduction to the Italian Economy* (London: Martin Robertson, 1974), pp. 250-55.

28. This conceptualization seems to be increasingly accepted within the PCI leadership. See Napolitano, *Intervista,* p. 49.

29. Ingrao, *Masse e potere,* p. 377.

30. Ingrao, p. 376.

31. Ingrao, p. 40.

32. Napolitano, p. 51

33. "The Political Resolution approved by the XIV National Congress of the PCI," *The Italian Communists*, March-May, 1975, p. 133.

34. Napolitano, *Intervista,* pp. 98-99.

35. Berlinguer, *Austerita occasione per trasformare l'Italia* (Roma: Editori Riuniti, 1977), pp. 47-52. Also Achille Occhetto, "Austerita, a sviluppo della democrazia," *Rinascita,* June 17, 1977.

36. Berlinguer, *Austerita,* p. 18.

37. Ingrao, *Masse e potere,* pp. 27-29. Also Occhetto, *op.cit.*

38. Andre Gorz argues this point in connection with the overall thrust of European Communist economic programs. See "Technology, Technicians, and

Class Struggle," in Gorz, ed., *The Social Division of Labor* (Atlantic Highlands, N.J., The Humanities Press, 1976), p. 162.

40. Habermas, *Legitimation Crisis,* pp. 43-46. Also Renate Mayntz, "Legitimacy and the Directive Capacity of the Political System," in Leon Lindberg, et. al. eds., *Stress and Contradiction in Modern Capitalism* (Lexington Mass.: D.C. Heath, 1975).

41. Nicos Poulantzas, *Political Power and Social Classes* (London: New Left Books, 1973), p. 218.

42. The classical and still unsurpassed analysis of this phenomenon, which seems even more valid today, is Herbert Marcuse's *Soviet Marxism* (New York: Vintage, 1957), especially chapters 1-5.

43. The concept of the "public sphere," following the work of Habermas, Oskar Negt, and Alexander Kluge, refers to the totality of political (and cultural) space available for the development of oppositional communities and movements, and is not reducible to discrete sets of institutions, the state, or the public *sector*. See Habermas, "The Public Sphere," *New German Critique*, fall 1974 and *Legitimation Crisis*, pp. 36-37 and 70, and Negt and Kluge, *Oeffentlichkeit und Erfahrung* (Frankfurt am Main, 1973), which is discussed at length by Eberhard Knodler-Bunte, "The Proletarian Public Sphere and Political Organization," *New German Critique*, winter 1975.

44. The PCI's approach to the middle strata is examined by Stephen Hellman, "The PCI's Alliance Strategy and the Case of the Middle Classes," in Donald L. M. Blackmer and Sidney Tarrow, eds. *Communism in Italy and France* (Princeton, N.J. Princeton University Press, 1975).

45. Andrew Feenberg, "From May Events to Eurocommunism", *Socialist Review* No. 37. For a more general discussion of the middle strata in the French context, see George Ross, "Marxism and the New Middle Classes," *Theory and Society*, March, 1978.

46. Tactical alliances with elements of the bourgeoisie must be differentiated from strategic formulations like those incorporating the new middle strata. Thus, Carrillo argues for a convergence between the PCE and the dynamic bourgeoisie who see fascism as an "obstacle to the development of modern capitalism in Spain...It is this that is bringing about an objective convergence between the revolutionary forces and this sector of Spanish capitalism...It is a question, then, of a momentary convergence, and it is clear that after this stage we are going to diverge." *Dialogue on Spain*, p. 169.

47. While technological rationality might furnish the instrumental requirements of legitimation, the need for a more purposive system of values—especially within the party itself—does not disappear. See Alvin W. Gouldner, *The Dialectic of Ideology and Technology* (New York: Seabury Press, 1976), p. 241. For Eurocommunism, of course, this purposive ideology is "Marxism," with its goals of democratization and social equality. It clearly exerts *some* impact on political commitments, but, as I have argued, this impact is limited by the opposite pull of rationalization.

48. The essays by Gorz and Steve Marglin ("What Do Bosses Do?") in Gorz, *The Social Division of Labor*, develop this point very effectively.

49. Gouldner refers to this formation as a distinct "technical political class." *Op. cit.* p. 231.

50. For example, Gian Franco Vene, *La Borghesia comunista* (Milano: SugarCo Edizioni, 1976). Some of Vene's arguments echo Milovan Djilas' thesis in *The New Class*. He associates the PCI's rightward move with its electoral appeals to the new middle strata, including "left" elements of the Church and the Christian

Democrats, and concludes that such "interclassism" has subverted the party's proletarian identity.

51. As in other realms of Eurocommunist theory, the PCI was first to reformulate the nature of party-union relationships, in the early 1960s. The rationale for this change can be found in Fernando Di Giulio, "La Politica, partiti, e il movimento sindicale," *Rinascita*, April 19, 1971 and "Unita sindicale e nuovo blocco di forze sociali e politiche," *Critica Marxista*, Nov.-Dec. 1970.

52. One might argue that "austerity" programs can *only* serve to strengthen bourgeois power during crisis, which of course would sharpen even further the contradictions of Eurocommunism. See Elmar Altvater, "L'Egemonia borghese e l'alternativa del movimento operaio," *Problemi del socialismo*, no. 5, 1977. Also Ernest Mandel, *From Stalinism to Eurocommunism* (London: New Left Books, 1978), ch. 6.

53. For example, Wolfgang Muller and Christel Neussus, "The Illusion of State Socialism and the Contradiction between Wage Labor and Capital," *Telos*, fall, 1975.

54. Ingrao, *Potere e masse*, pp. 385-386, argues that a dialectical relationship between "central" and "local" forms must characterize the democratic road, but he hedges by deferring the local structures to a future moment when socialist democracy can presumably be posed. More typical of PCI, and Eurocommunist thinking, is Napolitano, *Intervista*, p. 104, who argues that parliament must be the "basic center of decision-making."

55. Claudin, *Eurocommunism and Socialism.* p. 74.

56. This is a major theme of Arthur Rosenberg's classic, *Democracy and Socialism* (New York: Knopf, 1939), esp. pp. 355-363.

57. Claus Offe, "Political Authority and Class Structures," in *Critical Sociology* (New York: Penguin Books, 1976), p. 404. Italics mine.

58. The concept of alienated politics is elaborated by Alan Wolfe in his *The Limits of Legitimacy* (New York: The Free Press, 1977), ch. 9.

59. Maria Antonietta Macciocchi, *Letters from Inside the Italian Communist Party to Louis Althusser* (London: New Left Books, 1973), pp. 94, 135-136, 205, and 290-291. Macciocchi emphasizes the "spectacle" quality of electoral campaigns. These themes are also explored in Lucio Magri e Filippo Maone, "L'organizzazzione," *Il Manifesto*, September, 1969, pp. 29-32.

60. The most highly-institutionalized PCI machine is probably that of Bologna, where the party has governed since 1945. Its development is analyzed by Gianluigi Degli Esposti, *Bologna PCI* (Bologna: Il Mulino, 1966). See also Robert Evans, *Coexistence: Communism and its Practice in Bologna* (Notre Dame, Ind: University of Notre Dame Press, 1966).

61. In a special issue devoted to PCI politics, the revolutionary left periodical *Rosso* (June, 1976) extensively analyzed this containment of local movements—especially in the chapter "PCI e forze politiche," pp. 39-52.

62. Poulantzas, "Dual Power and the State," *New Left Review*, May-June, 1978.

63. See Lucio Magri, "Italy, Social Democracy, and Revolution in the West," *Socialist Revolution*, Nov.-Dec., 1977, pp. 109-112.

64. Peter Gay analyzes this problem in his *The Dilemma of Democratic Socialism* (New York: Collier Books, 1962), chs. 8 and 12. See also Mandel, *From Stalinism to Eurocommunism*, p. 35.

THE CONTRIBUTORS

JOANNE BARKAN is a New York journalist who lived in Italy for several years. Her articles on the Italian economic and political situation have appeared in a number of publications. She is the U.S. correspondent for *Il Manifesto* (a daily newspaper in Italy) and is a member of the New American Movement

LOUISE BEAULIEU is a poet from St. Jean, Quebec and a founder (along with Jonathon Cloud) of the Alternative Growth Institute in Ottawa. For several years she worked as a consultant on social policy issues for the Canadian government, mainly in the areas of youth programs, community employment, guaranteed income, and cultural affairs. She also was employed by the Advanced Concepts Centre of the Canadian Department of the Environment. She studied at the Institut d'Etudes Politiques in Paris.

FRED BLOCK is the author of *The Origins of International Economic Disorder*, a study of the rise and fall of the post-World War II global economic system. His most recent work attempts to develop a neo-Marxist theory of post-industrial transition. He teaches sociology at the University of Pennsylvania.

ANNARITA BUTTAFUOCO is involved in the Italian feminist movement and lives in Rome.

JONATHON CLOUD is a writer and itinerant student of human affairs who has travelled and lived in Mexico, France, New Zealand, and Canada. He studied psychology and sociology at Victoria University in Wellington, New Zealand and at York University in Toronto. He has worked in the areas of journalism, consumer advocacy, communications, and Third World development. He is the translator of Andre Gorz's *Ecology and Freedom* (1978), and has published several articles and reports. Presently he is involved in the Alternative Growth Institute.

SUZANNE COWAN teaches Italian language and literature at the University of California, Santa Cruz. She has lived and worked in Italy for several years, and has published articles on contemporary Italian culture, theater, and politics. She is now doing research on the development of theatre in Italy.

ANDREW FEENBERG teaches philosophy at San Diego State University. His main area of interest is Marxist philosophy and problems related to the role of technology in the transition to socialism. Among his recent publications is a chapter, "Transition or Convergence: Communism and the Paradox of Development," in Frederick Fleron Jr., ed., *Technology and Communist Culture*, and an article, "Remembering the May Events," *Theory and Society* (July, 1978). He has co-authored (with James Freedman) *The Changing Image of Socialism* (South End Press, forthcoming).

TEMMA KAPLAN is the author of *Anarchists of Andalusia, 1868-1903* (Princeton, 1978) and has been a long-time activist in the new left in Spain and the United States. She has been an editor of *Feminist Studies, Politics and Society,* and *Marxist Perspectives,* and has written for *Socialist Review* and *Radical America.* Her forthcoming book, *From Feudalism to Feminism,* explores the way in which women since the thirteenth century—have engaged in mass struggles to secure food for their children and win social services.

DIANA JOHNSTONE is a journalist who lives in Paris. Her articles on Western European politics—especially on Eurocommunism, feminism, European integration, and the new left—appear in many newspapers and periodicals in Europe and the U.S. She is a regular contributor to *In These Times.*

PAUL JOSEPH teaches sociology at Tufts University and is a member of the *Socialist Review* editorial collective. His study of U.S. intervention in Vietnam will soon be published by South End Press.

LOUIS MENASHE teaches Russian history at the Polytechnic Institute of New York, is Communist Affairs editor for *Marxist Perspectives,* and an associate of *Socialist Review.* His articles on Soviet history and politics have appeared in *IN These Times* and other publications.

JOSE RODRIGUEZ-IBANEZ studied sociology and law at the University of Madrid. His main fields of interest are political sociology, critical theory, and social psychology. He is the author of *Teoria critica y sociologia* and has published numerous articles in Spanish and U.S. journals and newspapers.

GEORGE ROSS teaches sociology at Brandeis. He studied at Williams college, the University of London, the University of Paris, and Harvard. He has written books on labor and politics in Britain and France, along with many articles on social movements and on Marxism and social theory. He is currently at work on a project that looks at the relationship between mass labor organizations and politics in France.

THE EDITORS

CARL BOGGS is a former political scientist who teaches sociology at UCLA. He is the author of *Gramsci's Marxism* (Pluto, 1976) and numerous articles on the Italian left, political movements, and Marxist theory and strategy. He is presently associated with the editorial boards of *Radical America, Socialist Review,* and *Theory and Society.* His work on the theory of Eurocommunist parties is being developed into a book for Westview Press.

DAVID PLOTKE is an editor of *Socialist Review.* He has written many articles on European politics, Marxist theory, and the American left. His current work is concerned with the development of American political parties in the post-World War II period.

THE POLITICS OF EUROCOMMUNISM

EDITED BY CARL BOGGS AND DAVID PLOTKE

In the last years of the 1970s, determined to escape from political irrelevance, the Communist Parties of France, Spain and Italy rode the waves of Eurocommunism to the gates of governmental power.

While there has been general agreement that Eurocommunism is an important and significant phenomenon, there has been less of a consensus about what it represents. While some establishment analysts applauded the Eurocommunist Parties' conversion to liberal democracy, many others denounced the whole business as a dangerous charade to deceive the naive.

Socialists have also been divided between those who see in the Eurocommunists' 'revolutionary pragmatism' an important new tradition of working-class radicalism and others who regard it as a further step on the road to reformism, social democracy or opportunism. *The Politics of Eurocommunism* attempts to set this debate on a firmer footing by bringing together major new contributions on all aspects of the Eurocommunist phenomenon by socialist scholars and activists of various persuasions from Spain, Italy, France and the United States.

The authors consider the origins of Eurocommunism in the post-war politics of Mediterranean Europe and the continuing process of de-Stalinization and its effects on relations between the Communist Parties and other social movements, parties and pressure groups in their own countries and on the policies of the countries of the Soviet bloc, the USA and the EEC. A concluding section reviews the historical significance of Eurocommunism and assesses its prospects in the 1980s.

Carl Boggs is Assistant Professor of Sociology at the University of California (Los Angeles) and is author of *Gramsci's Marxism*.

David Plotke is an editor of the American journal *Socialist Review* and has written widely on Eurocommunism and international socialism.

SOUTH END PRESS
Cover Design by Michael Prokosch

ISBN 0-89608-051-x